UPGRADING AND REPAIRING MICROSOFT® WINDOWS®

Second Edition

Scott Mueller
Brian Knittel

Contents at a Glance

800 East 96th Street
Indianapolis

Upgrading and Repairing Microsoft® Windows®, Second Edition

Copyright © 2009 by Pearson Education, Inc.

ISBN-13: 978-0-7897-3695-6
ISBN-10: 0-7897-3695-0

Library of Congress Cataloging-in-Publication Data

Mueller, Scott.
 Upgrading and repairing Microsoft Windows / Scott Mueller, Brian Knittel. -- 2nd ed.
    p. cm.
 ISBN 978-0-7897-3695-6
 1. Microsoft Windows (Computer file) 2. Operating systems (Computers)
I. Knittel, Brian. II. Title.
 QA76.76.O63M8444 2008
 005.4'46--dc22
                        2008036253

Printed in the United States of America

First Printing: September 2008

Trademarks

All terms mentioned in this book that are known to be trademarks or service marks have been appropriately capitalized. Que Publishing cannot attest to the accuracy of this information. Use of a term in this book should not be regarded as affecting the validity of any trademark or service mark.

Warning and Disclaimer

Every effort has been made to make this book and DVD as complete and as accurate as possible, but no warranty or fitness is implied. The information provided is on an "as is" basis. The authors and the publisher shall have neither liability nor responsibility to any person or entity with respect to any loss or damages arising from the information contained in this book or from the use of the DVD or programs accompanying it.

Bulk Sales

Que Publishing offers excellent discounts on this book when ordered in quantity for bulk purchases or special sales. For more information, please contact

U.S. Corporate and Government Sales
1-800-382-3419
corpsales@pearsontechgroup.com

For sales outside of the U.S., please contact

International Sales
international@pearson.com

Associate Publisher
Greg Wiegand

Acquisitions Editor
Rick Kughen

Development Editor
Todd Brakke

Managing Editor
Patrick Kanouse

Project Editor
Mandie Frank

Copy Editor
Margo Catts

Indexer
Ken Johnson

Proofreader
Mike Henry

Technical Editor
Mark Reddin

Publishing Coordinator
Cindy Teeters

Designer
Anne Jones

Table of Contents

About the Authors and Contributors

Scott Mueller is president of Mueller Technical Research (MTR), an international research and corporate training firm. Since 1982, MTR has produced the industry's most in-depth, accurate, and effective seminars, books, articles, videos, and FAQs covering PC hardware and data recovery. MTR maintains a client list that includes Fortune 500 companies, the U.S. and foreign governments, major software and hardware corporations, as well as PC enthusiasts and entrepreneurs. His seminars have been presented to several thousands of PC support professionals throughout the world.

Scott is best known as the author of the longest-running, most popular, and most comprehensive PC hardware book in the world, *Upgrading and Repairing PCs*, which has not only been produced in more than 18 editions, but has also become the core of an entire series of books.

Scott has authored many books for more than 20 years, including *Upgrading and Repairing PCs*, 1st through 18th editions; *Upgrading and Repairing Laptops*, 1st and 2nd editions; *Upgrading and Repairing PCs: A+ Certification Study Guide*, 1st and 2nd editions; *Upgrading and Repairing PCs Field Guide*; *Killer PC Utilities*; *The IBM PS/2 Handbook*; and *Que's Guide to Data Recovery*. Scott recently completed *Upgrading and Repairing PCs: Build a PC with Scott Mueller*, a 2-hour DVD and 100-page book, which shows viewers how to build a computer, step-by-step.

Contact MTR directly if you have a unique book, article, or video project in mind, or if you want Scott to conduct a custom PC troubleshooting, repair, maintenance, upgrade, or data-recovery seminar tailored for your organization:

Mueller Technical Research

3700 Grayhawk Drive

Algonquin, IL 60102-6325

847-854-6794

847-854-6795 Fax

Email: scottmueller@compuserve.com

Web: http://www.upgradingandrepairingpcs.com

http://www.scottmueller.com

http://forum.scottmueller.com

Scott's premiere work, *Upgrading and Repairing PCs*, has sold more than 2 million copies, making it by far the most popular and longest-running PC hardware book on the market today. Scott has been featured in *Forbes* magazine and has written several articles for *PC World* magazine, *Maximum PC* magazine, several newsletters, and the Upgrading and Repairing PCs website.

If you have suggestions for the next edition of this book, any comments about the book in general, or new book or article topics you would like to see covered, send them to Scott via email at scottmueller@compuserve.com or visit http://www.upgradingandrepairingpcs.com.

Scott has a forum exlusively for those who have purchased one of his books or DVDs. Visit http://forum.scottmueller.com to view the forum.

Brian Knittel has been a software developer for nearly 30 years. After doing graduate work in medical imaging technologies, he began a career as an independent consultant. An eclectic mix of clients has led to long-term projects in medical documentation, workflow management, real-time industrial system control, and most importantly, more than 15 years of real-world experience with MS-DOS, Windows, and computer networking in the business world. He is the author of *Windows XP Under the Hood: Hardcore Scripting and Command Line Power*, and is co-author of several other Que books including *Special Edition Using Microsoft Windows* editions covering XP Home, XP Professional, and Windows 2000 Professional. Brian lives in Albany, California, halfway between the tidal wave zone and the earthquake fault. He spends his free time snowboarding, restoring antique computers (check out www.ibm1130.org), and trying to perfect his wood-fired pizza recipes.

Mark Edward Soper has taught computer troubleshooting and other technical subjects to thousands of students from Maine to Hawaii since 1992. He is a longtime contributor to *Upgrading and Repairing PCs*, working on the 11ᵗʰ though 16ᵗʰ editions. He has contributed chapters to *Upgrading and Repairing Networks,* Second Edition, *Special Edition Using Microsoft Windows,* Millennium Edition, and *Special Edition Using Microsoft Windows XP* (both Home and Pro editions). Mark coauthored both the first and second editions of *Upgrading and Repairing PCs, Technician's Portable Reference,* and *Upgrading and Repairing PCs: Field Guide* and cowrote *Upgrading and Repairing PCs: A+ Study Certification Guide,* Second Edition. Mark also authored *Absolute Beginner's Guide to Home Networking, Absolute Beginner's Guide to A+ Certification* and currently is writing *Absolute Beginner's Guide to Home Automation*. He is a regular contributor to *Maximum PC* magazine.

Mark Reddin is a Microsoft Certified Systems Engineer (MCSE) and A+ Certified PC technician. In his younger days he enjoyed tinkering with computers during the time of the early Commodore and Atari systems (with all those wonderful games). Mark delved more seriously into computer technology during his undergraduate studies at Ball State University and has since been involved in the industry in various capacities. His experience with computers and networks has ranged from consulting to owning and operating a sales and repair shop. Additionally, he has been involved as both a technical and development editor with numerous Que publications over the past 5 years, including *Upgrading and Repairing PCs* and *How Computers Work*.

Dedication

To Emerson: Keep up the good work in school!

Acknowledgments

This new edition is the product of a great deal of additional research and development over the previous editions. Several people have helped me with both the research and production of this book. I would like to thank the following people:

First, a very special thanks to my wife and partner, Lynn. She used her creative and technical skills to shoot and produce the video that is included with this book. I'm extremely proud of her for all I've seen her accomplish. The dedication she has shown to her work has been inspiring. Thanks also to Mike Sundstrom, who runs Forum.ScottMueller.com in addition to helping with the videos and other projects.

I must give a *very* special thanks to Rick Kughen at Que. Through the years Rick is the number one person responsible for championing this book and the *Upgrading and Repairing* series. I cannot say enough about Rick and what he means to all the *Upgrading and Repairing* books.

I'd also like to thank Todd Brakke for once again doing the development editing for this edition. His excellent tips and suggestions really help to keep the material concise and up-to-date. Special thanks also go to Mandie Frank who helped tremendously with the project editing. I'd also like to thank all of the other editors, illustrators, designers, and technicians at Que who work so hard to complete the finished product and get this book out the door! They are a wonderful team that produces clearly the best computer books on the market. I am happy and proud to be closely associated with all the people at Que.

I would also like to say thanks to my publisher Greg Wiegand, who has stood behind all the *Upgrading and Repairing* book and video projects. Greg is a fellow motorcycle enthusiast, someday hopefully we can go riding together.

All the people at Que make me feel as if we are on the same team, and they are just as dedicated as I am to producing the best books possible.

I would also like to say thanks to Brian Knittel, Mark Soper, and Mark Reddin, who have all made considerable contributions and added their expertise to this book.

Many readers write me with suggestions and even corrections for the book, for which I am especially grateful. However some readers go the extra mile, and their contributions deserve a special mention. Of special note is Daniel Sedory, who made many helpful suggestions. Please keep those comments coming; I welcome any and all of your comments, and even your criticisms. I take them seriously and apply them to the continuous improvement of this book. Interaction with my readers is the primary force that helps maintain this book as the most up-to-date and relevant work available *anywhere* on the subject of PC hardware.

Finally, I would like to thank the thousands of people who have attended my seminars or sent me questions via email or my forum; you might not realize how much I learn from each of you and all your questions!

We Want to Hear from You!

As the reader of this book, *you* are our most important critic and commentator. We value your opinion and want to know what we're doing right, what we could do better, what areas you'd like to see us publish in, and any other words of wisdom you're willing to pass our way.

As an associate publisher for Que Publishing, I welcome your comments. You can email or write me directly to let me know what you did or didn't like about this book—as well as what we can do to make our books better.

Please note that I cannot help you with technical problems related to the topic of this book. We do have a User Services group, however, where I will forward specific technical questions related to the book.

When you write, please be sure to include this book's title and author as well as your name, email address, and phone number. I will carefully review your comments and share them with the author and editors who worked on the book.

Email: feedback@quepublishing.com

Mail: Greg Wiegand
            Associate Publisher
            Que Publishing
            800 East 96th Street
            Indianapolis, IN 46240 USA

Reader Services

For more information about this book or another Que title, visit our website at www.quepublishing.com. Type the ISBN (excluding hyphens) or the title of a book in the Search field to find the page you're looking for.

Introduction

Welcome to *Upgrading and Repairing Microsoft Windows, Second Edition*. This is the book for people who want to know more about how to use and support Microsoft Windows than most other books dare to detail. While covering all versions in many respects, this book devotes most coverage to Windows Vista and XP. Whether you want to install, manage, or troubleshoot the Windows operating system, this book goes far deeper than just the basics. Whether you support a large network of Windows machines, a few Windows PCs in a small office/home office environment, or just a single at-home system, this book can quickly turn you into an advanced Windows power user.

Is This Book for You?

Upgrading and Repairing Microsoft Windows, Second Edition is designed for people who want a thorough understanding of Windows and how it works without wasting time and pages on endless handholding through basic, everyday tasks. Each section fully explains management and troubleshooting issues related to Windows, including user management, networking, and security issues. Over the course of this book you'll develop a feel for what goes on behind the stylish graphical user interface so you can rely on your own judgment and observations and not some table of canned troubleshooting steps.

Upgrading and Repairing Microsoft Windows, Second Edition is written for people who will install, configure, maintain, and repair systems they use personally or in a corporate environment. To accomplish these tasks, you need a level of knowledge much higher than that of an average system user. You must know exactly which tool to use for a task and how to use the tool correctly. This book can help you achieve this level of knowledge.

Chapter-by-Chapter Breakdown

Chapter 1, "Windows Version History," examines the very beginnings of PC operating systems from DOS all the way through Windows XP and Vista, including the latest Service Packs. Microsoft operating systems have had quite a wild ride over the years and it's amazing to see how the operating system we all use almost every day has become what it is.

Chapter 2, "Windows Boot (Startup)," details the Windows startup process, including what takes place between power-up and the appearance of the Welcome screen. In addition, it includes detailed information about Windows services, which are processes that run in the background to provide support for Windows networking, searching, authentication, and management.

Chapter 3, "Installing Windows," explains procedures and issues regarding the preparation and installation of Windows. It includes detailed steps for baseline installations for single desktops as well as in a more complex networked environment.

Chapter 4, "Upgrading Windows," discusses how to upgrade Windows to a new version. You look at paths for upgrading existing systems to either Windows XP or Vista. Also shown are methods for migrating user settings and documents to new Windows computers.

Chapter 5, "Tweaking and Tuning Windows," shows you how to configure Windows for peak performance and usability, using the Windows configuration dialogs and special-purpose tools such as TweakUI and the Registry Editor. In addition, we'll give you a checklist you can use to identify and fix the most common Windows performance bottlenecks.

Chapter 6, "Networking Windows," tells you how to configure Windows to run a reliable and secure network at home or at the office. Whether you have two computers or two hundred, a network can immediately pay for itself—many times over—by letting you share printers, giving you access to files from any computer, and letting you share a single Internet connection among several computers.

Chapter 7, "Protecting and Securing Windows," covers the steps you can take to ensure your Windows PC is well protected from outside intrusion. Have you lost your administrator account password? Would you like some help protecting your computer from spyware and viruses? We'll help you learn how to recover lost passwords, use firewalls to block intruders, and protect your computer from viruses, spyware, and trojans. Learn how to take an active approach to security and harden your existing security to stop attacks before they start.

In Chapter 8, "Managing Windows," we cover the most important Windows management functions: adding and managing user accounts, hardware, device drivers, and hard disks. In addition, Chapter 8 gets down and dirty with Windows Backup, showing you how make essential backups of your precious data and how to restore those backups should the data on your hard drive be lost or corrupted.

In Chapter 9, "Windows Commands and Scripting," we cover Windows scripting essentials and the oft-forgotten-but-highly-useful world of the command prompt. The command prompt environment not only runs old MS-DOS programs, but also gives you access to a large number of efficient, concise, and powerful Windows management and operating tools. The chapter covers the general principles of command-line programs, configuration settings, and several important commands, as well as scripting and batch file procedures that you can use to automate complex jobs.

Chapter 10, "Windows File Systems," covers file systems. If you're currently running FAT32 drives and deciding whether to switch to NTFS, or if you just want to know everything there is to know about the file system, this is the place to look.

Chapter 11, "Windows Data Recovery," covers data recovery procedures. If you can't access your drive because of a corrupted master boot record (MBR) or volume boot record (VBR), you'll find information you can use to recover these sectors and regain access to your valuable data.

Chapter 12, "Windows Troubleshooting," looks at some of the more common problems encountered with Windows. Troubleshooting software is one part skill, one part craft, and one part knowing where to look for information. In this chapter, you'll look at how to identify Windows problems, and what tools and methods you should use to solve them. This chapter includes an extensive look at how to deal with a system that cannot stably boot, and how to use both the System Restore feature and the arcane but powerful XP Recovery Console and Vista Recovery Environment when you can't even log in to your user account.

This edition of *Upgrading and Repairing Windows* also includes online content that can be found at www.informit.com/title/9780789736956.

Appendix A, "Windows Tool Reference," describes several useful categories of Windows management, maintenance, configuration, monitoring, and data processing tools that you may not be familiar with. Most of them are not installed by Windows Setup but instead are hidden away in obscure folders on your Windows Setup CD-ROM. Several more are available from Microsoft via free download over the Internet, and some others must be purchased. In any case, we think you should know about all of them.

Appendix B, "Windows Command Reference," lists all the executable programs provided with Windows 9x/Me, NT/2000, and the various versions of XP and Vista, including application programs, services, system components, built-in commands, Control Panel applets, MMC Management snap-ins, and screen savers. You can browse this listing to find useful programs you might not be familiar with, or to help identify the many obscure programs that are run automatically by Windows.

Appendix C, "Remote Desktop and Remote Assistance," shows you how to set up the Windows Remote Desktop feature so that you can access your computer from anywhere in the world. It also includes information on third-party remote connection tools that offer alternatives to using Remote Desktop.

Getting the Most from This Book

Upgrading and Repairing Microsoft Windows, Second Edition is not a book that you read through once and never touch again. In fact, this is not a book that needs to be read straight through at all, although any Windows user will learn a great deal from doing just that.

This book is, in fact, a detailed and valuable reference that should be kept next to your PC (and your copy of the latest edition of *Upgrading and Repairing PCs*) at all times. The information shoehorned into every line of every page of this tome will help you put Windows to work the way it was meant to and keep it running for the long term.

Scott's Website—www.upgradingandrepairingpcs.com

Don't miss my book website at www.upgradingandrepairingpcs.com! Here, you'll find a cache of helpful material to go along with the book you're holding. I've loaded this site with tons of material, from video clips to monthly book updates. I use this spot to keep you updated throughout the year on major changes in both the PC hardware industry and the evolution of Windows. Each month, I write new articles covering new technologies released after this book was printed. These articles are archived so you can refer to them anytime.

You'll also find exclusive video clips available nowhere else!

I also use this site to tell you about some of the other fantastic *Upgrading and Repairing PCs* products, including

- *Upgrading and Repairing PCs*
- *Upgrading and Repairing PCs: Build a PC with Scott Mueller*
- *Upgrading and Repairing Laptops*
- *Upgrading and Repairing Servers*
- *Upgrading and Repairing Networks*

If you have technical questions, use my forum at http://forum.scottmueller.com. You can read the forum to see existing questions and answers, or sign up to post a question yourself.

Laptops have become the largest growing segment of PCs, and my new book *Upgrading and Repairing Laptops, 3rd Edition* covers these systems in great detail and is due out in spring 2008. Be sure to check the upgradingandrepairingpcs.com website for more information on all my latest books, videos, articles, and more!

Windows Version History

A Brief History of PC Operating Systems

Microsoft Windows has evolved considerably since it was first introduced in 1985. As is typical for evolutionary processes, its progress has been uneven and not always in the forward direction (Windows Me comes to mind). Still, despite the occasional misstep and an antitrust suit or two along the way, Windows today is mostly secure, reliable, easy to use, and completely ubiquitous.

To give you a picture of where we are now, consider that the original PCs from 1981–82 were able to fit an operating system, application software, and user data onto one or two 160KB single-sided floppy disks, a default Windows Vista installation occupies approximately 8GB of hard disk space before any user data or application software is added. This is a staggering amount of software! In fact, it's more than a typical IBM mainframe computer has, and mainframe software maintenance is a career in itself, requiring months if not years of training.

The fact that it is possible for anyone but a career computer engineer to use, manage, maintain, upgrade and repair a Windows PC is something of a minor miracle, mostly the result of two decades of effort by hardware manufacturers, software vendors, and Microsoft to incorporate a lot of that career engineer's knowledge into software that—to a large extent—can take care of itself. Still, there is a lot left for the user to take care of—that's why you purchased this book.

To get a clearer picture what Windows is now, it's useful to see how it evolved. In this chapter, we'll go through its history and examine its roots, which reach back well before the introduction of the PC as we know it today.

DOS History

A discussion of the different versions of Windows cannot be complete without also talking about DOS. This is because early Windows versions were an add-on or extension to DOS, and actually required DOS to be preinstalled on a system in order to run. Later Windows versions included DOS internally, which was gradually minimized until virtually all the legacy 16-bit DOS and Windows code was replaced by entirely new 32-bit and 64-bit code in Windows NT, Windows 2000, and later.

Before Windows existed, MS-DOS was the most popular operating system for PCs, and DOS continued to be the most popular OS from 1981 when the PC was introduced until well after 1995 and the appearance of Windows 95. All versions of Windows before Windows 95 actually required MS-DOS to be preinstalled on the system because many of those earlier versions of Windows were more of a DOS graphical user interface extension than a complete standalone operating system. And although Windows 95, 98, and Me were sold as standalone operating systems (no prior DOS required), they actually included MS-DOS and used portions of 16-bit DOS code. Windows 95 included MS-DOS 7.0, Windows 95B and 98 included MS-DOS 7.1, and Windows Me included MS-DOS 8.0.

Windows NT was the first truly standalone fully 32-bit version of Windows that wasn't based on MS-DOS. Because Windows 2000 and later versions are the successors of Windows NT, they are also not based on MS-DOS or 16-bit code in any way.

Even though later versions of Windows aren't based on MS-DOS or include 16-bit code in the internal workings, in many ways DOS still plays a role in running certain diagnostic or utility programs, or especially when partitioning and formatting certain types of disks and drives. For example, when you format a floppy disk as a bootable "system" disk by checking the Create an MS-DOS Startup Disk option, Windows XP and Vista automatically copies the MS-DOS 8.0 system files to the disk at the completion of the formatting process.

Evolution of DOS

When the IBM PC was announced on August 12, 1981, IBM indicated that three operating systems would be available for its new PC. They were

- IBM Personal Computer Disk Operating System ($40)
- Digital Research CP/M-86 ($240)
- SofTech USCD p-System w/Pascal ($695)

Of those three operating systems, only the IBM Personal Computer Disk Operating System (normally abbreviated as PC DOS, or just DOS) was immediately available. The other two operating systems weren't available until several months later, and were priced significantly higher as well. As you can imagine, due to both availability and price, it was pretty clear that the PC DOS operating system would be the one most people used on their new PCs.

Although IBM marketed and sold PC DOS as an IBM product, most people know that Microsoft actually supplied the core code of PC DOS to IBM in the form of MS-DOS. What many people don't know is that Microsoft first licensed, and then purchased MS-DOS from another company called Seattle Computer Products (SCP). One could say that Seattle Computer, Microsoft, and IBM were all intimately involved in the early development and evolution of DOS; however, when you go back far enough, all origins of DOS trace back to one man.

From 1978 through 1980 Tim Paterson worked for a small company called Seattle Computer Products developing computer hardware and software products. In June of 1978 Intel introduced the 8086 processor, and shortly thereafter Paterson designed an S-100 bus computer system using the 8086 for SCP. The hardware consisted of three S-100 cards; a CPU card, a CPU support card, and a memory card. These cards were designed to be installed in an S-100 chassis, and would then operate together as a complete 8086 computer system.

At that time Microsoft's BASIC-80 (Beginners All-purpose Symbolic Instruction Code for the 8080 processor) was one of the most popular programming languages for microcomputers, so it was only natural to port that language to the new 8086 processor. In May 1979 Paterson spent a week at Microsoft working with a programmer named Bob O'Rear to port Microsoft BASIC-80 to the new SCP 8086 system. The result was Microsoft BASIC-86, one of the first software packages available for the 8086 processor. BASIC-80 and BASIC-86 were unique at the time in that they included a built-in File Allocation Table (FAT) file system originally written by Bill Gates. This meant that they could run standalone; that is, with no operating system or other software required. Both the 8086 computer system and Microsoft BASIC-86 were completed and sold by Seattle Computer starting in November 1979.

While BASIC-86 would run standalone on the new 8086 computer, other languages would require an operating system in order to run. At the time Microsoft had been selling FORTRAN (FORmula TRANslation) and COBOL (Common Business Oriented Language) for CP/M systems using the Intel 8080 processor, and it wanted to port those operating systems to run in the 8086 like BASIC. Unfortunately that would not be possible without an operating system.

At the time, Digital Research's CP/M (Control Program for Microcomputers) was by far the most popular operating system for microcomputers, and everybody including Microsoft and SCP expected Digital Research to port CP/M over to the new 8086 processor. Unfortunately Digital Research was taking too long, so in April of 1980 Paterson got tired of waiting, and decided to write his own DOS for the 8086, calling it QDOS for Quick and Dirty Operating System. QDOS 0.11 was first released by Seattle Computer Products in August 1980. Paterson continued improving and refining QDOS, which SCP renamed 86-DOS and released in December 1980 as 86-DOS 0.33.

During the summer of 1980 IBM began working on Project Chess, which was the codename for the top-secret IBM PC project. Needing software for its new machine, IBM approached Microsoft to provide BASIC, FORTRAN, and COBOL for the PC. However, before IBM would divulge the details about the secret project, it required that Microsoft sign a very strict nondisclosure agreement. Once the agreement was signed, IBM discussed details about the new system. Original plans apparently called for an 8-bit processor; however, Bill Gates pushed for IBM to use the new 16-bit Intel 8086 instead, which would allow access to up to 1GB of RAM instead of the 64KB limit imposed by 8-bit processors. IBM ended up settling on the Intel 8088, which was essentially a lower-cost version of the 8086 that ran 8086 software.

Then the discussions turned to an operating system. Microsoft knew that BASIC-86 could run standalone on the new system, but Microsoft's other languages were designed to run under Digital Research's CP/M-80 operating system. IBM asked Microsoft if it could provide an OS as well, but that was a major undertaking, and Microsoft knew that Digital Research had already been working on CP/M-86. If Digital Research could provide CP/M-86, Microsoft could port its languages over and meet the tight IBM deadlines. So Microsoft told IBM to visit Digital Research and talk about CP/M-86 for the new PC.

Legend has it that when IBM went to visit Digital Research, Gary Kildall (the author of CP/M and principal of the company) stood them up and was out flying his plane. The truth is that Kildall was more of a programmer than a businessman, and he usually left his wife Dorothy McEwen in charge of any business dealings at DR, and the IBM meeting was no exception. The problem wasn't Kildall's presence so much as it was the restrictive nondisclosure agreement. When IBM presented DR with the same nondisclosure agreement that Microsoft had already signed, McEwen and the DR attorneys thought that the terms of the agreement were too strict and they refused to sign. Without a signed agreement, IBM could not divulge any information about its secret PC, so the deal with DR for CP/M-86 was essentially dead in the water.

At this point Microsoft realized that any delays in IBM finding an operating system for the new PC could give IBM reason to cancel the entire project, and consequently Microsoft's deal to provide the languages. In late September of 1980 Microsoft principals Bill Gates, Paul Allen, Steve Ballmer, and Kay Nishi met and decided that they should take the risk and try to provide not only the languages that IBM wanted for the new PC, but also the operating system as well. The problem was that they didn't have the time or manpower to develop a completely new operating system from scratch along with porting over their languages. Microsoft knew it needed a ready-made 8086 operating system, and from their past dealings with Tim Paterson at Seattle Computer Products, they knew just where to get one.

Microsoft made a call to SCP and quickly licensed 86-DOS for unlimited use by a "secret customer" for a one-time fee of $25,000, and in turn licensed the DOS to IBM for a one-time unlimited use fee of $80,000. Although this made a profit for Microsoft, to IBM this was quite a bargain, and would allow IBM to charge a relatively low fee for the operating system to its customers. In consideration of the low license fee, Microsoft bargained to retain the rights to license the operating system to other manufacturers as well. Microsoft believed it could make MS-DOS the industry standard for all PCs based on the 8086 or 8088 processor, and this type of deal would allow Microsoft to retain control over DOS. IBM and Microsoft signed what would probably become the most important deal in computer history on November 6, 1980.

Paterson continued work on 86-DOS at SCP, while at Microsoft Robert O'Rear took the code from Paterson and began modifying it to work on the prototype PC it had been sent. In April 1981 SCP released 86-DOS 1.0, and the very next month Paterson left SCP and was hired by Microsoft to work full time getting 86-DOS ready for Microsoft's still-secret customer. Although there were suspicions, it wasn't until Paterson arrived for work at Microsoft that he knew for sure the secret customer was IBM. Now at Microsoft, Paterson worked once again with Bob O'Rear, cleaning up the code and fulfilling IBM's demands for quality and features. They worked closely with several people at IBM, including David Bradley who was responsible for writing the ROM BIOS code used in the PC. Paterson and O'Rear finished the core of what IBM would call the Personal Computer

DOS (also called PC DOS) 1.0 in July 1980. IBM also wrote several additional utility programs to go with DOS 1.0, including the MODE, COMP, DISKCOMP, and DISKCOPY commands, as well as several demo programs in BASIC.

On July 27, 1981 (just over 2 weeks before the IBM PC and the new DOS would be officially introduced) Microsoft decided it would be best if it closed up any loose ends by purchasing 86-DOS outright from SCP for $50,000, thus giving Microsoft full ownership. One condition of the sale was that SCP could retain a perpetual royalty-free license to MS-DOS for itself. This license would later result in a legal battle that was eventually settled in 1986, with Microsoft paying SCP another $975,000 to purchase that license back. This meant that Microsoft essentially paid SCP just over $1 million dollars total for full ownership of MS-DOS, a very wise investment when you consider that in June of 1986 Microsoft estimated that half of its $61 million annual revenue came from MS-DOS licensing. MS-DOS licensing eventually turned into a multibillion dollar cash cow for Microsoft.

The IBM PC and PC DOS 1.0 were officially introduced on August 12, 1981, kicking off a family of personal computers that today we simply call PCs. Meanwhile, Paterson continued working at Microsoft on PC DOS 1.1 (which was called MS-DOS 1.25 by Microsoft). PC DOS 1.1 was released in June 1982 along with double-sided floppy drives for the PC. DOS 1.1 was also the first version licensed by Microsoft to other PC OEMs (Original Equipment Manufacturers) as MS-DOS 1.25. One of the first PC-compatible systems with MS-DOS was the Columbia Dataproducts Computer in July 1982, but many others soon followed.

Microsoft licensed MS-DOS to any OEM who wanted to make a system compatible with IBM, which eventually made Microsoft the largest software company in the world. While Windows is by far the most popular OS for PCs today, it wasn't until Windows 95 came out in 1995 that Windows went from being a loss-leader to becoming a huge hit. You could say that up until the release of Windows 95, MS-DOS paid all the bills.

After finishing PC DOS 1.1 (also known as MS-DOS 1.25) and doing initial planning on PC DOS 2.0, Paterson left Microsoft on April 1, 1982 and went back to work at Seattle Computer Products, while Mark Zbikowski took over the development of DOS at Microsoft. DOS 2.0 was virtually a complete rewrite of DOS and introduced many new features including hard disk support, hierarchical directories, and installable device drivers. Zbikowski also designed the executable (*.EXE) file format used in MS-DOS, and used his own initials as the two-byte signature "MZ" (4D5Ah), which can be found at the start of all *.EXE files. IBM wrote and added several utilities of its own including FDISK, TREE, BACKUP/RESTORE, COMP, DISKCOMP, DISKCOPY, MODE, and GRAPHICS, and the final product was eventually released by IBM as PC DOS 2.0 on March 8, 1983.

Paterson eventually left SCP again and went back to work at Microsoft; in fact, he worked for Microsoft at least three times: '81–'82, '86–'88, and '90–'98. Besides his initial work on DOS, Paterson worked on other projects such as Visual Basic and Java. Today Paterson runs his own company called Paterson Technology (www.patersontech.com). In 2001 Paterson gained additional fame as he built the "Hexidecimator" robot, which competed on the *BattleBots* TV show.

MS-DOS Versus PC DOS

With modern PCs having a very high level of standardization and compatibility, today it is easy to see how Microsoft can market complete packaged operating systems that will install and work unmodified on practically any PC you can purchase or build. Without the standardization and compatibility we have come to depend on, different specific "flavors" of a given operating system would be required for specific different hardware.

That is exactly how things were back in the early '80s when the IBM PC was introduced. Many of the Intel x86 processor–based PCs in the early '80s were not fully compatible with the IBM PC, and IBM's PC DOS would not run on those systems right out of the box. If a given system would not run PC DOS, the manufacturer could license MS-DOS from Microsoft and produce a custom version for its computer that would run.

For DOS versions up through 3.1 there were only private-labeled OEM versions such as PC DOS, Compaq DOS, Zenith-DOS, and so on. Private labeled DOS names and version numbers could vary, even for releases based on the same set of Microsoft code. For example, the code base that Microsoft internally called MS-DOS 1.25 was called IBM PC DOS 1.1 by IBM, and Columbia DOS 2.0 by Columbia Data Products.

In the early to mid '80s there were many systems that were partially compatible with the IBM PC, but which also differed from the PC in many ways. For example, the Texas Instruments Professional Computer used an 8088 processor, had the same 5.25-inch 360KB floppy drives as an IBM PC (and could read and write the same 360KB disks); however, it also had a different ROM BIOS, an internally different hardware and software interrupt structure, and a higher-resolution graphics processor. Because of the differences in system design, IBM's PC DOS would not boot and run on the TI PC.

As you learned in the previous section, the development of PC DOS was a cooperative project between Microsoft and IBM. Microsoft was responsible for producing the core system code, while IBM helped specify the functionality, did testing, and added several additional utility programs to the system to both enhance functionality as well as to work specifically with IBM's hardware. The development agreement between Microsoft and IBM allowed Microsoft to license the Microsoft-developed portions of the PC DOS product (essentially the core system code) to other OEMs, which Microsoft called MS-DOS. As such, MS-DOS was not a complete (finished) product; rather, it was only a core set of code that could be licensed by a computer manufacturer to run on its systems.

To actually have a finished version of MS-DOS for end users, a given computer manufacturer such as Texas Instruments would have to license the core MS-DOS code from Microsoft, test and if necessary modify that code to work properly on its hardware, write its own versions of any or all of the utility programs that IBM had written for PC DOS (as well as possibly write any additional utilities they wanted), and finally write and print the manuals, copy the disks, and package it all together into a finished retail product. If the manufacturer was Texas Instruments, the finished MS-DOS product might be called Texas Instruments DOS, and would only be guaranteed to run on the Texas Instruments computers for which it was designed.

As an end user, once you had the TI version of MS-DOS running on a TI PC, any program strictly written to interface with MS-DOS would work on the system. Unfortunately many programs at the time were designed to go around the operating system and talk directly to the hardware for certain functions in order to improve performance. For example, the popular Lotus 1-2-3 spreadsheet program accessed the IBM graphics hardware directly and would not work on the TI PC. For Lotus 1-2-3 to run on the TI PC, TI had to work with Lotus to produce a special version of the program rewritten to work with the modified graphics on its system.

Besides TI, many other manufacturers at the time were also producing systems that were not 100% compatible with the IBM PC, and therefore also had to license and then produce custom versions of MS-DOS specifically designed for those systems. Owners of those few systems that were 100% compatible with the IBM PC could simply purchase PC DOS from IBM and run that. For example, I used a Compaq Portable PC for a short time, and although Compaq did produce its own custom version of MS-DOS, I ran IBM's PC DOS instead, and it worked perfectly.

As time progressed, most computer manufacturers realized that producing systems that were 100% compatible with the IBM PC was necessary in order to run all the software that was becoming available for the IBM PC, which in turn became critical for success in the marketplace. Also, PC components such as motherboards became available, enabling smaller computer dealers or even individuals to build their own systems. Although an individual who built a 100% IBM-compatible system could simply go to the IBM dealer and purchase a copy of PC DOS, most of the smaller computer manufacturers (who were really just system builders or assemblers) did not want to bundle IBM DOS with their systems, nor did they have the capability to license MS-DOS from Microsoft, write the additional utilities, or produce the manuals and packaging to create a finished product.

What was needed was a generic but complete shrink-wrapped packaged product that a smaller computer manufacturer or assembler could buy from Microsoft and sell with its computers. To oblige, Microsoft wrote its own versions of the utilities provided by IBM in PC DOS, and in August 1986 released Microsoft MS-DOS 3.2, the first Microsoft labeled "shrink-wrapped" packaged version of DOS for smaller OEMs or system builders. This became known as the Microsoft OEM version. On the box, the labeling stated that it was "For Personal Computers Compatible with IBM Personal Computers." This version was technically not sold retail, but was sold through what became known as the Microsoft OEM System Builder program. In fact, later versions of the packaged MS-DOS product contained the statement "Not for retail sale except with a computer system" right on the box. Microsoft was afraid to sell MS-DOS retail because then it would have to support it on the myriad of different systems out there. Instead Microsoft sold it only to system builders, who were responsible for testing the DOS to work properly on their systems, and then providing any and all necessary support to the end user.

IBM and Microsoft had signed a JDA (Joint Development Agreement) in June of 1985 to collaborate on what was originally called Advanced DOS, but which would later be known as OS/2. Although the JDA was centered around OS/2, it also brought on a major change in DOS development. Starting with DOS 3.3, IBM became the main development center for DOS (both the core and the utilities) while Microsoft focused mainly on OS/2. As a result of the JDA, Microsoft gained the right to redistribute the PC DOS utilities written by IBM. This meant that PC DOS 3.3 and the Microsoft MS-DOS 3.3 OEM packaged product version that followed were now almost identical code, with only a few minor exceptions.

Note that many of the larger computer manufacturers continued to license MS-DOS and produce their own custom versions. For example, after the IBM and Microsoft versions of DOS 3.3 were released, Compaq released Compaq DOS 3.31, which included the implementation of support for larger than 32MiB hard disk partitions that would officially appear in DOS 4.0.

As with 3.3, DOS 4.0 was also initially developed at IBM and subsequently released by Microsoft. There were several bugs in the first release, and by the time the Microsoft OEM packaged version came out it had been updated to version 4.01.

During 1991 the joint development agreement between IBM and Microsoft fell apart, which resulted in IBM taking over full responsibility and development for OS/2, and primary development of DOS 5.0 became Microsoft's responsibility. The MS-DOS 5.0 OEM packaged version was released on June 6, 1991, five days before IBM released PC DOS 5.0. This was somewhat significant as up until DOS 5, PC DOS had always been on the market first, and in some cases with a fairly long lead over the same relative version of MS-DOS. For the first time Microsoft also began selling MS-DOS as a retail product in the form of a lower cost upgrade version.

The growing rift forming between IBM and Microsoft after the dissolution of their joint development agreement caused several different and somewhat confusing releases of DOS 6.x. For example, Microsoft developed MS-DOS 6.0 and released its OEM and upgrade versions first. Rather than merely introducing the same thing later, IBM made some changes and subsequently released PC DOS 6.1, skipping a version number in the process (there was no PC DOS 6.0). Microsoft then developed its next version and also skipped a number, calling it MS-DOS 6.2 to eliminate confusion with the IBM product (there was no MS-DOS 6.1). IBM followed suit and called its subsequent release PC DOS 6.3 (there was no PC DOS 6.2).

The last official standalone MS-DOS release from Microsoft was 6.22, while IBM subsequently released PC DOS 7.0 and finally PC DOS 2000 (7.1). IBM's PC DOS 2000 was the last official release of any standalone version of MS-DOS. Later versions of MS-DOS 7.0, 7.1, and 8.0 came with Windows 95, Windows 98, and Windows Me respectively; however, those DOS versions were never released separately as standalone products.

DOS Versions

Now that I have outlined a history of DOS from a market perspective, let's take a look at the actual nuts and bolts that constituted each version of DOS.

DOS 1.x

PC DOS 1.0 was introduced along with the IBM PC on August 12, 1981, and supported only single-sided 5.25-inch drives. Floppy disks were formatted using 8 sectors per track (one side, 40 tracks) resulting in a capacity of only 160KB when formatted. There was no support for hard disks at all, which were generally quite rare for personal computers at the time. DOS was a text-based operating system, hence there was no graphical interface. Unlike CP/M, 8-bit ASCII characters were supported because the PC came with IBM 8-bit ASCII in ROM. This allowed the use of line drawing and other special characters to draw boxes and such on the screen.

For anyone who used the CP/M operating system, DOS seemed pretty familiar. The "user interface," consisting of a prompt that indicated the logged drive, was very similar to CP/M. This similarity helped many people, including myself, make the transition from older CP/M systems to PC DOS a painless one.

When DOS 1.0 was introduced, it contained several commands and limited batch-processing facilities. About half of the commands were internally part of DOS, while the disk utilities were external assembly language programs. The commands in DOS at that time were

CHKDSK	DIR	FORMAT	RENAME
COMP	DISKCOMP	MODE	SYS
COPY	DISKCOPY	PAUSE	TIME
DATE	ERASE	REM	TYPE

DOS also came with interpretive BASIC, a text editor called EDLIN, a LINKer, a DEBUGger, and a series of BASIC programs. All of these programs were sold on one single-sided floppy diskette.

People immediately noticed that the IBM-PC and PC DOS could handle only single-sided diskettes. This was seen as a disadvantage at the time, and was an indication of the conservative nature of IBM. But everybody knew that a version supporting double-sided drives was coming. In reality very few PCs ended up being sold with DOS 1.0 as the PC was in pretty short supply for the first few months of its existence. It was really not until the early part of 1982 that just anybody could get one, and by then DOS 1.1 was available.

PC DOS 1.1 was introduced in May 1982. It was called 1.25 internally by Microsoft, and was later released by a number of OEMs under a variety of names and version numbers. DOS 1.1 supported double-sided drives with 8 sectors per track, resulting in a formatted capacity of 320KB. PC DOS 1.1 used 12KB of RAM, and was the last DOS written by Tim Paterson, based on the original Seattle Computer Products 86-DOS.

The major difference between DOS 1.0 and 1.1 is that the latter can operate double-sided drives. All of the external, and most of the internal commands, were rewritten to accommodate double-sided drives. There was still no explicit support for hard disks, but several manufacturers supplied kits with software patches to DOS that allowed a large disk to be used. Actually many different companies offering expansion products for the PC emerged at this time, and many of these products came with software that patched DOS directly. I remember being concerned about this because the compatibility problems were enormous. I was getting the feeling that PC DOS was to go the route of Apple DOS at the time in that it would become so patched and hacked up by the aftermarket as to cease to be any kind of standard. Anyone who remembers the old Apple DOS for the Apple II series can tell you the problems with this methodology. Fortunately IBM and Microsoft came to the rescue with a new version (DOS 2.0) that was so changed and improved that it brought all of this patching to an abrupt halt. There was no need to patch it if it could already do what you wanted, or be easily adapted with extensions rather than patches.

DOS 2.x

PC DOS 2.0 was introduced on March 8, 1983 (along with the IBM PC XT), and was virtually a complete rewrite over the previous versions. DOS 2.0 added many new features and functions (mostly derived from UNIX), including a tree-structured (hierarchical) file system, support for hard disk drives up to 16.76MB (15.98MiB) using FAT12, 5.25-inch 9-sector per track floppy formats resulting in 180KB/360KB for single/double sided drives, I/O redirection and piping, and background printing. Many new commands were added as well. PC DOS 2.0 used 24KB of RAM.

In achieving its objectives Microsoft tripled the size of DOS, and added 17 new commands. The major feature of DOS 2.0 was support for the use of a hard disk and a hierarchical file structure in order to support the new IBM PC-XT, which included a 10MB hard disk as a standard feature.

DOS 2.0 also increased the storage capacity of single-sided floppies from 160KB to 180KB, and double-sided floppies from 320KB to 360KB. This was achieved by increasing the number of sectors on each track of the disk from 8 sectors to 9. DOS 2.0 could also read and write any of the older formats, ensuring backward compatibility.

Another major feature of DOS 2.0 was support for device drivers. This meant that there was a provision for new software routines that supported various hardware and software to be installed into DOS directly. I like to think of this as software "slots" for adding components to DOS, without patching DOS directly.

IBM introduced PC DOS 2.1 on November 1, 1983 (along with the IBM PCjr). It added no new commands or functions, but fixed bugs and altered timing parameters for the half-height floppy drives used in the PCjr and IBM Portable PC. PC DOS 2.1 used 24KB of RAM, same as the previous version. For the most part, DOS 2.1 was considered a maintenance release from 2.0, with no new functionality added.

DOS 3.x

PC DOS 3.0 and 3.1 were both introduced on August 14, 1984 (along with the 286 processor–based IBM PC AT). Although both were introduced at the same time, only version 3.0 was available immediately while version 3.1 became available a few months later, in October 1984.

DOS 3.0 was basically an unfinished version of 3.1, designed to get the necessary support in place for the PC AT. DOS 3.0 added support for a virtual disk (VDISK) using memory greater than 1MB, and added FAT16 support for hard drives supporting a single partition of up to 32MiB (33.55 MB). DOS 2.x and earlier only supported FAT12, even on hard disks. Support was also added for high-density 1.2MB 5.25-inch floppy drives using 15 sectors per track. PC DOS 3.0 used 36KB of RAM.

PC DOS 3.1 was introduced on August 14, 1984 (same as 3.0), but wasn't made available to the public until October 1984. Because 3.0 was really an unfinished 3.1, IBM offered the first DOS upgrade (from 3.0 to 3.1) for $30. International keyboard support was added to 3.1, but the main additions were network printer and file redirection as well as file sharing support. This was designed to support the new IBM PC Network hardware and software that was also released at the same time. PC DOS 3.1 used 36KB of RAM.

PC DOS 3.2 was released on March 18, 1986 (along with the Token Ring Network interconnect program). DOS 3.2 supported the Token Ring Network, and added support for 3.5-inch double-density (720KB) floppy drives. The first 3.5-inch drives for PCs were coming in the PC Convertible, also the first IBM laptop computer (which was introduced less than a month later on April 2, 1986). DOS 3.2 also added the XCOPY and REPLACE commands. PC DOS 3.2 was the first DOS available on both 3.5-inch and 5.25-inch diskettes, and used 44KB of RAM.

After the release of PC DOS 3.2, Microsoft made the first non-specific OEM (generic) packaged version of MS-DOS available. The packaged version of MS-DOS 3.2 was designed for smaller system builders who did not have the ability to produce a finished product from the raw code supplied with the large-scale OEM licenses. As such, the OEM-packaged MS-DOS 3.2 was essentially the first release of MS-DOS available in Microsoft packaging from MS directly. This was also the beginning of Microsoft's OEM program for small system builders, and OEM versions of its software were only sold to OEMs, who then could only resell the software with a system.

Both IBM and Microsoft issued a minor release update to DOS 3.2 called 3.21. This new version was available free of charge if you had 3.2, and corrected problems with BASIC and the keyboard of the IBM Convertible PC, as well as some other minor bugs.

PC DOS 3.3 was released on April 2, 1987, along with IBM's line of PS/2 systems, more than a year after DOS 3.2. DOS 3.3 introduced the extended partition, which could internally support up to 23 sub-partitions (logical drives) of up to 32MiB (33.55MB) each. Combined with the primary partition on a disk, this allowed for a total of 24 partitions of up to 32MiB each, which would be seen by the operating system as logical drives C through Z. Support was also added for 1.44MB high-density 3.5-inch floppy drives.

DOS 3.3 also added support for nested batch file commands (using the new CALL command), and the DATE and TIME commands would finally update the CMOS RTC chip directly. Foreign language support was enhanced with support for code pages (alternate international character sets), and the FASTOPEN and APPEND commands were added as well. 128KB of RAM was advertised as the minimum memory required for DOS 3.3.

DOS 4.x

To take full advantage of FAT16 and allow for much larger drives and partition sizes, Microsoft collaborated with Compaq, and Compaq introduced Compaq DOS 3.31 in November 1987. Compaq DOS 3.31 was the first DOS to use 32-bit sector addressing internally and in the BPB (BIOS Parameter Block), which when combined with the 16-bit File Allocation Table (FAT16) file system, allowed for a single partition to be supported up to 2GiB in size.

The rest of the PC world followed suit on July 19, 1988, when IBM and Microsoft released PC/MS-DOS 4.0. The use of 32-bit sector addressing meant that FAT16 could now handle partition sizes up to 2GiB (2.15GB) using 64 sectors per cluster. DOS 4.0 also added support for Lotus,

Intel, Microsoft (LIM) Expanded Memory Support (EMS), as well as an optional graphical user interface shell. The MEM command was added. 256KB of RAM was advertised as the minimum memory required for DOS 4.0.

After the initial 4.0 release, IBM followed up with six sets of CSDs (Corrective Service Diskettes), each of them reporting 4.01 as the version. MS followed the IBM CSDs with some (but not all) of the 4.01 corrections and enhancements in the following MS-DOS 4.01 release.

DOS 5.x

After switching initial DOS development back to Microsoft, MS-DOS 5.0 was introduced by Microsoft on June 6, 1991, and PC DOS 5.0 was introduced by IBM on June 11, 1991.

MS-DOS 5.0 was a significant release in that for the first time Microsoft was feeling some competitive heat from Digital Research Corporation, which sold an alternative operating system called DR-DOS. Microsoft was compelled to add several additional useful features to MS-DOS 5.0, including a full-screen editor, significantly improved memory management, and an improved BASIC language interpreter.

By this point, too, it could be assumed that most PCs had an Intel 80286 or better processor, so DOS could take advantage of this processor's capability to "map" extended memory into unused parts of the upper 384KB address range visible to DOS. These memory segments were called *upper memory blocks*. In addition, programmers had by now figured out how to use a programming trick to gain access to the first 64KB of extended memory (called the *high memory block*) from real mode without using the mapping features. These two techniques let MS-DOS locate parts of itself, device drivers, and "terminate and stay resident" accessory programs outside the lower 640KB address range, leaving more of the precious lower 640KB memory range available to application programs. MS-DOS 5.0 thus introduced the DOS=HIGH,UMB configuration option and the loadhigh command.

Many commands were added, including HELP (online help), DOSKEY, SMARTDRV (disk cache), EDIT (full-screen editor), EXPAND (file extractor), FC (file compare), LOADHIGH/DEVICEHIGH (load resident programs or drivers into UMBs—Upper Memory Blocks), MIRROR (backup FAT and directory structures for later UNDELETE or UNFORMAT), QBASIC (a version of BASIC that works on all IBM and IBM-compatible hardware, without the requirement of an IBM ROM as with BASICA), RAMDRIVE (replaces VDISK), SETVER (report different DOS versions to "fool" older programs that check versions before running), UNDELETE (undelete files), and UNFORMAT (unformat disks/partitions). A full-screen editor called EDIT was added to DOS 5.0 in addition to the EDLIN line editor.

DOS 5.0 also added support for 2.88MB ED 3.5-inch floppies, and the FORMAT command used the media sense capability present in most 3.5-inch drives to automatically format 720KB, 1.44MB, or 2.88MB media to the correct capacity. 512KB of RAM was listed as the minimum memory requirement for DOS 5.0.

On November 11, 1991, Microsoft released DOS 5.0a to address data-corrupting bugs in the original DOS 5 CHKDSK and UNDELETE commands. IBM on the other hand was much more diligent in finding and reporting bugs, and released five sets of CSDs and two sets of IFDs (Interim Fix

Diskettes) between July 1991 and September 1992, fixing not only the CHKDSK and UNDELETE problems, but more than 50 other individual problems in DOS 5.

PC DOS 5.00.1 was introduced on April 28, 1992, and is the first IBM version specifically supported on non-IBM hardware (although previous versions ran on all PC-compatible systems). One change was that QBASIC was now included, which no longer depended on the ROM BASIC as with previous DOS versions.

Version 5.00.1 also added refreshed code that included the latest CSD fixes, as well as a new SETUP module that installed over all IBM and IBM-compatible PC/MS-DOS Versions 2.1 and higher, and even across a LAN.

PC DOS 5.02 was introduced on October 20, 1992. It incorporated all the previous DOS 5 fixes, as well as added APM (Advanced Power Management) support for laptops via the new POWER command. Also added were the INTERLNK and INTERSVR commands supporting file transfer between systems over a parallel or serial cable. Version 5.02 also added support for electrically ejectable/lockable drives and ISO screen fonts. IBM also released various retail bundles with 386Max & Stacker using the 5.00.1 package.

MS-DOS 6.x

Microsoft introduced MS-DOS 6.0 (codename Astro) on March 30, 1993. Again, in response to competitive pressure, Microsoft copied disk data compression technology created by Stac Corporation as the new DoubleSpace feature.

How DoubleSpace Worked

Essentially, the physical hard drive was given a high drive letter; G, for example. The compression driver created a "virtual" C: drive, and intercepted all activity directed at drive C. Data that applications wrote to files on drive C was compressed, and the compressed files were stored on the actual drive G. Likewise, when an application program attempted to read from drive C, the compression software would open the actual file on the physical drive G, uncompress the data as needed, and give it to the application program.

Microsoft introduced MS-DOS 6.2 (codenamed Elroy) in November 1993. It included bug fixes to the DoubleSpace (Stacker) disk compression as well as upgrades to the SCANDISK, DISKCOPY, and Smartdrive (disk cache) programs.

Later it was ruled that Microsoft illegally used the Stac Electronics Stacker disk compression, which it was forced to remove in a 6.21 release. Finally in 1994 Microsoft released MS-DOS 6.22, with disk compression added back in, but using different (noninfringing code) and renamed as DriveSpace. 6.22 was the last standalone version of MS-DOS released by Microsoft.

PC DOS 6.x

IBM introduced PC DOS 6.1 on June 19, 1993 as its version of MS-DOS 6.0, but with some improvements. IBM skipped the 6.0 release number to avoid confusion with Microsoft's 6.0 release, and to indicate to the public that IBM's version included more.

PC DOS version 6.1 included a library of integrated DOS utilities from other software vendors and IBM Research. The utilities included the following:

- Disk compression (licensed from Stac Electronics)
- Antivirus
- Full-screen backup
- New full-screen editor (called "E")
- Program scheduler

DOS 6.1 also included support for pen-based systems as well as PCMCIA (PC Card) slots in laptop systems, plus an automatic memory configuration program called RAMBoost.

IBM then released PC DOS 6.3 on April 27, 1994, and included the MSCDEX program for CD-ROM support, plus many minor updates to the various utility programs.

IBM continued to improve DOS, and released PC DOS 7.0. This was followed by PC DOS 2000, which was really 7.0 with updates added to fix certain Y2K issues. PC DOS 2000 was the last standalone version of DOS ever released, and can still be purchased from IBM today.

Windows 9x/Me DOS

Windows 95, 98, and Me all include subsets of MS-DOS as their base, and those versions offer enhancements over the standalone releases from both Microsoft and IBM.

The DOS included with Windows 95 is internally coded as MS-DOS 7.0, and includes support for long filenames. MS-DOS 7.1 was included with Windows 95B (OEM Service Release 2), Windows 98, and Windows 98SE (Second Edition), which added support for FAT32. Windows Me included MS-DOS 8.0, which had some bug fixes for supporting larger drives.

MS-DOS Alternatives

We mentioned earlier that IBM and several other PC manufacturers all sold customized versions of Microsoft's MS-DOS, and that there was a competitor called DR-DOS.

Gary Kildall, whom we left several pages ago spurning IBM's offer to create the operating system for the PC, went on to finish his 16-bit operating system, called CP/M-86. Kildall sued IBM and Microsoft for copying CP/M, and eventually reached a settlement whereby IBM agreed to offer CP/M-86 in addition to PC-DOS. And IBM did offer CP/M-86, for $240 a copy, versus $40 for PC-DOS. It didn't sell well.

By 1987, Kildall had abandoned the idea of promoting CP/M in the 16-bit world. Killdall's company Digital Research eventually produced a MS-DOS clone called DR-DOS, which never, as they say, made the big bucks, but did force Microsoft to significantly lower its prices and make enhancements to MS-DOS that otherwise might never have been made. Anyone who's used `edit` to edit a text file has Digital Research to thank. Digital Research also produced GEM, a graphical operating system that predated and competed with Windows—more on that shortly. DR-DOS ultimately did not survive, although various legal battles continued. In 2000, Microsoft paid

Digital Research's successor company a reputed $150–$200 million to settle suits over the licensing and marketing practices that drove DR-DOS under.

Besides DR-DOS, other operating systems came and went, or came and stayed, including these more popular ones:

- **OS/2**—IBM and Microsoft initially collaborated to create OS/2, a 32-bit protected-mode advanced operating system that was intended to eventually replace DOS. Later versions sported a user interface that served as the inspiration for Windows 95. It was incredibly reliable and seemed to be the future of PC operating systems, but in 1991 Microsoft and IBM parted ways. Microsoft went on to develop Windows NT, which begat Windows 2000 and XP (more on that in the next section). IBM doggedly tried keep OS/2 alive and didn't give up until mid-2005. It eventually found a niche as a network server operating system and as a host for industrial control systems. You may never have seen a computer running it, but you've probably been in buildings whose air conditioning systems were controlled by it. It's sad really—had the Microsoft/IBM partnership survived, we'd all be using OS/2 today, and we would probably have had 32-bit Windows reliability 10 years earlier.

- **UNIX**—Many versions of the UNIX operating system were developed for the PC architecture. UNIX was originally created as a "programmer's workbench" by computer scientists at AT&T's Bell Laboratories, and was given away free to universities during the 1970s and 1980s. The result was a generation of programmers who were trained in this elegant but somewhat cryptic environment. PC flavors of UNIX include AT&T licensees Xenix and SCO UNIX, and clones XINU, NetBSD, FreeBSD, Linux, and several others.

- **BeOS**—The BeOS was initially released in 1995 by Be Inc. to run on the BeBox computer, which featured dual PowerPC processors. Later versions were released to run on PowerPC-based Apple Mac systems as well as Power Computing Mac clones. In 1998 the BeOS was released in an x86 version that ran on PCs. The last official release was in 2000, and Be Inc. was acquired by Palm in 2001. Since then, a small number of enthusiasts have continued to develop, enhance, and run the BeOS.

- **Pick**—Pick was a database system that in some cases was packaged as a standalone operating system. It was one of the earliest multiuser systems for the PC architecture.

Other operating systems were developed, but have since faded to total obscurity.

The Evolution of Microsoft Windows

Well before Windows first appeared, the graphical user interface (GUI) revolution began in California's Silicon Valley. In 1968, computer pioneer Douglas Engelbart demonstrated a computer system created at Stanford Research Institute that incorporated a mouse, video display, hypertext links, word processing tools, and online help—all things that we'd insist upon on any computer today, but which were radical innovations at the time. For videos of the original 1968 demonstration, see (http://sloan.stanford.edu/MouseSite/1968Demo.html). Engelbert's spectacular lecture established—and delivered—the vision of the computer as a constant companion, "always available, and immediately responsive."

Researchers at Xerox Corporation's nearby Palo Alto Research Center (Xerox PARC) incorporated these concepts to create the MAXC computer in 1972, which included a high-speed bitmapped graphical display, a mouse, overlapping windows, and cut and paste capability. In 1973, Xerox created the more refined Alto, adding a laser printer and an early version of the Ethernet network (also PARC inventions). The Alto had a page-sized display, pull-down menus, icons, disk storage, WYSIWYG editing, email, typeset-quality printing, and network file sharing. Virtually all the technical elements of today's desktop computing paradigm were present.

If the Alto was such a magnificent invention, why have most people never heard of it? The reasons are threefold. First, Xerox corporate management didn't foresee that computers would eventually become as common as indoor plumbing, and decided that a computer meant for use by just one person was unmarketable. Second, the necessary processing and display hardware required for such a computer was *very* expensive at that time, so the Alto was far too expensive to become a viable mass-market product*. And finally, software was not yet considered patentable, so Xerox did not attempt to protect the Alto concept from being copied by others. So, the Alto was used internally at PARC, but never made it out the front door.

Although the Alto was never a commercial success, it profoundly influenced computer history. Most importantly, it caught the attention of Steve Jobs of Apple Computer. Jobs saw the Alto in 1979, and directed his staff to incorporate its concepts in the Lisa and Macintosh computers that were already under development. The result was the Apple Lisa, released in 1983 to no great fanfare, and the follow-on Apple Macintosh in 1984, which was a sensation.

The impact and utility of the graphical interface wasn't lost on developers in the PC world. Knowing that Apple was working on the Macintosh, Microsoft and its primary operating systems competitor Digital Research both began projects to develop a graphical operating system for the PC. Digital Research's GEM interface came to market first, in 1983. With GEM on the market, and a VisiCorp competitor named VisiOn and the Apple Macintosh soon to appear, Microsoft responded with a premature demonstration of Windows 1.0 at the Comdex computer industry trade show in November, 1983. This became infamous as the "smoke and mirrors demo," because Windows 1.0 did not actually run at the time; the demo was rigged. But it had its intended effect, and both developers and customers waited for Microsoft's GUI project rather than jumping on the GEM or VisiOn bandwagons. They waited, and waited, until November 1985, when Windows 1.0 was finally released.

While GEM and its early applications were far superior in look, feel, and performance to Windows 1.0 and 2.0 and the early Windows applications, market forces (and business practices that have kept Microsoft in hot water to this day) eventually pushed GEM into obscurity.

16-Bit Windows

Although its initial release was long delayed and underwhelming, Windows would eventually become the world's most popular operating system. Let's take a look how Windows has evolved since it was released in 1985.

In 1981, Xerox finally did release a commercial version of the Alto called the Star, but at nearly $17,000, its cost was three to four times that of a PC or CP/M-based computer. The Star sold only about 30,000 units, mostly in the technical documentation publishing market, where its graphical capabilities were unmatched by any other technology available at the time.

Windows 1.0

Development of a graphical user interface for the IBM PC began in 1981. The goals were multitasking ability, a graphical user interface, and device-independent screen and printer graphics; that is, application programs would not be required to know the details of how graphics were to be transmitted to each and every supported model of printer and display adapter. The original concept placed the menus at the bottom of the screen, but this was abandoned for drop-down menus and dialog boxes as seen on Xerox Alto and Macintosh.

Announced in 1983, Windows version 1.0 (the actual released version was 1.01) was not actually released until November 1985, and even then it did not realize its intended potential. In version 1.0, windows could not be positioned so that they overlapped, but could only be placed side-by-side. Its release really served just as a placeholder, to affirm to the marketplace that Microsoft did intend to release a graphical environment along the likes of Macintosh, GEM, and VisiOn.

While limited in performance and appearance, version 1.0 did include Windows Write and Windows Paint, Notepad, and smaller applications such as Clock, Calculator, Reversi (a game), CardFile, and Terminal (a serial data communications program). It required 256KB of memory, and could run from two double-sided double-density (360KB) floppy disks, or a hard disk. A program called the MS-DOS Executive served as a sort of file manager, and served as the program's shell. It ran entirely in real mode, and could not address memory past the 640KB limit imposed by the initial C architecture. Minor versions 1.03 and 1.04 were released between August 1986 and April 1987 with additional support for national languages, MS-DOS 3.2, more fonts and printers, and additional PC models.

Windows 2.0

Windows 2.0 was released in November 1987, and addressed many of the shortcomings of version 1.0. This release added icons to the interface metaphor, and supported overlapped windows. Version 2.0 required at least 512KB of memory, but could still be run from floppy disks. Version 2.1, released later, was the first to require a hard disk. Version 2.0 also introduced the Smartdrive disk cache and Dynamic Data Exchange (DDE) support, which allowed a level of automatic interaction between applications.

All program code still ran in "real mode," with a limit of 640KB of RAM directly addressable. However, on computers with enhanced memory, multiple applications whose total memory requirements exceeded 640KB could still be run. As Windows switched between applications it swapped program code and data modules between the lower 640KB and enhanced memory. When memory usage was pushed to the limit, program code modules were discarded from memory and reloaded from the hard disk when needed again. This caused a massive slowdown and the familiar sound of disk "thrashing," but it did work.

Windows 2.1, released in May 1988, permitted the use of mice from other manufacturers, and was the first version to require the use of a hard disk. A new version of the `himem.sys` driver learned the trick of using the first 64KB of extended memory for system code, freeing up memory for applications.

As with Digital Research's GEM windowing system, Windows was available as a "runtime-only" version that software vendors could bundle with application software. Windows version 2.11 was the last to be made available in this bundled format.

Windows 386

Windows 386 was released in 1987 as a specialized version of Windows 2 that required the use of an Intel 80386 processor. The 386 provided hardware support for virtual memory paging, more total system memory, and used the CPU's protected mode to gain direct access to extended memory. The processor also provided a "virtual 86" CPU mode that let Windows run several DOS applications at once, with preemptive multitasking between DOS applications and Windows. Preemptive multitasking gave each DOS application time to run, in round-robin fashion. The memory management and preemptive-multitasking of DOS applications that appeared in Windows 386 were carried forward into the "386 enhanced mode" of Windows 3.0.

Windows 3.0

Windows version 3.0 was a significant rewrite of Windows, and was released in May 1990. At this time there was a still a significant installed base of 80286-based computers, but 80386 and 80486 processors were found in virtually all newer computers, and it was time for Windows to start to take advantage of these processors' significant memory access improvements.

The 8088 processor used in the original IBM PC and its clones was capable of addressing at most 1MB of memory, due to the processor's design. Programs specified memory locations using two components: a 16-bit address value, and a 16-bit segment register. 16-bit values alone can specify at most 65,536 distinct addresses, but the segment register increased this many fold. When a program makes reference to a memory location, the processor automatically takes the value from a segment register, multiplies it by 10 (in hexadecimal, which is 16 in decimal), and adds the 16-bit address value to get a physical memory address.

Figure 1.1 shows an example. When fetching program instructions in real mode, the CPU uses the address stored in the Program Counter (PC) register, along with the value in the Code Segment (CS) register.

In this example, the programmer has loaded the CS register with 3000h (hexadecimal). With the PC register holding address 1447h, the processor will retrieve the next instruction from physical address 31447h. This scheme allows the processor to access at most 1MB of memory.

Note

Using a large segment value and a large address value, combined with the control over the A20 (21st address line) designed into the original IBM AT, the 1MB memory access limit could be raised by 64KB. This is what the **HIMEM.SYS** driver did for DOS and Windows. Today, it seems odd that programmers went to such trouble to gain access to just 64KB of memory, but it really did matter back then.

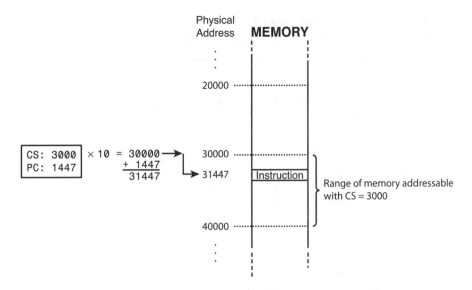

Figure 1.1 Instruction fetching in real mode.

Intel 80286 and later processors could use a more flexible memory access scheme called *protected mode*. In protected mode, the value of segment register was not used directly, but was instead used to select an entry from a table that contained 24-bit (80286 processors) or 32-bit (80386 or better) base address values, as shown in Figure 1.2. With the capability to add larger segment values, the protected mode scheme allows programs running on 32-bit processors access up to 4GB of physical memory.

Because 16-bit versions of Windows rely upon DOS and the computer's BIOS code to perform input/output operations, and DOS and the BIOS are real-mode programs, Windows needs to be able to rapidly switch the processor back and forth between protected and real mode. The 80286 could not be easily returned to real mode from protected mode. This is why Windows 1 and 2 were forced to rely solely on real mode.

The 80386 and later processors, however, could instantly be switched back and forth between real and protected mode, so with the advent of these processors, Windows 3.0 was completely redesigned to take advantage of protected mode's vastly larger potential memory space.

For compatibility with older computers, Windows 3.0 could be run in any of three modes:

- Real mode, with access to at most 1MB of memory.
- Standard mode, which put the CPU into protected mode, and increased the maximum directly usable memory to 16MB.
- 386 enhanced mode, which let the CPU use the 386 processor's hardware support for running multiple DOS programs at once. This mode had been developed and tested in Windows 386. The DOS multitasking came at a slight decrease in performance, so both standard and 386 enhanced modes were made available as options.

Real mode (DOS, Windows 1-2)

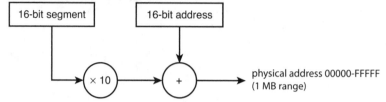

16-bit Protected mode (Windows 3)

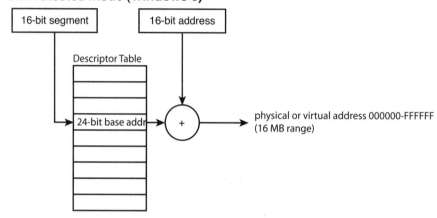

32-bit Protected mode (Windows 9x, NT)

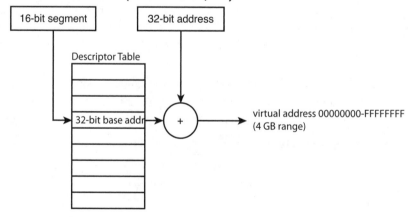

Figure 1.2   Intel CPU modes and memory access.

Windows 3.0 required 640KB of main memory plus at least 256KB of extended memory, and required MS-DOS 3.1 or better.

The Windows user interface was also significantly revamped. The MS-DOS Executive was replaced with Program Manager, which used icons to represent program groups, and File Manager, which was a graphical file system browser comparable to today's Windows Explorer. VGA graphics adapters were much more common by this point, and Windows graphical code was enhanced to support the use of more than the 16 primitive colors available in Windows 1 and 2. This made it possible for Windows to display photographic images for the first time.

While Windows 3.0's access to more memory was a huge improvement over Windows 1 and 2, protected mode introduced a new and soon to become annoying occurrence: the General Protection Fault. In real mode, buggy programs (or hardware drivers, or Windows components) that read from or wrote to incorrect memory addresses would often proceed as if nothing had happened, and only later might the system freeze up due to overwritten program code. Protected mode gave Windows the capability to detect when a program tried to access memory it wasn't supposed to (hence the word *protected*). Because there was nothing that Windows could really do to remedy the situation, it would just display the protection fault warning and terminate the program.

Unfortunately, when Windows 3.0 was first released, many application programs and drivers contained bugs that had never before been detected. Many were benign, but the protection mechanism couldn't know that. And, with much of Windows freshly rewritten, Windows itself contained countless bugs, too. Windows 3.0 quickly gained a reputation as being a phenomenally improved, but barely usable, operating system.

Windows 3.1

Microsoft released Windows 3.1 in April 1992, and for the first time, really got 16-bit Windows right. Most of the bugs were fixed, and developers had gotten their applications cleaned up. Even the General Protection Fault mechanism itself was improved, and was less often encountered. Some technical advances were made: Real mode support was dropped (for Windows itself; DOS applications were run in real or virtual 86 mode). TrueType scalable font support was added, as were extensions for multimedia support. Object Linking and Embedding (OLE) technology was released, which made it possible for applications to cooperate without knowing details about each other's internal operations. Windows 3.1 also included client-side networking support as a standard feature.

By this time, the market was way past ready for a reliable multitasking operating system, and Windows 3.1 sold one million copies in two months. Development of character-mode DOS applications virtually ceased, with WordPerfect Corporation being a notably—and fatally—late exception. The software industry focused almost entirely on Windows.

Windows for Workgroups

Windows for Workgroups (WFWG) was a product line based on Windows 3.1 that included file- and printer-sharing support built in at a small additional cost. This made it possible to build peer-to-peer networks with no additional software, and directly targeted Novell's NetWare and Artisoft's LanTastic products, which up until this point had the small office network market to themselves.

WFWG version 3.1 (based on Windows 3.1) was released in October 1992, and version 3.11 in November 1993.

Windows 3.11

Windows 3.11 was a bug-fix version, distributed as a free upgrade and installed on new computers, released in December 1993. This was the last issue in the 16-bit Windows product line.

For more details on each of the 16-bit Windows versions, see (http://support.microsoft.com/kb/32905).

The Windows 9x Family

By the mid-1990s, processor power had increased and memory prices had decreased dramatically since Windows' original release. The Internet had also sprung onto the world stage, from an academic tool to an instrument of global communication and commerce. (Windows 3.1 did not even include support for the TCP/IP network protocol used on the Internet—you had to purchase it from a third-party vendor or upgrade to 3.11.) Users' expectations likewise had grown with computers' capabilities, and desktop publishing, graphics editing, and multimedia applications had reached the point that 16-bit protected mode's 16MB memory was an obstacle.

The 32-bit Windows NT product line had become successful in the business market (more on this shortly), but it was not yet considered a viable product for the consumer market. The primary reason for this is that Windows NT did not include DOS, and provided no means for user programs to run in real mode. This meant that a huge number of games, multimedia programs, and other consumer and business applications would not run correctly under NT. It would be some time before those products faded away, so Microsoft created a new 32-bit Windows version based on DOS, rather than on the NT kernel. This would let developers write Windows programs that took advantage of the NT 32-bit Windows programming model, while DOS was still underneath to support so-called legacy applications.

Windows 95

Windows 95 was released in August 1995, as a consumer version of 32-bit Windows, meant to bring 32-bit architecture to the consumer market and hold its place while the Windows NT product line ripened to consumer readiness. Windows 95 was wildly successful, and its user interface (look and feel) is still available in Windows XP and Vista as the "Windows Classic" style today.

Windows 95 used Windows NT's 32-bit programming model, but most of the code was freshly written, not based on NT. Windows 95 uses the 32-bit protected mode made available by Intel 80386 and later processors, illustrated in Figure 1.2. Physically, the segment registers are still present and are still used by Windows itself, but with 32-bit addresses used throughout, application programs can access a 4GB memory address range without having to change the segment registers, and within a given program they can be ignored—they can use what is termed a "flat memory space." And because Windows 95 and its successors presume an Intel 80386 or later microprocessor, programs could take full advantage of several more efficient instructions that had been added to the Intel platform's instruction set since the original 8086 was released. It also required 4MB of memory as a minimum.

Note

Just because 32-bit software can *address* 4GB, doesn't mean you can actually use that much RAM in your system. If you were a PC user in the '80s or early '90s, you learned that in a system running a 16-bit OS, the hardware normally reserved the top 384KiB for video RAM, system ROM, and so on, leaving only 640KiB of available space for user RAM. Likewise, when running a 32-bit OS, the hardware normally reserves about 1GB, leaving only about 3GB remaining for user RAM. Think of it as the 32-bit version of the infamous "640K barrier."

You can break the 3GB barrier by running 64-bit Windows. Current 64-bit processors have an addressable memory limit of 1TB, while current 64-bit Windows x64 editions limit the usable RAM to 128GB. Unfortunately there are several driver and application compatibility issues to consider when switching to a 64-bit OS.

Perhaps the biggest improvement was the introduction of long filename support. The 8.3 filename structure (eight character filenames with a three character extension), which originally derived from the 1970s TOPS-10 operating system and used by CP/M and then MS-DOS, was finally left behind, and files could be named something like "My research notes on the history of DOS and Windows.doc" rather than DOSWHIST.DOC.

Windows 95 also included a significantly improved user interface. The Start button and taskbar appeared, and pop-up context menus (right-click menus) were introduced as a standard feature. DOS applications could be run inside of a window on the desktop and no longer needed to take over the entire screen as they did with Windows 3.1. Built-in networking support included TCP/IP connectivity, dial-up networking, and Internet Explorer and the entire operating system exhibited faster performance, due to the use of 32-bit drivers throughout.

Additional significant improvements included the following:

- 16-bit (Windows 3.1) applications could still be used, thanks to a "Windows-on-Windows" system that let the older application believe that it was running under the old operating system.

- Preemptive multitasking was implemented throughout, so that all Windows applications remained at least somewhat responsive even if one application attempted to use all available processing time.

- Windows 95 had the capability to terminate runaway applications without having to restart Windows to recover lost resources (limited memory space used by Windows to track a program's disk and graphics requirements).

- Support for Plug and Play meant that Windows could automatically recognize newly added hardware devices and either automatically install the appropriate drivers, or walk the user through the process of locating drivers, through the Add Hardware Wizard.

- The Windows Registry, a single database, was used to store system and application configuration information, rather than multiple text (.ini) files.

- Per-user settings. As an option, Windows 95 could be configured with separate logon names, passwords, desktops, and document folders for more than one user.

Windows 95 OSR2

In October 1996, Microsoft released an updated version of Windows 95 called OEM Service Release 2, or OSR2. The OEM part stands for Original Equipment Manufacturer, and indeed, OSR2 was made available only to system builders and computer manufacturers for sale with a new computer—it wasn't made available as an upgrade, although some parts could be downloaded as updates or hotfixes.

OSR2 included several significant improvements:

- Support for the FAT32 file system, which permits the use of partitions up to 2TB in size, and can break large disks into clusters of smaller size than FAT16 for more efficient use of space.

- Enhanced DriveSpace support for compression on volumes up to 2GB in size.

- Supported Zip drives, removable disk drives, "floptical" media, and detection of CD-ROM disc insertion and removal.

- Included Internet Explorer 3, Internet Mail and News reader, NetMeeting, and Personal Web Server. (Internet Explorer 4 was released as a later, separate update.)

- Support for the Intel MMX multimedia processor extensions.

- Support for Novell NetWare 4.0 networking software.

- Support for newer PCMCIA (PC Card) peripherals.

There was also a host of bug fixes in the release as well.

Subsequent OSR releases 2.1 in August 1997 and 2.5 in November 1997 added support for USB peripherals. USB support was not available as a download or update to Windows 95 or Windows 95 OSR2.

Windows 98

Windows 98 was released in June 1998. Windows 98 was a substantially improved version of the Win9x family, with the following major enhancements:

- Incorporated all the enhancements and fixes made to Windows 95 since its original release, including the FAT32 file system and 32-bit PC Card support.

- Improved USB support gave the ability to use USB keyboards and mice without specific drivers, as well as improved support for video devices and scanners. FireWire (IEEE 1394) support was added as well.

- Advanced Configuration and Power Interface (ACPI) support provided software control over system startup, shutdown, pause and suspend, and power consumption.

- Multiple monitor support gave users with more than one graphics adapter (or an adapter designed for multiple monitors) the ability to extend the Windows desktop across several monitors.

- Windows Update provided a web-based utility for downloading important security and bug fixes.

- Utilities included a disk defragmenter, Task Scheduler, Internet Explorer 4, and improved accessibility tools.

- Improved dial-up networking support included logon scripting, Remote Access Server (dial-in) support, and PPTP Virtual Private Networking.

- The Win32 Driver Model (WDM) made it easier for manufacturers to develop 32-bit device drivers for Windows 98 and subsequent versions.

- Windows Scripting Host provided a means of writing powerful application automation and data processing scripts in VBScript, JavaScript, and other languages.

In addition, subtle user-interface changes like the ability to right-click and drag a shortcut to the QuickLaunch bar or the Start menu made life easier for power users.

Windows 98 Second Edition

Windows 98 Second Edition was released in May 1999 on new computers, and was available as an upgrade as well. It included the following significant improvements:

- Hardware support included DVD-ROMs.

- Improved USB support.

- Internet Connection Sharing (ICS) permitted a Windows 98 SE computer to share a single dial-up or broadband connection with other computers over a network.

- Internet Explorer 5.0 was included.

- Windows Media Player was provided to play MP3 music files as well as several other audio and video formats.

- DirectX 6.1 was included to provide driver support for high-performance games and graphics adapters.

Y2K fixes were included as well.

Windows Millennium Edition

The end of the road for the Windows 9x product line was Windows Me, released in September 2000 to a highly unreceptive community and an enormous amount of criticism. Part of the problem was that Microsoft had promised that a true 32-bit operating system would succeed Windows 98, but a consumer-friendly (that is, game-friendly) version of Windows 2000 could not be created in time, and Windows XP was far off in the future. We can only surmise that Windows Me was produced as way to fish for income from upgrade sales, without having a real product to use as bait.

The marketing campaign stated Windows Me wasn't based on MS-DOS. In reality Windows Me started up with the assistance of MS-DOS just as its predecessors had. It was really just Windows 98 with the Exit to MS-DOS option removed from the Start menu and better-looking icons. The sys command was also deleted, so that bootable MS-DOS floppy disks could not easily be created.

Despite the elimination of easy access to DOS, Windows Me did include some improvements over 98SE:

- The Home Networking Wizard was added to simplify the task of joining several computers into a small local area network.

- Internet Explorer 5.5 was included.

- A code-signing system brought noncertified drivers to the user's attention during installation, to encourage the use of Microsoft-tested drivers, and hopefully minimize the number of problems caused by poor drivers.

- Windows Movie Maker encouraged home editing of digital video (although, at the time, disk space was still too expensive and processor power too limited for this to be practical).

- System Restore let Windows automatically back up system files before significant configuration changes, so that the changes could be rolled back if problems ensued.

- The Scanner and Camera Wizard greatly simplified the task of copying digital pictures from cameras to the hard disk.

The Windows 9x product line ended with Windows Me. Although it was visually slick, it never reached a level of reliability that made it truly acceptable to the business world. You just can't do business with a computer that crashes a couple of times a day (although some tried). Many users who tried Me immediately downgraded to Windows 98SE. Fortunately Windows XP was just around the corner. To get to that story we have to back up to the origin of Windows NT.

The Windows NT Family

The Windows NT family includes everything from the original release of Windows NT 3.1 to Windows Vista, and has become by far the most popular computer operating system in the world. This section details all the various releases in the NT family, which are summarized in Table 1.1.

Table 1.1   Windows NT Family Versions

Name	Codename	NT Version	RTM Build	Major Editions	Date Released
Windows NT 3.1	OS/2 3.0	3.1	528	Workstation Advanced Server	July 27, 1993
Windows NT 3.5	Daytona	3.5	807	Workstation Server	Sept. 21, 1994
Windows NT 3.51	Daytona update	3.51	1057	Workstation Server	May 30, 1995
Windows NT 4.0	Cairo	4.0	1381	Workstation Server	July 29, 1996
Windows 2000	NT 5.0	5.0	2195	Professional Server	Feb. 17, 2000
Windows XP	Whistler	5.1	2600	Home Professional Media Center	Oct. 25, 2001
Windows Server 2003	Whistler Server	5.2	3790	Web Standard Enterprise Datacenter	April 24, 2003
Windows Vista	Longhorn	6.0	6000	Home Basic Home Premium Business Enterprise Ultimate	Jan. 30, 2007

RTM = Release To Manufacturing
Build = Internal version number

The earliest beginnings of NT can be traced back to April 1987, when Microsoft and IBM announced a new operating system initiative called Microsoft Operating System 2, or OS/2. This was intended to be the platform to replace DOS, and would be a memory-protected, preemptively multitasked operating system, written from the ground up. Microsoft and IBM worked on the project jointly at first, but shortly after the release of Windows 3.0, the relationship soured, and eventually ended.

IBM and Microsoft each continued to work on OS/2 independently. IBM continued to develop OS/2 version 2 on its own. However Microsoft took the initial work on what was to have become OS/2 version 3, and began to move it in a different direction. In 1988, a team led by Dave Cutler, who was the architect of the RSX-11 and VAX/VMS operating systems for Digital Equipment Corporation, rechristened the project Windows NT, and redesigned and rewrote the kernel on which Windows NT was to be built.

Note

While Microsoft officially states that the name NT stands for New Technology, the actual origins of the name may be different. Mark Lucovsky (one of the original Windows NT developers) has stated publicly that the initial development of NT was targeted at the Intel i860 processor, which was codenamed the N10 (N-Ten) chip, and that the "NT" name for the OS was initially taken from the N-Ten chip. The i860 processor never became popular and was discontinued in the mid-90s, and while still in the early stages Windows NT development was shifted to the x86 processors used in PCs.

▶▶ To learn more about the kernel and internal structure of Windows, **see** "The Windows NT Kernel," **p. 58**.

Version 3.1

There never was an NT 1, 2, or even 3.0. The very first release of Windows NT in July 1993 was given version number 3.1 to match the contemporary 16-bit version of Windows also out at the time. (Magazines of that era claimed the number was also chosen to make it seem more likely to be reliable, as anyone knew that a ".0" release of anything was bound to be buggy.)

The user interface used in NT 3.1 was visually identical to that of the standard 16-bit Windows 3.1 but internally things were quite different. The entire system had been written from scratch in 32-bit code; no MS-DOS or Windows 3.1 code was used. From a programming standpoint, as mentioned earlier in the discussion of Window 9x, a "flat" 32-bit address space freed applications from having to manage 16-bit memory segment registers and their 64KB boundaries. The Windows API was modified to use 32-bit values in all communication between Windows and applications. This required Windows programmers to make some minor modification to their code in the process of developing applications for the new environment, but the effort required was surprisingly small. Device drivers were completely redesigned, and application programs were totally isolated; it was not possible for an errant application to mangle information stored in memory by other applications or by Windows itself. And, internally, Windows was made much more robust. For example, an errant application could be terminated, and all the memory, graphics, files, and other resources it had been using were automatically released and made available for reuse by other programs. These were, of course, not new features for operating systems in general, but it was huge improvement over MS-DOS and Windows 3.1.

Windows NT could still run MS-DOS applications, but MS-DOS itself was not present at all. A clever program called the Windows NT Virtual DOS Machine (NTVDM), using technology Microsoft licensed from Insignia Solutions Inc. that had originally been created to run MS-DOS applications on the Macintosh, provided DOS applications a "fake" or virtual DOS environment. NTVDM intercepted the DOS application's attempts to interact with DOS, the display adapter, and other hardware, and issued Windows NT requests to perform the desired functions. A similar (although less complicated) mechanism let Windows NT run 16-bit Windows applications without modification as well.

NT 3.1 was released July 1993 in two editions: NT Workstation, for use by an individual, and NT Advanced Server, which was basically the same operating system but with a different licensing scheme that allowed it to be used as a file server for larger organizations. All in all, the first version of Windows NT was 5 years in the making, from the point that David Cutler signed on to start the project, until the first public release.

Note

During Windows NT's development Microsoft had recognized that it would not be feasible to sell NT to the consumer market for some time yet…there were simply too many graphics-intensive games and strange, poorly written applications on the market, and NT's emulation system wasn't going to work very well with them. Thus, the Windows 95 project was initiated independently, to develop a version of 32-bit Windows that was still based on (and more compatible with) MS-DOS. It wasn't until Windows NT 5.1 (aka Windows XP) was released in 2001 that NT would finally be ready to go mainstream.

The intent was to build a highly reliable system by keeping the NT kernel small, and moving as much code as possible outside of the kernel so that bugs and crashes could be contained and not bring down the entire operating system. While this was a good concept, the initial version was unacceptably slow, and in subsequent versions, Microsoft moved more and more of the graphical interface program code into the kernel. There, it could run faster, but this brought increased risks that a bug in an errant driver or Windows module could take Windows down with it.

Windows NT 3.5

In September 1994, Microsoft released Windows NT 3.5, in both Workstation and Server editions. This version showed improved performance and reduced memory requirements, and was the first really usable version. Version 3.51 was released in June 1995 and included modifications to make it able to run applications designed for Windows 95.

Windows NT 3.5 servers could not only be licensed to provide shared file service to more than 10 simultaneous users, but could also act as domain controllers, offering authentication (password verification) services for corporate networks. This meant that user accounts could be managed in one place (the server) rather than on each individual workstation.

Windows NT 4.0 Workstation

By the time Windows NT 4.0 was released in July 1996, Microsoft had had time to not only significantly improve NT's performance and reliability, but also to incorporate the Windows 95 user interface, giving it a much more modern look and feel.

However, perhaps the most significant improvement was the addition of the NTFS file system. Up until this time, all versions of Windows used hard disks formatted with the FAT file system, which had been initially designed in the late '70s with only floppy disks in mind. FAT-formatted disks were unfortunately vulnerable to data loss due to crashes and power outages, and FAT provided no means of restricting access to files based on usernames, passwords, or other credentials.

Microsoft had worked with IBM to develop the High Performance File System (HPFS) for OS/2, and was able to apply lessons learned there to NTFS. The goals included

- **Reliability**—Protection of changes to directory entries and file sizes against loss due to crashes or power outages, by encapsulating them as "transactions."
- **Security**—Fine-grained control of who is allowed to create, read, modify, delete, or manage files and folders. An auditing system makes it possible to track who has succeeded or failed to make changes as well.
- **Capacity**—The capability to handle terabytes of disk capacity.
- **Efficiency**—Better use of disk space, smaller allocation units, and less I/O needed to read and modify disk structures.
- **Long filenames**—The capability to store filenames up to 255 characters.
- **Data spaces**—The capability to store parallel, separate sets of data for a given file. This is used, for example, to accommodate alternative filenames and extended directory information used by different operating systems served by an NT-based file server.

Windows NT 4.0 Workstation edition was meant as a highly reliable operating system for corporate PCs, while Windows NT 4.0 Server edition included additional networking services such as Windows Internet Naming Service (WINS), Dynamic Host Configuration Protocol (DHCP), Domain Name Service (DNS), Remote Access Service (RAS, a dial-up networking service), and others.

Windows 2000 Professional

Windows 2000 was also known as NT 5.0. Released in February 2000 after many delays, Windows 2000 was a significant advance in both functionality and reliability. It provided many advantages over Windows NT 4.0, just a few of which are listed here:

- FAT32 support in addition to NTFS and FAT16
- Windows 9x user interface (Start menu, taskbar, and so on)
- Microsoft Management Console (MMC) for many maintenance functions (although the split of functions between the Control Panel and the Computer Management MMC tools was somewhat arbitrary and confusing)
- Support for up to 4GB of RAM
- A unified driver model, shared with Windows Me, so that hardware vendors could supply a single driver that could be used on either operating system
- Greatly improved reliability

- NTFS improvements including reparse points, which give Windows 2000 the capability to redirect file accesses to alternative drives or servers, a UNIX-like mountable file system, and UNIX-like links (multiple directory entries for a single file)

- Dynamic disk support, which permits drive spanning and on-the-fly partition resizing

- Improved setup and software installation—fewer reboots required, and the Windows Installer service makes it easier to correctly uninstall or repair applications.

- Support for Plug and Play hardware, multiple monitors, USB, and FireWire

- Safe mode and Recovery Console boot options, to maintain and repair unbootable systems

- Active Directory, an enterprise management and security tool that allows very fine-grained delegation of management and security policy settings, automatic application deployment, and other services

- ACPI power management support, including suspend and hibernate modes, making it possible to use on laptops

Windows 2000 was released in several editions:

- Windows 2000 Professional, for individual users and systems with up to two processors. Windows 2000 Professional became the desktop operating system of choice for business users.

- Windows 2000 Server, supporting up to four processors in a single system.

- Windows 2000 Advanced Server, supporting up to eight processors and 64GB of RAM. At most 4GB of RAM is visible to any one application but if the motherboard is designed for it, Windows can use 36-bit virtual addressing to give more applications that much RAM.

- Windows 2000 Datacenter Server, supporting up to 32 processors and clustering, which links redundant servers to permit continuous operation should one fail.

Support for all the early non-Intel RISC processors (such as the DEC Alpha) was dropped and Windows 2000 was provided only in versions for the standard Intel x86 (IA-32) and Itanium (IA-64) architectures.

Windows XP

Released in October 2001, Windows XP officially eclipsed the Windows 9x product line and brought Windows NT to the consumer as well as the corporate environment. With XP, Microsoft finally managed to make NT reasonably compatible with the pool of remaining DOS games and applications (it helped that this pool had been dwindling over the years). Microsoft also made it simple enough to manage, and attractive enough to appeal to end consumers. It also didn't hurt that NT was a truly reliable operating system, much more robust than Win9x. This in itself is remarkable given how much Windows had grown. The original version of Windows fit on two floppy disks. Windows XP required about 2GB of disk space just to *install*. The massive amount of code can be seen in the number of lines of source code—the raw programming text typed by Microsoft's programmers—estimates of which are listed in Table 1.2.

Table 1.2   Lines of Code in Windows

Version (Millions)	Lines of Code
Windows NT 3.1	6
Windows NT 3.5	10
Windows 95	15
Windows NT 4.0	16
Windows 98	18
Windows 2000	30
Windows XP	40
Windows Vista	50

This is really a staggering amount of code, given that it's estimated that a typical programmer can produce about 100 lines of quality program code per day. If that's true, Windows XP is the product of 1,800 person-years of effort (assuming those persons get weekends off, and two weeks of vacation a year).

Windows XP introduced several enhancements over Windows 2000:

- Improved graphical design. Derided by some as "cartoony" at first, it has sort of grown on us.
- Simple File Sharing makes it easier for consumers and small offices to manage file security on a network and on a given computer when NTFS is used.
- System Restore, which performs automatic backups of system programs, components, and the Registry at regular intervals and before installing new applications.
- Fast User Switching makes it possible for several users to be logged on simultaneously, although only one person can use the computer at a time.
- Remote Desktop allows a user to view and control a Windows XP Professional computer over the Internet.

XP was released in two primary editions called Home and Professional. XP Professional is the everything-but-the-kitchen-sink desktop operating system and has a licensing allowance for two processors on the motherboard. XP Home Edition, which permits only one processor, had several features that were either restricted or removed. For example, Simple File Sharing cannot be disabled; the Power Users management group cannot be used; and File Encryption, Offline Files, Remote Desktop hosting, and domain membership are not available.

Other editions of XP would follow, mainly designed for specific types of hardware. These include XP Media Center Edition, Tablet PC Edition, and Professional x64 Edition.

Note

Microsoft does not count multicore or hyperthreading CPUs as multiple CPUs for licensing purposes. For example, both a true quad-core processor as well as a dual-core CPU with hyperthreading look like four CPUs to Windows but still count as a single *physical* processor for Windows licensing purposes, meaning that Windows XP Home Edition will support them.

Anytime there is a major new OS release there are bound to be bugs and problems that need to be fixed. Microsoft generally releases updates every month, which are fairly quick and easy to install. However, over time the cumulative number of updates grows, presenting problems for new installations, where often hundreds of megabytes of updates must be downloaded and installed. In addition, since many of the updates are security related, the system remains vulnerable during the time it takes for the updates to install. To make the update process easier, Microsoft periodically releases Service Packs for Windows, which generally combine all the fixes up to that point in a single update program. Service packs can be installed like an update, that is to update an OS that is already installed, or they can be merged or slipstreamed into the installation media, so that they are automatically present when the OS is initially installed.

Microsoft has released three major service packs for Windows XP, called Service Pack 1 (SP1), Service Pack 2 (SP2), and Service Pack 3 (SP3). The service packs are cumulative; that is, any newer service pack contains all necessary updates and fixes up to that point, as well as everything that was in previous service packs. This means that out of all the service packs that have been released, you only have to install the latest one.

Windows XP Service Pack 1/1a

Service Pack 1 for Windows XP was originally released on September 9, 2002, and then re-released on February 3, 2003 as SP1a. SP1a was the same as SP1 except it was modified to remove Microsoft's Java Virtual Machine (JVM) from Windows in order to comply with the results of a lawsuit with Sun Microsystems. Since that time users have been encouraged to install the updated JVM available for free from Sun at www.java.com.

SP1/1a consists of 321 individual fixes in a file that is over 128MB in size (SP1a). You can see the complete list in the following Microsoft Knowledge Base article:

> List of fixes in Windows XP Service Pack 1 and Windows XP Service Pack 1a
>
> http://support.microsoft.com/kb/324720

Besides the requisite fixes, the most notable new features in SP1 were USB 2.0 support, and 48-bit LBA (Logical Block Address) support for ATAPI disk drives, allowing hard disk drives larger than 137GB to be fully utilized. In addition, the Set Program Access and Defaults utility was added, allowing users to set the default applications for web browsing, email, media playing, and more.

Windows XP Service Pack 2

Service Pack 2 for Windows XP was released on August 6, 2004, and was considered by many an entirely new OS release since it was far more than just a few bug fixes and security patches. Unlike other service packs, SP2 replaced nearly all the OS files, and added several new features and improvements, upgrading the functionality of Windows XP in several areas. Many people felt that the number and scope of the improvements were such that Microsoft could have sold the result as a new OS version instead of giving it away as a free service pack (of course free is nice!). The most important additions in SP2 were

- An improved Windows firewall, which helps prevent malware damage and abuse to the system from over the Internet
- Windows Security Center, which detects and notifies the user of out-of-date antivirus protection and less-than-optimal security configurations
- Major improvements to Internet Explorer (such as a pop-up blocker) to prevent its being hijacked by malicious websites
- Support for the NX/XD (No eXecute/eXecute Disable) bit incorporated into newer processors to prevent buffer overflow attacks
- Greatly improved wireless networking management and controls
- Bluetooth support
- Improvements to Outlook Express to prevent its automatically displaying graphic and script content, which can install malware and notify spammers that their email has been read

In addition to the upgrades and improvements, SP2 incorporated 826 new individual fixes (*plus* all the fixes previously included in SP1) in a single file that is more than 272MB in size. The full list of fixes are detailed in the following Microsoft Knowledge Base article:

> List of fixes included in Windows XP Service Pack 2
>
> http://support.microsoft.com/kb/811113

Microsoft later released OEM versions of Windows XP media (primarily for system builders) with SP2b and SP2c included. These were not available as separately downloadable service packs, and were only included as integrated to the OEM installation CD media. The SP2b release included a non-security update (KB912945) related to a patent suit brought against Microsoft covering technology that allows browsers to automatically launch external files. This update prevents interacting with ActiveX controls from web pages until these controls are manually enabled. This update was later offered to all XP users via Windows Update.

OEM versions of Windows XP Professional with SP2c were released in September 2007. This update was only for XP Pro, and the only change was a modification that allowed more installation product keys in order to support the continued sale of Windows XP Professional through the scheduled end-of-life date of January 31, 2009.

Windows XP Service Pack 3

While SP2 was a fantastic addition to XP, and a virtual refresh of the entire OS, since it was released in August 2004, by late 2007 the number of cumulative updates over more than 3 years time had grown to hundreds of updates totalling well over a hundred megabytes of downloads. The large number of updates was making new installations of Windows XP quite a chore for many users, since after installing a system all of these updates would need to be downloaded from Microsoft Update. This was especially a problem for those with a dial-up internet connection. While it was possible for more sophisticated users to download the updates in advance and integrate them into the installation media directly, this capability was not necessarily easy or even known to most users. This prompted Microsoft to finally release Service Pack 3 for Windows XP.

Unlike the more radical changes and upgrades contained in the SP2 release, SP3 is more like a traditional service pack, including only the cumulative fixes to date. For example, new features such as Internet Explorer 7 and Media Player 11 are not included, and remain as optional updates that are separately installable. Of course SP3 also includes everything that was in SP1 and SP2, so as a whole the package is quite large at more than 340MB. More information on SP3 can be seen in the following Microsoft Knowledge Base article:

> Windows XP Service Pack 3
>
> http://support.microsoft.com/kb/936929

Windows Server 2003

In April 2003 Microsoft released the successor to Windows 2000 Server with the name Windows Server 2003. As a server OS, several of the services not essential to servers, such as video hardware acceleration, audio, and themes, are disabled by default.

Windows Vista

Windows Vista is the long coming successor to Windows XP, and the latest member of the Windows NT family. Development of Vista (codenamed Longhorn) began in May 2001, even before XP had been released. Longhorn was initially intended to be a minor step up from XP originally slated for release in 2003, however the project became much more ambitious, causing the feature list to both grow and shrink during development. In July 2005 Microsoft announced that the OS codenamed Longhorn would be called Windows Vista, and Vista was finally released in November 2006 to corporate and OEM customers, and in January 2007 to the public.

Although based on NT technology and a successor to XP, Vista adds many new features as well as a redesigned user interface that substantially changes the look and feel over previous versions. All the new visual styles run on a redesigned shell, with modifications to Windows Explorer and other components.

Highlights of the new features in Vista include the following:

New Visual Styles and User Interface:

- **Aero**—The Aero style features translucency effects on window borders and Flip 3D, where open windows can be viewed in a 3-dimensional rolodex form.
- **Standard**—The Standard interface is the same as Aero without the translucency and Flip 3D effects.
- **Basic**—The Basic interface is similar to Windows XP Luna.
- **Classic**—Offers the look and feel of Windows 2000.

Improved Security:

- **User Account Control**—Designed to limit the number of default user privileges to improve overall security and limit the effects of malware.

- **Parental Controls**—Allows control over websites, programs and games each standard user can access.

- **Firewall**—Now works two ways controlling both incoming and outgoing traffic.

Performance Boosting Technologies:

- **SuperFetch**—Caches frequently used applications in memory for quicker access.

- **ReadyBoost**—Uses USB flash memory devices as additional cache memory to increase system performance.

- ReadyDrive—Recognizes and utilizes the memory in hybrid drives, which are hard drives with integral flash memory to increase drive performance.

New and Updated Applications:

- *Sidebar*—A panel for Desktop Gadgets, small visual applications such as news, weather, slide shows, and so on.

- *Desktop Search*—A greatly improved search application.

- *Internet Explorer 7*—Updated web browser.

- *Media Player 11*—Updated media player.

- *Photo Gallery*—A photo and video library and management application.

- *Windows Defender*—An anti-spyware/malware application.

Other Improvements:

- Integrated DVD burning support

- Integrated speech recognition

- DirectX 10 graphics support

- New Games

Windows Vista demands much more of the hardware than previous versions. Table 1.3 lists the system requirements for Vista Capable and Vista Premium Ready systems. Premium Ready systems are defined as capable of running the Aero visual style.

Table 1.3   Windows Vista System Requirements

Component	Vista Capable	Vista Premium Ready (Aero Capable)
Processor	800MHz	1GHz
Memory	512MB	1GB
Graphics card	DirectX 9 capable	DirectX 9 capable with Pixel Shader 2.0 in hardware and WDDM driver support
Graphics memory	-	128MB RAM
HDD capacity/free	20GB/15GB	40GB/15GB
Optical drives	DVD-ROM	DVD-ROM

WDDM = Windows Driver Display Model

As with previous versions, the minimum hardware requirements are just that, the bare minimum, while most would recommend more capable hardware for improved performance.

Windows Vista Service Pack 1

Service Pack 1 for Vista was released in early 2008, and included updates in three main categories:

- Fixes—including all previously released updates
- Administrative improvements to the BitLocker Drive Encryption (BDE)
- Support for new features such as Direct3D 10.1 graphics, EFI (Extensible Firmware Interface) BIOS and the Extended File Allocation Table (exFAT) file system used by newer flash memory storage and consumer devices

Unlike previous service packs for other operating systems, SP1 for Vista cannot be integrated or slipstreamed into existing installation media. You must either acquire new media from Microsoft with SP1 already integrated, or install SP1 separately after installing Vista. When installing separately, you can either install the service pack via Windows Update (approximately 50MB download) or via a very large standalone executable installer (approximately 1GB download). To perform a new installation of Vista with SP1 already integrated will require obtaining a completely new install DVD from Microsoft with SP1 pre-loaded.

Because the Vista SP1 installation replaces so many files, Microsoft recommends a minimum of 7GB or 12GB of free space on the system partition for 32/64-bit versions respectively. Fortunately most of the additional drive space that is used during the SP1 install is regained when the installation is completed.

Windows Server 2008

In late 2007 Microsoft released the successor to Windows 2003 Server, called Windows Server 2008. Server 2008 is built on the same source code as Vista, and is basically Vista with services not essential to servers disabled or removed. For example, Windows Media Center only appears in Vista, while Active Directory or Windows Clustering only appear in Server 2008.

Alternative CPU OS Versions: Intel, Alpha, MIPS, and Motorola

Windows NT was originally designed so as not to be tied exclusively to the Intel CPU architecture used in PCs. Windows NT's design put the processor's unique setup and control instructions into the Hardware Abstraction Layer (HAL) software component. Most of the rest of Windows is written in high-level languages that have no explicit processor dependence. To run on a new processor, Microsoft or a hardware manufacturer merely had to write a new Hardware Abstraction Layer module and a compiler to convert the rest of the Windows code into machine instructions for the new architecture.

When NT was originally released, Microsoft supported four microprocessors:

■ Intel IA-32 (32-bit architecture, also known as x86), the base processor architecture in most PCs. x86-compatible CPUs are made by Intel, Advanced Micro Devices (AMD), VIA, and others.

■ Alpha AXP, a Reduced Instruction Set Computer (RISC) chip originally designed by Digital Equipment Corporation.

■ MIPS R4000, a RISC processor originally designed by MIPS Computer Systems, Inc.

■ PowerPC, yet another RISC processor designed by IBM.

In addition, some manufacturers developed their own versions of NT for still other architectures under licensing agreements from Microsoft.

Support for alternative architectures was short-lived. One reason for this is that Windows applications had to be compiled and tested for each CPU platform. MS-DOS applications could run thanks to an emulator program that was built into the Virtual DOS environment, but third-party Windows applications were in short supply. This was probably not the largest obstacle, though, as the alternative platforms were usually used primarily to run special-purpose applications.

The main problem facing the RISC chips is that the speed advantage they enjoyed over Intel chips eventually disappeared. While the RISC chips were originally worth the extra expense to get high performance for graphics workstations and servers, as Intel and graphics chip vendors caught up, the commodity PC became as powerful as the workstation at a vastly lower price. Political pressure from Intel and Microsoft also very likely factored into the decisions. Whatever the reasons were, the Alpha, MIPS, and PowerPC processors eventually succumbed to decreasing support and demand. Alpha chips are no longer manufactured, nor are MIPS processors, as such; the technology is still available and licensable to chip designers for inclusion in larger designs. IBM still makes PowerPC chips, but Windows support for the PowerPC ended after NT 4.0.

Windows XP and Vista 64-Bit Editions

The need for processors capable of handling far more than 4GB of memory has led to development of two 64-bit architectures. Intel originally developed and promoted a 64-bit architecture called IA-64 or Itanium, intended primarily for database and network server computers. Realizing the need for 64-bit extensions to the existing 32-bit x86 architecture, Advanced Micro Devices developed a 64-bit architecture called x64 or AMD-64. Intel then adopted this architecture for its processors as well, calling it Intel 64 or Extended Memory 64 Technology (EM64T). While both the Itanium and x64 architectures are supported by Microsoft, only the x64 architecture is supported for 64-bit user versions of Windows XP and Vista.

Thus, at the time this was written, Windows is available for three architectures:

■ IA-32 (x86 32-bit) for all versions of Windows XP and Vista

■ IA-64 (Itanium) for Windows Server 2003/2008

■ x64 (64-bit extensions to x86) for Windows XP, Vista, and Windows Server 2003/2008

Usage of the x64 versions of Windows XP and Vista should be very similar to the 32-bit versions with the following exceptions:

- 64-bit versions of Windows will run 32-bit Windows applications, but will not run 16-bit (Windows 3.1) applications, nor can they use 32-bit drivers (drivers written for the standard versions of Windows XP and Vista). This means that hardware support may be limited until vendors produce 64-bit driver versions, which will likely occur for selected new hardware only.
- MS-DOS applications cannot be run because they are 16-bit.
- DirectX graphics support does not take advantage of hardware graphics acceleration, so gaming performance will likely be less than satisfactory.

DirectX support may be improved in a future Windows version or in a future service pack.

Service Packs, Hotfixes, and Rollups

It's a given that operating systems and large software suites have bugs, and Windows is definitely a member of both categories. The Microsoft method of dealing with bugs in Windows has varied depending on the product line in question.

In the consumer Windows 9x product line, users were largely left on their own. Only the most severe security bugs were addressed, and even then, for the most part, computer owners had to take the initiative to visit Windows Update to download "Critical Updates." It took many years—and tens of millions of virus-infected computers—for Microsoft to develop an automated method of delivering security updates to Windows 9x users, and even then they had to download this updating mechanism themselves. Bugs that affected Windows functionality but not security were largely left unfixed, with the result that a typical Windows 9x could be expected to crash once a day, in heavy use. Patches called *hotfixes* were available as downloads from support.microsoft.com for some problems, but finding these was a job that required a high level of training and technological savvy.

However, Microsoft recognized from the start that operating system products sold to business customers had to have a level of support that rivaled that of other enterprise software vendors, so the Windows NT product line has enjoyed a much higher level of support. This is not a trivial or inexpensive undertaking because proper software quality management is expensive, time-consuming, and involves interactions with customers on several levels:

- Communicating known bugs to customers.
- Development and announcement of any possible short-term workarounds, and estimated delivery dates for complete fixes.
- Thorough testing of all software changes for possible negative interactions with existing hardware, software, and all previous updates (regression testing). If done properly, this involves testing installation and operation of all fixes on every possible combination of supported hardware and software, with and without every combination of other optional software components, versions, patches, updates, and fixes. Testing a single software change against all of these permutations takes an enormous effort.
- Timely release of individual fixes to customers who are encountering a given problem.

- Periodic bulk updates that combine all known and tested fixes, to simplify the maintenance job for the majority of customers who are not directly affected by each identified problem. This can be accomplished by releasing new operating system versions, or through an updating mechanism.

To meet these Microsoft has established a system for delivering updates for the Windows NT product line that includes Windows 2000, XP, and Vista, with five mechanisms:

- The Microsoft *Knowledge Base* contains reports on known problems and solutions, at support.microsoft.com.

- *Hotfixes*, interim patches that address known problems, which are made available for download at support.microsoft.com. Hotfixes are intended for use only by customers directly experiencing a given problem (due to, for example, a particular combination of hardware and software that exposes a given bug). They are not necessarily tested with every possible combination of hardware and software. Several hotfixes are typically posted every week.

- *Service packs* are cumulative updates of all hotfixes released since the operating system was original released. When Microsoft constructs a service pack, hotfixes are tested much more extensively. In addition, new functionality might be included, as we saw with the inclusion of Windows Firewall in Windows XP Service Pack 2, although Microsoft has stated that they expect this to be a rare occurrence.

  Service packs are generally tested internally by Microsoft, and then by major computer vendors, and then by large corporate clients and possibly the public, through a beta program, and may go through two or more beta versions before being finalized. Service packs have typically been released 6 months to 2 years apart.

Note

On Windows NT 4.0 and earlier, service pack installers copied only files for features in use, and the service pack had to be reapplied if an optional feature was subsequently installed. On Windows 2000 and later, installing a service pack installs files for all Windows features, whether they are in use or not. This ensures that if an optional Windows component is installed later, the updated version will be used.

Windows service packs include all fixes made since the product's initial release, so it's not necessary to install older Windows service packs before installing a newer Windows service pack. *This may not necessarily be true for service packs for other Microsoft products.*

- *Rollups*, which contain a significant set of hotfixes released since the last service pack. Rollups include only the most important hotfixes, ones likely to affect a large number of customers, and are tested for proper installation and correct operation together as a package. Testing is less extensive than for a service pack. Rollups are designed to make installation of important hotfixes easier, and to make them available in a timely fashion without the burden and expense of a full-scale service pack. Rollups are produced only on rare occasion.

- *Critical Updates* are patches that address a security risk to the average user. Critical Updates are typically given extensive testing, as they're considered mandatory for all customers. They are distributed through Windows Update, and now through the new Automatic Updates system so that all users will get them in a timely fashion. Critical Updates are typically released once a month on a Tuesday, unless they are considered urgent enough to be released immediately after testing.

■ *Optional Updates* are updates to Windows components, new versions of Windows applications, or new functions that have no direct security or usability impact, but which for some reason Microsoft feels it is important to distribute. They're made available through the Windows Update tool.

Now that Windows XP and Vista Home editions have brought NT to the consumer Windows product line, this level of support is available to the average consumer as well.

It's a matter of speculation what will happen to the frequency of issuance of service packs, as increased reliability coupled with a regular stream of bug fixes may prove to be a disincentive for purchasing upgrades to later operating systems.

Service packs can be obtained in several ways:

■ As standalone executables, either downloaded from Microsoft or available on disc for those with a slower Internet connection. If you have to update several computers, the service pack executable can be downloaded and stored on a shared network folder or removable media. This is also helpful for those with a slower Internet connection since the pack can be downloaded on another system that has a faster connection and installed via disc. These versions typically cover all flavors of the operating system for which they are intended. For example, the standalone executable Windows XP SP2 or SP3 updates all XP versions including XP Home Edition, Professional, Media Center Edition, and Tablet PC Edition. The same is true for Vista, the Windows Vista SP1 standalone executable will work on all versions from Home Basic to Ultimate. The only exception is that different service pack executables are required for different platforms, meaning that 32-bit versions use a different pack than 64-bit versions.

■ Via download from Windows Update. The update process first downloads a small tool that analyzes the user's Windows installation and determines which updated files are required. Just the files needed by the user's flavor for Windows are retrieved and installed. This is the easiest download format for users with just one or two computers.

In addition, service packs for Windows XP and earlier can be merged into the Windows installation setup files in an operation called *slipstreaming*. Organizations and vendors that install many copies of Windows can use this technique to construct updated Windows installation media. (In addition, a Windows Deployment Toolkit can be obtained from microsoft.com, which lets organizations pre-install applications and customizations onto new computers.) Unfortunately Windows Vista does not support slipstreaming, instead new media incorporating the service pack must be obtained from Microsoft.

Windows Boot (Startup)

System Layers

Startup—also known as *booting (from bootstrapping)*—is the process that occurs in the period between turning a computer on and being able to use it. With older systems taking a minute or more just to complete the POST (Power On Self Test), and older versions of Windows taking several minutes to load, booting a system was considered a real test of patience. With modern systems' POST times of 7 seconds or less, and newer versions of Windows such as Windows XP and Vista, the process has been sped up to the point that it can take as little as 30 seconds from power-on to the Windows desktop, and significantly less if you resume from Stand By or Hibernation. When things are working properly, most people aren't that concerned about the startup process, but when things go wrong, and either the process takes significantly longer than it used to, or especially if it fails at some point, you may have to take a deeper look at the startup process to see where things went wrong. For example, this might happen when you've installed a new hardware device (and driver) that causes Windows to crash upon startup, or if your computer has become infected with some sort of malware. Another good reason to investigate the startup process is to know the options and settings that are available to customize the process. A lot goes on in the seconds—or minutes—between pressing the power switch and seeing the welcome screen, and this chapter discusses it in detail.

When you investigate computer hardware and software you'll repeatedly encounter the concept of *layers*. Computers and their operating systems are amazingly complex constructions, but they have a very definite structure. When you use an application program like Microsoft Word, the application doesn't actually "know" how to read and write data from the hard disk, or how to draw letters on the screen. It relies on the graphics and file system support layers of the operating system to do these jobs for it; the operating system layers in turn rely on device driver software to handle the particular hardware devices in your computer, and the device drivers rely on the hardware to get the job done, as illustrated in Figure 2.1. The figure shows a vastly simplified picture of the software layers in Windows.

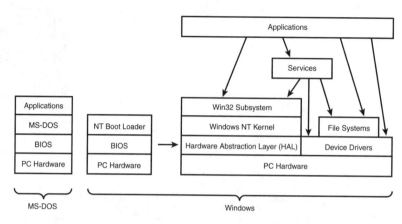

Figure 2.1   Windows has many layers of software between your application and the PC's hardware.

Hardware Layers

Ultimately, all the work your computer does is performed by hardware. The central processing unit (CPU) shuffles data around; calculates where to draw the letters, images, and lines on your display; interprets the data stored on your disks; and so on. Ancillary processors also do a considerable amount of work. Every hard disk, for example, has its own dedicated CPU that is responsible for not only moving the magnetic recording head back and forth across the disk surface and generating and interpreting the recorded signals, but also for caching and optimizing the flow of data between the disk and the system. Video cards have graphics processors that may have power rivaling the primary CPU, although their architecture limits them to special purpose processing tasks.

These independent devices must be controlled, coordinated, and managed by software. For the last 30 years or so, the first bit of software that runs when a microcomputer is turned on is called the BIOS.

BIOS

Basic Input Output System (BIOS) is a term that first appeared around 1976 as a component of Gary Kildall's CP/M operating system for the 8-bit Intel 8080 CPU. In early microcomputers, hardware devices were not well standardized, and the interface hardware for each computer's keyboard, display, and floppy disk drives required custom software. Loadable device drivers were not yet widely used, so to make it easier to produce a version of the operating system for a new computer model, the software drivers for the floppy drive, and serial interface or keyboard and display were stored in a separate software module; this way, the majority of the operating system and all application software could be left as is. Once the BIOS was loaded, the routine to read a character from the terminal was stored at one fixed, predetermined address, the routine to send a character to the terminal at another, and so on. CP/M and application programs could thus rely on these BIOS routines, and didn't have to directly deal with differences in hardware from one make of computer to another.

When IBM hired Microsoft to develop an operating system for the original IBM PC in 1980, CP/M quite literally served as the model, and the concept of BIOS came along with it in both name and function. On the IBM PC, the BIOS was stored in a read-only memory (ROM) chip so that it didn't need to be loaded from disk. Its first task on startup was to perform an extensive test of the computer's hardware, called the Power On Self Test, or POST. If a hardware failure was detected, the BIOS would display a code number that indicated which device had failed. If the POST was successful, the BIOS program ran a bootstrap loader routine that scanned floppy and hard disk drives looking for an operating system to load. The PC's BIOS chip also contained driver subroutines to display characters on the screen, read characters from the keyboard, and read and write blocks of data to and from blocks or sectors on the disk. MS-DOS, once loaded, added additional functions to create and manage a file system, which gave programs access to directories and files.

As the PC evolved into today's version, the BIOS evolved as well. Because of the limited space in ROM, additional BIOS-level subroutines (called *device drivers*) were loaded from disk drives into RAM. Modern PCs use the ROM BIOS solely for loading the OS and drivers; the BIOS in a modern system consists almost entirely of drivers loaded into RAM while the system is running. Even the ROM portion has evolved: Today's BIOS POST, setup, and bootstrap loader routines are stored not in a permanently programmed ROM chip, but in a reprogrammable Flash chip, so that the code can be updated. The original PC had only floppy drives for storage, and only a handful of other interfaces to manage. Today's BIOS faces hard disks with ATA, SATA, USB, FireWire, and SCSI interfaces; optical drives, PCI, PCI-Express, and AGP buses; various types of memory interfaces with different timing requirements; USB keyboards and mice; and a huge variety of graphics adapters. The ROM portion of the BIOS must be able to detect, initialize, and use (in at least a primitive way) all these devices in order to boot whatever operating system is being used. In addition, some older operating systems rely on the BIOS to enumerate (detect) the installed devices and assign them addresses and interrupts, using the Plug and Play mechanism. Newer Plug and Play OS can handle this without assistance from the BIOS.

Tip

If a failure occurs during the Power On Self Test before the video card is initialized, most BIOS make the PC speaker beep out a code that tells you what was wrong: memory error, missing display adapter, and so on. After the video is initialized, the POST will use more descriptive error messages on the screen instead, although these may be fairly cryptic as well. Some newer BIOS use voice prompts that literally *tell* you what's wrong, which can be a little disconcerting if you haven't heard it before. The POST also writes code numbers to a port on the bus that denotes the particular tests being performed. You can purchase a plug-in card called a *POST card* that displays these codes. If the POST fails, the last displayed code tells you where the failure occurred. A POST card can be helpful if the problem is so critical that neither beeps can be heard nor messages to the display can be seen.

Fortunately the BIOS in modern systems still contains 16-bit driver routines that allow you to run MS-DOS, and programs that rely solely on the BIOS and MS-DOS routines to interact with hardware can therefore still work.

ROM BIOS–based drivers are designed only to be run with the CPU in *real mode*, where the CPU acts like an Intel 8086 16-bit processor, there is a limit of 1MB of addressable memory, and, due to the design of the PC, only 640KB of the address range is actually usable. (The BIOS actually does briefly switch the CPU to protected mode during startup in order to test and initialize memory and some hardware, but the CPU is returned to real mode before the BIOS begins the process of loading an operating system.) Modern operating systems such as Linux and the 32-bit and 64-bit versions of Windows use the BIOS only to get the OS initially loaded; once their initial bits are loaded from the selected hard disk, the operating system loads 32-bit or 64-bit drivers and switches the CPU to 32-bit or 64-bit protected mode and takes over direct control of the hardware. These operating systems use the discrete, interchangeable software modules called device drivers.

Hardware Abstraction Layer

The hardware abstraction layer (HAL) is a special type of software that enables the same operating system to run on different types of hardware, such as single-processor, dual-processor, or multi-core processor-based computers, or computers using different types of power management. Windows NT, 2000, XP, and Vista include the HAL as part of the operating system kernel.

The standard HAL versions provided with Windows XP are listed in Table 2.1.

Table 2.1   Standard Windows XP HAL Versions

HAL Name	Original Filename	Used For
Advanced Configuration and Power Interface (ACPI) PC	halacpi.dll	A single-processor motherboard that complies with the ACPI configuration and power management specification.
ACPI Multiprocessor PC	halmacpi.dll	An ACPI-compliant multiprocessor motherboard with two or more CPUs installed (or with one or more dual-core or hyperthreading CPUs).
ACPI Uniprocessor PC	halaapci.dll	An APCI-compliant multiprocessor motherboard with one single core, non-hyperthreading CPU installed.
Compaq SystemPro Multiprocessor or 100% Compatible	Halsp.dll	A Compaq SystemPro or compatible server motherboard.
MPS Uniprocessor PC	halapic.dll	A non-ACPI–compliant multiprocessor motherboard with a single processor installed.
MPS Multiprocessor PC	halmps.dll	A non-ACPI–compliant multiprocessor motherboard with two or more processors installed.
Standard PC	hal.dll	A non-ACPI–compliant single-processor motherboard.
Standard PC with C-Step i486	(Not supported by Windows XP)	A PC with an Intel 486 C-step CPU. (This version of the 486 CPU has a bug that had to be dealt with by writing a custom HAL.)
Other		Custom HALs may be written and provided by computer manufacturers.

Note

Windows Setup detects your CPU and motherboard type during setup, and automatically selects the appropriate HAL version. The HAL module is copied to your `\windows\system32` folder with the name `hal.dll,` no matter which version was selected. If you need to force Setup to make another choice, visit support.microsoft.com and search for Knowledge Base Article 299340. This article describes a procedure that lets you manually choose a HAL version.

On Windows XP, Windows automatically switches between multiprocessor and uniprocessor HALs and kernels; you no longer need to reinstall Windows or use the Device Manager if you change the number of processors, for example, by enabling hyperthreading or installing a dual-core CPU.

On Windows XP and Vista, Windows automatically switches between multiprocessor and uniprocessor HALs and kernels; you no longer need to reinstall Windows or use the Device Manager if you change the number of processors, for example, by enabling hyperthreading or installing a dual-core CPU.

Vista reduces the total number of HAL types to include only `halacpi.dll` and `halmacpi.dll`, and both are copied to the hard drive on all installations. Vista does not support the other HAL types.

Because of the many HAL versions used by Windows XP, creating an image of Windows XP that will be used for installation on multiple systems should take place on a system that uses the same HAL as the target systems. The systems need not be identical, but both source and target systems should both have the same features (both supporting ACPI, both supporting multiple physical processors or multicore processors, and so on). If you create an image on a system that uses a different HAL than the target system, the target system may display a STOP 0x0000007b error after you apply the image and restart it.

Note

To learn the relationships between sysprep images of Windows XP and supported HAL types, see Microsoft Knowledge Base article 309283 at http://support.microsoft.com.

Windows Vista no longer uses different HAL drivers for systems. Instead, it uses a hardware-independent HAL that enables you to create a Windows Vista image and deploy it to any Windows Vista–compatible system, as described in Chapter 3, "Installing Windows." You no longer need to be concerned about mismatches between source and target hardware as with Windows XP or earlier Windows versions.

Note

If you support both 32-bit and 64-bit versions of Windows Vista, the only limitation you have is that you must create a 32-bit image for 32-bit processors (or 64-bit processors running the 32-bit version of Windows Vista) and a separate 64-bit image for 64-bit processors running the 64-bit version of Windows Vista. With Windows Vista SP1, a single image can be used for both 32-bit and 64-bit installations. Thus, it is no longer necessary to maintain separate 32-bit and 64-bit images.

Device Drivers

Device drivers are BIOS-level components written to manage specific hardware devices, and act as an interface between the device and the operating system. Although the driver is concerned with the intimate details of the particular make and model of hardware it's designed to control, it also shields the operating system from having to know these specific details. As far as Windows is concerned, the various categories of device drivers are just interchangeable parts, each doing the same job in exactly the same way.

For example, device drivers for graphic display adapters come in versions for each model of display adapter made, and there are dozens if not hundreds of these. Each one uses memory differently, has different mechanisms for setting resolution and update frequency, and so on. But as far as Windows is concerned, these hardware details are irrelevant; Windows can instruct the driver to shade a particular pixel on the screen a certain color, and the display adapter driver does whatever it has to do to make the hardware display that pixel. Likewise, the drivers for ATA and SATA hard disk interfaces shield Windows itself from the details of managing those devices; Windows can, for example, simply request logical block address number 63 from hard disk 0, and the disk driver will fetch it.

Part of the job of the operating system is to protect each of the system layers and user applications from interference by each other; this increases both security and reliability. On Windows NT–based operating systems like Windows XP and Vista, user-level programs are not allowed to directly access *any* system hardware; the processor instructions that initiate input/output activity are blocked (or in some cases are intercepted, and the action they would have performed is simulated by the operating system using calls to the appropriate device driver). The memory ranges that correspond to device hardware interfaces are not accessible.

The reason for these restrictions is primarily to give the operating system absolute control over the hardware in an environment where several applications could attempt to perform the same action at the same time. For example, with several applications running, it might happen that two of them would attempt to write data to the disk at the same time. If allowed to access the disk hardware directly, one application might instruct the disk to move its read/write head to a certain position and then to write data at that position. Another application could decide to do the same thing, and could move the disk head to a different location, while the first was still writing. The result would be a scrambled disk.

Device drivers themselves, however, must have unfettered access to the device hardware that they manage. The majority of them run in the context of the Windows kernel, where they are permitted to execute input/output instructions and hardware devices. And while each application program is allowed to access only a limited amount of memory dedicated for its use, device drivers have direct access to all of the PC's memory.

This total access carries some risk. A bug in a device driver can cause it to execute inappropriate instructions or memory accesses, leading Windows to conclude that its code *could* have become corrupted, and as discretion is the better part of valor, this causes an immediate halt: Windows displays the infamous Blue Screen of Death (BSOD), so named because the screen is blue with white error message text, and the system halts dead in its tracks and the only remedy is to cycle its power. Usually the BSOD indicates that a device driver caused the shutdown, but occasionally the bug corrupts some *other* driver or component, and...well, it's a nasty situation in any case.

But the advantage of a kernel driver is its faster performance. When the device driver is copying data between a hardware device and an application program, kernel mode makes it possible to copy the data in a single step. A user-mode driver would require a copy from the device to the driver's address space, and then another copy from the driver to the application.

File Systems and Filters

For storage devices such as hard disks, floppy disks, CDs, and DVDs, device drivers are used to manage the disk's physical controller hardware and to read and write data. However, the data on these devices is structured into files and folders, using any of several different file systems. For example, floppy disk data is organized using a file system called FAT-12, where FAT stands for File Allocation Table, and the 12 refers to the fact that the system is based on 12-bit numbers. The NT File System (NTFS) is used on larger volumes under NT-based operating systems such as XP or Vista, with PCs running Windows Me or older using FAT-32 and FAT-16 file systems. Many external drives also use FAT-32 to ensure read/write compatibility with Apple Mac systems, which cannot write to NTFS volumes. CDs, CD-Rs, CD-RWs, and DVDs use still other formats, and then there are flash cards, smart cards, and other devices.

In order to maintain independence between the software that operates the hardware and the software that interprets the data stored on it, there is an additional layer of software called file system drivers.

Here's how these layers work: An application program that wants to read a file from the disk passes its request to the Win32 subsystem. If the desired file is on a disk formatted with the NTFS file system, the NTFS file system driver works out exactly where on the disk the data is located. It asks the disk drive's driver to get it, the driver instructs the disk's hardware to move to a particular location and read it, and the data is passed back up through the same chain.

Now, added to this picture are other drivers called *filters* that position themselves in between any of the layers we've described so far. Filters can let requests move down through the layers and their results come back up, or they can intercept the flow of data and take some other action.

One use of the filter mechanism is to allow a developer to add support for some new feature, file system, or device that hasn't been conceived yet.

Another use of the filter mechanism is to add a security feature. For example, antivirus programs add filter drivers just above the file system drivers, where they intercept requests for reading data from your drives. When the data has been read, they can examine it all *before* any other program has a chance to see it, and can take appropriate action if they decide the data contains a virus program.

Services

Device drivers have unhindered, unprotected access to hardware. A great many of the internal functions of Windows don't need to have the kernel's unrestricted access, but they *do* need to run all the time, whether you're logged in or not, and they *may* need high privileges. Examples of these functions are the Automatic Update service, which downloads and installs critical Windows security patches, the Windows Firewall, which monitors all network activity and blocks attempts by outsiders to hack into your system, and the Print Spooler, which manages the flow of data to your printers.

Most operating systems provide a means of having programs run independently of any logged-on user. On UNIX and Linux, they're called *daemons*, and on Windows, they're called services. A Windows *service* is a program that can be started automatically when Windows starts up, and which provides some essential function. In most cases, services do their jobs without interacting with the keyboard, mouse, or display at all. It's possible, although uncommon, for a service for display a message on the screen. The Print Spooler is one service that does this—when a printer jams, the Print Spooler service pops up a message. But most do their job silently, and in the event of a problem usually just record an error message in the Windows Event Log.

We'll discuss services in greater detail later in the chapter.

The Startup Process

When a computer is powered up, all the various layers between the hardware and the visible interface have to be prepared, or *initialized*, from the bottom up. The hardware is initialized first. A circuit on the computer's motherboard sends a reset signal to each chip, module, and external hardware device, to set the hardware to a known state. The reset signal places the Intel or Intel-compatible processors used in Windows PCs in what is called *real mode*, in which the processor addresses memory by physical hardware addresses and in which there are no restrictions on memory or hardware access. The CPU then begins retrieving instructions from a fixed memory address, FFFF0 in hexadecimal. PC motherboards are constructed with a built-in ROM chip or electrically erasable and reprogrammable memory (flash) at that address. This chip contains a set of programs called the BIOS and its instructions initialize the computer, test its hardware, and load an operating system.

BIOS Startup

Two companies are responsible for the BIOS code used in most PCs: Phoenix Technologies (which sells Phoenix BIOS and Award BIOS) and American Megatrends (which sells AMI BIOS). The goings-on inside the BIOS, regardless of the source, are proprietary. Even the mechanism by which the BIOS is updated in flash is secret. However, although the specifics are not public, the boot process goes something like this:

1. A hardware reset puts the CPU in real mode, and it begins executing instructions starting at memory address FFFF0 hex, which is 16 bytes from the end of motherboard ROM, located in the first megabyte of address space.

2. The motherboard ROM BIOS contains a jump instruction at address FFFF0h, which moves the processor instruction pointer to the actual start of the ROM BIOS initialization routines (which can vary).

3. The initialization routine disables interrupts and any known hardware devices, so that any pending hardware operations initiated before reset will not disrupt the startup process, and sets the CPU's memory segment registers to access low memory. A stack is created for interrupt and subroutine data storage. Interrupt vectors (pointers to subroutines used to handle hardware service requests) are set in low memory for hardware and software interrupts.

4. The CPU's memory management registers are set and the CPU is switched to 32-bit protected mode so that it can detect, configure, test, and initialize memory beyond the 1MB real mode limit. Although early motherboards required you to manually enter memory timing settings, modern DIMM memory contains setup information that is read from the memory modules during startup.

5. The BIOS constructs in memory a list of all known hardware devices and their required interrupt, DMA, and I/O port requirements. Settings for non-Plug and Play ISA bus devices should have been entered into the BIOS setup screens by the user. Plug and Play devices are detected through a complex and peculiar mechanism: Bits on the computer's external bus are used to slowly pulse out serial data in a manner not unlike an old time Morse code telegraph system.

6. Some hardware devices respond not only to the CPU's I/O instructions but also have ROMs, hardware registers, and display buffer memory that is mapped into the standard memory range, and is readable and perhaps writable as if it were regular system memory. The BIOS scans memory at every 2,048 byte boundary for special "signature" values that mark the presence of a BIOS ROM. These are commonly found on SCSI disk adapters and network adapters so that the BIOS can boot from these nonstandard disks or from the network.

If found, the routines in these ROM are called and allowed to initialize their corresponding hardware, and if the user chooses, are used instead of the standard motherboard BIOS program to load the operating system at step 6.

7. If the BIOS is configured for a non–Plug and Play operating system, the BIOS assigns and configures interrupt, DMA, and I/O port addresses for all Plug and Play devices. For a Plug and Play operating system, resource allocation and initialization is left to the operating system.

8. Standard mass storage devices and any detected adapter option ROMs (disk or network) are searched in the user-configured order ("boot order"). The devices are initialized and scanned to find the first device that is online and contains a recognized file system with a valid bootstrap program. The bootstrap program is read from the device and control passes to that program to continue the initialization process.

Note

To read about Plug and Play and other hardware specifications, check out www.microsoft.com/whdc/resources/respec/specs.

When the BIOS or user selects the bootstrap device, a bootstrap loader is used to bring in the actual operating system.

Bootstrap Loaders

As the previous section discussed, the BIOS program stored on the motherboard contains the instructions your PC needs to start up, test itself, and access the keyboard, display, and mass storage devices. Because the BIOS can't know in advance what operating system you're going to use, or how or where that operating system is stored on your disks, or how it's to be read from disk and started up, an intermediate startup program is used, called a *bootstrap loader* or *OS loader*. This is a *very* small operating system–specific program that the BIOS can find and read into memory; the loader is then responsible for actually starting up your operating system. All bootable media use a standard layout so that the BIOS can find the loader.

Note

Disk organization and bootstrap structures are described in detail in Chapter 10, "Windows File Systems."

The BIOS begins the bootstrap process by reading the first 512 bytes stored on whatever startup disk is used, whether it's a floppy disk, hard disk, CD, DVD, USB flash drive, or other removable disk. This block of data is called the *boot sector* and it begins with the bootstrap loader specific to your operating system; it's placed there when you install the OS. It must end with the bytes 55 and AA (hexadecimal), so only 510 bytes are available for the boot program itself. The block is stored starting at address 7C00h and executed there.

Note

You can replace a missing or damaged master boot sector loader using the Windows Recovery `fixmbr` (XP) or `bootrec /fixmbr` (Vista) commands, discussed in Chapter 12, "Windows Troubleshooting."

The boot sector loader contains whatever instructions are necessary to

- Identify what file system is used on the disk media
- Locate and read into memory a secondary, larger, more comprehensive loader program called the *secondary loader*, which is stored elsewhere on the disk
- Transfer control to the secondary loader, which then continues the operating system's bootstrap process

Because the secondary loader program is not limited to 510 bytes in size, it can do the more sophisticated job of examining the disk's file system and directory structures. The process of locating the secondary loader depends on the medium and operating system in use:

- **Floppy disks**—The bootstrap loader in the first block of a bootable MS-DOS floppy disk contains a small program that interprets the disk's FAT-12 file system to locate files MSDOS.SYS and IO.SYS, which are stored as the first files on the disk (or IBMBIO.SYS and IBMDOS.SYS, in the early DOS versions distributed by IBM). These files are read into memory and contain the code needed to complete MS-DOS's initialization.

- **Hard disks**—The disk's first sector (called the *Master Boot Record* or MBR) contains, in addition to the bootstrap loader code, a table that indicates the location of one or more partitions on the disk. One partition is marked as the *active* partition. The first sector of the active partition is called the *Volume Boot Record* (VBR), and it contains the OS loader. The primary boot loader relocates itself in memory, calculates the disk location of the VBR, reads it into memory at address 7C00h, and runs it.

  When a disk is configured for booting by MS-DOS, Windows 9x, or Windows Me, the secondary boot loader in the VBR locates and reads in files MSDOS.SYS and IO.SYS. Early versions of MS-DOS required these files to be stored at fixed locations on the disk, but later versions are able to examine the FAT file system tables and root directory to locate these files wherever they were physically placed on the disk. (They can move if, for example, the system files are updated after other files have been stored on the disk.)

  For Windows XP, 2000, and NT, the secondary boot loader in the VBR determines whether the disk is formatted with the FAT or NTFS file system, and then locates and reads into memory the file ntldr, which is stored as a hidden file in the drive's root directory.

Note

You can replace a missing or damaged Windows XP or 2000 Master Boot Record using the Windows Recovery Console and the **fixmbr** command, discussed in Chapter 12. Windows Vista users should first run Windows Recovery Environment (Windows RE) and select the Startup Repair option to perform these and other startup repairs. However, if Startup Repair does not solve the problem, the command **bootrec /fixboot** can be run from the Windows RE command prompt to fix the boot record. These commands are also discussed in Chapter 12.

  For Windows Vista, the secondary boot loader in the VBR locates and reads into memory the bootmgr file, which is stored as a hidden file in the drive's root directory.

- **CDs and DVDs**—Bootable CDs and DVDs contain a data block called the *booting catalog*, which lists one or more bootable operating systems. For each bootable operating system, there is a corresponding block-by-block copy or *image* of an entire (and probably small) bootable hard drive partition. A BIOS that is capable of booting from CD or DVD drives makes it temporarily appear (to itself!) during a boot from CD that an additional hard drive had been detected during startup. Attempts to read data blocks from this virtual hard drive are turned into reads of the corresponding block in the recorded disk image. The standard first-sector boot program is read in from this disk image, and the normal hard disk boot process continues as described in the previous paragraph. The secondary and subsequent bootstrap programs don't actually need to "know" that a CD is being used. As long as they rely on the BIOS to read data from what they think is a regular disk drive, the BIOS can perform the necessary sleight-of-hand to get the data from the CD. This method is used on the Windows Setup CD and on bootable Linux distribution discs.

- **USB drives**—Most recent systems can be booted from USB flash memory or external hard disk drives, provided that the drive contains appropriate boot files and that the USB drive is placed first in the boot order. USB flash memory drives can emulate floppy disk drives or CD/DVD drives, depending upon the source of boot files you use to prepare them. Various utilities are available online for setting up USB drives as bootable drives.

- **Networks**—Some network adapters contain BIOS extension ROM (described earlier) that permit the computer to be booted over a LAN. Typically these ROM-based bootstrap programs broadcast to the network to locate a boot server. The boot server responds by selecting an appropriate boot disk image file, which it transmits to the booting computer. The network BIOS ROM stores this data in memory, and as with the CD boot process, modifies the BIOS's data tables to add a virtual hard or floppy disk. The normal boot process continues from there. The first sector of the image contains a bootstrap loader that uses standard BIOS calls to read subsequent data, which is retrieved from the disk image stored in memory. (And, not surprisingly, if the operating system that is being loaded overwrites the section of memory that contains the disk image before the bootstrap process is complete, it crashes.) Network booting can be used to perform Windows setup on a corporate network, or to load a "thin client" terminal program on a diskless computer. It's also commonly used on network-based computers such as Sun workstations.

The next few sections discuss how the Windows startup process continues.

Windows XP/2000/NT Startup

Although Windows 9x and Me computers actually boot up MS-DOS and then start up Windows, Windows NT and its descendents—Windows 2000 and XP—have a completely different startup mechanism.

For Windows NT and relatives, the bootstrap process begins as described previously. However, the active partition's secondary loader takes things in a different direction. The secondary loader determines whether the disk is formatted with the FAT or NTFS file system, and then locates and reads file `ntldr` from the root directory of the boot partition, and `ntldr` continues the boot process.

`ntldr` locates file `boot.ini`, also stored in the root folder of the boot partition. `boot.ini` contains a list of operating system choices, and optionally, multiple entries for Windows, each with different startup options specified, which can be used to recover from failures and for debugging purposes. If you install your operating systems carefully and in the right order, `boot.ini` can also contain entries that allow you to select among MS-DOS, Windows 9x, Windows 2000, XP, Linux, and possibly other operating systems. The section "Boot Options," later in this chapter, discusses `boot.ini` further.

For each operating system choice, `boot.ini` contains a file path that points to a Windows folder or to a folder that contains a file that contains an alternate secondary-boot sector. If there is more than one choice, `ntldr` displays a menu. If you make a selection, or if a timeout period elapses, `ntldr` starts the highlighted operating system. You can also press F8 during a very small time window during the startup process, which makes `ntldr` display the built-in Windows Advanced Options menu. This menu includes the option to boot in Safe mode, with a minimal set of drivers, along with several other startup options.

If MS-DOS, Windows 9x, or Windows Me is selected from the boot menu, `ntldr` reads a saved copy of the boot sector installed by the older OS (for example, `bootsect.dos`). The standard DOS or Windows 9x boot process continues from there.

For Windows NT, 2000, and XP, `ntldr` runs the program `ntdetect.com`, which collects information about the installed hardware. It performs some hardware detection itself and collects other information from tables left in memory by the BIOS. If multiple hardware profiles are loaded, at this point `ntldr` may also stop and display the Hardware Profiles/Configuration Recovery menu.

ntldr then locates files ntoskrnl.exe and hal.dll in the system32 folder under the selected Windows folder. These two files form the Windows *kernel*, the foundation on which the operating system is based.

Windows Vista Startup

Windows Vista, as mentioned previously in this chapter, no longer uses the ntldr and boot.ini files to control the startup process. Instead, Windows Vista uses a file called bootmgr (also known as the Windows Boot Manager). bootmgr reads the information stored in the Boot Configuration Database (BCD) store (a file called BCD) to determine how to boot the system.

On systems that use the traditional PC/AT BIOS, the BCD store is located in C:\Boot\. On systems that use extensible firmware interface (EFI), BCD is located in C:\EFI\Microsoft\Boot\.

The BCD store includes at least two objects:

- **A Windows Boot Manager object**—This displays startup options, including tools such as the Windows Memory Diagnostic, the operating system(s) installed, and how long the menu stays on screen before starting the default operating system. This portion of the BCD store is comparable to the [boot loader] section of Windows NT2000XP's boot.ini file. To display the startup menu, press the F8 key at system startup, as with previous versions of Windows.

- **One or more Windows boot loader objects**—BCD also stores a Windows boot loader object for each version of Windows Vista on a system. If the system includes a dual-boot configuration including Windows 2000 or Windows XP, BCD also includes an object that points to the location of ntldr.

bootmgr is started by the Master Boot Record of the primary partition. After it starts, it reads the BCD store to determine how to boot the system.

If the system is not configured as a dual-boot system (that is, Windows Vista is the only operating system) and the system is being started (cold boot) or restarted (warm boot), bootmgr launches winload.exe.

However, if the system is being awakened from hibernation, bootmgr launches winresume.exe instead. winresume reads the system state stored in the hiberfil.sys hibernation file created when the system was sent into hibernation and restores the system to that state.

If the system is configured as a dual-boot system, bootmgr displays a startup menu, prompting the user to select the operating system desired. If the user selects Windows Vista (or does not select any operating system before the delay timer expires), bootmgr launches winload.exe to start Windows Vista. If the user selects a legacy version of Windows, bootmgr launches the appropriate startup program, such as ntldr (Windows 2000 or XP).

Both winload.exe and winresume.exe are located in \%systemroot%\System32 (on most systems, %systemroot% is C:\Windows).

The Windows NT Kernel

Windows NT, 2000, XP and Vista are all based on a kernel layer that provides basic, fundamental services to mediate access to hardware, start and stop processes, control the CPU's hardware, manage multiple CPUs if present, manage memory, and so on. Differences between motherboard and CPU designs are handled by the kernel's hardware abstraction layer, which performs CPU hardware management functions for the kernel and higher levels of Windows, without requiring them to know the details of the particular hardware implementation.

The "NT kernel" is actually not "Windows." The Windows that you are familiar with, the graphical interface, is actually implemented in layers *above* the kernel. And in fact other operating system environments (subsystems) such as UNIX and OS/2 can also take advantage of the NT Kernel. For example, Microsoft provided an OS/2 subsystem that made it possible to run character-mode OS/2 programs on Windows NT and 2000, although it's not provided with Windows XP. The UNIX (actually, POSIX) subsystem provided with Windows NT and 2000 is now called Interix, and it's available as a free download for Windows XP Professional—see Appendix A, Windows Tool Reference," for more information.

In addition to loading the kernel and HAL into memory, ntldr locates and loads the Registry's component files. It examines the Registry for value HKEY_LOCAL_MACHINE\System\Select\Current or HKEY_LOCAL_MACHINE\System\Select\LastKnownGood, depending on the selected boot mode, and creates key HKEY_LOCAL_MACHINE\System\CurrentControlSet, which is an "alias" to HKEY_LOCAL_MACHINE\System\ControlSet*nnn*, where *nnn* is the value retrieved from Select.

It then examines key HKEY_LOCAL_MACHINE\System\CurrentControlSet\Hardware Profiles to see whether there multiple profiles are defined. If more than one profile is defined and is feasible to load, ntldr displays another menu on the console, and again, if the user does not make a selection, a default setting is used.

With the desired hardware profile determined, ntldr scans Registry key HKEY_LOCAL_MACHINE\System\CurrentControlSet\Services for entries with a Type value of 1, which indicates a kernel-level device driver. Drivers that are marked for boot time startup are loaded by ntldr. At this point, the Windows kernel takes over.

The kernel performs two initialization phases. In the first phase, a minimum of services are initialized: the HAL, the Memory Manager, the Object Manager, the Security Reference manager (which is ultimately responsible for all access control under Windows, including files, Registry keys, synchronization objects, and internal data structures), and the Process Manager. The display is now switched for the first time from the text mode set up by the BIOS to a graphics mode and the small Windows startup progress bar is displayed.

Now, all systems are reinitialized and the startup process starts in earnest. Device drivers and filter drivers are loaded, in the order specified by the Load Ordering list shown in Table 2.2, and the Session Manager Subsystem (SMSS) starts. It loads the Win32 subsystem (win32k.sys). At this point, it's fair to say that Windows itself, rather than just the generic kernel, is running. The second Windows graphical startup screen is displayed. The Windows Service Controller (`services.exe`) is started, and services are started, as described later in the chapter under Windows Services.

Table 2.2   Windows XP Driver, Filter, and Service Load Ordering

1. System Reserved	32. Pointer Port
2. Boot Bus Extender	33. Keyboard Port
3. System Bus Extender	34. Pointer Class
4. SCSI miniport	35. Keyboard Class
5. Port	36. Video Init
6. Primary Disk	37. Video
7. SCSI Class	38. Video Save
8. SCSI CDROM Class	39. File System
9. FSFilter Infrastructure	40. Event Log
10. FSFilter System	41. Streams Drivers
11. FSFilter Bottom	42. NDIS Wrapper
12. FSFilter Copy Protection	43. COM Infrastructure
13. FSFilter Security Enhancer	44. UIGroup
14. FSFilter Open File	45. LocalValidation
15. FSFilter Physical Quota Management	46. PlugPlay
16. FSFilter Encryption	47. PNP_TDI
17. FSFilter Compression	48. NDIS
18. FSFilter HSM	49. TDI
19. FSFilter Cluster File System	50. NetBIOSGroup
20. FSFilter System Recovery	51. ShellSvcGroup
21. FSFilter Quota Management	52. SchedulerGroup
22. FSFilter Content Screener	53. SpoolerGroup
23. FSFilter Continuous Backup	54. AudioGroup
24. FSFilter Replication	55. SmartCardGroup
25. FSFilter Anti-Virus	56. NetworkProvider
26. FSFilter Undelete	57. RemoteValidation
27. FSFilter Activity Monitor	58. NetDDEGroup
28. FSFilter Top	59. Parallel arbitrator
29. Filter	60. Extended Base
30. Boot File System	61. PCI Configuration
31. Base	

Finally, the Windows logon process, `winlogon.exe`, is started. `Winlogon.exe` displays the Welcome screen or logon dialog. At this point, a user can log on, although for a short time, Windows services not essential for logon such as the IIS web server are still loading.

The Logon Process

When you log on using the Welcome Screen or logon dialog (the only option on corporate networks), Windows checks the logon name and password against the local account database, or in the case of a domain logon, forwards the logon request to a domain controller for verification. Successful domain logons may be cached on the local computer to speed future logons.

Note

For more detailed information about the domain logon process, search microsoft.com for the Microsoft Technet article "How Interactive Logon Works."

The User Profile

When a user has successfully authenticated him- or herself, the user profile is loaded. The profile is a folder stored under Documents and Settings, and it contains several significant files and folders:

- The `ntuser.dat` and `ntuser.dat.log` files, the user's Registry hive file, and its transaction file (a file that helps protect against corruption should the system crash while the Registry is being updated). The user's Registry hive is loaded under `HKEY_USERS`, and an alias key named `HKEY_CURRENT_USER` is created that points to this data.

- The `Desktop` folder, which contains the user's personal desktop items. The contents of this folder and the Desktop folder under the `All Users` profile folder are combined and displayed on the user's desktop.

- The `Start Menu` folder, which contains the user's personal start menu items. The contents of the folder and the `Start Menu` under the `All Users` profile folder are combined and displayed on the user's Start menu.

- The `[My] Documents` folder contains the user's personal files. (Windows Explorer displays this folder's name as "[My] Documents" for the logged-on user, but as "*xxx*'s Documents," where *xxx* is another user's logon name, when displaying other users' profile folders—but the folder is actually still named `[My] Documents`, unless the name has been changed in the Registry.)

- `Cookies`, `Favorites`, `Local Settings`, `Application Data`, `[My] Recent Documents`, `NetHood`, `PrintHood`, and other folders contain data for specific applications including history lists, bookmarks, email files, and so on. These files may be moved to alternate locations in some cases.

The first time a user logs on to a given computer, a new profile folder is created. For local users, the new profile is a copy of the `Default User` profile folder. (A simple copy will not work, as Registry key and file permissions must be modified to match the user to whom the profile belongs. This is why user profiles must be managed from the System Properties dialog, using the User Profile management dialog.)

For users on a corporate domain network whose account is set up as a Roaming User Profile, the profile folder must be copied from a server. At logoff, changes will be copied back to the server, and on the next logon, only changes made to the network profile since the last local logon must be copied down again. The Windows File Replication Service manages this process. In this way, the user's settings and [My] Documents folder "follow" her on the network and are available at any computer. (On such networks, email is typically not stored locally on the computer, but is kept in a central mailbox repository and accessed over the network using IMAP or Exchange services.)

Policy

Group or Local Computer policy is applied next. Group Policy is a function of the Windows Server Active Directory system, and it is constructed from one or more sources, depending on the policy groups and/or containers to which the user and the computer itself are assigned. The resulting set of policy (RSOP) is transmitted to the computer from a domain server.

Policy is actually a set of Registry entries that add to, or supercede when overlapping regular Registry entries, and cannot be modified by the user using the Registry editor. Windows components and applications look at this combined set of Registry data for settings that restrict or enforce certain behavior. This feature is used not only to tighten security by limiting users' ability to make configuration changes, but also to ensure consistent and appropriate configuration for all users of an organization.

The User Environment

The environment variable list is created from the following sources, in the following order:

1. Automatic definitions created by the system, including USERPROFILE, USERNAME, and so on.

2. Set commands in `autoexec.bat` in the `%systemroot%` drive (usually C:\).

3. The system environment list, configured from the System properties dialog Advanced tab, and stored in the Registry under key `HKEY_LOCAL_MACHINE\SYSTEM\CurrentControlSet\Control\Session Manager\Environment`. Environment variables within definitions, such as `%USERPROFILE%`, are substituted if possible.

4. The user's personal environment list, configured from the System properties dialog Advanced tab, and stored in the Registry under key `HKEY_CURRENT_USER\Environment`.

If more than one source defines the same environment variable, the last definition is the one that is kept, with the exception of the PATH variable. If there are multiple definitions of PATH, the first definition is kept, a semicolon is added, and the additional definition is appended. This way, PATH accumulates all paths defined in the various sources. Changes to the first two sources take effect only after a reboot or on your next logon. Changes to the third and fourth sources take effect the next time you start a program; for example, on opening a new command prompt window.

Startup Programs

When the user profile has been loaded, `winlogon` starts the user's shell program, which is by default `explorer.exe`, the standard Windows Explorer program. When it recognizes that it is being run as the user's first application, however, it knows that it's being asked to act as the user's desktop shell, so it displays the desktop, taskbar, and Start menu.

Tip

If `explorer.exe` is terminated or crashes, `winlogon` *should* automatically start another copy. However, if your desktop icons and taskbar disappear and don't start coming back within a few seconds, you can help the process along by calling up Task Manager via the keyboard (press Ctrl+Alt+Del), viewing the Applications tab, clicking New Task, and entering **explorer** as the program name.

explorer.exe is the default shell, but another program could be used just as well, such as cmd.exe—which would give you a command prompt window with no Start menu—or perhaps a custom program of your own devising. The shell program is specified in the registry by the value Shell under the key HKEY_CURRENT_USER\SOFTWARE\Microsoft\Windows NT\CurrentVersion\ Winlogon. If this value is present, it is used to determine the user's shell program; otherwise, the same key and value under HKEY_LOCAL_MACHINE is read, which specifies the systemwide default. Be very careful if you decide to change the systemwide setting because you could render your system unusable if you specify an improper program.

Tip

I have seen spyware programs that exploit this Registry entry by adding a program name after **explorer.exe**. This leaves Explorer as the shell but also runs the spyware as soon as anyone logs on. To fix this, press F8 when Windows boots (see the discussion of Safe mode later in this chapter) and select Safe Mode with Command Prompt. Log on, run **regedit**, and repair the **Shell** Registry value. Remove the program from any other startup program entries in which it appears (see the discussion that follows), and delete the program's **.exe** file(s). Then, restart Windows.

While the desktop icons are being collected and displayed, startup scripts and startup programs are run from the following sources:

- Scripts specified by Group Policy (or Local Computer Policy) under User Configuration, Windows Settings, Scripts (Logon/Logoff), Logon.

- Logon script specified by the user profile (configurable, for example, under Computer Management, Local Users and Groups, Users, *username* Properties, Profile tab).

- Shortcuts, files, or programs in the All Users profile subfolder Start Menu\Programs\Startup. Shortcuts and programs are executed. Files are opened using the associated application.

- Shortcuts, files or programs in the user's profile, subfolder Start Menu\Programs\Startup.

- 16-bit Windows programs listed in \windows\win.ini under the [windows] section in run= entries and load= entries.

- Programs listed in Registry key HKEY_LOCAL_MACHINE\Software\Microsoft\Windows\CurrentVersion\Run.

- Programs listed in Registry key HKEY_LOCAL_MACHINE\Software\Microsoft\Windows\CurrentVersion\RunOnce.

- Programs listed in Registry key HKEY_LOCAL_MACHINE\Software\Microsoft\Windows\CurrentVersion\RunOnceEx.

- Programs listed in Registry key
  HKEY_CURRENT_USER\Software\Microsoft\Windows\CurrentVersion\Run.

- Programs listed in Registry key
  HKEY_CURRENT_USER\Software\Microsoft\Windows\CurrentVersion\RunOnce.

- Programs listed in Registry key
  HKEY_CURRENT_USER\Software\Microsoft\Windows\CurrentVersion\RunOnceEx.

This process can take anywhere from a few seconds to a minute or more, depending on what scripts are set to run and what programs are installed. After this point, the user is completely logged on and ready to work.

Note

Besides the **Shell** Registry entry and the list of startup program sources listed previously, there is one other method that I've seen spyware authors use to install and run programs in a sneaky manner: creating a bogus print monitor. Print monitors are DLLs (program library modules) loaded by the Windows printing system, and they run in the context of the currently logged on user. If a program appears in the Task Manager's Processes under your username, and you can't find it listed in any other startup location (the **Winlogon\Shell** value, the **Run** Registry entries and Startup folder under All Users and your own user account, and the **win.ini** file), look for a bogus print monitor entry under **HKEY_LOCAL_MACHINE\System\CurrentControlSet\Control\Print\Monitors**. Spyware can install a DLL here, Windows will load it, and it then starts the spyware application that you see in the Processes list. If you find such an entry, boot Windows in Safe Mode with Command Prompt, log on, run **regedit**, and delete the bogus key under **Monitors**. There will most likely be several start techniques in use, so you'll need to check carefully—see the "Shell" tip mentioned previously.

Windows Boot Options

As discussed in the previous sections, as Windows XP, 2000, or NT begins its startup process, it runs program ntldr, which examines the root folder of the boot drive for a file named boot.ini. Windows Vista runs bootmgr, which uses the boot configuration data store \Boot\BCD instead. These files contain entries for one or more different installations of Windows, and different versions of Windows and even different operating systems such as MS-DOS or Linux. In addition, a special set of disaster-recovery boot options is available called the Windows Advanced Options menu; this menu is your first recourse if some driver or other disaster prevents Windows from starting, and it's discussed later in this chapter. We'll discuss the various startup options in this section.

Note

If the **boot.ini** file is missing, **ntldr** will load the first Windows installation it can find, and if you use SCSI disks it may not be able to find any. If you see a message that **boot.ini** is missing, you should try to restore it from a backup. The Recovery Console can also help you re-create **boot.ini**, as discussed later in the chapter.

Boot.ini and the Boot Menu (Windows NT Through XP)

When ntldr is starting Windows, it examines the root folder of the boot drive for a file named boot.ini. The file contains a list of one or more operating system choices. If there is just one choice, ntldr proceeds to load the operating system. When you have multiple operating system choices, or if you install the Recovery Console on your hard disk, you will run into the boot menu, an example of which appears in Figure 2.2. This section discusses the boot menu and boot.ini.

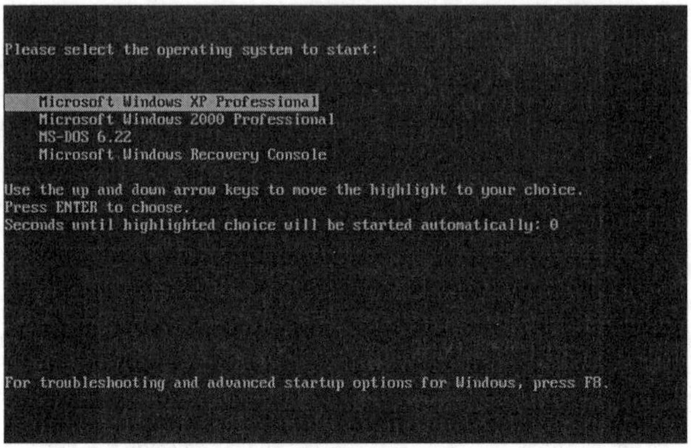

Figure 2.2 The Windows Boot menu lets you select from various operating systems and/or Windows installations.

Just to get us started, a boot.ini file for a system with several boot choices might look like this:

```
[boot loader]
timeout=5
default=multi(0)disk(0)rdisk(1)partition(2)\WINDOWS
[operating systems] ·
multi(0)disk(0)rdisk(1)partition(1)\WINDOWS="Microsoft Windows XP Professional"
➡    /fastdetect /NoExecute=OptIn
multi(0)disk(0)rdisk(1)partition(2)\WINDOWS="Microsoft Windows 2000 Professional"
➡    /fastdetect
C:\BOOTSECT.DOS="MS-DOS 6.22"
C:\CMDCONS\BOOTSECT.DAT="Microsoft Windows Recovery Console" /cmdcons
```

The [boot loader] section contains entries that control the behavior of the boot menu. The [operating systems] section contains entries for each bootable operating system, one line per entry. (The format of this book isn't wide enough to permit the lines to be printed as they appear in boot.ini; the symbol ➡ indicates that a line had to be split up to be printed. In the real boot.ini file, the text from /fastdetect on appears right after Professional.)

Boot Loader Options

The Boot Loader section can contain any of the entries listed in Table 2.3.

Table 2.3 *Boot.ini* **Boot Loader Section Options**

Entry	Description
timeout=*n*	Sets the time that **ntldr** waits for you to press a key while the boot menu is displayed to *n* seconds. If you don't press a key, the default operating system is booted. If you press any key, the countdown stops and **ntldr** waits for you to highlight an entry and press Enter.
	If timeout is set to 0, **ntldr** boots the default operating system without displaying the boot menu. If you set timeout to -1, **ntldr** always waits until you make a selection.
default=*location*	Sets the default operating system. The *location* text must match one of the location paths in the **[operating systems]** section. The location paths are the parts that appear to the left of the equal sign.

On Windows XP, you can change these settings most conveniently from the System Properties dialog, as discussed shortly.

Operating System Options

The [operating systems] section of boot.ini lists operating system boot choices, one per line, each with the format

```
location="description" options
```

The *description* text on the right side of the equal sign is placed between quotation marks. This is the text displayed as the boot menu choice when Windows starts, and it should be a descriptive name of the operating system and any special startup options that are attached.

The *options* are optional arguments placed after the description text, separated by single spaces, which can be used to control how the operating system starts. Options can be used, for example, to turn on startup logging, enable Safe mode, or let a software developer debug a device driver. The available options for Windows XP are listed in Table 2.4. Options that are not valid for Windows XP Professional x64 Edition include the notation "32-bit versions only."

Table 2.4 **Windows XP (32-bit)** *boot.ini* **Options**

Option	Description
/basevideo	Disables your selected video adapter, and instructs Windows to use a plain VGA adapter set to 640×480 resolution.
/bootlog	Creates a file named **ntbtlog.txt** in the root folder of the boot drive, listing all device drivers loaded, to help diagnose driver problems. The file may not be created if the kernel crashes before it can load the file system.
/burnmemory:*n*	Decreases the amount of memory available to Windows by *n* MB. Can be used to test Windows or application performance in impoverished circumstances. See also the **\maxmem** option.
/fastdetect	Prevents Windows from scanning your COM and LPT ports for devices, such as a serial mouse or printer ports. This option can speed up the boot process if you use a USB or PS2 mouse.

(continues)

Table 2.4   Continued

Option	Description
/fastdetect:*n*	Instructs Windows that you have a serial mouse connected to COM port number *n*. This option can speed up the boot process if you use a serial port mouse.
/maxmem=*n*	Specifies the maximum amount of RAM that Windows is allowed to use, where n is the number of MB. (See /burnmemory as well.)
/noexecute	Configures data execution prevention (DEP). To enable DEP at all times, add the option =alwayson. To enable DEP for the operating system and all processes, but allow administrators to disable DEP for specified executable files, add the option =optout (this is useful for solving problems with utility programs). To enable DEP only for operating system components, but enable administrators to enable DEP for executable files by using the Application Compatibility Toolkit (ACT), add the option =optin. To disable DEP completely, use the option =alwaysoff. Supported in Windows XP SP2 and later. These options are available only for 32-bit versions.
/noguiboot	Suppresses the graphical startup and progress bar that appears while Windows is booting. This is said to speed the boot process somewhat, but it results in a troublingly empty black screen during startup, unless you also specify /SOS.
/numproc=*n*	Limits the number of processors that Windows is to use to *n*; effective only on multiprocessor (or multicore) systems.
/safeboot:minimal	Starts Windows in Safe mode, with a minimal set of known "safe" drivers and services. See the later section on the Windows Advanced Options menu for more information about Safe mode.
/safeboot:minimal(*alternateshell*)	Starts Windows in Safe mode with a Command Prompt window instead of the usual desktop.
/safeboot:network	Starts Windows in Safe mode with networking support.
/safeboot:dsrepair	On a Windows domain controller server, starts Directory Services repair mode.
/SOS	Instructs ntldr to display the name of each driver it loads; this can help you identify which driver is crashing and preventing Windows from booting. Use with /basevideo for increased reliability.

Less Commonly Used Options

/HAL=*filename.dll*	Specifies a specific HAL module to load, rather than the one selected by Windows Setup. The file must be stored in \windows\system32. Specifying an alternative HAL may not work; see Microsoft Knowledge base article 309283. See also the /kernel option. It also may not be necessary: Windows XP automatically chooses between uniprocessor and multiprocessor HALs and kernels. Windows XP SP2 and later.
/kernel=*filename*	Specifies the kernel version to load, rather than the one specified by Windows Setup. The file must be stored in the \windows\system32 folder. This option is used primarily by device developers to select a "checked" debugging kernel.

Option	Description
/break	Sets a breakpoint (specified with the /debug parameter) to make the HAL wait until a debugger is connected. Note that system will crash with a BSOD if the /debug parameter is omitted.
/debug	Enables remote debugging of the Windows kernel or device drivers through a serial port or IEEE-1394 (FireWire) interface connected to a second computer (*remote debugging*). The debugger is activated immediately upon startup. USB debugging is also supported if the target system is running Windows Vista.
/crashdebug	Like /debug, but the debugger is not activated until a STOP (blue screen) occurs.
/debugport=*n*	Used with /debug or /crashdebug, specifies the COM port number to be used for debug communication.
/baudrate=*n*	Used with /debugport, sets the baud rate of the COM port used for kernel debugging to *n*, usually 9600 or greater.
/channel=*n*	Used with /debug, enables kernel debugging over an IEEE-1394 (FireWire) channel.
/nodebug	Disables kernel debugging; needed only when the installed Windows kernel has debugging enabled by default.
/redirect	The /redirect option applies to Windows Server 2003 only and is used to configure boot monitoring over a serial port for servers with no display adapters.
/3GB	Instructs the kernel to allow each application 3GB of *virtual* address space, with the kernel and kernel services mapped into 1GB, rather than the usual 2/2 split. Used primarily in Exchange Server installations.
/userva=*n*	Used in conjunction with /3GB; sets the amount of application virtual memory space to *n* MB rather than the default value of 3072 set by /3GB. Applies to Windows Server 2003 only.
/PAE	Instructs ntldr to load a Windows kernel that supports Physical Address Extension (an increased memory architecture) on Server computers. This option is ignored in Safe mode.
/nopae	Disables physical address extension (PAE); forces boot loader to load the non-PAE version of the Windows kernel. Supported in Windows XP SP2 and beyond. Disables PAE, except on 32-bit systems that include hardware-enabled data execution protection (DEP). On these systems, PAE is enabled when DEP is enabled. When DEP is disabled, PAE is also disabled.
/pcilock	Prevents Windows from managing interrupt addresses, I/O ports, and memory configuration for PCI devices, leaving the original BIOS settings in place. Using this option may make Windows fail to boot.

The *location* part of each [operating systems] line is a path to the Windows folder, or a specification for the boot sector of an alternative operating system.

For MS-DOS, Windows 95, 98, and Me, and the Recovery Console, the *location* is specified using a standard *drive:\path\filename* syntax specifying the name of a file that contains a copy of the boot loader originally stored in the first block of the boot partition by the alternative operating system. These original boot loaders are saved in a file by Windows Setup when it replaces an older operating system during installation. (For more information on performing upgrade installations of Windows XP, see Chapter 3, "Upgrading Windows.")

For Windows XP, 2000, and NT entries on Intel and Intel-compatible processors, the location path uses the unusual Advanced RISC Computing (ARC) path syntax rather than the expected `drive:\path` format used elsewhere in Windows. This is the tricky part.

Tip

To see the correct ARC pathnames for all of your hard drives, run the Recovery Console as described in Chapter 12, and type the **map** command.

In *most* cases, your Windows folder is `c:\windows` on an IDE or SATA disk drive. In this case, the ARC path is

```
multi(0)disk(0)rdisk(0)partition(1)\windows
```

But, ARC paths can take one of three forms. For drives that can be accessed through standard BIOS INT 13 calls, which includes IDE disks, SATA disks, and SCSI disks on controllers with modern BIOS extensions, thus the majority of drives on home/office computers, the format is

```
multi(c)disk(0)rdisk(n)partition(p)\foldername
```

> where: *c* is the disk controller number, counted from 0 up.
>
> *n* identifies the physical disk drive attached to this controller. For IDE drives this is 0 (master) or 1 (slave); for SATA drives this is a number from 0 to 3; and for SCSI drives this number can be between 0 and 15.
>
> *p* indicates the partition number on this physical drive, counted from 1 up.
>
> *foldername* is the name of the %systemroot% folder on this partition, usually windows or winnt.

For SCSI disks that the BIOS cannot access using INT 13 calls, and that require a separate driver (ntbootdd.sys, installed by Windows Setup), the syntax is

```
scsi(c)disk(n)rdisk(u)partition(p)\foldername
```

> where: *c* is the disk controller number, counted from 0 up.
>
> *n* specifies the physical disk drive attached to this controller. For SCSI drives this number can be between 0 and 15.
>
> *u* indicates the SCSI logical unit number (LUN) of the disk that contains the boot partition, typically 0.
>
> *p* indicates the desired partition number, counted from 1 up.
>
> *foldername* is the name of the %systemroot% folder on this partition, usually windows or winnt.

A third syntax is used when either of the following conditions is encountered:

- Windows is installed on a partition greater than 7.8GB in size or the ending disk cylinder number for the partition is greater than 1024, and, the system BIOS does not support extended INT 13 calls or they are disabled.

- The disk controller requires BIOS extensions, but they do not support extended INT 13 calls or they are disabled.

(In other words, the Windows partition is too large or too far into the disk to be reachable by non-extended BIOS functions.)

In this case, Windows Setup will have installed a driver named `ntbootdd.sys` in the boot drive's root folder, and the following syntax will be used in `boot.ini`:

`signature(s)disk(n)rdisk(0)partition(p)\foldername`

> where: *s* is an 8-digit hexadecimal number that matches a special identifying number written to the hard disk's Master Boot Record during Windows setup.
>
> *n* specifies the disk's physical drive number, counted from 0 on up.
>
> *p* indicates the partition number on the this physical drive, counted from 1 up.
>
> *foldername* is the name of the `%systemroot%` folder on this partition, usually `windows` or `winnt`.

During startup, `ntldr` must scan the *n*th disk on each controller until it finds the disk with the indicated signature value.

For more information about basic ARC syntax, see support.microsoft.com/kb/102873. For more information about the `signature()` syntax, see support.microsoft.com/kb/227704.

Selecting a Default Operating System

You could edit the `boot.ini` file manually to select the default operating system choice displayed on the boot menu, and the time that the boot loader waits if you make no selection, but there's an easier way. To set these options using a dialog box, follow these steps:

1. Log on as a Computer Administrator.

2. Click Start, and right-click [My] Computer. Select Properties.

3. Select the Advanced tab, and under Startup and Recovery click the Settings button.

4. The Startup and Recovery dialog will appear, as shown in Figure 2.3.

5. Select a default operating system from the drop-down list.

6. To speed up the Windows boot process when you're not attending to the screen, set Time to Display List of Operating Systems to a small number like 5 seconds.

7. Alternatively, to make Windows wait for you to make a selection no matter how much time passes, uncheck the box next to both of the Time to Display entries.

8. Click OK to save the changes.

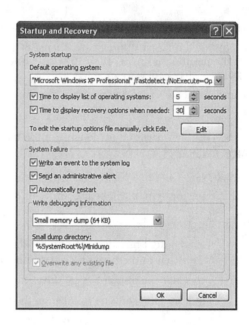

Figure 2.3   The Startup and Recovery dialog lets you select a default operating system and edit `boot.ini`.

Editing `boot.ini` Manually

If you want to delete boot menu choices or add options to one of the selections, on Windows XP you can use the `bootcfg` command-line program (this is distinct from the `bootcfg` Recovery Console command). Its use is described in Microsoft Knowledge Base article number 289022, at support.microsoft.com/kb/289022.

However, it's just about as easy to edit `boot.ini` directly. On Windows XP, open the Startup and Recovery dialog as described in steps 1 through 4 in the previous section. Then, click the Edit button. This will temporarily remove protections from `boot.ini` and will let you edit the file with Notepad. It would be prudent to save a copy of the contents of `boot.ini` before you make any changes. When you have made your changes, save the file and exit Notepad. The file protections will put be back in place automatically.

On Windows 2000 and NT, you must edit `boot.ini` from the command prompt. You must be logged on as a Computer Administrator. Open a Command Prompt window and type the following commands:

```
c:
cd \
attrib -s -h -r boot.ini
copy boot.ini boot.ini.bak
notepad boot.ini
attrib +s +h +r boot.ini
```

This procedure leaves a backup copy of `boot.ini` named `boot.ini.bak`. If you have to undo your changes, simply repeat the steps but reverse the `copy` command:

```
copy boot.ini.bak boot.ini
```

If you can't boot Windows at all, you can use the Recovery Console to repair `boot.ini` using the `bootcfg /rebuild` command, or you can create a `boot.ini` file on another computer and transfer it to your computer on a floppy disk.

Windows Vista Boot Configuration Data Store

During the process of starting Windows Vista, the `bootmgr` program uses the BCD store file (BCD) to configure and control the boot process. The BCD store file lists the operating system(s) available for booting and any additional diagnostic tools that can be run during the boot process. Unlike `boot.ini`, though, the BCD store file is not a plain-text file, a feature designed to protect Windows Vista startup from being easily hijacked by malware.

Understanding the Structure of the BCD Store File

The BCD store file is object oriented: It contains various objects, each with various elements that configure the object. For example, the first object listed is the Windows Boot Manager, which, as displayed by BCDEdit (the BCD store file viewer and editor provided by Windows Vista), looks like this:

```
Windows Boot Manager
--------------------
identifier              {9dea862c-5cdd-4e70-acc1-f32b344d4795}
device                  partition=C:
description             Windows Boot Manager
locale                  en-US
inherit                 {7ea2e1ac-2e61-4728-aaa3-896d9d0a9f0e}
default                 {7d36dfda-da5c-11db-bcb9-f957cd5e1116}
resumeobject            {7d36dfdb-da5c-11db-bcb9-f957cd5e1116}
displayorder            {7d36dfda-da5c-11db-bcb9-f957cd5e1116}
toolsdisplayorder       {b2721d73-1db4-4c62-bf78-c548a880142d}
timeout                 30
```

The BCD object name is "Windows Boot Manager," and all the entries that follow, such as identifier, device, and so on, are BCD elements. Note that many elements are identified by globally unique identifier (GUID) values (hex digits in curly brackets).

Any BCD store file also includes at least one Windows Boot Loader element, which points to a Windows Vista installation on the system. A typical Windows Boot Loader element resembles the following, as displayed by BCDEdit:

```
Windows Boot Loader
-------------------
identifier              {7d36dfda-da5c-11db-bcb9-f957cd5e1116}
device                  partition=C:
path                    \Windows\system32\winload.exe
description             Microsoft Windows Vista
locale                  en-US
```

```
inherit                {6efb52bf-1766-41db-a6b3-0ee5eff72bd7}
osdevice               partition=C:
systemroot             \Windows
resumeobject           {7d36dfdb-da5c-11db-bcb9-f957cd5e1116}
nx                      OptIn
```

As you can see from these objects, this system uses US-English as its locale (which configures it to use U.S. standard English and date/time/money settings), uses the C: drive as the system drive, locates Windows in the usual `\Windows` folder, and starts Vista using `winload.exe` in Windows' `system32` folder.

On a system with only Windows Vista installed, BCDEdit displays only these two objects. However, the BCD store file contains many additional elements. Here is the complete list of BCD store file objects from a typical Windows Vista installation:

```
Windows Boot Manager
--------------------
identifier             {9dea862c-5cdd-4e70-acc1-f32b344d4795}
device                 partition=C:
description            Windows Boot Manager
locale                 en-US
inherit                {7ea2e1ac-2e61-4728-aaa3-896d9d0a9f0e}
default                {7d36dfda-da5c-11db-bcb9-f957cd5e1116}
resumeobject           {7d36dfdb-da5c-11db-bcb9-f957cd5e1116}
displayorder           {7d36dfda-da5c-11db-bcb9-f957cd5e1116}
toolsdisplayorder      {b2721d73-1db4-4c62-bf78-c548a880142d}
timeout                30

Windows Boot Loader
-------------------
identifier             {7d36dfda-da5c-11db-bcb9-f957cd5e1116}
device                 partition=C:
path                   \Windows\system32\winload.exe
description            Microsoft Windows Vista
locale                 en-US
inherit                {6efb52bf-1766-41db-a6b3-0ee5eff72bd7}
osdevice               partition=C:
systemroot             \Windows
resumeobject           {7d36dfdb-da5c-11db-bcb9-f957cd5e1116}
nx                      OptIn

Resume from Hibernate
---------------------
identifier             {7d36dfdb-da5c-11db-bcb9-f957cd5e1116}
device                 partition=C:
path                   \Windows\system32\winresume.exe
description            Windows Resume Application
locale                 en-US
inherit                {1afa9c49-16ab-4a5c-901b-212802da9460}
filedevice             partition=C:
filepath               \hiberfil.sys
pae                    Yes
debugoptionenabled     No

Windows Memory Tester
---------------------
```

```
identifier              {b2721d73-1db4-4c62-bf78-c548a880142d}
device                  partition=C:
path                    \boot\memtest.exe
description             Windows Memory Diagnostic
locale                  en-US
inherit                 {7ea2e1ac-2e61-4728-aaa3-896d9d0a9f0e}
badmemoryaccess         Yes

Windows Legacy OS Loader
------------------------
identifier              {466f5a88-0af2-4f76-9038-095b170dc21c}
device                  partition=C:
path                    \ntldr
description             Earlier Version of Windows

EMS Settings
------------
identifier              {0ce4991b-e6b3-4b16-b23c-5e0d9250e5d9}
bootems                 Yes

Debugger Settings
-----------------
identifier              {4636856e-540f-4170-a130-a84776f4c654}
debugtype               Serial
debugport               1
baudrate                115200

RAM Defects
-----------
identifier              {5189b25c-5558-4bf2-bca4-289b11bd29e2}

Global Settings
---------------
identifier              {7ea2e1ac-2e61-4728-aaa3-896d9d0a9f0e}
inherit                 {4636856e-540f-4170-a130-a84776f4c654}
                        {0ce4991b-e6b3-4b16-b23c-5e0d9250e5d9}
                        {5189b25c-5558-4bf2-bca4-289b11bd29e2}

Boot Loader Settings
--------------------
identifier              {6efb52bf-1766-41db-a6b3-0ee5eff72bd7}
inherit                 {7ea2e1ac-2e61-4728-aaa3-896d9d0a9f0e}

Resume Loader Settings
----------------------
identifier              {1afa9c49-16ab-4a5c-901b-212802da9460}
inherit                 {7ea2e1ac-2e61-4728-aaa3-896d9d0a9f0e}
```

For information about the Windows Boot Manager and Windows Boot Loader objects, see the discussion of these objects earlier in this section.

The Resume from Hibernation object configures how Windows Vista wakes from hibernation. Note that Windows Vista uses winresume.exe, rather than winload.exe, for this task. Note also the location of the hibernation file (\hiberfil.sys).

The Windows Memory Tester object enables the tester to be made available on the boot menu that appears in a dual-boot configuration, or if the user presses the F8 key at startup to start the boot menu. If the Windows Memory Tester detects defective memory locations, they are stored in the location referred to by the RAM Defects object described later in this section.

The Windows Legacy OS Loader object is present whether a dual-boot configuration is installed or not. By default, it points to `ntldr` on the system drive, but if a version of Windows that does not use `ntldr` is present (such as Windows 9x or Me), this information would be changed to reflect the startup file used by the legacy version in use.

The EMS Settings object configures the Emergency Management Services remote access option.

The Debugger Settings object sets up the type of debugger connection that can be used if the boot process needs to be debugged. By default, Windows Vista is configured to use a serial connection on COM 1, but USB and 1394 ports can also be used for debugging.

Note

Windows Vista defaults to COM 1 even on legacy-free systems that do not include serial ports.

The RAM Defects object points to the location storing information about RAM defects detected with the Memory Diagnostic program.

The Global Settings object lists global settings that should be inherited (used) by all boot applications.

The Boot Loader Settings object lists global settings inherited by all boot loaders.

The Resume Loader Settings object lists global settings that should be used by all resume applications.

Note

The standard GUID values for the last three objects are listed in the Standard Inheritable Objects table located in the Microsoft reference document "Boot Configuration Data in Windows Vista." Use this document to explore BCD in more detail than is available here. It can be obtained from the Downloads section of www.microsoft.com.

End the elements in a BCD store file as listed here by using `BCDEdit.exe`, you must run BCDEdit with the optional switches `bcdedit /enum all /v`.

Using `BCDEdit.exe`

To enable you to view or change the contents of the BCD store file, Windows Vista includes a command-line program called `BCDEdit.exe`. To run BCDEdit, right-click the command prompt shortcut in the Start menu (by default, it's located in Accessories, but some systems might locate it in the first-level Start menu) and select Run as Administrator. Provide credentials as prompted. Type **bcdedit**, add any options desired, and press Enter.

If you run BCDEdit without any options, you will see a condensed version of the BCD store's contents, listing only the boot manager and boot loader sections.

To see the entire contents of BCDEdit, as shown in the previous section, use the command bcdedit /enum all /v.

The following command switches can be used with BCDEdit. Note that you must specify file names, GUID values, or other information with these commands.

Commands That Operate on a Store

/createstore	Creates a new and empty boot configuration data store.
/export	Exports the contents of the system store to a file. This file can be used later to restore the state of the system store.
/import	Restores the state of the system store using a backup file created with the /export command.

Tip

Because a damaged or lost BCD store file can prevent your system from starting, it's a very good idea to use the **BCDEdit /export** option to create a backup of your data store. For example, **BCDEdit /export c:\mybcdfile** creates a copy of your BCD store file in the root folder of C: drive under the name *mybcdfile*.

After you create the store file, copy it to a USB flash drive or a recordable CD for safekeeping.

The Windows RE Startup Repair function or the **Bootrec /rebuildBCD** command can be used to rebuild a missing or damaged BCD store file. For more information about using these tools, see Microsoft Knowledge Base article 927391, available from http://support.microsoft.com.

Commands That Operate on Entries in a Store

/copy	Makes copies of specified entries in the store.
/create	Creates new entries (as specified) in the store.
/delete	Deletes entries (as specified) from the store.
/? ID	Displays information about identifiers used by these commands.

Commands That Operate on Entry Options

/deletevalue	Deletes entry options (as specified) from the store.
/set	Sets entry option values (as specified) in the store.
/? TYPES	Lists datatypes used by these commands.
/? FORMATS	Lists valid data formats.

Commands That Control Output

/enum	Lists entries in the store.
/v	Command-line option that displays entry identifiers in full, rather than using names for well-known identifiers. Use /v by itself as a command to display entry identifiers in full for the ACTIVE type.

Note

Running **bcdedit** by itself is equivalent to running **bcdedit /enum ACTIVE**.

Commands That Control the Boot Manager

/bootsequence	Sets the one-time boot sequence (as specified) for the boot manager.
/default	Sets the default entry that the boot manager will use.
/displayorder	Sets the order in which the boot manager displays the multi-boot menu.
/timeout	Sets the boot manager timeout value.
/toolsdisplayorder	Sets the order in which the boot manager displays the tools menu.

Commands That Control Emergency Management Services for a Boot Application

/bootems	Enables or disables Emergency Management Services for a boot application.
/ems	Enables or disables Emergency Management Services for an operating system entry.
/emssettings	Sets the global Emergency Management Services parameters.

Commands That Control Debugging

/bootdebug	Enables or disables boot debugging for a boot application.
/dbgsettings	Sets the global debugger parameters.
/debug	Enables or disables kernel debugging for an operating system entry.

As you can see from this list of commands, you can use BCDedit to make temporary or permanent changes to the system's boot sequence.

Other methods for changing the contents of BCD included in Windows Vista include using the Boot tab of MSConfig or going through a Windows Management Instrumentation (WMI) interface. For more information, see the links available at http://msdn2.microsoft.com/en-us/library/aa362692.aspx.

Alternatives to BCDEdit

Although BCDEdit can be used to create, as well as view, boot configuration, its use of the command line and the need to specify some types of boot information in hexadecimal notation make it difficult to use. As an alternative, consider the use of a third-party BCD editor, such as VistaBootPRO, available from http://www.vistabootpro.org, or EasyBCD, available from http://neosmart.net.

Adjusting Boot Options with MSConfig

Instead of editing boot.ini in Windows XP or the BCD store file in Windows Vista, consider using the System Configuration utility, MSConfig.exe.

The Windows XP version of MSConfig.exe includes the BOOT.INI tab, which edits the BOOT.INI file for you. In the Windows Vista version, this tab is replaced by the Boot tab, which offers similar options for editing the BCD data store. Vista options are shown in parentheses in **bold**.

These switches are

- /SAFEBOOT (**Safe Boot**)—Sets the computer to always boot into Safe mode. You can choose additional switches for this option, including MINIMAL (normal Safe mode; **Minimal**), NETWORK (Safe mode with networking; **Network**), DSREPAIR (Directory Services Repair, normally only used on servers in an Active Directory environment; **Active Directory Repair**), and MINIMAL/ALTERNATE SHELL (Safe mode with command prompt, **Alternate Shell**).

- /NOGUIBOOT (**No GUI Boot**)—Disables startup animation.

- /BOOTLOG (**Boot log**)—Writes a detailed log of the boot process to a file named NTBTLOG.TXT.

- /BASEVIDEO (**Base video**) —Causes Windows to start up using a generic 640×480 VGA driver rather than the installed video driver (useful if the installed video driver isn't working or if your display has been configured to use an unsupported mode).

- /SOS (**OS boot information**)—Displays the driver filenames as each driver is loaded during startup (can help to pinpoint where Windows startup is bogging down); normally, this information is displayed only in Safe Mode, Safe Mode with Networking, or Safe Mode with Command Prompt startups.

At the bottom of the Boot Options section of the BOOT.INI or Boot tab is a button labeled Advanced Options. Four additional switches can be added to the Windows startup process via this button:

- /MAXMEM (**Maximum Memory**)—Enables you to set a limit on how much RAM Windows is able to access (can be used to test whether a RAM module is faulty, or to solve problems that may occur when using more than 2GB of RAM on a 32-bit installation).

- /NUMPROC (**Number of Processors**)—Lets you limit the number of processors Windows has access to on a multiprocessor system.

- /PCILOCK (**PCI Lock**)—Prohibits Windows from assigning IRQ resources to PCI-based hardware; the devices remain as configured by the BIOS settings.

- /DEBUG (**Debug**)—Starts Windows in debugging mode (this is used when you have a second system hooked up to debug the malfunctioning system).

The Boot Advanced Options on the Windows Vista version also includes this option:

- **Detect HAL**—Detects the hardware abstraction layer used by this installation.

You can run MSConfig at any time to change these options, rather than using a text editor with boot.ini or the arcane switches of BCDEdit. For other features of MSConfig, see the section "System Configuration Utility," in Chapter 12.

Windows Advanced Options Menu (Safe Mode)

If you experience problems after installing a new driver or hardware, or if you are plagued by virus or spyware software that can't be deleted while Windows is running, you can often boot

Windows in a special Safe mode that uses a very limited set of known-good device drivers, and very few additional services. In many cases Windows can be started in a degraded but functional mode in which you can then perform repairs. Windows also has boot options that keep a record of all drivers loaded to help you find which one is causing a problem.

You can access the special Windows Advanced Options menu for Windows XP or Vista by pressing F8 while Windows starts up. There are two ways to get to this menu:

- If your system doesn't pause at the boot menu, you'll have to plan your attack. Start Windows, and as soon as the screen indicates that the BIOS startup is finished, start pressing F8 rapidly and repeatedly. If this doesn't work, restart the computer again (you may need to power it off and back on, if Windows won't start or if you can't shut it down), and this time start pressing F8 as soon as something appears on the screen.

- If your system has multiple boot options, it will pause at the boot menu when Windows starts. You can press F8 while this menu is displayed.

The Windows Advanced Options menu for Windows XP will appear as shown in Figure 2.4.

Windows Vista's Advanced Boot Options menu is shown in Figure 2.5.

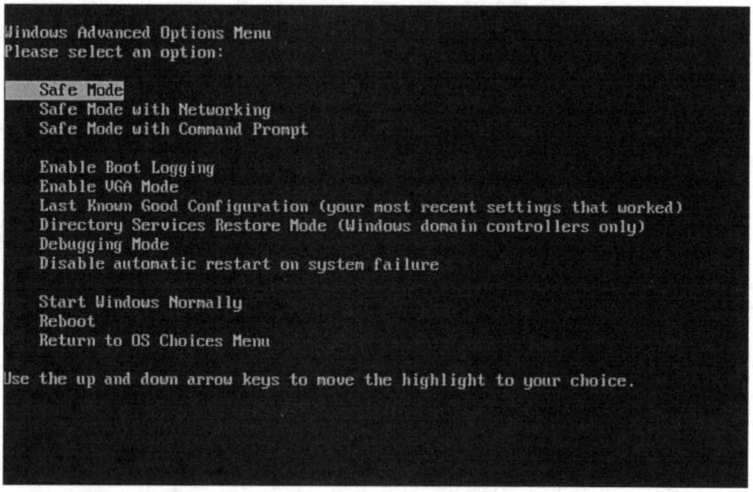

Figure 2.4   Press F8 during startup to display the Windows Vista (left) and XP (right) Advanced Options menu, which includes Safe mode.

The most common choices and their uses are as follows:

- If you have set your display adapter to a resolution or refresh rate that your monitor doesn't support, select low-resolution video (VGA Mode). This uses your normal graphics adapter driver but sets the resolution to 640×480 at a 60Hz refresh rate.

- If malware such as a virus or spyware is causing trouble and you can't delete it, or you are unable to install an antivirus or antispyware utility because of it, use Safe Mode.

- If you have made a device driver configuration change and Windows no longer works, try Last Known Good Configuration before trying System Restore.

- If you have installed a new driver and Windows no longer works, use Safe mode, and try to update, replace, or disable the driver. If this fails, use Safe mode and use System Restore to roll back your driver change. System Restore data is not saved in Safe mode, so you can't use System Restore to undo changes you've made in Safe mode. Windows Vista also supports running System Restore from Windows RE (see Chapter 12 for details).

- If a device driver is making Windows crash but you don't know which driver is causing it, select Enable Boot Logging. Then, after Windows crashes, restart in Safe mode. Use Notepad to examine the file `ntbtlog.txt` in your `\windows` folder, which will display a list of drivers that were loaded. There will be two boots' worth of drivers listed. The first part begins with the operating system version and file `ntoskrnl.exe`, and ends (hopefully) with the driver that crashed Windows. The second part of the listing starts with the operating system version and `ntoskrnl.exe` again. This second part was added when you rebooted in Safe mode, so your troublesome driver *should* be the one just above the second part. (You can also examine `ntbtlog.txt` by booting up the Recovery Console in Windows XP, or by starting Command Prompt from Windows RE with Windows Vista.)

  Delete `ntoskrnl.txt` after viewing it; otherwise it will just continue to grow and will be difficult to interpret.

- If your display adapter driver is crashing Windows, the previous technique won't help—the crash will probably occur before Windows starts writing the log file. In this case select Safe Mode, which uses a "plain vanilla" VGA display driver, and either update your display driver or use System Restore to roll back a previous one.

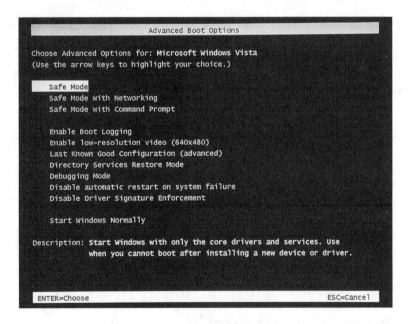

Figure 2.5   Press F8 during startup to display the Advanced Boot Options menu for Windows Vista.

All the selections in the Windows Advanced Options menu are described in the following sections.

Safe Mode

Safe Mode boots Windows with a limited set of display and disk drivers, and minimal services. The display driver used is for the original IBM PC VGA color adapter, which all current adapters can emulate, set to 640×480 resolution, which all current monitors can display.

Safe mode will often let you start Windows when viruses or adware keep it from starting, or prevent you from loading antivirus or antispyware software. It also usually works when you have a problematic driver or service that is crashing Windows. Start in Safe mode and use Driver Roll Back or System Restore to repair the problem.

Selecting Safe Mode with Windows XP is the same as adding options `/safeboot:minimal /sos /bootlog /noguiboot` to whatever standard options are specified in `boot.ini`, such as `/fastdetect`. To add comparable options to Windows Vista, use MSConfig. Refer to the section "Adjusting Boot Options with MSConfig" for details.

Safe Mode with Networking

Like Safe Mode, Safe Mode with Networking uses a small set of very basic drivers and minimal services. In addition, your network adapter driver is loaded and Windows networking services are started. Use this mode when you need to perform a Safe mode repair but you need files that are stored on a network server.

Selecting this mode is the same as adding options `safeboot:network /sos /bootlog /noguiboot` to the `boot.ini` entry. To add comparable options to Windows Vista, use MSConfig. Refer to the section "Adjusting Boot Options with MSConfig" for details.

Safe Mode with Command Prompt

Safe Mode with Command Prompt is the same as Safe Mode, except that when you have logged on, instead of running `explorer.exe` to display the standard Desktop, a Command Prompt window is opened. This can help circumvent problems that prevent Explorer from starting correctly.

Selecting this mode is the same as adding `/safeboot:minimal(alternateshell) /sos /bootlog /noguiboot` to the `boot.ini` entry in Windows XP. To add comparable options to Windows Vista, use MSConfig. Refer to the section "Adjusting Boot Options with MSConfig" for details.

Enable Boot Logging

This option adds the `/bootlog` option to your standard boot selection. This creates the file `ntbtlog.txt` (in whatever folder your copy of Windows is installed), and this log file lists every driver loaded during startup. See the discussion of boot logging earlier in this section.

Enable Low-Resolution Video (VGA Mode)

The Enable Low-Resolution Video (VGA) Mode selection performs a standard startup, but your existing video driver is reset to 640×480 resolution and a 60Hz refresh rate. This should fix things if you've selected an inappropriate video mode. It will *not* help if you have a bad or incorrect video driver installed. In that case, use Safe mode.

Enable VGA mode adds the `/basevideo` option to the default `boot.ini` options in Windows XP. To add the comparable option to Windows Vista, use MSConfig. Refer to the section "Adjusting Boot Options with MSConfig" for details.

Last Known Good Configuration

Last Known Good Configuration starts Windows using the `Last Known Good` section in the Registry. This is a copy of the service and device driver selections and settings that were in effect the last time Windows was able to start up normally. These settings are recorded when Windows starts, and are marked "Last Known Good" when Windows is then shut down normally.

Directory Services Restore Mode

This option is used only on a Windows Server Domain controller. It initiates a repair procedure.

Debugging Mode

The Debugging Mode option is used by device driver software developers to let a second computer monitor Windows kernel activity through a serial or IEEE-1394 port. Selecting this option is the same as adding `/debug` to the selected `boot.ini` entry in Windows XP. You should also add the `/channel` or `/debugport` and `/baudrate` options to the `boot.ini` entry before using this selection. To add comparable options to Windows Vista, use MSConfig. Refer to the section "Adjusting Boot Options with MSConfig" for details.

Disable Automatic Restart on System Failure

This option is available on Windows XP Service Pack 2 and later. It disables the Windows automatic restart-after-crash feature so that you can then restart Windows and see what the blue screen says when Windows crashes. It's a very welcome addition.

Disable Driver Signature Enforcement

Windows Vista x64 editions load a kernel-mode driver only if the kernel can verify the driver signature. This option disables load-time signature enforcement for a kernel-mode driver, which allows unsigned drivers or drivers with improper signatures to be installed, primarily for testing or driver development purposes. This setting is for the current session only, and does not persist across system restarts.

Start Windows Normally

This selection starts your default or selected operating system with no extra recovery options.

Reboot

This selection restarts the computer. This option is not available in Windows Vista.

Esc=Cancel or Return to OS Choices Menu

This selection returns to the boot menu, if it was displayed prior to your pressing F8.

Starting Windows Memory Diagnostic (Windows Vista)

Windows Vista includes the Windows Memory Diagnostic, which is discussed in detail in Chapter 12. It is available as a startup option from the Advanced Boot Options menu, although it is not listed as a selection.

To select the Windows Memory Diagnostic from the Advanced Boot Options menu shown in Figure 2.5, press Esc to display the Windows Boot Manager dialog. If you have a dual-boot configuration, make sure Microsoft Windows Vista is highlighted. Then press the Tab key to move the highlight to Windows Memory Diagnostic and press Enter. Windows Memory Diagnostic tests your system before booting Windows.

Installing a Multibooting System

Windows makes it reasonably easy to choose between several different operating systems or versions of Windows when you start up your computer. This process is called *multibooting*. There's not room in this book to go into multiboot setup in great detail. I will give you this bit of advice, however: To create a system that lets you choose between different Windows versions and older Windows versions, use the following guidelines:

■ If you want to be able to boot to MS-DOS, set up multiple disk partitions, or multiple disks. Format the first drive, or the first partition, with the FAT file system, using the MS-DOS setup floppy disk. This partition can be small—a few dozen to a few hundred megabytes should be sufficient. The maximum size supported by MS-DOS 5 and above is 2GB.

Install MS-DOS first. Then, install later versions of Windows.

■ If you want to boot Windows 95, 98, or Me, set up multiple disk partitions or multiple disks. For Windows 98 or Me, format a partition with the FAT32 file system to get more efficient disk utilization. Install these operating systems after MS-DOS and before Windows Vista, XP, 2000, or NT.

■ If you want to install multiple versions of Windows Vista, XP, 2000, or NT, install NT first, and then 2000, XP, and finally Vista. Install each of these onto *separate disk partitions*. Don't succumb to the temptation to install them in differently named folders on the same partition, as the Program Files folder name is fixed, and you will end up with mismatched versions of system utilities.

Install the latest service pack for Windows NT before installing Windows 2000, and the latest service pack for Windows 2000 before installing XP. This is necessary because each later version of Windows may upgrade your disks' NTFS version, and the service packs are necessary so that the older operating system can read the newer versions.

■ If you want to install older versions of Windows, such as Windows 9x or Me, Windows 2000 or Windows XP, and then Windows Vista, install the older version of Windows first, and then install Windows Vista. Install each of these onto *separate disk partitions*. And be sure to configure System Restore in Windows XP to ignore the system drive letter used by Windows Vista. Do this to prevent Windows XP's System Restore from deleting Windows Vista's restore points. For more information about System Restore in Windows XP and Vista, see Chapter 12.

■ MS-DOS can't read FAT32 or NTFS partitions, and Windows 95, 98, and Me can't read NTFS partitions. Older operating systems will skip over any partitions they can't read when assigning drive letters, so the disk drive letter assigned to a given partition may vary from one operating system to another.

■ If you want to be able to boot Linux, your best bet is to install either install Linux last and use a Linux boot loader, or install Vista last and use the Windows Boot Manager.

For more detailed information on setting up multibooting Windows installations, see *Special Edition Using Windows XP Professional, 3rd Edition*, and *Special Edition Using Microsoft Windows Vista*, both published by Que. Also, view Microsoft Knowledge Base article number 306559 at support.microsoft.com/kb/306559.

Windows Services

As mentioned earlier, services are programs that are run by Windows without the need for an interactive logon. They are not part of the Windows kernel, but are applications that nevertheless provide essential system functions.

Services can be configured to start automatically as soon as Windows starts up (this includes services like Remote Desktop and the Event Logging system); to start up manually, either by you, when you want it or more often, when requested by another service or application (this includes the CD Burning service); and a "disabled" setting that prevents the service from running at all.

Most Windows service programs are packaged as dynamic link libraries (.DLLs) rather than as standalone executable (.EXE) files. These are loaded and called by svchost.exe. Svchost is a small program that contains the code a service needs to interact with the Windows Service Controller, but none of the code to actually implement a service. Svchost calls functions in the service's dynamic link library to do whatever job the service requires. One running copy of svchost can load and manage any number of services. This reduces the amount of memory each service consumes: The DLL method requires a minimum of about 150KB of memory per added service, versus a minimum of about 800KB for each service contained in a separate .EXE file.

On a typical Windows installation, five to seven copies of svchost are started up (you can see them if you run the Task Manager and view the Processes tab), and collectively they manage several services. Windows Vista uses about 12 copies in a typical installation. However, they are not visible in the normal Processes window. To see the instances of svchost, click the Show Processes from All Users button and provide administrative credentials.

Many services rely on other services to do their job. These dependencies are tracked by Windows, and the relied-upon services are automatically started before their dependents. When Windows starts, the Service Controller program services.exe is started, and it uses the following procedure to start device drivers and services in an orderly fashion.

1. The Service Controller (services.exe) scans the Registry subkeys under HKEY_LOCAL_MACHINE\System\CurrentControlSet\Services. Each subkey lists the service name for each device driver, filter, and service. Entries with a Type value of 10 or 20 (hex) are services. The Service Manager creates a list of all items that have a start mode of System, Boot, or Automatic. All of these are started when Windows boots up.

Although the Service Controller starts many device drivers as well as services, we'll focus on services here.

2. Under each service's subkey are optional values named `Group`, `DependOnGroup`, and `DependOnService`. The Service Controller starts up services in the following order:

   - Services with a Group value are considered first, with groups started in the order specified by the Registry value `HKLM\SYSTEM\CurrentControlSet\Control\ServiceGroupOrder\List`.

   - Within each group, services with no dependencies are started first. Services with names listed in their `DependOnGroup` or `DependOnService` values are started only after, and only if, the named groups or services have successfully started.

   - Services with no group name are started last. Again, services with no dependencies are started first. Services with dependencies are started only after, and only if, the named groups or services have successfully started.

3. When the Service Controller is to start a given service, it examines the Registry value `HKLM\SYSTEM\CurrentControlSet\Services\Alerter\ImagePath`, which contains the name of the executable file to start and any additional command-line parameters to pass to it. The Service Controller starts the specified program using the designated account credentials (LOCAL_SYSTEM, LOCAL_SERVICE, NETWORK_SERVICE, or a specified user account).

4. When the service executable program starts up, it communicates to the Service Controller the name or names of any services it is designed to provide. In the future, if the Service Controller needs to start any other services that this executable program says it supports, it will not start a new copy of the program but will simply notify the existing process to start operating the additional service. This minimizes the number of separate processes required. (Presumably the Service Controller checks the definitions for any additional services to be sure that they point to the same executable; otherwise, a process could hijack other services and compromise the system.)

5. The Service Controller signals the service process to start operating the designated service. The service process communicates its progress back to the Service Controller, indicating that the service status is "Starting," and then "Started." If the service process fails to report its status within a limited amount of time (30 seconds by default, or more if the service has indicated that it may need more time), or if the service process crashes, the Service Controller considers it to have failed.

`Services.exe`, besides acting as the Service Controller for all services, implements two services by itself: the Event Log service, and the Plug and Play service, presumably because these are required during Windows startup before any other services are started.

For services packaged as DLLs run by `svchost.exe`, the `-k` parameter passed to an instance of svchost tells it what set of services the particular svchost instance is to support. The names are recorded in Registry key `HKLM\Software\Microsoft\WindowsNT\CurrentVersion\Svchost`. For example, when the first service whose `ImagePath` value has the command line `%SystemRoot%\System32\svchost.exe -k LocalService` is started, svchost examines value

HKLM\Software\Microsoft\WindowsNT\CurrentVersion\Svchost\LocalService, which contains
the REG_MULTI_SZ string

```
Alerter
WebClient
LmHosts
RemoteRegistry
upnphost
SSDPSRV
```

This instance of svchost.exe will inform the Service Controller that it manages these six services.
When the time comes to start one of the other five services, the Service Controller will not run
an additional copy of svchost.exe, but will instruct the appropriate already-running instance to
start the additional service.

For each service that svchost.exe is instructed to start, it examines Registry key
HKLM\System\CurrentControlSet\Services\servicename\Parameters value ServiceDll for the
name of a DLL file to load. It loads the designated DLL and calls routines within it that actually
perform the service functions. Table 2.5 lists the services implemented by the five or six instances
of svchost.exe started when Windows starts. (The same DLL might contain more than one service; each would have a different entry point function in the DLL.) The services themselves are
listed in detail in the next section.

Table 2.5   Svchost Service Groups in Windows XP

Svchost Group	Logon Account	Service Name
DcomLaunch	LocalSystem	DcomLaunch
HTTPFilter	LocalSystem	HTTPFilter
imgsvc	LocalSystem	StiSvc
LocalService	LocalService	Alerter LmHosts, RemoteRegistry, SSDPSRV, unphost, WebClient
netsvcs	LocalSystem	6to4, AppMgmt, AudioSrv, BITS, Browser, CryptSvc, DHCP, DMServer, ERSvc, EventSystem, FastUserSwitchingCompatibility, helpsvc, HidServ, Ias, Iprip, Irmon, LanmanServer, LanmanWorkstation, Messenger, Netman, Nla, Ntmssvc, NWCWorkstation, Nwsapagent, asauto, Rasman, Remoteaccess, Schedule, Seclogon, SENS, Sharedaccess, ShellHWDetection, SRService, Tapisrv, TermService, Themes, TrkWks, W32Time, winmgmt, WmdmPmSp, Wmi, wscsvc, wuauserv, WZCSVC, xmlprov
NetworkService	NetworkService	DnsCache
rpcss	NetworkService	RpcSs

Windows Vista also uses service groups, but includes different groups and combinations of service
names, as shown in Table 2.6.

Table 2.6   Svchost Service Groups in Windows Vista

Svchost Group	Logon Account	Service Name
DcomLaunch	LocalSystem	DcomLaunch, PlugPlay
imgsvc	LocalSystem	StiSvc
LocalService	LocalService	nsi, lltdsvc, SSDPSRV, upnphost, SCardSvr, w32time, EventSystem, RemoteRegistry, WinHttpAutoProxySvc, lanmanworkstation, TBS, SLUINotify, THREADORDER, fdrespub, netprofm, fdphost, wcncsvc, QWAVE, WebClient
LocalServiceNetworkRestricted		DHCP, eventlog, AudioSrv, LmHosts, wscsvc, p2pimsvc, PNRPSvc, p2psvc, WPCSvc, PnrpAutoReg
LocalServiceNoNetwork		PLA, DPS, BFE, mpssvc
LocalSystemNetworkRestricted		Hidserv, UxSms, WdiSystemHost, Netman, trkwks, AudioEndpointBuilder, WUDFSvc, irmon, sysmain, IPBusEnum, dot3svc, PcaSvc, CscService, wlansvc, UmRdpService, EMDMgmt, WPDBusEnum, TabletInputService
netsvcs	LocalSystem	AeLookupSvc, wercplsupport, Themes, CertPropSvc, SCPolicySvc, lanmanserver, gpsvc, IKEEXT, AudioSrv, FastUserSwitchingCompatibility, Ias, Irmon, Nla, Ntmssvc, NWCWorkstation, Nwsapagent, Rasauto, Rasman, Remoteaccess, SENS, Sharedaccess, SRService, Tapisrv, Wmi, WmdmPmSp, TermService, wuauserv, BITS, ShellHWDetection, LogonHours, PCAudit, helpsvc, uploadmgr, iphlpsvc, seclogon, AppInfo, msiscsi, MMCSS, ProfSvc, EapHost, winmgmt, schedule, SessionEnv, browser, hkmsvc, AppMgmt
NetworkService	NetworkService	CryptSvc, DHCP, TermService, KtmRm, DNSCache, NapAgent, nlasvc, WinRM, WECSVC, Tapisrv
NetworkServiceNetworkRestricted		PolicyAgent
regsvc		RemoteRegistry
rpcss	NetworkService	RpcSs
sdrsvc		Sdrsvc
secsvcs		WinDefend
swprv		swprv
termsvcs		TermService
wcssvc		WcsPlugInService
wdisvc		WdiServiceHost
WerSvcGroup		wersvc

Services often have to have wide-ranging privileges. For example, services that catalog (index) or back up the hard disk must be able to read any file on the disk, regardless of permission settings. (They, of course, must take responsibility for the data they collect, and release it only to authorized users.) Yet, one of the basic principles of computer and network security is to never give a program more than the minimum level of privilege it needs to get its job done. Therefore Windows runs services in the context of a user logon account, and the service gains only the privileges of its associated account. There are several "built-in" accounts provided with Windows that are never used for interactive logon, but solely to run services.

Most services are run under the LocalSystem account. This account can access any file or other secured object, and has *all* possible system privileges. It's the service's version of the Administrator account, and lets the service do whatever it needs, but it also is a problem if the service is compromised by a hacker, who could obtain full access to the entire system. When services are written correctly, they can usually be run under lower-privilege user accounts. Windows predefines two accounts for use by services:

> **LocalService**—This account has a reduced privilege level. Its file access rights can be controlled on NTFS file systems. When services under this account access the network, they do not present user credentials to other computers; they use anonymous access methods.

> **NetworkService**—This account is like LocalService but when it accesses the network, it uses the local machine account rather than anonymous access. On a domain network, this lets services run under NetworkService perform domain operations on behalf of another computer, such as replication.

Custom services may be installed with different user credentials.

Caution

Do not attempt to change the logon user account for a standard Windows service without explicit instructions to do so from Microsoft; changing a service's account or privileges may make it fail or may prevent Windows from starting.

List of Windows Services

This section lists the standard services provided with Windows XP and Vista. Not all of these services may be installed on a given system, depending on the optional software and hardware installed. The first line in each table row contains the service name in boldface, followed by the service's display name. Where DLL files are listed, the service is run from svchost.exe. These details are discussed in more detail later in the section.

Services with a Start mode of "Auto" are started when Windows boots, but may shut themselves down if they have no work to do. Services with a Start mode of "Manual" are usually started automatically by other services or applications when they are needed.

The list of Windows XP services includes:

- **6to4**—IPv6 Helper Service. Provides DDNS name registration and automatic IPv6 connectivity over an IPv4 network. (Installed with the IPV6 optional network protocol. The Tcpip6 item listed in the dependency list is a network protocol driver, not a service.)

Start mode:	Auto
Login account:	LocalSystem
DLL file:	`6to4svc.dll`
Dependencies:	RpcSs, Tcpip6, winmgmt

- **Alerter**—Notifies selected users and computers of administrative alerts.

Start mode:	Auto
Login account:	LocalService
DLL file:	`alrsvc.dll`
Dependencies:	lanmanworkstation

- **ALG**—Application Layer Gateway Service. Provides support for third-party protocol plug-ins for Internet Connection Sharing and Windows Firewall.

Start mode:	Manual
Login account:	LocalService
EXE file:	`alg.exe`

- **AppMgmt**—Application Management. Provides software installation services such as Assign, Publish, and Remove.

Start mode:	Manual
Login account:	LocalSystem
DLL file:	`appmgmts.dll`

- **aspnet_state**—ASP.NET State Service. Provides support for out-of-process session states for ASP.NET.

Start mode:	Manual
Login account:	NetworkService
EXE file:	`aspnet_state.exe`

- **AudioSrv**—Windows Audio. Manages audio devices for Windows-based programs.

Start mode:	Auto
Login account:	LocalSystem
DLL file:	`audiosrv.dll`
Load group:	AudioGroup
Dependencies:	PlugPlay, RpcSs

- **BITS**—Background Intelligent Transfer Service. Transfers files in the background using idle network bandwidth. Features such as Windows Update, Automatic Updates, and MSN Explorer depend on this service.

Start mode:	Manual
Login account:	LocalSystem
DLL file:	`qmgr.dll`
Dependencies:	RpcSs
Failure action:	Restart service after 60 seconds

- **Browser**—Computer Browser. Maintains an updated list of computers on the network and supplies this list to computers designated as browsers.

Start mode:	Auto
Login account:	LocalSystem
DLL file:	`browser.dll`
Dependencies:	lanmanworkstation, lanmanserver

- **cisvc**—Indexing Service. Indexes contents and properties of files on local and remote computers; used for desktop search and Internet Information Services Server Extensions searching.

Start mode:	Manual
Login account:	LocalSystem
EXE file:	`cisvc.exe`
Dependencies:	RpcSs

- **ClipSrv**—ClipBook. Enables ClipBook Viewer to store information and share it with remote computers. If the service is stopped, ClipBook Viewer will not be able to share information with remote computers.

Start Mode:	Disabled
Login account:	LocalSystem
DLL files:	`catsrv.dll` and `comsvcs.dll`, via COM+ and `dllhost.exe`
Dependencies:	NetDDE

- **COMSysApp**—COM+ System Application. Manages the configuration and tracking of Component Object Model COM+ components. Most COM+-based components depend on this service.

Start mode:	Manual
Login account:	LocalSystem
EXE file:	`dllhost.exe`
Dependencies:	RpcSs
Failure action:	Restart service after 1 second, 5 seconds

- **CryptSvc**—Cryptographic Services. Provides three management services: Catalog Database Service, which confirms the signatures of Windows files; Protected Root Service, which adds and removes Trusted Root Certification Authority certificates from this computer; and Key Service, which helps enroll the computer for certificates.

Start mode:	Auto
Login account:	LocalSystem
DLL file:	`cryptsvc.dll`
Dependencies:	RpcSs

- **DcomLaunch**—DCOM Server Process Launcher. Provides launch functionality for DCOM services.

Start mode:	Auto
Login account:	LocalSystem
DLL file:	`rpcss.dll`
Load group:	Event Log
Failure action:	REBOOT after 60 seconds

- **Dhcp**—DHCP Client. Manages network configuration by registering and updating IP addresses and DNS names.

Start mode:	Auto
Login account:	LocalSystem
DLL file:	dhcpcsvc.dll
Load group:	TDI
Dependencies:	Tcpip, AFD, NetBT

- **dmadmin**—Logical Disk Manager Administrative Service. Configures hard disk drives and volumes. The service only runs for configuration processes and then stops.

Start mode:	Manual
Login account:	LocalSystem
EXE file:	dmadmin.exe
Dependencies:	RpcSs, PlugPlay, dmserver

- **dmserver**—Logical Disk Manager. Detects and monitors new hard disk drives and sends disk volume information to Logical Disk Manager Administrative Service for configuration. Maintains configuration information for dynamic disks.

Start mode:	Auto
Login account:	LocalSystem
DLL file:	dmserver.dll
Dependencies:	RpcSs, PlugPlay

- **Dnscache**—DNS Client. Resolves and caches Domain Name System (DNS) names for this computer.

Start mode:	Auto
Login account:	NetworkService
DLL file:	dnsrslvr.dll
Load group:	TDI
Dependencies:	Tcpip

- **ERSvc**—Error Reporting Service. Allows error reporting for services and applications running in nonstandard environments.

Start mode:	Auto
Login account:	LocalSystem
DLL file:	ersvc.dll
Dependencies:	RpcSs

- **Eventlog**—Event Log. Enables event log messages issued by Windows-based programs and components to be viewed in Event Viewer. This service cannot be stopped. This service is provided directly by the Service Controller process.

Start mode:	Auto
Login account:	LocalSystem
EXE file:	services.exe
Load group:	Event log

- **EventSystem**—COM+ Event System. Supports System Event Notification Service (SENS), which provides automatic distribution of events to subscribing Component Object Model (COM) components.

Start mode:	Manual
Login account:	LocalSystem
DLL file:	es.dll
Load group:	Network
Dependencies:	RpcSs

- **FastUserSwitchingCompatibility**—Fast User Switching Compatibility. Provides management for applications that require assistance in a multiple user environment.

Start mode:	Manual
Login account:	LocalSystem
DLL file:	shsvcs.dll
Dependencies:	TermService

- **Fax**—Enables you to send and receive faxes, using fax resources available on this computer or on the network.

Start mode:	Auto
Login account:	LocalSystem
EXE file:	fxssvc.exe
Dependencies:	TapiSrv, RpcSs, PlugPlay, Spooler

- **helpsvc**—Help and Support. Enables Help and Support Center to run on this computer.

Start mode:	Auto
Login account:	LocalSystem
DLL file:	pchsvc.dll
Dependencies:	RpcSs
Failure action:	Restart service after 100 milliseconds

- **HidServ**—HID Input Service. Enables generic input access to Human Interface Devices (HID), which activates and maintains the use of predefined hot buttons on keyboards, remote controls, and other multimedia devices.

Start mode:	Auto
Login account:	LocalSystem
DLL file:	hidserv.dll
Dependencies:	RpcSs

- **HTTPFilter**—HTTP SSL. This service implements the secure hypertext transfer protocol (HTTPS) for the HTTP service, using the Secure Socket Layer (SSL).

Start mode:	Manual
Login account:	LocalSystem
DLL file:	w3ssl.dll
Dependencies:	HTTP

- **IISADMIN**—IIS Admin. Allows administration of web and FTP services through the Internet Information Services snap-in. Installed with IIS; not available on Windows XP Home Edition.

Start mode:	Auto
Login account:	LocalSystem
EXE file:	`inetinfo.exe`
Dependencies:	RpcSs, SamSs
Failure action:	Run repair program after 1 millisecond

- **ImapiService**—IMAPI CD-Burning COM Service. Manages CD recording using Image Mastering Applications Programming Interface (IMAPI).

Start mode:	Manual
Login account:	LocalSystem
EXE file:	`imapi.exe`

- **Iprip**—RIP Listener. Listens for route updates sent by routers that use the Routing Information Protocol version 1 (RIPv1).

Start mode:	Auto, when RIP network support is installed
Login account:	LocalSystem
DLL file:	`iprip.dll`
Dependencies:	RpcSs

- **irmon**—Infrared Monitor Service. Monitors an infrared (IrDA) interface for connections to other computers and devices; primarily used on laptops, PDAs, and printers.

Startup mode:	Auto
Login account:	LocalSystem
DLL file:	`irmon.dll`

- **lanmanserver**—Server. Supports file, print, and named-pipe sharing over the network for this computer. This service lets you share your folders and printers with other computers.

Start mode:	Auto
Login account:	LocalSystem
DLL file:	`srvsvc.dll`

- **lanmanworkstation**—Workstation. Creates and maintains client network connections to remote servers. This service lets you use folders and printers shared by other computers.

Start mode:	Auto
Login account:	LocalSystem
DLL file:	`wkssvc.dll`
Load group:	NetworkProvider

- **LmHosts**—TCP/IP NetBIOS Helper. Enables support for NetBIOS over TCP/IP (NetBT) service and NetBIOS name resolution.

Start mode:	Auto
Login account:	LocalService
DLL file:	`lmhsvc.dll`
Load group:	TDI
Dependencies:	NetBT, AFD

- **LPDSVC**—TCP/IP Print Server. Provides a TCP/IP-based printing service that uses the Line Printer protocol. Installed as part of Print Services for UNIX.

Start mode:	Manual
Login account:	LocalSystem
EXE file:	tcpsvcs.exe
Dependencies:	Tcpip, Spooler

- **Messenger** —Transmits "net send" and Alerter service messages between clients and servers. This service is used primarily for network administrators to notify users of system outages, or for the Performance Logs and Alerts service to notify system managers of system problems. It is not related to the Windows Messenger chat program. Starting with Windows XP Service Pack 2, this service is disabled by default because it was abused by spammers to post pop-up ads.

Start mode:	Disabled
Login account:	LocalSystem
DLL file:	msgsvc.dll
Dependencies:	lanmanworkstation, NetBIOS, PlugPlay, RpcSs

- **mnmsrvc**—NetMeeting Remote Desktop Sharing. Enables an authorized user to access this computer remotely by using NetMeeting over a corporate intranet.

Start mode:	Manual
Login account:	LocalSystem
EXE file:	mnmsrvc.exe

Note

This service can interact with the desktop.

- **MSDTC**—Distributed Transaction Coordinator. Coordinates transactions that span multiple resource managers, such as databases, message queues, and file systems.

Start mode:	Manual
Login account:	NetworkService
EXE file:	msdtc.exe
Load group:	MS Transactions
Dependencies:	RpcSs, SamSs

- **MSFtpsvc**—FTP Publishing. Provides FTP connectivity and administration through the Internet Information Services snap-in. Installed with IIS; not available on Windows XP Home Edition.

Start mode:	Auto
Login account:	LocalSystem
EXE file:	inetinfo.exe
Dependencies:	IISADMIN

- **MSIServer**—Windows Installer. The Windows installer service coordinates installation and removal of applications.

Start mode:	Manual
Login account:	LocalSystem
EXE file:	`msiexec.exe`
Dependencies:	RpcSs

- **MSMQ**—Message Queuing. Provides a communications infrastructure for distributed, asynchronous messaging applications. Installed with optional Microsoft Message Queuing network component.

Start mode:	Auto
Login account:	LocalSystem
EXE file:	`mqsvc.exe`
Dependencies:	MQAC, RMCAST, lanmanserver, NtLmSsp, RpcSs, MSDTC

- **MSMQTriggers**—Message Queuing Triggers. Associates the arrival of incoming messages at a queue with functionality in a COM component or a standalone executable program. Installed with optional Microsoft Message Queuing network component.

Start mode:	Auto
Login account:	LocalSystem
EXE file:	`mqtgsvc.exe`
Dependencies:	MSMQ

- **NetDDE**—Network DDE. Provides network transport and security for Dynamic Data Exchange (DDE) for programs running on the same computer or on different computers.

Start mode:	Disabled
Login account:	LocalSystem
EXE file:	`netdde.exe`
Load group:	NetDDEGroup
Dependencies:	NetDDEdsdm

- **NetDDEdsdm**—Network DDE DSDM. Manages Dynamic Data Exchange (DDE) network shares.

Start mode:	Disabled
Login account:	LocalSystem
EXE file:	`netdde.exe`

- **Netlogon**—Net Logon. Supports pass-through authentication of account logon events for computers in a domain.

Start mode:	Manual
Login account:	LocalSystem
EXE file:	`lsass.exe`
Load group:	RemoteValidation
Dependencies:	lanmanworkstation

- **Netman**—Network Connections. Manages objects in the Network and Dial-Up Connections folder, in which you can view both local area network and remote connections.

Start mode:	Manual
Login account:	LocalSystem
DLL file:	netman.dll
Dependencies:	RpcSs

Note

This service can interact with the desktop.

- **Nla**—Network Location Awareness (NLA). Collects and stores network configuration and location information, and notifies applications when this information changes.

Start mode:	Manual
Login account:	LocalSystem
DLL file:	mswsock.dll
Dependencies:	Tcpip, AFD

- **NtLmSsp**—NT LM Security Support Provider. Provides security to remote procedure call (RPC) programs that use transports other than named pipes.

Start mode:	Manual
Login account:	LocalSystem
EXE file:	lsass.exe

- **NtmsSvc**—Removable Storage. The Removable Storage service tracks and manages removable media such as tapes used for backups and archiving.

Start mode:	Manual
Login account:	LocalSystem
DLL file:	ntmssvc.dll
Dependencies:	RpcSs

- **ose**—Office Source Engine. Saves installation files used for Microsoft Office updates and repairs and is required for the downloading of Setup updates and Watson error reports. (Installed as part of Microsoft Office.)

Start mode:	Manual
Login account:	LocalSystem
EXE file:	ose.exe

- **p2pgasvc**—Peer Networking Group Authentication. Provides Network Authentication for Peer Group Members. Installed with optional Peer-to-Peer networking support.

Start mode:	Manual
Login account:	LocalService
DLL file:	p2pgasvc.dll
Dependencies:	p2pimsvc

- **p2pimsvc**—Peer Networking Identity Manager. Provides Identity service for Peer Networking. Installed with optional Peer-to-Peer networking support.

Start mode:	Manual
Login account:	LocalService
DLL file:	`p2psvc.dll`

- **p2psvc**—Peer Networking. Provides Peer Networking services. Installed with optional peer-to-peer networking support.

Start mode:	Manual
Login account:	LocalService
DLL file:	`p2psvc.dll`
Dependencies:	PNRPSvc, p2pgasvc

- **PlugPlay**—Plug and Play. Enables a computer to recognize and adapt to hardware changes with little or no user input. Stopping or disabling this service will result in system instability. This service is provided directly by the Service Controller process.

Start mode:	Auto
Login account:	LocalSystem
EXE file:	`services.exe`
Load group:	PlugPlay

- **PNRPSvc**—Peer Name Resolution Protocol. Enables serverless peer name resolution over the Internet. Installed with optional peer-to-peer networking support.

Start mode:	Manual
Login account:	LocalService
DLL file:	`p2psvc.dll`
Dependencies:	Tcpip6, p2pimsvc

- **PolicyAgent**—IPSEC Services. Manages IP security policy and starts the ISAKMP/Oakley (IKE) and the IP security driver.

Start mode:	Auto
Login account:	LocalSystem
EXE file:	`lsass.exe`
Dependencies:	RpcSs, Tcpip, IPSec

- **ProtectedStorage**—Protected Storage. Provides protected storage for sensitive data, such as private keys, to prevent access by unauthorized services, processes, or users.

Start mode:	Auto
Login account:	LocalSystem
EXE file:	`lsass.exe`
Dependencies:	RpcSs

Note

This service can interact with the desktop.

- **RasAuto**—Remote Access Auto Connection Manager. Creates a connection to a remote network whenever a program references a remote DNS or NetBIOS name or address.

Start mode:	Manual
Login account:	LocalSystem
DLL file:	rasauto.dll
Dependencies:	RasMan, TapiSrv

- **RasMan**—Remote Access Connection Manager. Makes and manages temporary network connections including modem dialup and PPPoE.

Start mode:	Manual
Login account:	LocalSystem
DLL file:	rasmans.dll
Dependencies:	TapiSrv

- **RDSessMgr**—Remote Desktop Help Session Manager. Manages and controls Remote Assistance.

Start mode:	Manual
Login account:	LocalSystem
EXE file:	sessmgr.exe
Dependencies:	RpcSs

- **RemoteAccess**—Routing and Remote Access. Offers routing services to businesses in local area and wide area network environments.

Start mode:	Auto
Login account:	LocalSystem
DLL file:	mprdim.dll
Dependencies:	RpcSs

- **RemoteRegistry**—Remote Registry. Enables remote users to modify Registry settings on this computer. If this service is stopped, the Registry can be modified only by users on this computer.

Start mode:	Auto
Login account:	LocalService
DLL file:	regsvc.dll
Dependencies:	RpcSs
Failure action:	Restart service after 1 second

- **RpcLocator**—Remote Procedure Call (RPC) Locator. Manages the RPC name service database.

Start mode:	Manual
Login account:	NetworkService
EXE file:	locator.exe
Dependencies:	lanmanworkstation

- **RpcSs**—Remote Procedure Call (RPC). Provides the endpoint mapper and other miscellaneous RPC services.

Start mode:	Auto
Login account:	NetworkService
DLL file:	`rpcss.dll`
Load group:	COM Infrastructure
Failure action:	REBOOT after 60 seconds

- **RSVP**—QoS RSVP. Provides network signaling and local traffic control setup functionality for QoS-aware programs and control applets.

Start mode:	Manual
Login account:	LocalSystem
EXE file:	`rsvp.exe`
Dependencies:	Tcpip, AFD, RpcSs

- **SamSs**—Security Accounts Manager. Stores security information for local user accounts.

Start mode:	Auto
Login account:	LocalSystem
EXE file:	`lsass.exe`
Load group:	LocalValidation
Dependencies:	RpcSs

- **SCardSvr**—Smart Card. Manages access to smart cards read by this computer.

Start mode:	Manual
Login account:	LocalService
EXE file:	`scardsvr.exe`
Load group:	SmartCardGroup
Dependencies:	PlugPlay

- **Schedule**—Task Scheduler. Enables a user to configure and schedule automated tasks on this computer.

SStart mode:	Auto
Login account:	LocalSystem
DLL file:	`schedsvc.dll`
Load group:	SchedulerGroup
Dependencies:	RpcSs

Note

This service can interact with the desktop.

- **seclogon**—Secondary Logon. Enables starting processes under alternative credentials.

Start mode:	Auto
Login account:	LocalSystem
DLL file:	`seclogon.dll`

Note

This service can interact with the desktop.

- **SENS**—System Event Notification. Tracks system events such as Windows logon, network, and power events. Notifies COM+ Event System subscribers of these events.

Start mode:	Auto
Login account:	LocalSystem
DLL file:	sens.dll
Load group:	Network
Dependencies:	EventSystem

- **SharedAccess**—Windows Firewall/Internet Connection Sharing (ICS). Provides network address translation, addressing, name resolution, and/or intrusion prevention services for a home or small office network.

Start mode:	Auto
Login account:	LocalSystem
DLL file:	ipnathlp.dll
Dependencies:	Netman, winmgmt

- **ShellHWDetection**—Shell Hardware Detection. Provides notifications for AutoPlay hardware events.

Start mode:	Auto
Login account:	LocalSystem
DLL file:	shsvcs.dll
Load group:	ShellSvcGroup
Dependencies:	RpcSs

- **SimpTcp**—Simple TCP/IP Services. Supports the following TCP/IP services: Character Generator, Daytime, Discard, Echo, and Quote of the Day. Installed with Simple TCP/IP Services optional networking component.

Start mode:	Auto
Login account:	LocalSystem
EXE file:	tcpsvcs.exe
Dependencies:	AFD

- **SMTPSVC**—Simple Mail Transfer Protocol (SMTP). Transports electronic mail across the network. Installed with IIS; not available on Windows XP Home Edition.

Start mode:	Auto
Login account:	LocalSystem
EXE file:	inetinfo.exe
Dependencies:	IISADMIN, Eventlog

- **SNMP**—SNMP Service. Includes agents that monitor the activity in network devices and report to the network console workstation. Installed with the SNMP optional networking component.

Start mode:	Auto
Login account:	LocalSystem
EXE file:	snmp.exe
Dependencies:	Eventlog

- **SNMPTRAP**—SNMP Trap Service. Receives trap messages generated by local or remote SNMP agents and forwards the messages to SNMP management programs running on this computer. Installed with the SNMP optional networking component.

Start mode:	Manual
Login account:	LocalService
EXE file:	snmptrap.exe
Dependencies:	Eventlog

- **Spooler**—Print Spooler. Loads files to memory for later printing.

Start mode:	Auto
Login account:	LocalSystem
EXE file:	spoolsv.exe
Load group:	SpoolerGroup
Dependencies:	RpcSs
Failure action:	Restart service after 60 seconds

Note

This service can interact with the desktop.

- **srservice**—System Restore Service. Performs system restore functions. To stop service, turn off System Restore from the System Restore tab in [My] Computer, Properties.

Start mode:	Auto
Login account:	LocalSystem
DLL file:	srsvc.dll
Dependencies:	RpcSs

- **SSDPSRV**—SSDP Discovery Service. Enables discovery of UPnP devices on your home network. Installed with the Internet Gateway Device Discovery and Control Client optional networking component.

Start mode:	Manual
Login account:	LocalService
DLL file:	ssdpsrv.dll
Dependencies:	HTTP

- **stisvc**—Windows Image Acquisition (WIA). Provides image acquisition services for scanners and cameras.

Start mode:	Auto
Login account:	LocalSystem
DLL file:	`wiaservc.dll`
Dependencies:	RpcSs

- **SwPrv**—MS Software Shadow Copy Provider. Manages software-based volume shadow copies taken by the Volume Shadow Copy service. This service provides crucial support required by backup programs.

Start mode:	Manual
Login account:	LocalSystem
DLL file:	`swprv.dll`, via COM+ and `dllhost.exe`
Dependencies:	RpcSs

- **SysmonLog**—Performance Logs and Alerts. Collects performance data from local or remote computers based on preconfigured schedule parameters; then writes the data to a log or triggers an alert.

Start mode:	Manual
Login account:	NetworkService
EXE file:	`smlogsvc.exe`

- **TapiSrv**—Telephony. Provides Telephony API (TAPI) support for programs that control telephony devices and IP-based voice connections on the local computer and, through the LAN, on servers that are also running the service.

Start mode:	Manual
Login account:	LocalSystem
DLL file:	`tapisrv.dll`
Dependencies:	PlugPlay, RpcSs

- **TermService**—Terminal Services. Allows multiple users to be connected interactively to a machine as well as the display of desktops and applications to remote computers. The service provides the underpinning of Remote Desktop (including RD for Administrators), Fast User Switching, Remote Assistance, and Terminal Server.

Start mode:	Manual
Login account:	LocalSystem
DLL file:	`termsrv.dll`
Dependencies:	RpcSs

- **Themes**—Provides user experience theme management.

Start mode:	Auto
Login account:	LocalSystem
DLL file:	`shsvcs.dll`
Load group:	UIGroup
Failure action:	Restart service after 60 seconds

- **TlntSvr**—Telnet. Enables a remote user to log on to this computer and run programs, and supports various TCP/IP Telnet clients, including UNIX-based and Windows-based computers.

Start mode:	Manual
Login account:	LocalSystem
EXE file:	`tlntsvr.exe`

- **TrkWks**—Distributed Link Tracking Client. Maintains links between NTFS files within a computer or across computers in a network domain.

Start mode:	Auto
Login account:	LocalSystem
DLL file:	`trkwks.dll`
Dependencies:	RpcSs

- **UMWdf**—Windows User Mode Driver Framework. Enables Windows user mode drivers.

Start mode:	Auto
Login account:	LocalService
EXE file:	`wdfmgr.exe`
Dependencies:	RpcSs

- **upnphost**—Universal Plug and Play Device Host. Provides support to host Universal Plug and Play devices.

Start mode:	Manual
Login account:	LocalService
DLL file:	`upnphost.dll`
Dependencies:	SSDPSRV, HTTP
Failure action:	Restart the service immediately

- **UPS**—Uninterruptible Power Supply. Manages an uninterruptible power supply (UPS) connected to the computer.

Start mode:	Manual, or Auto if a UPS is installed
Login account:	LocalSystem
EXE file:	`ups.exe`

- **VSS**—Volume Shadow Copy. Manages and implements Volume Shadow Copies used for backup and other purposes. This service provides crucial support required by backup programs.

Start mode:	Manual
Login account:	LocalSystem
EXE file:	`vssvc.exe`
Dependencies:	RpcSs

- **W32Time**—Windows Time. Maintains date and time synchronization on all clients and servers in the network.

Start mode:	Auto
Login account:	LocalSystem
DLL file:	`w32time.dll`
Failure action:	Restart service after 60 seconds

- **W3SVC**—World Wide Web Publishing. Provides web connectivity and administration through the Internet Information Services snap-in. Installed with IIS; not available on Windows XP Home Edition.

Start mode:	Manual
Login account:	LocalSystem
EXE file:	`inetinfo.exe`
Dependencies:	IISADMIN

- **WebClient**—Enables Windows-based programs to create, access, and modify Internet-based files.

Start mode:	Auto
Login account:	LocalService
DLL file:	`webclnt.dll`
Load group:	NetworkProvider
Dependencies:	MRxDAV

- **winmgmt**—Windows Management Instrumentation. Provides a common interface and object model to access management information about operating system, devices, applications, and services. Most Windows management tools require this service.

Start mode:	Auto
Login account:	LocalSystem
DLL file:	`wmisvc.dll`
Dependencies:	RpcSs, Eventlog
Failure action:	Restart service after 60 seconds

- **WmcCds**—Windows Media Connect (WMC). Serves shared multimedia content to Universal Plug and Play devices. Installed as an optional downloadable extension to Windows Media Player.

Start mode:	Manual
Login account:	NetworkService
EXE file:	`mswmccds.exe`
Dependencies:	RpcSs, upnphost, WmcCdsLs

- **WmcCdsLs**—Windows Media Connect (WMC) Helper. Monitors the network for new UPnP Media Renderer devices.

Start mode:	Manual
Login account:	LocalSystem
EXE file:	`mswmcls.exe`
Dependencies:	RpcSs

- **WmdmPmSN**—Portable Media Serial Number Service. Retrieves the serial number of any portable media player connected to this computer. If this service is stopped, protected content might not be downloaded to the device.

Start mode:	Manual
Login account:	LocalSystem
DLL file:	`mspmsnsv.dll`

- **Wmi**—Windows Management Instrumentation Driver Extensions. Provides systems management information to and from drivers.

Start mode:	Manual
Login account:	LocalSystem
DLL file:	`advapi32.dll`

- **WmiApSrv**—WMI Performance Adapter. Provides performance library information from WMI "HiPerf" providers.

Start mode:	Manual
Login account:	LocalSystem
EXE file:	`wmiapsrv.exe`
Dependencies:	RpcSs

- **wscsvc**—Security Center. Monitors system security settings and configurations. (Windows XP Service Pack 2 and later.)

Start mode:	Auto
Login account:	LocalSystem
DLL file:	`wscsvc.dll`
Dependencies:	RpcSs, winmgmt

- **wuauserv**—Automatic Updates. Enables the download and installation of critical Windows updates. If the service is disabled, the operating system must be manually updated at the Windows Update website.

Start mode:	Auto
Login account:	LocalSystem
DLL file:	`wuauserv.dll`

- **WZCSVC**—Wireless Zero Configuration. Provides automatic configuration for the 802.11 adapters.

Start mode:	Auto
Login account:	LocalSystem
DLL file:	`wzcsvc.dll`
Load group:	TDI
Dependencies:	RpcSs, Ndisuio

- **xmlprov**—Network Provisioning Service. Manages XML configuration files on a domain basis for automatic network provisioning.

Start mode:	Manual
Login account:	LocalSystem
DLL file:	`xmlprov.dll`
Dependencies:	RpcSs

The list of Windows Vista services includes

- **AeLookupSvc**—Application Experience. Processes application compatibility cache requests for applications as they are launched.

Start Mode:	Automatic
Login Account:	Local System
DLL File:	`aelupsvc.dll`

- **ALG**—Application Layer Gateway Service. Provides support for third-party protocol plug-ins for Internet Connection Sharing.

Start Mode:	Manual
Login Account:	Local Service
EXE File:	`alg.exe`

- **Appinfo**—Application Information. Facilitates the running of interactive applications with additional administrative privileges. If this service is stopped, users are unable to launch applications with the additional administrative privileges they may require to perform desired user tasks.

Start Mode:	Manual
Login Account:	Local System
DLL File:	`appinfo.dll`

- **AppMgmt**—Application Management. Processes installation, removal, and enumeration requests for software deployed through Group Policy. If the service is disabled, users are unable to install, remove, or enumerate software deployed through Group Policy. If this service is disabled, any services that explicitly depend on it fail to start.

Start Mode:	Manual
Login Account:	Local System
DLL File:	`appmgmts.dll`

- **AudioEndpointBuilder**—Windows Audio Endpoint Builder. Manages audio devices for the Windows Audio service. If this service is stopped, audio devices and effects do not function properly. If this service is disabled, any services that explicitly depend on it fail to start.

Start Mode:	Automatic
Login Account:	Local System
DLL File:	`Audiosrv.dll`

- **Audiosrv**—Windows Audio. Manages audio for Windows-based programs. If this service is stopped, audio devices and effects do not function properly. If this service is disabled, any services that explicitly depend on it fail to start.

Start Mode:	Automatic
Login Account:	Local Service
DLL File:	`Audiosrv.dll`

- **BFE**—Base Filtering Engine. The Base Filtering Engine (BFE) is a service that manages firewall and Internet Protocol security (IPsec) policies and implements user mode filtering. Stopping or disabling the BFE service significantly reduces the security of the system. It also results in unpredictable behavior in IPsec management and firewall applications.

Start Mode:	Automatic
Login Account:	Local Service
DLL File:	`bfe.dll`

- **BITS**—Background Intelligent Transfer Service. Transfers files in the background using idle network bandwidth. If the service is disabled, any applications that depend on BITS, such as Windows Update or MSN Explorer, are unable to automatically download programs and other information.

Start Mode:	Automatic (Delayed Start)
Login Account:	Local System
DLL File:	`qmgr.dll`

- **Browser**—Computer Browser. Maintains an updated list of computers on the network and supplies this list to computers designated as browsers. If this service is stopped, this list is not updated or maintained. If this service is disabled, any services that explicitly depend on it fail to start.

Start Mode:	Automatic
Login Account:	Local System
DLL File:	`browser.dll`

- **CertPropSvc**—Certificate Propagation. Propagates certificates from smart cards.

Start Mode:	Manual
Login Account:	Local System
DLL File:	`certprop.dll`

- **clr_optimization**—Microsoft .NET Framework NGEN v2.0.50727_X86.

Start Mode:	Manual
Login Account:	Local System
EXE File:	`mscorsvw.exe`

- **COMSysApp**—COM+ System Application. Manages the configuration and tracking of Component Object Model (COM)+-based components. If the service is stopped, most COM+-based components do not function properly. If this service is disabled, any services that explicitly depend on it fail to start.

Start Mode:	Manual
Login Account:	Local System
DLL File:	`dllhost.exe`

- **CryptSvc**—Cryptographic Services. Provides four management services: Catalog Database Service, which confirms the signatures of Windows files and allows new programs to be installed; Protected Root Service, which adds and removes Trusted Root Certification Authority certificates from this computer; Automatic Root Certificate Update Service, which retrieves root certificates from Windows Update and enables scenarios such as SSL; and Key Service, which helps enroll this computer for certificates. If this service is stopped, these management services do not function properly. If this service is disabled, any services that explicitly depend on it fail to start.

Start Mode:	Automatic
Login Account:	Network Service
DLL File:	`cryptsvc.dll`

■ **CscService**—Offline Files. The Offline Files service performs maintenance activities on the Offline Files cache, responds to user logon and logoff events, implements the internals of the public API, and dispatches interesting events to those interested in Offline Files activities and changes in cache state.

Start Mode:	Automatic
Login Account:	Local System
DLL File:	cscsvc.dll

■ **DcomLaunch**—DCOM Server Process Launcher. Provides launch functionality for DCOM services.

Start Mode:	Automatic
Login Account:	Local System
DLL File:	rpcss.dll

■ **DFSR**—DFS Replication. Replicates files among multiple PCs, keeping them in sync. On a client, it is used to roam folders between PCs; on a server, it is used to provide high availability and local access across a wide area network (WAN). If the service is stopped, file replication does not occur, and the files on the server become out of date. If the service is disabled, any services that explicitly depend on it do not start.

Start Mode:	Manual
Login Account:	Local System
EXE File:	DFSR.exe

■ **Dhcp**—DHCP Client. Registers and updates IP addresses and DNS records for this computer. If this service is stopped, this computer does not receive dynamic IP addresses and DNS updates. If this service is disabled, any services that explicitly depend on it fail to start.

Start Mode:	Automatic
Login Account:	Local Service
DLL File:	dhcpcsvc.dll

■ **Dnscache**—DNS Client. The DNS Client service (dnscache) caches Domain Name System (DNS) names and registers the full computer name for this computer. If the service is stopped, DNS names continue to be resolved. However, the results of DNS name queries are not cached and the computer's name is not registered. If the service is disabled, any services that explicitly depend on it fail to start.

Start Mode:	Automatic
Login Account:	Network Service
DLL File:	dnsrslvr.dll

■ **dot3svc**—Wired AutoConfig. This service performs IEEE 802.1X authentication on ethernet interfaces.

Start Mode:	Manual
Login Account:	Local System
DLL File:	dot3svc.dll

- **DPS**—Diagnostic Policy Service. The Diagnostic Policy Service enables problem detection, troubleshooting, and resolution for Windows components. If this service is stopped, diagnostics no longer function. If this service is disabled, any services that explicitly depend on it fail to start.

Start Mode:	Automatic
Login Account:	Local Service
DLL File:	dps.dll

- **EapHost**—Extensible Authentication Protocol. The Extensible Authentication Protocol (EAP) service provides network authentication in such scenarios as 802.1x wired and wireless, VPN, and Network Access Protection (NAP). EAP also provides application programming interfaces (APIs) that are used by network access clients, including wireless and VPN clients, during the authentication process. If you disable this service, this computer is prevented from accessing networks that require EAP authentication.

Start Mode:	Manual
Login Account:	Local System
DLL File:	eapsvc.dll

- **ehRecvr**—Windows Media Center Receiver Service. Windows Media Center Service for TV and FM broadcast reception.

Start Mode:	Manual
Login Account:	Network Service
EXE File:	ehRecvr.exe

- **ehSched**—Windows Media Center Scheduler Service. Starts and stops recording of TV programs within Windows Media Center.

Start Mode:	Manual
Login Account:	Network Service
EXE File:	ehsched.exe

- **ehstart**—Windows Media Center Service Launcher. Starts Windows Media Center Scheduler and Windows Media Center Receiver services at startup if TV is enabled within Windows Media Center.

Start Mode:	Automatic (Delayed Start)
Login Account:	Local Service
DLL File:	ehstart.dll

- **EMDMgmt**—ReadyBoost. Provides support for improving system performance using ReadyBoost.

Start Mode:	Automatic
Login Account:	Local System
DLL File:	emdmgmt.dll

- **Eventlog**—Windows Event Log. This service manages events and event logs. It supports logging events, querying events, subscribing to events, archiving event logs, and managing event metadata. It can display events in both XML and plain text format. Stopping this service may compromise security and reliability of the system.

Start Mode:	Automatic
Login Account:	Local Service
DLL File:	wevtsvc.dll

- **EventSystem**—COM+ Event System. Supports System Event Notification Service (SENS), which provides automatic distribution of events to subscribing Component Object Model (COM) components. If the service is stopped, SENS closes and cannot provide logon and logoff notifications. If this service is disabled, any services that explicitly depend on it fail to start.

Start Mode:	Automatic
Login Account:	Local Service
DLL File:	`es.dll`

- **Fax**—Fax. Enables you to send and receive faxes, utilizing fax resources available on this computer or on the network.

Start Mode:	Manual
Login Account:	Network Service
EXE File:	`fxssvc.exe`

- **fdPHost**—Function Discovery Provider Host. Host process for Function Discovery providers.

Start Mode:	Manual
Login Account:	Local Service
DLL File:	`fdPHost.dll`

- **FDResPub**—Function Discovery Resource Publication. Publishes this computer and resources attached to this computer so they can be discovered over the network. If this service is stopped, network resources are no longer published and they are not discovered by other computers on the network.

Start Mode:	Automatic
Login Account:	Local Service
DLL File:	`fdrespub.dll`

- **FontCache3.0.0.0**—Windows Presentation Foundation Font Cache 3.0.0.0. Optimizes performance of Windows Presentation Foundation (WPF) applications by caching commonly used font data. WPF applications start this service if it is not already running. It can be disabled, although doing so degrades the performance of WPF applications.

Start Mode:	Manual
Login Account:	Local Service
EXE File:	`PresentationFontCache.exe`

- **gpsvc**—Group Policy Client. The service is responsible for applying settings configured by administrators for the computer and users through the Group Policy component. If the service is stopped or disabled, the settings are not applied and applications and components are not manageable through Group Policy. Any components or applications that depend on the Group Policy component might not be functional if the service is stopped or disabled.

Start Mode:	Automatic
Login Account:	Local System
DLL File:	`gpsvc.dll`

■ **hidserv**—Human Interface Device Access. Enables generic input access to Human Interface Devices (HID), which activates and maintains the use of predefined hot buttons on keyboards, remote controls, and other multimedia devices. If this service is stopped, hot buttons controlled by this service no longer function. If this service is disabled, any services that explicitly depend on it fail to start.

Start Mode:	Manual
Login Account:	Local System
DLL File:	`hidserv.dll`

■ **hkmsvc**—Health Key and Certificate Management. Provides X.509 certificate and key management services for the Network Access Protection Agent (NAPAgent). Enforcement technologies that use X.509 certificates may not function properly without this service.

Start Mode:	Manual
Login Account:	Local System
DLL File:	`kmsvc.dll`

■ **idsvc**—Windows CardSpace. Securely enables the creation, management, and disclosure of digital identities.

Start Mode:	Manual
Login Account:	Local System
EXE File:	`infocard.exe`

■ **IKEEXT**—IKE and AuthIP IPsec Keying Modules. The IKEEXT service hosts the Internet Key Exchange (IKE) and Authenticated Internet Protocol (AuthIP) keying modules. These keying modules are used for authentication and key exchange in Internet Protocol security (IPsec). Stopping or disabling the IKEEXT service disables IKE and AuthIP key exchange with peer computers. IPsec is typically configured to use IKE or AuthIP; therefore, stopping or disabling the IKEEXT service might result in an IPsec failure and might compromise the security of the system. It is strongly recommended that you have the IKEEXT service running.

Start Mode:	Automatic
Login Account:	Local System
DLL File:	`ikeext.dll`

■ **IPBusEnum**—PnP-X IP Bus Enumerator. The PnP-X bus enumerator service manages the virtual network bus. It discovers network-connected devices using the SSDP/WS discovery protocols and gives them presence in PnP. If this service is stopped or disabled, presence of NCD devices is not be maintained in PnP. All PnP-X-based scenarios stop functioning.

Start Mode:	Manual
Login Account:	Local System
DLL File:	`ipbusenum.dll`

■ **iphlpsvc**—IP Helper. Provides automatic IPv6 connectivity over an IPv4 network. If this service is stopped, the machine has only IPv6 connectivity if it is connected to a native IPv6 network.

Start Mode:	Automatic
Login Account:	Local System
DLL File:	`iphlpsvc.dll`

- **KeyIso**—CNG Key Isolation. The CNG key isolation service is hosted in the LSA process. The service provides key process isolation to private keys and associated cryptographic operations as required by the Common Criteria. The service stores and uses long-lived keys in a secure process that complies with Common Criteria requirements.

Start Mode:	Manual
Login Account:	Local System
EXE File:	lsass.exe

- **KtmRm**—KtmRm for Distributed Transaction Coordinator. Coordinates transactions between MSDTC and the Kernel Transaction Manager (KTM).

Start Mode:	Automatic (Delayed Start)
Login Account:	Network Service
DLL File:	msdtckrm.dll

- **LanmanServer**—Server. Supports file, print, and named-pipe sharing over the network for this computer. If this service is stopped, these functions are unavailable. If this service is disabled, any services that explicitly depend on it fail to start.

Start Mode:	Automatic
Login Account:	Local System
DLL File:	srvsvc.dll

- **LanmanWorkstation**—Workstation. Creates and maintains client network connections to remote servers via the SMB protocol. If this service is stopped, these connections will be unavailable. If this service is disabled, any services that explicitly depend on it will fail to start.

Start Mode:	Automatic
Login Account:	Local Service
DLL File:	wkssvc.dll

- **lltdsvc**—Link-Layer Topology Discovery Mapper. Creates a Network Map, consisting of PC and device topology (connectivity) information, and metadata describing each PC and device. If this service is disabled, the network map does not function properly.

Start Mode:	Manual
Login Account:	Local Service
DLL File:	lltdsvc.dll

- **lmhosts**—TCP/IP NetBIOS Helper. Provides support for the NetBIOS over TCP/IP (NetBT) service and NetBIOS name resolution for clients on the network, therefore enabling users to share files, print, and log on to the network. If this service is stopped, these functions might be unavailable. If this service is disabled, any services that explicitly depend on it fail to start.

Start Mode:	Automatic
Login Account:	Local Service
DLL File:	lmhsvc.dll

- **Mcx2Svc**—Windows Media Center Extender Service. Enables Windows Media Center Extender devices to locate and connect to the computer.

Start Mode:	Disabled
Login Account:	Local Service
DLL File:	Mcx2Svc.dll

- **MMCSS**—Multimedia Class Scheduler. Enables relative prioritization of work based on system-wide task priorities. This is intended mainly for multimedia applications. If this service is stopped, individual tasks resort to their default priority.

Start Mode:	Automatic
Login Account:	Local System
DLL File:	mmcss.dll

- **MpsSvc**—Windows Firewall. Windows Firewall helps protect your computer by preventing unauthorized users from gaining access to your computer through the Internet or a network.

Start Mode:	Automatic
Login Account:	Local Service
DLL File:	mpssvc.dll

- **MSDTC**—Distributed Transaction Coordinator. Coordinates transactions that span multiple resource managers, such as databases, message queues, and file systems. If this service is stopped, these transactions do not occur. If this service is disabled, any services that explicitly depend on it fail to start.

Start Mode:	Manual
Login Account:	Network Service
EXE File:	msdtc.exe

- **MSiSCSI**—Microsoft iSCSI Initiator Service. Manages Internet SCSI (iSCSI) sessions from this computer to remote iSCSI target devices. If this service is stopped, this computer is unable to log in or access iSCSI targets. If this service is disabled, any services that explicitly depend on it fail to start.

Start Mode:	Manual
Login Account:	Local System
DLL File:	iscsiexe.dll

- **msiserver**—Windows Installer. Adds, modifies, and removes applications provided as a Windows Installer (*.msi) package. If this service is disabled, any services that explicitly depend on it fail to start.

Start Mode:	Manual
Login Account:	Local System
EXE File:	msiexec.exe

- **napagent**—Network Access Protection Agent. Enables Network Access Protection (NAP) functionality on client computers.

Start Mode:	Manual
Login Account:	Network Service
DLL File:	qagentRT.dll

- **Netlogon**—Netlogon. Maintains a secure channel between this computer and the domain controller for authenticating users and services. If this service is stopped, the computer may not authenticate users and services and the domain controller cannot register DNS records. If this service is disabled, any services that explicitly depend on it fail to start.

Start Mode:	Manual
Login Account:	Local System
EXE File:	lsass.exe

- **Netman**—Network Connections. Manages objects in the `Network and Dial-Up Connections` folder, in which you can view both local area network and remote connections.

Start Mode:	Manual
Login Account:	Local System
DLL File:	`netman.dll`

- **netprofm**—Network List Service. Identifies the networks to which the computer has connected, collects and stores properties for these networks, and notifies applications when these properties change.

Start Mode:	Automatic
Login Account:	Local Service
DLL File:	`netprofm.dll`

- **NetTcpPortSharing**—Net.Tcp Port Sharing Service. Enables sharing of TCP ports over the net.tcp protocol.

Start Mode:	Disabled
Login Account:	Local Service
EXE File:	`SMSvcHost.exe`

- **NlaSvc**—Network Location Awareness. Collects and stores configuration information for the network and notifies programs when this information is modified. If this service is stopped, configuration information might be unavailable. If this service is disabled, any services that explicitly depend on it fail to start.

Start Mode:	Automatic
Login Account:	Network Service
DLL File:	`nlasvc.dll`

- **nsi**—Network Store Interface Service. This service delivers network notifications (for example, interface addition/deleting and so on) to user-mode clients. Stopping this service causes loss of network connectivity. If this service is disabled, any other services that explicitly depend on this service fail to start.

Start Mode:	Automatic
Login Account:	Local Service
DLL File:	`nsisvc.dll`

- **p2pimsvc**—Peer Networking Identity Manager. Provides identity service for peer networking.

Start Mode:	Manual
Login Account:	Local Service
DLL File:	`p2psvc.dll`

- **p2psvc**—Peer Networking Grouping. Provides peer networking grouping services.

Start Mode:	Manual
Login Account:	Local Service
DLL File:	`p2psvc.dll`

- **PcaSvc**—Program Compatibility Assistant Service. Provides support for the Program Compatibility Assistant. If this service is stopped, the Program Compatibility Assistant does not function properly. If this service is disabled, any services that depend on it fail to start.

Start Mode:	Automatic
Login Account:	Local System
DLL File:	pcasvc.dll

- **pla**—Performance Logs & Alerts. Performance Logs and Alerts collects performance data from local or remote computers based on preconfigured schedule parameters, and then writes the data to a log or triggers an alert. If this service is stopped, performance information is not collected. If this service is disabled, any services that explicitly depend on it fail to start.

Start Mode:	Manual
Login Account:	Local Service
DLL File:	pla.dll

- **PlugPlay**—Plug and Play. Enables a computer to recognize and adapt to hardware changes with little or no user input. Stopping or disabling this service results in system instability.

Start Mode:	Automatic
Login Account:	Local System
DLL File:	umpnpmgr.dll

- **PNRPAutoReg**—PNRP Machine Name Publication Service. This service publishes a machine name, using the Peer Name Resolution Protocol. Configuration is managed via the netsh program command p2p pnrp peer.

Start Mode:	Manual
Login Account:	Local Service
DLL File:	p2psvc.dll

- **PNRPsvc**—Peer Name Resolution Protocol. Enables serverless peer name resolution over the Internet. If disabled, some peer-to-peer and collaborative applications, such as Windows Meetings, may not function.

Start Mode:	Manual
Login Account:	Local Service
DLL File:	p2psvc.dll

- **PolicyAgent**—IPsec Policy Agent. Internet Protocol security (IPsec) supports network-level peer authentication, data origin authentication, data integrity, data confidentiality (encryption), and replay protection. This service enforces IPsec policies created through the IP Security Policies snap-in or the command netsh ipsec. If you stop this service, you may experience network connectivity issues if your policy requires that connections use IPsec. Also, remote management of Windows Firewall is not available when this service is stopped.

Start Mode:	Automatic
Login Account:	Network Service
DLL File:	ipsecsvc.dll

- **ProfSvc**—User Profile Service. This service is responsible for loading and unloading user profiles. If this service is stopped or disabled, users can no longer successfully log on or log off, applications may have problems getting to users' data, and components registered to receive profile event notifications do not receive them.

Start Mode:	Automatic
Login Account:	Local System
DLL File:	profsvc.dll

- **ProtectedStorage**—Protected Storage. Provides protected storage for sensitive data, such as passwords, to prevent access by unauthorized services, processes, or users.

Start Mode:	Manual
Login Account:	Local System
DLL File:	lsass.exe

- **QWAVE**—Quality Windows Audio Video Experience. Quality Windows Audio Video Experience (qWave) is a networking platform for audio video (AV) streaming applications on IP home networks. qWave enhances AV streaming performance and reliability by ensuring network quality-of-service (QoS) for AV applications. It provides mechanisms for admission control, runtime monitoring and enforcement, application feedback, and traffic prioritization.

Start Mode:	Manual
Login Account:	Local Service
DLL File:	qwave.dll

- **RasAuto**—Remote Access Auto Connection Manager. Creates a connection to a remote network whenever a program references a remote DNS or NetBIOS name or address.

Start Mode:	Manual
Login Account:	Local System
DLL File:	rasauto.dll

- **RasMan**—Remote Access Connection Manager. Manages dial-up and virtual private network (VPN) connections from this computer to the Internet or other remote networks. If this service is disabled, any services that explicitly depend on it fail to start.

Start Mode:	Manual
Login Account:	Local System
DLL File:	rasmans.dll

- **RemoteAccess**—Routing and Remote Access. Offers routing services to businesses in local area and wide area network environments.

Start Mode:	Disabled
Login Account:	Local System
DLL File:	mprdim.dll

- **RemoteRegistry**—Remote Registry. Enables remote users to modify Registry settings on this computer. If this service is stopped, the Registry can be modified only by users on this computer. If this service is disabled, any services that explicitly depend on it fail to start.

Start Mode:	Manual
Login Account:	Local Service
DLL File:	regsvc.dll

- **RpcLocator**—Remote Procedure Call (RPC) Locator. Manages the RPC name service database.

Start Mode:	Manual
Login Account:	Network Service
EXE File:	`locator.exe`

- **RpcSs**—Remote Procedure Call (RPC). Serves as the endpoint mapper and COM Service Control Manager. If this service is stopped or disabled, programs using COM or Remote Procedure Call (RPC) services do not function properly.

Start Mode:	Automatic
Login Account:	Network Service
DLL File:	`rpcss.dll`

- **SamSs**—Security Accounts Manager. The startup of this service signals other services that the Security Accounts Manager (SAM) is ready to accept requests. Disabling this service prevents other services in the system from being notified when the SAM is ready, which may in turn cause those services to fail to start correctly. This service should not be disabled.

Start Mode:	Automatic
Login Account:	Local System
EXE File:	`lsass.exe`

- **SCardSvr**—Smart Card. Manages access to smart cards read by this computer. If this service is stopped, this computer is unable to read smart cards. If this service is disabled, any services that explicitly depend on it fail to start.

Start Mode:	Manual
Login Account:	Local Service
DLL File:	`SCardSvr.dll`

- **Schedule**—Task Scheduler. Enables a user to configure and schedule automated tasks on this computer. If this service is stopped, these tasks do not run at their scheduled times. If this service is disabled, any services that explicitly depend on it fail to start.

Start Mode:	Automatic
Login Account:	Local System
DLL File:	`schedsvc.dll`

- **SCPolicySvc**—Smart Card Removal Policy. Allows the system to be configured to lock the user desktop upon smart card removal.

Start Mode:	Manual
Login Account:	Local System
DLL File:	`SCardSvr.dll`

- **SDRSVC**—Windows Backup. Provides Windows Backup and Restore capabilities.

Start Mode:	Manual
Login Account:	Local System
DLL File:	`SDRSVC.dll`

- **seclogon**—Secondary Logon. Enables starting processes under alternate credentials. If this service is stopped, this type of logon access is unavailable. If this service is disabled, any services that explicitly depend on it fail to start.

Start Mode:	Automatic
Login Account:	Local System
DLL File:	seclogon.dll

- **SENS**—System Event Notification Service. Monitors system events and notifies subscribers to COM+ Event System of these events.

Start Mode:	Automatic
Login Account:	Local System
DLL File:	sens.dll

- **SessionEnv**—Terminal Services Configuration. Terminal Services Configuration service (TSCS) is responsible for all Terminal Services and Remote Desktop–related configuration and session maintenance activities that require SYSTEM context. These include per-session temporary folders, TS themes, and TS certificates.

Start Mode:	Manual
Login Account:	Local System
DLL File:	sessenv.dll

- **SharedAccess**—Internet Connection Sharing (ICS). Provides network address translation, addressing, name resolution and/or intrusion prevention services for a home or small office network.

Start Mode:	Disabled
Login Account:	Local System
DLL File:	ipnathlp.dll

- **ShellHWDetection**—Shell Hardware Detection. Provides notifications for AutoPlay hardware events.

Start Mode:	Automatic
Login Account:	Local System
DLL File:	shsvcs.dll

- **slsvc**—Software Licensing. Enables the download, installation, and enforcement of digital licenses for Windows and Windows applications. If the service is disabled, the operating system and licensed applications may run in a reduced function mode.

Start Mode:	Automatic
Login Account:	Network Service
EXE File:	SLsvc.exe

- **SLUINotify**—SL UI Notification Service. Provides Software Licensing activation and notification.

Start Mode:	Manual
Login Account:	Local Service
DLL File:	SLUINotify.dll

- **SNMPTRAP**—SNMP Trap. Receives trap messages generated by local or remote Simple Network Management Protocol (SNMP) agents and forwards the messages to SNMP management programs running on this computer. If this service is stopped, SNMP-based programs on this computer do not receive SNMP trap messages. If this service is disabled, any services that explicitly depend on it fail to start.

Start Mode:	Manual
Login Account:	Local Service
EXE File:	snmptrap.exe

- **Spooler**—Print Spooler. Loads files to memory for later printing.

Start Mode:	Automatic
Login Account:	Local System
EXE File:	spoolsv.exe

- **SSDPSRV**—SSDP Discovery. Discovers networked devices and services that use the SSDP discovery protocol, such as UPnP devices. Also announces SSDP devices and services running on the local computer. If this service is stopped, SSDP-based devices are not discovered. If this service is disabled, any services that explicitly depend on it fail to start.

Start Mode:	Manual
Login Account:	Local Service
DLL File:	ssdpsrv.dll

- **stisvc**—Windows Image Acquisition (WIA). Provides image acquisition services for scanners and cameras.

Start Mode:	Manual
Login Account:	Local Service
DLL File:	wiaservc.dll

- **swprv**—Microsoft Software Shadow Copy Provider. Manages software-based volume shadow copies taken by the Volume Shadow Copy service. If this service is stopped, software-based volume shadow copies cannot be managed. If this service is disabled, any services that explicitly depend on it fail to start.

Start Mode:	Manual
Login Account:	Local System
DLL File:	swprv.dll

- **SysMain**—Superfetch. Maintains and improves system performance over time.

Start Mode:	Automatic
Login Account:	Local System
DLL File:	sysmain.dll

- **TabletInputService**—Tablet PC Input Service. Enables Tablet PC pen and ink functionality.

Start Mode:	Automatic
Login Account:	Local System
DLL File:	TabSvc.dll

- **TapiSrv**—Telephony. Provides Telephony API (TAPI) support for programs that control telephony devices on the local computer and, through the LAN, on servers that are also running the service.

    Start Mode: Manual
    Login Account: Network Service
    DLL File: tapisrv.dll

- **TBS**—TPM Base Services. Enables access to the Trusted Platform Module (TPM), which provides hardware-based cryptographic services to system components and applications. If this service is stopped or disabled, applications are unable to use keys protected by the TPM.

    Start Mode: Manual
    Login Account: Local Service
    DLL File: Win32_Tpm.dll

- **TermService**—Terminal Services. Enables users to connect interactively to a remote computer. Remote Desktop and Terminal Server depend on this service. To prevent remote use of this computer, clear the check boxes on the Remote tab of the System Properties control panel item.

    Start Mode: Automatic
    Login Account: Network Service
    DLL File: termsrv.dll

- **Themes**—Themes. Provides user experience theme management.

    Start Mode: Automatic
    Login Account: Local System
    DLL File: shsvcs.dll

- **THREADORDER**—Thread Ordering Server. Provides ordered execution for a group of threads within a specific period of time.

    Start Mode: Manual
    Login Account: Local Service
    DLL File: mmcss.dll

- **TrkWks**—Distributed Link Tracking Client. Maintains links between NTFS files within a computer or across computers in a network.

    Start Mode: Automatic
    Login Account: Local System
    DLL File: trkwks.dll

- **TrustedInstaller**—Windows Modules Installer. Enables installation, modification, and removal of Windows updates and optional components. If this service is disabled, install or uninstall of Windows updates might fail for this computer.

    Start Mode: Manual
    Login Account: Local System
    EXE File: TrustedInstaller.exe

- **UI0Detect**—Interactive Services Detection. Enables user notification of user input for interactive services, which enables access to dialogs created by interactive services when they appear. If this service is stopped, notifications of new interactive service dialogs no longer function and there may no longer be access to interactive service dialogs. If this service is disabled, both notifications of and access to new interactive service dialogs no longer function.

Start Mode:	Manual
Login Account:	Local System
EXE File:	`UI0Detect.exe`

- **UmRdpService**—Terminal Services UserMode Port Redirector. Allows the redirection of printers/drives/ports for RDP connections.

Start Mode:	Manual
Login Account:	Local System
DLL File:	`umrdp.dll`

- **upnphost**—UPnP Device Host. Enables UPnP devices to be hosted on this computer. If this service is stopped, any hosted UPnP devices stop functioning and no additional hosted devices can be added. If this service is disabled, any services that explicitly depend on it fail to start.

Start Mode:	Automatic
Login Account:	Local Service
DLL File:	`upnphost.dll`

- **UxSms**—Desktop Window Manager Session Manager. Provides Desktop Window Manager startup and maintenance services.

Start Mode:	Automatic
Login Account:	Local System
DLL File:	`uxsms.dll`

- **vds**—Virtual Disk. Provides management services for disks, volumes, file systems, and, hardware array objects such as subsystems, luns, controllers, and so on.

Start Mode:	Manual
Login Account:	Local System
EXE File:	`vds.exe`

- **VSS**—Volume Shadow Copy. Manages and implements Volume Shadow Copies used for backup and other purposes. If this service is stopped, shadow copies are unavailable for backup and the backup may fail. If this service is disabled, any services that explicitly depend on it fail to start.

Start Mode:	Manual
Login Account:	Local System
EXE File:	`vssvc.exe`

- **W32Time**—Windows Time. Maintains date and time synchronization on all clients and servers in the network. If this service is stopped, date and time synchronization are unavailable. If this service is disabled, any services that explicitly depend on it fail to start.

Start Mode:	Automatic
Login Account:	Local Service
DLL File:	`w32time.dll`

- **wbengine**—Block Level Backup Engine Service. Engine to perform block-level backup and recovery of data.

Start Mode:	Manual
Login Account:	Local System
EXE File:	`wbengine.exe`

- **wcncsvc**—Windows Connect Now - Config Registrar. Acts as a registrar, issues network credential to Enrollee. If this service is disabled, Windows Connect Now - Config Registrar does not function properly.

Start Mode:	Manual
Login Account:	Local Service
DLL File:	`wcncsvc.dll`

- **WcsPlugInService**—Windows Color System. The WcsPlugInService service hosts third-party Windows Color System color device model and gamut map model plug-in modules. These plug-in modules are vendor-specific extensions to the Windows Color System baseline color device and gamut map models. Stopping or disabling the WcsPlugInService service disables this extensibility feature, and the Windows Color System uses its baseline model processing rather than the vendor's desired processing. This might result in inaccurate color rendering.

Start Mode:	Manual
Login Account:	Local Service
DLL File:	`WcsPlugInService.dll`

- **WdiServiceHost**—Diagnostic Service Host. The Diagnostic Service Host service enables problem detection, troubleshooting, and resolution for Windows components. If this service is stopped, some diagnostics no longer function. If this service is disabled, any services that explicitly depend on it fail to start.

Start Mode:	Manual
Login Account:	Local Service
DLL File:	`wdi.dll`

- **WdiSystemHost**—Diagnostic System Host. The Diagnostic System Host service enables problem detection, troubleshooting, and resolution for Windows components. If this service is stopped, some diagnostics no longer function. If this service is disabled, any services that explicitly depend on it fail to start.

Start Mode:	Manual
Login Account:	Local System
DLL File:	`wdi.dll`

- **WebClient**—WebClient. Enables Windows-based programs to create, access, and modify Internet-based files. If this service is stopped, these functions are not available. If this service is disabled, any services that explicitly depend on it fail to start.

Start Mode:	Automatic
Login Account:	Local Service
DLL File:	`webclnt.dll`

- **Wecsvc**—Windows Event Collector. This service manages persistent subscriptions to events from remote sources that support WS-Management protocol. This includes Windows Vista event logs, hardware, and IPMI-enabled event sources. The service stores forwarded events in a local event Log. If this service is stopped or disabled, event subscriptions cannot be created and forwarded events cannot be accepted.

Start Mode:	Manual
Login Account:	Network Service
DLL File:	`wecsvc.dll`

- **wercplsupport**—Problem Reports and Solutions Control Panel Support. This service provides support for viewing, sending, and deletion of system-level problem reports for the Problem Reports and Solutions control panel.

Start Mode:	Manual
Login Account:	Local System
DLL File:	`wercplsupport.dll`

- **WerSvc**—Windows Error Reporting Service. Enables errors to be reported when programs stop working or responding and allows existing solutions to be delivered. Also allows logs to be generated for diagnostic and repair services. If this service is stopped, error reporting might not work correctly and results of diagnostic services and repairs might not be displayed.

Start Mode:	Automatic
Login Account:	Local System
DLL File:	`WerSvc.dll`

- **WinDefend**—Windows Defender. Scan your computer for unwanted software, schedule scans, and get the latest unwanted software definitions.

Start Mode:	Automatic
Login Account:	Local System
DLL File:	`mpsvc.dll`

- **WinHttpAutoProxySvc**—WinHTTP Web Proxy Auto-Discovery Service. WinHTTP implements the client HTTP stack and provides developers with a Win32 API and COM Automation component for sending HTTP requests and receiving responses. In addition, WinHTTP provides support for auto-discovering a proxy configuration via its implementation of the Web Proxy Auto-Discovery (WPAD) protocol.

Start Mode:	Manual
Login Account:	Local Service
DLL File:	`winhttp.dll`

- **Winmgmt**—Windows Management Instrumentation. Provides a common interface and object model to access management information about operating system, devices, applications and services. If this service is stopped, most Windows-based software does not function properly. If this service is disabled, any services that explicitly depend on it fail to start.

Start Mode:	Automatic
Login Account:	Local System
DLL File:	`WMIsvc.dll`

- **WinRM**—Windows Remote Management (WS-Management). Windows Remote Management (WinRM) service implements the WS-Management protocol for remote management. WS-Management is a standard web services protocol used for remote software and hardware management. The WinRM service listens on the network for WS-Management requests and processes them. For the WinRM Service to listen over the network, you need to use the winrm.cmd command-line tool or go through Group Policy to configure it with a listener. The WinRM service provides access to WMI data and enables event collection. Event collection and subscription to events require that the service be running. WinRM messages use HTTP and HTTPS as transports. The WinRM service does not depend on IIS but is preconfigured to share a port with IIS on the same machine. The WinRM service reserves the /wsman URL prefix. To prevent conflicts with IIS, administrators should ensure that any websites hosted on IIS do not use the /wsman URL prefix.

Start Mode:	Manual
Login Account:	Network Service
DLL File:	WsmSvc.dll

- **Wlansvc**—WLAN AutoConfig. This service enumerates WLAN adapters and manages WLAN connections and profiles.

Start Mode:	Manual
Login Account:	Local System
DLL File:	wlansvc.dll

- **wmiApSrv**—WMI Performance Adapter. Provides performance library information from Windows Management Instrumentation (WMI) providers to clients on the network. This service runs only when Performance Data Helper is activated.

Start Mode:	Manual
Login Account:	Local System
EXE File:	WmiApSrv.exe

- **WMPNetworkSvc**—Windows Media Player Network Sharing Service. Uses Universal Plug and Play to share Windows Media Player libraries to other networked players and media devices.

Start Mode:	Manual
Login Account:	Network Service
EXE File:	wmpnetwk.exe

- **WPCSvc**—Parental Controls. This service enables Windows Parental Controls on the system. If this service is not running, Parental Controls does not work.

Start Mode:	Manual
Login Account:	Local Service
DLL File:	wpcsvc.dll

- **WPDBusEnum**—Portable Device Enumerator Service. Enforces group policy for removable mass-storage devices. Enables applications such as Windows Media Player and Image Import Wizard to transfer and synchronize content that uses removable mass-storage devices.

Start Mode:	Automatic
Login Account:	Local System
DLL File:	wpdbusenum.dll

- **wscsvc**—Security Center. Monitors system security settings and configurations.

Start Mode:	Automatic (Delayed Start)
Login Account:	Local Service
DLL File:	`wscsvc.dll`

- **WSearch**—Windows Search. Provides content indexing and property caching for file, email, and other content (via extensibility APIs). The service responds to file and email notifications to index modified content. If the service is stopped or disabled, Explorer is not able to display virtual folder views of items, and searches in Explorer fall back to item-by-item slow search.

Start Mode:	Automatic
Login Account:	Local System
EXE File:	`SearchIndexer.exe`

- **wuauserv**—Windows Update. Enables the detection, download, and installation of updates for Windows and other programs. If this service is disabled, users of this computer cannot use Windows Update or its automatic updating feature, and programs cannot use the Windows Update Agent (WUA) API.

Start Mode:	Automatic (Delayed Start)
Login Account:	Local System
DLL File:	`wuaueng.dll`

- **wudfsvc**—Windows Driver Foundation - User-mode Driver Framework. Manages user-mode driver host processes.

Start Mode:	Manual
Login Account:	Local System
DLL File:	`WUDFSvc.dll`

Your computer may also have several services not listed in these tables because third-party drivers and application software may install additional services. For example, my ThinkPad laptop has several nonstandard services installed because of the additional drivers and applications came preloaded:

Access Connections Main Service (includes a helper application), and AC Profile Manager Service—`AcSvc.exe`, `SvcGuiHlpr.exe`, `AcPrfMgrSvc.exe`. Installed by the ThinkVantage Access Connections application, which manages wired and wireless network connections.

Atheros Configuration Service—`acs.exe`. Installed as part of the Atheros wireless network adapter driver.

Bluetooth Service—`btwdins.exe`. Installed as part of the Broadcom Bluetooth driver software.

IBM KCU (Keyboard Customizer Utility) Service—`TpKmpSvc.exe`. Installed as part of the ThinkVantage Keyboard Customizer Utility software.

Intel Graphics Service Module—`igfxsrvc.exe`. Installed as part of the Intel chipset integrated graphics drivers.

System Update and TVT (ThinkVantage Technologies) Scheduler Services— SUService.exe, tvtsched.exe. Installed by the ThinkVantage System Update application, which automatically checks for and installs system updates.

ThinkPad PM (Power Management) Service—ibmpmsvc.exe. Installed as part of the ThinkPad laptop power management drivers.

User Profile Hive Cleanup Service—uphclean.exe. An optional Microsoft service to improve Windows XP shutdown performance.

In addition, other services may be installed as part of Windows in order to support nonstandard hardware.

Tip

If you don't recognize a service installed on your system, check www.sysinfo.org, which has an extensive database of programs and services found on Windows computers, including third-party applications, spyware, adware, and virus programs. It also might help to perform a Google search on the name of the unrecognized executable file.

Using the Services Manager

You can start, stop, configure, and monitor the status of services using the Services management snap-in, which appears in the Computer Management console. To open it, right-click [My] Computer and select Manage. In the left-hand pane, open Services and Applications, and then select Services. The management console is shown in Figure 2.6.

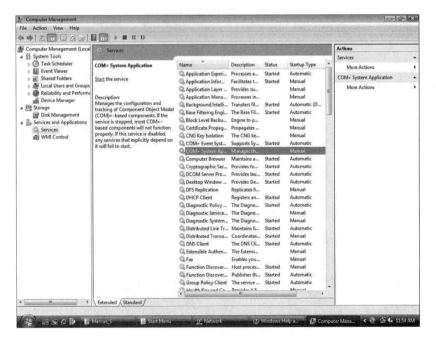

Figure 2.6 The Services management console lets you start, stop, and configure services.

Note

If you are using Windows 2000 or XP Professional, you can start, stop, and restart services using a Power Users account. Windows Vista administrators can start, stop, and restart services. Standard users must provide administrator credentials when prompted.

To change a service's configuration, you must be logged on as a Computer Administrator. Alternatively, open the Control Panel, select Performance and Maintenance, open Administrative Tools, right-click Computer Management, and select Run As. Select The Following User, and enter an Administrator account and password.

By default, services are listed in alphabetical order by their display name, although as usual for this type of display you can click on a column heading to sort by other column values, such as Status or Startup Type.

To start, stop, or restart (stop and then start) a given service, you can right-click it and select one of these actions from the pop-up menu.

To configure a service, double-click it, or highlight it and right-click Properties. The Service Properties dialog appears as shown in Figure 2.7.

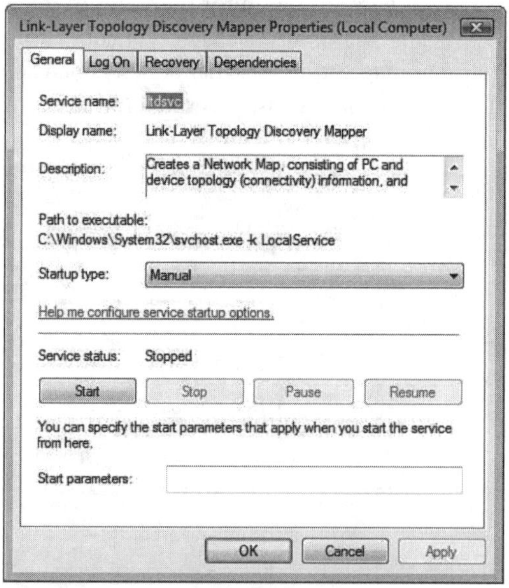

Figure 2.7 The Service Properties dialog lets you configure service startup options.

The dialog has four tabs, from which you can perform the following maintenance tasks:

- **General**—View the path to the service's executable file; set the startup type to Disabled, Manual, or Automatic; start, stop, pause, or resume the service; add additional command-line parameters used when the service is started.

- **Log On**—Set the user account used to run the service; enable or disable the service in each defined hardware profile.

- **Recovery**—Specify actions to be taken if the service fails (crashes or quits unexpectedly), which range from taking no action, restarting the service, rebooting the computer, or running a specified program.

- **Dependencies**—On this display-only tab you can see the services that depend on the selected service (its dependents), and the services on which the selected service depends (its antecedents).

In practice, you will almost never need to manage a service in any way other than to disable services that you do not want to use. Most Windows services are required for normal day-to-day use and should not be disabled. The one exception is the Indexing service in Windows XP. If the following holds:

- You are not running Internet Information Services on your computer, or you are not using any search functions provided by the Server Extensions on your website

  and

- You use an alternative desktop search program like the Windows Desktop Search by Microsoft or the Google Desktop Search, or you rarely perform keyword searches in the Windows Search window

then you can safely disable the Indexing service in XP, which eliminates its annoying tendency to perform massive amounts of disk activity when you're trying to get real work done. To do this, right-click Indexing Service in the list, select the General tab, and set Startup Type to Manual.

Windows Desktop Search is an optional Windows XP version of the improved search functionality found in Windows Vista. Visit http://www.microsoft.com/windows/products/winfamily/desktopsearch to download.

Managing Services from the Command Line

On Windows NT through Vista you can also use the `net` command to start and stop services from the command line. The command

```
net start servicename
```

starts a service, while

```
net stop servicename
```

stops it. The *servicename* must be one of the service names listed in boldface in the "List of Windows Services" section (earlier in this section), or a service's long Display name, enclosed in quotation marks if it contains spaces.

Windows has a more powerful command-line service management tool called `sc`, which can start, stop, report on, install, delete, or reconfigure services. To get a list of active services, type

```
sc query
```

For a list of all installed services, type

```
sc query type=service state=all
```

For information about a single service, type

```
sc queryex servicename
```

If you are logged on as a Computer Administrator, sc can also manage services on another computer. For example, to view the status of services on a computer named \\bobspc, you could type

```
sc \\bobspc query
```

For a list of all sc commands, type the command sc with no arguments.

Device Drivers and the *sc* Command

Windows device drivers are actually very similar to services in that they are executable programs run by the system with no direct connection to the keyboard or display. In fact, the configuration settings for both types of system components are stored in the same part of the Registry under HKEY_LOCAL_MACHINE\System\CurrentControlSet\Services, and only the type and start values serve to distinguish one from the other. The primary difference between the two component types is that drivers are run within the Windows NT kernel and have hardware access, whereas services are user-level programs.

The similarity between them is especially notable when you investigate the sc command. sc can list information about device drivers as well as services, and can change their startup options as well. Surprisingly, it's much easier to see a list of the device drivers that are loaded by your system using sc than it is using the Device Manager GUI program. For example, to display a list of device drivers, type the command

```
sc query type=driver
```

Installing Windows

Preinstallation Considerations

There is a little-known rule called the five P's that goes like this: Proper Preparation Prevents Poor Performance. Keep this rule in mind as you read this chapter. Before undertaking the installation of Windows XP Professional or Windows Vista, there are several factors that you need to consider regardless of the scope and size of the deployment. Whether you are rolling out 5,000 copies of Windows to an entire organization using sophisticated deployment methods such as ghosting or Remote Installation, or simply installing it on your home computer, the same issues still require your attention *before* the installation process begins.

In this chapter, you look at each of the following items in more depth, and get a feel for how they affect an installation of Windows XP Professional or Windows Vista and how they will impact the computer, both now and into the future:

- System requirements
- Hardware and software compatibility
- Transferring files and settings
- Network configuration
- File system considerations
- Type of installation to perform

When working through this chapter, it might be helpful to build a checklist. For an example, see Figure 3.1.

Without any further ado, let's get right into the meat of this chapter and start off by looking at the system requirements for installing Windows XP Professional and Windows Vista.

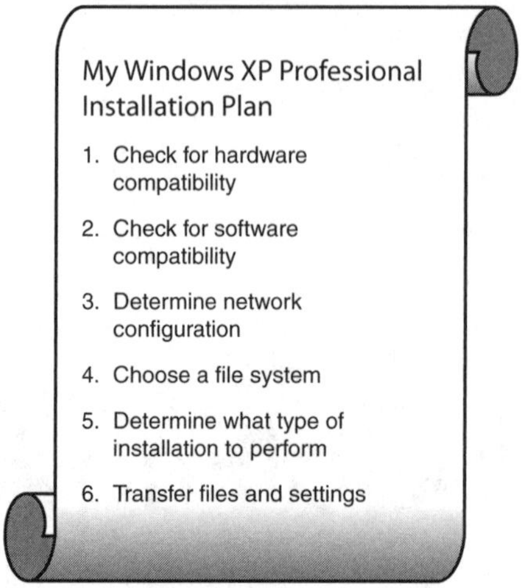

My Windows XP Professional
Installation Plan

1. Check for hardware
   compatibility

2. Check for software
   compatibility

3. Determine network
   configuration

4. Choose a file system

5. Determine what type of
   installation to perform

6. Transfer files and settings

Figure 3.1 My Windows XP Professional installation notes page.

System Requirements for Windows XP Professional

Although the system requirements for Windows XP Professional were fairly formidable when it was first introduced in 2001, by today's standards any system built in the last four years or so is fully capable of running Windows XP Professional. (Windows XP Home requirements are a bit less stringent.)

The official system requirements to support installation of Windows XP Professional are presented in Table 3.1. Although Windows XP Home is not quite as demanding as Professional, these minimums still apply.

Table 3.1 Hardware Requirements to Install Windows XP Professional

Minimum Requirements	Recommended Requirements
Pentium (or compatible) 233MHz or higher processor	Pentium II (or compatible) 300MHz or higher processor
64 megabytes (MB) of RAM	128MB (4GB maximum) of RAM
2 gigabyte (GB) hard disk with 650MB of free disk space	1.5GB of free disk space
Video graphics adapter (VGA) or higher display adapter	Super VGA (SVGA) display adapter and Plug and Play monitor
Keyboard, mouse, or other pointing device	Keyboard, mouse, or other pointing device
CD-ROM or DVD-ROM drive (required for CD installations)	CD-ROM or DVD-ROM drive (12× or faster)
Network adapter (required for network installation)	Network adapter (required for network installation)

Multiple (and Multicore) Processors

Windows XP Professional, like its predecessor Windows 2000 Professional, is capable of handling up to two CPUs and provides support for symmetric multiprocessing. In addition, XP Pro sees dual-core CPUs and Intel processors that feature hyperthreading as two physical CPUs. Likewise, processors with more than two cores are seen as the same number of physical CPUs as there are cores.

System Requirements for Windows Vista

Windows Vista requires much more powerful hardware, although the exact hardware requirements vary a bit with the Vista edition selected. Table 3.2 lists the requirements for Windows Vista Home Basic and for Windows Vista Home Premium/Business/Ultimate editions.

Table 3.2   Hardware Requirements to Install Windows Vista

Windows Vista Home Basic	Windows Vista Home Premium, Business, Ultimate Eitions
1GHz 32-bit (x86) or 64-bit (x64) processor	1GHz 32-bit (x86) or 64-bit (x64) processor
512MB of system memory	1GB of system memory
20GB hard disk (15GB available space)	40GB hard disk (15GB available space)
DirectX 9 graphics support	DirectX 9 graphics support
32MB graphics memory	WDDM driver
	128MB graphics memory
	Pixel Shader 2.0 in hardware
	32 bits per pixel color support
DVD-ROM drive	DVD-ROM drive
Audio output	Audio output
Internet access	Internet access
Single physical CPU (supports multicore CPUs)	Single or dual physical CPUs (supports multicore CPUs)

Of course, knowing the hardware requirements to support a successful installation (and later operation) of Windows is just one small part of the battle. Sticking to your plan of action, as outlined in the list in the first section of this chapter, you need to look at hardware and software compatibility issues, both of which can cause you some annoyance and lack of functionality or, at worst, bring your installation of Windows to a screeching halt.

Checking Hardware and Software Compatibility

Verifying that your current hardware supports an installation of your preferred Windows version is critical to getting Windows correctly installed and running smoothly. Verifying the existing software installed on your computer when performing an upgrade installation is just as vital—Windows can get pretty particular when it comes to dealing with previously installed software.

There are a couple of means at your disposal when it comes to verifying hardware and software compatibility for the installation of Windows XP or Vista. The first of these is the Hardware Compatibility List (HCL).

Note

Currently, Microsoft provides the Hardware Compatibility List for Windows Vista and Windows XP at a single website, http://winqual.microsoft.com/hcl/Default.aspx (you must use Internet Explorer to view this list). Select the Windows Vista tab to search for Windows Vista–compatible hardware, and the Windows XP tab to search for Windows XP–compatible hardware.

For more information on the Windows XP and Windows Vista Upgrade Advisors, refer to Chapter 12, "Windows Troubleshooting."

Known Compatibility Issues for Windows XP

If you are installing Windows XP as an upgrade to systems that are still running Windows 2000, Windows 98, or Windows Me with software of similar vintage, there are a few software compatibility issues to watch out for:

- Old versions of Roxio Easy CD Creator (specifically versions 4 and 5) do not work with Windows XP. Although Roxio provides updates to Easy CD Creator 5 to fix compatibility problems, you will probably want to uninstall either version 4 or 5 and install the latest version, Easy Media Creator 10, or a comparable CD/DVD-mastering program from another vendor, such as Nero or Sonic.

- The NetBIOS Extended User Interface (better known as NetBEUI) is no longer supported for networking in Windows XP. Although Microsoft provides an installable version of NetBEUI on the Windows XP CD in the Valueadd\MSFT\Net\NetBEUI folder, NetBEUI is provided only for troubleshooting. NetBEUI, if present, is automatically removed when upgrading older Windows versions to Windows XP. For networking in either a workgroup or domain configuration, you should be using TCP/IP. If you must install NetBEUI, see Microsoft Knowledge Base article 301041, located at http://support.microsoft.com/default.aspx?scid=kb;en-us;301041, for more information.

- To solve compatibility issues with pre-Windows XP applications, Microsoft has supplied several application compatibility updates. Many are included in Service Pack 2. The most recent is included in Service Pack 3, and can also be installed prior to the availability of Service Pack 3. See Microsoft Knowledge Base article 884130, available at http://support.microsoft.com/default.aspx?scid=kb;en-us;884130 for more information about the latest compatibility update.

If you use Windows XP with recent and current applications, there are no software compatibility issues to worry about.

Known Compatibility Issues for Windows Vista

Although Windows Vista can use many programs and drivers made for Windows XP, it uses a substantially different internal design than any previous Windows version. As a consequence, there are many more compatibility issues for Windows Vista than for Windows XP:

- You need to remove some programs before upgrading an existing XP installation to Windows Vista. These programs include antivirus, antispyware, backup, and other utility programs. Some of these programs can be reinstalled, but others are not compatible with Windows Vista and must be replaced.

- Other programs must be updated after Windows Vista is installed.

- Some devices are not compatible with Windows Vista.

- Some devices require updated drivers to be compatible with Windows Vista.
- After installing Windows Vista, but before installing software, you should also install application compatibility updates for Windows Vista.

Fortunately, Microsoft has developed several tools for determining compatibility. These include

- The Windows Vista Upgrade Advisor (designed for use on individual PCs); see Chapter 12 for details.
- The Microsoft Assessment and Planning Solution Accelerator (designed for use on networked computers).
- The Application Compatibility Toolkit version 5 or greater (designed for use on networked computers).

Note

Windows Vista, like Windows XP, does not support NetBEUI. However, Windows Vista does not include an installable NetBEUI protocol stack. With Windows Vista, NetBEUI is definitely history.

If you are planning to add Windows Vista–based systems to a network based on NetBEUI, you must move the network to TCP/IP (or another supported protocol) before you can add the Vista computers to that network.

Using the Microsoft Assessment and Planning Solution Accelerator

The Microsoft Assessment and Planning Solution Accelerator, available from http://www.microsoft.com/technet/solutionaccelerators/hardwareassessment/wv/default.mspx, is designed to determine which computers on your network are ready to run Windows Vista, Microsoft Office 2007, Windows Server 2008, or Microsoft Virtual Server 2005 R2. It can analyze computers running any of the following operating systems (32-bit versions only):

- Windows Vista and Vista SPI
- Windows XP Professional
- Windows Server 2003 (including R2)
- Windows Server 2008

It supports both Active Directory domains and workgroups, and uses Windows Management Instrumentation (WMI) technology to gather information. It can also find network printers and computers using Simple Network Management Protocol (SNMP). It uses Microsoft Word 2003 SP2 or 2007 and Microsoft Excel 2003 SP2 or 2007 to generate reports. During the installation process, it installs SQL Server 2005 Express Edition if it is not already present.

Note

SQL Server 2005 Express Edition is also used by the Application Compatibility Toolkit. Therefore, you should install and run the Microsoft Assessment and Planning Solution Accelerator first.

After installation, you are prompted to enable Remote Administration and File and Printer Sharing to run on each computer on the network. If you use Windows Firewall, use the Exceptions menu (see Figure 3.2) to enable these options; if you use a third-party firewall, see the documentation for the product for details.

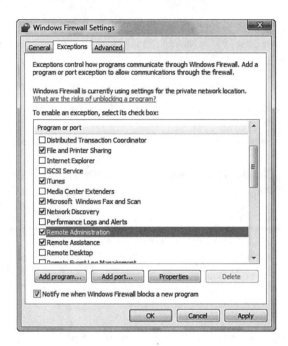

Figure 3.2   Configuring Windows Firewall to permit Remote Administration and File and Printer Sharing to run.

When you run the tool, you can specify computers by IP address range, domain, or workgroup. The tool generates a detailed report in Microsoft Excel format and an overview in Microsoft Word format.

Using the Application Compatibility Toolkit Version 5

The Application Compatibility Toolkit is available from the Microsoft Download Center. It can be used to determine application compatibility for new operating systems, Windows updates, or a new version of Internet Explorer, and can also provide compatibility fixes for many problems. Supported clients include

- Windows XP with Service Pack 2
- Windows Vista
- Windows Server 2003 with Service Pack 1
- Windows 2000 with Service Pack 4 and Update Rollup 1

The Application Compatibility Toolkit includes the following components:

- The Application Compatibility Manager is used to create and configure data collection packages and the databases used to store collected information. These are distributed as .exe files (default) or as .msi installation files as desired. After a system is analyzed, the manager analyzes and reports compatibility information.

- The Standard User Analyzer looks for applications that behave differently when run in Administrator or Standard modes because of the new User Account Control feature in Windows Vista.

- The Compatibility Administrator is used to apply application fixes to programs that are not fully compatible, as determined by the Application Compatibility Manager and the Standard User Analyzer.

- The Internet Explorer Compatibility Test Tool tests websites and web-based applications for behaviors not compatible with Internet Explorer 7. It does not work with Windows 2000.

- The Setup Analysis Tool checks installation programs for problematic behaviors such as installation of kernel mode drivers, 16-bit components, GINA DLLs, and modification of resource-protected files or Registry keys.

The Application Compatibility Toolkit uses Microsoft SQL Server or the free Microsoft SQL Server 2005 Express Edition installed by the Windows Vista Hardware Assessment Tool.

Note

For an overview of the Application Compatibility Toolkit and detailed instructions for performing each step of the analysis, download the Zip file **ACT_Step_by_Step_Guides** from the Microsoft Download Center. It contains the following documents: **ACT_Configuration_and_Troubleshooting**, **ACT_Step_By_Step**, **ACT_Phase1_Collecting_Data**, **ACT_Phase2_Analyzing_Issues**, and **ACT_Phase3_Testing_and_Mitigating_Issues** in Adobe PDF and Microsoft XPS formats.

Application Updates for Windows Vista

Application updates for Windows Vista are normally delivered via Windows Update, but you can download them manually and install them immediately after you install Windows Vista. The most recent application update as of this writing is the December 2007 application update, available from http://support.microsoft.com/kb/943302/. If this update is superseded by a more recent update, follow the link provided in the body of the article for the updated version. This update improves support for dozens of business and personal applications, and includes previous application updates.

With issues of system requirements and compatibility out of the way, you'll next take a look at the methods Windows XP and Windows Vista provide for migrating crucial information to a new Windows XP or Windows Vista installation.

Migrating Files and Settings to New Installations

If you want to bring existing data and settings from an existing Windows installation to your new installation, you now have more options than ever before. You can still perform an upgrade installation (as detailed in Chapter 4, "Upgrading Windows") and take your chances with compatibility issues and other problems, you can procure a third-party utility to perform this task for you, or you can use a Microsoft-provided tool to make the move for you.

Windows XP can use the Files and Settings Transfer Wizard (FSTW) and the User State Migration Tool (USMT), whereas Windows Vista users can use USMT or Windows Easy Transfer and Windows Easy Transfer Companion.

Note

These sections are intended only to introduce the capabilities of these two tools. For specific instructions on using these tools, see Chapter 4.

The Files and Settings Transfer Wizard (Windows XP)

The Files and Settings Transfer Wizard is provided on the setup CD-ROM. You can run the Files and Settings Transfer Wizard on any computer, or create a Files and Settings Transfer Wizard floppy disk if you want and use that instead. The Files and Settings Transfer Wizard can migrate a user's files and settings from any Windows OS from Windows 95 and Windows NT 4.0 and newer to Windows XP.

By design, the Files and Settings Transfer Wizard is built to transfer settings for Microsoft applications, such as Internet Explorer, Outlook, Outlook Express, and the Office suite. The settings that are migrated fall into these four major groups:

- **Appearance**—Items such as wallpaper, colors, sounds, and the location of the taskbar.
- **Action**—Items such as the keyboard key repeat rate, double-click settings, and so on.
- **Internet**—Settings that control how your browser behaves, including home page, favorites or bookmarks, cookies, security settings, proxy settings, and dial-up settings.
- **Mail**—Settings for Outlook or Outlook Express, such as mail servers, accounts, signature file, views, mail rules, contacts, and your local mail file.

Files can be selected for movement by type, such as .doc or .xls; by folder; or specifically by name. The Files and Settings Transfer Wizard automatically moves many of the most common file types for you during the process; however, you can add or remove folders, file types, or specific files from the transfer should you want to.

The Files and Settings Transfer Wizard can also transfer settings for selected third-party applications. The Files and Settings Transfer Wizard only transfers the user's settings; it will not transfer or install the applications themselves. In order for these settings to be successfully transferred, the applications must be installed on the target computer *before* the settings are migrated to it using the Files and Settings Transfer Wizard. For more information on using this wizard, see Chapter 3.

The User State Migration Tool

The User State Migration tool is the IT Administrator's version of the File and Settings Transfer Wizard. However, unlike File and Settings Transfer Wizard, USMT version 3.0 and above works with Windows Vista as well as Windows XP. USMT can perform all the functions of the File and Settings Transfer Wizard, but USMT is made to run from the command line, in environments where you will be migrating a number of users. In contrast, the File and Settings Transfer Wizard runs with a graphical wizard interface, and is intended only for one-off, user-driven migrations.

Because this tool is more useful when performing multiple installations in a networked environment than it is for standalone installations (although it can be used for this purpose if you prefer), full detail on using this tool is covered as part of performing automated installations in the section "Using the User State Migration Tool," p. 196.

Windows Easy Transfer

In Windows Vista, Windows Easy Transfer is used to transfer files and settings from an individual PC, replacing the Files and Settings Transfer Wizard used in Windows XP. Windows Easy Transfer can be used to transfer files and settings from Windows XP or Windows Vista–based systems, and files from Windows 2000–based systems. Windows Easy Transfer can be started from the Windows Vista DVD (select Transfer Files and Settings from Another Computer) or from a USB flash memory drive you create on a Windows Vista–based system (select Run Windows Easy Transfer from the AutoPlay menu).

Note

If you want to transfer data from a Windows XP or Windows 2000 computer and you do not have a Windows Vista DVD available, you can download Windows Easy Transfer from the Windows Vista: Windows Easy Transfer page at http://www.microsoft.com/windows/products/windowsvista/buyorupgrade/easytransfer.mspx.

Windows Easy Transfer supports both direct transfers between old and new systems by means of a network or Windows Easy Transfer cable connection, as well as transfers to an intermediate storage device such as an external hard disk, removable media, recordable or rewritable CD, or network share. Before starting the transfer from the source system, make sure that you have closed all applications and saved any open data files.

Note

Before transferring files and settings to a new computer or installation, you should install the applications whose settings you are transferring. You can perform this step manually. However, if you are using a direct network or Windows Easy Transfer cable to transfer between a Windows XP and a Windows Vista system, you can use the Windows Vista Easy Transfer Companion to transfer applications as well as files and settings. See the Windows Vista: Windows Easy Transfer page at http://www.microsoft.com/windows/products/windowsvista/buyorupgrade/easytransfer.mspx for the link to the file and instructions.

During the transfer process, you must identify the method you are using for transfer:

- Easy Transfer cable
- Network connection
- CD, DVD, or other removable media (including external hard disks)

If you choose the network connection, you are prompted to use the network connection for a direct transfer or to copy files to and from a network location.

For direct network transfers, a Windows Easy Transfer key (password) is required. Select No, I Need a Key, and you will be provided with a key. Record the alphanumeric value given; you will need to use it to complete the transfer process (see Figure 3.3).

If you select removable media, external hard disk, or network location, you are prompted to specify a network location (it can be a network path or a drive letter and folder). You can also add a password for protection. You will be prompted to provide a USB flash memory drive for use by the Easy Transfer software.

Figure 3.3   Windows Easy Transfer provides an alphanumeric key to protect your direct network transfer.

Use the Select User Accounts, Files and Settings to Transfer dialog to view the locations and settings to transfer. Clear check marks to deselect selected items. You can also add files, folders, and drives to transfer. The lower-right side of the dialog lists the total size of the transfer.

After selecting items to transfer, the Review Selected Files and Settings dialog appears. You can select additional locations to transfer before starting the transfer process.

If you selected the option to transfer to a network location or to an external hard disk, the transfer process starts. If you selected the option to transfer to removable media (including CDs), you are prompted to insert each cartridge or disc. If the media is not formatted, you are prompted to format the media before continuing.

To complete the transfer process, specify the location of the transferred files, or, for a direct network transfer, provide the Windows Easy Transfer key received earlier in the process. For other types of transfers, specify the location of the files and settings being transferred; provide a password if prompted. Before the process can be completed, you must specify the user account on the new computer or installation to use as the target for the transfer. If you are transferring from removable media or CD, provide media in the order it was used. At the end of the transfer process, a summary appears, listing the user accounts, files, folders, program, and systems settings transferred (see Figure 3.4). For details, click Show Me Everything That Was Transferred. This report can be saved to disk or printed.

Now, as you work your way down the preinstallation preparation path, your next stop is network configuration information—you will look at this in the next section.

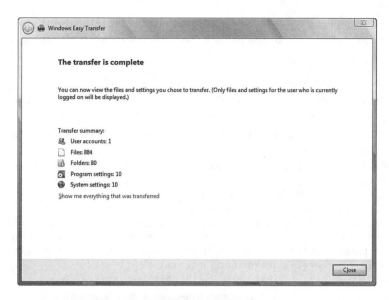

Figure 3.4 Windows Easy Transfer provides an overview of the items transferred.

Getting the Network Configuration

After you've determined what your hardware and software compatibility picture looks like, you are well on your way to being ready to install Windows on your computer. Of the major factors to consider before installing Windows, knowing the proper configuration of a networked PC is essential.

If the computer on which Windows will be installed is not connected to a network, you can skip this section. By *network*, I mean a formal (managed) network consisting of servers and client workstations that has a common naming system, uses an IP address assignment system, and uses network user accounts for access to resources. If this sounds exactly like your Windows NT 4.0 or Windows 2000/Server 2003 domain–based network, well then, that's because it is.

As you have likely guessed from this description, this scenario does not apply to a typical peer-to-peer small office or home network that does not employ servers or systems that just connect to the Internet.

If your network uses a peer-to-peer arrangement without using a centralized database for the storage of user accounts and permissions, you are operating in what is called a *workgroup*. The first piece of network information you need is either the workgroup name (for example, mygroup) or the domain name (such as netserverworld.com or netserverworld.local). You can always install Windows initially in a workgroup arrangement and then join a client/server domain after installation.

If you are upgrading a computer that is already participating in a network environment, the following list of items should be recorded on your checklist *before* starting the upgrade process:

- The computer name.

- The domain or workgroup name, as previously mentioned.

- Many networks use dynamic configuration for TCP/IP address information. However, if these are assigned manually for your network, you'll need this information.

- The username and password of an account with permissions to add or create computer accounts.

- If you are using connection-specific DNS suffixes in addition to a primary DNS suffix, you should record all DNS suffixes. For example, if your primary DNS suffix is netserverworld.com and you ping a computer by machine name server01, your computer will look for server01.netserverworld.com. If you are also using connection-specific DNS suffixes, such as newportnews on a connection, the computer will look for server01.netserverworld.com and server01.newportnews.netserverworld.com. This can affect how your computers locate other computers in the network, so pay close attention to these settings. Figure 3.5 shows this information.

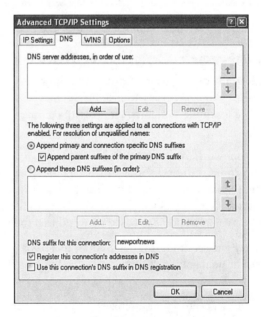

Figure 3.5   The connection-specific DNS suffix affects how your computer searches out other computers on the network.

Of course, you will need all the appropriate hardware and cabling, too...but that's kind of a given here! When you have all the network configuration information you need, be sure to write it down in a safe place so that it will be available during the installation process.

Note

If you're looking for more detailed information on Windows networking concepts and configuration, see Chapter 6, "Networking Windows."

Now that you've gotten the network configuration information you need for the installation, let's take some time to look in depth at choosing your file system, including the pros and cons of each file system.

Choosing a File System

Windows XP can be installed on one of two file systems (FAT32 or NTFS), but Windows Vista can be installed only on the NTFS file system. If you are installing Windows XP, the choice of a file system is not one to be taken lightly. Unlike most other configurable items in your Windows XP installation, the file system is one that can be changed only one time after installation, and only in one direction using Microsoft-supplied utilities.

▶▶ You can perform additional file system conversions by using third-party tools. To learn more about file systems in general and converting file systems, see Chapter 10, "Windows File Systems."

For a clean installation of Windows XP, you will have to make a choice between using the FAT32 or NTFS file system. On an upgrade installation from Windows 98, you could possibly even face an existing FAT16-formatted partition because Windows 98 supported the FAT32 file system but did not automatically invoke it—you had to convert to FAT32 after the fact.

Table 3.3 provides a quick comparison of the FAT16, FAT32, and NTFS file systems.

Table 3.3   File System Comparison

	FAT16	FAT32	NTFS
Supported operating systems	All versions of Windows, MS-DOS, and OS/2.	Windows 95 OSR2, Windows 98, Windows Millennium Edition, Windows 2000, Windows XP, and Windows Vista.	Windows NT 4.0 SP4 or later can access files and folders. Windows 2000 uses NTFS 5.0 XP; Server 2003 and Vista use NTFS 5.1.
Volume sizes	Maximum size is limited to 4GB (using a 64KB cluster size). In MS-DOS, Windows 95, Windows 98, and Windows Me the maximum size is 2GB because the largest cluster size supported is 32KB.	Minimum size is 512MB, maximum size is 2TB. In Windows XP Professional, Vista, and Windows 2000, the maximum size a FAT32 volume can be is 32GB.	Minimum volume size (recommended) is 10MB. Maximum volume size (recommended) is 2TB, although much larger sizes are possible.
Floppy disk usage?	No	No	No
Removable storage usage?	Yes	Yes	Yes, but not recommended.

(continues)

Table 3.3   Continued

	FAT16	**FAT32**	**NTFS**
Maximum file size	Maximum file size is 4GB minus 1 byte.*	Maximum file is size 4GB.	Maximum file size 16TB minus 64KB.
Files per volume	65,536 (2^{16} files).	Approximately 4,177,920.	4,294,967,295 (2^{32} minus 1 files).
Supports NTFS 5.0 features?	No	No	Windows 2000 and Windows XP fully support the advanced features of NTFS 5.0. Windows NT 4.0 SP4 supports access only, but not the advanced features.

On Windows NT/2000/XP; with Windows 9x/Me, 2GB

During the installation process, you may be asked to make a file system selection from the menu shown in Figure 3.6.

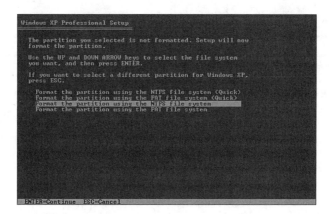

Figure 3.6   Selecting a file system during setup; you can convert FAT to NTFS later if you want.

You will be given this choice only when dealing with an unformatted volume. If you have a volume that is currently formatted with FAT16 or FAT32, you will be given the opportunity to convert or format it to the NTFS file system. Converting an existing file system is part of performing an upgrade installation of Windows XP or Vista, as covered in Chapter 4.

Take the Easy Road

If you are concerned about system stability, you can always make use of the FAT file system during installation of Windows XP. After you've verified that the installation has taken without any stability problems, you can then convert the file system to NTFS.

By installing Windows XP in this way, you can still make use of a variety of DOS boot disks and utilities. On a new installation using new hardware certified for Windows XP, this is probably not going to be a required step.

You cannot change your file system using Microsoft utilities after Windows XP Professional has been installed unless you are converting from FAT16 or FAT32 to NTFS. To revert the file system back to FAT32, you must use a third-party application such as Norton PartitionMagic (http://www.symantec.com/partitionmagic/). The real question you must answer when making the decision about which file system to use is this: Will this computer be used to multiboot another operating system that requires the FAT file system? If your answer is yes then you need to keep at least the System partition (the partition that holds the system files needed to start the computer) formatted as FAT16 or FAT32, depending on what other operating system you will have installed on the computer. You can format your Boot partition that will hold Windows XP Professional with NTFS if you like, but any data on it will be inaccessible to the other operating systems installed on the computer.

File System Misconception

A common misconception that people have about using the NTFS file system is that their files will not be available for access over the network when using a client operating system such as Windows 95 or Windows 98. The only time files on an NTFS volume are inaccessible to a legacy client is when the files reside in a different volume on the same computer in a multiboot arrangement and the legacy operating system is running. When files are accessed across the network, File and Printer Sharing for Microsoft Networks performs the magic in the background that allows FAT16- and FAT32-based operating systems access to files located on an NTFS volume.

It's always preferred to use the NTFS file system as often as possible, except where you must make the Windows XP Professional volume available to other operating systems installed on the same computer. Should you decide against using NTFS, you will miss the following features, just to name a few:

- **NTFS file and folder permissions**—Using NTFS permissions you can control access to every file on an NTFS volume. You can configure permissions at each level of the directory structure to meet your needs for allowing and/or preventing access to files and folders. However, don't get NTFS permissions confused with share permissions—they are two entirely different items, each requiring consideration both individually and as a pair.

Note

By default, Windows XP Professional uses Simple File Sharing, which does not support NTFS file and folder permissions.

To enable NTFS file and folder permissions, open the Tools menu in Windows Explorer, select Folder Options, click the View tab, and clear the check box for Use Simple File Sharing (Recommended).

- **The Encrypting File System**—Using a public/private key pair, EFS provides strong cryptographic encryption of files and folders that is extremely resistant to attack and compromise. EFS is completely transparent to the user, and in Windows XP supports multiple user access to an encrypted file. The only downside to using EFS is that its usage is mutually exclusive with NTFS compression. EFS is not supported in Windows XP Home.
- **File compression**—The NTFS file system supports encryption on both files and folders. NTFS uses a *lossless compression* algorithm, which ensures that no data is lost when compressing and decompressing data. *Lossy compression*, such as that used in many video and audio file formats, cannot be used with files that require exact data, such as spreadsheets or

document files where data losses due to compression will render the file corrupt and unusable. As previously mentioned, compression is mutually exclusive with EFS encryption.

- **Disk space quota management**—Using disk quotas enables you to control the amount of data that users can store on your NTFS volumes. Quota control is on a per-volume basis and can be configured with custom quotas for select users as desired. The disk quota system enables you to determine when users are nearing their limits and automatically prevent usage after a user has reached his defined quota limitation.

- **Volume mount points**—You can finally escape the 26-volume limit on a computer by using volume mount points. Think of it as mapping a path to a hard drive or CD-ROM to a folder on an NTFS volume; thus a new hard drive you've installed to hold user data can be mounted as C:\UserDocs or whatever name you choose.

If you are installing Windows Vista, there are no file system decisions to make: It can be installed only on a drive formatted with NTFS. If you are performing a clean install to an empty hard disk, Vista formats the hard disk as part of the installation process. However, if you are performing an upgrade installation of Windows Vista, you must convert the boot volume to NTFS before you can install Vista.

To convert the system (boot) drive in Windows XP from a FAT32 (or FAT) file system to NTFS, close all running applications, open the command prompt window (click Start, Run, CMD, and click OK), and use the following command:

```
convert C:/FS:NTFS
```

Perform the conversion before starting the upgrade process. To convert other drives to NTFS, use the same command, but replace C: with the drive letter you want to convert.

When you've made your file system choice, you are ready to move onto the next item of consideration: the decision about what type of installation to perform.

Installation Types

Deciding on the type of installation to perform is dictated by many factors, such as the following:

- Is there an operating system currently installed? If so, do you want to preserve settings and configurations, or start from scratch?
- Will the installation be performed interactively or remotely?
- How many computers are to be installed at a single time?
- Is your network arranged in a domain model using Active Directory?

These are many of the questions that lead to the answer for the larger question: What type of installation will you be performing? There are three distinct possibilities and each of them is explored in the following sections.

Upgrade Installations to Windows XP

Windows XP Professional supports direct upgrades from Windows 98, Windows Millennium Edition, Windows NT 4.0 Workstation, Windows 2000 Professional, and Windows XP Home Edition. If you are currently running any other operating system, including Windows NT 3.x

Workstation, Windows 95, or Windows 3.x, you will need to perform a clean installation because upgrading from these vintage operating systems is not supported.

Note

Although we assume that most readers of this book are using Windows XP Professional, you might want to note that you can also upgrade Windows 98 and Me (but not Window 2000 Pro or NT4) to XP Home Edition.

An upgrade installation is most useful in cases where you have customized user settings that you want to preserve. This option, however, does not always work flawlessly, especially if you are upgrading from an operating system other than Windows 2000 Professional or Windows XP Home Edition due to the differences in the Registry structure and the startup process.

Should you decide to upgrade an existing Windows 98 or Windows Millennium Edition installation to Windows XP (and you allow a backup to be made during installation), you will be able to later uninstall Windows XP and effectively revert your computer back to the state it was in immediately preceding the Windows XP upgrade. The ability to uninstall is contingent on the following factors, however:

- The volume on which Windows XP is installed cannot be converted from the FAT32 file system to the NTFS file system.
- You cannot create or delete any volumes on the computer.
- You must not delete the backup files that are created during Windows XP installation. Thirty days after installation, you will be prompted to delete these files. If you do not intend to revert back to your old OS, there's no reason not to delete them.

The easiest process is to upgrade from an installation of Windows 2000 Professional or Windows NT 4.0 Workstation to Windows XP Professional. Windows XP Professional shares a common operating system structure and core with these two operating systems, including device driver requirements and Registry structures. If you upgrade a Windows NT 4.0 Workstation installation that is installed on an NTFS-formatted volume, the file system will be automatically upgraded from NTFS 4.0 to NTFS 5.0 as part of the installation process. If the file system is FAT, you will be presented with the option to upgrade to NTFS during the installation.

When upgrading from older Microsoft operating systems, there are a few possible glitches to be aware of. The following list details some items of concern when upgrading from Windows 98 or Windows Millennium Edition to Windows XP:

- System tools such as ScanDisk and DriveSpace will not be upgraded in Windows XP. Windows XP brings along its own version of ScanDisk, and NTFS compression replaces legacy compression utilities such as DriveSpace.
- Client software for other network types cannot be upgraded during an upgrade to Windows XP. The only exception to this rule is that if Novell Client32 is installed, the setup routine will detect it and replace it with a newer version of Client32 from the Windows XP Setup CD-ROM. After the installation of Windows XP is complete, you can install additional network clients through the properties sheet for a particular network connection.

- Some applications might not run properly under Windows XP due to the fact that the Windows XP Registry is arranged differently than the Windows 98 or Windows Millennium Edition Registry. In some cases, *migration packs* can alleviate this problem. A migration pack (or upgrade pack) is simply a set of new application and library files for a specific application that enables it to run in a newer, more advanced environment than it was originally designed for.

- Some applications might not run properly under Windows XP if they attempt to make calls to APIs that don't exist in Windows XP. In some cases, migration packs can alleviate this problem. In other cases, you will need to remove the application from your computer. The Windows Upgrade Advisor typically identifies these applications for you.

- Some applications might not run properly under Windows XP if they install different files under different operating systems. In this case, you reinstall the application following the upgrade to attempt a fix.

- Applications that directly access hardware or use custom file filters will most likely not run correctly under Windows XP. The most common cases of these types of problems are related to CD-ROM–burning software and antivirus software. You will need to obtain updated versions of these types of applications for use with Windows XP.

There are additional issues to watch for if you upgrade from Windows NT 4.0 Workstation to Windows XP:

- File system filters written for Windows NT 4.0 will not work with Windows XP due to the upgrade in NTFS. This is commonly seen in antivirus software.

- Networking software written for Windows NT 4.0 will not run on Windows XP if it attempts to use the Windows NT 4.0 TCP/IP or IPX/SPX protocol stacks.

- Custom power management solutions written for Windows NT 4.0 are not compatible with Windows XP and are not required due to Windows XP's native support for ACPI (Advanced Power Configuration Interface) and APM (Advanced Power Management).

- Custom Plug-and-Play solutions written for Windows NT 4.0 are not compatible with Windows XP and are not required because Windows XP provides full Plug-and-Play support natively.

- Fault-tolerant disk arrangements, such as disk mirrors, are not supported in Windows XP. Windows 2000 Server and Windows .NET Server support disk mirroring and striping. Windows XP does, however, support RAID arrays hosted by onboard or add-on PATA, SATA, and SCSI host adapters.

Should you have an unsupported upgrade path or decide that you would rather perform a clean installation, but do not want to lose all of your personalized settings, don't despair. You can transfer a large majority of your personalized settings (and even your document files) by using either the Files and Settings Transfer Wizard or the User State Migration Tool. Full details on performing an upgrade installation of Windows XP and use of these tools can be found in Chapter 4.

One last point about upgrade installations before you move on to clean installations: You cannot perform upgrade installations over the network using Remote Installation Services—RIS supports only clean installations.

Upgrade Installations to Windows Vista

You can upgrade to Windows Vista from any edition of Windows XP (including Media Center and Tablet PC editions) or from Windows 2000. However, upgrades to Windows Vista differ in several ways from upgrades to Windows XP:

■ Upgrade versions of Windows Vista are intended for use only on systems that contain a previous version of Windows eligible for upgrading; there is no provision for inspecting a CD from a previous version to determine eligibility for the upgrade as with Windows XP and previous versions. Although an in-place upgrade uses the same folder name as the previous folder, during the upgrade process, the existing Windows folder is moved to a folder called Windows.old.

■ Some upgrade paths to Windows Vista do not support an in-place upgrade (Microsoft's term for starting the installation from within the existing operating system). In such cases, you must install Vista to a new folder and reinstall applications you used previously.

■ Different editions of Windows Vista have different upgrade paths. Table 3.4 lists the upgrade paths available to Windows Vista editions available at retail.

Table 3.4   Upgrade Paths to Windows Vista

Upgrade From	Vista Home Basic	Vista Home Premium	Vista Business	Vista Ultimate
Windows 2000	Clean install	Clean install	Clean install	Clean install
Windows XP Home	In-place upgrade	In-place upgrade	In-place upgrade	In-place upgrade
Windows XP Media Center	Clean install	In-place upgrade	Clean install	In-place upgrade
Windows XP Tablet PC	Clean install	Clean install	In-place upgrade	In-place upgrade
Windows XP Professional x64	Clean install	Clean install	Clean install	Clean Install

As you can see from Table 3.4, you might need to perform a clean install to upgrade your system. To perform a clean install, either to an unused portion of your hard disk, creating a dual-boot configuration, or to an empty hard disk, with an upgrade DVD, you need to follow this procedure. It essentially installs Windows Vista twice—once without the product key or activation to create a location for the second installation (with product key and activation) to use:

1. Start your system using the Windows Vista DVD.

2. From the opening dialog, select Install Now. Note that the choices you make over the next few steps are critical.

3. Do **not** enter the product key when prompted.

4. Be sure to **clear** the Automatically Activate check box. Click Next.

5. Answer **No** when asked whether you want to enter a product key now.

6. **Select** the Windows Vista edition you are installing.

Caution

Keep in mind that the product key you enter later in the process determines what product you bought. With the initial release of Windows Vista, if the key doesn't match the Windows Vista edition, you won't be able to run your installation of Windows Vista when you activate it—and you'll need to start over. With an installation of Windows Vista SP1, you can still run Windows Vista if you can't activate it, but you will see an advisory message on the desktop that you are not running a legal copy of Vista.

7. After selecting the correct product, click the check box and click Next.

8. Accept the license terms and click Next.

9. Click Custom (Advanced) for the installation type.

10. You can delete or resize partitions as desired. Do *not* remove a partition containing data unless you've already backed it up with Windows Easy Transfer or another backup program. To remove a partition, select it and click Drive Options (Advanced). Click Delete, and then OK to remove it. Even if you have only one partition, by deleting it, you remove your old Windows installation and the space it uses.

11. Select the partition or unallocated space you want to use for the Windows installation. Click Next.

12. The installation proceeds normally.

13. After the installation is complete and Windows Vista boots, start the Windows Vista setup program (setup.exe) from the DVD.

14. Select Install Now from the opening dialog.

15. When prompted, enter your product key and click Next.

16. Accept the license terms and click Next.

17. Select Upgrade as the installation type and click Next.

18. The installation completes normally.

Clean Installations

Clean installations are the easiest to perform and should result in the least amount of work at installation time. A clean installation is required in any of the following situations:

- You have an unsupported upgrade path.
- There is no operating system currently installed on the computer.
- The computer has more than one partition, and you want to configure the computer to support multibooting.
- You are performing installations across the network using Remote Installation Services.
- You prefer to perform a clean installation—so as to "start over with a clean slate," rather than risk encountering some of the issues that can crop up from performing an upgrade installation of Windows XP. Windows Vista is designed to minimize problems that could be caused by upgrades.

When performing a clean installation, there are really no problem areas to watch for in general. The most common problem that people run into is trying to install Windows XP Professional onto a computer in which the CD-ROM is not El Torito–compliant (it does not support booting from the CD-ROM drive). In this case you will need to acquire the Windows XP Setup Boot Disk creation utility (`makebt32.exe`) by visiting MSKB# 310994, at http://support.microsoft.com/default.aspx?scid=kb;en-us;310994. The `makebt32.exe` utility will enable you to create a set of setup boot floppy disks; however you will need to have six disks in Windows XP instead of the four disks you needed for Windows 2000 Professional. Note that you must select the appropriate boot disk set for your Windows XP Professional installation: There are separate boot disk sets for original Windows XP, Service Pack 1, and Service Pack 2. When Service Pack 3 is introduced in 2008, expect to see a listing for Service Pack 3 as well. Windows XP Home users also obtain boot disks from this same URL.

Note

If Microsoft has released service packs past the one integrated into your Windows XP installation disc, or if you are using a Windows XP installation disc produced before Service Pack 1 was released, you should install the most recent service pack after completing your initial installation. You can do that before or after using the Files and Settings Transfer Wizard described previously in this chapter and further detailed in Chapter 4.

Windows Vista users must have a bootable DVD (or CD) drive to perform a clean installation; Windows Vista does not support installation from floppy disks. Although Windows Vista is sold at retail only on DVD media, CD media can be obtained from the Windows Vista Alternate Media website at http://www.microsoft.com/windowsvista/1033/ordermedia/default.mspx. This website can also be used to buy 64-bit installation DVDs. (Only Windows Vista Ultimate comes with both 32-bit and 64-bit installation DVDs in the retail package.)

You'll find a step-by-step guide through the process of performing a clean installation of Windows XP or Windows Vista later in this chapter.

Repair Installations

A repair installation (also known as an in-place upgrade) is used to fix a damaged Windows installation. A repair installation preserves your existing Windows configuration while replacing corrupt files and repairing incorrect settings. Both Windows XP and Windows Vista support repair installations, but the methods used are different.

Performing a Repair Installation of Windows XP

Before you start a repair installation of Windows XP, follow these steps:

1. Make a backup copy of your data files (stored in \Documents and Settings*Username* for each user of your PC) before performing a repair installation in case of problems.

2. Determine the size of the hard disk used for the Windows installation and the release of Windows XP you will be using for the repair installation. If you are performing a repair installation from an original Windows XP CD *and* the hard disk containing Windows XP is

larger than 137GB, you could experience data loss because the original release of Windows XP does not support hard disks larger than 137GB. Files stored on hard disk sectors beyond 137GB will be corrupted after the repair installation is completed because the original release of Windows XP cannot access those sections of the drive. Windows XP SP1 and above support 48-bit LBA mode, enabling support for hard disks larger than 137GB. If your Windows XP CD includes SP1 or SP2, you do not need to be concerned about the size of the hard disk.

To prevent data loss if you are using an original Windows XP CD for a repair installation, create an installation source that includes the original Windows XP installation files and SP2 updates. This process is known as *slipstreaming*. Microsoft Knowledge Base article 828930 discusses this process. If you are performing the repair installation from CD, you may prefer to create a slip-stream CD based on your original Windows XP CD and SP2 updates. See the following websites for details:

- http://www.winsupersite.com/showcase/windowsxp_sp2_slipstream.asp
- http://www.helpwithwindows.com/WindowsXP/winxp-sp2-bootcd.html

If you want to add SATA and/or RAID drivers to the CD, see http://www.maximumpc.com/article/How-To--Slipstream-your-XP-installation for details.

Follow this procedure to perform a repair installation of Windows XP:

1. Check the \Windows\system32 folder to determine whether a file called Undo_guimode.txt is present. Remove this file before continuing because if it is present, data loss could result. See Microsoft Knowledge Base article 312369 at http://support.microsoft.com for details.

2. Locate the Windows Product Activation files wpa.dbl and wpa.bak from the \Windows\system32 folder and copy them to a floppy disk or USB flash drive for safekeeping.

3. Back up each user's My Documents files (stored in \Documents and Settings*Username*).

4. Disconnect USB devices other than the USB mouse and keyboard. USB flash drives, hard drives, scanners, printers, and other devices can interfere with a repair installation.

5. Start the system with the Windows XP CD or slipstream CD (if necessary), or with Windows XP boot disks.

6. The Windows XP Setup program asks you whether you want to set up Windows, repair Windows, or quit. Press Enter to select the Set up option.

7. After you accept the license agreement, the setup program searches for previous Windows installations.

8. When the setup program detects your existing Windows installation, it displays the location (usually C:\Windows) and asks whether you want to repair it or install a fresh copy. Select the existing installation and press R to repair it.

9. The installation process continues until completed.

10. Download and install the most recent Windows XP service pack, whether through automatic updates, Windows Explorer, or manually. This step is necessary because changes made by service packs are undone when you perform a repair installation of an earlier revision. This step is not necessary if you are performing a repair install from a CD containing the most recent service pack.

11. Reconnect USB devices.

Repair Installation Help and How-To

Many websites provide repair installation tutorials. Some of the most useful include the following:

Microsoft Knowledge Base article 315341, available at http://support.microsoft.com

http://www.michaelstevenstech.com/XPrepairinstall.htm (includes very important warnings)

http://support.gateway.com/s/SOFTWARE/MICROSOF/7509595/Install/Install06.shtml (includes illustrations)

Performing a Repair Installation of Windows Vista

To perform a repair installation of Windows Vista, start the system and start the installation from within Windows. Essentially, Windows Vista performs an "upgrade" of itself when started this way. Just as with a standard Windows Vista upgrade installation, the existing (damaged) Windows installation is moved to a folder called Windows.old. The new installation will retain most of your existing settings and you will be able to run your installed programs.

If you are unable to perform a repair installation from within Windows Vista, install a fresh copy to a new folder. You will need to reinstall your applications.

Note

If Windows Vista stopped working after you installed new hardware or a new application, you may be able to solve the problem by running System Restore and restoring the system to its previous configuration. You can run System Restore from the Windows Recovery Environment (Windows RE). For details, see Chapter 12.

If running System Restore does not fix the problem, run a repair install of Windows Vista.

Using Installation Switches for a Windows XP Installation

Depending on your needs and the type of installation you are performing, you can modify the behaviors and actions of the Windows XP Setup routine by using various switches. Depending on how you are installing Windows XP, there are two methods you can use to call the Setup routine: by using the winnt.exe command or by using the winnt32.exe command. Some typical reasons to use switches include unattended installations, using Dynamic Update, installing the Recovery Console, and changing the location for the installation source files, to name a few.

winnt32.exe

Let's look first at the more useful, and likely, winnt32.exe command. The winnt32.exe command can be used to perform a clean installation or an upgrade installation of Windows XP. You can run the `winnt32.exe` command at the command prompt from any computer running one of the following operating systems:

- Windows 95
- Windows 98
- Windows 98 Second Edition
- Windows Millennium Edition
- Windows NT 4.0
- Windows 2000
- Windows XP

Using `winnt32.exe` from Windows 95

You cannot upgrade from Windows 95 to Windows XP. An installation started from Windows 95 using the `winnt32.exe` command can be only a clean installation.

For more information about supported upgrade paths, see the "Upgrade Installations to Windows XP" section earlier in this chapter.

The `winnt32.exe` command has the following syntax and switches, as detailed in Table 3.5:

```
winnt32 [/checkupgradeonly] [/cmd:command_line] [/cmdcons]
[/copydir:{i386|ia64}\FolderName] [/copysource:FolderName]
[/debug[Level]:[FileName]] [/dudisable]
[/duprepare:pathname] [/dushare:pathname] [/m:FolderName]
[/makelocalsource] [/noreboot] [/s:SourcePath]
[/syspart:DriveLetter] [/tempdrive:DriveLetter]
[/udf:id [,UDB_file]] [/unattend[num]:[answer_file]]
```

Table 3.5   **winnt32.exe Switches**

Switch	Description
`/checkupgradeonly`	Checks your computer for upgrade compatibility with Windows XP. When used with the `/unattend` switch, no user input is required. If used without the `/unattend` switch, the results are displayed on the screen and you can save them as desired. The default location is a file named **upgrade.txt** located in the %systemroot% folder.
`/cmd:command_line`	Instructs Setup to carry out a specific command before the final phase of setup.
`/cmdcons`	Installs the Recovery Console as a startup option on a functioning x86-based computer. You can only use the `/cmdcons` option after normal setup is finished.
`/copydir:{i386|ia64}\FolderName`	Creates an additional folder within the folder in which the Windows XP files are installed. You can use `/copydir` to create as many additional folders as you want.
`/copysource:FolderName`	Creates a temporary additional folder within the folder in which the Windows XP files are installed. Unlike the folders `/copydir` creates, `/copysource` folders are deleted after Setup completes.

Switch	Description
/debug[Level]:[FileName]	Creates a debug log at the level specified. The default log file is C:\systemroot\Winnt32.log, and the default debug level is 2. The log levels are as follows: **0** represents severe errors, **1** represents errors, **2** represents warnings, **3** represents information, and **4** represents detailed information for debugging. Each level includes the levels below it.
/dudisable	Prevents Dynamic Update from running. This option disables Dynamic Update even if you use an answer file and specify Dynamic Update options in that file.
/duprepare:pathname	Carries out preparations on an installation share so that it can be used with Dynamic Update files that you downloaded from the Windows Update website.
/dushare:pathname	Specifies a share on which you previously downloaded Dynamic Update files (updated files for use with Setup) from the Windows Update website.
/m:FolderName	Specifies that Setup copies replacement files from an alternative location. Instructs Setup to look in the alternative location first, and if files are present, to use them instead of the files from the default location.
/makelocalsource	Instructs Setup to copy all installation source files to your local hard disk. Use /makelocalsource when installing from a CD to provide installation files when the CD is not available later in the installation.
/noreboot	Instructs Setup to not restart the computer after the file copy phase of Setup is completed so that you can run another command.
/s:SourcePath	Specifies the source location of the Windows XP files. To simultaneously copy files from multiple servers, type the /s:SourcePath option multiple times (up to a maximum of eight). If you type the option multiple times, the first server specified must be available, or Setup will fail.
/syspart:DriveLetter	On an x86-based computer, specifies that you can copy Setup startup files to a hard disk, mark the disk as active, and then install the disk into another computer. When you start that computer, it automatically starts with the next phase of Setup. You must always use the /tempdrive parameter with the /syspart parameter.
/tempdrive:DriveLetter	Directs Setup to place temporary files on the specified partition. For a new installation, Windows XP is also installed on the specified partition.
/udf:id [,UDB_file]	Indicates an identifier (**id**) that Setup uses to specify how a Uniqueness Database (UDB) file modifies an answer file (see the /unattend entry). If no UDB file is specified, Setup prompts the user to insert a disk that contains the $Unique$.udb file.
/unattend	Upgrades your previous version of Windows 98, Windows Millennium Edition, Windows NT 4.0, or Windows 2000 in unattended Setup mode. All user settings are taken from the previous installation, so no user intervention is required during Setup.
/unattend[num]:[answer_file]	Performs a fresh installation in unattended Setup mode. The specified **answer_file** provides Setup with your custom specifications. **num** is the number of seconds between the time that Setup finishes copying the files and when it restarts your computer.

▶▶ To learn more about using the Windows Upgrade Advisor, **see** "Checking Hardware and Software Compatibility," **p. 131**.

Winnt32 on Itanium-Based Computers

If you run the `winnt32.exe` command on an Itanium-based computer, the command must be run from the Extensible Firmware Interface (EFI) or from Windows XP. Also, the `/cmdcons` and `/syspart` switches are not available, and options relating to upgrades are also not available.

For more information on EFI, see the article "Extensible Firmware Interface" in the Microsoft Windows Server Tech Center at http://technet2.microsoft.com/windowsserver/en/library/4b35160a-4e27-4258-9e8b-e2088f8a757a1033.mspx?mfr=true.

Winnt.exe

The second, and less often used, way to invoke Setupp is by using the `winnt.exe` command. The `winnt.exe` command can be used from the command prompt of even the oldest operating systems, such as Windows 95, Windows 3.x, and MS-DOS. These operating systems are not upgradeable to Windows XP Professional.

The `winnt.exe` command has the following syntax and switches, as detailed in Table 3.6:

```
winnt [/s:SourcePath] [/t:TempDrive] [/u:answer file]
[/udf:ID [,UDB_file]] [/r:folder][/rx:folder][/e:command]
[/a]
```

Table 3.6   winnt.exe Switches

Switch	Description
/s:SourcePath	Specifies the source location of the Windows XP files. The location must be a full path and can use UNC locations.
/t:TempDrive	Directs Setup to place temporary files on the specified drive and to install Windows XP on that drive.
/u:answer file	Performs an unattended Setup using an answer file. If you use /u, you must also use /s.
/udf:ID [,UDB_file]	Indicates an identifier (ID) that Setup uses to specify how a Uniqueness Database (UDB) file modifies an answer file (see /u). If no **UDB_file** is specified, Setup prompts you to insert a disk that contains the **$Unique$.udb** file.
/r:folder	Specifies an optional folder to be installed. The folder remains after Setup finishes.
/rx:folder	Specifies an optional folder to be copied. The folder is deleted after Setup finishes.
/e:command	Specifies a command to be carried out just before the final phase of Setup.
/a	Enables accessibility options.

Using Installation Switches to Install Windows Vista

Windows Vista uses an installation program called `Setup.exe`, rather than `winnt.exe` or `winnt32.exe` as in Windows XP. `Setup.exe` also features various installation switches. Some typical reasons to use switches include unattended installations, disabling the use of Dynamic Update, and changing the location for the installation source files, to name a few.

`Setup.exe` has the following switches and syntax. These are described in more detail in Table 3.7:

```
setup.exe [/1394debug:channel [baudrate:baudrate]]
[/debug:channel [baudrate:baudrate]] [/dudisable]
[/emsport: {com1 | com2 | usebiossettings | off} [/emsbaudrate:baudrate]]
[/m:folder_name] [/noreboot] [/tempdrive:drive_letter]
[/unattend:answer_file]
[/usbdebug:hostname]
```

In Table 3.7, italic text indicates variables you should replace with the appropriate values for your situation.

Table 3.7 *Setup.exe* Switches

Option	Description
[/1394debug:*channel* [baudrate:*baudrate*]]	Enables kernel debugging over an IEEE 1394 (FireWire) port while Windows is running and during the windowsPE configuration pass of Windows Setup.
	channel
	The debugging channel. The default value is **1**.
	[baudrate:*baudrate*]
	Specifies the baud rate to use while transferring data during debugging. The default is **19200**. Other options include **115200** or **57600**.
	Example:
	`setup.exe /1394debug:1 /baudrate:115200`
[/debug:*channel* [baudrate:*baudrate*]]	Enables kernel debugging over a serial communications (COM) port while Windows is running and during the windowsPE configuration pass of Windows Setup.
	channel
	The debugging channel. The default value is **1**.
	[baudrate:*baudrate*]
	Specifies the baud rate to use while transferring data during debugging. The default is **19200**. Other options include **115200** or **57600**.
	Example:
	`setup.exe /debug:1 /baudrate:115200`
[/dudisable]	Disables Windows dynamic update during Windows Setup. Only original Windows Setup files are used to install Windows. This option disables dynamic updates even if the DynamicUpdate option is specified in an unattended Windows Setup answer file.
	Example:
	`setup.exe /dudisable`
[/emsport: {com1 | com2 | usebiossettings | off} [/emsbaudrate:*baudrate*]]	Enables or disables Emergency Management Services (EMS) during Windows Setup and after the server operating system has been installed. EMS allows remote administration of Windows 2003 Server.

(continues)

Table 3.7   Continued

Option	Description
	Options:
	com1
	Enables EMS over COM1. Supported for x86 systems only.
	com2
	Enables EMS over COM2. Supported for x86 systems only.
	usebiossettings
	Uses the setting specified in the BIOS. For x86 systems, the value from the Serial Port Console Redirection (SPCR) table is used. For Itanium-based systems, the Extensible Firmware Interface is used. If no SPCR table or EFI console device path is specified in the BIOS, **usebiossettings** will be disabled.
	off
	Disables EMS. If EMS is disabled in Windows Setup, you can later enable EMS by modifying the boot settings. For more information, see the Resource Kits for the Windows Server 2003 family.
	[/emsbaudrate:*baudrate*]
	Specifies the baud rate to use while transferring data during debugging. The default is **19200**. Other options include **115200** or **57600**.
	Example:
	`setup.exe /emsport:COM1 /emsbaudrate:115200`
[/**m:***folder_name*]	Specifies Setup to copy alternative files from an alternative location. This option instructs Setup to look in the alternative location first, and, if files are present, to use them instead of the files from the default location.
	folder_name
	The name and location of the folder containing the replacement files. *folder_name* can be any local drive (not UNC path) location.
	You must know where the files will be installed on the Windows installation. All the additional files must be copied to a OEM folder in your installation sources or in the ***folder_name***. The OEM structure provides a representation of the destination installation disk. For example,
	OEM\$1
	maps to %SYSTEMDRIVE%; for example, drive C.
	OEM\$$
	maps to %WINDIR%; for example, C:\windows\.
	OEM\$progs
	maps to the program files directory.
	OEM\$docs
	Maps to the Documents and Settings folder.
	Example:
	To copy an updated C:\program files\messenger\msmsgs.exe file into the Windows installation, create the following folder structure on the installation source

Option	Description
	(pro\sources\$OEM$\\$progs\messenger\msmsgs.exe) by using the **Setup** command:
	`pro\sources\setup.exe /m`
	If you replace a file protected by Windows file protection, you must also copy the updated file to the local sources to be installed with Windows (C:\windows\i386). The filename must be the same as what is used in Windows Setup. For example, add this file and folder structure to your OEM directory:
	`pro\sources\$OEM$\$$\i386\msmsgs.ex_`
	If you use files that are not on an installation share, specify the folder name. For example,
	`setup.exe /m:C:\OtherFiles`
	where C:\OtherFiles is your customized OEM directory.
	For example,
	`C:\OtherFiles\$$\i386\msmsgs.ex_`
	For more information about running a command during Windows Setup, see "Unattended Windows Setup Reference" at http://technet2.microsoft.com/WindowsVista/en/library/d7fb3680-6824-4bdf-9e16-76450f1b73a31033.mspx?mfr=true.
	If you make resource changes in your replacement files, you must add the updated MUI files to the installation.
[/noreboot]	Instructs Windows Setup not to restart the computer after the down-level phase of Windows Setup completes. The **/noreboot** option enables you to execute additional commands before Windows Vista restarts. This suppresses only the first reboot. Subsequent reboots, if required, are not suppressed.
	Example:
	`setup.exe /noreboot`
[/tempdrive:*drive_letter*]	Instructs Windows Setup to place temporary installation files on the specified partition. For an upgrade, the **/tempdrive** option affects only the placement of temporary files; the operating system is upgraded in the partition from which you run the **Setup.exe** file.
	drive_letter
	The partition to copy installation files to during Windows Setup.
	Example:
	`setup.exe /tempdrive:P`
[/unattend:*answerfile*]	Enables unattended Windows Setup mode. You can also specify a value for **answerfile**. If you specify a value for **answerfile**, Windows Setup applies the values in the answer file during installation. If you do not specify a value for **answerfile**, Windows Setup upgrades your existing version of Windows. All settings are taken from the previous installation, so minimal user intervention is required.
	answer_file
	The file path and filename of the unattended Windows Setup answer file. The paths to an answer file can be a local or UNC path.

(continues)

Table 3.7   Continued

Option	Description
	Example:
	`setup.exe /unattend:\\server01\share\` `unattend.xml`
`[/usbdebug:hostname]`	Sets up debugging on a USB port. Debug data is effective on the next reboot.
	hostname
	The name of the computer to debug.
	Example:
	`setup.exe /usbdebug:VistaTest01`

Clean Install Procedures

A clean install of Windows XP and Windows Vista is typically performed on a new (empty) hard disk. However, it can also be performed on a system that contains an existing operating system. In such cases, unpartitioned disk space (or an existing partition that can be reused) is the target. The following sections discuss the procedures to use for Windows XP and Windows Vista.

Windows XP Clean Install

Performing a clean installation of Windows XP Professional will take about 30–90 minutes, depending on your particular hardware. The setup process consists of several steps, which fall into two phases: the text-mode phase and the GUI-mode phase.

▶▶ To learn more about installing Windows XP Professional by using unattended installation methods, **see** "Automated Deployments," **p. 177**.

To perform a clean installation of Windows XP Professional, follow the process outlined here:

1. Power on your computer and insert the Windows XP Professional Setup CD-ROM into the CD drive. If your computer is not capable of booting from the CD drive, you need to create and use the Windows XP Professional Setup floppy disks, as detailed previously in the section "Installation Types."

2. When prompted onscreen, press any key (or the specific key required) to boot the computer from the CD-ROM.

3. After Setup briefly examines your computer's hardware, you are prompted to press F6 if you have any third-party drivers that require loading, such as RAID, SCSI, or SATA device drivers.

Note

You must install third-party device drivers for storage devices from a floppy disk. If your system's RAID, SATA, or SCSI host adapters are integrated into the motherboard's South Bridge or I/O Controller Hub and the motherboard vendor provides chipset drivers on a CD, you need to copy the appropriate drivers to a floppy disk.

4. At the next screen, you are prompted to press F2 if you are performing an Automated System Recovery (ASR). Just sit on your hands and let Setup do its thing here.

5. For the next few minutes, Setup will load the files required to perform the installation. If you have an older, slower computer, this is a good time to grab a cup of coffee!

6. When you are presented with the Welcome to Setup screen, press Enter to continue on with the setup process.

7. Before you can install Windows XP, you must accept the End-User License Agreement. Press F8 to accept this agreement and continue forward with the installation process.

8. From the screen shown in Figure 3.7, you can create and delete partitions on your hard drives. Additionally, you need to select the partition on which you will install Windows XP. After selecting the partition on which to install Windows XP, press Enter to continue.

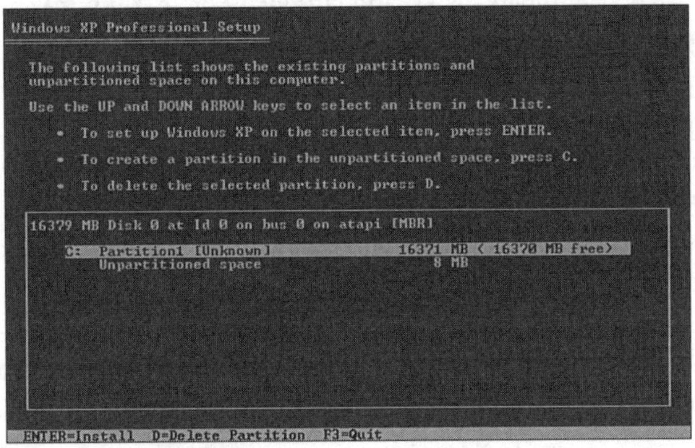

Figure 3.7   Selecting the installation partition.

9. On the next screen, you need to select the file system with which to format the selected partition. If you are installing on a partition that was previously formatted with FAT16 or FAT32, options to convert the file system are also present. In most clean installations, the NTFS file system is preferable, so consider using it. After making your file system selection, press Enter to continue.

▶▶ For more guidance on choosing a file system, **see** "Choosing a File System," **p. 141**.

MBR Versus GPT

MBR (Master Boot Record) and GPT (Globally Unique Identifier Partition Table) refer to types of hard disk arrangement. The MBR method is the old standby...it has been around since the days of old. The GPT method is new to Windows with the 64-bit edition of Windows XP Professional. The article "Windows and GPT FAQ" located at http://www.microsoft.com/whdc/device/storage/GPT_FAQ.mspx discusses GPT disks at length.

10. After the formatting process is complete, Setup examines your hard drives and then progresses to copying the required installation files.

11. After the files have been copied from the installation source to their correct locations on the hard drive, the installation must be initialized.

12. After initialization has completed, the computer prompts you for a restart. This is the last step of the text-mode phase. If you are prompted to "hit any key" to boot from your CD-ROM on the subsequent startup, *do not* do so; your installation will continue from the hard drive.

13. After the computer restarts, you are presented with the GUI phase of Setup. Your screen may flash or go blank several times during the GUI phase—this is normal.

14. After some time (and after the small progress bar at the bottom-left side of the screen moves to 100%), you are presented with your first configuration opportunity: the Regional and Language Options page. In most cases, you will want to simply click Next to accept the default values. Should you need to perform a custom configuration, you can change many settings, such as numbers, dates, and currencies or Text Input Languages and keyboard layouts. When you have finished with your selections, click Next to continue.

15. From the Personalize Your Software page, you can enter your name and organization. At a minimum, you must enter a name. You cannot use the name "Guest" or "Administrator." You do not have to enter an organization. After entering your information, click Next to continue.

16. From the Your Product Key page, enter your 25-digit CD key. Click Next to continue after entering your CD key.

17. From the Computer Name and Administrator Password page, you need to enter a unique computer name (that is, no other device on the network should have the same name) and the Administrator password. After entering this information, click Next to move ahead.

18. From the Date and Time Settings page, configure the appropriate date, time, and time zone settings. If you are in a daylight saving time area, be sure to place a check in the Automatically Adjust Clock for Daylight Savings Changes box. Click Next to continue.

19. After Windows XP Setup performs some more work, you are presented with the Networking Settings page, as shown in Figure 3.8. If this computer is participating in a domain-based network with DNS servers, DHCP servers, and/or WINS servers, you will want to select the Custom Settings radio button. If you are setting up this computer to participate in a workgroup or as a standalone computer, you can pretty much rest safely with the default selection of Typical settings. Either way, click Next to move on.

20. If you selected the Custom Settings option in step 19, you are presented with the Networking Components page. From here you can install, uninstall, and configure protocols, services, and clients. Because most configuration centers around the TCP/IP protocol, you should look at that. Selecting Internet Protocol (TCP/IP) and clicking Configure opens the Internet Protocol (TCP/IP) Properties page. Clicking the Advanced button opens the Advanced TCP/IP Settings page, shown in Figure 3.9, which lets you specify many TCP/IP-related settings, including DNS servers, DNS suffixes, WINS servers, NetBIOS over TCP/IP, and TCP/IP filtering among other settings. After you've made your advanced configuration, click OK to close the Advanced TCP/IP Settings page. Click OK to close the Internet

Protocol (TCP/IP) Properties page and then click Next after making all configuration entries. (You can change network properties at any time after installation completes, should you need to, so don't worry about it now.)

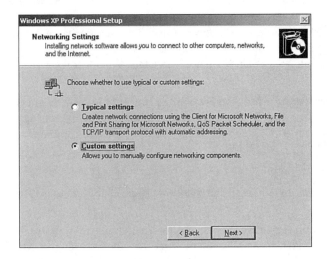

Figure 3.8   Configuring the networking settings.

Alternate Configuration

New in Windows XP, the Alternate Configuration tab of the Internet Protocol (TCP/IP) Properties page enables you to configure an alternative (secondary) TCP/IP setup for those times when a DHCP server is not found. This is a great benefit to portable computer users who would like their portable computer to default to a second set of preconfigured TCP/IP settings when not connected to the corporate network. These settings could be for a branch office or a home network.

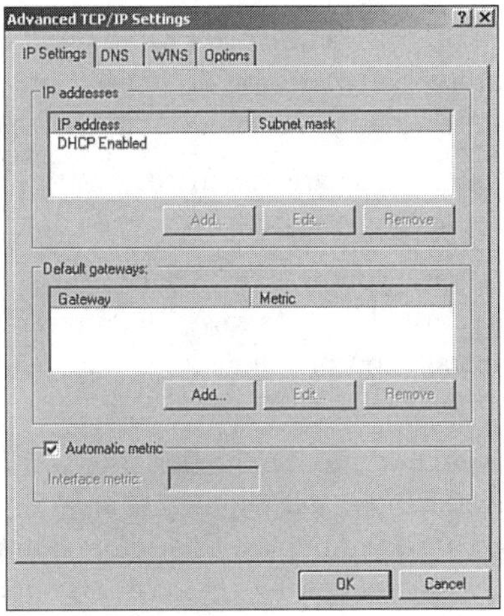

Figure 3.9   The Advanced TCP/IP Settings page.

21. From the Workgroup or Computer Domain page, you need to supply either the workgroup name or domain name into which you will be placing this computer. If you are installing a standalone computer, you can pick any name you want for the workgroup. If you are installing a computer in a workgroup, ensure that you enter the correct workgroup name. Either way, you should select the No option. If you want to join the computer to a domain at this time, you need to supply the username and password of a user who has privileges to add computers to the domain. You can also add the computer to a domain after installation is complete (which is what we do later). Whatever your selection is, click Next to continue.

22. Windows Setup performs more configuring and file copying at this point, including installing the Start menu, registering components, saving settings, and lastly, removing temporary files. After Setup completes this phase, the computer restarts again.

23. After the restart, the Windows XP Professional splash screen appears while Setup completes the installation process.

24. On the Welcome to Microsoft Windows page, click Next to get down to the last stages of Setup.

25. After Windows quickly checks your Internet connectivity status, it progresses to the Will This Computer Connect to the Internet Directly or Through a Network page. If you are using a modem for a dial-up Internet connection, you will most likely want to select the No, This Computer Will Connect Directly to the Internet option. If you are part of a network, you should select the Yes, This Computer Will Connect Through a Local Area Network or Home Network option. Click Next after making your selection to continue. (Here, you select the Yes option.)

26. From the Ready to Activate Windows? page, you need to decide whether you are going to activate your installation at this time via the Internet. This is the easiest option by far, and thus the option we use here. For more information on product activation, see the "Product Activation" section later in this chapter. After making your selection, click Next to continue. If you will not be activating at this time, skip to step 28.

27. From the Ready to Register with Microsoft page, select either to register or not register your Windows XP Professional software. You do not have to register your software to perform product activation. After making your selection, click Next to continue.

28. After activation completes, you are presented with the Who Will Use This Computer? page. Enter at least one user account, and click Next to continue.

29. When all is said and done, you receive a Thank You! page informing you of what has been accomplished, such as installing Windows XP Professional, activating it, and so on. You've just completed the installation of Windows XP Professional! Click Finish to complete the process.

30. After a few moments of disk activity, the first user you configured in step 28 is logged in to the computer. At this time, you *must* configure a strong password for this user account because the password box is empty. Do this before doing anything else. The password can most easily be changed by using the User Accounts applet located in the Control Panel. To change the password from the User Accounts applet, simply select the user and choose Create a Password.

What Makes a Strong Password?

According to Microsoft, a strong password is one that has the following characteristics:

- Is at least 7 characters long. The most secure passwords are those that are between 7 and 14 characters long.

- Contains characters from each of the following three groups: letters (A, B, C...a, b, c), numbers (0, 1, 2), and symbols (!, #, %, and so on).

- Has at least one symbol character in the second through sixth positions.

- Is significantly different from prior passwords.

- Does not contain your name or username.

- Is not a common word or name, such as family or pet names.

- Does not contain your address, phone number, license plate number, or any other common-knowledge item.

You can use the Password Checker located at http://www.microsoft.com/protect/yourself/password/checker.mspx to test the strength of your password (this site does not record passwords).

31. At this point, you are finished. You can go on to add the computer to a domain, as detailed in step 32, or stop here...the choice is up to you.

32. From the System applet in the Control Panel, switch to the Computer Name tab. Click the Change button to open the Computer Name Changes page, as shown in Figure 3.10. From here you can change the computer name and workgroup or domain membership. Enter the domain name information and click OK. You need to supply the username and password for an account that is authorized to add computers to the domain. The username should be in the *user@domain.com* format. After you have joined the domain, a restart is required to complete the process.

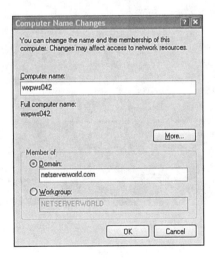

Figure 3.10 Joining a domain.

Now that Windows XP is installed, the next step is to install updates and service packs. You should perform these tasks before you install any applications or other devices, such as printers, scanners, or all-in-one units. Depending on your system configuration, you might use Windows Update to install service packs and updates, or you might install already-downloaded packages from a network server. Contact your system administrator for details.

As you will learn in the following section, the clean install process for Windows Vista is substantially different than for Windows XP—and easier to perform.

Windows Vista Clean Install

A Windows Vista clean install takes about 45 minutes. Because the install process is a staged process, configuration steps take place at the start and end of the process, rather than throughout the process as with Windows XP.

1. Power on your computer and insert the Windows Vista DVD into the DVD drive.

2. When prompted onscreen, press any key (the spacebar will do nicely) to boot the system from the DVD (your system may refer to the drive as the CD drive).

3. After Vista loads files, it prompts you to select the install language, time and currency formats, and keyboard or input method. If the defaults are not correct, make your choices (see Figure 3.11), and then click Next.

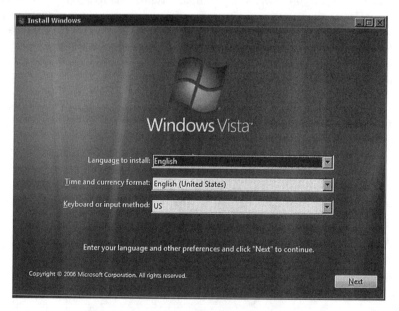

Figure 3.11   Vista's first install dialog prompts you for language, format, and keyboard settings.

4. Click Install Now to continue installation.

5. Vista prompts you to enter the product key. You should do so at this time *unless* you are performing a clean install using an upgrade DVD.

▶▶ For more information, **see** "Upgrade Installations to Windows Vista," earlier in this chapter, on **p. 147**.

6. Check the Automatically Activate Windows box below the product key if you don't want to activate the product later. Click Next to continue.

Tip

If you're not sure whether the system you're using for Vista is going to be suitable, make sure that the automatic activation check box is cleared. There's no need to rush this step. As with previous versions, you have 30 days before you must activate Vista.

7. Review the license terms, click I Accept, and then click Next to continue.

8. Select Custom (Advanced) as the installation type.

9. On the Where Do You Want to Install Windows? dialog, click Next if you want to use the entire hard disk as a single partition.

BitLocker Drive Preparation Considerations

Windows Vista Ultimate and Enterprise editions include support for BitLocker full-disk encryption. Originally, it was necessary to manually partition the hard disk during installation to create the 1.5GB partition used to store Vista boot files and BitLocker encryption files and a separate encrypted partition for Windows Vista and all users' data files. However, Microsoft now offers the BitLocker Drive Preparation tool to enable you to repartition the hard disk after installing Windows Vista.

Windows Vista Ultimate users can download this tool via Windows Update; it's one of the Vista Ultimate Extras. Windows Vista Enterprise users can obtain this tool from Microsoft Customer Support Services. For more information about this tool, see the Microsoft Knowledge Base article 930063 available from http://support.microsoft.com.

If you prefer to partition your hard disk manually before installing Vista, see the following article for a procedure that uses a script that can be executed from a USB key: http://www.windowsecurity.com/articles/Best-practice-guide-how-configure-BitLocker-Part1.html

Windows Vista SP1 supports BitLocker disk encryption for volumes other than the system volume, enabling you to encrypt a separate data drive letter. If you are installing Windows Vista from original version media and are planning to create a separate volume (drive letter) for user data, upgrade to Windows Vista SP1 before running the BitLocker Drive Preparation Tool and setting up BitLocker.

10. If you want to partition only part of the hard disk for use by Windows Vista, to create separate Windows/application and data partitions, or to remove existing partitions (and the data they contain), click Advanced.

11. To create a disk partition for Vista, click New (refer to Figure 3.12) and, in the size field that appears, enter the size of the desired partition in MB; then click the Apply button next to the field.

Note

If you want to place your data on a drive other than the system drive, you need to allocate at least 30GB or more for Windows Vista and your applications, and use the rest of your hard disk for a separate data drive. As soon as you start Windows Vista, you need to configure Windows Vista to use the data drive for user folders.

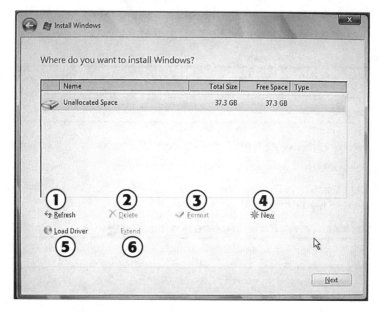

1. Refreshes drive display (use after loading drivers for unrecognized drives)
2. Deletes the selected partition
3. Formats the selected partition
4. Creates a new partition
5. Loads drivers for unrecognized media
6. Enlarges selected partition

Figure 3.12 Advanced hard disk preparation options. Some options here are disabled until after you create a disk partition.

Tip

Vista uses binary MB (1024MB=1GB), not decimal MB (1000MB=1GB). Thus, if you want to create a 40GB (binary) partition for Vista, enter 40960MB or use the arrows to scroll to the partition size you want.

12. To increase the size of the partition you specified in step 11, click Extend (refer to Figure 3.12), and enter the size you want. Click Apply, and a warning dialog appears, reminding you that you can't undo this particular option. Click OK and the partition is extended.

Tip

Unpartitioned hard disk space can be partitioned after Windows Vista starts by using its Disk Management tool. You can also extend your Windows system volume into unpartitioned space with Disk Management.

If you need to shrink a partition, rather than expand it, exit the installation process and use a third-party partition-resizing program such as Partition Commander or Partition Magic.

13. If the target drive is not visible to Vista, click Load Driver and provide the driver files needed for the RAID, SATA, or other host adapter. Windows Vista can use drivers on USB, CD, or DVD media. Click OK after inserting the media. After loading the drivers for your hard disk or disk array, click the Refresh button to display your drive. Create the partition as desired.

14. Select the partition you created in the previous steps and click Next. The Installing Windows display appears.

15. After Vista is installed, you are prompted to enter your username and password, provide a password hint (optional), and select a picture for the administrator account (see Figure 3.13). Click Next to continue.

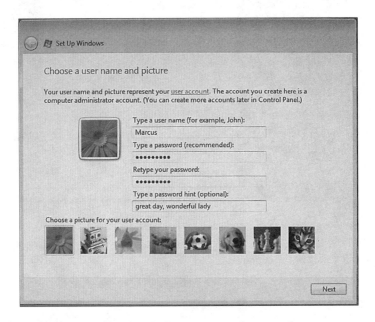

Figure 3.13   Setting up the administrator's username and password.

16. Keep the computer name created by Vista (it's based on your username) or change it. Select a desktop background and click Next to continue.

17. The Help Protect Windows Automatically dialog appears. Choose the setting you prefer.

18. Specify the time zone and adjust the date and time as necessary. Click Next to continue.

19. Click Start on the Thank You dialog to start Windows Vista. The Welcome Center dialog appears.

20. To join a domain or a workgroup, click Show More Details to display the System Properties sheet in Figure 3.14.

21. Click Change Settings, and provide administrator credentials when prompted. Click the Network ID button to join a domain or workgroup by running a wizard. To rename the computer or change the current domain or workgroup, click the Change button shown in Figure 3.15.

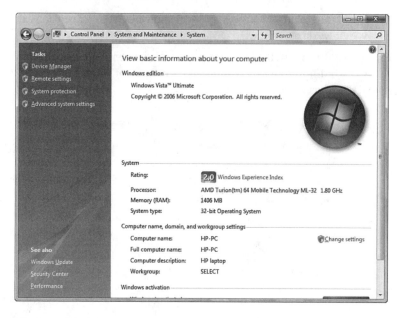

Figure 3.14   Windows Vista's System Properties sheet.

Figure 3.15   The Computer Name tab in the Windows Vista System Properties sheet is also used for changing domain or workgroup network settings.

Now that Windows Vista is installed, the next step is to install updates and service packs. You should perform these tasks before you install any applications or other devices, such as printers, scanners, or all-in-one units. Depending on your system configuration, you might use Windows Update to install service packs and updates, or you might install already-downloaded packages from a network server. Contact your system administrator for details.

Multibooting Other Operating Systems

If you need to maintain continued access to other operating systems, one method for doing so is to install Windows XP Professional or Vista in a multiboot situation with one or more other operating systems, including other instances of Windows XP or Vista. Installing in a multiboot situation encompasses either an upgrade installation or clean installation as well—the same rules and caveats apply. The chief difference is in the formatting of the System partition—the place where the files required to start up the computer are loaded. The only real trick to successfully installing Windows XP Professional or Vista into a multiboot arrangement without using a third-party boot manager is that the newest version of Windows being installed must also be the last operating system installed. As a rule, you should always install Microsoft operating systems from oldest to newest. So, if you had a new computer, for example, and you wanted to install Windows Vista, Windows XP Professional, and Windows 98 on it, you would first install Windows 98, and then next install Windows XP Professional, and lastly install Windows Vista.

A multiboot arrangement can use either multiple partitions or the same partition with different folders for different operating systems, depending on the operating systems, file systems, and other features each uses.

Using Multiple Partitions

If you are planning on multibooting with an older operating system that does not recognize the NTFS file system, such as Windows 98, you need to ensure that the System partition used by the older version of Windows is never formatted or converted to the NTFS file system.

To avoid this possibility, make sure that the hard disk used by the computer has adequate free (unpartitioned) space that can be used by the new operating system. If the entire capacity of the hard disk is already assigned to the current operating system, but the operating system is not using all the space, determine how much space on the system drive the current operating system is using: With Windows XP, open My Computer, right-click the C: drive, select Properties, and the used and free space are displayed. With Windows Vista, select Computer, select C: drive, and the used and free space are displayed.

Windows XP needs a minimum of 650MB of free space for installation on a 1.5GB or larger hard disk, whereas Windows Vista needs a minimum of 15GB of free space on a 40GB or larger hard disk. Much more space than that should be allocated for applications and updates: I recommend making sure that you have at least 20GB of space you can allocate for Windows XP or at least 40GB you can allocate for Windows Vista. If you have at least this much space or more not in use, you can use your existing hard disk for a dual-boot configuration.

To shrink the size of the existing partition, you can use a third-party program such as Norton Partition Magic, V-com Partition Commander Professional, and others. After shrinking the existing partition (make sure that you leave adequate space for swapfiles, data files, and additional programs you might install), leave the remainder of the disk space unallocated.

When you install Windows XP or Windows Vista, use the unallocated space as the location for the installation. If you want to share data files with the legacy Windows version, make sure that the location for the data files uses the FAT32 file system. This could be the drive letter used by the legacy Windows version, or an additional drive letter you create.

▶▶ For more information on partitioning a hard disk, **see** "Disks, Partitions, and Volumes," **p. 597**.

Note

If you need to migrate your existing Windows 9x or Me installation to a larger hard disk so that you will have room for installing Windows XP or Windows Vista, keep in mind that the largest hard disk you can install without running into the 48-bit LBA limitation (137GB) is 120GB. To use larger hard disk drives, you must have a 48-bit LBA driver compatible with your motherboard chipset, or use an ATA/IDE host adapter that plugs into a PCI slot and includes 48-bit BIOS and driver support. To learn more about the 137GB limit, see the section "Drive Capacity Limitations" in Chapter 10, p. 615.

If you are primarily interested in maintaining access to an older version of Windows for running specific programs or providing help desk services, consider using Virtual PC 2007 or a third-party virtualization environment and installing the legacy Windows version into a virtual machine running under Windows XP Professional or Vista. A virtual machine does not require you to reboot your system, runs in a window alongside current applications, and operates in the same basic manner as a standalone installation of Windows. See "Using Virtual Machines," this chapter, p. 171, for details.

When you install Windows Vista, do not attempt to convert the basic disk into a dynamic disk. Dynamic disks do not support multiboot configurations; only one operating system can "own" a dynamic disk or dynamic disk array.

If you need to use a dynamic disk but need access to older operating systems, consider installing them into virtual machines created with Microsoft Virtual PC 2007 or third-party VM managers such as VMWare and others.

Using a Single Partition

If you want to install a multiboot configuration of Windows 2000 and Windows XP, keep in mind that both support the NTFS file system. By installing Windows 2000 Professional first, updating it to SP4 and installing all other updates, and then creating a new folder (such as C:\WinXP) for Windows XP and using that folder for your installation, you can create a multi-boot configuration without repartitioning your hard disk.

What about Windows XP and Windows Vista in the same partition? The problem with installing both into the same partition is that Windows XP's System Restore feature deletes Windows Vista's restore points. For details, see Microsoft KB article 926185, available at http://support.microsoft.com. Windows Vista's restore points, unlike Windows XP's, can contain shadow copy information for retrieving older copies of files, so losing Windows Vista restore points affects your ability to retrieve older file versions as well as the ability to "walk back" your Windows Vista configuration to an earlier time.

To prevent this from happening, you need to install Windows XP first, install Windows Vista into a separate partition (see "Using Multiple Partitions" earlier in this chapter), and then configure Windows XP's System Restore feature sothat it will not monitor the partition (drive letter) used by the Windows Vista installation or other folders containing data files that are monitored by Windows Vista's System Restore feature.

Using a Third-Party Boot Loader

If you are using some sort of third-party boot loader, its files create and control the boot menu and operating system selection process. You also gain the ability to install more than one instance of a Windows 9x operating system when using a third-party boot loader.

Some boot loaders to consider include

- **BootMagic** (included as part of the Norton PartitionMagic application)—See the Symantec website, http://www.symantec.com/, for more information.
- **OS Selector** (included as part of Acronis Disk Director Suite)—See the Acronis website, http://www.acronis.com/, for more information.
- **System Commander**—See the Avanquest website at http://vcom.avanquest.com/ for more information.

Most Linux distros include GRUB, a boot loader for Linux and other operating systems.

Note

You can install only one instance total of Windows 3.x, Windows 95, Windows 98, or Windows Millennium Edition on a computer without using a third-party boot loader application or a virtual machine environment such as Virtual PC 2007.

Using Virtual Machines

One major disadvantage of traditional multiboot configurations is that you cannot switch between operating systems without shutting down the current operating system and restarting your system. If you need access to multiple operating systems at the same time, this is time-consuming and tedious. As an alternative, consider the use of a virtual machine environment such as Microsoft Virtual PC 2007 or one of the products of VMWare. A virtual machine environment is also useful for maintaining access to legacy programs that do not run under Windows XP or Windows Vista by running them under their native operating systems.

A virtual machine environment enables you to run additional operating systems in separate windows, each isolated by the virtualization software from the other operating systems in use. Essentially, each virtual machine operates as if it has exclusive access to the system's hardware, although you may have two, three, or many more operating systems running in different virtual machines at the same time.

Two approaches can be used for using virtual machines. You can use a virtual machine environment that uses a desktop operating system as a host, such as Microsoft Virtual PC 2007, available from http://www.microsoft.com/windows/products/winfamily/virtualpc/default.mspx. This is a suitable solution for experimenting with virtual machines or for occasional use of legacy software running under a virtual machine. This approach has some limitations.

- You must start the host operating system before you can start a virtualized guest operating system.

- The host operating system uses a substantial chunk of computer resources, plus each guest operating system running requires additional computer resources.

- The performance of the guest operating system is limited by available resources.

However, if you want to use virtualization as a full-time solution for legacy operating systems and applications or to reduce the number of physical systems in use, you should consider a virtual machine server that hosts all operating systems you want to use, such as Microsoft Virtual Server, available from http://www.microsoft.com/windowsserversystem/virtualserver/default.aspx or VMWare's VMWare Server, available from http://www.vmware.com/products/server/. A virtual machine server has a smaller memory and resource footprint than a desktop host will, enabling virtually all the physical machine's resources to be available for virtual machines.

Creating a New Virtual Machine with Virtual PC 2007

Microsoft Virtual PC 2007 is available in separate 32-bit and 64-bit versions to support 32-bit and 64-bit editions of Windows XP Professional, Windows XP Tablet Edition, Windows Vista Ultimate, Windows Vista Business, and Windows Vista Enterprise. After Virtual PC 2007 (VPC 2007) is installed, run the Virtual PC Console application to set up a new virtual machine or to run an existing virtual machine. Each virtual machine configuration is stored as a .vmc file, and each virtual hard disk file is stored as a .vhd file.

To create a new virtual machine with VPC 2007, follow these steps:

1. Start the program.

2. Click New from the Virtual PC Console dialog to start the New Virtual Machine Wizard.

3. Click Next from the opening dialog.

4. From the Options dialog, select Create to create a virtual machine with the settings you prefer. Other options include Use, which uses default settings to create a virtual machine, or Add to add an existing virtual machine (.vmc) to your system (see Figure 3.16).

5. Enter the name of the virtual machine you want to install. It is installed in the My Virtual Machines folder (a subfolder of the current user's [My] Documents folder) by default. To change the default, click Browse and select a location.

6. Select the operating system. VPC 2007 has preconfigured definitions for Windows 98, NT Workstation, 2000, XP, Vista, OS/2, NT Server, 2000 Server, and Server 2003. If you want to install a different operating system, select Other. Note that each operating system has different memory and virtual disk specifications. Click Next to continue.

7. Specify the amount of RAM to use for the VM. A default amount is listed, or you can change the size by selecting Adjusting the RAM and using a slider control to make changes. Click Next to continue.

Figure 3.16 Creating a new virtual machine with Virtual PC 2007.

8. Specify whether to use an existing virtual hard disk or create a new one. Each virtual machine should be stored in its own virtual hard disk (.vhd) file. Click Next.

9. Enter the name of the virtual hard disk. Use a meaningful name, such as the name of the operating system or the name of the legacy application for which it will be used. If you need to adjust the size of the virtual hard disk, change the size listed. Click Next.

10. Click Finish. The new virtual machine appears in the Virtual PC Console.

Starting a New Virtual Machine

After you create a new VM with Virtual PC 2007, it appears in the Virtual PC Console. To start it, select its icon and click Start. The VM displays startup messages, and then attempts to boot from any available boot devices. Until you install an operating system, the only available boot device in the default configuration is the default PXE boot agent.

Installing and Using a Virtualized Operating System

Installing an operating system to a VPC VM requires you to insert the appropriate bootable installation media into a drive available to VPC when you start the VM. If the VM attempts to boot from the PXE boot agent, press Esc to stop the boot process, make sure that the bootable media is inserted, anmd then press the spacebar to boot from the media.

Note

Virtual PC 2007 can use internal hard disks and CD/DVD drives. Although it supports some types of USB devices, it does not support USB or FireWire hard disks or flash memory drives.

For example, if you need to install Windows 2000, Windows XP, or Windows Vista, you would use bootable CD or DVD installation media with a valid license. However, if you need to install MS-DOS, Windows 95, or Windows 98, you would use the appropriate startup floppy disk.

Figure 3.17 shows the installation of Windows 2000 inside a virtual machine hosted by Virtual PC 2007. Note the live thumbnail view of the VM within the Virtual PC Console at top left.

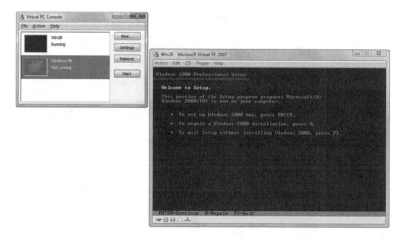

Figure 3.17   Installing Windows 2000 into a VM created by Virtual PC 2007.

Disk formatting and partitioning and other activities performed by the operating system's installation program do not change the physical hard disk hosting the VM, but change only the virtual hard disk (.vhd) file used by the VM.

After the installation is complete, the operating system runs inside the virtual machine. You can minimize the VM to the taskbar, run it in a window, or maximize it. The Virtual PC Console lists Running for each VM in use and displays a real-time thumbnail of each running VM.

To stop a running VM, select it and then open its Action menu. Click Close, and choose from these options:

- **Shut down**—Shuts down the current session, the operating system, and the VM. Use this option when you are finished using a VM, or if you need to manage the VM.
- **Save state**—Saves the current machine state, enabling the VM to be brought back with all open windows in a few seconds. Similar to the hibernate feature in a nonvirtualized VM.
- **Cancel**—Cancels operation; VM continues to run.

Managing VMs with Virtual PC 2007

You can use the operating system's own management tools (such as config.sys and autoexec.bat in MS-DOS or Control Panel in Windows) to configure the operating system instance running in a VM. However, to manage the VM itself, select the VM in the Virtual PC Console and click the Settings button.

Note

If you want to manage all settings for a VM, shut it down first. Some settings cannot be altered while a VM is running.

Figure 3.18 lists the settings available for a typical VM (in this case, a VM running Windows 2000). To change a setting, click it in the left pane, and use the right pane to specify a different value. After making changes, click OK to save them.

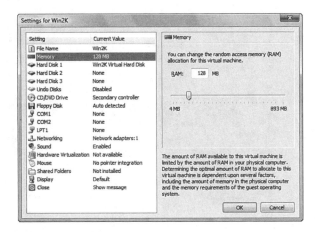

Figure 3.18   Adjusting the memory size allocated to a VM with Virtual PC 2007.

To view the properties of a running VM, right-click the VM in Virtual PC Console and select Properties, or open the VM's Action menu and select Properties. A four-tabbed properties sheet appears. The General tab lists the guest operating system, the version of Virtual Machine Additions in use, processor emulation and features in use, whether hardware assisted virtualization is in use, and the video mode. The Memory tab lists the total amount of system memory used by the VM. Note that video RAM and code cache use memory in addition to the memory size allocated to the VM itself. The Statistics tab lists performance for the IDE and ethernet controllers and the video frame rate. The Advanced tab lists active command-line options and the optimization level in use. Figure 3.19 shows typical examples of these tabs.

To add additional capabilities to a VM running under Virtual PC 2007, start the VM, open the Action menu in the VM window, and select Install or Update Virtual Machine Additions. Virtual Machine Additions are supplied as part of Virtual PC 2007, and provide the following features:

- Drag and drop
- Folder sharing
- Integrated mouse
- Optimized video drivers
- Time synchronization
- Clipboard sharing

- Improved operating system performance
- Dynamic resizing of the virtual machine window, which automatically adjusts the size of the guest operating system desktop
- Sound driver compatible with Windows Vista

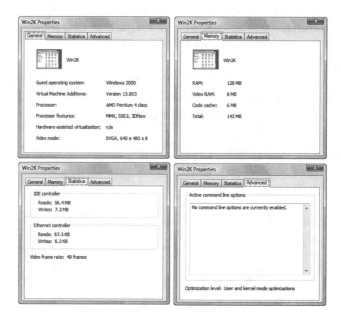

Figure 3.19   General, Memory, Statistics, and Advanced tabs for a VM running under Virtual PC 2007.

Note

You must log in to the operating system running in the VM as an administrator to install Virtual Machine Additions.

Virtual Machine Additions designed for Virtual PC 2004 can be installed into VMs running operating systems that can run under Virtual PC 2007, but are no longer supported, including MS-DOS, Windows 95, and NT Workstation 4.0. To install DOS Virtual Machine Additions, see Microsoft Knowledge Base article 833146. To install Windows Virtual Machine Additions, see Microsoft Knowledge Base article 887790.

Clean Install Summary

The User State Migration Tool, discussed in this chapter, and Files and Settings Transfer Wizard, discussed in the next chapter, can also aid you in migrating your settings and files from an old computer to a new computer. Should you decide later that you want to take advantage of the NTFS file system on an upgrade installation, you can easily convert the file system without losing a single file.

Installation Problems with Windows

Although about 99% of all installations should go smoothly, problems can and do happen. Some of the more common issues that you may see during an installation of Windows XP or Windows Vista include the following:

- You see `Stop 0x0000000A irql_not_less_or_equal` appear on the screen. This error is usually due to hardware or hardware drivers that are not compatible with Windows XP. Ensure that all your hardware is listed on the Hardware Compatibility List and that you have the most up-to-date drivers for your installed hardware. MSKB# 311564, located at http://support.microsoft.com/default.aspx?scid=kb;en-us;311564, has more information on this error.

- You get an error such as `Setup cannot copy the file *file_name*. Press X to retry, Y to abort` when attempting to perform the installation. This error can be caused by many problems such as a dirty or damaged CD-ROM or DVD-ROM disc, viruses, or damaged RAM installed on your computer. If possible, attempt to perform the installation using a different CD-ROM or DVD disc, and verify that all installed hardware in your computer is working properly, and that you do not have any viruses. Also, certain third-party applications that may be installed (if performing an upgrade installation) can cause this error to appear. MSKB# 310064, located at http://support.microsoft.com/default.aspx?id=kb;en-us;310064, has more information on this type of error.

- You are unable to start Windows Vista after installing an earlier version of Windows as a dual-boot configuration on a system already running Windows Vista. Windows Vista does not use `boot.ini` to control its boot process, but a new Boot Configuration Database (BCD) store. When you install an older version of Windows on a Windows Vista system, the BCD and other system files are overwritten, preventing Windows Vista from starting. To fix this error, you need to restore the BCD and other boot files. See MSKB #919529, available at http://support.microsoft.com/kb/919529, for details. Keep in mind that if you want to dual-boot an older version of Windows and Windows Vista, you should install the older version first. If this is not possible, you must use a third-party boot manager to avoid damaging the Windows Vista installation.

- You receive this error: `NTLDR is missing. Press any key to restart.` This error is usually caused by running an upgrade installation of Windows XP over a Windows 9*x* installation that resides on a FAT32 hard drive with an incorrect geometry configuration. To fix this error, you will need to correct the hard drive geometry configuration. MSKB# 314057, located at http://support.microsoft.com/default.aspx?scid=kb;en-us;314057, has more information on this error.

Should you encounter problems during your installation of Windows XP Professional or Windows Vista, a quick search on the Microsoft website will usually turn up the required information. To perform advanced searches, visit the Microsoft Advanced Search page at http://search.microsoft.com/advanced_search.asp.

Automated Deployments

If you're planning to deploy Windows XP or Windows Vista to a number of systems, you're probably considering automating the installation process. And if you're not, you should be. Automating a deployment may take a bit of development time up front, but it saves time in the long run when compared to manually installing a large number of systems. Automation ensures consistency by removing most of the opportunities for human error.

So, who should use automated deployment? Well, if you're a home user, and you're only planning on installing Windows on that old machine your kid uses to surf the Web, you probably just want to run with the standard out-of-the-box install process. But if you happen to have 50 such kids, if you need to frequently install the same base configuration on a system or two for testing purposes, if you configure Windows XP or Windows Vista systems for resale, or if you're developing a deployment scenario for an organization's IT department, you'll definitely want to consider automating. A number of options are available when automating the installation of Windows XP, which are listed as follows and illustrated in Figure 3.20:

- **Scripted install from CD or Distribution Share**—This is the most basic type of automated install. Setup runs using the usual `winnt.exe` or `winnt32.exe` installer, and a preconfigured answer file is passed in from a command-line switch. The answer file supplies the information that would normally have to be entered manually.

- **Scripted install using boot CD**—In this process, the system boots from the install CD, and Windows XP Setup reads an answer file from the A: drive.

- **System image prepared with Sysprep**—With this scheme, you install and configure one system to your exact specifications, and use a *disk image* (an exact duplicate of a system drive) to deploy identical copies to a large number of systems.

- **Remote Installation Services (RIS)**—This more sophisticated method for deploying Windows XP over the network involves booting from a network interface card (NIC), ROM, or ROM emulator disk.

Windows Vista also supports automated installations, but some of the methods differ from those used by Windows XP. For example, RIS is no longer used, having been replaced by Windows Deployment Services. Windows Vista uses XML files to control various installation procedures, rather than TXT or INF files. Also, the setup program is now known as `Setup.exe`, replacing `winnt.exe` and `winnt32.exe`.

Adding and Using the Deployment Tools for Windows XP

As with Windows 2000, the deployment tools for Windows XP are in the `DEPLOY.CAB` file under the \SUPPORT\TOOLS directory of the installation CD. Extract these files to a directory of your choice. For the sake of future reference, we'll assume that the files have been extracted to C:\DEPLOYTOOLS.

Note

While in this directory, it wouldn't hurt to install the Support Tools by running **Setup.exe**. Select Complete Installation for the full toolset. The Support Tools are unsupported utilities included to provide support personnel and experienced users with handy tools for diagnosing and resolving computer problems. About 70 executables and 6 script files are documented in the supporting files included with the install.

Not all the included support tools are listed in the Support Tools Help (this Help file shows under the Support Tools program group after installing the tools). For a full list, be sure to read \SUPPORT\TOOLS\README.HTM.

Scripted Install from CD or Distribution Share

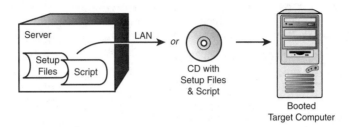

Scripted Install Using Boot CD

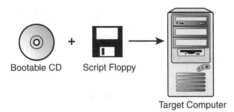

Scripted Install prepared with Sysprep

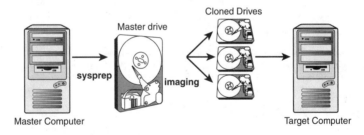

Remote Installation Services (RIS)

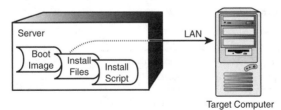

Figure 3.20   Four scenarios for automatic deployment of Windows XP.

Let's look at some of the key files you have under C:\DEPLOYTOOLS:

- DEPLOY.CHM—Windows Help file for the Microsoft Windows XP Corporate Deployment Tools User's Guide. This Help file contains a great deal of useful information. To view it, double-click its icon, or type **start deploy.chm** at the command prompt.

- SYSPREP.EXE—Executable used to prepare a system for disk imaging.

- SETUPCL.EXE—When preparing a system for disk imaging, this executable must be included in the SYSPREP folder with the SYSPREP.EXE and SYSPREP.INF files.

- SETUPMGR.EXE—This is the Windows Setup Manager Wizard. It will run through a series of questions, resulting in a properly formatted answer file suitable for framing.

- REF.CHM—This Windows Help file provides full documentation for all sections used in answer files. In addition, you can find a couple of sample answer files under both the Unattend.txt and the Sysprep.inf sections. Many of the sections listed in this Help file are not exposed by the Windows Setup Manager Wizard.

Using Interactive Answer Files for Installation of Windows XP

The answer file is the cornerstone of any automated installation routine. If you used answer files under Windows 2000, the concept and purpose haven't changed: The answer file provides the answers for both the text mode setup and GUI mode setup portions of the install, relieving end users or technicians from manually completing this repetitive task. Naturally, this speeds up the install process, increases the accuracy over manual data entry, and serves as a form of documentation. The basic structure of the file is the same for a CD-based unattended install, an over-the-network scripted install, an RIS-based install, or an OS image using SYSPREP.

Note

The procedure in the next section can vary if you have a Windows CD slipstreamed with Service Pack 2.

Creating an Answer File with Windows XP

Creating an answer file can be as easy as running a wizard or as complex as manually creating the entire file in Notepad. Personally, I prefer the wizard to create the initial file and Notepad for post-wizard tweaking. To start the Windows Setup Manager Wizard, go to the C:\DEPLOYTOOLS directory and run SETUPMGR.EXE.

Note

You do not have to run the Setup Manager Wizard under Windows XP. It will run on Windows 2000, allowing you to create distribution share points and answer files for Windows XP without having XP installed.

Let's walk through using the wizard to create a complete answer file for a fully automated CD-based installation of Windows XP Professional. If you're following along in the wizard, this should take about 30 minutes to complete. I'm not going to take up space with screen shots, but I will identify and explain all the screens you should expect to see:

1. The first screen is the welcome screen for the wizard. Click Next.

2. The second screen, New or Existing Answer File, lets you select between creating a new file or modifying an existing file. Select Create a New Answer File and click Next.

Note

The Help button becomes active after you reach the second screen of the Setup Manager Wizard. The Help files in the Windows XP Setup Manager are very well developed and provide excellent on-the-spot information if you find yourself questioning the intricacies among multiple options. Be aware that there are different versions of the wizard that may display variations in the options explained here. If you are using a CD that is slipstreamed with SP2, there will be no help button and some of the options will vary.

3. Next is the Product to Install screen. On this screen, select whether to create a file to use with a Windows unattended installation, a Sysprep install, or an install using Remote Installation Services. For our purposes, select Windows Unattended Installation and click Next.

4. The fourth screen, Platform, is where you select between Windows XP Home Edition, Windows XP Professional, and Windows 2003 Server versions. Note that the wizard was released before the server family officially changed names to Windows .NET Server (unless you have a CD with SP2). Select Windows XP Professional and click Next.

5. On the screen titled User Interaction Level, decide how automated the automated install process should be. Table 3.8 details the different options for this screen. After reviewing the table, select Fully Automated and click Next. If using retail media, you actually need to select Hide Pages or Read Only for the user interaction level, which I'll explain further in Step 11.

Table 3.8   Automated Install Interaction Levels

Interaction Level	Description
Provide defaults	Questions posed by Windows Setup are filled in with defaults provided by the answer file, but the user is able to review or change any answers you have supplied.
Fully automated	If you select this option, you must supply all required answers in the answer file. Windows Setup will not prompt the user for any answers, and setup will complete with no action required from the user. If you select this option, the wizard will require you to answer all necessary questions.
Hide pages	Any page for which all answers are provided by the answer file will not be displayed. If an answer is missing, the page will be displayed and the user will be prompted to fill in the blanks.
Read only	If you provided answers for questions posed by Windows Setup, the page will still be displayed, but the end user cannot change the answers you have provided. The user will be prompted for any answers left out of the answer file.
GUI attended	The text mode portion of install is automated, but the user must manually complete the graphical portion of Windows Setup.

6. On the sixth screen, select whether to create a distribution folder or run the installation from a CD. If you select the option to create a distribution folder, the Setup Manager Wizard will prompt you to insert a Windows XP CD from which it can copy the required files. For now, select No, This Answer File Will Be Used to Install from a CD.

7. On the License Agreement screen, check the box to accept the EULA. Click Next.

8. The remainder of the screens will prompt for answers to the questions normally presented by the graphical portion of Setup. The first of these asks for a name and organization. Enter your name and organization, and click Next.

Note

If you plan to use the option for automatic computer naming (see step 12), you must enter an organization name at this screen.

9. You should see the Display Settings panel. Here, configure the default colors, screen area, and refresh frequency. Sticking with the Windows default for all three options is the safe bet, but if you want different options and know your target hardware will support the exact configuration you select, feel free to adjust accordingly. When done, click Next.

10. Select your time zone and click Next.

11. The next screen is Providing the Product Key. If you're using retail media, you won't really get much use out of this screen; leave it blank and manually enter the product key at this point in each installation. In addition, you'll probably need to go back and select Hide Pages or Read Only for the user interaction level on step 5. If you have your volume license media and volume license product key (refer to the first section of this chapter), this is where you enter it. Enter a product key, and click Next.

12. In the Computer Names screen, click the check mark next to Automatically Generate Computer Names Based on Organization Name at the bottom of the screen. This lets you use the same answer file for any number of systems without naming conflicts. Automatically generated computer names are composed of the first word of the organization name, followed by a hyphen and a randomly generated alphanumeric string.

13. The next screen prompts you for the Administrator password. Unlike previous versions of Windows, you have the option of encrypting the password in the answer file. In Windows 2000 and earlier, the password was stored as clear text, which meant that anyone who found your answer file could compromise your local administrator passwords. Enter your password in both boxes, select the option to encrypt, and click Next.

Note

When using a disk image, you must clear the Administrator account's password on the system used to make the master image. If you do not, setting the password in the answer file (**SYSPREP.INF**, in this case) will have no effect, and the target systems will retain the same local administrator password as on the master system.

14. In the Networking Components screen, select Typical Settings to configure your machine for standard settings (TCP/IP using DHCP for addressing, File and Print sharing for Microsoft Networks, and the Client for Microsoft Networks). Click Next.

Note

If you are in a small office or home office environment, rather than setting up a server just to use as a DHCP server, I recommend the Etherfast Cable/DSL Router from Linksys (www.linksys.com). It one-port, four-port, and eight-port versions, all of which can uplink into a hub. Not only do these devices provide full DHCP services for up to 253 clients, but also they act as both an Internet gateway to a broadband connection and as a hardware-based firewall to protect your internal network from outside influences.

15. On the Workgroup or Domain screen, select the option for Windows Server Domain. During mass-production installations, you probably won't want to manually set up domain computer accounts in advance, so enter your domain name in the requisite blank, and select the option to create a computer account in the domain during installation. Enter a username and password with rights to add a computer to the domain. If you do not have an accessible domain to use for this, are setting up standalone workstations, or use workgroups instead of domains in your organization, you can select the option for Workgroup and provide a workgroup name.

Note

Strangely enough, even though you can use encryption for the local administrator account password, it is not an option for this area. That means the account information you enter here will be stored in the answer file in clear text. For this reason, it is recommended that you do *not* use a domain administrator's account to join computers to the domain. You might want to create a special domain account that does not have permission to log on as an interactive user but does have permission to create computer accounts in the domain, and enter the account information in these spaces.

16. On the Telephone screen, fill in your country, area code, and the number to access an outside line. Select whether your phone system uses pulse or touch-tone, and enter any number sequence required to access an outside line. When you've filled out all the boxes, click Next.

17. On the Regional Settings screen, select Use the Default Regional Settings for the Windows Version You Are Installing. Click Next.

18. The Languages screen provides an opportunity to install additional default language groups. For now, stick with the defaults and click Next.

19. On the Browser and Shell Settings screen select Use Default Internet Explorer Settings and click Next.

20. On the Installation Folder screen, specify where to install Windows XP. By default, Windows XP uses Windows as the folder name. If you want Windows to install to the same location as Windows NT 4.0 or Windows 2000, select the option labeled This Folder and enter `Winnt`. For now, let's stick with the default, a folder named Windows, and click Next.

21. If you want, you can automatically install network printers after the first user logon. You'll configure the default printers at this screen, the Install Printers screen. To use this feature, enter a network printer UNC in the form *\\servername\printername*, and click Next. If you don't have any network printers, leave this blank. It is not required for a successful fully automated setup.

22. The next screen, Run Once, lists commands to run after the user logs in for the first time. Any printers you added on the previous screen will show up here as `AddPrinter` `\\server\share`. Do not change anything on this screen; click Next. Any additional commands can be manually added to the script later.

23. After installation, the final screen in this section, Additional Commands, allows you to run commands that do not require a user to be logged on. Commands entered here will execute before the Windows Logon screen shows up the first time. For the purposes of this walkthrough, do not add anything at this screen; click Finish.

24. Windows Setup Manager prompts you for the location and filename under which to save your answer file. Save your file somewhere you can find it, with the filename `Winnt.sif`.

25. In the final window, Setup Manager Complete, available, click the X in the upper right to close the dialog.

You should now have a complete answer file named `Winnt.sif`. If you open the file in a text editor, it should look a little like the following:

Note

If you copy the following sample file for your own use, I strongly recommend changing the product key I've used to a valid product key for the media you are planning to use. The listing shows a Microsoft-provided generic product key that's suitable for testing purposes only. Refer to http://www.microsoft.com/technet/prodtechnol/winxppro/deploy/default.mspx for a full list of generic Windows XP product keys. These keys are blocked from activation at the Microsoft clearinghouse. If you use one of the generic keys, you will have approximately 14 days to experiment with and test your system before Windows will require activation.

```
;SetupMgrTag
[Data]
    AutoPartition=1
    MsDosInitiated="0"
    UnattendedInstall="Yes"

[Unattended]
    UnattendMode=FullUnattended
    OemSkipEula=Yes
    OemPreinstall=No
    TargetPath=\WINDOWS

[GuiUnattended]
    AdminPassword=eadb1736119939abdd99a9b993edc9a87a44c42236119ae1893bd142a2bbaead
    EncryptedAdminPassword=Yes
    OEMSkipRegional=1
    TimeZone=20
    OemSkipWelcome=1

[UserData]
    ProductID=DR8GV-C8V6J-BYXHG-7PYJR-DB66Y
    FullName="Jeff Ferris"
    OrgName="Ferris Technology Networks"
    ComputerName=*

[TapiLocation]
    CountryCode=1
    Dialing=Tone
    AreaCode=512

[GuiRunOnce]
    Command0="rundll32 printui.dll,PrintUIEntry /in /n \\printserver01\laser"
```

```
[Identification]
    JoinDomain=FERRISTECH
    DomainAdmin=ComputerAddAccount
    DomainAdminPassword=ferristechCA

[Networking]
    InstallDefaultComponents=Yes
```

Customizing the Answer File

To modify an existing answer file, you have two options: First, you can take the easy way out by rerunning the Setup Manager Wizard. After starting the wizard, select Modify an Existing Answer File on the second wizard screen. The rest of the process is the same as in the walk-through under the "Creating an Answer File" section in this chapter. Answers already provided by the existing answer file will show up in the proper locations as you go through the wizard. Change what needs changing, resave the file, and you're good to go. You'd probably want to use the wizard when making major changes to your answer file, such as when changing from a domain to a workgroup model.

Your second option is to modify the answer file using a text editor. Most of the answer file options are fairly self-explanatory, and the REF.CHM file from the DEPLOY.CAB contains full documentation for all sections, keys, and options in case you need additional guidance. I'd document everything for you here, but it would translate to about 150 pages of text that wouldn't be indexed and couldn't be searched (unlike the Help file), and you'd probably fall asleep reading through it all anyway. You'd probably prefer using a text editor to modify an answer file when changing things such as the username (FullName=<*answer*>), the organization name (OrgName=<*answer*>), or the username and password used to join a computer account to the domain (DomainAdmin=<*answer*> and DomainAdminPassword=<*answer*>).

If you are going to use the answer file installation method with standard retail Windows XP licenses, you will need to either edit the product ID in the answer file each time you use it, or you must delete the product ID line from the answer file so that the setup program will prompt for a unique product ID for each installation.

Changing the Answers in a SYSPREP.INF File

After you've created a **SYSPREP.INF** file, saved it in the SYSPREP directory, executed Sysprep, and created your image, the **SYSPREP.INF** file becomes a permanent part of that image. So, if you need to make changes to something in the answer file, you must create a new image, update the **SYSPREP.INF** file, and rerun Sysprep.

Suppose that you need to change the answer file for only a couple of systems. You wouldn't want to go through the whole reimaging process just to change some of the options in the answer file. Fortunately, there's a rarely documented out. Simply make the changes to your **SYSPREP.INF** file, and save **SYSPREP.INF** to the root of a floppy disk. Apply your image to a target system and boot the target system. As soon as the system starts to boot, insert the floppy disk containing the updated **SYSPREP.INF** in the A: drive. The Windows XP Setup Wizard will use the answer file on the floppy disk to override the settings specified in the Sysprep file stored with the image.

Putting an Answer File to Use

Four main types of installations can be performed using an answer file. The name of your answer file will be different depending on the type of install you intend to use it for. Table 3.9 lists the four standard filenames for answer files, as well as their purpose and location.

Table 3.9   Types of Answer Files

Filename	Purpose
RISETUP.SIF	Automate the setup wizard for RIS-based installs. You'll put this file in the \I386\Templates subdirectory of the folder created for any RIS image.
SYSPREP.INF	Provides answers for the SYSPREP Mini-Setup Wizard. **SYSPREP.INF** should be placed in the C:\SYSPREP directory before running **SYSPREP.EXE** to prepare a drive for imaging.
UNATTEND.TXT	Provides responses for the installation process when running an install using **winnt** or **winnt32** from a network share or from a command-line–initiated installation from the CD. This file can actually have any name and can be saved in any location that you will be able to access while running the install.
WINNT.SIF	Provides answers for the setup wizard when installing by booting to the Windows XP CD. Save this file to the root of a floppy, and insert the disk right after the installation starts from the bootable Windows XP CD.

Local and Network-Based Unattended Installation

With the answer file created in the "Creating an Answer File" section earlier in this chapter, you might have noticed that the Setup Manager Wizard created a batch file in the same directory as your answer file. This batch file can kick off a Windows XP install from a machine that is already running Windows 95, Windows 98, Windows Me, Windows NT, Windows 2000, or Windows XP. The install will take advantage of the answer file as long as you leave both the batch file and the answer file in the same directory. By default, answer files created to install from the Windows XP CD expect to find your Windows XP CD in the D: drive. If your CD-ROM uses a different drive letter, you must edit the batch file using Notepad to reflect the correct drive letter.

You may remember a point in the walk-through under "Creating an Answer File" (step 6) where the Setup Manager Wizard asked whether to create an answer file to install from CD, or to create or modify a distribution folder. You selected the option to install from CD. Had you selected the distribution folder option, the batch file would point to the UNC to which the install files were copied. Additionally, from within Windows 95/98/Me/NT/2000/XP, you could manually run the installation using the answer file with the winnt32.exe command and the optional /unattend switch, using the following syntax:

```
<path_to_install_files>\winnt32 /unattend:filename
```

If you want to complete an over-the-network installation from a system without an operating system, you need to create a DOS-bootable disk capable of connecting to the network and map a drive to the location of the shared Windows XP install files. Instead of running winnt32.exe as when running a local or network install from Windows 95/98/Me/NT/2000/XP, use the winnt.exe command. To use the answer file, the full command will be

```
Winnt /s:install_source_directory /u:answerfile_name
```

Unattended Install from the Bootable Windows XP CD

Caution

The following paragraph starts a fresh unattended install of Windows XP Professional. This *will* wipe your drive clean. And after you've started, you can't go back. *Do not* attempt to run the bootable CD setup process unless you are willing to clear the primary drive on the target machine.

In the walk-through in the "Creating an Answer File" section of this chapter, the answer file was named WINNT.SIF, allowing it to be used to run a fully automated installation simply by booting from the Windows XP Professional install CD. To make this work, you don't need to worry about the batch file. Just copy WINNT.SIF to the root of a floppy disk. Go to your target system, insert the Windows XP Professional CD in the CD-ROM drive, and boot to the CD.

As discussed in the "Licensing Issues" section earlier in this chapter, you must use volume license media and a volume license product key to use the same product key on multiple systems. If you're not using volume license media with a volume license product key, you must either update the Product ID line in the WINNT.SIF file before loading each different system or leave the Product ID line out of the WINNT.SIF so that the system will prompt for the key during the Mini-Setup Wizard.

Note

If Setup isn't starting when you attempt to boot to the CD, check two things: First, ensure that your system boot order is configured with the CD-ROM as the first boot device under your system BIOS. Second, pay close attention while booting your system. If you have no operating system, Windows Setup will start on its own. If, however, an active partition with a bootable OS exists, at one point booting to the CD will prompt you with "Press any key to continue booting from CD." Press the Any key at this point. Look closely, the label for the Any key—usually the long key at the bottom center—frequently falls off before a keyboard leaves the factory.

As soon as your system starts to read the CD and recognizes it as bootable, insert the floppy disk containing the answer file into the A: drive. After a few minutes, Setup will prompt you to partition and format the drive. This is a safety mechanism to give you one last chance to back out of the install before wiping out your system. After partitioning the disk, you should be able to sit back and relax for about 45 minutes while Windows XP Professional completes installation to your system without prompting you to answer any additional questions.

Now, I know what some of you may be thinking: Hey! If this is automated why is Setup asking for my input before it partitions and formats the disk?

Although you selected Fully Automated in the Setup Manager Wizard, the partitioning and formatting of the disk does not complete without user interaction unless you know about this rarely documented trick: Open your WINNT.SIF file in Notepad, and add the following two lines under the (Unattended) section header:

```
FileSystem = ConvertNTFS
Repartition = Yes
```

If you find that this isn't working for you and booting from the Windows XP CD still runs a normal setup, make sure that you've named your answer file WINNT.SIF and saved it to the root of the A: drive. Windows Setup will not check for any other filename, and it will not check in any other location. In addition, double-check that you're getting the disk inserted as soon as the system starts to boot from the CD, or Windows Setup will not read the answer file.

If you're having difficulty getting the disk inserted at the right time, you could go into your system BIOS and disable booting from floppy, or move the floppy drive to the end of your boot order. You should then be able to leave the floppy disk containing the WINNT.SIF file in your drive from the beginning of the boot process.

Remote Installation Services

If you are familiar with using RIS under Windows 2000, not much has changed with the upgrade to Windows XP. RIS is an optional server-side service provided with Windows 2000 Server and Windows Server 2003 that enables you to deploy Windows XP to a new system by booting to the NIC using an NIC with a Preboot Execution Environment (PXE) boot ROM enabled.

Other than booting client systems using a PXE boot ROM rather than a network boot disk, installing Windows XP using RIS is similar to installing over the network from a network share point. All files are copied over the network to the client station, and Windows XP runs a full install.

From an infrastructure perspective, RIS requires a TCP/IP-based network that uses a DHCP server, a Windows 2000–compliant DNS service conforming with both RFC 2052 and RFC 2136, and Active Directory to provide client authorization and configuration information to the RIS server during the client install process. If you are still using Windows NT 4.0 Server DNS, it does *not* support the required protocols. If using UNIX BIND, versions 8.1.2 and later support the required protocols.

To add a Windows XP Professional installation to your RIS server, follow the same procedure as adding a Windows 2000 Professional image, but using the source files and answer file for Windows XP. Remember, you can create the RISETUP.SIF answer file by using the Setup Manager Wizard and selecting the option to create an install for RIS on the third screen of the wizard.

Note

For full details on setting up and configuring RIS under Windows 2000, see the Remote Installation Services chapter excerpt from the New Riders title, *Windows 2000 Deployment and Desktop Management*, available online at http://technet.microsoft.com/en-us/library/Bb742501.aspx.

Windows Installation Tools for Windows Vista

Microsoft has rolled out a variety of installation tools exclusively for Windows Vista, including Windows Deployment Services and the Windows Automated Installation Kit (Windows AIK). These new tools are covered in the following sections.

Using Windows Deployment Services for Windows Vista

Windows Vista uses Windows Deployment Services (WDS) as a replacement for RIS. The requirements for WDS are similar to those for RIS, except that WDS supports Windows Server 2003 or Windows Server 2008; it is not supported on Windows 2000 Server.

WDS can run in three modes: a legacy mode that emulates RIS (available only on Windows Server 2003), mixed mode supporting both OSChooser and Windows PE boot images (available only on Windows Server 2003), or native mode on Windows Server 2003 and Windows Server 2008.

Note

For full details on setting up and configuring WDS under Windows Server 2003, see "Windows Deployment Services Update Step-by-Step Guide for Windows Server 2003," available from the Deployment section of the Windows Vista Technical Library at http://technet2.microsoft.com/WindowsVista/en/library/.

Using the Windows Automated Installation Kit

You can install Windows Vista automatically by using the Windows AIK. Windows AIK (see Figure 3.21) enables you to perform unattended Windows Vista installations, capture Windows images with ImageX, and create Windows PE images. Windows AIK is available from the Downloads section of the Microsoft website.

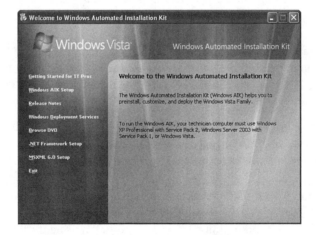

Figure 3.21 The Windows AIK opening dialog can be used to install the program, support files, and to access documentation.

Note

Windows AIK is distributed as an IMG file. The image must be burned to a DVD for installation. You may need to rename the file extension to ISO to enable some DVD-burning applications to use it.

Windows AIK is designed to use the WIM Windows Image file format used for Windows Vista. The WIM file format reduces network traffic to make network installation faster.

How Windows Vista Automated Installation Differs from Windows XP

Windows Vista uses a single answer file, `Unattend.xml`, to guide an automated installation. The Windows System Image Manager (Windows SIM) component of Windows AIK is used to generate the answer file and to create distribution shares and configuration sets.

Other new features in Windows AIK include

- A new version of Sysprep, which is used to prepare a new Windows installation for deployment.

- ImageX, a new command-line tool for capturing, modifying, and applying file-based disk images

Overview of Supported Installation Methods for Windows Vista

There are three methods for performing an automated installation of Windows Vista:

- Installing from a Windows Vista product DVD, using an answer file created with Windows SIM

- Installing from a configuration set created with Windows SIM

- Installing from an image created with Windows SIM, Sysprep, or ImageX

To help understand how the process works, the following sections discuss the third option. For information on other options, see the Windows AIK documentation.

Installing the Windows AIK

After you create the Windows AIK DVD from the downloadable image file, insert the DVD into a computer running Windows XP SP2, Windows Server 2003 SP1, or Windows Vista. The computer you use for the installation is referred to as the "Technician computer" in Windows AIK documentation.

If Windows AutoPlay program doesn't open the disc automatically, double-click it in My Computer to open the Welcome dialog shown in Figure 3.21. Before you run Windows AIK setup, perform the following tasks as necessary:

- If you have not used Windows AIK before, click the Getting Started for IT Pros link, which opens an RTF (Rich Text Format) document containing an illustrated overview of the process of using AIK. Save this document or print it, and review it before continuing.

- If the computer is not running MSXML 6.0, install it using the link provided. You cannot install Windows AIK unless MSXML 6.0 is already installed on the system.

- If the computer is not running Microsoft .NET Framework 2.0, install it using the link provided. You cannot install Windows AIK unless MSXML 6.0 is already installed on the system.

- Click the Release Notes link to open a Readme file. Note any documentation errors or workarounds that might apply to your situation. This file also contains a link to the latest version online.

After performing any or all of these steps as necessary, click the Windows AIK Setup link to start the installation process. By default, the program is installed in C:\Program Files\Windows AIK\, but you can select a different folder if desired. The program uses slightly over 1GB of disk space. It can be installed for use by all users, or the current user only.

Creating an Answer File with Windows AIK

To create an answer file, follow these steps:

1. Insert the Windows Vista DVD into the technician computer. If the Install Windows dialog appears, close it. Explore the Windows Vista DVD using [My] Computer. Navigate to the \sources folder.

2. Copy install.wim to a folder on the technician computer.

3. Start Windows System Image Manager (Windows SIM). It's located in the Microsoft Windows AIK program group.

4. Select File, Select Windows Image.

5. Navigate to the folder containing install.wim and click Open.

6. Select the version of Windows Vista for which you are creating the answer file and click OK.

7. If a catalog does not already exist for the Windows Vista version you selected, click Yes to create a catalog (you must create a catalog for each version of Windows Vista).

8. The catalog file is generated. After the catalog file is created, it is displayed in the Windows Image section of Windows SIM.

9. Click File, New Answer File. The Answer File section of the dialog lists components and packages.

10. Click the Component node in the Windows Image pane. Available components are displayed. Expand components as needed until all components are visible.

11. Right-click each component you want to add to your answer file and select the configuration pass where it will be installed. As each component is added to your answer file, the Answer File section is populated. Figure 3.22 shows a typical answer file being created.

Note

If you want to create an answer file for a basic unattended installation, follow the guidelines in the GETTING_STARTED_ITPRO.rtf file to select components and values for the answer file.

12. Continue by configuring the Answer File: Select each component in the answer file, and use the Settings section of the Properties sheet for the component to select the setting and value desired. For most values, a pull-down menu listing valid choices is provided. When an alphanumerical value must be entered, type it in using the keyboard. Context-sensitive help is provided below the Settings dialog.

13. Next, validate the answer file. Click Tools, Validate Answer File. Errors (if any) are listed in the Messages pane. To correct errors, select the node in the Answer File window and enter the correct information in the Settings portion of the properties sheet.

Figure 3.22 Creating an answer file with Windows SIM.

14. Repeat step 13 until the message No Warnings or Errors appears in the Messages pane.

15. Click File, Save Answer File, and use the filename `Autounattend.xml`.

16. Copy `Autounattend.xml` to a floppy disk or USB flash memory drive.

Note

If you are creating an answer file for systems using a volume-licensed edition of Windows Vista, be sure to read the document "Windows Vista Volume Activation 2.0 Step-by-Step Guide," available from http://technet.microsoft.com/en-us/windowsvista/bb335288.aspx. This document discusses how to specify product keys in the answer file under different activation scenarios.

Running an Unattended Installation Using the Answer File

The next step in the process is to build a master installation using the answer file and your Windows Vista product DVD. Use a system with a blank hard disk as the installation target.

1. Insert the floppy disk or plug in the USB flash memory drive containing `Autounattend.xml`.

2. Insert the Windows Vista DVD.

3. Turn on the target system.

4. Boot the system from DVD.

5. Setup starts automatically. Unless you omitted answers to some setup questions, the installation runs automatically. Provide any information not included in the answer file when prompted.

Note

If the installation process prompts you for information, note which screens are displayed. You can go back to the technician computer and add information to the **Autounattend.xml** answer file to improve future installations.

Creating a Master Installation from an Unattended Installation

If you need to install Windows Vista on only a few computers, you might prefer to use the **Autounattend.xml** file and the Windows Vista DVD as described in the previous section for each installation. However, if you need to deploy Windows Vista on many systems, particularly in a network environment, you will want to convert the unattended installation into a master installation that can be imaged for reuse:

1. After the unattended installation is complete and the administrator has logged on to the Windows Vista GUI, open a command prompt window with cmd or the command prompt option in the Accessories menu.

2. Type the command **c:\windows\system32\sysprep\sysprep.exe /oobe /generalize /shutdown** and press Enter. This command prepares the Windows installation for imaging and shuts down the computer.

Creating the Windows PE CD

Before you can create a product image from the master installation, you need to return to the technician computer and create a bootable Windows PE CD.

Here's an overview of the process. For details, see the document GETTING_STARTED_ITPRO.rtf supplied as part of Windows AIK.

Note

If you are using Windows XP on the technician computer, I recommend you download and install the Open Command Window Here (**CmdHere.exe**) PowerToy, available from http://www.microsoft.com/windowsxp/downloads/powertoys/xppowertoys.mspx. You can use it to open a command prompt session on any folder.

1. Run the copype.cmd script to create a local Windows PE build directory. Figure 3.23 shows a typical example of this command in action.

2. Copy ImageX (used to capture the image from the master installation) to the build directory.

3. Create a configuration file for ImageX (optional) and store it in the ISO folder inside the build directory. This file, called wimscript.ini, is used to exclude files and folders from the image created by ImageX.exe.

4. Create an image (.iso) file of the Windows PE RAM CD, using the oscdimg tool. Be sure to type the command into the command window, rather than trying to cut and paste it from a document such as GETTING_STARTED_ITPRO.rtf because cut/paste or copy/paste do not work.

5. Burn the image to a CD using a CD-mastering program such as Nero or Roxio Easy Media Creator.

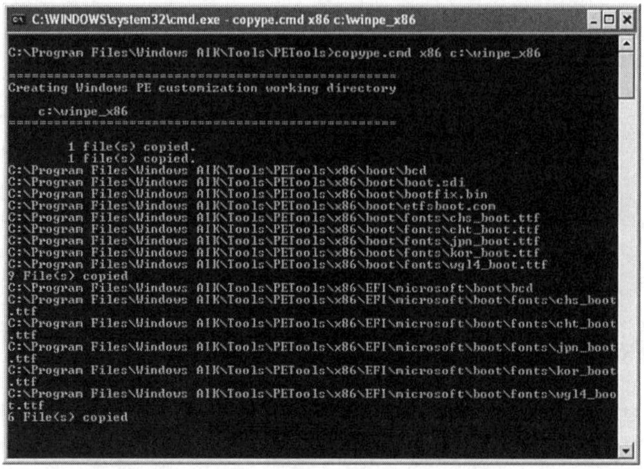

Figure 3.23   Creating a local Windows PE build directory (folder) with the copype.cmd script.

The contents of the CD should include

- Root folder—ImageX.exe, WIMSCRIPT.ini, bootmgr
- SOURCES folder—BOOT.wim
- BOOT folder—ETFSBOOT.com, BOOT.sdi, BOOTFIX.bin, BCD, and FONTS folder
- BOOT\FONTS folder—CHS_BOOT.ttf, CHT_BOOT.ttf, JPN_BOOT.ttf, KOR_BOOT.ttf, and WGL4_BOOT.ttf
- EFI folder—MICROSOFT folder
- EFI\MICROSOFT folder—BOOT folder
- EFI\MICROSOFT\BOOT folder—BCD, FONTS folder
- EFI\MICROSOFT\BOOT\FONTS folder—CHS_BOOT.ttf, CHT_BOOT.ttf, JPN_BOOT.ttf, KOR_BOOT.ttf, and WGL4_BOOT.ttf

If you added additional options, additional files and folders may be present on your bootable CD.

Using the Windows PE CD to Capture the Image

The Windows Vista installation image you capture in this step is used as the source for Windows Vista installations. To capture the image, follow these steps:

1. After the Windows PE CD is created, use it to boot the master installation computer. If necessary, configure the master installation computer so that it boots from the CD first.

2. If the boot options menu appears, select Windows Setup [EMS] as the program to run. Windows PE loads its workfiles into a RAMdisk using drive X:.

3. A command prompt window opens automatically.

4. Change to the D: drive.

5. Change to the folder containing imagex.exe.

6. Use this command to create an image of the Vista installation on the C: drive in the root folder of the C: drive: `imagex.exe /compress fast /capture c: c:\myimage.wim "my Vista Install" /verify`

Deploying the Image via the Network

You can deploy the image captured in the previous step via the network. First, the image must be copied to a network folder mapped to a drive letter. Then, the image must be copied to each computer on the network and applied to each computer.

To place the image on a network share for use by other computers, follow these steps:

1. Use the Net Use command prompt to map a network folder to a drive:
   `net use y: \\network_share\images`

2. Copy the image to the mapped drive: `copy c:\myimage.wim y:`

To deploy the image on the network folder to other computers, follow these steps:

1. Start each computer with the Windows PE disc you created.

2. Use DiskPart from the command prompt to create a disk partition matching the disk partition size in the original image. This example creates a 20GB partition:

   ```
   diskpart
   select disk 0
   clean
   create partition primary size=20000
   select partition 1
   active
   format
   exit
   ```

3. Copy the image from the network share:

   ```
   net use y: \\network_share\images
   copy y:\myimage.wim c:
   ```

4. Use ImageX to apply the image to the hard disk:

   ```
   d:\tools\imagex.exe /apply c:\myimage.wim 1 c:
   ```

Installation Tools for Windows XP and Windows Vista

In addition to providing unattended installation tools designed either for Windows XP or Windows Vista, Microsoft also offers cross-platform installation tools that work with either Windows version. These include Systems Management Server and the User State Migration Tool, both of which are covered in the following sections.

Systems Management Server

If so inclined, you can use Microsoft Systems Management Server (SMS) to deploy a Windows XP or Windows Vista upgrade. The question is, should you? To be honest, I've tried it (with Windows XP), and I don't like it. Part of the problem is that you can deploy Windows XP or

Windows Vista via SMS only if doing an upgrade. You cannot use SMS to deploy a clean installation of Windows XP or Windows Vista. So rather than telling you *how* to use SMS to deploy a Windows XP or Windows Vista upgrade, I'm going to tell you why you probably *shouldn't*.

Note

If, after reading the rest of this section, you still want to attempt an upgrade to Windows XP or Windows Vista using Microsoft SMS, refer to the Microsoft-provided documentation at http://technet.microsoft.com/en-us/sms/bb676794.aspx. SMS 2003 Service Pack 3 supports Windows Vista as well as Windows XP. To learn what's new in this version of SMS, see http://technet.microsoft.com/en-us/sms/bb676774.aspx.

When planning for a mass-scale operating system upgrade, I usually opt to develop a single clean install process to use for all systems in an environment, rather than developing one install process for people who need a clean install and an additional upgrade process for systems that can handle the upgrade. Upgrading an operating system tends to result in a number of difficult-to-diagnose technical inconsistencies; a clean install does away with any questions. I'm sure that if you've been working with any Microsoft operating system for very long, you've eventually reinstalled just to improve system performance, get rid of unneeded files, and start with a clean slate. Major operating system upgrades provide an excellent opportunity for a wide-scale cleanup of all systems in an organization.

Using the User State Migration Tool

Unless you're lucky enough to be running in a fully managed environment with roaming user profiles and all unique user data stored on the network, you need to find a way to migrate the settings and documents from the old systems to the new. The User State Migration tool (USMT) helps with this endeavor.

Compared to the Files and Settings Transfer Wizard (XP) or the Windows Easy Transfer Tool (Vista), which are GUI-based and end-user-oriented, the USMT is powerful, complex, and intended for administrators and advanced support personnel. The same thing that makes the User State Migration Tool so powerful is what makes it so complicated to most people: Its arcane command-line interface that relies on INF (in version 2.6 and earlier) or XML files (in version 3.0) to control the migration process.

The latest version of the USMT is available from the Microsoft Download Center. Version 3.0.x works with both Windows XP and Windows Vista, so it can be used in place of the USMT found on the Windows XP Setup CD-ROM. USMT 3.0 can be used to migrate from Windows 2000, Windows XP, or Windows Vista to Windows XP or Windows Vista. If you need to support migrations from earlier operating systems to Windows XP, use the version of USMT included with Windows XP in the \VALUEACC\MSFT\USMT folder.

Note

Before installing USMT 3.0.x on a Windows Vista–based system, see Microsoft Knowledge Base article 929761, available from http://support.microsoft.com. The update discussed in this article may already have been installed on the system via Windows Update, or it can be installed manually.

As with earlier versions, version 3.0.x includes two executable files: SCANSTATE.EXE and LOADSTATE.EXE. However, version 3.0.x no longer uses default INF files. Instead, it uses three default XML files: MigApp.xml, MigUser.xml, and MigSys.xml. These files can be modified as needed.

Table 3.10 explains the primary files and their purposes in more detail.

Table 3.10   The Core USMT 3.0.x Files Explained

File	Description
SCANSTATE.EXE	Collects user data and settings based on the information contained in Migapp.xml, Migsys.xml, and Miguser.xml.
LOADSTATE.EXE	Applies the collected user state data on a computer that has a clean installation of Windows XP Professional.
Migapp.xml	Used to collect application settings; can be modified to customize a migration.
Migsys.xml	Used to collect system settings, such as fonts, accessibility settings, and Internet Explorer settings, among others; can be modified to customize a migration.
Miguser.xml	Used to collect personal settings and files from the My Pictures, My Documents, and other user-specific folders; can be modified to customize a migration.

USMT and Upgrade Installations

The User State Migration Tool does not support the application of collected settings to computers that have been upgraded from a previous operating system. Install Windows XP or Windows Vista in a clean installation before attempting to use the USMT.

Out of the box, USMT migrates the following files and settings:

- Accessibility
- Classic desktop
- Cookies folder
- Dial-up connections
- Folder options
- Fonts
- Internet Explorer settings
- Mouse and keyboard settings
- My Documents folder
- My Pictures folder
- Network drives and printers
- Office settings
- Outlook Express settings and store
- Outlook settings and store
- Phone and modem options

- Regional options
- Screen saver selection
- Sounds settings
- Taskbar settings

As mentioned previously, the User State Migration Tool's `.xml` files are highly customizable. By modifying the `.xml` files in the USMT directory, you can change the files and settings that USMT will migrate in order to fit your specific needs.

Customizing the `.xml` Files

For complete online documentation for the USMT, including information on customizing the `.xml` files that control the migration process in the USMT, see "User State Migration Tool 3.0" in the Windows Vista Technical Library, located at http://technet2.microsoft.com/WindowsVista/en/library/.

As mentioned previously, the User State Migration Tool consists of two executable files, three migration `.xml` files, and several supporting `.dll` files. The migration process takes place in just four major steps, just the same as when using the Files and Settings Transfer Wizard. Additionally, the information provided for the Files and Settings Transfer Wizard in the "Before Starting the Transfer" section as detailed in the next chapter apply to using the USMT as well.

Let's run through a quick data and settings migration using the default `.inf` files. To accomplish this task, you need a "used" system with a configured user profile directory, a server (or a workstation on which you can create a data share), and a clean system to which to copy the user state.

1. On the server, create a shared directory called USMT. If you are using version 3.0.x, install the USMT you downloaded to this directory (for version 2.6, copy the entire USMT directory from the \VALUEADD\MSFT\ directory of the Windows XP Installation CD into this directory). Create a subdirectory named DATA.

2. Log on to the "used" system and map the U: drive to the USMT share on your server.

3. Open the command prompt. Switch to the U:\USMT directory, and type the command **SCANSTATE U:\DATA**.

4. You will see the line ScanState is running.... Wait. When ScanState finishes, you will see the line The tool completed successfully.

5. Move to the clean system and map the U: drive to the USMT share on your server.

6. Open the command prompt. Switch to the U:\USMT directory, and type the command **LOADSTATE U:\DATA**.

7. You will see the line LoadState is running.... Wait. When LoadState finishes, you'll be back at the command prompt, and you should have the same data and settings as on the system from which SaveState was run.

Using USMT for a Single System Transfer

You don't have to use USMT in a client/server environment. If you just want to migrate data between a handful of systems, use the following steps instead:

1. On the source computer, logged on as the user in question, run the ScanState file to copy the settings to an intermediate storage location. This can be done via script, shortcut, or manually.

2. Prepare the target computer with a clean installation of Windows XP Professional or Windows Vista. There are no restrictions on performing Remote Installations or other automated deployment methods.

3. On the target computer, logged on as the *local* administrator, run the LoadState file to apply the user's settings. This, again, can be done using a script, a shortcut or a scheduled task using the local administrator's credentials.

4. The user logs on to her account and the process is completed.

Using the default settings, that's really all there is to it. Of course, there are any number of switches you can use with the executable files to further modify how USMT works. The ScanState program's syntax varies with the version of ScanState used. If you use the version supplied with Windows XP Professional (version 2.6), the syntax used is

```
scanstate [/c /i input.inf]* [/l scanstate.log]
  [/v verbosity_level] [/f] [/u] [/x] migration_path
```

For ScanState 3.0.x, more options are available:

```
scanstate [StorePath] [/i:[Path\]FileName] [/o] [/v:VerbosityLevel] [/nocompress]
[/localonly]
[/encrypt /key:KeyString|/keyfile:[Path\]FileName] [/l:[Path\]FileName]
[/progress:[Path\]FileName] [/r:TimesToRetry] [/w:SecondsBeforeRetry] [/c] [/p]
[/all]
[/ui:[DomainName\]UserName]|LocalUserName]
[/ue:[DomainName\]UserName]|LocalUserName]
[/uel:NumberOfDays|YYYY/MM/DD|0] [/efs:abort|skip|decryptcopy|copyraw]
[/genconfig:[Path\]FileName] [/targetxp] [/config:[Path\]FileName] [/?|help]
```

The LoadState program has the following syntax in version 2.6:

```
loadstate [/i input.inf]* [/l loadstate.log] [/v #]
  [/f] [/u] [/x] migration_path
```

Version 3.0 adds many syntax options:

```
loadstate StorePath [/i:[Path\]FileName] [/v:VerbosityLevel] [/nocompress]
[/decrypt /key:KeyString|/keyfile:[Path\]FileName] [/l:[Path\]FileName]
[/progress:[Path\]FileName] [/r:TimesToRetry] [/w:SecondsToWait] [/c] [/all]
[/ui:[[DomainName\]UserName]|LocalUserName]
[/ue:[[DomainName\]UserName]|LocalUserName]
[/uel:NumberOfDays|YYYY/MM/DD|0] [/md:OldDomain:NewDomain]
[/mu:OldDomain\OldUserName:[NewDomain\]NewUserName] [/lac:[Password]] [/lae] [/q]
[/config:[Path\]FileName] [/?|help]
```

The option switches supported by these versions of ScanState and LoadState are explained in Table 3.11. In Table 3.11, italics indicate variables that you need to replace with the correct information for your situation.

Table 3.11   ScanState and LoadState Switches

Switch	Description	Supported Version(s)	ScanState	UserState
/c	In version 2.6, instructs programs not to stop on filename too long errors. These errors are logged in the **Longfile.log** log file for later analysis. In version 3.0, instructs programs not to stop on nonfatal errors. If a progress log (see **/progress** switch) is in use, errors are logged there.	2.6, 3.0	Yes	Yes
/f	A troubleshooting switch that specifies that files will be migrated; not normally used.	2.6	Yes	Yes
/i:*Path\ FileName(s)*	Specifies the **.inf** (v2.6) or **.xml** (v3.0) file (or multiple **.inf** or **.xml** files) that is to be used to define the settings that are to be collected for transfer.	2.6, 3.0	Yes	Yes
/l:*Path\FileName*	Specifies the file to log errors that may occur during the process.	2.6, 3.0	Yes	Yes
/u	A troubleshooting switch that specifies that user settings will be migrated; not normally used.	2.6	Yes	Yes
/v	Enables verbose output. With version 2.6, use the format: **/v #**, substituting **1** (least verbose) to **7** (most verbose) for the **#** symbol. With version 3.0, substitute **0** (least verbose), **1, 4, 5, 8, 9, 12,** or **13** (most verbose) for the # symbol. Other values (up to 15) are mapped to supported values.	2.6, 3.0	Yes	Yes

Switch	Description	Supported Version(s)	ScanState	UserState
/x	A troubleshooting switch that specifies that no files or settings will be migrated; not normally used.	2.6	Yes	Yes
migration_path	Specifies the path to the location to which files should be written. You must have the appropriate NTFS and share permissions to this location.	2.6	Yes	Yes
StorePath	Folder to use for files and settings.	3.0	Yes	Yes
/o	Overwrites existing data in store.	3.0	Yes	No
/encrypt	Use with /key and /keyfile options to encrypt the files and settings storefile: /key:KeyString KeyString identifies encryption key (use quotes around KeyString if it contains a space); can be up to 256 characters long; at least 8 characters recommended. /keyfile: FilePathandName FilePathandNAME specifies a text (.txt) file containing the encryption key.	3.0	Yes	No
/nocompress	This option disables file compression (on by default) and saves store to a hidden folder called 'File' at \StorePath\USMT3. Useful for testing or for checking store contents for viruses, but not recommended for production operation.	3.0	Yes	Yes
/genconfig: Path\FileName	Generates the optional Config.xml file. This switch does not create a store file. Use it on the source computer.	3.0	Yes	No

(continues)

Table 3.11   Continued

Switch	Description	Supported Version(s)	ScanState	UserState
`/config:` `Path\Filename`	Specifies the `Config.xml` file you want to use to create the store (see `/genconfig:` switch to create this file)	3.0	Yes	Yes
`/targetxp`	Use when the destination computer runs Windows XP to create a store or when running `/genconfig`.	3.0	Yes	No
`/localonly`	Migrates only files on the local computer's internal storage; does not migrate files on external drives or mapped network drives.	3.0	Yes	No
`/progress:` `Path\FileName`	Creates the progress log (optional) on the specified path and filename; cannot use *StorePath* for this information	3.0	Yes	Yes
`/r:` *Times2Retry*	Specifies number of times to retry (default is three) when an error occurs in saving the user state to a server. Use this option when network latency, rather than connectivity problems, are an issue.	3.0	Yes	Yes
`/w:`*Seconds* *BeforeRetry*	Specifies how long to wait (in seconds; default is one second) before retrying a network operation.	3.0	Yes	Yes
`/p`	Creates a file called `USMTSIZE.TXT` in *StorePath*. This file estimates the amount of space that will be used if the `/nocompress` option is used (requires `/nocompress`). The estimate is usually twice the disk space needed, except when calculating disk space	3.0	Yes	No

Switch	Description	Supported Version(s)	ScanState	UserState
	requirements when migrating from x86-based computers running Windows XP. Lists cluster (allocation units) in the first column, store size for each in the second column. Use the value matching the cluster or allocation unit size of your network drive.			
/?, /help	Displays help.	3.0	Yes	Yes
/all	Migrates all users on the computer (default).	3.0	Yes	Yes
/ui:*DomainName* *UserName* or *DomainName* \"*User Name*" or *LocalUserName*	Migrates specified users in domain or local system; requires /ue or /uel switches.	3.0	Yes	Yes
/uel:*NumberOfDays* or *YYYY*/*MM*/*DD* or 0	Migrates only users who have logged on to the computer in the specified period; 0 migrates only users currently logged on and users with loaded profiles; date specification migrates only users who have logged on during the date specified or more recently.	3.0	Yes	Yes
/ue: *DomainName* *UserName* or *DomainName*\ "*User Name*" or *LocalUserName*	Excludes specified users from migration. Supports * wildcard.	3.0	Yes	Yes
/efs:abort	ScanState stops with error if an EFS file is found on the source computer (default).	3.0	Yes	No
/efs:skip	Forces ScanState to ignore EFS files.	3.0	Yes	No
/efs:decryptcopy	Decrypts file and copies it; ScanState fails if file cannot be decrypted.	3.0	Yes	No

(continues)

Table 3.11   Continued

Switch	Description	Supported Version(s)	ScanState	UserState
/efs:copyraw	Copies encrypted files. Files are not accessible on destination computer until EFS certificates are migrated. A destination computer running Windows Vista automatically migrates certificates, but a destination computer running Windows XP must migrate certificates manually. **Cipher.exe** can be used for this task.	3.0	Yes	No
/q	Runs LoadState without administrative credentials; migrates only settings for current user; can migrate only to folders the user has credentials to use.	3.0	No	Yes
/md:*OldDomain: NewDomain* or *LocalComputer Name:NewDomain*	Specifies the new domain for the user. Can use * wildcard in *OldDomain*.	3.0	No	Yes
/mu:*OldDomain\ Old Username: NewDomain\ NewUserName*	Specifies a new username for the specified user. Specify new domain name only if the user is in a different domain.	3.0	No	Yes
/lac:*Password*	Creates local (nondomain) account and provides password specified (optional).	3.0	No	Yes
/lae	Enables local account created with /lac.	3.0	No	Yes

Windows Copy Protection

To discourage copying and distribution of unlicensed copies of Windows XP and Windows Vista, Microsoft has developed a variety of copy protection features. Unlike the copy protection features used by some games and DVDs, these do not involve alterations to the physical media, but instead use two major mechanisms that involve interaction between authentication servers at the Microsoft website and individual Windows-based PCs:

■ Product Activation

■ Windows Genuine Advantage

Product Activation for Windows XP

Product Activation, or Microsoft Product Activation (MPA) as it has become known, was not exactly a welcome addition in Windows XP. However, it was not introduced in Windows XP; it existed in late versions of Office 2000, all versions of Office XP, and Visio 2002. MPA works to stop casual copying of software by tying the hardware profile of a computer to software installation.

In the next sections, you are going to take an in-depth look at Product Activation, including the different activation scenarios that exist, how Product Activation works and what information it transmits to Microsoft, how Product Activation will affect you, and the new Product Activation features added in Windows Vista.

When dealing with Product Activation, there are three scenarios that can occur. Without exception, you should fall into one of these three scenarios:

- Retail box purchases
- OEM installations
- Volume licensing

Retail Box Purchases

Retail box purchases of Windows XP present the most complex and confusing situation when it comes to dealing with Product Activation. Product Activation depends on submission of the Installation ID to Microsoft. The *Installation ID* is a unique number generated from two different pieces of information about a computer: the Product ID number and a hardware hash. The Installation ID has been designed to ensure anonymity in that no personally identifying information is ever transmitted to Microsoft. Instead, the Installation ID serves to deter and prevent software piracy by preventing installations of Windows XP Professional that violate its license.

The Product ID uniquely identifies one and only one copy of Windows XP, and is created from the Product Key used during the installation of Windows XP. Each retail copy of Windows XP has a unique Product Key, and thus every Product ID generated from a valid Product Key is also unique. Additionally, as in the past, the Product ID is used by Microsoft for support calls. You can view your Product ID by looking at the General tab of the System applet in the Control Panel (alternatively, you can access this applet by right-clicking on My Computer and selecting Properties from the context menu).

Product Keys and Product IDs

The practice of using Product Keys and Product IDs is not new to Windows XP. Microsoft, like many other software vendors, has been using Product Keys for many years to license software. Likewise, the practice of using a Product ID to validate an installed product has been around for a while as well.

The hardware hash is an eight-byte value generated from information taken from 10 different components inside the computer and that is run through a mathematical calculation. The hash process is one way and thus this information cannot be reverse-engineered to yield any specific details about the computer from which it was obtained. The hardware hash also uses only a portion of each individual component hash value, thus further increasing user anonymity and preventing Microsoft from collecting any personally identifying information during the process of implementing Product Activation. Hardware hashes are discussed at greater length in the "How Windows XP Product Activation Works" section later in this chapter.

OEM Installations

A large majority of users acquire Windows XP in the process of purchasing a new computer. These customers don't need to take any action because Windows XP Professional is preloaded onto the new computer already. OEMs can preactivate Windows XP as part of the setup and configuration process before the new computer ever leaves the manufacturer. The overwhelming majority of new computers that feature Windows XP are preactivated by the OEM before shipping. The chief difference between how OEMs license Windows XP comes in how they choose to implement Product Activation.

System Locked Preinstallation

Many OEM computers come with a system restore CD-ROM that allows the user to perform a complete reinstallation or repair of the installed software components, including the operating system. In this way a specific CD-ROM can be tied to a specific system BIOS, thus preventing the CD from being used to install Windows on any other computer. Although OEM CD BIOS locking is not new, it has been expanded and now features integrated Product Activation. This method of protecting the software product is called *System Locked Preinstallation*, or *SLP*.

When SLP is implemented, the information stored in the BIOS is what protects against casual piracy such as installing the product on another computer. No communication is required with the Microsoft activation center, and thus the hardware hash value is required to be calculated. This form of Product Activation relies entirely on the BIOS information matching the SLP information at boot time. Because no hardware hash is calculated, you could thus change out every piece of hardware in the OEM computer without the need for reactivation of Windows XP Professional. In cases where the motherboard must be replaced, this could also be done without reactivation as long as the replacement motherboard was from the same OEM and contained the proper BIOS. Should a different motherboard that has nonmatching BIOS information be installed in the OEM computer, the Windows XP installation would then require reactivation within 30 days via the Internet or telephone call.

Using Standard Product Activation

If desired, an OEM can also activate a Windows XP installation in the same way that retail purchase versions are activated. OEM computer installations activated using the standard Product Activation methods have all the same restrictions that retail purchase versions of Windows XP Professional do.

No OEM Product Activation

Some OEMs may choose to not activate Windows XP at all. Newly purchased OEM computers that fall under this category require Product Activation by the consumer using the standard Product Activation methods, either via the Internet or by telephone call to Microsoft.

Volume Licensing

The simplest of all scenarios occurs when dealing with Windows XP Professional licenses acquired through one of the Microsoft volume licensing agreements, such as Microsoft Open License, Enterprise Agreement, or Select License. Such installations do not require activation.

Windows XP Professional installations that are performed using volume licensing media and volume licensing keys (VLK) have no Product Activation, hardware checking, or limitations on product installation or disk imaging.

Licensing Lingo

For more information on Microsoft volume licensing and the various programs, see the Microsoft Licensing home page located at http://microsoft.com/licensing/.

How Windows XP Product Activation Works

As mentioned previously, the hardware hash and the Product ID are the two parts that make up the Installation ID. The Product ID is directly tied to the Product Key supplied with the Windows XP retail product. OEMs usually supply the Product Key with media they ship with new computers. Of the Product ID and the hardware hash, only the hardware hash truly identifies a particular computer enough for Product Activation's purposes. Thus, the hardware hash is of some concern to you because it ultimately controls how Product Activation functions and whether or not activation is required on an installation.

Table 3.12 lists the hardware components that are used in calculating the hardware hash and the length of the data (in bits) that makes up the hardware hash. The hardware hash value comprises two 32-bit double words, for a total of 64 bits (or 8 bytes) worth of data.

Table 3.12 Hardware Hash Components

Component	Length of Hash Value (in Bits)
Volume serial number	10
Network adapter MAC address	10
CD-ROM/DVD-ROM/CD-RW identifier	7
Graphics display adapter	5
Amount of installed RAM (various ranges)	3
CPU type	3
CPU serial number	6
Hard drive serial number	7
SCSI controller serial number	5
IDE controller serial number	4
Docking capability	1
Hardware hash version (version of algorithm used)	3

The first four components make up the first double-word value, with the rest of the list making up the second double-word value. With the exception of the amount of installed RAM and the hardware hash version, selected bits of an MD5 hash are used to calculate all other values.

The value for a docking-capable computer also includes PCMCIA cards because using either a docking station or PCMCIA cards can cause hardware to appear and disappear. This can lead to the appearance of devices being changed when they are simply not present at that time—such as when a portable computer is undocked.

The possible values for the installed RAM value are listed in Table 3.13. As of the time of this writing, the hardware hash value is always set to a value of 001 decimal, which is a hex value of 0x01. If a component is not installed, such as a SCSI host adapter, the value returned in the hardware hash is a zero value.

Hex, Huh?

Hexadecimal, or more commonly hex, uses the numbers 0–9 and the letters A–F to form a base-16 numbering system. The 0x in front of a hex value simply notates it as a hexadecimal value.

For a great primer on hexadecimal numbering, see the Intuitor Hexadecimal Headquarters located at http://www.intuitor.com/hex/.

Table 3.13   RAM Amounts and Corresponding Hash Values

Amount of RAM Installed	Value
Less than 32MB	1
32MB–63MB	2
64MB–127MB	3
128MB–255MB	4
256MB–511MB	5
512MB–1023MB	6
More than 1023MB	7

As an example, the processor serial number is 96 bits in length. When Product Activation performs the hash calculation on that 96-bit value, it returns a 128-bit–long value. Of these 128 bits in the hash value, only 6 bits of data are actually used in the hardware hash value that forms part of the Installation ID.

Six bits provides 64 different combinations (2^6); thus for the millions of computers in existence, only 64 possible processor hash values are possible. As only a fraction of the original data is used in the Product Activation calculation, the data cannot be reverse-engineered, as previously mentioned. The processor serial number can never be determined from these six bits of data; the same holds true for all the other components on which Product Activation performs hashes. In this way, the hardware hash has purposely been designed by Microsoft to ensure that the user's privacy is respected at all times.

Perfect Privacy?

Although Microsoft has gone to great lengths to ensure that your private information stays private at all times, no process is perfect, and Product Activation is no exception. For more alternative views on the security of Product Activation, see the Fully Licensed FAQ on Product Activation at http://www.licenturion.com/xp/fully-licensed-faq.txt.

During the installation of Windows XP, the hardware hash is calculated. These eight bytes of data, when combined with the Product ID (nine bytes) make up the Installation ID. When Product Activation is conducted via the Internet, these 17 bytes of data are sent to the Microsoft activation servers in binary format, along with header information, over a secure sockets (SSL) connection.

The activation process requires three steps when completed over the Internet:

1. A handshake request, which establishes the connection between the Windows XP Professional computer and the Microsoft activation servers.

2. A license request, in which the Windows XP Professional computer asks for a PKCS10 digital certificate from the Microsoft activation servers.

3. An acknowledgement request, in which the Microsoft activation servers transmit a signed digital certificate activating the installation.

If the Internet activation succeeds, Product Activation is complete and does not again become an issue unless you exceed the maximum number of allowed changes, as detailed in the "Number of Changeable Items" section.

Should Internet activation not be feasible or desirable, telephone activation is possible as outlined in the following process:

1. Locate the appropriate telephone number by selecting the country from which you are calling.

2. Provide the 50-decimal digit Installation ID to the Microsoft representative.

3. Enter in the corresponding 42-decimal digit Confirmation ID as supplied by the Microsoft representative.

For More Information...

For more information on Product Activation, including how the hardware hash values are calculated for each hardware component, see the Fully Licensed website at http://www.licenturion.com/xp/.

Number of Changeable Items

After Windows XP has been activated, the hardware hash is rechecked at every user logon event. This serves to reduce another prevalent form of software piracy—that of disk cloning. *Disk cloning* is an asset to administrators looking to quickly deploy multiple copies of Windows XP, but is illegal for anyone who doesn't have the required Product Keys. In most legal cases, disk cloning is done with a volume license copy of Windows XP Professional, using a Volume License Key, which does not require Product Activation in the first place.

When Windows XP performs its hardware check, it is looking for changes in the hardware configuration of the computer. If a substantially different configuration is detected, reactivation is required. The actual number of components that will result in a reactivation scenario is discussed shortly. The hardware check at login is done after the SLP BIOS check, should the SLP BIOS check fail. As long as an OEM computer is using a genuine replacement motherboard from the OEM containing the correct BIOS data, all other components in an OEM computer activated using the SLP BIOS method can be changed out without requiring reactivation of Windows XP.

The number of hardware items that it takes to achieve "substantially different" configuration (in Microsoft speak) is dependent on two things: whether the computer has a network adapter at the time of Windows XP activation, and whether the computer is dockable (this also includes the presence of PCMCIA slots), as outlined in Table 3.14.

Table 3.14   Number of Changed Components to Require Reactivation

Network Adapter Status	Docking Capability	Number of Changed Components to Require Reactivation
None installed at the time of Windows XP activation	No	4 or more
Installed at the time of Windows XP activation and subsequently changed	No	4 or more
Installed at the time of Windows XP activation and not changed	No	6 or more
None installed at the time of Windows XP activation	Yes	7 or more
Installed at the time of Windows XP activation and subsequently changed	Yes	7 or more
Installed at the time of Windows XP activation and not changed	Yes	9 or more

To help explain Table 3.14, two scenarios might be helpful:

- A computer has a network adapter installed at the time of Windows XP activation. You later change the motherboard, CPU, video adapter, and CD-ROM drive. Additionally, you add more memory and a second hard drive.

  Reactivation is not required in this instance because only five components have been changed: motherboard, CPU, video adapter, CD-ROM, and RAM (amount). The addition of a second hard drive is not of significance to Product Activation. If you were to change six or more hardware components, reactivation would be required.

- A computer has no network adapter installed at the time of Windows XP Professional activation. You later change the motherboard, CPU, video adapter, and CD-ROM drive. Additionally, you add more memory and a second hard drive.

  Reactivation is required in this instance because five components have been changed: motherboard, CPU, video adapter, CD-ROM, and RAM (amount). When you change four or more hardware components, reactivation is required.

If a single device is changed repeatedly, such as a video adapter that is changed from the original one to new adapter A and later to new adapter B, this is evaluated as only one change. Either the current hardware is the same as when activation was completed or it's not. Windows XP doesn't care how many changes have been made in the interim. Adding components after activation that were not present at the time of activation also has no impact on the hardware hash and is ignored by Windows XP during its check to determine whether reactivation is necessary. Microsoft has also built two additional loopholes into Product Activation for power users who frequently reinstall Windows XP or who frequently change the hardware configuration of their computers. Windows XP can be reinstalled and subsequently reactivated on the same computer an infinite number of times. In cases where the hardware configuration has changed enough to require reactivation, Microsoft allows a maximum of four reactivations per year on "substantially different" hardware—this should be enough to keep most power users happy as they continually tweak their systems. Both of these reactivation events can occur over the Internet instead of requiring a phone call.

Windows Vista Product Activation with MAK and KMS

The basic process of activating computers running retail or upgrade versions of Windows Vista is similar to that used for Windows XP. However, Windows Vista includes a new activation requirement for volume licenses, Volume Activation 2.0.

Volume Activation 2.0 offers two types of keys for systems using a volume-licensed edition of Windows Vista:

- Multiple Activation Keys (MAK)
- Key Management Service (KMS)

MAK supports two activation methods:

- MAK Independent Activation, in which each computer contacts Microsoft individually for activation
- MAK Proxy Activation, in which one computer contacts Microsoft to activate a group of computers that require activation

MAK Product Keys can be configured before or after the installation of Windows Vista, using any of the following methods:

- Activation section of the computer's properties sheet
- Running a script
- During installation with Setup.exe or Windows Deployment Services with the Unattend.xml answer file

MAK activation is a one-time process unless substantial changes to hardware take place. In such cases, the computer(s) with substantial hardware changes would need to be reactivated. In addition to Internet and phone activation methods, you can also use the Volume Activation Management Tool (VAMT), available from www.microsoft.com/downloads.

KMS is designed for situations in which an organization prefers to run activation locally and has at least 25 Windows Vista client computers consistently connecting to the organization's network. A server running the KMS service can support hundreds of thousands of clients, so the service can be co-hosted with other services. KMS activation, unlike MAK activation, must be renewed every 180 days to maintain activation. By default, KMS clients attempt connection every two hours to the KMS host until they are activated, and then attempt connection every seven days until successful, at which point their 180-day activation is renewed. The connection frequency for both events can be changed from the defaults.

For more information about configuring Windows Vista volume licenses with MAK and KMS, see the Windows Vista Volume Activation Technical Guidance Home Page at http://technet.microsoft.com/en-us/windowsvista/bb335280.aspx.

Windows Genuine Advantage for Windows XP and Vista

As a secondary method to discourage software piracy, Microsoft has created the Windows Genuine Advantage (WGA) authentication service for Microsoft Windows XP and Microsoft Windows Vista. (Microsoft Office also uses WGA, but its features vary and are not discussed in this section.)

When a user of Windows XP attempts to download designated "Genuine Windows" updates from the Microsoft Download Center or optional (nonsecurity) updates from Windows Update, the WGA server checks to see whether the system has been validated. If not, users running Internet Explorer are prompted to install an ActiveX control that is used to validate Windows. Users running Mozilla Firefox are prompted to install a WGA validation browser plug-in that provides the same features as the ActiveX control used by Internet Explorer for WGA validation.

This control checks for various types of counterfeiting methods, duplicate license keys, and so forth. If the system passes the validation checks, the WGA ActiveX control stores a license file to indicate the validation has taken place so that the system does not require revalidation in the future.

Note

To validate Windows XP systems that are configured to block installation of ActiveX controls or if you use other web browsers, use the "Validate Now" program available from http://www.microsoft.com/genuine/downloads/RunHTA.aspx?displaylang=en.

Windows Vista includes integrated support for Windows Genuine Advantage; no ActiveX control or plug-in is necessary.

Troubleshooting Nonvalidated Installations

If your Windows XP system does not pass validation, this problem could be caused by several issues:

- Using an individual license that is in use by another system, or is a volume license key that the user does not have the right to use. Some common causes include a reinstallation of a previously validated Windows XP system using a copy of Windows XP with a different license number, or installing the same copy on more than one system owned by a particular user.

- Using a counterfeit copy of Windows XP—The Microsoft How to Tell website (available from a link at http://www.microsoft.com/genuine/downloads/FailureScenarios.aspx) can be used to determine whether a particular copy of Windows XP is legitimate.

- Purchasing a copy of Windows on a used computer—Microsoft recommends running the validation tool on the computer before you purchase it whenever possible.

Microsoft estimates that about 80% of failed validations can be traced to these and similar causes. However, it is also possible to have validation fail for other reasons, including problems with Microsoft's WGA validation servers. To rerun validation and to receive a report indicating why your system can't be validated (if validation fails), use the Validate Now button on the Microsoft Genuine Advantage Support page at http://www.microsoft.com/genuine/selfhelp/support.aspx. To troubleshoot problems with WGA, see the Windows Genuine Advantage Solution Center at http://support.microsoft.com/ph/9860.

How Windows Genuine Advantage Changes with Vista SP1

With the original version of Windows Vista, Windows Genuine Advantage takes some drastic steps if it determines that a nongenuine copy of Windows Vista is in use: Those systems lose access to ReadyBoost, Windows Aero, and Windows Defender, as well as access to downloads and nonsecurity updates through Windows Update. Plus, the lower-right corner of the display also states This copy of Windows is not genuine. If Windows Vista is not activated within 30 days, the system goes into a reduced functionality mode that permits you to run only the IE web browser for 60 minutes at a time, or permits you to boot the system into Safe Mode.

Because WGA servers sometimes go offline and have sometimes mistaken driver changes for hardware changes, many Windows Vista users have seen their operating systems incorrectly labeled as not authentic and lost major functionality.

As a consequence, Windows Vista SP1 makes major changes in how WGA and product activation work. Systems that fail WGA checks or are not activated will no longer lose functionality. Instead, you will see an hourly pop-up message that you need to activate or validate your copy of Windows Vista and the system wallpaper will change to black.

The next chapter discusses performing an installation of Windows XP or Windows Vista as an upgrade to a system with a previous version of Windows already installed. It may be tempting to skip over this chapter should you not intend to perform an upgrade installation; however, this chapter also includes crucial information on how to migrate key user data and applications from an existing installation to a new one as well as information on installing Windows XP Service Pack 2 or Windows Vista.

Upgrading Windows

Windows XP Upgrade Installations

Chapter 1, "Windows Version History," introduced you to the various versions of Windows, past and present, and briefly mentioned the features of Windows XP and Windows Vista. Large numbers of individuals and companies still have older versions of Windows running on their computers.

In Chapter 3, "Installing Windows," we talked about baseline Windows XP and Windows Vista installation concepts and features as well as how to perform clean and professional installations of the Windows XP and Windows Vista operating system. In this section I cover how to perform an upgrade Windows XP installation, in which Windows XP replaces a previous Windows OS without first removing all data from the system drive and starting from scratch. Later in this chapter I'll tackle Windows Vista upgrade installations, as well as how to migrate an existing installation and handle the installation of service packs.

An upgrade installation is most useful in cases where you have customized user settings that you want to preserve. This option, however, does not always work flawlessly, especially if you are upgrading from an operating system other than Windows 2000 Professional or Windows XP Home Edition (to XP Pro) due to the differences in the Registry structure and the startup process.

Stability issues aside, if you allow Windows XP to back up the existing operating system during the upgrade, you can later uninstall Windows XP and effectively revert your computer back to the state it was in immediately preceding the Windows XP upgrade. The ability to uninstall is contingent on the disk volume being FAT32 and not NTFS, that you have not created or deleted any disk volumes on the system, and that you do not delete any backup files created during the upgrade installation process.

Deciding Whether an Upgrade to Windows XP Is Worthwhile

Most individuals and companies acquire Windows XP installed on a new computer. However, existing computers running older versions of Windows may be present in many organizations. Although users of older versions of Windows would like to take advantage of the improved capabilities of Windows XP, upgrades are not always feasible. First and foremost, there is the significant cost of new software and its licenses. In addition, you need to take into account the following:

- Many older computers lack the hardware resources required to run Windows XP.
- You cannot upgrade all operating systems directly to Windows XP.
- Upgrading a large number of computers on a network involves a considerable investment in time and money.
- Applications running on existing computers may not be compatible with Windows XP.

Available Upgrade Paths

Possible upgrade paths for computers running older Windows operating systems depend on the operating system currently installed as well as the version of Windows XP you plan to install. Table 4.1 outlines the available upgrade paths.

Table 4.1 Available Windows XP Upgrade Paths

Operating System	Upgrading to Windows XP Home Edition	Upgrading to Windows XP Professional
Windows 98/Me	Can upgrade directly.	Can upgrade directly.
Windows NT 4.0 Workstation or Windows 2000 Professional	Cannot upgrade. You must perform a clean installation.	Can upgrade directly.
Windows XP Home Edition	–	Can upgrade directly.
Windows 3.1x/95	Upgrade to Windows 98, and then upgrade to Windows XP.	Upgrade to Windows 98, and then upgrade to Windows XP.
Windows NT 3.x Workstation	Cannot upgrade. You must perform a clean installation.	Upgrade to Windows NT 4.0, and then upgrade to Windows XP.
Windows NT/2000 Server	Cannot upgrade. You must perform a clean installation.	Cannot upgrade. You must perform a clean installation.

You should note that although dual upgrade paths described in Table 3.1 for Windows 3.1x/95/NT 3.x computers are theoretically possible, most computers running these older operating systems do not have the required hardware for running Windows XP. Should you need to upgrade such an older computer to Windows XP, it is preferable to perform a clean installation of Windows XP as described in Chapter 3, after you have upgraded the hardware to an appropriate level.

In addition, it is not possible to upgrade any non-Windows computers (Linux, UNIX, MS-DOS, OS/2, and so on) to Windows XP. You must perform a clean installation of Windows XP on these computers.

Verifying System Compatibility

The Windows XP compatibility tool enables you to create a compatibility report that identifies any problems with hardware or software on a computer that is to be upgraded to Windows XP. You can run this compatibility tool from the Windows XP CD-ROM by following these steps:

1. Insert the Windows XP (Home Edition or Professional) CD-ROM.

2. From the Welcome to Microsoft Windows XP screen, select the Check System Compatibility link.

3. Select the Check My System Automatically link. Follow the prompts to update setup files (if necessary). Once that's complete, the advisor starts.

Tip

You can also test your computer's Windows XP compatibility by opening a command prompt or the Run dialog box and typing the following: **d:\i386\WINNT32 /CHECKUPGRADEONLY** (where d: is the drive containing the Windows XP CD-ROM).

4. After a minute or two, the Microsoft Windows Upgrade Advisor displays a list of items that may not be compatible with Windows XP, as shown in Figure 4.1. If no incompatible items are found, it informs you of this fact.

5. To obtain additional information on any item, select it and click More Details. To save a copy of the compatibility report, click Save As, type the name of the file to be saved in the dialog box that appears, and then click Save. Click Finish to close the Microsoft Windows Upgrade Advisor.

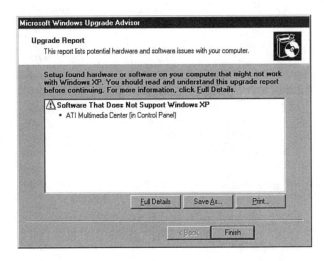

Figure 4.1 The report produced by the Microsoft Windows Upgrade Advisor notifies you of any hardware or software that may not work properly on Windows XP.

Items that may be included in the upgrade report shown in Figure 4.1 include the following:

- Incompatible software that may require upgrade packs, or applications that are not compatible with the Control Panel in Windows XP. If you cannot obtain upgrades, you may need to remove the application using Control Panel Add/Remove Programs before upgrading to Windows XP. If you do not remove these applications, you may receive an error message when upgrading to Windows XP. See Knowledge Base article 891891, available at http://support.microsoft.com for more information.

- Incompatible entries in MS-DOS files such as `Autoexec.bat` and `Config.sys`.

- Plug and Play hardware devices that are incompatible with Windows XP Professional or require additional files.

Note

When run on Windows NT 4.0, the Microsoft Windows Upgrade Advisor may not provide the option to download upgraded Setup files. If this happens, simply continue the earlier procedure from step 3.

Note that if you do not have a Windows XP CD available and are wondering whether your computer will support an upgrade, the Windows XP Upgrade Advisor is available from Microsoft at http://www.microsoft.com/windowsxp/pro/upgrading/advisor.mspx.

Upgrade Scenarios

After you have run the Microsoft Windows Upgrade Advisor and ascertained that you want to perform an upgrade installation of Windows XP, you are ready to proceed. The following section looks at upgrading computers running Windows 98, Windows NT 4.0, and Windows 2000 to Windows XP.

Before Upgrading to Windows XP

After you are satisfied that an upgrade is worthwhile, you should perform several additional preliminary tasks. The following tasks are suggested, and depend on the current operating system on the computer:

- Back up your data before upgrading, in case something goes wrong during the upgrade. The easiest way to perform the backup is to simply copy the data folders to another disk or computer because the Windows 98/Me backup and restore utilities are not compatible with those in Windows XP.

- Check the availability of BIOS upgrades from the BIOS manufacturer's website. If upgrades are available, you should install them before upgrading your computer. Otherwise, machines with older BIOS versions may not shut down or restart properly. Furthermore, if the computer is not Advanced Configuration and Power Interface (ACPI)–compatible, you may need a BIOS upgrade.

- Turn off power management features so that they do not activate during upgrade. You can do this from the Power Options applet in Control Panel.

- Use an antivirus program that has been updated with the most recent antivirus signatures to scan the computer to ensure that the computer is free of viruses. In addition, use an antispyware program to scan for and remove malicious software such as spyware, adware, and rootkits. After you have completed this task, remove or disable these programs because antivirus programs can interfere with the upgrade process.

■ Ensure that all hardware is listed in the Windows Hardware Compatibility List (available online at http://www.microsoft.com/whdc/hcl/default.mspx). You can use Device Manager on a Windows 98/Me/2000 computer or Windows NT Diagnostics on a Windows NT 4.0 computer to print out a list of all hardware components. Also check with hardware manufacturer websites for updated device drivers.

■ If you have used programs such as DriveSpace or DoubleSpace to compress partitions on computers running Windows 98 or Windows Me, you should decompress these partitions before upgrading to Windows XP, and then remove the compression utilities. On the other hand, it is not necessary to decompress files or folders on Windows NT or Windows 2000 computers that have been compressed using Windows NT/2000 NTFS compression.

■ If the Microsoft Windows Upgrade Advisor tool has identified software applications as being incompatible with Windows XP, upgrade or remove these programs. Software manufacturers may have released upgrade packs or newer versions that enable older programs to work properly with Windows XP, and with Windows XP SP2 in particular.

■ Ensure that the latest service pack is installed on your computer. In particular, Windows NT 4.0 computers must be running at least SP5 and preferably SP6a.

■ Ensure that no unnecessary programs are running when you are ready to begin the upgrade. Access the Task Manager or the Windows 98/Me Close Program dialog box, and close any programs that should not be running.

■ Windows XP does not support volume sets or stripe sets created on basic disk volumes in Windows NT 4.0 or Windows 2000. If you are upgrading a Windows NT 4.0 computer that contains volume sets or stripe sets, you should back up their contents and delete them before upgrading. If you are upgrading a Windows 2000 computer, convert the disks containing these volumes to dynamic storage. For more information on disk volumes in Windows XP, refer to Chapter 8, "Managing Windows," and Chapter 10, "File Systems."

Note

Because Windows XP is more architecturally similar to Windows NT/2000 than to Windows 98/Me, you generally have fewer application compatibility problems when upgrading a Windows NT or 2000 computer to Windows XP, relative to Windows 98/Me.

Upgrading a Windows NT 4.0 or 2000 Computer

After you have ensured that your computer meets all hardware requirements for Windows XP Professional and that you have performed all required preliminary tasks, you are ready to perform the actual upgrade. Remember that you cannot upgrade a computer running Windows NT 4.0 or 2000 to Windows XP Home Edition; you must upgrade to Windows XP Professional. In addition, you cannot upgrade a computer running a server version; you must perform a fresh install.

Note

Microsoft also makes an upgrade version of the Windows XP CD-ROM. Use of this version is nearly identical to the procedure displayed here, except that the option for New Installation (Advanced) is not present.

To upgrade a Windows 2000 Professional computer to Windows XP Professional with SP2, follow this procedure. Note that an upgrade from Windows NT 4.0 Workstation proceeds in a similar manner:

1. Insert the slipstreamed Windows XP/SP2 CD-ROM.

2. If the Welcome to Microsoft Windows XP screen does not appear, double-click the CD-ROM drive in Windows Explorer and then double-click the Setup icon.

Note

You can also upgrade by accessing the installation files from a distribution share located on a server on the network. To do so, use My Network Places (or Network Neighborhood in Windows NT 4.0) to map a drive to the distribution share. Then open the Run dialog box and type **x:\i386\winnt32.exe**, where x is the drive letter you used when mapping to the distribution share.

3. On the Welcome to Microsoft Windows XP screen, click Install Windows XP.

4. The Welcome to Windows Setup dialog box (see Figure 4.2) provides a choice of installation type. Select Upgrade (Recommended) to begin the upgrade, and then click Next. You would select New Installation (Advanced) to completely replace your current version of Windows or to create a dual-boot system.

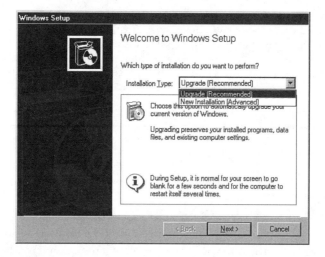

Figure 4.2   The Welcome to Windows Setup screen provides a choice between upgrading to Windows XP and performing a new installation.

5. The License Agreement screen appears. Read the license agreement, click I Accept This Agreement, and then click Next.

6. The Your Product Key screen appears. Type the 25-character alphanumeric product key and then click Next.

7. The Get Updated Setup Files dialog box appears and enables you to use Dynamic Update to obtain updated Setup files. If you have an Internet connection, you should select Yes,

Download the Updated Setup Files. Otherwise, select No, Skip This Step and Continue Installing Windows. Click Next to continue.

8. Installation files are copied and the computer restarts. This takes up to a minute, and involves copying of files to a separate folder on the computer's hard drive. At this point, no change has been made to the old operating system.

9. Press Enter to accept the default of Windows XP Professional Setup from the boot menu.

10. If prompted, insert the Windows XP Professional CD-ROM and press Enter. Then insert the Windows XP Professional Service Pack 2 CD-ROM and press Enter again. This may happen more than once. If informed that Setup cannot copy a file while the Windows XP Professional CD-ROM is in the drive, switch to the Windows XP Professional Service Pack 2 CD-ROM and press Enter.

11. Setup examines the computer's disks, and text-mode file copying proceeds for 5 to 10 minutes, and then the computer reboots again.

12. Windows XP Setup obtains its additional setup parameters from the previous Windows NT/2000 installation. This can take up to 40 minutes. You are asked for additional information only if Setup cannot obtain a required piece of information. You may be prompted for the original CD-ROM as described in step 10.

13. When installation has completed, the computer reboots and displays the Welcome to Microsoft Windows screen. Click Next.

14. The Help Protect Your PC screen (see Figure 4.3) enables you to turn on Automatic Updates, which enables the operating system to check for updates on a regular basis. You should select the Help Protect My PC by Turning on Automatic Updates Now option. Then click Next.

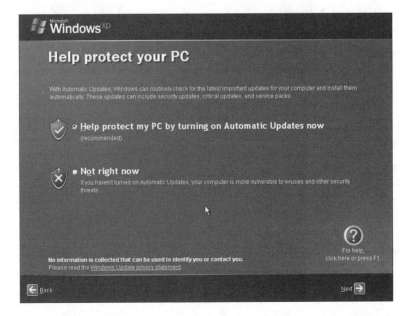

Figure 4.3 The Help Protect Your PC screen enables you to turn on Automatic Updates.

15. The Let's Activate Windows page appears and prompts you to perform Windows Product Activation (WPA). The options available and the procedure for performing WPA were discussed in Chapter 2.

16. Similar to the option presented during an original installation, enter your name and the names of any other users in the Who Will Use This Computer? page. You might not see this page when upgrading from Windows 2000 Professional. Click Next and then click Finish.

17. The logon page appears. Click your username to begin.

Note

When you upgrade from Windows NT 4.0 to Windows XP, user files and documents are stored in the `C:\WINNT\Profiles\%username%` folder for each user, rather than in the Windows XP default of `C:\Documents and Settings\%username%`. Unlike a new installation of Windows XP, the default desktop contains icons for My Documents, My Computer, and My Network Places.

Upgrading a Windows 98 Computer

As with a Windows NT 4.0 or 2000 computer, once you have performed all preliminary steps, you are ready to proceed with upgrading to Windows XP, either Home Edition or Professional. Upgrading a computer running Windows 98/Me is similar. Perform the following steps:

1. Insert the slipstreamed Windows XP/SP2 CD-ROM (or access a distribution share as described previously).

2. If the Welcome to Microsoft Windows XP screen does not appear, double-click the CD-ROM drive in Windows Explorer and then double-click the Setup icon.

3. On the Welcome to Microsoft Windows XP screen, click Install Windows XP.

4. As with Windows NT or 2000, the Welcome to Windows Setup page (refer to Figure 4.3) offers a choice of upgrading or performing a new installation. To upgrade your computer, select Upgrade (Recommended) and then click Next.

5. Accept the license agreement, and then click Next.

6. Type the Windows product key in the spaces provided, and then click Next.

7. Setup displays an Upgrade Report screen that informs you of possible compatibility issues with your computer (see Figure 4.4). If you have performed a proper assessment of system compatibility issues as described earlier in this chapter, you should not receive any additional warnings. Select the default of Show Me Hardware Issues and a Limited Set of Software Issues, and then click Next.

8. The Get Updated Setup Files screen (see Figure 4.5) enables you to download the updated Setup files from the Microsoft website. If you have an Internet connection, you should select this option. Otherwise select the No option. Then click Next.

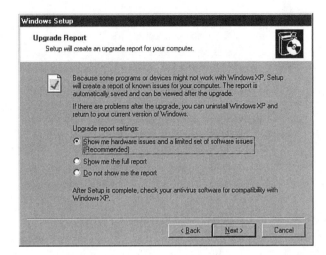

Figure 4.4   When upgrading from Windows 98/Me, Windows XP Setup enables you to create an upgrade report.

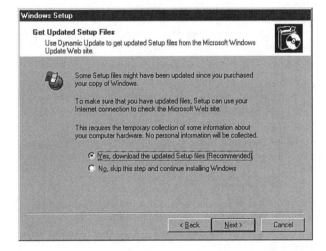

Figure 4.5   The Get Updated Setup Files screen enables you to download updates to the Windows XP Setup files.

9. Setup copies the installation files and restarts the computer. Select the default of Windows XP Professional (or Home Edition) Setup from the boot menu that is displayed. File copying continues and the computer reboots again. Installation proceeds with the Setup program gathering information from the previous Windows installation.

10. The computer reboots and displays the Welcome to Microsoft Windows screen. Click Next and follow the same instructions as provided in steps 13 to 15 of the procedure for upgrading Windows NT.

11. After you have entered the names of users, the Password Creation dialog box asks for passwords for new Windows XP accounts. Type and confirm a password for these accounts, and then click OK. Each of the listed accounts receives the same password, which you can later change from the Control Panel User Accounts applet.

12. Log on to Windows with the username and password supplied in step 11.

Similar to an upgrade from Windows NT, the upgraded desktop contains icons for My Documents, My Computer, and My Network Places. Windows creates a Documents and Settings folder with subfolders for each user who has logged on to the computer. However, documents stored in the C:\My Documents folder remain in this folder and are not moved to the new location of My Documents (C:\Documents and Settings\%username%\My Documents).

Troubleshooting a Failed Upgrade

Many problems that occur during upgrading an older Windows installation are similar to those you might encounter when installing Windows XP for the first time, as discussed in Chapter 3. You may also encounter one of the following problems:

■ Programs or services that are running may interfere with the upgrade process. As mentioned earlier in this chapter, use the Windows NT/2000 Task Manager or the Windows 98/Me Close Program dialog box to close unnecessary programs. You can also use the Msconfig.exe utility to choose Selective Startup, clear the check boxes associated with programs that start automatically, and then restart the computer. This procedure is also known as *clean booting*. Knowledge Base article 192926 provides additional information.

■ If Selective Startup does not work, you may need to start your computer in Safe mode (Windows 98/Me/2000). You can then run the Winnt32.exe command to begin upgrade. If your CD-ROM does not function in Safe mode, refer to Knowledge Base article 194846 for assistance.

■ You may receive messages informing you that Setup cannot copy a file. This may be the result of hardware problems such as an over-clocked processor or damaged memory. Try copying the contents of the Windows XP CD-ROM to a folder on the hard drive and installing from this location.

■ Incompatible hardware may result in the setup program failing to respond ("hanging") or a Stop message (blue screen error) appearing. Refer to the suggestions presented earlier in this chapter for checking system compatibility. Also refer to Knowledge Base article 310064 and other articles referenced therein.

■ If you are installing Windows XP to an SATA (Serial ATA) hard disk that uses an add-on host adapter or a discrete host adapter chip on the motherboard, the drive will not be recognized during installation if you don't install the appropriate driver when prompted. See "Windows XP Clean Install," Chapter 3, p. 158, for details.

■ An upgrade error related to the setup catalog may appear when you are attempting to upgrade Windows 98, Me, or XP Home Edition to Windows XP Professional. This problem may occur if the Setup routine fails to delete all files in the Windows\System32\Catroot2 folder. You can overcome this problem by starting a command prompt and renaming the Catroot2 subfolder. For additional information, refer to Knowledge Base article 307153.

Uninstalling Windows XP

When you upgrade a computer running Windows 98/Me to Windows XP Home Edition or Professional, the Setup routine automatically saves a copy of the Windows XP removal files to the Windows folder. These files enable you to later revert to the previous operating system if desired. The Add or Remove Programs applet in Control Panel contains a Windows XP Uninstall option that restores the previous operating system without changing any data you have created since upgrading to Windows XP. However, you may need to reinstall any applications that were installed or modified since you upgraded to Windows XP because these applications will not have the correct Registry entries for Windows 98/Me. Likewise, if you have removed any applications while running Windows XP, Start menu shortcuts will be present after you revert to Windows 98/Me. Simply delete these shortcuts if this happens.

Caution

If you have upgraded from Windows 98 or Windows Me and think you may want to revert to your previous operating system, do not convert your hard disk to the NTFS file system or upgrade the disk to dynamic storage. If you do, the option to uninstall Windows XP is no longer available. Refer to Chapter 10, "Windows File Systems," for more information on file systems in Windows XP.

Follow these steps to uninstall Windows XP:

1. Click Start, Control Panel, Add or Remove Programs.

2. As shown in Figure 4.6, the Add or Remove Programs applet will contain a Windows XP Uninstall entry. Select this entry and click Change/Remove.

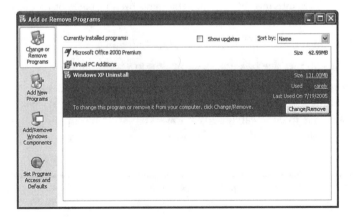

Figure 4.6   If you have upgraded from Windows 98/Me, you can uninstall Windows XP from the Add or Remove Programs applet in Control Panel.

3. Select Uninstall Windows XP from the options in the Uninstall Windows XP dialog box that appears, and then click Continue. Note that if the removal files are not present or have been deleted, it will not be possible to uninstall Windows XP. In this case, the Uninstall Windows XP option will not appear.

Tip

To delete the older OS files, follow the first three steps of this procedure, and then select the Remove the Backup of My Previous Operating System option, and click Continue.

4. The Windows XP Uninstall dialog box (see Figure 4.7) informs you of the programs that have been installed or modified since you installed Windows XP. You will need to reinstall these programs after you complete uninstalling Windows XP. Click Continue to uninstall Windows XP or Quit to cancel.

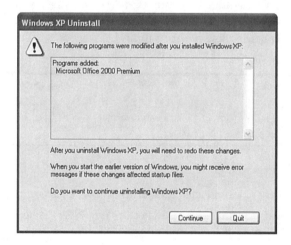

Figure 4.7   You are informed of programs that have been installed or modified since installing Windows XP.

5. Click Yes in the confirmation message box that appears.

6. An Uninstall message box appears and Windows XP shuts down.

7. The computer reboots and Windows uninstallation proceeds. When the computer reboots a second time, the previous Windows operating system will start. Note that the Documents and Settings folder created by Windows XP is still present and may contain documents created while Windows XP was running.

Tip

If you are unable to start Windows XP properly after upgrading from Windows 98/Me, you may be able to uninstall Windows XP from the Safe Mode with Command Prompt advanced startup option. See Knowledge Base article 308233 for more information.

Windows Vista Upgrade Installations

Windows Vista, like Windows XP, can be installed as an upgrade to previous operating systems as well as a clean installation to an empty hard disk. However, there are numerous differences between a Windows XP upgrade installation and a Windows Vista upgrade installation. For one, you will notice many improvements over Windows XP upgrade installations:

- A Windows Vista upgrade installation, although it migrates applications and settings from the previous version, does so without retaining old drivers and DLL files from Windows XP. The result is that a Windows Vista upgrade installation runs as efficiently as a clean install.

- A Windows Vista upgrade installation uses only the NTFS file system, enabling advanced security features such as group and user access control and EFS file/folder encryption (not supported in Windows Vista Home Basic/Premium editions). FAT32 is supported only for data drives.

- A Windows Vista upgrade installation uses a staged image-based design, meaning that you can start the installation and it runs with minimal user interaction. You don't need to enter configuration information several times during the setup, making for an easier installation.

There are, however, a few shortcoming to performing an upgrade installation of Windows Vista:

- A Windows Vista upgrade installation can take substantially longer than a clean install, in part because of the migration of applications and data files. During the file copy process, a message appears advising you that an upgrade can take "several hours" to finish.

- A Windows Vista upgrade installation uses more disk space than a clean install because the previous version of Windows occupies some disk space.

- The official method to revert to Windows XP after upgrading to Windows Vista involves a number of manual steps, rather than just a Control Panel option as in Windows XP. Also, some systems do not have the Windows.old folder necessary to revert to Windows XP after an upgrade to Vista.

Note

Although an upgrade installation does take more time than a clean install, by the time you factor in installation of applications and restoration of data to the clean installation, the difference might not be significant in some cases. If you are planning to migrate a large number of similar systems from Windows XP to Windows Vista, you might want to compare the overall time it takes with each installation method (including reinstallation of programs and restoration of data files) before deciding which one to use.

Deciding Whether an Upgrade to Vista Is Worthwhile

Most individuals and companies acquire Windows Vista installed on a new computer. However, a large established base of existing computers running Windows XP is present in nearly all organizations. Although Windows Vista offers new security, networking, multimedia, and system management features, upgrades are not always feasible. In addition to the significant cost of new software and its licenses, the following might also influence your decision:

- Many older and some recent computers lack the hardware resources required to run Windows Vista efficiently or at all. Such systems might also lack the capability to run the 3D Aero desktop or other premium features.

- You cannot upgrade all operating systems directly to Windows Vista.

- Upgrading a large number of computers on a network involves a considerable investment in time and money.

- Applications running on existing computers may not be compatible with Windows Vista.

Available Upgrade Paths to Windows Vista

Possible upgrade paths for computers running older Windows operating systems depend on the operating system currently installed, as well as the version of Windows Vista you plan to install. Table 4.2 outlines the available upgrade paths.

Table 4.2   Available Windows Vista Upgrade Paths

Windows Version	Vista Home Basic	Vista Home Premium	Vista Business	Vista Ultimate
Windows XP Home	Yes	Yes	Yes	Yes
Windows XP Professional	No	No	Yes	Yes
Windows XP Media Center Edition	No	Yes	No	Yes
Windows XP Tablet Edition	No	No	Yes	Yes

If you own Windows 2000 Professional or Windows XP Professional x64 Edition, you can purchase and install the upgrade editions of Windows Vista Business or Ultimate, but you must perform a clean install.

▶▶ For information about performing a clean install, **see** "Installing Windows," **p. 129**.

Verifying System Compatibility for Windows Vista

The Windows Vista Upgrade Advisor enables you to create a compatibility report that identifies any problems with hardware or software on a computer that is to be upgraded to Windows Vista.

Note

The Windows Vista Upgrade Advisor not only checks your system to see whether it can run any edition of Windows Vista, but also compares the requirements for each edition of Windows Vista, so you can use it to determine whether your Vista system is ready for a Windows Anytime Upgrade, using the Windows Anytime Upgrade disc. The Windows Anytime Upgrade disc is available from many stores that sell Windows Vista retail product or direct from Microsoft.

If you want to run the Windows Vista Upgrade Advisor before purchasing Windows Vista, go to http://www.microsoft.com/windows/products/windowsvista/buyorupgrade/upgradeadvisor.mspx and follow the instructions in the following text, starting with step 4.

You can run this compatibility tool on any 32-bit version of Windows XP (or Windows Vista) from the Windows Vista DVD by following these steps:

1. Insert the Windows Vista DVD.

2. From the opening (Install Windows) screen, select the Check Compatibility Online link. Note: You must have a working Internet connection to check compatibility.

3. Internet Explorer opens the Windows Vista: Upgrade Advisor website.

4. Connect and turn on any external USB or other devices before continuing.

5. Click the Download Windows Upgrade Advisor link to open the Download page.

6. Click Download to continue.

7. The File Download—Security Warning dialog appears. To run the upgrade advisor now, click Run. The installation package is about 6.6MB. (If you want to run the Upgrade Advisor later, or transfer the installation file to other machines, click Save and specify a folder.)

8. Click Run when prompted.

9. Click Next to start the installation process.

10. Select I Agree to agree to the license agreement, and click Next.

11. Click Next to accept the default installation location, or click Browse to select another location.

12. By default, a desktop shortcut is created. To prevent a shortcut from being created, click Don't Create Desktop Shortcut. Click Next.

13. Click Close to close the install program and start the Upgrade Advisor. The Upgrade Advisor checks for updates and installs them before continuing.

14. To scan your system, click Start Scan. During the scan, you can review a check list of Windows Vista features by edition or view major features and benefits of each edition, using the buttons at the bottom of the scan window.

15. When the scan is complete (it takes less than 5 minutes on most systems), click See Details.

16. The Upgrade Advisor recommends a Windows Vista edition (highlighted in the left pane) and it checks compatibility in three areas: system requirements (can your hardware run Windows Vista?), devices (are your devices supported by Windows Vista?), and programs (will your programs run under Windows Vista?).

17. Click any of the See Details buttons to open the multi-tabbed Report Details dialog (Figure 4.8 shows the Devices tab). To save the report, click Save Report. To print the report, click Print Report.

Tip

If you prefer compatibility information about a different Windows Vista edition than the one selected by Upgrade Advisor, select it from the left pane in step 16, or use the back arrow to return to this dialog and select it after step 17. If you are considering an upgrade to a higher version (such as Ultimate instead of Home Premium or Business), you might see more issues to deal with compared to the original report.

Figure 4.8 Windows Vista Upgrade Advisor's Devices tab lists any device issues you need to deal with before installing Windows Vista.

The Report Details dialog provides a convenient way to review possible issues with your system and helps you prepare to upgrade to Windows Vista:

- The System tab reports any issues with system configuration, such as not enough memory or available hard disk space.

- The Devices tab reports any devices that need driver updates or have other problems.

- The Programs tab reports any programs that are not compatible with Vista or might need to be uninstalled before an upgrade to Vista.

- The Task List tab places issues described in other tabs into one of two lists: Things You Need to Do Before Installing Windows Vista, and Things You Need to Do After Installing Windows Vista.

When you print the report or save it to disk, each tab becomes a section of the report. The Task List portion of the report from a typical system is shown in Figure 4.9.

Note

Before upgrading to Windows Vista, go to Windows Update to install critical updates for your system. After upgrading to Windows Vista, also go to Windows Update to install critical updates.

Upgrading from Windows XP to Windows Vista

After you have run the Microsoft Windows Upgrade Advisor and determined that you want to perform an upgrade installation of Windows Vista, you are ready to proceed.

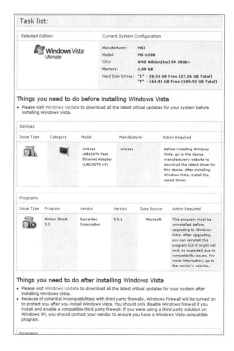

Figure 4.9   Windows Vista Upgrade Advisor's Task List tab makes it easy to determine what you need to do before and after installing Windows Vista.

Before Upgrading to Windows Vista

After you are satisfied that an upgrade is worthwhile, you should perform several additional preliminary tasks. The following tasks are suggested, and depend on the current operating system on the computer:

- Back up your data before upgrading, in case something goes wrong during the upgrade. You can use Windows XP's NT Backup or Backup Wizard, a third-party program compatible with Windows XP and Vista, or Windows Vista's Windows Easy Transfer program. Be sure to back up files that may be stored in the hidden `Username\AppData` folder, such as the Outlook Express email store.

Tip

Although Windows Vista's File and Folder Backup utility is not compatible with Windows XP's NT Backup, you can download the Windows NT Backup—Restore Utility from the Downloads section of Microsoft.com after you install Windows Vista. This utility enables Windows Vista to read and restore NT Backup files created with Windows XP or Windows Server 2003. It is available in 32-bit and 64-bit versions.

You must enable the Removable Storage Service in Vista before using this program. To enable it, open Control Panel, Programs, Programs and Features, select Turn Windows Features On or Off, click the check box for Removable Storage Management, and click OK.

■ Check the availability of BIOS upgrades from the BIOS manufacturer's website. If upgrades are available, you should install them before upgrading your computer. Otherwise, machines with older BIOS versions may not properly support all Windows Vista features, including power management.

■ Turn off power management features so that they do not activate during upgrade. You can do this from the Power Options applet in Control Panel.

■ Use an antivirus program that has been updated with the most recent antivirus signatures to scan the computer to ensure that the computer is free of viruses. In addition, use another program such as the Microsoft Windows Defender (http://www.microsoft.com/athome/security/spyware/software/default.mspx) or a third-party tool to scan for and remove malicious software such as spyware, adware, and rootkits. After you have completed this task, remove or disable these programs because antivirus programs can interfere with the upgrade process.

■ Download updated device drivers for devices that were identified by Upgrade Advisor as needing updates. If you are unable to locate native Windows Vista drivers, keep in mind that you can use Windows XP drivers for most device categories. Note that you must provide a driver after Windows Vista installation for any devices tagged by Upgrade Advisor, even if the device was running under Windows XP, and you must use a Windows XP device driver!

■ If the Windows Vista Upgrade Advisor tool has identified software applications as being incompatible with Windows Vista, upgrade or remove these programs. Software manufacturers may have released upgrade packs or newer versions that enable older programs to work properly with Windows Vista.

Note

It may be possible to run certain older applications in compatibility mode after you have upgraded to Windows Vista; see Chapter 12, "Windows Troubleshooting," for further details.

■ Ensure that the latest service pack and updates are installed on your computer.

■ Ensure that no unnecessary programs are running when you are ready to begin the upgrade. Access the Task Manager dialog box, and close any programs that should not be running.

■ Create an image backup of your Windows XP installation, using Norton Ghost, Acronis True Image, or another program of your choice. Make sure that you can restore this backup if necessary if you want to go back to XP after the Windows Vista upgrade.

Caution

Although the Windows Vista upgrade process is supposed to save your previous version of Windows in a folder called `Windows.old`, this doesn't always happen, particularly on systems with limited disk space. So, ensure that you make your own image backup first! Without an image backup or the `Windows.old` folder, you cannot revert to your previous Windows XP installation after upgrading to Windows Vista. Instead, you need to perform a clean install of Windows XP, reinstall your applications, and restore your data.

Upgrading a Windows XP Computer to Windows Vista

After you have ensured that your computer meets all hardware requirements for Windows Vista and that you have performed all required preliminary tasks, you are ready to perform the actual upgrade.

To upgrade a Windows XP computer to Windows Vista, follow this procedure:

1. Insert the Windows Vista DVD (or CD) into the computer.

2. If the Install Windows dialog does not appear, double-click the DVD drive icon in Windows Explorer and then double-click the Setup icon.

Note

You can also upgrade by accessing the installation files from a distribution share located on a server on the network. To do so, use My Network Places to open the shared folder. Then double-click the Setup icon in the root folder.

3. On the Install Windows screen, click Install Now.

4. When prompted, click Go Online to Get the Latest Updates for Installation. If you select this option (recommended), your computer must stay connected to the Internet during the entire setup process.

5. Vista prompts you to enter the product key. You should do so at this time *unless* you are not certain you plan to keep Windows Vista on this system (for example, you are installing it for testing purposes or it's a marginal hardware platform).

6. The Automatically Activate Windows box below the product key is checked. Clear the box if you are not entering the product key at this time. Click Next to continue.

Tip

If you're not certain that the system you're using for Vista is going to be suitable, make sure the automatic activation check box is cleared. There's no need to rush this step. As with previous versions, you have 30 days before you must activate Vista.

7. If you do not enter your product key in step 5, a pop-up dialog box appears asking you to enter your product key now. Click Yes if you decide to get it over with, or No if you're not ready to enter it.

8. If you do not enter your product key in step 5 or step 7, you must select your edition of Windows Vista. Make sure that you select the edition you purchased. Select it, click the I Have Selected check box, and click Next.

9. The License Agreement screen appears. Read the license agreement, click I Accept This Agreement, and then click Next.

10. Select Upgrade as the installation type, and click Next. Use the Advanced option if you prefer to set up Windows Vista as a dual-boot configuration (see Chapter 3 for details).

11. Before continuing, Window Vista performs a compatibility check. If any potential problems are detected, a window displaying details or a link to details appears. Make note of any problems, and then click Next to continue. Windows Vista begins to copy files.

12. After the file copy, expansion, and feature setup processes are completed, the system reboots.

13. After the system reboots, the Help Protect Windows Automatically dialog appears. Use Recommended Settings is selected by default. This setting automatically installs both important and recommended updates.

Note

The Recommended Settings and Install Important Updates Only settings cause a system running original Windows Vista (also known as *Vista RTM*) to reboot after installing system updates (to complete updates). If you want to control when updates are installed (and when the system reboots), select Ask Me Later. You can then use the Windows Security Center to select the option to download updates automatically, but install them only when you specify.

One of the improvements in Windows Vista SP1 is support for hotpatching, which means that most system updates that formerly would have required reboots to complete no longer require the system to be rebooted. This improvement results in more uptime and fewer problems with remote access, backup, or other critical operations being interrupted by reboots.

14. Specify the time zone and adjust the date and time as necessary. Click Next to continue.

15. Click Start on the Thank You dialog to start Windows Vista. After a brief pause, the system performs a series of performance tests to create the Windows Experience Index. After these tests are complete, the Windows Vista desktop appears and displays the Welcome Center.

16. If any hardware on your system does not have a Vista-compatible driver, you are prompted to provide a driver for each item.

Now that the upgrade to Windows Vista has been completed, the next step is to install updates and service packs. You should perform these tasks before getting back to work. Depending upon your system configuration, you might use Windows Update to install service packs and updates, or you might install already-downloaded packages from a network server. Contact your system administrator for details.

Troubleshooting a Failed Upgrade to Windows Vista

Many problems that occur during the upgrade of a Windows XP installation to Windows Vista are similar to those you might encounter when installing Windows Vista for the first time, as discussed in Chapter 3. You may also encounter one of the following problems:

- Programs or services that are running may interfere with the upgrade process. As mentioned earlier in this chapter, use the Windows XP Task Manager to close unnecessary programs before starting the upgrade. You can also use the Msconfig.exe utility to choose Selective Startup, clear the check boxes associated with programs that start automatically, and then restart the computer. This procedure is also known as *clean booting*. Knowledge Base article 316434 provides additional information.

- If you did not uninstall incompatible software before starting the upgrade process, it halts and displays a message indicating which program needs to be uninstalled (see Figure 4.10). To avoid this problem, be sure to run the Windows Vista Upgrade Advisor and follow the instructions on the Task List before starting the upgrade.

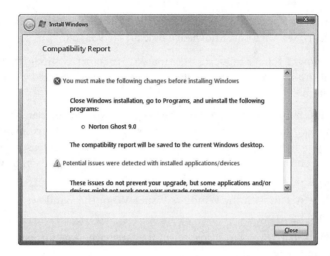

Figure 4.10   See problems in the Compatibility Report? Your upgrade to Windows Vista cannot be completed until you solve them.

- You may receive messages informing you that Setup cannot copy a file. This may be the result of hardware problems such as an over-clocked processor or damaged memory. Make sure that your processor is running at its rated speed (see your system or motherboard manual for details). To test memory for errors, download the Windows Memory Diagnostic from http://oca.microsoft.com/en/windiag.asp, install it to a floppy disk or CD, use it to boot the computer, and start the testing process. If the processor is not overclocked and the memory test indicates system memory is working correctly, try copying the contents of the Windows Vista DVD to a folder on the hard drive and installing from this location.

- Incompatible hardware may result in the setup program failing to respond ("hanging"), or a Stop message (blue screen error) appearing. Refer to the suggestions presented earlier in this chapter for checking system compatibility.

Reverting to Windows XP After Upgrading to Windows Vista

One of the unpleasant surprises many Windows XP users discovered when they first upgraded to Windows Vista was that there was no easy way to revert to Windows XP. For some reason, Microsoft did not provide an option in Programs (Vista's equivalent to Windows XP's Add/Remove Programs) to revert to Windows XP automatically. This is surprising because many (but not all) Windows Vista upgrades from Windows XP preserved the old Windows XP installation in a folder called Windows.old.

If the Windows.old folder exists, you can manually revert to Windows XP after upgrading to Windows Vista. The procedure, documented in detail in Microsoft Knowledge Base article 933168, available at http://support.microsoft.com, requires you to use the Windows Recovery Environment's Command Prompt feature to replace the Windows Vista installation files with files from Windows.old, rename the saved boot.ini file, and replace the boot sector from Windows

Vista with the saved Windows XP boot sector. The basic steps are listed here. If you have questions or problems, see Microsoft Knowledge Base article 933168.

1. Use Windows Explorer to locate the `Windows.old` folder. It should be located in the root folder of the system drive (normally C:). If the `Windows.old` folder is not present, you cannot continue.

2. Check the amount of free space on the system drive and compare it to the space used by the `Windows.old` folder. In most cases, the `Windows.old` folder is smaller than the free space on the system drive. However, if the `Windows.old` folder is at least two times larger than the free space on the system drive, you cannot restore the old version of Windows unless you remove unwanted files first.

3. Restart the system with the Windows Vista DVD or the Windows Recovery Environment disc.

4. From the Install Windows dialog, select the language, time format, currency, and input method and click Next.

5. Click Repair Your Computer.

6. From the System Recovery Options window, select your Windows Vista installation and click Next.

7. Click Command Prompt. This opens the command prompt window.

8. Type `c:` and press Enter.

9. Type `ren Windows Windows.Vista` and press Enter.

10. Type `ren "Program Files" "Program Files.Vista"` and press Enter.

11. Type `ren "Users" "Users.Vista"` and press Enter.

12. Type `ren "Documents and Settings" "Documents and Settings.Vista"` and press Enter.

13. Type `move /y c:\windows.old\windows c:\` and press Enter.

14. Type `move /y "c:\windows.old\program files" c:\` and press Enter.

15. Type `move /y "c:\windows.old\documents and settings" c:\` and press Enter.

16. Type `D:\boot\bootsect /nt52 c:` and press Enter. (If the DVD drive is a different drive letter, replace D: with the appropriate drive letter.)

17. Type `c:` and press Enter.

18. Type `attrib boot.ini.saved -s -h -r` and press Enter.

19. Type `ren"boot.ini.saved""boot.ini"` and press Enter.

20. Type `attrib boot.ini +s +h +r` and press Enter.

21. Type `exit` and press Enter. This command closes the command prompt window.

22. Click Restart.

23. After the system reboots, Windows XP restarts.

If your system does not have a `Windows.old` folder but you created an image of your Windows XP installation, you can use the image to revert to Windows XP. However, if your system does not have a `Windows.old` folder and you did not create an image of your Windows XP installation, you must reinstall Windows XP as a clean install to revert to Windows XP. See Chapter 3 for details.

Migrating Existing Installations

Existing networks often contain an entire series of computers running older operating systems that need to be upgraded to Windows XP or Windows Vista. Often these computers are replaced by newer ones containing a factory installation of Windows XP or Windows Vista. You may need to migrate user settings, applications, and documents to new computers so that users can continue working as they would have on the old computers. We look at these issues in this section.

Moving to a New Drive

As storage costs decrease and space requirements increase, it makes sense to migrate to the newer, high-capacity hard disks. You can upgrade an older Windows operating system at the same time you install a new hard disk by any of several means: You can use a disk-copying utility from the hard disk vendor or a third-party tool such as Acronis True Image to move your data to a new drive before upgrading; you can upgrade your operating system on the existing drive and add a new hard disk that holds your data after the upgrade is completed; you can add a new hard disk before upgrading and perform a clean installation of Windows XP or Windows Vista on the new disk.

Installing a New Hard Disk

If you install a new hard disk, modern Windows versions will automatically recognize the disk when you restart your computer. To move or copy Windows system files to the new disk, you need to use a third-party tool.

Note

It may seem easier to use the Windows Advanced Boot Options menu (accessed by pressing F8 during bootup) to boot to a command prompt. However, starting up your PC this way still uses a few Windows system files on the hard disk to bring up the command prompt. To copy or move these files you need to boot your computer without referencing *any* files on the system disk.

Using a Vendor-Supplied Disk-Cloning Program

Some hard disk vendors provide a hard disk installation and drive-copying (cloning) utility, on a floppy disk, on a CD packaged with a retail-boxed hard disk, or as a download from the vendor's website. These utilities enable you to copy the contents of one hard disk to another, even if the new hard disk is larger than the old hard disk. If you need to clone a Windows Vista installation, make sure that the hard disk utility supports Windows Vista. Hard disk–cloning tools currently offered by hard disk vendors include

- Seagate's Disc Wizard powered by Acronis and similar Maxtor MaxBlast 5 (both available from www.seagate.com) are compatible with Windows Vista and Windows XP. You can use either Disc Wizard or MaxBlast 5 as long as your system contains at least one Seagate or Maxtor hard disk drive (Seagate owns Maxtor).

- Western Digital's Data Lifeguard Tools version 11.2 is compatible with Windows XP only (an updated version will support Windows Vista). See www.wdc.com for updates. You can use Data Lifeguard Tools as long as your system contains at least one Western Digital hard disk.

Note

If you need to copy the contents of a hard disk to another hard disk, and the vendor of your new hard disk does not supply a disk-copying utility, you can use the utility provided by your old hard disk's vendor as long as it works with your version of Windows. Alternatively, you could use a program such as Acronis True Image or Norton Ghost to clone your old hard disk's contents to a new hard disk. The newest version of Disc Wizard (as well as MaxBlast 5) includes special versions of Acronis True Image.

Installing Windows XP as a Dual-Boot Configuration

You can also install Windows XP or Windows Vista on the new hard disk from the Windows version on the first disk. This creates a *dual-boot* system in which you can start either version of Windows. To install Windows XP with SP2 on the new disk, proceed as follows:

1. Insert the slipstreamed Windows XP/SP2 CD-ROM (or access a distribution share as described previously).

2. If the Welcome to Microsoft Windows XP screen does not appear, open My Computer, navigate to the CD-ROM drive, and double-click the Setup icon.

3. Click Install Windows XP.

4. In the Welcome to Windows Setup dialog box (refer to Figure 4.2), select New Installation (Advanced), and then click Next.

5. Click I Accept This Agreement, and then click Next.

6. On the Your Product Key page, type the product key and then click Next.

7. If necessary, modify any of the options provided in the Setup Options page, and then click Next.

8. On the Get Updated Setup Files dialog box, leave the default of Yes, Download the Updated Setup Files (Recommended) selected, and then click Next. If you are not connected to the Internet, select No, Skip This Step and continue installing Windows.

9. Setup copies files to your hard disk. This takes several minutes, after which your computer shuts down and restarts.

10. After the computer restarts, it displays the text-based Welcome to Setup page. Press Enter to proceed with installing the dual-boot system.

11. Setup displays information similar to that shown in Figure 4.11, from which you can select the partition on which you want to install Windows XP and the file system with which you want to format it. Use the arrow keys to make a selection, and then press Enter.

12. Setup copies files to the Windows installation folders, and restarts into GUI-mode Setup.

13. The remainder of the installation proceeds in a fashion similar to that of a clean Windows installation described in Chapter 3. You are asked for the same information as described in that chapter.

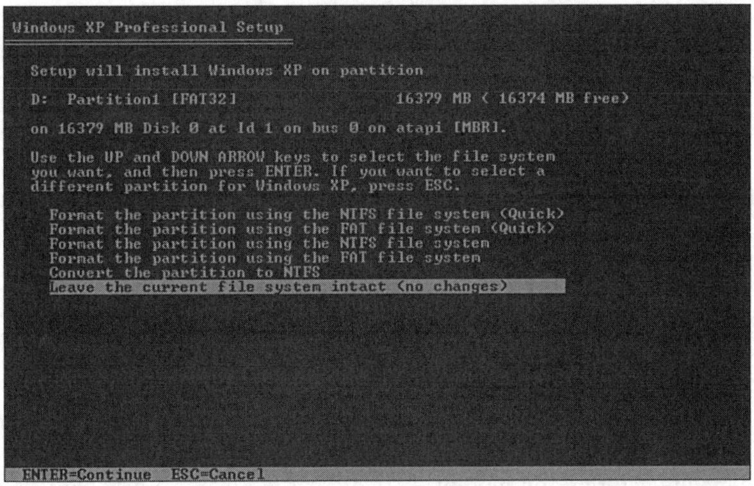

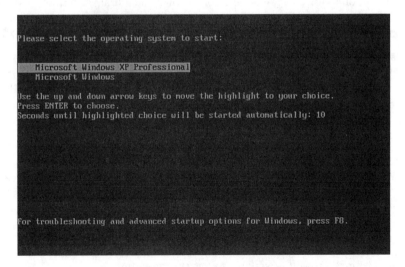

Figure 4.11 When creating a dual-boot system, Setup provides a choice of partitions and formatting options.

After installation completes, you can boot your computer into either operating system. On startup, the computer displays a menu called the *boot loader* (see Figure 4.12), which enables you to select either operating system.

Figure 4.12 On a dual-boot system, the boot loader menu enables you to select which operating system you want to run.

Installing Windows Vista as a Dual-Boot Configuration

When installing Windows Vista as a dual-boot configuration, start the installation process from within your existing version of Windows. Follow the instructions provided for an upgrade installation until you reach step 10. At step 10, choose Custom (Advanced) as the installation option. Specify the empty hard disk as the installation target and create a partition on the disk. You can use all or a portion of the hard disk. The remainder of the installation process continues as with an upgrade installation.

When you perform a dual-boot installation, you are prompted to select the country or region, time and currency, and keyboard layout just before entering the username and password, rather than at the beginning of the process as you do with a standard clean install. After these options are selected, the remainder of the process is the same as in a clean install.

When you restart the system, you see a boot loader menu similar to the one in Figure 4.12.

Using Partition Management Programs

Partition management programs, such as Norton Partition Magic (supports Windows XP) and Acronis Disk Director Suite 10 (supports Windows XP and Windows Vista), enable you to organize and modify partitions on multiple hard disks. You can add a new hard disk to a computer running any Windows operating system and move the contents of your old hard disk to a partition on the new one. You can also create, move, split, merge, and convert disk partitions including those formatted with NTFS rapidly. You can even recover deleted partitions and the data they contain.

For more information about Norton Partition Magic, see www.symantec.com. For more information about Acronis Disk Director Suite 10 or to download a trial version, see www.acronis.com.

Moving a Windows Installation to a New Motherboard

Moving a Windows installation to a new motherboard can range anywhere from being relatively simple to being fiendishly complicated. Basically, if you are moving to a motherboard that uses the same chipset and mass storage drivers, your installation will work properly. However, if your new motherboard uses a different chipset and different mass storage drivers, you need to follow special procedures to enable it to run.

Moving a Windows XP Installation to a New Motherboard

If you see a Stop 0x0000007B INACESSIBLE_BOOT_DEVICE error (also known as a *Stop 07B error*) when you move your installation to another motherboard, the old and new motherboards do not use the same mass storage drivers. Microsoft recommends a couple of different procedures for moving an existing Windows XP installation to a new motherboard. These procedures are provided in Microsoft Knowledge Base article 824125. Here's an outline of the basic procedure.

If the original motherboard is working, follow this procedure:

1. Start an installation of Windows XP by booting from the Windows XP CD.
2. Select Upgrade as the installation type.
3. Follow the onscreen instructions until the system begins to restart.
4. Turn off the system *immediately.*

5. Swap motherboards (or move the installed hard disk to the new host machine). Be sure to plug the drive into the same host adapter and position as on the original machine, such as primary adapter, master drive; secondary adapter, master drive; and so on.

6. If you moved the hard disk to a different machine, make sure that you move the Windows XP CD and insert it before continuing.

7. Restart the system; the "upgrade" continues, installing a new hardware abstraction layer (HAL), chipset, and other drivers as needed.

8. Reinstall service packs and other updates after the installation is complete.

Note

If your system is now running Windows XP SP2 or later, but was originally set up using Windows XP RTM or SP1, you can save time by creating a slipstream CD containing the latest service pack files and using it as an installation source. This is especially important if you originally used Windows XP RTM and have moved to a hard disk larger than 120GB. Windows XP RTM cannot properly manage larger hard disks, and data residing on disk areas beyond 137GB could be corrupted. For a detailed tutorial for slipstreaming Windows XP with SP2 files, see http://www.winsupersite.com/showcase/windowsxp_sp2_slipstream.asp. For a Service Pack 3 (SP3) version, see http://www.winsupersite.com/showcase/xpsp3_slipstream.asp.

If the original motherboard has failed and the hard disk is now connected to a new motherboard, follow this procedure to perform a repair installation:

1. Restart the system with the Windows XP CD.

2. When the system displays To Set Up Windows Now, Press Enter, perform this step.

3. Select your Windows XP installation from the list of installations.

4. Press R when the message To Repair the Selected Windows Installation, Press R appears.

5. Follow onscreen instructions to complete the repair installation.

6. After the repair installation is complete, reinstall any service packs or hotfixes you had previously installed.

Moving a Windows Vista Installation to a New Motherboard

Although Microsoft provides a couple of official methods for moving an existing Windows XP installation to a new motherboard, it does not offer comparable options for Windows Vista owners. The "official" message from Microsoft MVPs on some forums is that a clean installation is necessary. However, other users' experiences suggest it might work in some cases.

In an article called "How to install a new motherboard without reinstalling Windows," the ArsTechnica website (http://arstechnica.com/journals/hardware.ars/2007/09/04/how-to-install-a-new-motherboard-without-reinstalling-windows) suggests a method for manually replacing a chipset-specific hard disk and video drivers with generic drivers in Control Panel and removing references to hidden devices in Device Manager as a way to create a "hardware-agnostic" Windows configuration that can be moved to a new motherboard. The methods discussed in this article are specific to Windows XP, but also appear to work for Windows Vista. The main reason to use this method is to preserve a customized Windows installation that includes many installed applications.

Your best option is to maintain frequent file and folder backups, so if you need to move your installation in case of a motherboard failure that you will be able to do so. However, before you determine that you must perform a clean install, use the Startup Repair option provided by the Windows Recovery Environment. Some users have had success with this option.

Moving Data to a New System

New computers are getting more economical all the time. Rather than taking the time and expense to upgrade an existing computer to Windows XP or Windows Vista, it often makes sense to simply purchase a new computer with your preferred version of Windows already loaded. You can continue to use the old computer as a backup, recycle it, or donate it to a charitable organization. Organizations exist that will refurbish donated computers for schools, for example.

Windows XP includes two tools for migrating user data, applications, and settings to new computers:

- **User State Migration Tool (USMT)**—Enables network administrators to migrate settings on a large number of old computers to new Windows XP computers in a corporate setting.
- **Files and Settings Transfer Wizard**—Provides a simple means of migrating data and settings on one computer in a home or small office environment. We discuss the Files and Settings Transfer Wizard in a later section.

Windows Vista includes Windows Easy Transfer and Windows Easy Transfer Companion.

User State Migration Tool

Using the USMT, you can rapidly and easily transfer user documents and settings at the time of deploying new Windows XP Professional computers in a corporate setting. This tool enables you to migrate files and settings from source computers running Windows 95, Windows 98, Windows Me, Windows NT 4.0, or Windows 2000 to new Windows XP Professional computers. An updated version of USMT also works with Windows Vista. The following are several advantages of USMT:

- Technicians spend less time in migrating files and settings for users.
- It improves employee productivity by preventing help desk calls and reducing the amount of time wasted searching for missing files or reconfiguring the new desktop.
- Administrators can provide customized settings such as unique Registry modifications.
- Users become productive more rapidly because they can become familiar with the new operating system faster.
- Users express an improved overall sense of satisfaction with migrating to the new operating system.

▶▶ For more information on the use of this tool, **see** "Using the User State Migration Tool," **p. 196**.

Files and Settings Transfer Wizard

Microsoft provides the Files and Settings Transfer Wizard for transferring user settings, files, and folders to a new computer or to a clean Windows XP installation on an existing computer. It is the simplest means of transferring this information when only a few computers are affected, or when individual users are migrating information on their computer. It is automatically installed when you install or upgrade to Windows XP.

Before you start the transfer process using the Files and Settings Transfer Wizard, you should pay particular attention to the following list of potential trouble spots:

- Before attempting to transfer files to the target computer, ensure that the appropriate user account has been created and configured with the required NTFS permissions to allow access to the location where the transfer image will be located. If the transfer image is to be located on a network share, ensure that the share permissions are also correctly configured to support access.

- Before attempting to transfer files to the target computer, ensure that any special or specific folder paths that exist in the user's profile on the old computer are created on the new computer. This will help to alleviate problems with orphaned folders and files during the transfer process. Make sure that these folders have the required NTFS and share permissions applied to them as well.

- When performing the transfer process, ensure that you are logged in as the user whose files and settings you are transferring. Although this is a minor annoyance on the source computer, it can be a great catastrophe on the target computer if you are logged in under the wrong user account.

- Ensure that the location where the transfer image file will be located has enough available space to support the operation. You will need between 50MB and 600MB per user that you migrate using the Files and Settings Transfer Wizard. Table 4.3 provides some recommended guidelines for space availability.

- After the transfer process is complete, you will have to manually delete the transfer image file and folders.

Space Race

The estimates given in Table 4.3 are fairly realistic. I used more than 700MB to transfer my primary user profile and about 6MB to transfer a new (and unused) user profile. Plan ahead and ensure that you have plenty of empty disk space before starting to use the Files and Settings Transfer Wizard!

Table 4.3   Estimated Space Requirements When Using the Files and Settings Transfer Wizard

Type of User	Space Required
Desktop user storing email on server	50–75MB
Desktop user with local email storage	150–400MB
Laptop user	150–300MB

The best practice is to pad these values somewhat as well, just for safety, by adding 25%–50% to them depending on the average user type in your organization.

The process to use the Files and Settings Transfer Wizard is broken down into two separate phases, as you might expect. You will need to first gather the files and settings from the source computer and then apply them to the target computer.

Musical Windows

It is possible to use the Files and Settings Transfer Wizard to transfer a user's files and settings from a Windows XP computer and then apply these settings back to the same computer, either following a new installation of Windows XP or into a new user account.

Collecting Files and Settings from the Source PC

To transfer files and settings from the source computer, follow this procedure:

1. Log in to the source computer using the user account that you want to transfer files and settings from. If this computer is not a Windows XP computer, insert the Windows XP Professional Setup CD-ROM and proceed to step 2. If this computer is a Windows XP computer, you can launch the Files and Settings Transfer Wizard by clicking Start, Programs, Accessories, System Tools, Files and Settings Transfer Wizard, and then jump to step 4 of this procedure.

2. If this computer is not a Windows XP Professional machine, click Perform Additional Tasks on the Welcome to Microsoft Windows XP screen.

3. From the screen shown in Figure 4.13, select Transfer Files and Settings. Alternatively, you can navigate to the Support\Tools folder on the Windows XP Professional Setup CD-ROM and double-click the FASTWIZ.EXE file.

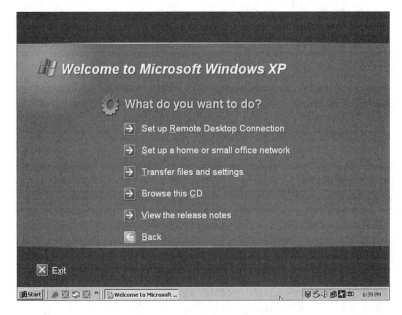

Figure 4.13 Starting the Files and Settings Transfer Wizard from the Windows XP Professional Setup CD-ROM.

4. After making your selection, the Files and Settings Transfer Wizard will open.

5. Click Next to dismiss the opening screen of the Files and Settings Transfer Wizard.

6. If prompted, select Old Computer and click Next.

7. On the Select the Transfer Method page, shown in Figure 4.14, configure the transfer method you want to use, and click Next to continue. In most cases, you will want to use a network location for your transfer image because the size can quickly grow past the capability of most removable storage media. Should you desire to use the direct cable connection, you will need to connect a null modem serial cable between the old computer (source) and the new computer (target) and follow through the prompts given in the wizard.

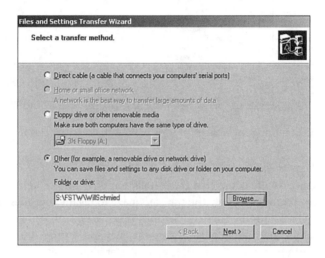

Figure 4.14 Selecting a location to place the transfer image.

8. On the What Do You Want to Transfer? page, select to transfer Settings Only, Files Only, or Both Files and Settings. If you want to configure additional transfer settings, place a check in the Let Me Select a Custom List of Files and Settings When I Click Next check box. Click Next to continue. If you are not custom-configuring your transfer settings, skip to step 10 of this procedure.

9. If you are custom-configuring your transfer settings, you can use the buttons shown in Figure 4.15 to modify the transfer settings. After you have customized the transfer settings, click Next to continue.

10. The Install Programs on Your New Computer page will show you a listing of what the Files and Settings Transfer Wizard thinks you need to install on the target computer before applying the transfer image. Click Next to continue.

11. The Files and Settings Transfer Wizard will now collect data and write it to the transfer image file. While this occurs, you can monitor the progress on the Collection in Progress page.

12. After the Files and Settings Transfer Wizard has completed, a summary page will appear telling you to now move to the new computer and apply the transfer image. Click Finish to close the Files and Settings Transfer Wizard.

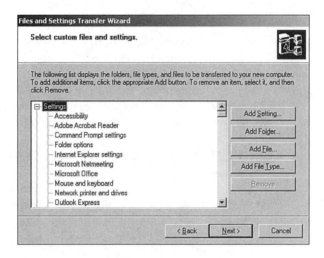

Figure 4.15   Customizing the transfer process ensures that you get exactly what you want.

Applying Files and Settings to the Target Computer

After you have successfully completed the installation of Windows XP Professional onto your new computer, you can then apply the transfer image to regain your files and settings. However, before you jump back into the Files and Settings Transfer Wizard, you *must* install all of your applications that you transferred settings for—the Files and Settings Transfer Wizard transfers only files and settings, not applications. If you transfer your settings and then install the application, you stand a good chance of having your settings overwritten during the install process.

To apply your files and settings to the target computer, follow this procedure:

1. Log in to the target computer using the user account that you want to restore the files and settings for.

2. If you've placed your transfer image on a network drive, map the network drive to the local computer and ensure that the user account has the required NTFS and share permissions.

3. Launch the Files and Settings Transfer Wizard either from the Start menu or from the Windows XP Professional Setup CD-ROM.

4. The Files and Settings Transfer Wizard opening page will be displayed. Click Next to continue.

5. On the Which Computer Is This? page, select New Computer and click Next to continue.

6. Because you have already collected your transfer files and settings, select I Don't Need the Wizard Disk on the Do You Have a Windows XP CD? page, shown in Figure 4.16. Click Next to continue.

7. On the Where Are the Files and Settings? page, select the location where you placed your transfer image in the previous procedure. Click Next to continue.

8. The Files and Settings Transfer Wizard will now transfer and apply the files and settings to the target computer. You can monitor the progress on the Transfer in Progress page.

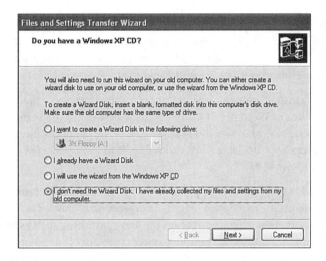

Figure 4.16   Telling the Files and Settings Transfer Wizard how to do its job!

9. After the Files and Settings Transfer Wizard has completed, a summary page will inform you of any errors or orphaned files that have been created during the process. Click Finish to close the Files and Settings Transfer Wizard.

10. You will receive the following message: `You need to log off for the changes to take effect. Do you want to log off now?` Select Yes and log back on to the account to see whether the transferred files and settings have taken effect.

If you have only one user or a small number of users to migrate settings for, the Files and Settings Transfer Wizard is the best way to go. However, should you need to migrate settings for a large number of users, or need extremely granular control over what gets transferred, the User State Migration Tool is for you.

Windows Easy Transfer

Windows Vista uses Windows Easy Transfer rather than the Files and Settings Transfer Wizard to move files and settings from a Windows XP (or Windows Vista) system to a Windows Vista system. (Windows Easy Transfer can also transfer files, but not settings, from a Windows 2000 system.)

Windows Easy Transfer can be used to create a backup of the information on a Windows XP computer before you perform an upgrade installation, and it can also be used to move files and settings from a computer you are redeploying (or retiring) to a new Windows Vista computer. For detailed information about using Windows Easy Transfer, see "Windows Easy Transfer," Chapter 3, p. 137.

Note

If it is not convenient to set up a Windows Easy Transfer USB flash drive for a Windows XP system on your Windows Vista system, you can download Windows Easy Transfer from the Microsoft Download Center website. Go to www.microsoft.com/downloads and search for Windows Easy Transfer for Windows XP.

Windows Easy Transfer Companion

If you are preparing to redeploy or retire a computer running Windows XP SP2 and need to move its applications to a computer running Windows Vista, you can download Windows Easy Transfer Companion, available from the Microsoft Download Center website.

Windows Easy Transfer Companion works only in a direct-connect mode between systems running 32-bit versions of Windows (it cannot be used between systems running a 32-bit and a 64-bit version of Windows, or between 64-bit versions). The connection can be via a network or the USB Easy Transfer Cable available from various vendors (and packaged with some systems preinstalled with Windows Vista).

Although Windows Easy Transfer Companion has successfully transferred a wide variety of business, educational, utility, game, and security programs (see Knowledge Base article 931696 for details), it cannot transfer programs that do not have installers, such as some plug-ins or self-contained utilities. Antivirus and operating system monitoring programs as well as operating system utilities cannot be transferred, either. A specific list of programs on the old system that cannot be transferred to the new system appears during the transfer process.

For a link to the download and more information, go to Knowledge Base article 931696, available at http://support.microsoft.com.

Moving Applications

When migrating user documents and settings to new Windows XP computers, an important segment of the task is that of migrating applications. When more than a few users are involved, the manual task of reinstalling applications on every new computer becomes extremely time-consuming and labor-intensive. Fortunately, there are ways to automate this process.

Including Applications with New Installations of Windows XP

Microsoft makes available several methods of performing bulk installations of Windows XP on new computers that include applications. Two methods of automated installation that enable you to include applications are the System Preparation Tool (Sysprep) and Remote Installation Services (RIS).

Sysprep

The *System Preparation Tool*, *Sysprep*, enables you to create an image of a typical installation of Windows XP Professional, including SP2 and a standard set of applications that can be deployed to multiple destination computers. This tool, found in the `Deploy.cab` file in the `Support\Tools` folder of the Windows XP Professional CD-ROM, prepares a reference computer for imaging using a cloning application such as Norton Ghost or Symantec Drive Image.

To use Sysprep, you first install and configure a reference computer with Windows XP Professional, SP2, and the required set of applications including standard application settings. You then run `Sysprep.exe` on this computer to remove computer-specific information such as security identifiers (SIDs). The computer will shut down automatically. Finally, you reboot the computer with a floppy and run the cloning application. You can store the image thus created on a shared folder, from which the target computers can connect and install the Windows XP image.

RIS

Remote Installation Services, or *RIS*, enables you to deploy Windows XP Professional images containing applications and other configuration parameters on an Active Directory–based network that includes Dynamic Host Configuration Protocol (DHCP) and Domain Name System (DNS). Images can contain items such as applications and desktop settings, and users can install these images themselves from any computer equipped with a Preboot Execution Environment (PXE)–compatible network interface card (NIC).

RIS is available as a component on servers running Windows 2000 Server or Windows Server 2003. You set up a series of remote installation shared folders on the server, and then create images of Windows XP Professional installations containing the required settings and applications. RIS includes a Remote Installation Preparation Wizard that you run on the Windows XP computer, which performs a series of copy steps (see Figure 4.17) that places the image on the appropriate subfolder on the server.

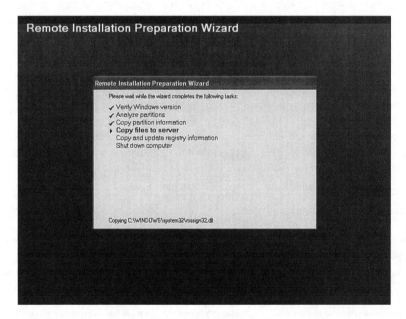

Figure 4.17 The Remote Installation Preparation Wizard prepares the image of the reference computer and copies it to the server.

A remote user who needs to install Windows XP can use the Client Installation Wizard, which is a text-based wizard that guides the user through the process of installing Windows XP. A computer with a PXE-compatible NIC automatically connects to the RIS server and downloads the wizard. The user then logs on to the domain and follows the steps presented by the wizard to install Windows XP Professional, complete with all service packs, hotfixes, and applications, without further involvement by the user.

Tip

If you need to use RIS to install Windows XP on computers that are not equipped with a PXE-compatible NIC, you can create a remote boot floppy disk at the RIS server. This disk enables a client computer to boot and access the RIS server.

Using Group Policy

On a Windows 2000 Server, Windows Server 2003, or Windows Server 2008 domain, you can use Group Policy to distribute software to all computers, both new and existing. This provides a means to push required software out to users and computers at the next reboot or logon. A user receiving a new computer merely needs to start the computer and log on to the domain to receive a complete set of software. You can create policies that apply to the entire domain or to an organizational unit (OU) containing a subset of computers or users requiring specific applications, such as line-of-business applications required by a specific department. Besides installation of software on new computers, you can use software installation policies to automatically update software or remove outdated software from all computers affected by the policy.

Group Policy enables you to deploy software by any of three methods:

- **Assigned to computers**—Software is installed on all computers affected by the policy the next time the users restart their computers.
- **Assigned to users**—Software intended for a specific set of users is installed on the users' computers the next time they log on.
- **Published to users**—Optional software is advertised to users the next time they log on, and a user can install it from the Control Panel Add or Remove Programs applet.

Use of Group Policy for software deployment involves creating one or more shared folders on a software distribution server, copying the software installation files, and creating a Group Policy object (GPO) that specifies the software packages to be installed (see Figure 4.18). Software installation files should include Windows Installer package (`.msi`) files.

Using Windows Easy Transfer Companion to Transfer Applications

If you are preparing to redeploy or retire a computer running Windows XP SP2 and need to move its applications to a computer running Windows Vista, you can use Windows Easy Transfer Companion, available from the Microsoft Download Center website. For more information on obtaining Windows Easy Transfer Companion, see "Windows Easy Transfer Companion," p. 248.

Programs on the old system are placed into three categories by Windows Easy Transfer Companion: programs that transfer well, programs that transfer with possible limitations, and programs that cannot be transferred (see Figure 4.19). By default, all programs in the first category are selected for transfer; you can uncheck programs you don't want to transfer. Programs in the second category can be selected for transfer as desired. The Save Report button can be used to save a report for analysis or reference.

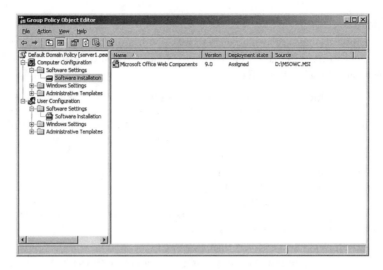

Figure 4.18   Using Group Policy in Windows Server 2003 to deploy a software package.

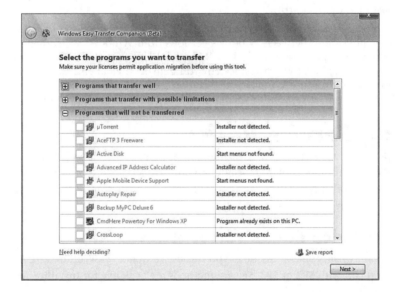

Figure 4.19   Viewing the Windows Easy Transfer Companion report of programs that will not be transferred.

Note

Windows Easy Transfer Companion is still a beta product as of spring 2008.

Third-Party Tools

Several third-party tools are available that assist you in moving applications from computers running older operating systems to new Windows XP and Windows Vista computers. The following describes a few of the available tools:

- CellarStone Inc. (www.cellarstone.com) markets StepUpPro, which is a PC migration tool that transfers user settings, data, and applications from a source computer running Windows 95/98/Me/2000/XP to a new Windows 2000 or Windows XP computer. It provides a wizard-based interface that guides you through the process of a direct migration from the source computer to the destination computer.

- KBOX by Kace Software (www.kace.com) is a hardware-based enterprise software management appliance. Although KBOX devices do not migrate applications *per se*, it enables you to view the software installed on all machines on the network, and distribute software to a new or upgraded computer. Users can fix certain problems with the software on their computers without administrator assistance.

- Altiris Migration Suite (www.altiris.com; Altiris is now owned by Symantec) is a comprehensive product designed for migrating computers to Windows XP or Windows Vista, including software migration. It works on networks of all sizes and offers services such as inventorying, upgrade assessment, computer backup, cloning, network configuration, and post-migration reporting.

- PCmover by Laplink Software (www.laplink.com) is designed to move data, user profiles, and applications between Windows versions from Windows 95 through Vista to a new computer running Windows XP or Windows Vista. PCmover also supports Mac Boot Camp (Apple's Mac/Windows dual-boot environment) and Parallels (Apple's virtualization environment for hosting Windows XP/Vista on a Mac). PCmover supports transfers via direct USB, network, or removable media.

Installing Service Packs

When performing either a clean or upgrade installation of Windows XP or Windows Vista, it is, under most circumstances, vital that one of your first actions is to go to the Windows Update website and install any available service packs for your operating system. The following sections discuss how to install these service packs.

Installing Service Packs for Windows XP

This section explains several methods you can use to upgrade a Windows XP RTM or SP1 system to be compliant with SP2 or SP3. Several methods are available for installing SP2 or SP3 on existing Windows XP computers:

- Manual installation of SP2 or SP3 and additional updates
- Use of Automatic Updates or Windows Update
- Using Group Policy to deploy SP2 or SP3 to computers in a domain or OU
- Use of Windows Server Update Services (WSUS) to deploy SP2 or SP3 to network computers

Note

The procedures discussed were originally developed for SP2, but should also work with SP3 when it is introduced. SP3 includes all previous Windows XP service packs, and should be installed on pre-SP3 systems. Any changes specific to Windows XP SP3 will be published on Microsoft's website.

Manual Installation of SP2 or SP3

You can download SP2 or SP3 from the Microsoft website or order it on CD-ROM. The download may be in the form of an ISO image (an image file representing a one-to-one copy of the files or folders, which can be burned to a CD-ROM using commercial CD-burning software), or it may be an .exe file (Microsoft has used both methods). The CD is available for free and upgrades any version of Windows XP. Its use is a simple means of upgrading computers when only a small number of computers are involved.

Perform the following procedure to manually install SP2 or SP3:

1. To install from CD: Insert the Windows XP SP2 or SP3 CD-ROM. Click Continue when the Welcome page appears. To install from a download (.exe file): Navigate to the folder containing the download and double-click the .exe file.

2. CD installation: SP2 or SP3 displays a page that introduces its new features and provides a link to further information about installation. To proceed with installation, click Install Now. Download (.exe) installation: After files are extracted, click Next to continue.

3. The Windows XP Service Pack 2 or Service Pack 3 Setup Wizard appears. Follow the instructions presented. The installation procedure also takes several minutes.

4. When the completion page appears, click Finish to restart your computer.

Using Automatic Updates or Windows Update to Download SP2 or SP3

You can configure your computer to automatically download updates from the Automatic Updates tab of the System Properties dialog box (right-click My Computer and choose Properties). After you have done this, your computer will download SP2 or SP3 automatically, including only those files required for your specific installation. You will receive a notification that SP2 or SP3 is ready to install; the installation procedure is similar to that described for manual installation from the CD-ROM.

You can also download and install SP2 or SP3 from the Microsoft Windows Update web page (http://windowsupdate.microsoft.com). This page checks the version of Windows running on your computer and provides a list of available updates that will include SP2 or SP3. As with Automatic Updates, only the required components of SP2 or SP3 will be downloaded. Again the installation procedure is similar to that already described.

Using Group Policy to Deploy SP2 or SP3

Group Policy is an efficient means of deploying SP2 to a large number of Windows XP Professional computers in an Active Directory domain. You can deploy SP2 or SP3 to all computers in the domain or an OU by creating a software installation policy that assigns SP2 to the required computers.

Use the following procedure to prepare an installation share and create a GPO for SP2 deployment:

1. While logged on to a server running Windows 2000 Server or Windows Server 2003 as an administrator, create and share a folder named XPSP2.

2. Copy all files in the Windows XP SP2 CD-ROM to this share.

3. From a command prompt, navigate to this folder and type **XPSP2 -X** to extract the service pack files.

4. Click OK to create a subfolder named I386 in the XPSP2 shared folder and extract the service pack files to this subfolder.

5. Access the Active Directory Users and Computers console, right-click the domain or OU containing the computers on which SP2 will be installed, and click Properties.

6. On the Group Policy tab of the Properties dialog box that opens, select an appropriate GPO and click Edit. Alternatively, you can click New to create a new GPO and then click Edit.

7. In the Group Policy Object Editor console, expand the Software Settings node under Computer Configuration, right-click the Software Installation subnode, and choose New, Package.

8. In the Open dialog box that appears, select My Network Places and navigate to the I386\Update subfolder of the XPSP2 share, select Update.msi, and then click Open.

9. Click OK to accept the deployment method of Assigned. As shown in Figure 4.20, the Group Policy Object Editor console displays the service pack with the path to its installation files.

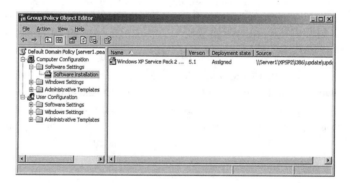

Figure 4.20   Deploying SP2 by means of Group Policy.

After you have completed this procedure, users merely need to shut down and restart their computers to install SP2. The SP2 installation process takes several minutes on each client computer, after which the computer automatically shuts down and restarts. To deploy SP3, through Group Policy, follow the same procedure, but start with a CD containing SP3 create a folder called XPSP3 in step 1, switch to that folder in step 2, and use the command XPSP3 –X in step 3. Point to this folder in place of the SP2 folder as needed.

For detailed information on the use of Group Policy to deploy SP2, refer to the article "Managing Windows XP Service Pack 2 Features Using Group Policy" at http://www.microsoft.com/technet/prodtechnol/winxppro/maintain/mangxpsp2/mngintro.mspx.

Using WSUS to Deploy SP2 or SP3

WSUS is the successor to Software Update Services (SUS), which is installed on a server running Windows 2000 Server SP4, Windows Server 2003, or Windows Server 2008 and provides patches and other software updates to client computers on the network. You can either download the SP2 or SP3 files from the Microsoft website or copy them from the SP2 or SP3 CD-ROM to make them available to all client computers that have been configured to obtain their updates from the network SUS or WSUS server.

For detailed information on the use of SUS or WSUS to deploy SP2, refer to the article "Deploying Windows XP Service Pack 2 Using Software Update Services" at http://www.microsoft.com/technet/prodtechnol/winxppro/deploy/xpsp2sus.mspx.

Uninstalling SP2 or SP3

Should you find that some component or application fails to work properly after installing SP2 or SP3, you can remove it from Control Panel Add or Remove Programs. Perform the following procedure:

1. In the Control Panel Add or Remove Programs applet, select the Windows XP Service Pack 2 entry and click Remove.

2. The Windows XP Service Pack 2 Removal Wizard opens and warns you about actions you should perform to protect your computer. Click Next to proceed.

3. The wizard performs a series of cleanup actions that include inspecting the current configuration, stopping and restarting processes, deleting files, and updating the Registry. These actions take several minutes. To stop the removal, click Cancel.

4. The wizard informs you when these actions have been completed. Click Finish to restart your computer.

Installing Service Packs for Windows Vista

Windows Vista Service Pack 1 (Vista SP1) can be installed via download, through Automatic Updates or Windows Update, via Group Policy, WSUS, or System Center Configuration Manager 2007.

This section explains several methods you can use to upgrade a Windows Vista RTM system to be compliant with Vista SP1. These include

- Manual installation of Vista SP1 and additional updates
- Use of Automatic Updates or Windows Update
- Use of WSUS to deploy Vista SP1 to network computers
- Use of Windows Deployment Services
- Use of SMS 2003 or System Center Configuration Manager

Before installing Vista SP1, make sure that you perform the following tasks:

- Plug your portable computer into an AC power source to avoid power loss during the installation.
- Close and open programs and files.
- Run File and Folder Backup, or your preferred backup program, to back up files, folders, and settings.
- If your antivirus program prevents changes to system files, disable it temporarily, but be sure to re-enable it after completing installation.

Manual Installation of Vista SP1

Perform the following procedure to manually install Vista SP1:

1. Download the appropriate version of Vista SP1 (32-bit or 64-bit) from the Microsoft Download Center.

2. Navigate to the location of the download using Computer Explorer and double-click it.

3. A security warning appears. Click Run to continue.

4. Provide administrator credentials if prompted to do so by User Account Control.

5. The Welcome to Windows Vista Service Pack 1 dialog appears. Click Next to continue.

Note

Make sure you have adequate free disk space before continuing. The 32-bit version of Vista SP1 requires 7GB of free disk space; the 32-bit version requires 13GB of free disk space.

6. Review the license terms, click the I Accept the License Terms checkbox, and click Next to continue.

7. Click Install to install the service pack. Installation may take up to one hour, and the system restarts automatically several times during the process.

8. At the end of the process, you will be prompted to log back in to Windows Vista as you normally do.

Using Automatic Updates or Windows Update to Download Vista SP1

To configure your computer to automatically download updates, open Control Panel, Security, click the Turn Automatic Updating On or Off link, and make sure the Install Updates

Automatically option is selected. Adjust the time as desired. After you have done this, your computer will download Vista SP1 automatically, including only those files required for your specific installation. You will receive a notification that Vista SP1 is ready to install; the installation procedure is similar to that described for manual installation.

Note

You cannot receive Vista SP1 via Automatic Updates or Windows Update unless the following updates are performed first: KB937287 and KB938371 must be installed on all Vista editions, whereas KB935509 must also be installed on Vista Enterprise and Ultimate editions only. To determine whether these updates have been installed, open Control Panel, Programs, Programs and Features, and View Installed Updates. Look up the KB articles at http://support.microsoft.com for details and download links.

Using WSUS to Deploy SP1

Windows Server Update Services version 2.0 with Service Pack 1 or WSUS 3.0 with Service Pack 1 can be used to deliver SP1 and other software updates via network connections to client computers running Windows Vista.

Before using WSUS to deploy Vista SP1, client computers need to install the KB947821 update available from the Microsoft Download Center, and Windows Server 2003 computers running WSUS need to install the KB938759 update. After these updates are installed, make sure that the WSUS server is configured to synchronize Vista service packs.

For detailed information on the use of WSUS to deploy Vista SP1, refer to Scenario 4 in the Windows Vista Service Pack 1 Deployment Guide available at http://technet2.microsoft.com.

Deploying Vista SP1 with Windows Deployment Services

Vista SP1 can be deployed by using Windows Deployment Services (WDS). This method uses either a customized install image captured from a reference computer or the `install.wim` image from a DVD that contains the integrated image of Windows Vista SP1.

For detailed information on the use of WDS to deploy Vista SP1, refer to Scenario 5 in the Windows Vista Service Pack 1 Deployment Guide available at http://technet2.microsoft.com.

Deploying SP1 with SMS or System Center Configuration Manager

Vista SP1 can also be deployed by using System Center Configuration Manager 2007, System Center Essentials, or SMS 2003.

For detailed information on the use of these options to deploy Vista SP1, refer to Scenario 6 in the Windows Vista Service Pack 1 Deployment Guide available at http://technet2.microsoft.com.

Note

Vista SP1 cannot be delivered automatically via Windows Update or other automatic deployment methods to computers that have drivers that are not compatible with Windows Vista SP1. For a list of these drivers and the recommended updates, as well as other reasons that Windows Update might not deliver SP1, see KB948343 at http://support.microsoft.com.

Uninstalling Vista SP1

Should you find that some component or application fails to work properly after installing Vista SP1, you can remove it from Control Panel's Programs category.

1. Open the Control Panel Programs category and select Programs and Features.

2. Click the View Installed Updates link.

3. Select Service Pack for Microsoft Windows (KB936330) and click Uninstall.

4. Follow the onscreen prompts to complete the removal.

Making Vista SP1 Installation Permanent

After you have used Vista SP1 on your system and tested your applications and utilities, you may decide that you no longer need the option to uninstall it. To make it permanent, use the vsp1cln.exe utility. To use this utility, do the following:

1. Restart the computer.

2. After Windows restarts, click Start, type **cmd** in the Start Search box.

3. When cmd.exe appears, right-click it and select Run as Administrator, and click Continue.

4. Provide administrator credentials as prompted by User Account Control.

5. Type vsp1cln.exe and press Enter.

6. The following message appears:

```
This operation will make Windows Vista Service Pack 1 permanent on this
computer. Upon completion you will not be able to remove Windows Vista
Service Pack 1 from this system. Would you like to continue (Y/N):
```

7. Press Y to remove the files replaced by Vista SP1. 600–800MB of disk space will be freed up for use, depending upon the Vista edition in use.

8. Type Exit to close the command prompt window.

Note

If you receive an error message when you run **vsp1cln.exe**, see Microsoft KB949472, available at http://support.microsoft.com.

Tweaking and Tuning Windows

Configuration Settings

When you install Windows XP or Vista, or turn on a new computer that has one of these versions of Windows preinstalled, you'll find that it works pretty darn well right out of the box. There are several reasons for this. First, modern computer hardware is *really* fast, and many things that used to cause irritating delays have sped up to the point that they're barely noticeable.

Second, PC hardware standards have evolved and matured, and virtually all hardware you can buy now is compliant with various standards for Plug and Play operation, intervendor operation, and so on. The software standards for driver architecture have stabilized to the point that almost all drivers install themselves automatically, configure the hardware automatically, tune themselves for best performance automatically, and don't leave much for you to worry about. Drivers for the new generation of 64-bit processors may take a while to become ubiquitous, but other than that, I haven't seen a piece of basic hardware not work instantly upon installation in at least five years. If you've already followed the advice in *Upgrading and Repairing PCs* for selecting and connecting your computer's hardware, there's not a lot left for you do on the configuration front.

Finally, the minimum requirements for the hardware on which Windows can run have increased to the point that Windows no longer has to keep its default settings tuned for computers far below our current expectations. For example, Windows now assumes that your display can handle at least 800×600 resolution, rather than the minimum 640×480 standard that dates back to 1987. If it detects that your monitor can work at a higher resolution (and with a modern Plug and Play monitor, it *can* detect that), it automatically switches up to a higher resolution, depending on your monitor's size and native resolution.

So, if adequate raw performance was your only concern, you wouldn't need this chapter. That's why this chapter is focused on *usability*, which encompasses not only raw performance, but also ease of use, efficiency, "friendliness," and other subjective attributes. This chapter is about making the *experience* of using Windows more pleasant and efficient, removing impediments to effective use, and in general, making Windows better fit your way of working and thinking. It's a very noble idea.

However, what helps one person work faster may not help you at all, and vice versa, so you'll have to test the ideas presented here to see which ones will work for you. Effective tuning depends on what *you* do frequently and personal taste. I've found that the biggest paybacks come from tiny improvements in activities that I perform over and over, rather than large improvements in things that I do rarely. If you use Microsoft Word frequently, shaving a half-second off the time it takes to be able to start using Word may help more than making a once-a-month tune-up run in 15 minutes instead of 30. If you frequently log on and off, minimizing the number of automatic-startup programs is something you will want to focus on. If you frequently use a few applications or certain network resources, you can really help by giving yourself instant access to those resources, even at the expense of others.

Note

Although it's helpful to adjust the GUI tools for better usability, remember that you can often perform a job with the command line much faster than you can with a GUI interface. And you can set up command line "aliases" to abbreviate common functions. For example, on my system I just have to type the letter *n* and press Enter to start Notepad, which takes only a fraction of a second. For more about using and configuring the command line, see Chapter 9, "Windows Commands and Scripting."

Finally, it's worth considering that there is a trade-off involved when you make customizations. The more you customize, the less your computer will look and act like other Windows computers. If you frequently work with other peoples' computers, or if other people often use your computer, major changes in the way the Windows interface works can actually slow you down. You'll have to stop and hunt around for the right way to do something that you're used to doing by habit, and it's irritating.

So, with the philosophy out of the way, let's go over some Windows configuration settings that you might be able to use to make your use of your computer more effective and pleasant. At the end of the chapter "Tuning for Maximum Performance," I'll summarize the most important recommended settings.

An Apology in Advance

Before I start to dig into tweaking and tuning Windows, I want to mention that Microsoft went nuts changing the user interface for the Control Panel on Windows Vista. Most of the Control Panel applets and configuration dialogs that you're used to from Windows 95 through XP are still there and are mostly unchanged, but *getting* to the familiar settings has changed drastically, and in my opinion, confusingly. Because this book covers both Windows XP and Vista, we thus have to describe two procedures for pretty much everything in this chapter: one for XP, and another for Vista. You might find it a bit irritating, and I apologize in advance, but in the end I hope it will help you become fluent in both XP and Vista. I suspect that you'll find yourself working with both operating systems for many years to come.

Display Settings

As I mentioned earlier, Windows automatically takes good advantage of modern high-resolution displays. There are, however, some settings you can do to get better performance and make the display easier on your eyes.

Adjusting Resolution and Refresh Rate

It's likely that your monitor can handle several different screen resolutions. The higher the resolution, the finer the detail Windows can display, and the more information you can display on the screen at once. This is a more important issue with CRT monitors, and less so with LCD monitors. If you have an LCD monitor, be sure to read the additional information on resolution settings after this section.

To adjust the screen resolution on XP, right-click the desktop, select Properties, and select the Settings tab. On Vista, right-click the desktop, select Personalize, and then click Display Settings.

The dialog's appearance may change depending on whether you have one monitor (see Figure 5.1) or multiple monitors (see Figure 5.2; these are the XP versions, but the dialogs on Vista are nearly identical). The procedures for making adjustments are the same in either case, except that in the case of multiple monitors you must click on one of the monitor icons to indicate which monitor's settings you want to change.

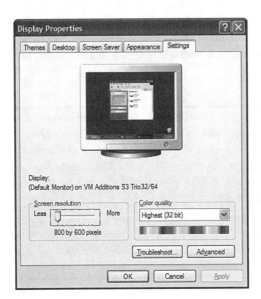

Figure 5.1 Display Properties Settings Page for a single monitor.

Figure 5.2 Display Properties Settings Page for dual monitors.

A display's resolution is the number of pixels or dots drawn on the screen, horizontally and vertically. The optimum resolution for different monitor sizes has proven to be that which gives you about 86 to 96 pixels per inch (also called dots per inch, or dpi), or equivalently, a *dot pitch* of about 0.27 mm. The resolution can be decreased to make the display elements bigger and easier to read—those of us over 40 understand this well. For various monitor sizes, the typical maximum resolution is listed in Table 5.1.

Table 5.1   Typical Maximum Display Resolution for Various Monitor Sizes

Diagonal Size	Resolution
15" standard	1024×768
17-19" standard	1280×1024
17-19" widescreen	1440×900
21-23" standard	1600×1200
21-22" widescreen	1680×1050
23-28" widescreen	1920×1200
30" widescreen	2560×1600

Some monitors can be set for higher resolutions than this, but the dot pitch will be significantly lower than .27mm and possibly difficult to read.

To adjust the monitor's resolution, drag the Resolution slider to the left or right. In most cases, Windows will offer only choices that it knows the graphics card can generate *and* that the monitor can accept. When you have made a selection, click Apply and wait for Windows to switch to the new display mode. If the screen does not become readable within 5 to 10 seconds, press the Esc key.

Tip

Do not press the Enter key if you cannot read the screen. If you do, Windows locks in the nonfunctional setting. If this happens, and you need to fix this without resetting your computer and losing work in progress, try this: Press the Esc key 10 times. Press Windows+D. Move the mouse in the direction that takes it away from the taskbar. Right-click the mouse and press the letter R. On XP, press Shift+Tab once wait a moment, press the right arrow key five times, and then press Alt+S; on Vista, press Alt+Y, wait a moment, and then press Alt+R. Now press the left arrow key five times, and then press Alt+A. This should set the resolution to its minimum setting.

If this doesn't work, you'll have to reset or cycle the power on your computer. When the BIOS screen appears, press F8 until you see the Windows Advanced Options menu. On XP, select Enable VGA mode; on Vista, select Enable Low-Resolution Video. This starts Windows with your current display driver set to 640×480 resolution. You can then reset the resolution to something appropriate.

Note

Some display adapters will let you set the screen resolution higher than is physically displayable. In this case, part of the desktop will be hidden, and it will "pan" when you move the mouse to the edge of the screen. If you see this happen and don't like it, just reduce the resolution setting.

If you have a CRT monitor, it's best to adjust the refresh rate—the rate at which the display is repainted on the screen—to around 70Hz or higher if your monitor is capable of it. LCD monitors are fine at 60Hz, but CRTs at this speed have a faint flicker, more noticeable in your peripheral vision than at the center of your field of vision, that can give you a headache or cause eye strain.

To adjust the screen refresh rate on XP, open the Display Properties Settings tab, and click the Advanced button; on Vista, view the Display Settings control panel and click Advanced Settings. Select the Monitor tab, and select a higher refresh rate from the drop-down box. I typically use 70 or 72Hz for CRT monitors because most can handle this without problems, and 60Hz for LCD monitors. Again, most modern monitors are Plug-and-Play–capable and tell Windows what rates they can accommodate, but if you select too high a rate on a non–Plug-and-Play monitor, you can make the display inoperative, and can actually burn out your monitor. Click Apply after changing the rate, and be prepared to press Esc if the display doesn't come back within 5 to 10 seconds.

Resolution Issues on LCD Monitors

If you have a flat-panel LCD monitor, it's best to always run it at its native hardware resolution. LCD monitors can be fed a lower resolution signal, but the pixels on an LCD screen are physical, and can't simply be drawn farther apart as they can be on a CRT display. The LCD monitor or its driver must internally expand a lower resolution display to the higher, physically determined resolution. The result is that at lower resolution settings, the screen will always be slightly blurry.

If your aim is to make desktop elements, icons, and text larger and more readable, you might consider leaving the resolution at its native setting (the resolution that the monitor's hardware uses) to get the sharpest display, and instead ask Windows to draw larger elements and text, as discussed in the next section.

If you have an LCD monitor, be sure to read the section on font smoothing and ClearType later in this chapter.

Adjusting Text, Icon, and Window Element Sizes

If you find the items on the screen difficult to read or see, you can either lower the screen resolution, which makes everything larger but blurrier, or ask Windows to make the elements themselves larger while keeping a crisper, high screen resolution. Changing screen resolution was discussed in the previous section. Here's how to change the size of Windows' menus and text labels:

1. Right-click the Desktop, and select Properties on XP or Personalize on Vista.

2. Save the current screen settings so that if you're unhappy with the results, you can back the changes out. On XP, select the Themes tab, or on Vista, click Theme. Click Save As, and enter the name **Original Display Settings**. Click Save.

3. On XP, select the Appearance tab, change the Font Size drop-down to Large Fonts, and click Apply to view the new text size. The text in the dialog won't change but the desktop and Start menu will. You can also try the Extra Large Fonts setting. You can also enlarge not only fonts, but all Windows elements, using this procedure:

a. Right-click the Desktop and select Properties.

b. Select the Settings tab and click the Advanced button.

c. Select the General tab and make a note of the DPI setting. It's usually set to 96dpi, although some monitors may cause Windows to use a larger or smaller value. Select Custom Setting, and then drag the ruler left and right to adjust the scaling value. Start by entering a number about 1.2 times the original value. Release the mouse to see a sample of the new text size for menus and icons, and adjust again if desired. When you're satisfied, click OK, and then restart Windows.

d. You may need to repeat this procedure more than once. Experiment with the DPI setting at a higher value and the Font Size setting (discussed previously) at both the Normal and Large Fonts settings.

On Vista, the process is slightly different. In the left Tasks pane, click Adjust Font Size, and approve the User Account Control dialog. Select Larger Scale, and click Apply to check the results. You can also click Custom DPI and use your mouse to drag the ruler's tick marks left and right to change the font size. Release the mouse to see a sample of the new text size for menus and icon labels. Adjust again if necessary. Click OK when you're finished and check the results after Windows restarts.

4. If want to back out all the changes you made, go back to the Themes tab, open the Theme drop-down, select the entry that says Original Display Settings Without "(Modified)", and click OK.

With this change, application programs won't necessarily know to make their displays more readable, but many have settings that will enlarge the display. You can zoom the display in Microsoft Word, alter your email program's default font size, and so on.

Configuring Multiple Monitors

Windows quite nicely supports the use of two or more monitors; Windows can stretch your desktop across up to 16 of them. Sixteen may be overkill, but even two 15" monitors, with about the same area as one 21" monitor, make it easier to stretch out several application windows. And you should see what three 21" monitors in a row looks like!

To get a multiple monitor setup, you'll need to install multiple display adapters, use a display adapter that supports more than one monitor (a "dual head" or "quad head" adapter), or both. These days display adapters that support more than one monitor are increasingly common. Conversely, adding multiple adapters to a PC can be both difficult and cost prohibitive.

Note

Be careful when buying additional adapters. Most motherboards support just one high-speed PCI-Express (PCI-E) or AGP bus adapter, and any additional adapters must be PCI. Some motherboards have two or more PCI-E slots. On these motherboards, you'll get the best performance if you use two or more PCI-E adapters.

Some motherboards support a feature called Scalable Link Interface (SLI). SLI lets gaming programs use the graphics processing power of two identical nVIDIA-based PCI-E adapters to generate a single display. You can switch SLI mode on and off in software. Be aware that that when SLI mode is enabled, only one monitor will be active. Other manufacturers, such as ATI, have their own proprietary methods for using multiple graphics adapters.

Some laptops also support multiple monitors. The method varies between manufacturers; some require you to make a Control Panel setting (enable DualView), but on some you must use a function key to scroll between display modes. You want the one that enables both monitors with separate displays.

Tip

Some higher-performance display adapters come with advanced control panels that supercede the Windows display control panel. You should check the instructions for configuring your display adapter before using the procedures in this section. For example, some drivers for adapters based on nVIDIA chips want to set up and handle multiple-monitor configurations themselves. If you want to have Windows do it as described here, you have to instruct the nVIDIA driver to enable DualView display mode before Windows will recognize that multiple monitors are installed.

To enable the multiple monitor feature, connect your monitors to the display adapter connectors, turn them on, and then boot up Windows. The initial boot screen will appear on one monitor, or perhaps all the monitors connected to the primary adapter card.

When Windows starts, log on,and right-click the desktop. On XP, select Properties, and then view the Settings tab. On Vista, select Personalize, and then select Display Settings. The display will appear like that in Figure 5.2. To activate additional displays, click on the numbered monitor icons and check Extend My Windows Desktop Onto This Monitor; then click Apply. (If additional icons don't appear, you may need to select them in the Display drop-down list.)

It's important to arrange the monitor icons in the Settings dialog exactly as the monitors on your desk are arranged so that your mouse will move between the monitors in the right order. Click the Identify button to display numerals on your monitors. If necessary, rearrange the icons in the Settings dialog to appear in the same physical order, and then click Apply. The mouse should now move smoothly from monitor to monitor, left to right (or top to bottom, if you've stacked your monitors vertically). To eliminate any vertical jumping as the mouse crosses between the monitors, move the icons slightly up or down to exactly match the exact physical arrangement of your monitors, and click Apply to test the smoothness of the mouse movement. To move an icon one pixel at a time, click it, and then use the Up Arrow or Down Arrow key. You must click Apply before testing the adjustment.

Tip

If your computer has multiple monitors and you connect to the computer using Remote Desktop, you may find that an application seems to be running, but you can't make its window appear. What's happened is that it's positioned off-screen, where it would be if there were a second monitor. To move it into view, right-click the application's button in the taskbar. If Move is grayed out, click Restore, and then right-click again. Select Move, and press and hold down the left or right arrow key to bring the window into view.

Also, if you have monitors set to different screen resolutions, you may find that application windows and dialogs can open up with the title bar and menu out of view. To move them fully into view, select the window (click it anywhere), press Alt+spacebar followed by the letter M, and then use the arrow keys to move the window into view. Press Enter to lock in the new position.

Getting the Highest Quality Drivers

Although CPU speeds increase only fractionally from year to year, the special-purpose Graphical Processing Units (GPUs) built into display adapters are being improved in leaps and bounds and their processing speeds now reach into the *teraflop* (trillion floating-point operations per second) range. In fact, some researchers are now exploiting graphics adapters' blazing mathematical computation speeds to perform scientific calculations at supercomputer rates, with the main CPU left to handle mundane tasks such as shuffling data and performing I/O.

If you have a pricey high-speed graphics display adapter, perhaps because you're into computer games or graphical design, you should know that the drivers provided by Microsoft with Windows usually (a) are more reliable and (b) perform more slowly than drivers provided directly by the adapter's manufacturer. The reason is that Microsoft's drivers usually undergo more rigorous testing before being released as part of the Windows Setup CD or Windows Update, but they are also usually written to the lowest-common-denominator capabilities of the manufacturer's product line, and may not take best advantage of built-in acceleration capabilities.

The Microsoft drivers are the ones you'll get if you simply install your new graphics adapter and start up Windows. The manufacturer's drivers must usually be installed from a CD, or downloaded from the manufacturer's website. My experience is that new drivers for high-end graphics adapters are released fairly frequently, so you may want to make a note to check for updates every two or three months, at least until the updates for your model taper off.

When you test an upgrade to your drivers, you can usually use Driver Roll Back if you encounter a problem, but problems with graphics drivers sometimes make Windows completely unbootable. Frequently, what you will observe is that Windows makes it partway through its startup process, something flashes briefly on the screen, it goes black, and the boot process starts over. This repeats indefinitely. Or, the boot process may halt with white text on a blue background—this is the infamous Blue Screen of Death. If you've just installed a new graphics adapter, power off your computer, unplug it, remove the new adapter and/or replace the original one, and then power back up. If Windows boots successfully, download and install an updated driver before attempting to reinstall the new adapter.

▶▶ For more on testing an upgrade to your drivers, **see** "Updating Device Drivers", **p. 458**.

If Windows continues to fail to boot even without new hardware, you'll need to boot Windows in a special VGA mode, where it expects nothing but the most primitive graphics capability. Immediately after your system BIOS message flashes on the screen during bootup, start pressing the F8 key repeatedly until the Advanced Boot Options menu appears. (For more information about the Advanced Boot Options menu, see Chapter 2, "Windows Boot.") Select Enable VGA Mode and press Enter. This should let you get in, albeit at 640×480 resolution. Then perform a driver roll back or update your device driver.

Note

As you might guess, you're most likely to run into problems with the most up-to-date drivers for the latest, most expensive graphics adapters. Welcome to the leading edge of technology.

Font Smoothing and ClearType

You've probably noticed that with computer displays, as the size of displayed text get smaller and smaller, its appearance gets more and more jagged. The reason is that the curves and diagonal lines in the typeface are being drawn with a very limited number of square pixels on the screen, and the size of those pixels is fixed by the resolution of the monitor. At a certain point, your eye no longer glosses over the square edges, and you start to notice them. Figure 5.3(b) shows what happens to the letter *D* when it's drawn so small that it's just seven pixels high—the boxy pixels in the curved part are quite noticeable.

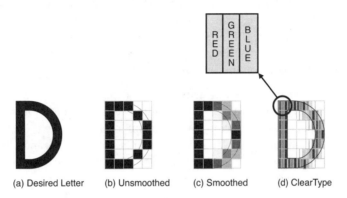

| (a) Desired Letter | (b) Unsmoothed | (c) Smoothed | (d) ClearType |

Figure 5.3   Font Smoothing and ClearType use shading to reduce jagginess.

Windows can help reduce this jagginess using a technique called *antialiasing*, or *font smoothing*, illustrated in Figure 5.3(c). Instead of being drawn only all-black or all-white, each pixel is shaded to the degree that it would have been filled in by the shape of the desired letter. If the shape would have filled in only half of the area of the pixel, it's displayed at half intensity. You can see that the jagginess is greatly diminished, but the shape also becomes blurred. (Hold the book at arm's length to get the best view of the pixel effects in the figure.) It's a trade-off, and whether it's worthwhile or not is a judgment that you have to make for yourself. To change the setting, open a document or web page with a small typeface. Then do the following:

- On XP, right-click the desktop, select Properties, select the Appearance tab, and then click Effects.

- On Vista, right-click the desktop, select Personalize, and select Window Color and Appearance. If the control panel displays a row of colored icons, click Open Classic Appearance Properties for More Color Options. In the Appearance Settings dialog, click Effects.

Then check or uncheck Use the Following Method to Smooth the Edges of Screen Fonts, with the drop-down box set to Standard. Click OK, and then click Apply, and see what you think of the effect. Switch back and forth a few times to see which display you prefer.

If you have an LCD monitor, you can choose between two different methods of smoothing fonts. The full-pixel method shown in Figure 5.3(c) is available on both CRT and LCD monitors. A second smoothing method trademarked by Microsoft as *ClearType* is available only for LCDs and takes advantage of the fact that each pixel on an LCD monitor is laid out as a set of vertical stripes of red, green, and blue, as illustrated in Figure 5.3(d). When the antialiasing concept is applied to each of these subpixels independently, the horizontal resolution for text is effectively tripled, and the blurred areas around curves are much smaller.

You could switch the effect on and off using the drop-down list on the Effects dialog that you used to turn smoothing on and off, but there's a much better way. Microsoft has released a ClearType Tuning program that displays a series of text samples using different degrees of smoothing, and lets you decide which you like best. (It's a lot like a visit to the ophthalmologist: "Which looks better, A or B?") After several comparisons, this tuning utility is able to set some ClearType smoothing options that aren't reachable directly, and the result can be a much improved display. There are two versions of the tuning tool. One is delivered as an ActiveX component in a web page, which can be used on either Vista or XP. The other is a downloadable, standalone XP PowerToy application. (Microsoft says that this PowerToy doesn't work on Vista, but I've tried it and it seems fine. Still, the online version works just as well, so that's the one to use.)

To use the online version of the tuner, visit microsoft.com and search for ClearType Tuner. Select the Windows ClearType Tuner link. When prompted to enable and/or install the ClearType Tuning Control published by Microsoft Corporation, click Continue or Install. After the ClearType Tuner web page is displayed, you should be able to check and uncheck the Turn On ClearType box and immediately see the difference. Then, with the box checked, click Next to go through the tuning process.

When the tuning process is finished, if you don't like ClearType, you can disable it. Just start the tuner again, uncheck Turn On ClearType, and close your web browser. Personally, I have ambivalent feelings about ClearType. Although the smoothing effect is quite remarkable, to my eyes ClearType text is too thin and blurry, and has an odd "unstable" quality—it seems to swim around a bit.

Note

Some applications such as Adobe Acrobat 8 and Internet Explorer 7 control font smoothing within their displays independently of the Display properties setting. So, if this procedure described in this section doesn't affect the display in one or more of your applications, look through the application's Preferences settings.

Note

For a comprehensive and interesting article on the concepts behind antialiasing and ClearType, with excellent illustrations, check out www.grc.com/ct/cleartype.htm. The nifty downloadable "Free and Clear" program lets you experiment with subpixel rendering and zoom in on the results. It's really fun.

Updating DirectX

Although most Windows applications place fairly low demands on the display system, putting up fairly static displays and updating them relatively infrequently, interactive games and video displays are very graphics intensive. Game players pay big bucks for *fps*, or *frames per second*, which is a measure of how fast the hardware and software can generate new images as the scene changes and objects move. Under about 30fps, the image flickers and motion is noticeably jerky. Beyond 30fps, faster updates aren't noticeable, and the extra processing power can be put to work by reconfiguring the game to generate more complex, detailed images.

The problem is that the software overhead that Windows places between applications and the graphics hardware in order to foster good cooperation, nicely rendered text, and cleanly overlapping windows can slow down a game program or DVD video player and hinder its capability to crank out images. Enter *DirectX*, a set of application software interfaces (drivers, really) that give applications direct, faster access to underlying display hardware, while still presenting a consistent software interface for all graphic card makes and models. DirectX provides hardware-independent image-rendering and sound-producing tools that applications and games can rely on; these can take advantage of the hardware adapters' built-in computing capabilities, but are guaranteed to work—if slowly—even on inexpensive adapters without hardware acceleration.

Microsoft updates DirectX on a schedule independent of its updates to Windows, and although some software setup CDs come with a version of DirectX, if you play video-intensive games or watch movies on your computer you're better off getting the latest DirectX package directly from Microsoft. To find out what version of DirectX is installed on your computer, click Start. On XP, click Run, and then type **dxdiag** in the command box. On Vista, type **dxdiag** in the Search box. Then press Enter. If prompted, click Yes to let dxdiag connect to the Internet to verify the digital signatures on your system's DirectX drivers. Finally, on the System tab, near the bottom of the System Information list, you should see an entry labeled DirectX Version. At the time this was written, the latest version of DirectX for Windows XP was version 9.0c, and the latest version of DirectX for Windows Vista was version 10.1 (it's installed as part of Windows Vista Service Pack 1).

DirectX updates are usually not security-related fixes, so they will not be delivered through Automatic Updates, nor will they appear in the High Priority section in Windows Update. DirectX *might* appear in Windows Update's Optional section. To check, click Start, All Programs, Windows Update. Select Custom updates, and view any entries in the "Software, Optional" category. Check and install DirectX if it appears.

If Windows Update doesn't offer you the latest DirectX package, you can also download and install the latest version from www.microsoft.com/directx.

Menu Accelerator Keys

In all versions of Windows prior to Windows XP, Window menus used underscores (as in File) to indicate Alt key shortcuts. For touch typists, these so-called *menu accelerators* can save a lot of time and trouble; it's much easier to type Alt+F, Alt+A than to take your hands off the keyboard, reach for the mouse and click File, Save As, and then go back to the keyboard to enter a filename. And you didn't even have to memorize these shortcuts; they were always displayed on the screen.

By default, however, current versions of Windows hide the telltale underscores until you press and release the Alt key. Unless you think to press the Alt key, you won't even know that the shortcuts are available, or which menu functions even have them. To make Windows display accelerators by default, on XP right-click the Desktop, select Properties, view the Appearance tab, click Effects, uncheck Hide Underlined Letters, and click OK. On Vista, open the Control Panel, select Appearance and Personalization, and then select Underline Keyboard Shortcuts and Access Keys, under Ease of Access Center. Scroll down and check the box under Make It Easier to Use Keyboard Shortcuts, and then click Save. Some applications, such as Word, control the appearance of menu accelerators themselves and are not affected by this setting.

Start Menu Settings

Windows Vista and XP use a Start menu, shown in Figure 5.4, that differs significantly from the Start menu in previous versions of Windows. Although some of the changes may please the casual user, not all of them contribute to efficiency and greater usability. The self-reorganizing Recent Application list is one example. Although a "most recently used" list for applications sounds like a good idea, and it may be for some users, it drives me crazy to have menu items appear and disappear and move around by themselves; usually I'm already moving my mouse to a favorite item before I can even read the menu titles, and I hate a moving target. Luckily, the Start menu and its submenus are eminently configurable. In this section, I'll list some changes you may want to make. To customize the Start menu, right-click the Start button and select Properties. From the Start Menu tab, you can elect to use the original Windows 2000–style Start menu by selecting Classic Start Menu. However, the new style Start menu can be much handier, so you may want simply to customize it instead. Click Customize, and investigate the following options:

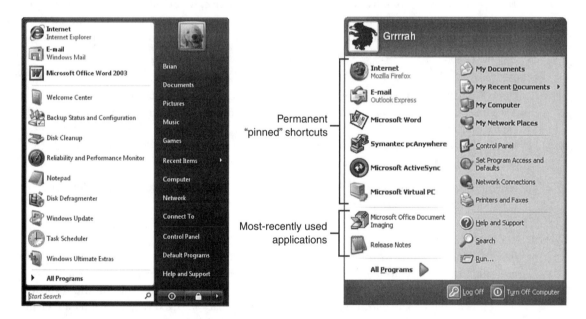

Figure 5.4   The Customizable Start menu, Vista (left) and XP (right) versions.

- You can eliminate the ever-changing most-recently used program icons in the bottom-left part of the menu by changing Number of Programs on Start Menu to 0. Or you can adjust the number of recent applications listed to another number.

- You can control whether Internet (web browser) or email icons are displayed, and what applications are launched.

- You can add your own preferred program shortcuts to the fixed upper-left part of the Start menu by locating items in the Start menu, holding down the right mouse button, and dragging them to the desired position in the main Start Menu panel. To remove an item from the fixed area, right-click the icon and select Remove from This List.

There are some other options that you can set directly on the Vista version of the dialog. On XP, you have to select the Advanced tab to get to these:

- In the large list of optional Start menu selections, you can determine whether items such as Control Panel and [My] Documents appear. You can also specify whether items such as Network [Connections] act as links, which when clicked open the associated window, or as menus, which when opened display a submenu.

- Favorites adds an item to the Start menu that, opened, lists all of your web browser bookmarks.

- You can elect to show or hide entries for Help and Support, Network Places, Printers, the Run command dialog, Search, and so on.

- The System Administrative Tools entry is especially helpful to set. By default it's disabled entirely. Select Display on the All Programs menu to enable the Administrative Tools submenu. (It's always available from the Control Panel in any case.)

- If you want, you can disable the list of most-recently opened documents. On Vista, view the Start menu's Properties dialog and uncheck Store and Display a List of Recently Opened Files. On XP, view the Start Menu's properties page, click Customize, select the Advanced tab, and uncheck List My Most Recently Opened Documents.

Once you've removed any unwanted Start menu features, you can add desired startup items of your own.

Organizing Menus for Efficient Use

Although menus that reorganize themselves can hinder you by short-circuiting your natural tendency to (eventually) learn where menu items are, you *can* move menu items to more convenient places and have them stay put.

Simply open the Start menu, hold down the right mouse button, and select and drag a menu item to a new position. A thin black line will appear where the menu will land if you release the mouse button. If the menu item above the mouse pointer has submenus, the submenus will open and if desired, you can move the menu item into the submenu.

Remember that the entire contents of the All Programs menu is actually a set of shortcuts stored in two folders: one containing your personal shortcuts and one containing shortcuts common to every user on the system. The contents of the two folders are merged to create the list of submenus and shortcuts that you see on the Start menu. On XP, these folders are \Documents and Settings*your_login_name*\Start Menu and \Documents and Settings\All Users\Start Menu, respectively. On Vista, the folders are \Users*your_login_name*\AppData\Roaming\Microsoft\ Windows\Start Menu and \ProgramData\Microsoft\Windows\Start Menu, respectively. Subfolders in these folders appear as submenus under All Programs, and any items in these folders are the menu items.

Creating QuickLaunch Icons

The taskbar has a place that can hold tiny icons for favorite applications or folders, called the QuickLaunch menu. The selected applications can be launched with a single click without even opening the Start menu, and the icons don't clutter up your desktop. I strongly suggest that you customize your QuickLaunch menu by following these steps:

1. Right-click the taskbar. If Lock the Taskbar is checked, uncheck it and right-click the taskbar again.

2. Select Toolbars, and check QuickLaunch.

3. If necessary, enlarge the QuickLaunch menu and/or adjust the height of the taskbar to make room for the QuickLaunch buttons. Some people keep dozens of icons in it, but I like to keep it down to fewer than 10; any more and I have trouble finding them more quickly there than I could in the Start menu.

4. Right-click any icons you don't want to have there, and select Delete.

5. Populate the QuickLaunch menu with icons from your desktop or Start menu. To get items from the Start menu, locate the desired Start menu item, right-click and hold the button down, and drag the icon to the desired position on the QuickLaunch menu. When you release it, select Copy Here from the menu that pops up. (If you inadvertently select Move Here, it will disappear from its original location in the Start menu. Immediately right-click the desktop and select Undo Move to fix this.) You can also open Windows Explorer and Alt+drag a shortcut to a favorite folder to the QuickLaunch menu. Be sure to use the Alt key while dragging, otherwise you will copy the folder's contents.

6. When you've added icons for your most common applications, resize the QuickLaunch menu down to the minimum necessary size, and if you want, relock the taskbar.

Some surprisingly big-name software applications install icons in your QuickLaunch menu whether you want them there or not, and occasionally reinstall them even after you've deleted them. It's arrogant and rude, but they do it anyway. You may have to weed your QuickLaunch menu from time to time.

Internet and Email Options

You have control over which programs are launched when you use the Internet or email icons on the Start menu. If you've installed an alternative web browser or email program and want to use it as your primary program from the Start menu, right-click the Start menu, select Properties, and click Customize. At the bottom of the dialog you can select from among the web browsers and email programs installed on your computer. (Non-Microsoft applications must have registered themselves correctly in order to appear in this list.) Microsoft products may not be available if you or your computer manufacturer disabled them—click Start, All Programs, and then on XP select Set Program Access and Defaults, or on Vista select Default Programs, to show or hide applications.

Changing the applications displayed as the Internet and email programs in the Start menu changes the programs launched from the QuickLaunch menu as well.

Tuning System Properties

The System Properties dialog provides one-stop shopping for a whole bunch of important system environment settings.

On XP, to open this dialog, right-click My Computer and select Properties, or open the Control Panel, select Performance and Maintenance, and open the System icon. You may need to be logged on as an Administrator to change many of the settings. (Alternatively, you can use runas to run cmd.exe as an administrator, and then type **start sysdm.cpl** to open the dialog.)

On Vista, User Account Control made it necessary to package administrative and nonadministrative features in separate programs, so access to various System Properties settings is maddeningly spread all over the Control Panel. However, you can use this neat trick, which works for all but one of the settings I'll describe shortly: Click Start, type **sysdm.cpl** in the Search box, press Enter, and then approve the User Account Control dialog. You can then select the various tabs just as you did on XP.

You can make the following adjustments from this dialog, shown in Figure 5.5:

Figure 5.5 You can make numerous adjustments from the System Properties dialog.

- **Computer Name** tab—Computer description, computer name, workgroup or domain network type, workgroup or domain name. These items are covered in Chapter 6, "Networking Windows."

- **Hardware** tab—Launch Device Manager, enable/disable installation of unsigned drivers, use of Windows Update during driver installation, and on XP only, management of hardware profiles (sets of different hardware configurations). These items are covered in Chapter 8, "Managing Windows."

- **Advanced** tab—Performance (CPU scheduling) adjustments, user profile management, system startup/crash recovery options, environment variables, configuration of crash reporting to Microsoft. User profiles and environment variables are covered in Chapter 8, and the remaining items are covered in the following sections.

- **System Protection or System Restore** tab—Selection of protected drives. This feature is covered in Chapter 8 and in Chapter 12, "Windows Troubleshooting." Chapter 12 deals with using System Restore to fix a nonbootable system.

- **Automatic Updates** tab—(XP only) Configuration of automatic update download and installation. On Vista, Automatic Updates are configured in the Control Panel. These items are covered in the following sections.

- **Remote** tab—Configuration of access to this computer via Remote Assistance and Remote Desktop. This tab is covered in Chapter 6.

You must be logged on as a Computer Administrator to change most of these settings, although any user can change his own personal Environment Variables list. Administrators (and Power Users on XP Professional) can change the default operating system in the startup and recovery options, virtual memory settings, visual effects, error reporting, and driver signing options.

Application Performance Settings

There are some settings you can use to adjust Windows performance. Virtual memory settings are the most important, and to a lesser extent, you can also instruct Windows to give slightly greater emphasis to either running programs or creating a smooth visual display.

To adjust these performance settings, on XP, right-click My Computer and select Properties. On Vista, click Start, right-click Computer, select Properties, and then Advanced System Settings. Select the Advanced tab, and click the top Settings button under Performance.

In the unlikely event that your computer will be running as a server of some sort, and is to expend as much of its processing power as possible running a constant CPU-intensive workload, you can disable Windows' slicker graphical features. On the Performance Options dialog, select the Visual Effects tab and check Adjust for Best Performance. If the processing is to be done by a service rather than an application launched on the desktop, select Background Services.

If your computer will be reading and writing a large amount of data using relatively small programs, you can tune Windows for faster I/O by selecting System Cache. This can take away from application memory space, so you should compare performance with and without this setting; a reboot is required to put the change in effect.

Virtual Memory and Page File Settings

The Windows virtual memory system works by writing data that won't fit into RAM—and data that could fit in RAM but that hasn't been used recently—onto the disk in what's called a *page file.*, For efficient operation, the page file should be unfragmented and positioned either on its own separate physical disk drive (preferably a disk that's seldom used) or on the Windows disk, but not on a drive that's really just an alternative partition on the same physical drive as the Windows installation drive.

▶▶ To determine what your system's RAM and page file requirements should be, **see** "How Much Memory Is Enough?" **p. 315**.

To configure page file sizes and locations, you must be logged on as a Computer Administrator. On XP, right-click My Computer and select Properties to open the System Properties dialog. On Vista, click Start, right-click Computer, select Properties, and then Advanced System Settings. Select the Advanced tab, and click the top Settings button under Performance. Select the Advanced tab and click the Change button under Virtual Memory. The page file configuration dialog appears as shown in Figure 5.6. On XP, the Automatically Manage Paging File Size for All Drives check box is not present.

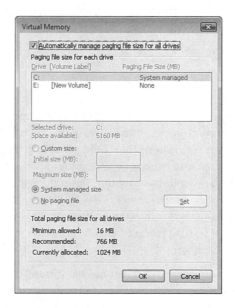

Figure 5.6 The Virtual Memory dialog lets you specify the location and size of page files.

After first installing Windows, there will probably be a page file located on drive C: (or the boot drive) with the System Managed Size option selected. You can create page files on more appropriate, faster drives and either leave the original file as is, or delete it.

To create a new page file, uncheck Automatically Manage Paging File Size on All Drives (if this check box is present), select a drive letter in the upper part of the dialog, and select either Custom Size or System Managed Size. If you want to prevent the page file from fragmenting, create it on a freshly formatted or defragmented drive and set a custom initial size at 1.5 to 3 times the amount of physical RAM installed in your computer. To prevent the page file from growing or fragmenting, set its maximum size at the same amount. The new file will be created and used immediately.

If you are not sure what your system's memory demands will be, leave the page file set to System Managed Size and let Windows manage it.

To delete a page file, select a drive letter in the upper part of the dialog and select No Paging File. The file will be freed and deleted when you restart Windows.

Note

Page files are created in the root folder of the selected drive(s) with the name **pagefile.sys**, with the System and Hidden attributes. The file will be locked and unreadable as long as Windows is running.

The disk defragment utility provided with Windows can't defragment your page file. The job can't be done while Windows is running, so it has to be done early in the boot process. You can do it with **PageDefrag**, a free stand-alone page file and Registry defragmenting utility, available at technet.microsoft.com. (PageDefrag is one of the fantastic tools Microsoft acquired along with SysInternals.com.) Many commercial defragmenters can do the job as well. Be sure to verify this capability before you purchase one.

For some tips on selecting appropriate page file settings, see "Placing the Page File" later in this chapter.

Data Execution Prevention

Windows Vista and Windows XP Service Pack 2 and later support a feature called Data Execution Prevention (DEP) that prevents programs from replacing the original, intended machine instructions in memory with new instructions that could perform malicious acts. This feature became necessary when virus writers and hackers began exploiting bugs in software that can result in program instructions being written in memory that was supposed to hold just program data. These are often referred to as *buffer overrun exploits* or *stack overflow exploits*. If the program's path through memory eventually takes it into the malicious code, the injected instructions can do anything *you* can do; that is, the program has your privileges, can access any file you can, can infect other programs, and so on.

Data Execution Prevention uses two different mechanisms to guard against this type of attack: First, it uses Windows software mechanisms to prevent programs from writing any new instructions into sections of memory that were originally designated as holding instructions. Second, it uses CPU hardware mechanisms to prevent programs from executing instructions in memory that was originally designated as holding only data. The second form of protection is the stronger of the two, but it is only available with some CPU chips, including all 64-bit processors from AMD and Intel, Intel's Pentium D and Pentium 840 Extreme Edition processors, and AMD's Sempron processors. This second mechanism is called *Execute Disable* or *ED* by Intel, and *No Execute* or *NX* by AMD, and it's used when available whenever Data Execution Prevention is enabled in Windows.

Note

On a corporate network, Data Execution Prevention is probably enabled and managed by the network Group Policy. Individual applications that are known to be safe but which modify their own executable instructions on purpose can be marked to opt out of protection using the Application Compatibility Toolkit. For more information about this mechanism, see www.microsoft.com/windows/appcompatibility/default.mspx.

By default, when Windows Vista or XP Service Pack 2 (or later) is installed, DEP is enabled only for Windows components themselves. To protect all applications, on XP, right-click My Computer and select Properties to open the System Properties dialog. On Vista, click Start, right-click

Computer, select Properties, and select Advanced System Settings. Then select the Advanced tab, and click the top Settings button under Performance. Select the Data Execution Prevention tab, shown in Figure 5.7.

Figure 5.7 Enabling Data Execution Prevention.

To enable DEP for all applications, select Turn On DEP for All Programs and Services Except Those I Select. (If this option is greyed out, your CPU does not support DEP.)

If you change Data Execution Prevention settings, you'll need to restart Windows. When enabled for all applications, you may find that an application that used to work now fails with a dialog box that says "Data Execution Prevention—A Windows security feature has detected a problem and closed this program." In this case, you should contact the manufacturer's tech support to see whether this is a known issue or if an update is available.

If you determine that the application is actually safe but just happens to require the capability to write modified instructions in order to work, you can instruct Windows to disable DEP for this application. Back in the DEP setup dialog (refer to Figure 5.7), click Add, and then browse to select the .exe file that corresponds to the application in question. Click OK to save it in the list of exceptions.

Caution

If you enable Hardware Data Execution Prevention and have a flaky device driver, the driver may prevent Windows from booting. Use the following procedure to recover.

If Windows halts with a blue screen, or reboots repeatedly when you restart it after enabling hardware DEP (or after updating a device driver when hardware DEP is enabled), one of your device drivers is executing code from "No Execute" memory and terminating. Use one of the following methods to disable DEP. First, try to boot Windows in Safe mode:

1. When your computer's BIOS startup screen appears, press F8 repeatedly until Windows' Advanced Startup Options menu appears. Select Safe Mode and press Enter.

2. When Windows has started, log on as a Computer Administrator, go back to the Data Execution Prevention setup tab, and disable hardware protection. Restart Windows to test.

If Windows won't even boot in Safe mode, you'll need to take the more drastic step of manually editing the boot configuration file on the hard drive that contains Windows. To do this on Windows XP, follow these steps:

1. If you have multiple versions of Windows installed, boot into an alternative version and try to perform steps 2 through 7 in another version. If that fails, remove the hard drive from your computer and install it in another computer, which, if your Windows partition uses NTFS formatting, must be running Windows Vista, XP, or 2000. If you need to change the drive's master/slave jumpers, be sure to make a note of the original setting before changing them.

2. Start up the alternative operating system or computer, and view My Computer to identify the drive letter that is assigned to your original Windows installation drive; let's say it's E. (If a different drive letter is assigned, use that letter instead of E in the next step.)

3. Open a command prompt window and type the following commands:

```
e:
attrib -r -h -s boot.ini
notepad boot.ini
```

4. In Notepad, locate the line under [operating systems] that has /NoExecute=OptIn, /NoExecute=OptOut, or /NoExecute=AlwaysOn in it. If the current setting is OptOut, carefully change it to read OptIn. If it currently says OptIn, change it to read AlwaysOff.

5. Save boot.ini (Alt+F, Alt+S) and close Notepad (Alt+X).

6. Type the following command:

```
attrib +r +h +s boot.ini
```

7. Shut down the computer. If you moved your hard disk to another computer in step 1, remove the hard drive, reset the master/slave jumpers if you changed them, put it back in your computer. Finally, restart Windows.

On Vista, recovery is less cumbersome. If you have only one operating system installed, use these steps:

1. Boot from your Vista setup DVD.

2. Select your language and keyboard.

3. Click Repair Your Computer.

4. Select your Vista installation and click Next.

5. Select Command Prompt.

6. Type the command **bcdedit /set {default} nx optin**.

7. Close the command prompt window, and then click Restart.

If you have other operating systems installed, you should be able to boot into another OS and use a GUI-based BCD editor to reconfigure the \boot\bcd store on your Vista installation.

Finally, when Windows boots successfully, log on as a Computer Administrator and check the event log for an indication of which driver failed during startup. Update it or roll it back before enabling hardware DEP again.

Setting Environment Variables

Environment variables are used by Windows to communicate the locations of certain folders to application programs. Environment variables are set through the System Properties dialog, but the process can be somewhat tricky, especially for the PATH variable.

▶▶ For instructions on managing environment variables, **see** "Setting Default Environment Variables," **p. 535**.

System Startup Options and Crash Recovery

The Startup and Recovery Options dialog lets you specify what operating system choices are available when your computer boots, and what action Windows should take when Windows itself crashes and cannot continue. To set these options on XP, right-click My Computer and select Properties to open the System Properties dialog. On Vista, right-click Computer, select Properties, and select Advanced System Settings. Then select the Advanced tab, and click the Settings button under Startup and Recovery.

If Windows crashes due to a bad device driver, hardware failure, or software error in an internal part of Windows itself, it will halt without performing a proper shutdown. It will usually display the now infamous Blue Screen of Death, which displays code numbers indicating the type of failure detected. What happens next depends on the options selected in the System Failure section of the Startup and Recovery dialog, which you can see in Figure 5.8.

By default all three options are checked:

- **Write an Event to the System Log**—Information about the crash is stored in memory, and when Windows restarts, if it is able to progress far enough that the system event logging service starts, the information will be recorded in the event log. The entry will not be written if the PC is shut off before Windows restarts, or if Windows fails to find the crash information left in memory when it restarts.

- **Send an Administrative Alert**—Like the preceding option, when Windows restarts, if it is able to detect that it had previously crashed, it will send an intercomputer message to any logged-on administrators. Unless you're on a network and actually use alerts, you can disable this option. (This option is not available on Windows Vista.)

- **Automatically Restart**—If this option is unchecked, Windows displays the blue screen after a crash, and the PC will have to be restarted using its reset button (or power switch) to reboot. If this option is checked, the blue screen will be displayed for only an instant, and Windows will automatically restart. This can be problematic if you never get to see what's wrong.

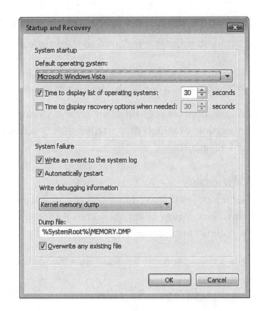

Figure 5.8 The Startup and Recovery Options dialog lets you specify boot crash restart behavior.

I recommend that for a server or other computer that must run unsupervised all the time, you check Automatically Restart, but for all other uses, uncheck Automatically Restart. Otherwise, after a crash, you will likely never get to see the information displayed on the blue screen, and if Windows is crashing before you have a chance to log on, you'll only be able to watch it boot up, crash, reboot, crash, over and over.

Note

If Windows does crash and restart in an endless loop, try pressing F8 repeatedly as soon as the reboot starts. On Vista, select Disable Automatic Restart on System Failure. Then select Start Windows Normally.

On XP, it's a bit harder. When you are in the Advanced Boot Options menu, select Safe Mode. When Windows has started up, open the Startup and Recovery dialog as discussed previously and uncheck Automatically Restart. Then restart Windows, and you should be able to see what the blue screen says.

If Safe mode doesn't work, remove the disk drive from the computer, install it in another computer running Windows XP (or Vista), and use the Registry Editor to mount the hive file `\windows\system32\config\system` on the crashed computer's hard drive (see "Editing a Hive File" later in this chapter for instructions). Find key `SYSTEM\Select` in the mounted hive. Locate value `Current` and note the number. Open key `System\ControlSet00n`, replacing *n* with the number you saw in value `Current`. Locate key `Control\CrashControl`. Edit value `AutoReboot` and change its value to 0. Shut down the computer, remove the drive, reinstall it in the original computer, and power it up. You should now be able to see what the blue screen says. If you don't have another computer you can use for this, you can add another hard drive to your original computer, install Windows on that drive, and then use this procedure to edit the Registry of the original drive.

The Write Debugging Information option can make Windows store a copy of the contents of memory in a disk file after a crash (assuming that the disk hardware and file system drivers are still operative). I recommend that you set this option to (none) unless requested to change it by a tech support person, or unless you are a device driver developer and need to use debugging tools to analyze the crash dumps. Saving crash dumps takes time and disk space and a complete memory dump can take a *very* long time.

Tip

Chapter 12 has more information on working through Blue Screen of Death issues.

Error Reporting

Windows has an application error reporting feature that collects information about the circumstances of application failures and Windows crashes and sends them back to Microsoft headquarters over your Internet connection. The purpose is to gather statistics about the types of crashes that occur, and enough information to identify what part of the program had the problem. Some people worry that it may invade their privacy (I don't), but it's a voluntary program, and it can help lead you to solutions for some types of system problems. And it helps everyone in the long run. The idea is that over time, statistical fingers will point toward the most error-prone programs, and with the necessary repairs, this will lead to improvements in future releases and service packs. Furthermore, if you enable error reporting, you can check on the status of your previous crashes. For more information, see "Problem Reports and Solutions," p. 788.

It makes sense to let error reporting send Microsoft reports about failures in Windows itself and in Microsoft applications. Vendors of most big-name applications obtain crash report information from Microsoft as well, so it's probably worth reporting other commercial applications. It usually doesn't make sense to report errors in applications you develop yourself or those from your own company, unless you've registered with Microsoft to pick up the information, so you can either elect not to send them when an error box pops up, or you can tell Windows not to even offer to report these applications.

Note

To obtain Windows error reporting logs for applications you've developed, go to www.microsoft.com/whdc/maintain/StartWER.mspx to begin the registration process.

To change the error reporting settings on XP, right-click My Computer and select Properties to open the System Properties dialog. Select the Advanced tab, and click the Error Reporting button at the bottom. In the Error Reporting dialog, you can disable error reporting entirely, or enable it for Windows itself, application programs, or both. For more detailed control over which programs are reported, click Choose Programs.

In the Choose Programs dialog, you can select All Programs to report everything, or All Programs in This List to report only Microsoft products or selected programs of your own choosing; click the Add button and locate the .exe files of any applications you want to include by name. You can also exclude specific programs using the list at the bottom of the dialog. Click Add to locate specific programs.

Note

When programs are listed for inclusion or exclusion, only the filename itself is recorded, not the full path. Thus if `AIM95.EXE` is listed, any program file named `AIM95.EXE` will be included or excluded no matter what folder it resides in.

On Vista, the problem reporting system has been significantly beefed up. To configure it, right-click Start, Control Panel, System and Maintenance. Under Problem Reports and Solutions, select Choose How to Check for Solutions, and then select Advanced Settings. In the Advanced Settings dialog, you can instruct Windows to enable or disable reporting for your account or for all accounts on your computer. You can also specify applications for which you don't want Windows to track problems. (Note that XP lets you list specific applications that you do or don't want to report, but Vista has no "include" list. When Problem Reporting is enabled, all applications are reported, except those listed in the block list.)

Note

When an error report is sent, it includes the name of the application that crashed, and a minimal amount of data copied from the memory stack. This stack data could conceivably contain a tiny bit of confidential information. It's very unlikely, but if you're seriously concerned about this, you should instruct Windows to never to send reports *before* you start using your computer for sensitive work.

Configuring Automatic Updates

Automatic Updates is a mechanism with an awkwardly plural-sounding name by which Microsoft or corporate network managers distribute critical security updates to Windows users. Fixes sent by this means are considered so important for adequate security in the hostile Internet environment that Microsoft prefers that you configure it to download and install the updates, and if necessary even restart your computer, without your having to be involved at all. I agree that most computers should be configured to accept these automatic updates and restarts. (An exception should be made for servers and workstations that perform critical services that must not be interrupted.) By default, Automatic Updates obtains updates from Microsoft's own servers. In a corporate environment, network managers can set up their own Windows Update servers so that they can test out new updates before they're delivered to throughout the organization (for more information on this, search technet.microsoft.com for "Windows Server Update Services").

There are four levels of Automatic Updates protection to which you can subscribe:

- **Automatic**—Windows will query Microsoft or your corporate network servers every day or on a specified day of the week, or whenever Internet access is available. It will download the updates when they become available, and will install the updates at a designated time, if the computer is on at that time, or the next time you shut the computer down, or when you log on as an administrator and open the Update Notification icon in the taskbar, whichever occurs soonest. This is the option recommended by Microsoft.

- **Download updates**—Windows will download the updates automatically, but will not automatically install them until you ask for them to be installed. You will be prompted to do this when you log on as an administrator; a balloon tip will pop up from the taskbar informing you that updates are ready to install.

- **Notify me**—Windows will not download updates automatically. You will have to log on as an administrator to receive the pop-up notification that updates are available for download and activate the pop-up icon to begin the download process.

- **Turn off**—Windows will neither download nor notify you of the availability of updates. This option should be used only on a corporate network where the administrators will take responsibility for all updates, but no Automatic Updates server is installed locally.

In most cases the Automatic method is best, for as long as your computer is turned on and has frequent Internet access, you will get these critical security fixes within hours or days of their release. The Download Updates option is recommended only if your computer is running important services and cannot be allowed to shut itself down for a restart without your consent and supervision, and you will be sure to log on as a computer administrator frequently so that you see the update notification.

To modify the Automatic Updates settings on XP, right-click My Computer and select Properties to open the System Properties dialog. Select the Automatic Updates tab, and make the appropriate selection. Click OK to save the change. On Vista, click Start, Control Panel, Security. Then, under Security Center, select Turn Automatic Updating On or Off.

Vista lets you not only choose how to receive critical updates, but gives you two additional options. By default, both are checked on installation:

- **Include recommended updates when downloading, installing or notifying me about updates**—This option lets Windows install "Recommended" updates as well as "Critical" security updates. "Recommended" updates are not security-related, but provide new or altered functionality. The category can include new versions of Windows Media Player, the .NET Framework, Root Certificate updates, and so on.

- **Use Microsoft Update Service**—This option lets Windows Update download security fixes for Microsoft Products other than Windows, such as Office. With the box unchecked, Automatic Updates uses the Windows Update service, and downloads only updates to Windows itself.

It is quite important that the vast majority of Windows computers do use Automatic Updates so that in the future there will not be large numbers of unprotected, vulnerable computers for software viruses and worms to prey upon. Keeping the number of vulnerable systems under a certain critical mass will help minimize the number of virus storms that occur.

Managing Startup Programs

Besides ensuring that your computer has adequate memory, one of the next best ways to improve your subjective experience of Windows' speed is to make the logon process faster. The logon process can be greatly slowed by large numbers of programs that are launched automatically upon logon; the desktop and Start menu don't respond until all the login programs have been activated.

Keeping the list of startup programs short is a constant struggle, however. To hide the fact that many common programs are poorly written and bloated in size, software vendors have taken to stealthily having Windows start them up when you log on, where they remain hidden. If you later launch the application, its window pops right up because it was actually already running in the background. The software vendors fool you into thinking that their products are fast, and that it's the Windows logon process that is slow. What's even worse, because you have to wait for their clunky software to start up *every time you log on*, even if you rarely actually use the application, over time they waste hours of your time to make their program start up 10 or 20 seconds faster. And, like virus authors, they usually have their software rigged to keep adding itself back as a startup program even after you've told it not to, especially after software updates. It's shameful, and what's amazing is that the vendors that practice this include large companies such as Apple (QuickTime Player and iTunes), Microsoft (Windows Messenger), and Real Audio (Real Player).

So, to avoid ongoing theft of your time, you need to know how startup programs are run, how to find them, and how to manage them.

There are several places to specify programs that are to be run upon logon:

- Shortcuts in the `Startup` folder in the `All Users Start Menu` folder, usually `\Documents and Settings\All Users\Start Menu\Startup` on XP, and `\ProgramData\Microsoft\Windows\Start Menu` on Vista.

- Shortcuts in the `Startup` folder in your personal `Start Menu` folder, usually `\Documents and Settings\`*your logon name*`\Start Menu\Startup` on XP, and `\Users\`*your logon name*`\AppData\Roaming\Microsoft\Windows\Start Menu` on Vista.

- Values in the following Registry keys:
  `HKEY_LOCAL_MACHINE\Software\Microsoft\Windows\CurrentVersion\Run`
  `HKEY_LOCAL_MACHINE\Software\Microsoft\Windows\CurrentVersion\RunOnce`

  `HKEY_LOCAL_MACHINE\Software\Microsoft\Windows\CurrentVersion\RunOnceEx`

  `HKEY_CURRENT_USER\Software\Microsoft\Windows\CurrentVersion\Run`

  `HKEY_CURRENT_USER\Software\Microsoft\Windows\CurrentVersion\RunOnce`

  `HKEY_CURRENT_USER\Software\Microsoft\Windows\CurrentVersion\RunOnceEx`

- Commands in logon scripts specified through Group Policy or Local Security Policy, on Windows XP Professional or Vista Business, Enterprise, or Ultimate.

- On Vista, tasks set up in the Task Scheduler with triggers set for logon, startup, connect to user session, and so on.

▶▶ Two other potential sources of startup programs are the `Winlogon\Shell` Registry value and print monitors. For more information, **see** "Startup Programs," **p. 61**.

You can manually scan through these locations using Windows Explorer and the Registry Editor, or you can use the msconfig tool described in the next section. In some cases the program being run will be obvious but in other cases you will need to do some research to determine what the startup program is. I've found that a Google search on the name of the `.exe` file (for example, something like `ssmmgr.exe`) will usually lead me to a clue, although there are now dozens of fairly useless websites that simply contain pages for all known programs, with advertising and links to very dubious "antispyware" products. Another good site to check out is www.sysinfo.org/startuplist.php. There you can search a database of known good and bad programs.

Some programs definitely should be run at startup. These include special purpose printer monitors, certain backup applications, antivirus and antispyware user interfaces, PDA synchronizers, and such programs. Even programs like Apple's Quicktime player startup program `qttask.exe` might be worth allowing to remain active as startup programs *if* you use these applications during nearly every logon session.

Some programs can be cajoled into at least temporarily removing themselves as startup programs. QuickTime Player, for example, has a Preferences setting under its Browser Plug-In category called "QuickTime System Tray Icon." Unchecking this *appears* to remove the `qttask.exe` startup program (for a while, at least, until the next update to QuickTime Player).

However, you should still check the Run Registry entries after doing changing the program's startup preferences because many programs still leave a startup entry in place in order to check with the manufacturer for software updates; if no updates are found, the program quits without creating a System Tray icon. (QuickTime Player is one of the programs that does this.) This stealth tactic still takes up a significant amount of your time *every time you log on*, so if you find that a program keeps its Run startup entry after you've disabled its "quick start" feature, and you really do want to prevent it from running, delete the associated Run entry (and send a complaint to the software vendor).

If you decide to manually eliminate a startup program, it can't hurt to make a note of the corresponding entry before you delete it, in case you want to manually restore it later. Deleting startup programs requires deleting shortcuts from the Startup folder (or moving them out of the Startup folder), or deleting specific Registry values using the Registry editor. (Editing the Registry is discussed later in this chapter.)

msconfig

To quickly see what programs are run when you log on and to test what happens without them, use msconfig, a utility provided with both Windows XP and Vista. To start msconfig on XP, log on as a computer administrator, click Start, Run, and then enter **msconfig**. To run it from the command line, type **start msconfig**. If you are not currently logged on as a computer administrator, open Windows Explorer and browse to `\Windows\PCHEALTH\Binaries`. Right-click `msconfig.exe` and enter administrator credentials. On Vista, just type **msconfig** into the Start menu's search box, press Enter, and confirm the User Account Control prompt. The Vista version of the program is shown in Figure 5.9.

Figure 5.9   msconfig lets you test Windows with and without startup programs.

The program's main window is shown here. On the General tab, you can select what sets of programs Windows starts up at boot time and when you log on:

- The Boot or `boot.ini` tab controls which version of Windows is run at boot time, and what diagnostic options are enabled. (`boot.ini` is discussed in detail in Chapter 2.)
- Services are started when Windows starts.
- Startup items, discussed earlier in this section, are run when you log on, from Registry values and Startup folder shortcuts.
- `win.ini` and `system.ini` entries are also processed when you log on; usually these contain only entries inserted by 16-bit Windows applications. (This applies to Windows XP only.)

The Diagnostic Startup mode loads an absolute minimum number of drivers and services. Selective Startup lets you individually control which programs and services are run at startup and logon.

Individual services and startup programs can be disabled using check boxes on the other five tabs. For a minimal startup that preserves the ability to perform maintenance, Microsoft recommends that you do *not* disable the following services:

- Cryptographic Services
- Event Log
- Logical Disk Manager
- Help and Support
- Plug and Play
- Remote Procedure Call (RPC)
- System Restore Service
- Windows Management Instrumentation

msconfig does not permanently disable services or delete entries that initiate startup programs. It simply inhibits them temporarily, and in fact when you log on while items are disabled, you will see a dialog box warning you of this. msconfig is meant to be used to identify which services or startup programs are causing specific problems by process of elimination so that you can then disable or delete the service or program by the usual means, and use msconfig to restore "normal startup" operation.

Tip

`Msconfig` comes preinstalled on Windows[md]so it's always available[md]but you can download a much better tool called `Autoruns` from Microsoft's website. Autoruns knows about a number of additional mechanisms that Windows uses to start programs, including printer drivers and Explorer extensions. To get it, visit microsoft.com and search for "Autoruns for Windows."

Antispyware and Antivirus Programs

As I discuss in more detail in Chapter 7, "Protecting and Securing Windows," if your computer is infected with spyware or viruses, you will likely not be able to remove their associated startup programs nor their executable files for more than a few seconds at a time. They're devious. Use a good antispyware or antivirus program to clean and protect your computer.

Be very careful when researching antispyware and antivirus programs on the Internet, however. The Web is filled with bogus advertisements and "reviews" for products that actually *install* spyware and viruses on your computer. Remember that no reputable software vendor would *ever* advertise with a pop-up ad, offer to scan your computer for viruses for free over the Internet, or use an ad that looks like a Windows error dialog box saying "Your computer is unprotected!"

Tip

If you do want to have a go at removing spyware manually, boot Windows in Safe mode with Command Prompt; this prevents all Startup programs from running, even the desktop GUI, so you'll have a better chance of deleting the executables and the startup entries. Also, many spyware programs deliberately attack any setup programs they believe to be antispyware installers. If your antispyware program's installer hangs up or crashes, reboot in Safe mode and try to install it again.

Most viruses and spyware programs use several different means to get themselves running when you log on, so, if you find an entry that's starting a dubious program, don't just delete that one entry and assume that the problem is fixed.

Internet Explorer

Internet Explorer (IE) is a significant application and, assuming that you don't use an alternative browser, you probably open it more than any other application on your computer. It has a little startup system of its own that you can tune to minimize the time it takes for IE to open and become available.

First off, Microsoft and nearly every computer manufacturer seem to think that it is *their website* that you want to visit every time you open a copy of IE, but they're wrong. You can control where IE goes when it opens. If you really do visit the same site nearly every time you open IE, set that page to be your start page: visit the page. If the Internet Explorer menu is not visible, press and release the Alt key. Then click Tools, Internet Options and under Home Page, click Use Current. If you're like me, though, and head off to visit all sorts of random pages, set IE to display a blank screen when it opens: Click Tools, Internet Options, Use Blank. This will save you a few seconds every time you open IE.

Tip

If you use Internet Explorer's menu frequently and don't like its little disappearing act, you can make it remain permanently visible. Press and release Alt to make it appear, and then click View, Toolbars, and check Menu Bar.

Furthermore, if you type an invalid URL, you probably *don't* want to send the mistyped entry to Microsoft for its recommendation of what you ought to view. Open the Internet Options dialog, select the Advanced tab, scroll down to Search from the Address Bar, and select Do Not Search from the Address Bar. You may have to reset this option from time to time because Microsoft occasionally changes it back to its preferred setting.

Also, software vendors and ISPs seem very interested in installing add-on toolbars and "browser helper" agents into IE, which you pay for with your time every time IE starts and has to load them. Click View, Toolbars and disable any toolbars you don't want or use. Click Tools, Manage Add-Ons to disable any browser plug-ins that you don't recognize, don't want, or don't use.

TweakUI and TweakVI

TweakUI is a program that you can download for free from Microsoft, and it's a veritable Swiss Army knife for Windows configuration. TweakUI lets you configure many Windows features that aren't adjustable from standard Windows dialogs or control panels. I'll give you a tour in this section, but I recommend that you download and install a copy—you may find that something I've passed over as uninteresting is just what you've been looking for. For information on obtaining and installing TweakUI for Windows XP, see "PowerToys for Windows XP" on page A14.

TweakUI works on Windows 2000 and XP, but not on Vista, and for some reason Microsoft seems not to be interested in making a Vista version. For Vista, you can use TweakVI, a commercial product, which you can get from www.tweakvi.com. The free version performs plenty of useful functions, and you can purchase additional features if you wish. (If you install it, I strongly urge you not to let it disable User Account Control.)

Table 5.2 lists the categories of adjustments TweakUI can make, with a brief description of the items available in each category. For each item, you can see a fairly detailed description by clicking on the name of the item as opposed to its check box, although in a few cases this also toggles the check box. Where there are several categories of options, you can also click the ? button at the upper-right corner of the window, and then click the item's name. (If the Description text doesn't change, the same description applies to all the displayed items.)

Table 5.2   Adjustments Available via TweakUI

Category	Adjustments
About	None.
Tips	None; here you can view the tips that Windows offered to show you the first time you logged on, which you didn't read but instead clicked "Don't show these ever again." These tips refer to Windows itself, not TweakUI.
General	Beep-on-error, menu animation and fading.
Focus	Focus-stealing prevention, taskbar flashing.
Mouse	Speed, double-click, and drag sensitivity.
Hover	Balloon-tip hover sensitivity.
Wheel	Mouse-wheel sensitivity.
X-Mouse	"Activation follows mouse" option.
Explorer	Double-click action, scrolling, search behaviors.
Shortcut	Visual appearance of shortcut icons.
Colors	Colors for compressed, tracked, encrypted files.
Thumbnails	Image quality and size for Thumbnail view.
Command Keys	Assignments for special keyboard function keys such as email and speaker volume.
Taskbar	Balloon tips.
Grouping	Grouping of multiple copies of applications into a single toolbar button.
XP Start Menu	Applications that can be added to Frequently Used Programs list.

Category	Adjustments
Desktop	Visibility of icons for IE, Recycle Bin, My Computer, Documents, Network Places.
First Icon	Order of My Desktop/Computer icons.
My Computer	Visibility of icons for Control Panel, mobile devices, other special displays.
Special Folder	Location of files held for burning to CD.
AutoPlay	None; reminds you how to enable/disable autoplay and select autoplay applications.
Handlers	Autoplay players and actions, associated commands, and media types.
Control Panel	Visibility of Control Panel icons.
Templates	Document types for New context menu.
Internet Explorer	Toolbar background.
Search	Search shortcut keywords for Address field.
View Source	Program used to display page source.
Command Prompt	Filename and directory completion keys, word separators recognized by Ctrl+Left, Right.
Logon	Parsing of `autoexec.bat` for `SET` commands.
Unread Mail	Notification of new mail on Welcome screen.
Repair	None; repairs missing or incorrect desktop icons.

Using TweakUI to...

As you can see in Table 5.2, there are quite a few adjustments you can make with TweakUI. Here are a few that I find interesting, keeping in mind my earlier comments about the trade-off between making Windows easier to use versus the irritation of finding that everyone's computer behaves differently.

Speed Up XP's Menus

Although XP's fading menus are nice, and perhaps easier on the eyes than the older instant-pop-up kind, I don't like waiting for them, and on some computers, they're too slow and jerky. You can eliminate all fades and UI animation from TweakUI's General page by unchecking Enable Combo Box Animation, Enable List Box Animation, Enable Menu Animation, Enable Menu Fading, and Enable Tooltip Fade. Leave Window Animation (that swoopy thing windows do when you minimize and reopen them) checked; it's too helpful to disable.

Tip

You can make the same adjustments on Vista manually. Click Start, right-click Computer, select Advanced System Settings, and then click the Settings button under Performance. Select Adjust for Best Performance to nix all graphical slickness, or just uncheck the three Fade and two Slide items.

Hide or Show Desktop Icons

You can use the standard desktop Display Properties dialog to hide or show icons for My Computer, My Documents, and so on, but TweakUI can also make the Recycle Bin disappear. I prefer to have a completely clean desktop and hide Recycle Bin because I always press the Del key to delete files anyway. This is a per-user setting.

Perform Instant Searches from Internet Explorer

You can add a special form of shortcut to Internet Explorer that lets you perform searches from the Address bar. For instance, I defined "gg" as a shortcut for Google searches, so I can type **gg Windows XP tweakui** in the Address field to perform a Google search for the words Windows XP tweakui.

To define a prefix, open TweakUI, select Internet Explorer, and Search in TweakUI, and click Create. Enter a desired prefix and the query URL with %s in place of the search words, and click OK to save. The next time you start Internet Explorer, the prefix will be available. Here are some ways you can use this feature:

Google Search: gg *words to find*

> Prefix: gg
> URL: http://www.google.com/search?q=%s

Yahoo! Search: yy *words to find*

> Prefix: yy
> URL: http://search.yahoo.com/search?p=%s

United Parcel Service Package Tracking: ups 1z2345678901234567

> Prefix: ups
> URL: http://wwwapps.ups.com/WebTracking/
> processInputRequest?TypeOfInquiryNumber=T&InquiryNumber1=%s

FedEx Package Tracking: fedex 1234567890

> Prefix: fedex
> URL: http://www.fedex.com/Tracking?tracknumbers=%s

To design your own prefix URL, perform a search, take the URL from the results page, and replace the query words you had typed in with %s. (Be sure to prefix the URL with http://, or it doesn't work.) This search method works only with websites that transmit the query string in the URL; not all of them do.

Tip

It's hard to enter these shortcuts manually. To install these search shortcuts on Vista, it's best to enter them on a Windows XP computer using TweakUI, and then export the Registry key **HKEY_CURRENT_USER\Software\ Microsoft\Internet Explorer\SearchUrl** to a **.reg** file, and import the **.reg** file on Vista.

Enable Filename and Directory Completion

If you use the command prompt a lot, you can save a lot of typing if you take advantage of filename and directory completion. When you're entering a command line, by default, if you press the Tab key, Windows will take whatever you've typed so far and perform a directory search to see whether any file or folder names match. If one or more does, Windows finishes typing it for you; successive Tabs scroll through other matching files. You can designate a separate key to be used only to match folder names using TweakUI's Command Prompt page. I use Ctrl+D.

Most Windows settings (and in fact, all the settings made by TweakUI) are controlled by entries in the Windows Registry, and you may run into articles on various websites that tell you how to adjust many of the same settings by editing the Registry. It's neither necessary nor advisable to do so when a nifty, comprehensive graphical tool such as TweakUI can do the job. However, there may on rare occasion be times when you need to make Registry changes directly. The next section covers this process.

Other Useful XP PowerToys

Besides the TweakUI PowerToy, you may want to download and install some or all of the others. I've found several of them to be very helpful:

- **Open Command Window Here**—This PowerToy adds an Open Command Window Here context menu option on file system folders, giving you a quick way to open a command window (`cmd.exe`) preset to use the selected folder.
- **Alt-Tab Replacement**—With this PowerToy, when you press Alt+Tab to switch between applications, in addition to seeing the icon of the application window you are switching to, you will also see a preview of the window and its contents. This helps particularly when multiple sessions of an application are open.

Microsoft has an additional tweaking tool for Windows XP Media Center Edition 2005 and later called TweakMCE. You can get it by searching www.microsoft.com for "Tweak MCE." It lets you alter remote control settings, skip and replay times, user interface options, and more. It also lets you adjust MCE for plasma and LCD displays.

Vista Tweaking Tools

In addition to TweakVI, which I mentioned previously, there are other third-party tools that you might want to have on hand to help tune and tweak Windows Vista:

- **Vista Boot Pro**—If you multiboot your computer (that is, if you have it set up to let you select which operating system to use at startup), you'll definitely want to get the free tool Vista Boot Pro from www.vistabootpro.org. It's a GUI tool that lets you edit Vista's boot configuration data.
- **EasyBCD**—This is another boot configuration editor tool, available from www.neosmart.net. EasyBCD has some advanced tools to let you configure the boot managers for Linux and Mac OS X (in case you're running Windows Vista on an Intel-powered Mac).

The Windows Registry

The Windows XP Registry is the central repository in which Windows and most Windows applications store configuration information, such as hardware settings, software configuration, licensing and registration data, associations between filename extensions and applications, and user preferences.

For most of your daily tasks with Windows, you will never need to touch the Registry. Almost everything you'll ever need to configure that shows up in the Registry can be handled through a Control Panel applet, application option dialogs, or, as discussed in the last section, tweaking tools such as TweakUI. But there are some adjustments that can only be made through direct Registry settings, so you should know the basics of safe Registry editing.

There are hundreds of websites offering advice about performance improvements you can gain by altering Registry settings. My advice is to *ignore these entirely*. My experience is that much such advice is either out of date, specific to other versions of Windows or very particular situations (but not yours), or flat-out wrong. (As a perfect example, while writing the previous section, I tried a Registry hack that purported to make the TweakUI XP Power Toy appear in the Control Panel, and it did do that, but it also made Explorer crash every time I clicked on a Control Panel icon.) There are, however, times when Registry editing is necessary; usually on the advice of a Microsoft Knowledge Base article, tech support person, or a helpful book like this one.

Structure of the Registry

The Registry is a specialized database that is organized a lot like the files and folders on your hard disk. The Registry contains *values*, which can be compared to files, and values are stored in a hierarchical structure of *keys*, which can be compared to folders. There are five *top-level keys*, under which all the Registry's keys reside. Logically, then, each top-level key contains a plethora of related keys, subkeys, values, and data. The top-level keys (in order of appearance) are as follows:

- **HKEY_CLASSES_ROOT (HKCR)**—This contains file association data. For example, when you click on a file ending in .txt, the .txt subkey contains the information that tells Windows to display the file using Notepad. HKEY_CLASSES_ROOT also contains the configuration information for COM and ActiveX objects and document type/MIME type associations. HKCR is actually a combined view of two other Registry sections: HKEY_LOCAL_MACHINE\Software\ Classes, which contains systemwide default application associations, and HKEY_CURRENT_USER\ Software\Classes, which contains user-specified preferences for application associations. If any keys appearing in both locations are in conflict, the settings specified under HKEY_CURRENT_USER appear.

- **HKEY_CURRENT_USER (HKCU)**— This is another virtual top-level key that actually references the subsection of HKEY_USERS pertaining to the currently logged-on user.

- **HKEY_LOCAL_MACHINE (HKLM)**— This stores all hardware and machine-specific setup information for your computer. For example, this key lists every device driver to load, all of your hardware's settings, all services and service configurations, and any software setup and configuration data that is common to all users.

- **HKEY_USERS (HKU)**— This contains a subkey for each user of the computer, as well as subkeys for built-in hidden accounts used for system services. Under each user's key, Windows stores user-specific information such as file locations, display preferences, software preferences, and recently accessed file lists. These keys are only loaded when the associated user is logged on. When you're logged on, your HKEY_USERS subkey appears as the content of HKEY_CURRENT_USER.

- **HKEY_CURRENT_CONFIG (HKCC)** —This is another virtual top-level key whose contents are actually the contents of HKEY_LOCAL_MACHINE\System\CurrentControlSet\Hardware Profiles\Current. This key is the selected hardware configuration specific to your current hardware profile.

Note

When referencing the Registry via a script or command-line utility—as well as in much of the documentation available for the Registry—the parent Registry hives are often referred to only by their three- or four-letter standard abbreviations. The accepted abbreviations are listed in parentheses behind their associated full names in the preceding list.

Physically, the Registry's data is stored in a small collection of files called *hives*. For each hive file there is corresponding file called a *change log*, which protects against corruption from system crashes. Most hive files can be found in folder %*systemroot*%\System32\Config. The Registry hive used to store per-user preference settings is named ntuser.dat (with corresponding change log file NTUSER.DAT.LOG), and is stored in each user's profile folder, which on XP is by default %*systemdrive*%\Documents and Settings*username* and on Vista is %*systemdrive*%\Users\ *username*. This hive's data is loaded as a subkey under top-level key HKEY_USERS when a user logs on, and the same data appears under top-level key HKEY_CURRENT_USER when the user is the current primary user.

Another file, UsrClass.dat (and UsrClass.dat.LOG), can be found a bit deeper under each user profile in %*systemdrive*%\Documents and Settings*username*\Local Settings\Application Data\Microsoft\Windows on XP, and in %*systemdrive*%\Users*username*\AppData\Local\ Microsoft\Windows on Vista. This second hive holds the list of keys that *add to* and *override* systemwide settings that are specified in the HKEY_CLASSES_ROOT key. This feature makes it possible for users to have individualized document type/application associations (which used to be applied throughout the system) and for individual users to have customized application and ActiveX/COM object installations.

Note

You can see a complete listing of the full paths to all currently loaded Registry hives under HKEY_LOCAL_MACHINE\ SYSTEM\CurrentControlSet\Control\hivelist.

Backing Up and Restoring the Registry

Before diving into Registry modifications, I'll talk about backing them up. Every computer book I've seen (including those I've written) stresses these facts:

1. There is no Undo key in the Registry Editor.

2. Improper changes to the Registry can keep Windows from booting, or can make subsystems fail to work.

3. You should always perform a system backup, or at least back up the entire Registry before you make *any* changes to the Registry.

In the spirit of full disclosure, I have to tell you that items 1 and 2 are completely true, and I've never followed the advice of item 3 myself. Maybe I'm an idiot, maybe the warnings are a bit too strident, or maybe it's something in between. But, especially with Windows System Restore feature to do all of the work for you, there's really no good excuse for not taking a few extra moments to protect yourself against a preventable bad outcome.

You can back up the Registry in Windows XP in five ways: You can back it up as part of a regular disk backup; you can selectively back up portions of the Registry by exporting the keys with the Registry Editor; you can create a System Restore Point; you can use the command-line application REG.EXE; or you can use a special-purpose Registry backup program.

I'd recommend using the Restore Point method, which is described under Creating Restore Points in Chapter 8, "Managing Windows," (p. 502). The other methods are rather more time-consuming, but I'll describe them here because they have other uses besides backing up and restoring the Registry.

Exporting and Importing Registry Files with the Registry Editor

The Registry Editor allows you to selectively export anything from a single subkey to an entire Registry key. The principal use for this feature is to let you save modified Registry keys or values to a file that you can then import on other computers to quickly deploy the same modification. As a secondary use, if you're performing significant Registry modifications, this is a good way to ensure that you can figure out what the original values were if you need to back out your changes.

To back up a key including all subkeys and values, follow these steps:

1. Click Start. On XP, click Run, type **regedit**, and click OK. On Vista, type **regedit** into the Search box, press Enter, and then confirm the User Account Control prompt.

2. Select the key you want to back up from the list in the left pane.

3. Select File, Export.

4. In the Common File dialog, select a directory and enter the filename where you would like to save the exported Registry entries.

5. Select Selected Branch in the Export Range option box, and click Save.

Because this is a plain-text file, you can open it in Notepad to see the contents. I often use this method to deploy changes to several computers: I make limited Registry changes on a single system, export the change as a .reg file, edit the file down to just the modified entries, move the file to a network folder, and import the file on other machines.

Importing a Registry file exported through the Registry Editor is just as straightforward as exporting:

1. Click Start, Run, type **regedit**, and click OK.

2. Select File, Import.

3. In the Common File dialog, enter the filename containing the data you want to import.

4. Select Open.

Importing a Registry setting through the Registry Editor overwrites existing keys or values and adds missing keys or values, but it does *not* delete extra keys or values that are not contained in the Registry file. However, you can use a Registry file to explicitly specify subkeys or values to delete. I'll show you how in the section "Deploying Registry Settings with .reg Files," later in this chapter.

Note

You can also import .reg files without manually starting up the Registry editor. Just locate the .reg file in Explorer and double-click. Alternatively, you can type **start** *filename.reg* or **regedit** *filename.reg* at the command prompt. (You'll get a prompt verifying that you indeed want to import the Registry data.) The command line **regedit** */s* *filename.reg* imports a Registry file without any confirmation. You can't back out of the import after you've done it, so be very sure that you know what you're importing when you use a .reg file this way.

Command-Line Registry Modifications with reg.exe

A command-line Registry manipulation tool called reg.exe is included with Windows XP and Vista. This tool is useful for adding or deleting Registry values from the command line. Numerous functions are available in reg.exe, including bulk Registry exporting and importing.

To save a Registry key using reg.exe, use the following syntax:

```
reg export rootkey\subkey filename
```

This saves the entire subkey and any values or subkeys it contains. For rootkey, you can use the abbreviations HKLM, HKCU, HKCR, HKU, or HKCC. *Subkey* must be the full name of a Registry key under the selected root. *Filename* is the name of the file to which you want to save the exported data.

To import a Registry key using reg, use the following syntax:

```
reg import filename
```

When importing, *filename* can be any file created by reg export, from the regedit Registry Editor's Export command, or created manually with a text editor.

The reg command can also set, delete, and extract Registry values. For example, the command line

```
reg add HKCU\Software\MyCompany /v ValueName /t REG_DWORD /d 0xff
```

sets the DWORD value ValueName in the key HKEY_CURRENT_USER\Software\Company\Keyname to the hex value FF. What makes the reg command interesting is that it can also operate on remote computers, over the network, if you have administrative rights on that computer. Only keys HKEY_LOCAL_MACHINE (HKLM) and HKEY_USERS (HKU) are accessible remotely. (The Remote Registry service must be running on the remote computer for this to work. And on Vista, User Account Control prevents anyone but a domain administrator from accessing the Registry using reg.)

Note

You can do quite a few things with **reg**. Use the command **reg** */?* for a complete usage syntax of the command.

Editing the Registry

The primary interface to the Registry, the Registry Editor, displays a representation of the Registry using an interface that is similar to the familiar layout of folders and files as viewed through Windows Explorer. To run it, click Start. On XP, click Run, type **regedit**, and press Enter. On Vista, type **regedit** into the Search box, press Enter, and then confirm the User Account Control prompt.

Figure 5.10 shows a Registry Editor window. The left pane contains the five top-level keys. The status bar along the bottom displays the full path of the currently selected key. I've expanded the HKEY_CURRENT_USER and HKEY_LOCAL_MACHINE keys to show the first round of subkeys beneath each. The right pane shows values assigned to the key selected in the left pane.

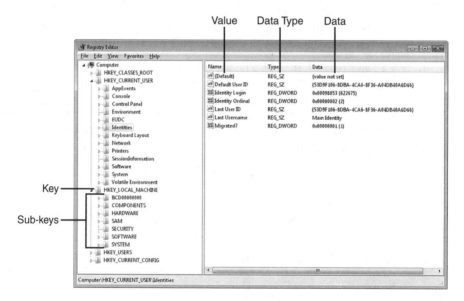

Figure 5.10   The Registry Editor: unfiltered access to your system's configuration database.

Just as a disk's folders can contain subfolders, and in each there may be files as well, Registry keys can contain subkeys, and each key can contain *values* as well. Most Registry editing tasks consist of locating one or two existing values and changing them. Occasionally, you will need to add new values or subkeys; it is impossible for you to add a new top-level Registry key.

The five main value data types in the Registry are as follows:

- **REG_DWORD**—This is a single hexadecimal or decimal number. You can select decimal or hexadecimal display when you're editing a particular value.
- **REG_BINARY**—This is a block of binary data displayed in the REGEDIT interface in hexadecimal format.
- **REG_SZ**—This is a plain-text string of alphanumeric characters.
- **REG_MULTI_SZ**—This is similar to REG_SZ, but it can contain multiple lines of text.

- **REG_EXPAND_SZ**—This is similar to REG_SZ, but the string can contain environment variables such as %SYSTEMROOT% or %USERNAME%. When a program requests such a value from Windows, the environment values are automatically substituted in before the program sees the data.

There are other data types, but they are rarely encountered, and never need to be edited by hand.

To open the Registry Editor, click Start, Run, type **regedit** in the Open field, and click OK. You can dig through the top-level keys into subkeys in the left pane. Values associated with each key are displayed in the right pane.

To change the data associated with a value, double-click the value and change the value data in the resulting dialog. For numeric (DWORD) values, you can select a decimal or hexadecimal display; use whichever mode is more convenient for you.

Keep in mind that all changes are final. There is no Undo. If you delete a key or value, the only way to put it back is to manually re-add it or restore it from backup.

Caution

Here's that strident warning again: Editing the Registry can change the configuration of your system. Therefore, by nature, it is a potentially dangerous task. Do not directly manipulate the Registry when using a GUI setting can do the same job, and never blindly fiddle with the Registry unless you are aware of what the potential consequences are.

Some Registry-based settings take effect immediately; others require a restart of an associated application or a reboot of the system.

Editing the Registry Remotely

If you need to edit the Registry of a system other than your own, you can connect to a Registry over the network. To perform this function on a workgroup network, three conditions must be met:

- The remote computer must have an account with the same logon name and password as the account you're currently using.
- The account on the remote computer must be a computer administrator account.
- Simple File Sharing must be disabled on the remote computer. This means that the remote computer cannot be running Windows XP Home Edition, but it can be running Windows XP Professional with Simple File Sharing disabled. Windows 2000 Professional or a Server version are editable as well. On Vista, Password Protected Sharing must be turned on.

And in any case, the Remote Registry service must be running on the remote computer. By default, it's set for manual startup on most Windows computers, so you need to take steps in advance of needing it to change its startup mode to automatic if you will need to use it in your organization. Also, on Vista, User Account Control prohibits remote access to HKEY_LOCAL_MACHINE, except for domain administrators.

If your network meets these conditions, in the Registry Editor, simply click File, Connect Network Registry, and enter the computer name for the remote system in the resulting dialog. The remote computer's HKEY_CURRENT_USER section will not be displayed.

Editing a Hive File

At some point you may find that you need to edit the Registry of a Windows system that cannot boot. To edit a dead system's Registry, you can install its boot drive in another computer and use that computer's Registry Editor to mount and edit the Registry files on the added disk. Once the hard drive from the dead computer is running in a new computer, follow these steps:

1. Log on as a computer administrator and start regedit.

2. Select HKEY_USERS in the left pane, and from the menu, select File, Load Hive.

3. In the Load Hive (open file) dialog, click My Computer, open the drive that came from the dead computer, and browse to the file corresponding to the Registry section that you need to edit (see Table 5.3). Click Open.

4. For a key name, enter **xxx** or something clearly not normal.

5. Browse into key xxx and make the necessary changes, as shown in Figure 5.11.

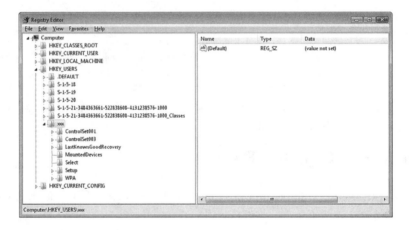

Figure 5.11   Editing a Registry hive mounted from another computer's disk.

6. Hightlight xxx under HKEY_USERS in the left pane and from the menu select File, Unload Hive. Confirm by checking Yes.

Now you can shut down Windows and return the hard disk to the original computer.

Table 5.3   Hive Files for Various Registry Sections

Registry Section	Hive File
HKEY_CLASSES_ROOT (look at subkey Classes)	\windows\system32\config\software
HKEY_CURRENT_USER	\Documents and Settings*username*\ntuser.dat
HKEY_LOCAL_MACHINE\Hardware	(None, this is created dynamically when Windows boots)
HKEY_LOCAL_MACHINE\SAM	\windows\system32\config\sam

Registry Section	Hive File
HKEY_LOCAL_MACHINE\Security	\windows\system32\config\security
HKEY_LOCAL_MACHINE\Software	\windows\system32\config\software
HKEY_LOCAL_MACHINE\System	\windows\system32\config\system

Alternatively, if the disk in the dead system has more than one partition, you can leave the disk in the original computer, and install a fresh copy of Windows into an alternative partition. Boot that copy of Windows and locate and edit the hive files from the original partition.

Deploying Registry Settings

When a Registry change has to be made in several computers, it can be impractical to visit each one and manually make the changes. On a corporate domain network, Registry settings can easily be deployed through Active Directory. If you don't have a domain network, there are still some ways to quickly install Registry changes in multiple computers.

Deploying Registry Settings with .reg Files

The easiest method for distributing Registry settings is through the use of a .reg file. You saw how to export and import .reg files earlier in this chapter, in the section "Exporting and Importing Registry Files with the Registry Editor" (p. 294), but in that section you were exporting an entire Registry key. Let's take a look at using .reg files to deploy a limited group of settings.

In the earlier example, you selected the top-level Registry key and exported the entire thing to a .reg file. If you viewed the resulting file in the Registry Editor, you probably noticed fairly significant and unruly content. That is because the .reg file contained all keys, subkeys, values, and data in the branch of the Registry that you exported. Let's manually create a .reg file that adds a key and some values to HKEY_CURRENT_USER. Create the following file in a plain-text editor, such as Notepad:

```
Windows Registry Editor Version 5.00

[HKEY_CURRENT_USER\My Settings]
@="this is the default value"
"ValueName1"="String Value"
"ValueName2"="String Value"
"ValueName3"=dword:0000002a
```

Save this file as mysettings.reg. To import the settings, follow these steps:

1. Double-click the mysettings.reg file.

2. You see a pop-up confirmation message that asks Are you sure you want to add the information in c:\mysettings.reg to the Registry? Click Yes to import the file.

3. You then receive a confirmation box stating Information in C:\mysettings.reg has been successfully entered into the Registry. Click OK.

Alternatively, to import the settings without any prompting or confirmation, issue the command

```
regedit /s mysettings.reg
```

After you import the .reg file, open the Registry Editor (Start, Run, regedit). Expand HKEY_ CURRENT_USER, and you should see a subkey named My Settings that contains values as displayed in Figure 5.12.

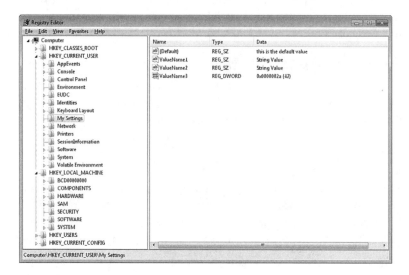

Figure 5.12 The Registry key and values created by mysettings.reg.

Note

Importing a **.reg** file by double-clicking it is pretty straightforward, but what about those two confirmation boxes? What if you don't want your users to know that you are importing Registry settings? And what's more, you don't want them having an opportunity to reject the setting by clicking No on the confirmation dialog. Fortunately, you can silently install a Registry file from the command line using the following command:

```
regedit /s mysettings.reg
```

Add a line like the preceding to a logon or startup script, and you can quickly, easily, and silently deploy Registry settings to users and computers throughout your environment.

Deploying Registry settings using .reg files overwrites existing keys, values, or data and adds missing keys, values, or data. .reg files do *not* delete extra keys, values, or data that are in the Registry but not in the Registry file. To delete information in the Registry, you must use regedit, remove the key using a script (as demonstrated in the next section), or explicitly define the keys or values you want to delete within the .reg file. To demonstrate, I show you how to manually create two .reg files to manipulate values created under the HKEY_CURRENT_USER\My Settings key created earlier in this section.

First, create the following file in a plain-text editor, such as Notepad, and save the file as WhackOneValue.reg:

```
Windows Registry Editor Version 5.00

[HKEY_CURRENT_USER\My Settings]
"ValueName2"=-
```

Notice the minus (-) sign where the data normally goes for the value. This directs the Registry Editor to delete the associated name and data pair when you run or import the .reg file. After you run WhackOneValue.reg, open the Registry Editor. You no longer find ValueName2 under HKEY_CURRENT_USER\My Settings. Note that if you had the Registry Editor open when you ran the script, you might need to press F5 to refresh the display before seeing the effect of the script.

Next, create the following file in Notepad and save the file as WhackMySettings.reg:

```
Windows Registry Editor Version 5.00

[-HKEY_CURRENT_USER\My Settings]
```

Notice the minus (-) sign in front of HKEY_CURRENT_USER. This directs the Registry Editor to delete the following key when you run or import the .reg file. After you run WhackMySettings.reg, open the Registry Editor. You no longer find the My Settings key under HKEY_CURRENT_USER. Again, if you had Registry Editor open when you ran the script, you might need to press F5 to refresh the display before seeing the effect of the script.

Deploying Registry Settings with VBScript

Managing the Registry with VBScript is amazingly straightforward using the RegRead, RegWrite, and RegDelete methods against the WScript.Shell object.

Note

For full downloadable Windows Scripting Host documentation in the Windows Help File format, see the Microsoft Developers Network Scripting resources at http://msdn.microsoft.com/scripting.

The following code listing creates a Registry subkey named My Settings under the HKEY_CURRENT_USER key. The script uses the RegWrite method to populate the default value, plus three additional values under the new subkey. Each new value is populated with data. After populating the key, values, and data, the script displays the data values by reading the Registry with the RegRead method. Enter the following lines of code into a plain-text editor, such as Notepad, and save the file as mysettings.vbs.

```
Set myReg = CreateObject("WScript.Shell")
key =  "HKEY_CURRENT_USER\My Settings"

'Write the keys
myReg.RegWrite key & "\",              "this is the default value"
myReg.RegWrite key & "\Boolean Value", "True"
myReg.RegWrite key & "\String Value",  "Upgrading and Repairing", "REG_SZ"
myReg.RegWrite key & "\DWORD Value",   42, "REG_DWORD"
```

```
'Read the keys
WScript.Echo "Default Value: " & myReg.RegRead(key & "\")
WScript.Echo "Boolean Value: " & myReg.RegRead(key & "\Boolean Value")
WScript.Echo "String Value:  " & myReg.RegRead(key & "\String Value")
WScript.Echo "DWORD Value:   " & myReg.RegRead(key & "\DWORD Value")
set myReg = Nothing
```

After you type the command `cscript mysettings.vbs`, open the Registry Editor (Start, Run, regedit). Expand `HKEY_CURRENT_USER`, and you should see a subkey named My Settings, containing values created by the script.

To demonstrate the use of the `RegDelete` method—and to clean up the useless Registry key created previously—create a script file named `delkey.vbs` containing the following five lines.

```
'Delete the keys
Set myReg = CreateObject("WScript.Shell")
key =  "HKEY_CURRENT_USER\My Settings"
myReg.RegDelete key & "\"

Set myReg = Nothing
```

After you run the command `cscript whackmysettings.vbs`, open the Registry Editor. You should no longer see the `My Settings` key under `HKEY_CURRENT_USER`. If you had Registry Editor opened when you ran the script, you might need to press F5 to refresh the display before seeing the effect of the script.

Because `startup`, `shutdown`, `logon`, and `logoff` scripts can all be written using VBScript, the previous samples give you an easy way to deploy scripted changes to the Registry of any systems on which you control the related script policies.

Caution

Often, deploying settings through `startup`, `shutdown`, `logon`, or `logoff` scripts is your only way to distribute Registry edits now that `.reg` and `.vbs` files effectively function as a sort of poor man's virus for virus authors who can't afford compilers. You definitely don't want to get your users in the habit of opening `.vbs` or `.reg` attachments from their email. In fact, many corporate email scanners automatically delete attachments of these types, and Outlook XP automatically blocks both types of attachments. Therefore, a user might not even be able to open or run `.vbs` or `.reg` files if you don't deploy them through the system scripts.

Managing Windows Services

Services are programs that are started independently of your logging on. For the most part, they are started up in a specific sequence when Windows boots up, and they perform their jobs without directly interacting with the keyboard, mouse, or display. Services are used to perform such tasks as indexing your hard disk for faster searching, managing various types of storage devices, providing networking functions, and more. On other operating systems, they might be called *daemons* or *background processes*. Services are described in detail in Chapter 2. Here, I'll cover the tools used to manage them.

Managing Services with the GUI

Figure 5.13 shows the Services management tool from which you can manage the services available on your computer. (The services themselves are described in Chapter 2.) You must be logged on as a computer administrator, or on Windows XP Pro, as a Power User.

To open the Services management tool, right-click My Computer and select Manage; then in the left pane, open Services and Applications, and select Services. Alternatively, you can type `services.msc` at the command prompt, in the run dialog, or on Vista, in the Start menu's search box.

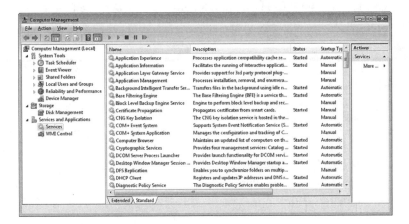

Figure 5.13 The Services management tool allows you to monitor and change the status of services.

The columns in the management display list the name of each service, a description of its purpose, its current status, its startup type, and its logon account. The Status column can display any of the following values:

(blank)	The service is not running (is stopped).
Starting	The service is starting up but is not yet operational.
Started	The service is operational.
Stopping	The service is in the process of shutting down.
Pausing	The service is in the process of suspending its activity.
Paused	The service is running, but has been instructed to suspend activity.
Continuing	The service is resuming normal activity after having been paused.

The startup type can have any of the following values:

Automatic	The service is started automatically as Windows boots up. Services with no dependencies are started first, followed by any services that depend on them.
Manual	The service is not started unless requested to by an application, another service, or by a Services management tool.
Disabled	The service has been designated as disabled and will not be started under any circumstances.

Services can run in the context of a user account in order to control the privileges they have; for best security, a service should run with only the privileges it absolutely needs, and no more, in order to limit the damage it could do should it crash or get compromised by a hacker. Most of the standard services run under the Local System context, which means they have total privileges, but some are run using the special built-in Network Service or Local Service user accounts. These accounts do not appear in the account manager. Other special services could conceivably be configured to standard user accounts.

On Windows Vista, a special account name called a Principal is available for each service. This is not a logon account, but it can be used in Security (permissions) settings for files, Registry keys, and other resources to tighten security.

Note

Each installed service registers with Windows the names of any services that it requires to get its job done. These are called *dependencies*, and as it starts services during the boot process, Windows first starts services that have no dependencies, and only when depended-upon services are operational does it start up dependent services. This process is automatic.

Current Status and Startup Options

To manage or monitor a service, double-click it in the Services list, or right-click and select Properties (see Figure 5.14).

Figure 5.14   A service's Properties page lets you specify startup, logon, and failure recovery settings.

On the General tab, you can perform the following maintenance tasks:

- Start, stop, pause, resume, or restart the service. Restarting a service stops it and then immediately starts it again. It's like "rebooting" the service. This can be especially useful in cases where you need to restart a service that is not working, or has failed and is consuming 100% of the CPU doing nothing (I have seen the Printer Spooler service do this), or is working with corrupt data (for example, restarting the DNS Client clears stale entries from the local DNS cache).

- View the command line that is used to run the service. You will see that many services use the program svchost.exe; this is a shell program that interacts with the service management system. The real work is performed by a Dynamic Link Library (DLL) whose name is stored in the Registry. See Chapter 2 for more information on svchost.exe.

- Set the startup type to automatic, manual, or disabled. This can be useful in cases where you want to prevent a service from starting for one reason or another.

Caution

Disabling a service also disables any dependent services, which you can view using the Dependencies tab.

Note

Some services don't accept the Stop or Restart functions; they'll be grayed out. If such a service is not functioning correctly, you will probably have to restart Windows itself to get the service going again.

Log On Account

On the Log On tab, you can define the login account used for the service. This is most useful when you are configuring additional third-party services or services for a very specific task where you want to confine the service to an account that has only the specific privileges it requires to perform its function. Do not change the logon account for standard services.

Note

If you specify an account and password to be used by a service, and later change the account's password, you must come back to the Services snap-in and re-enter the logon password for the service.

From this tab, on XP, you can also specify whether the service is to be run in each of the computer's hardware profiles. (Windows Vista doesn't let you manually create hardware profiles.)

Crash Recovery Options

The Recovery tab, shown in Figure 5.15, lets you specify actions to be taken if the service fails, that is, it crashes or stops unexpectedly. The options for the first, second, and subsequent crashes can be set separately, and the following choices are available:

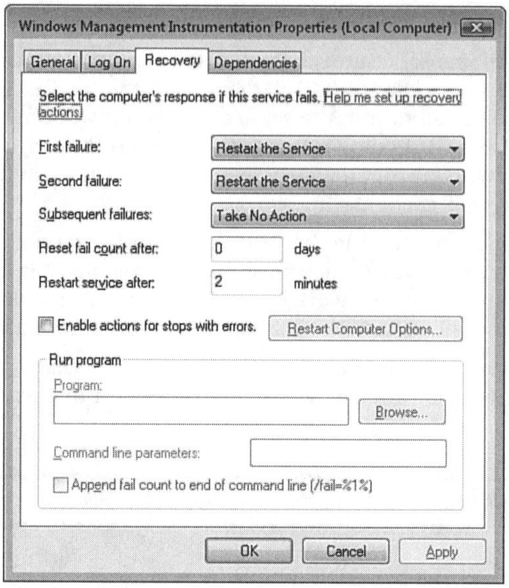

Figure 5.15 The Recovery tab lets you determine what Windows should do if the service crashes.

Take No Action—A note will be written to the event log, but that's all. The service will be left unavailable.

Restart the Service—Windows will attempt to restart the service.

Run a Program—Windows will run the program specified in the Properties dialog that can take any action you want.

Restart the Computer—Windows will shut down and restart.

In addition, you can specify the time frame over which successive failures are considered sequential.

This configuration scheme is meant primarily for servers or computers that run unattended and perform some critical function. It might be reasonable to attempt to restart a service once, but if it fails again shortly afterward, something is probably seriously wrong, and it may make more sense to try something else, perhaps reboot Windows, or perhaps run a program that invokes a repair procedure or sends a text page to a network administrator.

View Dependencies

Finally, on the Dependencies tab, you can view the service's dependency tree. This is the list of other services that a given service requires to do its job, and the list of services that depend on this service to do their jobs. If you start a service that has dependencies, the other services will be started first. If you shut down a service that has dependents, the dependents will be shut down first.

Managing Services on Another Computer

Network managers frequently have to manage large numbers of computers, and it's often inefficient to have to physically visit them when there's trouble. Like most Windows management utilities, the Services management console can request to manage services for a remote computer over the network.

To manage another computer's services using the GUI, right-click the icon at the top of the list in the upper-left pane of the management window (it will be labeled Computer Management or Services, depending on how you opened the window), and select Connect to Another Computer. Enter the name of the other computer, or click Browse to select it from your workgroup or domain. You must have an account on the remote computer with the same login name and password as the account you're currently using, or you must have a domain logon valid on that computer. And on Vista, because of User Account Control, this feature is not available when UAC is enabled, except to domain administrators.

You can also manage services on other computers using the sc command discussed in the next section.

Managing Services from the Command Line

You can manage services through the command-line interface as well as the GUI; in some cases, the command line can be faster and easier.

There are two ways to do this. The first is with the net command. The commands net start *servicename* and net stop *servicename* start and stop a service on the local computer. If the service name has spaces in it, you must enclose the name in quotation marks ("), and you can specify either the service's display name (the name listed in the Services management display), or the shorter service key name.

▶▶ For a list of service key names, **see** "List of Windows Services" on **p. 87**. The service key names are in boldface.

These commands can be used to quickly and easily restart a service. For example, if you had recently accessed a network host by its DNS name and the host's IP address is now changed, or if the host was offline but is now online, your computer's DNS cache will still hang on to the out-of-date address or the failure result for several minutes. Restarting the DNS service will make it discard the old, incorrect information and refresh itself. You can do this with

```
net stop dns
net start dns
```

A more powerful command-line service management utility is sc, which can manage services on other computers, change service settings, and list information about installed services.

However, to manage services with sc, you must know the service's service key name, which is usually not the name displayed in the Services management window. You can use sc to get a list of all installed services and their service key names, or you can refer to the list of Windows services in Chapter 2 for the names of common Windows services; the key names are printed in boldface.

Here are some sample uses of the sc utility:

■ Print a list of all services installed on the local computer, including their Automatic/Manual/Disabled setting and their service key names (labeled SERVICE_NAME)

```
sc query
```

■ Print a list of services installed on another computer named otherhost:

```
sc \\otherhost query
```

■ Restart the IIS web server service on computer otherhost:

```
sc \\otherhost w3svc stop
sc \\otherhost w3svc start
```

To get a listing of sc's full command syntax, type these three lines in a command prompt window:

```
sc ? >x.txt
y
notepad x.txt
```

(You will not be prompted for the y line.) Open the Windows Help and Support Center and search for sc for details on each subcommand.

Running Your Own Program as a Service

Developing a Windows service program requires a fair bit of effort and programming skill. In addition to writing code to do whatever job the service has to do, you must add extra code that lets the service program communicate with the Windows service manager so that the service can be started, stopped, and communicate its status and dependencies to the manager.

Still, in some cases it's nice to be able to have a program run when Windows boots up and have it stay running 24×7, whether you're logged on or not, and no matter what else is going on. And, in fact you can do this, using a utility program from the Windows 2000 Resource Kit that runs a program of your choice as if it were a service; the utility takes care of communicating with the service manager, and runs your program using a specified command-line when the service manager starts it up. Your program can be a Windows application, command-line program, batch file, Windows Script Host script, database application, or a program written in another scripting language such as Perl. I've used this method to create a web server database back-end written in the FoxPro database language, and an interface to the SpamAssassin spam-filtering program written in Perl.

A program that is to act as a service needs to function with no interaction from the keyboard, mouse, or screen. To communicate with the outside world, it can create and listen on network sockets, or it can scan a specified directory every so many seconds for the appearance of files. It should *not* run in an endless loop waiting for work to do, or it will slow performance of your computer. Instead, it should use Windows synchronization tools such as events, or at least it should "sleep" for periods of time in order not to consume any CPU power when it's idle. Test the program from the command line to be sure it works before trying to run it as a service.

Then, when you are ready to install it as a service, follow these steps.

Caution

Running a program as a service this way has some risks. In fact, Windows Defender reports the presence of Srvany as a risk every time it runs. If a hacker replaces the program that the service manager starts up, the bogus program will run with whatever privileges the service would have run with. You should follow the steps listed here to ensure that your service is safe from hacking.

1. Log on as a computer administrator.

2. Download the Windows 2000 Server or Windows Server 2003 Resource Kit Tools package from microsoft.com, as discussed in Appendix A. Install the package.

3. Click Start, All Programs, and find the new Resource Kit Tools entry. Open the Resource Kit Tools help file, and search for srvany. On the srvany page, there are several links to other pages that you'll need to read: Installing Srvany, Running an Application as a Service, Starting and Stopping a Service, and Srvany Notes. You may want to print these documents.

4. Create a special user account to be used just for your service, and set a password for it.

5. Create a special folder for the service's files on a drive that is formatted with the NTFS file system (do *not* use a FAT-formatted disk). For these instructions, I'll assume that the folder is C:\myservice.

6. In the Resource Kit tools folder under Program Files, locate files instsrv.exe and srvany.exe. Copy instsrv.exe, srvany.exe, the program file(s) for your service, and any data files it needs to the service's folder (c:\myservice in this example).

7. Set NTFS permissions for this folder so that only administrator, and the new user account have access to it. Use the Advanced button to reset permissions on all objects in the folder. (On XP, Simple File Sharing must be disabled in order to set permissions.)

8. Open a command prompt window and change to the service's folder, for example, with cd /d c:\myservice.

9. Choose a name for your service; it must be different from any other service, and should describe in a word or two what the service does.

10. Follow the instructions for installing srvany as a service, and for creating the Application and AppParameters values that specify your program and its command line parameters. Table 5.4 lists the correct application values for various types of programs; replace the filename in italics with the appropriate filename for your program.

11. Create the AppDirectory value and set it to the full path of your service's folder.

12. When the service has been installed, open the Services management tool, locate your service, and use the Log On tab to specify that it's to run under the special user account.

Now, you should be able to start the service and press Ctrl+Alt+Del to see that the associated program appears in the Windows Task Manager's Processes display. If it doesn't, it may be exiting prematurely, or there may be a problem starting the service. In the latter case, there should be a record in the event log.

Table 5.4   *Application* and *AppParameters* Values for Various Types of Service Programs

Program Type	Registry Value	Setting
Standard `.exe`	Application AppParameters	`c:\`*path...*`\myprogram.exe` *any needed parameters*
Batch file	Application AppParameters	`c:\windows\system32\cmd.exe` `/c c:\`*path...*`]\mybatch.bat`
Script	Application AppParameters	`c:\windows\system32\cscript.exe` `c:\`*path...*`]\myscript.vbs`

Monitoring Your System to Identify Bottlenecks

Sometimes you get the feeling that your computer is not performing at full capacity. The indication might anything from a momentary lag between typing and having characters appear on the screen, to applications taking far too long to open when you start them. Sometimes these slowdowns can be caused by momentary network outages, the automatic installation of Windows Updates downloads, or the Windows Indexing Service deciding that the middle of your workday is a good time to scan through every document on your disk. Sometimes they fix themselves and don't occur again. But sometimes they don't, and you need to know how to find the source of the problem.

Using the Task Manager

The first place I go when my computer is acting sluggish is the Task Manager. Type Ctrl+Alt+Del to open it, view the Processes tab, and click the title of the CPU column twice to show the processes using the greatest percentages of available CPU cycles.

Note

On Vista, by default the Task Manager does not show system services. And if you are logged on to XP via Remote Desktop, you might only be able to see processes running in your remote session. To view all active processes on Vista, you can just click the Show Processes from All Users button and User Account Control takes it from there. On XP, you must run the Task Manager as a computer administrator and check Show Processes from All Users. If you don't want to log off and back on as an administrator to do this, open a command prompt window and type **runas /user:Administrator taskmgr**.

If a single task is consuming a large percentage of the CPU, it's either very busy, or it's stuck in an infinite loop doing nothing. It's difficult to tell which, sometimes. One helpful indicator is the amount of disk activity the program is doing. Click View, select Columns and check PID, I/O Read Bytes, and I/O Write Bytes, and click OK. The result is shown in Figure 5.16.

Watch the I/O Read Bytes and I/O Write Bytes numbers. If they are increasing, the program is actively reading and writing data. A program that is consuming nearly 100% of the CPU (50%, if you have a dual-core processor), with no I/O activity is probably hung up; a program that is using a large CPU percentage and is also performing I/O is just working hard.

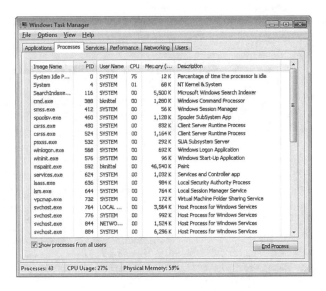

Figure 5.16   Task Manager display showing %CPU usage and total disk activity.

If you suspect that a program is hung up, you can try to terminate it from the Task Manager. Select the program in the list and click End Process. In most cases, this will have no effect, so the next step is to open a command prompt window. If you are using Vista or Windows XP Professional, type the command `taskkill /pid nnn` with the number from the process's PID column in place of *nnn*. If you are using XP Home Edition, try the command `tskill`, although it may not work. Hopefully you had previously downloaded installed the Resource Kit Tools described in Appendix A, and can type `kill /f nnn` which is more likely to work.

Using the Performance Monitor

Windows has a tool called Performance on XP, and Reliability and Performance on Vista, which lets you plot and monitor all sorts of internal measurements inside Windows, view recorded performance data, and configure management alerts to be sent when system measurements stray from preset bounds. This can help you identify what processes and services are occupying your computer's time, and can help you measure disk, network, and other input/output activity.

To start the Performance console on XP, type `perfmon.msc` at the command line, or choose Start, All Programs, Administrative Tools, Performance. You'll get the console shown in Figure 5.17. The tool labeled System Monitor lets you watch a real-time graph of selected system measurements such as disk read bytes per second, transmitted network packets per second, free disk space in bytes, and so on. Performance Logs and Alerts lets you record these quantities in a log file for subsequent plotting, and can send administrative users an online message if a selected measurement goes over or under a threshold.

On Vista, type `perfmon.msc` at the command line (or Start Menu search box), or click Start, All Programs, Administrative Tools, Reliability and Performance Monitor. The Vista version has a tool named Performance Monitor that is identical in usage to XP's System Monitor, but is far more elegantly displayed, as shown in Figure 5.18. Vista doesn't provide the Performance Logs and

Alerts tool, but does have diagnostic tools labeled Data Collector Sets and Reports. These two are discussed in Chapter 12.

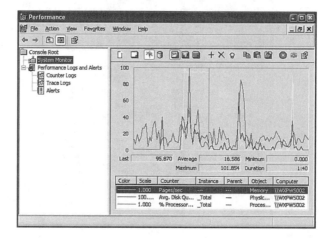

Figure 5.17   XP's Performance console can provide a wealth of tuning information.

Note

If Administrative Tools doesn't appear under All Programs in your Start menu, right-click the Start button, select Properties, click Customize and on XP, select the Advanced tab. Locate System Administrative Tools in the list of Start Menu items, and select Display on the All Programs Menu. Click OK twice to close the dialogs and Administrative Tools will now be available.

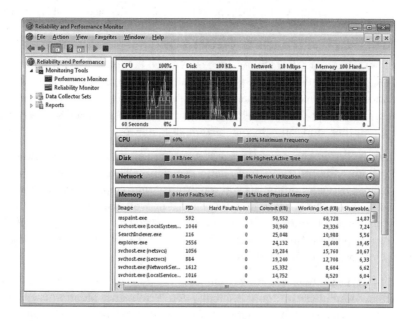

Figure 5.18   Vista's Reliability and Performance console has vastly improved graphics and report formatting.

Using System Monitor/Performance Monitor

The System Monitor (shown previously in Figures 5.19 and 5.20) enables you to view statistical data either live or from a saved log. You can view the data in three formats: graph, histogram, or report. Graph data is displayed as a line graph; histograms are incorrectly named and are actually just bar graphs; and reports are text-based displays that show the current numerical information available from the statistics.

To add counters to the graph, click the "+" icon above the plot area. This opens the Add Counters dialog box shown in Figure 5.19. At the top of the dialog box, you can elect to obtain statistics from the local machine or from a remote machine. This is useful when you want to monitor a computer elsewhere on your network. Under the computer selection is a pull-down list naming the performance objects that can be monitored. Which performance objects are available depends on the features (and applications) you have installed on your server. The selections on this dialog make more sense if you understand the terms *object*, *counter*, and *instance*:

- An *object* is the software or device being monitored, such as memory or processor.

- A *counter* is a specific statistic for an object. For instance, Memory has a counter called `Available Bytes`, and a processor has a counter called `% Processor Time`. Counters are the actual numerical measurements that you will be observing.

  On XP, after you select an object from a drop-down list, related counters appear in a separate list box. On Vista, objects and counters are in the same list box. Click on the v marker to the right of an object name and its counters are displayed.

- An *instance* is the specific occurrence of an object you are watching. For example, in a multiprocessor server with two processors, or a single CPU system with dual cores or hyperthreading, you have three instance selections: `0`, `1`, and `Total` or `All Instances`. 0 and 1 are the two separate CPUs or cores, which you can monitor separately. The third choice gives a graph that shows the sum of the counter values for all instances together.

Windows defines hundreds of objects and counters, and application programs and add-on services can add their additional objects and counters. These performance counters enable you to monitor statistics relating to that application from the Performance Monitor.

Counters are the actual statistical values that you want to monitor. For example, if you choose to monitor the processor, you can watch for the average processor time and how much time the processor spent performing non-idle activity. In addition, you can watch for %user time (time spent executing user application processes) versus %privileged time (time spent executing system processes).

To the right of the counter list is the instances list. In most cases where instances are listed, selecting Total will give you the most useful results.

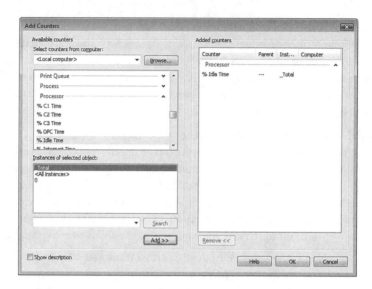

Figure 5.19   Use the Add Counters dialog box to add counters to the System Monitor.

Using XP's Performance Logs and Alerts

Using the Performance Logs and Alerts section of the Performance Monitor, you can log counter and event trace data. Additionally, you can create alerts triggered by performance that can notify the administrator of critical changes in monitored counters to give advance warning of impending problems. The following three items are located in the Performance Logs and Alerts section of the Performance Monitor:

- *Counter logs* enable you to record data about hardware usage and the activity of system services from local or remote computers. You can configure logging to occur manually or automatically based on a predefined schedule. If you desire, continuous logging is available, but it consumes large amounts of disk space quickly. You can view the logs in System Monitor or export the data to a spreadsheet or database program, such as Microsoft Excel and Microsoft Access, respectively.

- *Trace logs* are used to record data as certain activity, such as disk I/O or a page fault, occurs. When the event occurs, the provider sends the data to the log service.

- *Alerts* can be set on a specific counter defining an action to be performed when the selected counter's value exceeds, equals, or falls below the specified setting. Actions that can be set include sending a message, running a program, and starting a log. However, on most systems, the "message" selection is not terribly useful; the alert messages are sent through an archaic pop-up notification system called the Messenger service (not related to Windows Live Messenger), and this service is disabled by default on XP and absent from Vista. Alert messages are used primarily on corporate networks.

Tuning for Maximum Performance

In this section you'll learn some specific settings you can make to tune Windows for peak performance. Of course there are always trade-offs to be made, and you'll have to make personal judgments as to whether a feature is worth its cost in computer time, whether it should be disabled to gain speed, whether you should spend more money to speed your computer with better hardware, *or* gain speed through software settings and feature sacrifices.

Installing Sufficient Memory (RAM)

The single most important thing you can do to make sure your computer runs at top speed it to make sure that you have enough main memory (RAM) installed. Here's why: Windows uses a system called *virtual memory* to let applications use pretty much as much memory as they want, even if they want to use more memory than the system has available. The shortfall is made up by using space in a hidden disk file called the *page file* to store data that won't fit into main memory. When a program wants to access a memory location that previously wasn't able to fit into RAM, Windows freezes the application, finds a block of memory that hasn't been recently accessed, writes its contents to the page file (*pages it out*), reads the frozen application's data off of the disk and into this memory block (*pages it in*), and then lets the application continue. At some point the application whose memory was paged out will need to use it again, so the same thing happens in reverse. Applications never know that this shuffling is taking place; they just run sluggishly.

This decades-old technique lets multiple applications share limited memory, and lets an application run even if it needs more memory than the computer has. The virtual memory system has been made as efficient as possible, but it has a cost: Reading data from and writing to the hard disk can be *millions* of times slower than reading from or writing to RAM. Each time Windows has to stop to move memory in or out of the page file, it delays the frozen application by several tens of milliseconds at least, and if this happens several dozen times a second, the application slows to a crawl. There's even a technical term for this: *thrashing*, which means expending a lot of effort and getting little done. If you ever used Windows 95 or 98 on an old computer with 32MB of memory, you know well what this is like. And even a current computer with 512MB of memory can start thrashing if you load in a big video clip for editing.

The good news is that even while Windows and applications have bloated to the point that they require hundreds of megabytes just to boot up, memory has gotten so cheap that there's virtually (ha!) no reason to suffer with a computer that's having to page data to disk.

How Much Memory is Enough?

So, how much memory is enough? You can actually do some calculations to find out. After going through a demanding work session, type Ctrl+Alt+Esc to open the Task Manager, and select the Performance tab. Under the graphs are some numbers listing amounts of memory. On Windows XP, the numbers are displayed in KB (thousands of bytes), and this is what they indicate:

- **Physical Memory, Total**—The amount of RAM you've installed in your computer, less any borrowed by a low-end shared memory motherboard-based graphics adapter.

- **Physical Memory, System Cache**—The amount of physical RAM being used just to speed up file operations by holding the contents of frequently-used files. Windows automatically adjusts the size of the cache to optimize performance.

- **Physical Memory, Available**—The amount of memory that is either totally unused or could be taken away from the system cache if needed by applications.

- **Commit Charge, Total**—The amount of *virtual* memory in use by Windows, drivers, services, and applications; in other words, the amount of memory your system *thinks* it's using at this moment, and this can be larger than the amount of physical memory.

- **Commit Charge, Peak**—The largest Total Commit Charge since Windows was last booted.

- **Commit Charge, Limit**—The amount of physical memory plus the current size of the page file; this is the most virtual memory that could be in use at once. If necessary, Windows will increase this quantity automatically by enlarging the page file(s), if the page file(s) can be increased in size.

- **Kernel Memory, Total**—The amount of memory occupied by the Windows kernel and its data structures.

- **Kernel Memory, Paged**—The portion of the kernel's memory total that can be paged out to disk if necessary.

- **Kernel Memory, Nonpaged**—The portion of the kernel's memory total that cannot be paged out, but which must remain resident in RAM at all times.

On Vista's Task Manager display, the numbers are organized somewhat differently than on XP. They're also displayed in MB (millions of bytes). Here are the quantities you have to obtain so that you can calculate how much memory you need:

- **Physical Memory, Total**

- **Kernel Memory, Nonpaged**

- **Page File**—The first number listed is the Commit Charge Peak. The second number is the Commit Charge Limit.

Now, here's how to use these numbers:

- If the Commit Charge Peak is equal to the Commit Charge Limit, your page file filled up at some point, and either had to be extended, which means it's now fragmented and slowing you down, or it has reached its maximum size, which means you've pushed your computer to the proverbial wall and held it there. Check the page file settings to see whether your total page space is limited in size to this amount. If so, you should increase the limit. You may also want to use a third-party disk defragmenter that is able to defragment your page file. Alternatively, move the page file to a different physical disk drive with more room and less fragmentation.

- Calculate the approximate amount of "working memory" in your system by calculating (0.9 × Physical Memory Total) – Kernel Memory Nonpaged.

- If this working memory amount is *greater* than Commit Charge Peak, you have sufficient memory installed in your computer. (Of course, having more wouldn't slow it down any.)

- If the working memory amount is *less* than the Commit Peak, calculate the shortfall as Commit Charge Peak – working memory. (If you're using numbers in KB from Windows XP, divide this shortfall amount by 1,024 to get the number of MB that you need to add.)

  You can account for some of the shortfall by assuming that Windows will take memory from the system cache. But, system performance really suffers if the cache falls below, say,

300MB. So, if the shortfall is larger than 300MB, you definitely should add additional RAM. You may have to replace your current memory modules or add additional modules, depending on what you have now; *Upgrading and Reparing PCs* goes into these details.

Here's an example. From my XP computer, I recorded the following numbers:

Physical Memory Total	1048096KB
Physical Memory, System Cache	502420KB
Commit Charge Limit	2520816KB
Commit Charge Peak	649472KB
Kernel Memory Nonpaged	19288KB

The interpretation is

- Commit Charge Peak is much less than Commit Charge Limit, so the page file is currently large enough.
- Working memory is (0.9 × 1048096) – 19288 = 923988KB.
- 923988 is greater than the Commit Charge Peak of 649472, so there is sufficient RAM.

Now, on an XP computer with only 512MB (524,288K) of memory installed, the results would have been different:

- Working memory = (0.9 × 524288) – 19288 = 452571KB.
- The system cache size is reported as 325292KB.
- The working memory is less than the Commit Charge Peak, with a shortfall of (649472 – 452571) = 196900KB, or 192MB.

In this case, Windows would have to either decrease the size of the cache, or would have to start paging applications and data. Either way, performance would suffer. The indication in this case would be that I would have to add at least 192MB of memory to prevent memory paging from slowing me down. You can live with some paging, of course, but it definitely drags performance down. This is why, despite Microsoft's recommendation of a 256MB minimum, 512MB is a *functional* minimum memory size for Windows XP.

Let's do the same exercise for my Vista Ultimate Edition computer, with *no* applications having been run since boot-up. Here are values from the Task Manager:

Physical Memory, Total	511MB*
Physical Memory, Cached	318MB
Commit Charge Limit	1700MB
Commit Charge Peak	473MB
Kernel Memory, Nonpaged	24MB

I actually have 512 MB of RAM installed, but Windows reports 511. It's nothing to worry about.

Now, from these numbers we can draw these conclusions:

- The Commit Charge Peak is much less than Commit Charge Limit, so the page file is large enough.

- Working memory is $(0.9 \times 511) - 24 = 435MB$.

- 435 is less than the Commit Charge Peak of 473, so there is not sufficient RAM to hold all of Windows and the active services and applications. There is a small shortfall of 38MB.

- Windows would have taken the shortfall from the cache if it thought that this would be a better use of memory, so the paged-out memory likely holds Windows components and services that are dormant.

Because many Windows services are only infrequently called upon to perform their job, it's not really a terrible thing if Windows has to make some of them spend most of their time out on the page file, rather than keeping them in RAM. However, I hadn't run even one application when I took these measurements. So, you can see here that Windows Vista Ultimate pretty much fills up 512MB of RAM just by itself, before you do *anything*, so more memory than this is really necessary to get good performance. This is why 1GB is the recommended minimum memory size for all versions of Vista beyond Home Basic.

Placing the Page File

If the preceding calculation shows that you need to increase the size of your page file, consider where you should put the page file for best performance. Paging needs to be as fast as possible. You can configure Windows to put page files on more than one drive, and you can set maximum and minimum page file sizes or let Windows manage the size automatically, as discussed earlier in this chapter. Here are the things you should consider to make the most efficient page file setup:

- Your total page file size should be 1.5 to 3 times the amount of physical memory in your computer; tending toward the smaller factor if you are sure that you have adequate physical RAM, and toward the larger if you know you don't. Don't allocate less than 512MB of page file space.

- If Windows is reading or writing to the page file, it means that some application, or Windows itself, is frozen and waiting for the disk operation to complete. Reading and writing data to and from disk is slow enough, but having to mechanically reposition the little recording head that swings back and forth across the disk surface is even slower, thus costlier. Therefore, you don't want your page file to get fragmented, forcing Windows to move the recording head all over the disk to pick up the scattered data. As soon as you install Windows, set a very large minimum page file size, 2 or 3 times the amount of physical memory in your computer, so that this block is allocated all in one piece.

- If your page file grows during normal operation, the Windows Defragmenter can't put the pieces back together. (The page file can be defragmented only during the boot process before Windows starts up.) Only third-party applications such as PerfectDisk and Diskeeper can do this.

- The best place to put a page file is on a fast disk drive that is *physically* separate from your primary Windows disk drive, preferably one used only occasionally for other purposes. This way, the disk's recording head will be positioned once and left in the location of the page file. The disk drive should be an internal SATA drive, internal or external fast SCSI drive, or an IDE drive *not* on the same controller cable as a CD-ROM or DVD drive.

- The second best place to put a page file is on the same drive as Windows.

- The *worst* place to put a page file is in a separate partition on the same physical disk as your Windows drive. In this case, the disk's recording head has to travel a large distance every time it needs to switch between the page file and an operating system file.

- If you have several otherwise equally desirable choices, dig into the specifications for the disk drives involved, and place your page file on the disk with the lowest track-to-track positioning time and the highest data transfer rate.

Defragment the Disk

Another key factor in achieving top performance is the speed at which data can be moved between your computer's CPU and its hard disk. Having the latest high-speed disk interface hardware won't help you if your files and data are widely scattered across the disk. Disk data gets scattered, or fragmented, over time, and to maintain peak disk performance, you should periodically run a disk defragmenting utility.

Windows XP and Vista come with a defragmenting tool that is discussed in Chapter 8. However, it's not the sharpest knife in the drawer, so to speak, and you can get *much* better disk performance improvements if you buy a better "defragger" and run it on a regular schedule. Check out Raxco's PerfectDisk (www.raxco.com) and Diskeeper Corporation's Diskeeper (www.diskeeper.com, with just one k).

▶▶ To learn more about defragmenting, **see** "Defragmenting for Greater Speed," **p. 475**.

Note

If you use a virtual machine environment such as VMWare or Microsoft Virtual PC, you should be sure to not only defragment the drive that holds your virtual hard disk files on the host computer, but also to defragment each virtual disk's contents from within the virtual machines, that is, inside the guest operating systems. Be aware that the licensing terms of third-party defragmenters may require you to purchase separate licenses for the host and guest installations, even through they are all installed on one physical computer. Also, you may want to see whether you can purchase a defragmenter that provides native support for virtual disk content defragmenting from the host side (that is, a defragmenter that can mount and defragment the contents of a virtual disk image). For example, Raxco's PerfectDisk 2008 for VMWare can do this for VMWare disk images.

Note

To help Windows XP and Vista meet the goal of booting in under 30 seconds, there is a special service that automatically runs every few weeks or so, which identifies the files Windows uses when it boots, and reorganizes them on the disk so that they're placed in the order in which they're used, in consecutive unfragmented disk blocks. This helps reduce boot time but doesn't speed up subsequent disk operations.

Disk Interface Tuning

Having data neatly organized on disk won't help if the pipeline between the disk and the CPU is restricted. IDE (also called ATA or PATA) hard drives can achieve the highest transfer rates if they transfer data directly into the memory on your motherboard using Direct Memory Access (DMA), but they can be prevented from doing this if they share a controller cable with a slower Zip disk, optical, or other ATA disk device. To verify that your disk drives are using DMA transfers, log on as a computer administrator, right-click My Computer and select Manage, and open the Device Manager. Locate the entries for any IDE-type disk controllers. You will have to open the items in the tree view to find them (see Figure 5.20 for the Windows XP version).

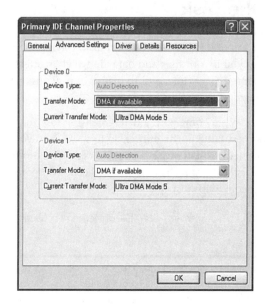

Figure 5.20   Verify that your disk controller channels are using DMA.

On Windows XP, find the channel entry that connects to your Windows hard drive, such as Primary IDE Channel; double-click it and select the Advanced Settings tab, and examine the current transfer mode for each device. Disk devices should be using a DMA mode, not Programmed I/O (PIO), which requires the CPU to intervene in transferring every byte to and from the device. Higher DMA transfer modes are faster. Transfer modes and rates for standard parallel ATA devices are listed in Table 5.6. If a disk is listed as using a mode that is slower than the disk drive's peak transfer rate, you may have incorrectly arranged or cabled disks, or an inadequate disk controller.

Table 5.6   IDE Disk Transfer Modes and Rates

Mode	Also Called	Maximum Transfer Rate, MBps
Ultra DMA Mode 6	UDMA/133 or Ultra ATA/133	133
Ultra DMA Mode 5	UDMA/100 or Ultra ATA/100	100
Ultra DMA Mode 4	UDMA/66 or Ultra ATA/66	67
Ultra DMA Mode 3		44

Mode	Also Called	Maximum Transfer Rate, MBps
Ultra DMA Mode 2	UDMA/33	33
Ultra DMA Mode 1		25
Ultra DMA Mode 0		16.7
DMA Mode 2	Multiword DMA mode 2	16.7
DMA Mode 1	Multiword DMA mode 1	13.3
DMA Mode 0	Multiword DMA mode 0	4.2
PIO Mode 4		16.7
PIO Mode 3		11.1
PIO Mode 2		8.3
PIO Mode 1		5.2
PIO Mode 0		3.3

Repeat this check for any other channels that connect to hard drives. If DMA transfers are prevented by a slower device on the same channel as a disk, you may want to reconfigure the hardware so that slower devices are on a separate channel.

On Vista, it's very unlikely that the fastest available DMA mode is not being used already. You can check the current mode by viewing the IDE channel properties dialog as just described for XP. You can't select the mode on Vista, however. You can only enable or disable DMA with a check box.

What to Enable and Disable

Earlier in the chapter you read about ways to eliminate unwanted startup programs run when you log on and when you start Internet Explorer.

In addition, you can disable some Windows services and graphical functionality to gain additional performance. There aren't many such items that make the trade-off worthwhile, but we'll cover a few of them here.

Graphical Niceties

You can make Windows' responses to menu operations somewhat snappier by disabling some of the shading, shadows, and smooth-scrolling features that have crept into the Windows user interface. You can see a list of optional graphical effects in the Display Properties dialog, Settings tab, and Effects button, and the TweakUI PowerToy discussed earlier in this chapter also has check boxes that you can use to disable graphics effects.

On my computer, I've disabled the fade-in of pop-up submenus, which occasionally seems to take more time than I would like it to, and font smoothing, which I don't like.

Unnecessary Services

You may find tips on supposedly helpful websites that suggest that you disable a long list of services, but in most cases, services that aren't used, or which are only infrequently used, are simply paged out of RAM and don't really affect system performance at all. Disabling services might slightly speed up Windows' startup time, but even this has a minimal benefit because Windows offers the Welcome screen early in the process. While you're entering your password, less essential services continue to start. So, disabling services has very minimal benefit, except in one instance.

The only truly egregious CPU and disk hog in the Services list is the Indexing service. If you don't use the search for keywords within files option in the standard Windows Search utility, or if you use a more advanced search tool like Google Desktop Search instead, you can disable the Indexing service using the Services management utility discussed earlier in the chapter.

If you do need to use the Indexing service because you use search functions in web pages hosted by Internet Information Service on your computer, you can restrict Indexing Service so that it searches only web content and not your entire disk. As a computer administrator, open the Computer Management window, open the Indexing service entry under Services and Applications, and dig down to System, Directories. Delete the entry for C:\ and for any other drive root folders. This will prevent the indexing of your disks for general searches. Leave the other entries, and all entries under the web branch, alone.

If you installed the Internet Information Services web server suite on XP out of curiosity but don't use it, this is another candidate to be disabled.

Improving Startup and Logon Time

Finally, here is a quick list of things you can do to shorten the time it takes Windows to start up and let you log on.

DHCP

If your network connection(s) are configured to obtain an IP address automatically (that is, to use DHCP), be sure that there is a functioning DHCP server on your network. On corporate networks, your network router infrastructure provides the DHCP service, or it's provided by a service on a server computer such as one running Windows Server. On a home network, DHCP service is usually provided by your home router, or by a computer running Windows Internet Connection Sharing service. If the DHCP service is not available when your computer starts up, it can delay startup. If this is a common and unavoidable occurrence, either configure your network connection to use a static IP address or set up a DHCP server.

In the same vein, disable any network connections that you don't use. For example, if your computer has two network adapters but you use only one, disable the disconnected adapter. Just right-click it in the Network Connections window and select disable. On XP, disable the 1394 (Firewire) connection.

Network Connections

If you map network shared folders to drive letters, be sure to use the Reconnect at Logon option only on shared folders that you are sure will always be available every time you start up your computer—likewise for drives mapped with the net use command-line utility. If the drive is unavailable when you log on, this can delay the appearance or responsiveness of the desktop, Windows Explorer, and File Open/Save dialogs. To prune the dead wood out of your mapped drive list, open Windows Explorer. On Vista, press and release the Alt key. Then click Tools, Disconnect Network Drive. Select any drive that is shown as disconnected and that you no longer need, and click OK.

External Disks

If your computer has USB and/or FireWire drives attached to it, and you notice that Windows startup is significantly delayed, try disconnecting or turning off the drives before starting up your computer. It may be that one or more of your drives has an unusual partitioning arrangement that throws Windows off if it's detected during startup.

Antivirus Programs

If you have an antivirus and/or antispyware program installed on your computer, and startup appears to be slow, try disabling or uninstalling the program and restart. If startup is much faster, you've identified the culprit. Complain to the vendor, and check the vendor's support website for updates that may remedy the problem. Remember, antivirus programs are typically revised every year, and the one that won the speed trophy last year may be this year's nominee for the glue factory. Before purchasing any computer protection software, check the reviews for the exact product version(s) you're considering.

Also, on Vista, the \windows folder has better security than on XP, so you may be able to cut startup and logon times by instructing your antivirus program not to perform real-time checks on files in the \windows folder and its subfolders. In this case, be sure to schedule routine scans of the entire hard disk so that if an infection does occur in \windows, you'll eventually hear about it.

Defragmentation and Disk Organization

Be sure to scan through this chapter and follow the advice on speeding up your hard disk by setting up a speedy page file, and by getting a disk defragmenting utility that does a better job than the one that comes for free with Windows. Speeding up disk access can significantly improve Windows' responsiveness.

Startup Programs

Programs that start up automatically every time you log on can really slow down the logon process. It makes you think Windows itself is slow, but the problem is really caused by third-party software vendors. For tips on thinning the startup herd, see "Managing Startup Programs" on page 283.

Tip

If you frequently use shared folders on other computers via your network, you might be tempted to create shortcuts to these folders and put them on your desktop. This does make it convenient to get to the networked folders, but if the remote computer is offline or otherwise unreachable, it can cause huge delays when you try to view pictures. The symptom is that the desktop, the task bar, and Windows Explorer lock up entirely for up to 30 seconds. The solution is to move the network folder shortcuts into a subfolder and open it only when you need to use the network folders.

Networking Windows

Setting Up a Network

In this chapter, we're assuming that you are creating or adding to a network for a home or small office network, which in Microsoft's jargon is called a *workgroup network*. That said, much of this material still applies to corporate-style domain networks as well. There just isn't room in this book to cover every nuance of creating that type of network.

Windows has all the software you need already built in, but you *may* need to purchase some additional hardware components:

- An Ethernet (wired) or wireless network adapter for each computer. Virtually all new desktop and laptop computers have an Ethernet adapter built onto the motherboard, and many laptops have wireless networking built in as well, so you may not have to purchase these.

- For a wired network, an Ethernet switch or hub, or a cable/DSL sharing router with a built-in switch, and CAT-5 cables to run from each computer to the switch, as shown in Figure 6.1.

- For a wireless network, a wireless router or access point. This router or access point usually also has jacks for Ethernet connections so that wired connections can be made as well, if desired, as shown in Figure 6.2.

Here are the steps you'll want to follow:

- Get whatever extra hardware you need. The next section gives you a brief overview of the types of available hardware.

- Install your network adapters and cabling. I won't cover this part in detail in this book. (If you need more information on selecting and installing network hardware, refer to *Upgrading and Repairing Networks* or *Upgrading and Repairing PCs*, both published by Que.)

- If you are creating a wireless network, install your access point or wireless router according to the manufacturer's instructions.

- Set up Windows to use your network, as described under "Configuring a Workgroup Network," later in this chapter.

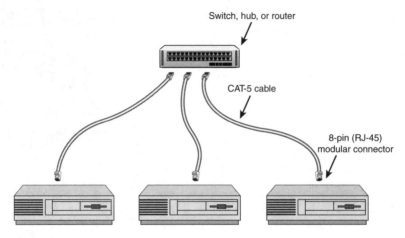

Figure 6.1   A basic wired Ethernet network, using CAT-5 cabling.

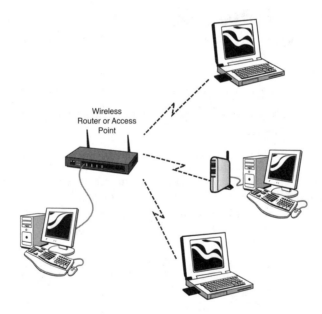

Figure 6.2   A wireless network with an access point or wireless Internet sharing router, and optional wired Ethernet connections.

If you're not already familiar with network hardware, the next section gives a quick overview of what's available. If you already have your hardware, skip ahead to "Wireless Networking" or if you're building a wired Ethernet network, "Configuring a Workgroup Network."

Network Hardware

Hardware for computer networking was once *very* expensive, but today networking hardware costs as little as $5 to $40 per computer. When you consider that a network can let you share a single printer between two or more computers, or share a single high-speed Internet connection, a network can pay for itself the first day you set it up.

This section gives you a quick run-through of the various types of network hardware you can use to tie your computers together.

Wireless Versus Wired

A network lets your computers "talk" to each other. They can do this through wires or through radio signals, using one of the following types of networks:

- **Ethernet** uses a physical cable to connect the computers. Ethernet networking runs at either 10 million bits per second (Mbps), 100Mbps, or 1000Mbps (1Gbps). 100Mbps is the most common speed at present. (10Gbps Ethernet is coming, but it's not something the average home user needs to worry about yet.)

- **Wireless** or Wi-Fi networking sends data through radio signals over the air. Wireless networking doesn't require you to string cables between your computers, but it's less reliable (that is, it may stop working for a few seconds every once in a while, disrupting a long download or file transfer), and the signal sometimes has problems passing through walls and floors. Wireless networking comes in several flavors named after standards published by the International Association of Electrical and Electronics Engineers (IEEE). The wireless network types for home and small offices are named 802.11b, which runs at up to 11Mbps, 802.11g, which runs at up to 54Mbps, and 802.11n, which can run at up to 200Mbps or more and has better signal strength. "Up to" is the key phrase there. In real-world use, you'll get at most half of the rated maximum speed, and if signal quality is low, much less. Still, wireless speeds are fine for surfing the Internet, and if you have 802.11n, even big file transfers should perform well.

  Most current equipment is 802.11g. At the time this was written, the 802.11n standard was not yet finalized, although several manufacturers are presently selling "*pre-n*," that is, uncertified products that are *not* guaranteed to work well with products from other manufacturers. (They will presumably be upgradable via software when the final specification is made, but until the standard is finalized in late 2008, buy this stuff at your own risk.)

In addition to Ethernet and wireless, there are two lesser-used wired network types that don't require you to run new cables because they use your existing household wiring:

- **Powerline** networking sends data via radio signals sent through your electrical wiring, using adapters that plug into wall outlets. Powerline networking runs at 10Mbps, which is a bit slow by today's standards—it can take hours to back up a large hard disk over a 10Mbps connection. But it would be fine for sharing an Internet connection.

- **Phoneline** sends data via radio signals sent through your telephone wiring, using adapters that plug into telephone jacks. (All the jacks must be connected to the same telephone extension.) Phoneline networking also runs at relatively slow 10Mbps.

You can set up a network using any of these hardware types, and you can even mix and match the types if you want, using access points or devices called *bridges* to connect the different network types together. Wired Ethernet connections are the least expensive, the fastest, the easiest to set up, and the most reliable, but it can be annoying to have to run the cables around. So for example, you might use Ethernet connections to hook up several computers in close proximity, and then use a wireless access point or a powerline/Ethernet bridge to extend the network to a computer in another room.

Network Interface Adapters

Whatever type of network(s) you decide to use, you'll need a network interface adapter for each computer. Adapters come in several forms: internal (PCI) cards for desktop computers, PCMCIA cards for laptops, and USB adapters for either desktops or laptops. I'll briefly discuss each adapter type here:

- **Ethernet**—Typical internal adapters are PCI cards. These can cost as little as $5 each. USB and PCMCIA adapters are available for laptops at a slightly higher cost. Better yet, many desktops and most laptops have Ethernet built in already, so in most cases no add-on adapter is needed. Ethernet adapters are labeled "10/100Mbps" or "10/100/1000Mbps," meaning that they can run at any of the listed speeds, depending on the capability of the hub into which they're plugged.

- **Wireless**—There are some internal PCI adapters for desktops. Most are USB, for either desktops or laptops, or PCMCIA for laptops. Some manufacturers make PCI cards for desktops into which you plug a PCMCIA wireless network adapter. Many laptops have wireless built in, so no add-on adapter is needed. If you need to buy an adapter for a desktop, I recommend the USB variety because you can easily move these around to get the best signal reception.

- **Powerline**—Typically packaged as a box that plugs into a wall outlet and connects to your computer through a USB cable. Some adapters have Ethernet connectors instead, which you would connect to an Ethernet adapter in your computer, or to a hub.

- **Phoneline**—Typically internal (PCI) cards or external USB devices.

Cabling

If you are making a wired Ethernet network, you have to run a cable from each computer to the nearest hub (hubs are discussed in the next section). Ethernet cable is also called Unshielded Twisted Pair (UTP) cable because it looks like ordinary telephone cable, with four pairs of wire twisted together inside the cable's jacket. However, it's specially manufactured for computer use, and the electrical properties of the wire are very strictly controlled. UTP cable for networking use is rated according to the highest data speed that it's designed to carry, as listed in Table 6.1.

Table 6.1   Ethernet Cable Ratings

Ethernet Speed	Minimum Cable Rating
10MBps (10BASE-T)	CAT-3
100MBps (100BASE-T)	CAT-5
1000MBps (1000BASE-T)	CAT-5, but CAT-6 or CAT-5e is recommended

Even if you have only older, slower 10Mbps equipment, I recommend that you use at least CAT-5 cabling for all Ethernet networks.

Ethernet cables can't be cut and spliced in the normal way. If you need to connect cables from end to end, you *must* use CAT-5 certified plugs and jacks.

You can purchase premade CAT-5 cables (called *patch cables*) in varying lengths from computer stores or online. You can also purchase bulk cable, connectors, and a connector crimping tool and make your own, although that's beyond the scope of this book.

Be aware that the maximum length for Ethernet cabling is 100m (330 feet). If you have computers farther apart than this, you have to place the hub somewhere between them, or use multiple hubs in sequence, so that no single cable is more than 100m long. For a really long run, you may have to use fiber optic cable or wireless networking.

If your only goal is to connect two computers together with Ethernet, you can connect the two computers directly to each other, using a special cable called a *crossover cable*, which routes the send and receive data wires so that the cable can connect one Ethernet adapter directly to another. In most cases, however, you use regular Ethernet patch cables to connect each computer to a central hub or switch, as discussed in the next section.

Hubs and Switches

If you use a wired Ethernet network and have more than two computers or other devices, you need one or more switches or hubs. These devices route the signals between the computers. Hubs and switches serve the same purpose, so for the rest of this chapter, I'll just use the term *hub*. (See the sidebar "Switch? Hub? What's the Difference?" for an explanation of the two terms.)

A simple wired network was shown in Figure 6.1. If you have two or more groups of computers, separated by some distance, you can simplify your cabling job by using more than one hub, with just a single cable running between them, as shown in Figure 6.3.

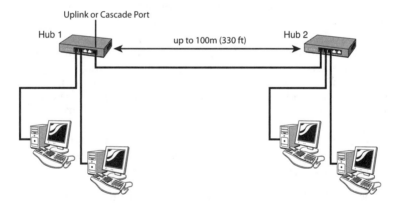

Figure 6.3 A more complex Ethernet network with more than one hub.

Hubs can generally adapt themselves to the various Ethernet speeds supported by the computers that you attach to them. Thus, they're marketed as "10/100Mbps" or "10/100/1000 Mbps." Most network adapters are rated 10/100, so these run at the higher 100Mbps speed when connected to a 10/100 hub. Higher-end desktops, some laptops, and most Macs usually have 10/100/1000Mbps adapters. If you have two or more computers with these high-speed (Gigabit) adapters, get a 10/100/1000 hub; otherwise, 10/100 is fine.

If you are going to be using wireless networking in addition to Ethernet, and/or you'll be sharing a DSL or cable Internet connection, you may not need to purchase a hub at all because most wireless access points and DSL/cable sharing routers have a hub built in. Check for this before you spend the money on a standalone Ethernet hub.

Switch? Hub? What's the Difference?

The difference between a hub and a switch is subtle and almost irrelevant today. Here's the difference: Hubs are brainless devices. When a data packet arrives on any of its ports, it transmits the data back out on all its other ports. Thus, only one connected computer at a time can transmit data. A switch, on the other hand, has some processing power built in. It pays attention to the data that passes through it, and learns the physical network addresses of the computer(s) connected to each of its ports. When it receives a data packet addressed to a specific computer, it sends the packet out only through the port that leads to that computer. Thus, the other ports aren't clogged up with unnecessary data, and the switch can support several simultaneous independent "conversations" between its ports, each running at full speed.

Today, as I mentioned, the distinction is effectively irrelevant because the processing power and signal-handling circuits needed to build switches are available in a single, inexpensive silicon chip. As a result, there is no extra manufacturing cost involved, so nobody makes plain old hubs anymore. Today, all Ethernet hubs made are actually switches.

Wireless Access Points

Wireless networks function in one of two ways:

- In an *ad hoc* network, the computers that participate in the network communicate directly to each other through their antennas.

- In an *infrastructure* network, a device called an *access point* serves as a sort of referee. Each networked computer transfers data to the access point, which then relays it to the other computers. Access points also provide a means of connecting the wireless network to a wired Ethernet network so that wired-in computers can communicate with the wireless ones. Additionally, an access point makes it easy to connect a high-speed Internet connection to the network, where it can be shared by all the computers.

I don't discuss creating *ad hoc* networks in this chapter, but I do want to mention that Vista's Windows Meeting Space collaboration tool can automatically set up a temporary *ad hoc* wireless network to let a group of computers share files and applications during a meeting.

For the purpose of this book, I recommend that if you want to set up a wireless network for your home or office, you should set up an infrastructure network, by purchasing an 802.11g or 802.11n (or pre-n) access point that has both a wired Ethernet switch and Internet connection-sharing router capability built in.

Gateways and Routers

A *router* is a device that transmits data between two or more *separate* networks. Routers serve much the same function as post offices, which examine the mail they collect, deliver what they can, and forward the rest on to other post offices for *them* to deliver. A router doesn't get involved when data is being sent from one computer to another on the same network. But when data is intended for a computer on some other connected network, it's the router's job to forward the data from one network to another, to still others if need be, until it reaches its destination.

In corporate environments, routers are used to connect the local networks in separate offices or workgroups. In the home and small office, a router can connect your personal network to the Internet, which after all is nothing more than a bunch of networks just like yours, all connected together. (Tens of millions qualifies as a bunch, yes?) Routers that are specially designed to perform this Internet connection service are often called *Internet gateways*, or *connection-sharing routers*. Although routers intended for corporate use can cost thousands of dollars, home/small office connection-sharing routers can cost as little as $10, up to about $100 for models that include an 801.11n wireless network access point in the same unit. Connection-sharing routers have one 10Mbps or 10/100Mbps Ethernet socket that is used to connect to your DSL or cable modem. This is called the *WAN port*. (WAN stands for *Wide Area Network*.) Most sharing routers also include a 10/100 Ethernet switch (hub) for up to four wired Ethernet connections. These are labeled LAN ports. You can tack on additional switches or hubs if you need to connect more computers to the Internet.

Tip

If you have cable or DSL Internet service, I strongly recommend that you use a router (wired or wireless) to share the Internet connection with your network, rather than using Windows Internet Connection Sharing. These inexpensive ($10 to $40) devices simplify setup and provide increased security against hackers.

If you're setting up new DSL or cable Internet service, you may not even need to purchase a separate connection-sharing router. Your ISP may be able to give you a DSL or cable modem that has a sharing router built in.

The next section discusses wireless networking. If you're going to set up a standard, wired Ethernet network, you can skip ahead to "Configuring a Workgroup Network."

Wireless Networking

Wireless networking has become much faster, more reliable, and *much* less expensive year by year. At the time this book was written, 802.11g adapters cost about $40 per computer, less when on sale or with a rebate, and a wireless router costs about the same. The next generation of 802.11n (WiMax) equipment, when its specifications are finalized in late 2008, promise even faster speeds and greater range. The Multiple-Input Multiple-Output (MIMO) technology promises to extend the range of wireless networking from the current effective limit of about 100 feet indoors to considerably more.

If you do want to install a wireless network, you need to know that security risks are involved:

■ If you don't enable wireless security, any passerby can connect to your network.

■ If you use the old WEP encryption option, a motivated passerby can still easily connect.

■ With Windows Simple File Sharing enabled on XP, or Password Protected Sharing disabled on Vista, anyone who is able to connect can read or modify your shared files. (Simple File Sharing is discussed later in this chapter.)

■ Even without Simple File Sharing, anyone who connects could send spam or viruses from *your* Internet connection.

So, wireless security is important, but fortunately, it's not that difficult to manage.

Note

This section tells how to configure wireless networking for Windows Vista and Windows XP Service Pack 2 or later in a home or small office. If you are using an earlier version of Windows, consult the manual provided with your hardware for setup instructions.

Caution

If you want to set up an "open" wireless hotspot to freely share your Internet connection with friends, neighbors, customers, or the world, that's great, but you must not use file and printer sharing on the same network. If you use a wireless network for your own file sharing, configure your network with wireless security (preferably WPA) enabled, and then plug into it a second wireless router, set with a different SSID and a different channel, and disable wireless security only on that second network.

Wireless Network Basics

Wireless networking (Wi-Fi) transmits data on the same 2.2GHz radio frequency band used by wireless telephones, microwave ovens, and other consumer products. Many people are familiar with using Wi-Fi to connect to the Internet at airports, cafes, hotels, and the like. You can also use it, rather than cabled Ethernet networking, to connect your computers at home or the office. Wi-Fi has become common enough that in most urban and suburban neighborhoods you'll probably find that your computer can pick up three or four networks operated by your neighbors. To be able to distinguish your network's signal from other peoples', and to secure your network, you must make four choices when you set it up:

- A SSID (Service Set Identifier), a short name that you give your network, up to 32 characters in length. This could be your last name, company name, a pet's name, or whatever makes sense to you.

- An encryption type, which consists of a choice of protocol, and "strength" of the code used to secure the network against eavesdropping. The choices, in order of increasing security, are none, WEP 40-bit (also called 64-bit), WEP 128-bit (also called 104-bit), WPA, and finally WPA2, which is the most secure as of the time this was written. I'll discuss encryption schemes in more detail shortly.

- An encryption key, which is a string of hexadecimal digits—that is, the numbers 0 through 9 and the letters A through F. Some wireless networking software lets you generate a key from an ordinary text password, but this method may not work when you use equipment from different manufacturers.

- A channel, which selects the frequency used to transmit your network's data. In the U.S., this is a number between 1 and 11; the numbers may be different in other countries. The channel is set by your wireless access point. In the U.S., the most common channels used are 1, 6, and 11. Change the channel from its default setting only if you find that several other networks in your area use the same channel; if in doubt, try channel 6.

- MAC-level security, which lets you specify which network adapters can connect to your router. MAC-level security is cumbersome to set up and does nothing to repel a really determined hacker, so I won't discuss it further.

Wireless Network Security

When you are using a traditional, hard-wired network, your data is fairly safe from prying eyes because the signal is contained with the wires, and someone would have to physically connect to your wiring to steal information or freeload on your Internet connection. (Of course, if corporate spies or government agencies get involved, all bets are off.) Wireless networks, on the other hand, broadcast information over a range of at least hundred feet and up to hundreds of yards, and anyone passing with a computer could receive those signals.

To let you limit others' ability to read your data and use your network bandwidth, wireless networking manufacturers have come up with schemes to encrypt (scramble) the data sent on the wireless signal so that only someone possessing a secret code (key) can connect to, send, and read data from the network. The first such scheme was named Wired Equivalent Privacy, or WEP, but this name turned out to be just a bit overoptimistic—WEP security can be broken in just a few hours with a single computer and some freely available software. WEP was strengthened by extending the length of the secret key from 40 to 128 binary bits, but because of its design flaws, this didn't help all that much. The networking industry devised a new encryption protocol called Wi-Fi Protected Access, or WPA, which is *much* more secure than WPA, and the latest, new-and-improved security scheme is called WPA2, for WPA version 2. WPA and WPA2 are very secure as long as you choose a truly random key, as we'll discuss shortly.

Do you really have to worry about your network being broken into? *Maybe* not, but you can't really tell because the "enemy" is most likely someone you don't know and will never see. And although someone might "just" be after a free Internet connection, someone who'd deliberately break into your network could very well want to do things that could get *you* in hot water if the activity is traced back to your Internet connection: send spam, share copyrighted music and video, purchase items with stolen credit card numbers, exchange illegal pornography, communicate with terrorists, commit espionage, or who knows what? So you really do need to at least try to make this difficult; with luck anyone trying to tap into your network will move on to look for an easier target. (It's like locking your front door. Intruders can still break a window to get in, but you at least have to force them to break the window.)

The problem with wireless security is that the same scheme has to be used by all access points and computers on the network. If even one of your devices doesn't support WPA2 or WPA, you're stuck using the relatively insecure WEP. If your access point or router doesn't support WPA2 or WPA, you may be able to install updated firmware to get it—visit the manufacturer's website to check. Furthermore, if you have an older version of Windows on your network, you might have to settle for WEP. Here is a list of the various schemes supported by different versions of Windows:

- **Vista** (all versions)—Has built-in support for WPA2, WPA, and WEP.
- **XP Service Pack 3**—Has built-in support for WPA2, WPA, and WEP.
- **XP Service Pack 2**—Has built-in support for WPA, and WEP. You can add WPA2 support with a hotfix. Visit support.microsoft.com and search for KB893357.
- **Earlier versions of Windows**—Previous versions of Windows (Windows Me, 9x, 2000, and XP without SP2) support WEP, but not WPA. The manufacturer of your computer's wireless network adapter *may* be able to provide an updated driver that includes WPA support.

Select the best security method supported by *all* your network gear, including any access points or routers. For example, if your access point and all computers support WPA2, use WPA2. Otherwise, if all support WPA, use WPA. Use WEP only if you have one or more devices that can't manage WPA. And be sure to use a truly random key when you set up the network.

Creating a Random Encryption Key

In actual use, a key is a string of binary ones and zeroes, ranging from 40 to 256 bits or more in length, looking like this: 1100101000111010110101010001110101001010. That's just 40 bits, and you can imagine how hard it would be to type something like this correctly into a router and several computers. Usually, then, keys are expressed in the shorter hexadecimal notation, where each group of four bits is represented by the digits 0 through 9 and the letters A through F. The same 40-bit key in "hex" looks like this: CA3AD51D4A, which is much more manageable. A 128-bit WEP key* takes 26 hex characters, like this: 9552DCF6069263823BFFA19957.

Even this shorthand form of the key can be tedious and difficult to type correctly, so most wireless equipment manufacturers—and Windows itself—let you enter a key using a *passphrase* instead. A passphrase is a word or short phrase that the software converts into numbers, which it scrambles and from which it then extracts the necessary bits for the key. For WPA, which uses 256 bits for the key, most devices and drivers require a passphrase—there usually isn't even the option of specifying the key as 64 hex characters.

On the surface, passphrases appear to make things easier but they can actually introduce some serious problems. With WEP, not every device driver or access point uses the same mathematical scheme to derive the key. The same passphrase typed into Windows and into your access point could produce a different set of bits, and if that happened, your wireless connection would not work. WPA doesn't have this particular problem because the formula for turning the passphrase into a key is part of the standard, but it shares another problem with WEP: Any wireless encryption scheme can be broken if the intruder can guess your passphrase. Freely available WEP- and WPA-attacking software comes with a huge list of names, numbers, and words to try. If your passphrase is in the attacker's dictionary, he can connect in just a few minutes.

So although it's tempting to use your pet's name or your house number as a passphrase, to make a really secure network, you need to create a truly random key. This means that if you're using WPA or WPA2, you should create a 63-character random text string. If you *have* to use WEP, create a 26-digit random hex number. Save this random key in a text file, and use it to copy and paste the key into each of your computers and your router's setup screen. This is a bit more work than typing just "fluffy," but it's necessary if you want your network to be protected against intrusion.

The WEP protocol automatically adds 24 bits to the key you specify. For 128-bit security, you are asked to specify only 104 bits of key, thus only 26 hex characters. Similarly, 64-bit WEP requires only 40 bits, or 10 hex characters for its key.

The Wireless Network Setup Wizard provided with Windows XP and Vista can generate and install a truly random key for you. We discus this wizard in the next section. You can also create a randomly key manually, using these steps:

1. If you're using WPA, visit www.grc.com/passwords.htm and press the F5 key to refresh the web page. Under 63 Random Alpha-Numeric Characters, select all the text in the box, right-click, and select Copy. (You're best off using all 63 characters in this key, but you could shorten it and still have pretty decent security. Just don't use fewer than about 20 characters or so.)

   If you're using WEP, visit www.andrewscompanies.com/tools/wep.asp. Click on the Generate 128-bit Key button. Under Generated Key, select the text in the Hex box, right-click, and select Copy.

2. Click Start, [All] Programs, Accessories, Notepad. Click Edit, Paste.

3. Click File, Save As, and save the file with the name `Wireless key` in your [My] Documents folder, or better yet, to a removable USB drive, so that you can carry it around to your other computers.

4. Print this file and keep the hard copy in a safe place.

Now you can copy and paste in this key when Windows asks you for your wireless key. When you're configuring your wireless router or access point, paste this key into the device's configuration software or web page.

Setting Up a Wireless Network Access Point

When you set up a wireless router or access point, you are setting up what is called an *infrastructure network*. Before you start, you should read the previous three sections: "Wireless Network Basics," "Wireless Network Security," and "Creating a Random Encryption Key," which go over the choices you'll have to make along the way.

Note

You may see web pages that tell you to have your access point hide (not broadcast) its SSID for increased security, but this is useless advice. Cracking programs can determine your SSID whether it's broadcast or not.

There are three main ways to set up a new wireless router in your home or office:

- Use a special setup or "wizard" program provided by the manufacturer.
- Set up the access point manually, following the manufacturer's instructions.
- Use the Wireless Network Setup Wizard provided with Windows XP and Vista.

I'd suggest that you read the manual that comes with your router to see whether it comes with its own setup program. If it does, and if its instructions make sense and seem easier than what follows in this section, by all means use it and see whether it works. If you elect not to use it, try the Wireless Network Setup Wizard, described in the next section. As a last resort, configure the router manually, as described later in this chapter.

Using the Wireless Network Setup Wizard

The easiest way to set up a wireless network is to use the built-in wizards provided with Windows XP and Vista. These tools not only help you generate a truly secure, random key, they may also be able to automatically configure your wireless router or access point.

Tip

If your wireless router supports Microsoft's Windows Connect Now (Rally) technology, Windows can set up the router automatically, saving you a lot of time and trouble. Some routers have a USB port for this purpose, and others can do it through the network. So, before you start, if you can, connect your computer's Ethernet adapter to the wireless router using a CAT-5 patch cable. This gives the wizard the best chance of successfully configuring the router without you having to lift a finger. If your router has a USB port on it, you may also want to have a USB flash drive on hand, in case you need it later in this procedure.

Because the details vary greatly, I describe the XP and Vista wizards separately.

Windows Vista

If at least one of your computers has Windows Vista, use Vista to set up your wireless network, and then add the XP computer(s) later. To run the Vista wizard, follow these steps:

1. Click Start, Control Panel. Select Network and Internet, and then under Network and Sharing Center, select Connect To a Network.

2. Select Set Up a Connection or Network. Select Set Up a Wireless Router or Access Point, and then click Next.

3. Click Next and confirm the User Account Control prompt.

4. If you are asked Do you want to turn on network discovery for all public networks? click No, Make the Network I Am Connected to a Private Network.

5. If Windows can connect to and can configure the router directly through the network, it offers to do so. Select that option and follow the wizard's prompts to complete the setup procedure.

   If Windows can't directly control the router, it offers two other choices: Configure This Device Manually, or Create Wireless Network Settings and Save to USB Flash Drive. Even if your router doesn't have a USB flash drive port, select the Create option.

6. Enter the name (SSID) you selected for your network and click Next.

7. If *all* your computers and other wireless devices support WPA encryption, accept the proposed random passphrase and click Next.

   If *any* of your computers or other wireless devices doesn't support WPA (your TiVo, for instance), you must use WEP encryption. Click Show Advanced Network Security Options, and select WEP. A random WEP key is generated. Click Next to proceed.

8. If you have already set up file and printer sharing, select Keep the Custom Settings I Currently Have and click Next. You can also make one of the following selections here:

   ■ **Do Not Allow File and Printer Sharing**—Prevents other computers from accessing files and printers shared by your computer.

- **Allow Sharing with Anyone with a User Account and Password for This Computer**—Enables File and Printer Sharing by your computer, using Password Protected Sharing.

- **Allow Sharing with Anyone on the Same Network as This Computer**—Enables File and Printer Sharing by your computer, with Password Protected Sharing turned off.

Password Protected Sharing is described later in this chapter under "Simple File Sharing" (p. 356). Make the desired selection and click Next.

9. Plug a removable (USB) flash drive into your computer if you haven't done so already, and wait for it to be recognized. If a `What do you want to do with the contents of this drive?` prompt appears, or if an Explorer window opens, close it. Then, in the Wireless Wizard, select the drive under Save Settings To, and click Next. This copies a file containing wireless setup information and a setup program that can install these settings on Windows on XP and Vista. We talk more about this in a moment.

10. When the copying process is complete, click Print Network Settings to make a hard copy of the setup information. You many need this to configure your router, and you also need it as a backup of your network setup information. (Be sure to keep it in a safe place.) Click Next.

11. Windows prompts you to configure your access point and other computers. Windows might be able to configure your router directly over its Ethernet connection, if you made that connection as suggested in the earlier Tip. If it can't do that, and if your router has a USB slot, plug the flash drive that was prepared in step 9 into your router. Within 30 seconds, the router should blink its lights three times. This indicates that its wireless security settings have been configured. (Its Internet connection haven't been configured or changed, however, so you have to take care of that part separately.)

If your router doesn't have a USB port, you have to configure it manually as described later in this section.

After the router is configured, you can take the USB flash drive to your other Vista and XP computers to configure them. Simply log on using a Computer Administrator–type account, and plug in the flash drive. This should run the setup program that the wizard put on the drive. You don't need to use the instructions in the next section to set up your XP computers—the setup program on the flash drive takes care of XP as well as Vista computers.

When all your other computers have been set up, if you want, you can bring the flash drive back to the original Vista computer and have the setup wizard erase the security information from the flash drive. This is up to you. You can always configure other computers manually by using the Network Settings printout you made in step 10. Finally, if you are using your wireless router to share a high-speed Internet connection, open the router's setup web pages and set up your Internet connection. I'll give a brief outline of this process later in this section under "Configuring a Wireless Router Manually."

Windows XP

If you don't have any Windows Vista computers, you can set up a new wireless network by using the Wireless Network Setup wizard provided with Windows XP, following these steps:

1. Start by logging on to a Computer Administrator account. Open My Network Places from the Start menu. In the Network Tasks list, select Set Up a Wireless Network for a Home or Small Office. When the wizard appears, select Set Up a New Wireless Network.

2. In the first screen, enter a name for your wireless network, select Automatically Assign a Network Key, and indicate that you want Windows to create a random key for you. Also, if *all* your wireless equipment supports WPA encryption, check the Use WPA box at the bottom of the screen. Then click Next, and Next again to proceed.

3. If you have a USB flash memory drive, or a USB-connected digital camera memory card reader that presents the memory cards as disk drives, select Use a USB Flash Drive. (You can also use a floppy disk, if you want, with this setting.) Alternately, you can also choose to copy the wireless settings manually. Make your selection and click Next.

4. If you chose to use the USB device, Windows asks you to insert the device. Plug it in and wait a moment. If Windows displays a What Do You Want to Do with This Drive dialog, or if an Explorer appears, close it. Then, select the corresponding drive letter. (You can also select your floppy drive here.) Click Next and Windows copies the necessary files.

   After Windows copies the files, remove the flash drive and take it to your router and/or other computers to configure them. If your router has a USB port, plug in the flash drive. Within 30 seconds the router should flash its lights three times to indicate that its wireless security settings have been configured. (Its Internet connection isn't configured or changed by this process, however, so you have to take care of that part separately.) If your router doesn't have a USB port, you'll configure it manually in a later step.

5. Configure your other Windows XP and Windows 9x computers:

   ■ If you're using a USB device, plug the device into the computer. The Wireless Network Setup Wizard should run automatically and add the computer to the wireless network.

   ■ If you're using a floppy disk, insert the disk in each computer, and use My Computer or Windows Explorer to locate and double-click the SetupSNK.EXE file. This adds the computer to the wireless network.

   ■ To add computers manually, wait until after the next step when you have a printout of the network settings. I discuss the manual procedure later under "Joining a Wireless Network."

6. Return to the original Windows XP computer, reinsert the flash drive, and Click Next in the Wireless Network Setup Wizard. Then click Print Network Settings to get a copy of the settings. This opens a window in Notepad. Click File, Print to get a hard copy. You definitely want to have this as a backup, and it will help you to configure your router if you have to configure it manually. Finally, click Finish.

7. If you have to configure your router manually, follow the instructions provided by the router's manufacturer and use the information on the printout you just made. The manual setup procedure is roughly outlined in the next section, "Configuring a Wireless Router Manually."

If you later need to add more computers to the network, you can rerun the wizard on the computer you started with, and it will walk you through the process of reinstalling the setup software on your USB drive, or reprinting the instruction sheet. Or, you can follow the procedure in the next section to join them to the network manually.

After all your computers have joined the wireless network, skip the next section and continue with "Configuring a Workgroup Network."

Configuring a Wireless Router Manually

If your router can't be configured automatically through the network or a USB flash drive, you have to configure it manually. The details, of course, vary from one manufacturer to another, so you have to read the instructions for your particular device. The manual procedure goes something like this:

1. Connect one of your computers to the access point's Ethernet port, using a CAT-5 patch cable, and power up the access point.

2. Note the IP address that is assigned to your computer's Ethernet adapter. To find this, view the Network Connections folder. (On XP, get there from Control Panel. On Vista, open the Network and Sharing Center and select Manage Network Connections.) Right-click Local Area Connection, and select Status. Click Details, and note your [IPv4] IP address. This will be something like 192.168.1.23.

3. Open Internet Explorer, and in the Address bar type your IP address, but change the last number to 1. In this example, I'd type 192.168.1.1. Then, press Enter.

4. You should be prompted to enter a username and password. The default name and password are described in your router's manual.

5. Set up the router's Internet connection. For cable Internet, you typically select the DHCP (automatic) option, and for DSL, you usually need to select the PPPoE option, requiring a username and password, but this varies from one ISP to another. Your ISP will have provided you with this setup information, and most are willing to talk you through setting up your wireless access point if you call the customer support line.

Note

You usually have to click OK or Save Changes after making a change on any of the router's setup pages, before you proceed to another page.

6. Select the Wireless Networking setup page and enter your chosen network name (SSID). Select WPA or WEP security. If there is a "key index" selection, select 1. In the box for the first key value, paste in the hexadecimal key you generated in the previous section.

This is *usually* all you have to do to get an access point up and running. After you have saved the last set of changes, you may need to restart your router. As soon as it's restarted, you should be able to disconnect the Ethernet cable and connect wirelessly.

Joining a Wireless Network

When your home or small office wireless network has been configured and you're ready to start using your computer(s), or, if you are taking your computer into someone's work or home and want to use the wireless network there, you have to take some steps to be able to use the network. You can use the Wireless Network Setup Wizard discussed in the previous section, or you can connect to and use the network by following this manual procedure. (The figures here show the Windows XP versions. The dialogs are slightly different on Vista, but the procedure is the same.)

1. In the notification area at the bottom corner of your screen, locate the Wireless Connection icon (shown here to the left). Double-click it.

2. Windows displays a list of the names (SSIDs) of the wireless networks that it "hears," as shown in Figure 6.4. Click on the network you want to use and click Connect.

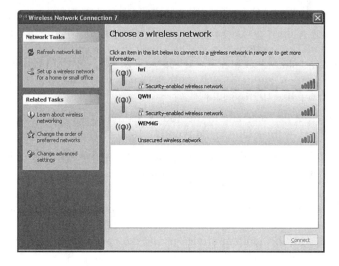

Figure 6.4   Windows displays the names of the networks whose signals it can receive.

Note

If the network you want to use doesn't appear, it could be because the signal is too weak. Also, some people prevent their routers from broadcasting SSID names over the airwaves. (This doesn't really provide much extra security; hackers can find the network anyway.) If the network you want to use isn't broadcasting its SSID, you have to enter the information manually.

3. Windows determines what type of security the network is using, and if the network is encrypted, prompts you to enter the network key. If the network uses WPA security, enter the passphrase, which is a string of letters, numbers, and/or punctuation. Be sure to enter it *exactly* as given to you. If the network uses WEP security, enter the 10- or 26-hex digit key.

Note

If you are using a wireless connection on a corporate network, your wireless configuration can and should be managed by your network administrators. Most likely, your administrator has installed a security "certificate" file that identifies your computer as one authorized to use the wireless network. And it's also likely that you won't have to configure any manual settings to use the network.

On Vista, you are asked whether the network is public or private. Take care answering this question! If you are in a public Wi-Fi hotspot such as a library, café, or business center, or even a client's office perhaps, select Public. File and printer sharing are disabled so that other computers on the network can't probe and possibly infect your computer with viruses. Select Private only if the wireless network was secured with a password or key, and you are sure that all the other computers on the network can be trusted.

After the wireless connections are made, you can continue setting up the rest of your network, as described in the following section.

Note

Microsoft has some experimental software available (for XP only) that lets you connect to more than one wireless network at the same time. If this sounds interesting, check out http://research.microsoft.com/netres/projects/virtualwifi/. No promises that it will work, but if you like to play around at the bleeding edge of technology, it's worth checking out.

Configuring a Workgroup Network

After your network hardware has been installed, whether it's wired or wireless, the next step is to make sure that Windows' networking software is set up correctly. This procedure is different for XP and Vista, so I'll go through the steps for each operating system separately. If you have both XP and Vista computers on your network, they'll work together just fine, as long as you set up both types using the following instructions. I cover XP first, then Vista.

After you've set up basic networking, you may want to make some optional settings. So after covering initial setup for XP and Vista, the remainder of this section covers the following topics:

- IP addressing options
- Networking with Windows 9x and Me
- Designating a master browser
- Providing a shared Internet connection

You may want to review all these topics before starting to set up your network.

Setting Up a Network on XP

Windows XP comes with a Networking Setup Wizard program that can automatically configure file sharing and Internet access for each of the computers on your network. The wizard lets you make a few basic choices, but otherwise takes care of all the technical details for you. You have to run this wizard at least once, whether you want to or not. For security reasons, Windows doesn't enable file and printer sharing until this wizard has been run at least once.

Note

If you're going to use Microsoft's Internet Connection Sharing to share an Internet connection over your LAN, configure the computer that will be sharing its Internet connection first. Establish and test its Internet connection, and only then configure the other computers. Internet Connection Sharing is discussed later in this chapter.

To start the wizard on XP, click Start, Control Panel, Network and Internet Connections, and Set Up or Change Your Home or Small Office Network. Read the "Checklist for Creating a Network" if you want, and then click Next. Follow the wizard through the following steps.

Select a Connection Method

The wizard asks you to select a statement that best describes your computer. The choices can be confusing, so consider them each carefully. They are

- **This Computer Connects Directly to the Internet. The Other Computers...Connect...Through This Computer**—Choose this if you want this computer to share its Internet connection with the rest of your LAN using Windows Internet Connection Sharing, which is discussed later in the chapter. *This* computer will connect to the Internet through a dial-up modem or a cable/DSL modem. In the latter case, you'll need two network adapters in this computer: one for the LAN connection and one to connect to the DSL or cable modem. In any case, be sure that you've already configured and tested your Internet connection before setting up the LAN.

- **This Computer Connects to the Internet Through Another Computer on My Network or Through a Residential Gateway**—Choose this if your network has a hardware Internet connection-sharing router, or if you've set up some *other* computer to share its connection with Internet Connection Sharing.

  Also, use this choice if your LAN has routed Internet service, such as that provided by a DSL, cable, ISDN, or Frame Relay router connected to your network hub, *and* the router for that service has been configured to filter out Windows networking traffic, which we'll discuss later in this chapter.

To get to the next three options, click Other. These alternatives are as follows:

- **This Computer Connects to the Internet Directly or Through a Network Hub. Other Computers on My Network Also Connect [this way]**—Select this if your computer uses its own dial-up or direct DSL/cable Internet connection, but you do *not* want to use Windows's Internet Connection Sharing to share the connection with the rest of your LAN.

  Also, use this selection if you use "multiple-computer" cable Internet service with no router. (I strongly urge you not to use this sort of connection—please read "Providing Shared Internet Access" later in this chapter for important warnings.)

- **This Computer Connects Directly to the Internet. I Do Not Have a Network Yet**—You would use this choice if you had a direct Internet connection (that is, a cable or DSL modem that uses a network adapter), but no LAN. Because you're setting up a LAN, this choice probably isn't appropriate.

  You *do* want to use this choice if you are setting up a network *only* to use a shared Internet connection, and don't want to share files with other computers. This might be the case if you are sharing an Internet connection in an apartment building or other public space, for instance. In this case, this choice indicates that you consider your network to be as untrustworthy as the Internet itself.

■ **This Computer Belongs to a Network That Does Not Have an Internet Connection**—Select this if your computer will connect to the Internet using dial-up networking or AOL, or if your computer will never connect to the Internet.

Make the appropriate selection and click Next.

Select Your Internet Connection

If you chose one of the "This computer is directly connected to the Internet" choices, Windows presents a list of options for making that connection, listing your network adapters and your configured dial-up connections. Choose the connection that is used to reach the Internet and click Next. If you use a dial-up or PPPoE connection (frequently used with DSL service), choose the appropriate dial-up connection. Otherwise choose the network adapter that connects to your broadband modem.

Give This Computer a Description and Name

Enter a brief description of the computer (such as its location or primary user) and a name for the computer. Choose a name using just letters and/or numbers with no spaces or punctuation. Each computer on your LAN must have a different name.

If you're hard pressed to come up with names, try the names of gemstones, composers, Impressionist painters, or even *Star Wars* characters, as long as Mr. Lucas' lawyers don't hear about it. I use the names of islands in the Indonesian archipelago—with more than 25,000 to choose from there's little chance of running out of unique names!

Some Internet service providers, especially cable providers, require you use a name that they provide. (If you have a hardware connection-sharing device hooked up to your cable modem, enter that name into the hardware device and use any names you want on your LAN.)

Name Your Network

Choose a name for your network workgroup. This name is used to identify which computers should appear in your list of network choices later on. All computers on your LAN should have the same workgroup name. The wizard puts MSHOME into the name field, but I strongly suggest that you change it to WORKGROUP, which is the default on both earlier and later versions of Windows.

Caution

If you run the wizard again, it tries to change your workgroup name back to MSHOME. Be sure to change it back to WORKGROUP.

Also: The workgroup name *must* be different from all the computer names.

File and Printer Sharing

The wizard asks whether you want turn file and printer sharing on or off. Select Turn On File and Printer Sharing unless your network will contain computers that you don't trust; that is, computers in a public area, computers on a public wireless network, computers whose users you don't know, and so on. (If you later change your mind, or move your computer from one network to another, you can turn file sharing on or off using the Exceptions tab on the Windows Firewall control panel.)

Ready to Apply Network Settings

The wizard lets you review your selections. Click Next to proceed.

You're Almost Finished...

You need to run the wizard on all the computers on your LAN at least once. If all the computers use Windows XP, select Just Finish the Wizard, and then run the wizard on each of your other computers. If you have computers running versions of Windows 95, 98, Me, NT, or 2000, you can create a disk that lets you run the wizard on these older machines, or you can use your Windows XP CD-ROM on these computers.

To use a disk, choose Create a Network Setup Disk, and insert a blank, formatted floppy disk. If you ran the wizard earlier and just changed some of the settings, choose Use the Network Setup Disk I Already Have, and reinsert the setup disk you created earlier. Otherwise, choose Just Finish the Wizard; I Don't Need to Run the Wizard on Other Computers.

Caution

Don't use this network setup disk on computers running Windows Vista.

Note

If you need to adjust the computer or workgroup name later, log on as a Computer Administrator, right-click My Computer, select Properties, and view the Computer Name tab. You can use a name-assignment wizard by clicking Network ID, or you can enter the information manually by clicking Change.

Now, continue with the next section to review the IP addressing choices made on your network, as discussed in the section titled "IP Addressing Options."

Setting Up a Network on Vista

Surprisingly, Windows Vista does not have a network setup wizard to walk you through setting up file sharing for a home or small office network. If you've just set up a wireless network, the procedure I described earlier under "Wireless Networking" took care of the wireless connection itself. But, after the wireless connection is set up, or if you've just installed a wired Ethernet or HomePNA (phoneline) network, you have to check or change a few other settings before you can share files and printers on your new network.

If your network is going to be used only to share an Internet connection, you don't need to perform these steps. But, if you do want to share files and/or printers among the computers on your network, you must check the following settings:

- Ensure that each computer has the same workgroup name.
- Enable file and printer sharing.
- If you use a third-party firewall product, permit file and printer sharing data to pass through the firewall.

I take you through these steps in detail in the following sections.

Each computer on the network must have a unique computer name. In addition, each computer has a workgroup name that should be the same on each of your computers. I recommend that you use WORKGROUP as the workgroup name—yes, it's unimaginative, but most Windows computers come with this name preset, so we'll go with it.

To check the workgroup name on your Vista computers, click Start, right-click Computer, and select Properties. The workgroup name is shown under the heading Computer Name, Domain and Workgroup Settings. If any computer has a different workgroup name, click the Change Settings button and approve the User Account Control prompt. When the System Properties dialog appears, click Change and type WORKGROUP under the Workgroup button. Click OK, and then let Windows restart.

Tip

If your network has computers running other versions of Windows, be sure that they use WORKGROUP as the workgroup name as well. If you use the Network Setup Wizard on an XP computer, be careful: It will try to change the workgroup name to MSHOME. At the appropriate step in the wizard, change the name back to WORKGROUP.

Enable File and Printer Sharing

To enable File and Printer Sharing on Vista, click Start, Control Panel. Select Network and Internet, and then Network and Sharing Center, shown in Figure 6.5.

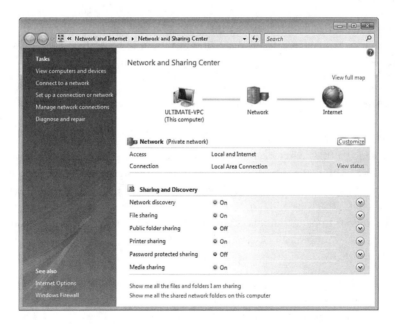

Figure 6.5 The Network and Sharing Center lets you control Vista's sharing features.

The first thing to note is the network type that you originally selected when you started Windows after installing your network. When you connect Vista to any network, wireless or wired, it probes the other devices on the network to see whether it's been connected to the same network before, or if the network is new. The first time Vista is connected to a new network, it asks you whether the network is Public or Private. If you label the network Public, it's considered to be "dangerous" in that you wouldn't want to trust other users to see the contents of your computer, and so file sharing, network device discovery, and other services are disabled on that network connection. If you label the network Private, network services such as file sharing can be enabled.

So before you can share files, check the label next to your network's name (which is usually just Network). If the label is Public, click the word Customize. Check Private, click Next, confirm the User Account Control prompt, and then click Close.

Now, check the following settings:

- **Network Discovery**—Should be On.
- **File Sharing**—Should be On.
- **Public Folder Sharing**—The Public Documents folder is used for files that you want all users on your computer to be able to see and use. Set Public Folder Sharing feature to On if you want the Public Documents folder to visible to other users on your network as well.
- **Printer Sharing**—Should be On.
- **Password Protected Sharing**—I discuss this feature in more detail later in this chapter under "Simple File Sharing."
- **Media Sharing**—Set to On if you have a library of music and video that you want to make available to other users and to media playback devices on your network (such as the Roku Soundbridge).

If you need to change any of these settings, click the small v in the circle to the right of the feature name and change the setting. You will probably need to confirm a User Account Control prompt.

At this point, file and printer sharing is ready to go. There is one more step only if you've added a third-party firewall program to your computer.

Open Firewall

If you've added a third-party network firewall program to your computer, just setting File and Printer Sharing On may not be enough to let other computers "see" your computer or use any folders or printers you share. You may need to take extra steps to open your firewall to Windows file sharing data. You'll have to check the manufacturer's instructions for the specifics, but what you want to do is to permit inbound and outbound Windows File Sharing data traffic. If your firewall requires you to specify TCP and UDP port numbers, be sure that the following protocols and ports are open:

> UDP port 135
> UDP port 136
> TCP port 137
> TCP port 445

Open these ports to other computers on your same network (same subnet).

IP Addressing Options

Windows uses TCP/IP as its primary network protocol. Each computer on the network needs to have a unique IP address assigned to it. There are three ways that IP addresses can be assigned:

- Manually, in what is called *static* IP addressing. You would select an address for each computer and enter it manually.

- Dynamically, through the DHCP service provided by Internet Connection Sharing, a Windows NT/200x server, or a hardware connection-sharing router.

- Automatically, though Windows' Automatic Private Internet Protocol Addressing (APIPA) mechanism. If Windows computers are configured for dynamic IP addressing but there is no DHCP server present, Windows automatically assigns IP addresses. This is the least desirable option.

By default, a newly installed network adapter will be set up for dynamic addressing. I recommend that you do *not* rely on APIPA to configure your network. In my experience, it can cause horrendous slowdowns on your computers. If you don't have a device or computer to provide DHCP service, configure static TCP/IP addresses.

Configuring Dynamic (DHCP) IP Address Assignment

By default, Windows sets up newly installed network adapters to use dynamic IP address assignment, so for new adapters, you don't need to take any additional configuration steps.

Note

If you used static addressing in the past, just view the properties page for your network adapter, select Internet Protocol (TCP/IP), click Properties, and set both the IP Address and DNS settings to Obtain an Address Automatically.

You will need a computer or hardware device to provide DHCP service (which provides configuration information) to all your other computers. This is provided automatically by any Windows computer that runs Windows Internet Connection Sharing (there can be at most one such computer on a network), by the addition of an Internet connection-sharing router, or a wireless access point that includes an Internet connection-sharing feature. (Alternately, you could run the DHCP service on a Windows Server computer. These operating systems can be used on workgroup networks as well as domain networks, although setting them up is beyond the scope of this book.)

If you are using Windows Internet Connection Sharing, it assigns IP address 192.168.0.1 with a network mask of 255.255.255.0 to the network adapter in the sharing computer. Other computers should be configured for dynamic addressing and receive addresses from 192.168.0.2 on up.

If you are configuring a hardware Internet Connection Sharing router, you may need to enable and configure its DHCP server. Usually, the DHCP feature is enabled by default, so you do not need to configure it. If you do, you can use the following settings:

DHCP Server:	**Enabled**
Server IP address:	192.168.0.1
DHCP starting address:	192.168.0.100
Number of addresses:	100
DNS server(s):	(As provided by your ISP)

Some routers prefer to use a different subnet (range of network addresses)—for instance, 192.168.1.x. Whichever range you use, be sure to use the same subnet range for any static IP addresses you assign. There is more information on setting up IP address ranges in the online Appendix C, "Remote Desktop and Remote Assistance" in the discussion of enabling Remote Desktop.

Configuring Static IP Addresses

You'll want to set up static (fixed) IP addresses for some or all of your computers in three situations:

- If your network has no shared Internet connection and no router, you'll want to assign static IP address for all your computers, so you won't be slowed down by the Automatic IP configuration mechanism.

- If you have computers that you want to reach from the Internet—for example, one or more computers that you want to be able to use via Remote Desktop—you'll want to assign a static IP address at least to those computers; the others can have their IP addresses assigned automatically.

- If you have network-attached printers or print servers, you'll need to assign static IP addresses to these devices. You need to enter these addresses when you're setting up Windows to use the printers.

The goal in assigning static IP addresses is to ensure that each computer on your network has a unique IP address, shared by no other, and that all the other TCP/IP setup information is the same on every computer.

I suggest you make a worksheet that lists the setup information for your network. Determining what settings to use depends on the type of network you have, which will be one of the following three choices:

- If your network does not have a router, *and* you are not using Windows Internet Connection Sharing, use the following values for your computers:

IP Address:	192.168.0.x, where x is a number from 200 on up
Network Mask:	255.255.255.0
Gateway Address:	Leave blank
DNS Server:	Leave blank

- If your network has a router, connect it and turn on one of your computers. Be sure that the router is configured and working, according to the manufacturer's instructions, and be sure that you can view web pages from the attached computer. Then click Start, All Programs, Accessories, Command Prompt. In the command prompt window, type **ipconfig /all** and press Enter. Make a note of the IP address, network mask, gateway address, and DNS server listed in the window. (On Vista, ignore the IPv6 information, and ignore the information for networking adapters that have the word *Tunnel* or *Teredo* in their name.)

Then use the following values for any computers and devices that need a static IP address:

IP Address: *a.b.c.x*, where *a.b.c* are the first three numbers of the IP address you saw in the Command Prompt window, and *x* is a number from 200 on up. This might end up being something like 192.168.1.200.

Network Mask: As noted in the Command Prompt window, usually 255.255.255.0.

Gateway Address: As noted in the Command Prompt window, usually something like 192.168.0.1.

DNS Server: As noted in the Command Prompt window, usually the DNS addresses supplied by your ISP, or in some cases the same as the gateway address.

■ If you are using Windows Internet Connection Sharing, use the following values for those computers and devices that need a static IP address:

IP Address: 192.168.0.*x*, where *x* is a number from 200 on up

Network Mask: 255.255.255.0

Gateway Address: 192.168.0.1

DNS Server: 192.168.0.1

I suggest that you then list on your worksheet all your computers and any printer devices. Next to each, write down "automatic" if you are letting the computer get its address automatically, or write down the IP address that you will be setting manually. This way you can keep track of which numbers have been used already. The finished worksheet might look something like this:

```
My Network:
Information from command prompt window:
IP Address:      192.168.0.2    (so: all IP addresses will start with 192.168.0)
Network Mask:    255.255.255.0
Gateway Address: 192.168.0.1
DNS Servers:     10.11.12.13
                 10.21.22.23

My IP Address assignments:
java             192.168.0.200  (want to access from Internet with Remote Desktop)
sumatra          automatic
bali             automatic
HPJetDirect      192.168.0.201  (print server)
```

With this worksheet in hand, configure each computer or device that requires a static IP address.

To assign an IP address to a computer running Windows XP, use the following steps:

1. Log on as a Computer Administrator.

2. Open the Network Connections window. Right-click the entry or icon for your LAN adapter (usually labeled Local Area Connection) and select Properties.

3. Select Internet Protocol (TCP/IP) and click Properties.

4. On the General tab, enter the selected IP address, subnet mask, default gateway, and one or two DNS server IP addresses, as shown in Figure 6.6.

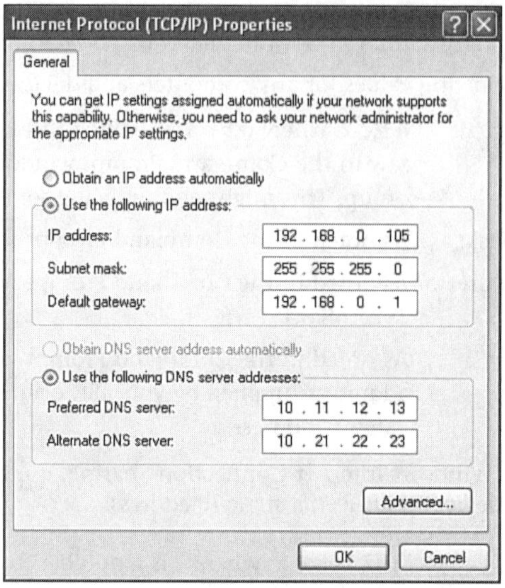

Figure 6.6   Enter static IP address information on the General tab.

5. You can configure your preferred Internet domain name (called the *preferred DNS suffix*) on the Network Identification page in the System Properties dialog. To get there, right-click [My] Computer and select Properties, or select Advanced, Network Identification in the Network Connections window. View the Computer Name tab, click Change, and then click More.

You can also enter a preferred Internet domain name for each individual network or Internet connection. You might want to use your company's domain name on the network connection, and your ISP's domain name on a dial-up connection. To do this, view the network connection's properties dialog, click the Advanced button, select the DNS tab, and enter the domain name under DNS Suffix for This Connection, as shown in Figure 6.7.

Also, if your ISP has provided you with more than two DNS server addresses, click Add to enter additional addresses on this same tab.

6. Unless your network's DNS server supports dynamic IP address registration, uncheck Register This Connection's Addresses in DNS.

7. Click OK to close the dialogs.

On Vista, follow these steps:

1. Click Start, right-click Network, and select Properties.

2. Select Manage Network Connections.

3. Locate the icon corresponding to your LAN adapter. It is probably named Local Area Connection or Wireless Connection. Right-click this icon and select Properties.

4. Confirm the User Account Control prompt.

5. Select Internet Protocol Version 4 (TCP/IPv4) and click Properties.

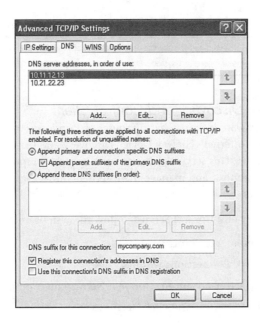

Figure 6.7   Enter per-connection DNS information on the connection's Advanced Properties DNS tab.

Then follow the steps previously described for assigning an IP address on Windows XP, starting at step 4.

Configuring Additional Useful Network Services

Besides the TCP/IP protocol and network services that are installed by default with Windows, you may want to install some additional services manually as part of your network setup.

Link Level Topology Discovery (LLTD) for XP

Windows Vista includes a network map feature that shows a diagram of the devices and computers on your network. The map is constructed from data collected by the Link Level Topology Discovery (LLTD) protocol. Vista comes with LLTD software preinstalled, but to get it in XP you must have Service Pack 3 installed. Thus, if you have computers running both Windows Vista and XP Service Pack 2 on your network, the XP SP2 computers don't show up on Vista's Network Map.

To install LLTD support on XP without installing Service Pack 3, perform the following steps on each of your XP computers:

1. Visit microsoft.com and search for "KB922120." Select the search result titled "Download Details: Link Layer Topology Discovery (LLTD) Responder (KB922120)."

2. Click Continue to perform Windows license validation.

3. Download and then run the small installer program.

Note

At the time this was written, LLTD responder software was not available for Windows Server versions, Mac OS X, or Linux, so computers running these operating systems also do not appear as connected computers in Vista's network map.

Internet Gateway Device Discovery and Control Client

If you are using a hardware Internet-sharing router or Windows Internet Connection Sharing, you should install the Internet Gateway Device Discovery and Control Client on all your Windows XP computers. This service places an icon in each computer's Network Connections folder that lets users monitor and manage the Internet connection that is hosted on the sharing computer or the router.

To install the Discovery and Control Service, follow these steps on each XP computer:

1. Log on as a Computer Administrator.

2. Open the Network Connections window.

3. From the menu, select Advanced, Optional Networking Components.

4. Select Networking Services and click Details.

5. Check both Internet Gateway Device Discovery and Control Client and UPnP User Interface, and click OK.

6. Click Next.

When this service has been installed, an icon appears in your Network Connections window for your router or other network devices. You can double-click this icon to open the device's setup and control page. What appears varies from device to device, but it's usually the device's built-in setup web page.

Universal Plug and Play

If you use a hardware connection-sharing router or Internet Connection Sharing, you may also want to consider enabling a feature called Universal Plug and Play (UPnP). UPnP provides a way for software running on your computer to communicate with the router. Here's what UPnP can do:

- It provides a means for the router to tell software on your computer that it is separated from the Internet by Network Address Translation. Some software—Remote Assistance and the video and audio parts of Windows Messenger in particular—ask the computer on the other end of the connection to establish a connection back to your IP address. On a network with a shared connection, however, the IP address that the computer sees is not the public IP address that the shared Internet connection uses. UPnP lets software such as Remote Assistance find out what its public IP address is. It also provides a way for the router to suggest alternate port numbers if several computers on the network want to provide the same service (for example, if several users send Remote Assistance requests).

- It provides a means for software running on the network to tell the router to forward expected incoming connections to the correct computer. Remote Assistance and Windows Messenger again are two good examples. When the computer on the other end of the connection starts sending data, the router does not know to send it to your computer. UPnP lets UPnP-aware application programs automatically set up forwarding in the router.

■ UPnP provides a means for printers and perhaps other types of as-yet-undeveloped hardware devices to announce their presence on the network so that Windows can automatically take advantage of the services they provide.

UPnP has a downside, however: It has no built-in security mechanism, so any program on any computer on your network could potentially take control of the router and open "holes" for incoming connections (and there are already some viruses and Trojan horses that take advantage of this). However, Windows Firewall or your third-party firewall package will still provide some protection. Windows Firewall warns you if an undesired program prepares to receive incoming network connections, and this cannot be disabled as long as you are not using a Computer Administrator user account. In addition, most third-party firewalls inform you if an unrecognized program requests either incoming or outgoing network connections. UPnP abuse is not yet a serious problem. If you use Remote Assistance or Windows Messenger, the benefits that UPnP provides mostly outweigh the risks.

To use UPnP, you must enable the feature in your router. It's usually disabled by default. If your router doesn't currently support UPnP, you may have to download and install a firmware upgrade from the manufacturer. Most routers now do support UPnP.

On Windows XP, UPnP is enabled by default. If you have a UPnP router or Windows Internet Connection Sharing running on your network, the Network Connections screen should display an icon for the router as shown in Figure 6.8.

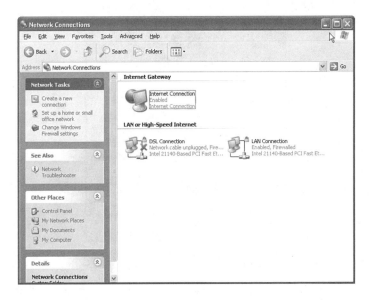

Figure 6.8   If your router supports UPnP, an Internet Gateway icon should appear in Network Connections.

Note

If the icon doesn't appear, click Advanced, Optional Networking Components, select Networking Services, and click Details. Be sure that Internet Gateway Device Discovery and Control Client is checked. While you're here, check UPnP User Interface as well—this enables support for future UPnP devices.

Then, on the task list, click Change Windows Firewall Settings. View the Exceptions tab and be sure that UPnP Framework is checked.

On Vista, UPnP is controlled by the Network Discovery setting, which is enabled by default on private networks and disabled on public networks. To manually control Network Discovery on Vista, follow these steps:

1. Click Start, Control Panel.

2. Select the Network and Internet link, and then select Network and Sharing Center.

3. At the bottom of the page, check the setting for Network Discovery. To change it, click the round v button, select Turn On or Turn Off Network Discovery, click Apply, and then confirm the User Account Control prompt.

When UPnP is working, on XP you should see an icon for your router or gateway under the title Internet Connection in the Network Connections window. If you right-click this icon and select Status, you'll see a dialog similar to the one shown in Figure 6.9, displaying the status of the router's connection. If your Internet service uses a connection-based system such as PPPoE or standard dial-up service via a modem, this dialog may display a button that lets you connect to and disconnect from your ISP.

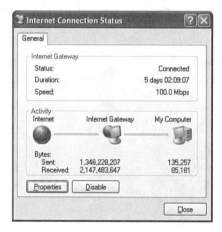

Figure 6.9 Router status displayed via UPnP.

Click Properties and then Settings to display a list of network services for which the router is forwarding incoming connections to computers on your network. This list shows only forwarding settings made via UPnP. Services you've forwarded using the setup screens on your router, such as Remote Desktop, as discussed in the online Appendix C, do not appear here and new settings should not be made here—they usually disappear when the router is reset.

On Vista, the icon appears in the Network Map in the Network and Sharing Center. All you can do with it is select Properties, and from the properties log, View Device Web Page. (The capability to monitor port forwarding is not available on Vista.)

Designating a Master Browser

Windows uses a database of known online computers to build the display known variously as Network Neighborhood, Computers Near Me, or View Workgroup Computers. The database is managed by a software service called the Browser Service. It runs on one of your computers, which is designated the "master browser." The master browser is selected by an automatic election held by the computers on the network. In addition, on a larger network some computers may be elected as backup browser servers.

Note

Vista adds an additional mechanism called the Link Level Discovery Protocol, which we discuss in the next section, but it still uses the Browser Service as well.

When you are running a network with different versions of Windows, or if your computers don't all have the exact same list of protocols installed, this service sometimes malfunctions: The election goes haywire (perhaps because of the Windows equivalent of the hanging chad), or the database is filled incorrectly, or other problems occur. The result is that the Network Neighborhood display doesn't function correctly even though the computers clearly can communicate with each other (for example, one can map network drives to folders shared by the invisible computers).

If you find that this occurs on your network, you may want to force the master browser service to run on a designated Windows XP or Vista computer that is always left on. This can help stabilize the list of local computers.

To make this work you have to configure one computer to always be the master browser, and configure all the other computers never to offer to be the master. To make these settings on a computer running Windows Vista, XP, 2000, or NT you have to edit the Registry key `HKEY_LOCAL_MACHINE\System\CurrentControlSet\Services\Browser\Parameters`. Two values can be altered (refer to Chapter 5, "Tweaking and Tuning Windows," for more details on editing the Registry):

Value	Possible Settings
IsDomainMasterBrowser	True—This computer will be the master browser
	False—Master is determined by election
MaintainServerList	No—Never serve as master
	Yes—Ask to be the preferred master
	Auto—Offer to be master if needed

If you want to force one computer to be the master browser in all circumstances, set the `IsDomainMasterBrowser` value to `True` on that computer and `False` on all others. If you want to set one computer to be the preferred browser, but let others step in if the master is unavailable, just set the `MaintainServerList` key to `Yes` on the preferred computer, and be sure to turn it on before the others.

Simple File Sharing

Although most home users are typically happy letting anyone at any computer read or modify any file, business users need to restrict access to files with payroll, personnel, and proprietary information. Windows Vista, XP, and their predecessors, Windows NT and Windows 2000, were designed with business use in mind, so they require usernames and passwords for identification, and have a security system that lets computer owners restrict access to sensitive files on a user-by-user and file-by-file basis on each computer.

Unfortunately, on a Windows workgroup network, there is no centralized list of authorized usernames. This makes maintaining control of who is and isn't permitted to access network files on each computer difficult. Here's why: When you attempt to use a file or printer shared by another computer, Windows sends your username and password to the other computer. In versions of Windows *prior* to XP,

- If the username and password matched a user account already set up on the other computer, Windows used that account's permission settings to determine whether to grant you access to the file.

- If the user information didn't match, Windows prompted you to enter a username and password that the other computer would recognize.

- If you failed to provide a valid password, the remote Windows computer gave you the permissions assigned to the Guest account, which was usually disabled or didn't have permission to access the resource you wanted.

The advantage of this system was that it let you determine precisely which users could access specific files and printers. The disadvantage was that it required you to set up identical user accounts for each network user on every computer, and then grant these users permissions to view and modify shared files and folders.

Smaller business and home users found this security setup cumbersome to use and difficult to set up properly. This pushed people into sharing accounts and passwords, and otherwise avoiding good security practices, just to get the network to work. That's a risky approach, so Microsoft gave Windows XP a feature called *Simple File Sharing*. On Vista, the corresponding feature is called Password Protected Sharing, but the sense of having it turned on or off is reversed from XP. Here's how the features correspond:

XP	**Vista**
Simple File Sharing *Enabled*	Password Protected Sharing *Off*
Simple File Sharing *Disabled*	Password Protected Sharing *On*

When Simple File Sharing is enabled (or on Vista, when Password Protected Sharing is off),

- Network users are always given access to shared folders and printers, without being prompted for a username or password. They are automatically granted access to files and folders, using the permissions granted to the Guest account, even if Guest is disabled for direct logins.

- On XP only, the Security properties tab that is normally used to assign per-user permissions to files and printers is not displayed, even for files that are stored on a drive formatted with the NTFS file system. Files stored in directories in a user's profile folder (My Documents, for example) are automatically set up to permit access only by the owner, and files stored elsewhere are set up to permit access by anyone.

- Windows automatically assigns appropriate security permissions to folders and printers when you share them. If you check Allow Network Users to Change My Files, all network users can read, write, rename, or delete the contents of the shared folder. If you don't check this option, network users can view but not modify the contents.

The result is that with Simple File Sharing in effect, anyone who connects to your computer through the network has access to all shared files, folders, and printers shared by the computer, with no security enforcement of any kind. This has the advantage of eliminating all worries about having to manage accounts and passwords on multiple computers, but it does mean that you have to keep in mind these points:

- You don't get to pick and choose who gets access and who doesn't. Everyone gets access to every shared resource.

- If you have an unsecured wireless network with no WEP or WPA security key, anyone driving by your home or office can not only connect to your network, but also see and/or modify your shared files.

- On XP, the Shared Documents folder that appears under My Computer is automatically set up as a shared folder, the idea being that any files you place in it are available not only to other users on your computer, but to other users anywhere on your network. On Vista, you can control whether the Public Documents folder is shared on the network from the Network and Sharing Center.

In the end, it's a reasonable trade-off, as long as you keep in mind the fact that all shared files and folders are available to anyone who can connect to your network. You should also keep in mind that

- Simple File Sharing is always used on XP Home Edition, and cannot be disabled. This means that anyone can use any resource shared by a computer running XP Home Edition.

- Simple File Sharing is optional on XP Professional, when the computer is part of a workgroup network. It's enabled by default when Windows is installed, but you can disable it if you want to use user-level security on files and/or shared resources.

- Simple File Sharing is always disabled on an XP Professional or Vista computer that is joined to a domain network. User-level security is always used in this case.

- Simple File Sharing applies only to the resources shared by the computer running Windows XP and Vista. If you use XP to use folders shared by a computer running some other operating system, such as Windows Me or Mac OS X, that operating system's security system is used.

On an XP Professional computer that is not a member of a domain network, the Simple File Sharing feature can be disabled from the Tools, Folder Options, View tab in any Windows Explorer window, as shown in Figure 6.10. You must be logged on as a Computer Administrator to change the setting.

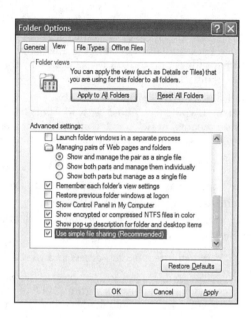

Figure 6.10 Simple File Sharing is enabled by default; disable it to use the old Windows NT/2000 access control system on a peer-to-peer network.

To change the Password Protected Sharing setting on Vista, follow these steps:

1. Click Start, Control Panel, Network and Internet, Network and Sharing Center.

2. Click the small round v button next to Password Protected Sharing. Click Turn On or Turn Off Password Protected Sharing as desired.

3. Click Apply, and then confirm the User Account Control prompt.

Tip

If you disable Simple File Sharing, remote users have to supply a username and password valid on your computer to use a shared resource on your computer. In this case, it vastly simplifies things if you set up an identical account for each user on each of your computers. For each user, pick a username and password, and use that same name and password on every computer.

Also, on XP if Simple File Sharing is disabled, your computer displays different dialog boxes when you go to share a folder, and you'll have access to the Security properties page on folders and printers. You can see both versions in the next section.

Sharing Resources

After your network is working, each computer can share selected resources—that is to say, folders and printers. The purpose of sharing is to make these folders and printers available to other computers, where they look and act *exactly* like folders on your own hard drive and printers connected to your own computer. This section briefly describes how to make resources available to other computers on the network.

Sharing Folders and Drives

By default, on a workgroup network Windows XP automatically shares the My Documents folder in the All Users profile folder; this is the folder that is listed as Shared Documents in My Computer.

Vista has a corresponding feature, but you must enable it. To do so, click Start, Control Panel, Network and Internet, Network and Sharing Center. If Public Folder Sharing is shown as Off, click the round v button next to it and select Turn On Public Folder Sharing.

Caution

Do not enable Public Folder Sharing if you are at an Internet café or on any other public network.

To make a file available to other users, simply drag it to the [Shared or Public] Documents folder on your computer, and users on other computers can locate it on the network and read or copy it. In many cases, having this one shared folder might be sufficient.

Sharing Folders on XP

You can share other folders as well. To do so, locate the folder in Windows Explorer and right-click it. From here, the procedure differs somewhat depending on whether you're using XP or Vista.

On XP, select Sharing. If you have Simple File Sharing enabled, the dialog in Figure 6.11 will appear.

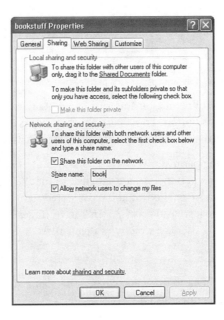

Figure 6.11   To share a folder, check Share This Folder on the Network and enter a share name.

Check Share This Folder on the Network and enter a share name, a name of up to 14 characters with no punctuation characters other than the underscore (_) or hyphen.

On an XP Professional computer on a workgroup network with Simple File Sharing enabled, or on a Windows XP Home Edition computer, you see a check box labeled Allow Network Users to Change My Files. If you do not check it, network users can view and copy the files, but they cannot modify or delete them.

On an XP Professional computer with Simple File Sharing disabled, or on a domain network, the Sharing tab appears as shown in Figure 6.12.

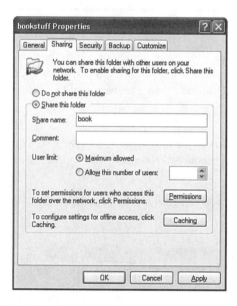

Figure 6.12 When Simple File Sharing is not active, there are more specific permission controls.

In this case, you can control permissions to read and write files on a per-user or per-group basis by clicking the Permissions button. These permissions work as *additional restrictions* to any imposed by NTFS file security, if the folder is on a drive formatted with NTFS.

For example, if the sharing permissions grant read/write access to Everyone, the file is still protected by whatever per-user permissions are assigned to the file; a network user simply has the same rights to the file that he or she would have if seated right at the computer. If the sharing permissions give Everyone just Read access, users can read files *if* the NTFS permissions let them, but in any case no network user can modify or delete files.

Sharing Folders on Vista

On Vista, after right-clicking a folder, select Share. The dialog shown in Figure 6.13 appears. By default, your own user account is listed.

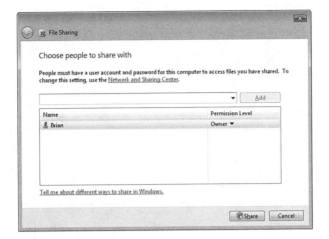

Figure 6.13   The File Sharing Wizard in Windows Vista.

- If Password Protected Sharing is turned on, use the drop-down list to select one or more other user accounts or group names (including the helpful catch-all Everyone), and click Add to give permission to read and/or save files in the shared folder.

- If Password Protected Sharing is turned off, add Everyone to the sharing list; this is the only entry that matters for network access.

As soon as one or more names are listed in the People to Share With list, you may adjust their Permission Level settings by selecting one of the following choices:

- **Owner, Co-Owner**—Can read, modify create, delete, rename, and change permissions on files.

- **Contributor**—Can read, modify create, delete, and rename files.

- **Reader**—Can read but not write, modify, or delete files.

Note

These permission settings do two things: They are used to add access rights (NTFS file permissions) to the folder, which are used for users who log on directly at the computer, *and* they are used for over-the-network access.

Click Share to finish the sharing process. After a folder has been shared, to adjust its sharing settings, view its Properties page and select the Sharing tab. The settings are nearly identical to those described previously for XP, so I won't repeat that discussion here.

Sharing Folders from the Command Line

From the command line, you can share a folder or drive with the command

```
net share sharename=drive:\fullpath
```

For example,

```
net share music=c:\musicfiles
```

or

```
net share cddrive=d:\
```

and can cancel a share with the command

```
net share sharename /delete
```

Note

You can prevent a share from being displayed when other users browse the network by adding a dollar sign ($) to the share name. For example, the share name **secret$** will not appear in the My Network Places display. This won't deter a motivated hacker, but it does discourage casual browsing. To use a resource that's been hidden this way, you have to explicitly use its name. For example, you can open *computername**sharename*$ in Windows Explorer or you can map a network drive to this network path.

Note

Administrators may be used to using the built-in whole-drive shares that are automatically created for each disk drive on a Windows NT/2000/XP computer, for example, C$. However, these shares are available only to Computer Administrator users. You cannot reach these administrative shares on a Windows XP computer that has Simple File Sharing enabled because all network access takes place through the Guest user account.

You can also share entire drives by viewing and right-clicking the drive icon in [My] Computer. This is a great way to make a DVD-ROM, CD-ROM, floppy disk, or other disk available to all users on a network. In the case of DVD and CD drives, you can read but not write to these disks.

Sharing Printers

You can share any printer that is controlled by your computer. This includes printers directly cabled to your computer and printers driven using LPR or other direct network protocols.

To enable printer sharing, do the following:

1. Choose Start and view the Printers and Faxes folder.

2. Right-click the printer icon and choose Sharing, or select Properties and then select the Sharing tab.

3. Select Share This Printer, and enter a network name for the printer, as shown in Figure 6.14. Enter up to 14 characters, avoiding punctuation characters.

4. If your network has only Windows Vista/XP/2000 32-bit computers, click OK, and you're finished. Other network users can now use the shared printer.

Otherwise, continue to the next section to add extra printer drivers for other operating systems.

Installing Extra Printer Drivers

If you have computers running other versions of Windows or other CPU types, you can load the appropriate printer drivers for those operating systems now, and network users will receive them automatically when they connect to your printer. This step is optional, but it's a friendly thing to do.

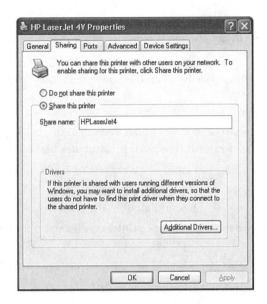

Figure 6.14 Enabling sharing for a printer.

View the Sharing tab in your printer's Properties dialog box and select the Additional Drivers button. Windows displays a list of supported operating systems and CPU types. The XP version is shown in Figure 6.15. (By the way, "Intel" refers to any Intel or compatible chips, such as those made by AMD or VIA/Cyrix.) On Vista, you can install only XP-/Vista-compatible drivers, in 32- and 64-bit flavors.

Figure 6.15 You can install drivers for additional operating systems or CPUs to make it easy for network users to attach to your printer.

Check the boxes for operating systems you want to support and click OK. Windows then goes through these one by one and asks for the appropriate driver disks. You can find these drivers on the original installation disks for the alternative operating system, or often on disks provided with the printer, which might contain support for many operating systems on the same disk.

When installed, the alternative drivers are sequestered in your Windows folder and delivered to users of the other operating systems when they elect to use the networked printer.

Setting Printer Permissions

If you're on a domain network or have chosen to disable Simple File Sharing, you can control access to your shared printers with three security attributes that can be assigned to users or groups:

Permission	Lets User or Group
Print	Send output to the printer
Manage Printers	Change printer configuration settings, and share or unshare a printer
Manage Documents	Cancel or suspend other users' print jobs

You can use the Security tab in the printer's Properties dialog box to alter the groups and users assigned each of these permissions. The CREATOR OWNER name applies to the user who submitted a given print job.

You probably don't have to change the default permission settings unless you want to limit use of the printer by outside users in a domain environment only. In this case, delete Everyone, and add specific groups with Print permission.

Sharing Fax Modems and Other Devices

The software provided with Windows does not permit you to share a data modem, fax modem, scanner, or other input/output device over your network. You may find it as annoying as I do that the Windows Fax service is built to provide shared fax sending and receiving for a network, but the sharing capability is disabled in Windows XP and Vista.

If you want to be able to send faxes through a single phone line from several networked computers, the Windows Fax service on Windows 2000 Server or Windows Server 2003 *can* be shared. You can also purchase a third-party fax sharing program such as Symantec WinFax.

Shared scanners are a more complex matter. Some printer/scanners have network capability built in. (This isn't even a high-end feature anymore. The Brother all-in-one laser printer/scanner/copier I bought for $99 has it.) With network capability, anyone on the network can use the scanner from his own desk. But this may not really be necessary. Because a scanner has to be connected to one of your computers anyway, and you will need to stand there to put pages into the scanner, you can simply save the scans to a network shared folder and later pick up the files from another computer.

Avoiding Firewall Issues

If you find that you cannot access shared folders or printers on another network computer, or if other users cannot access resources that are shared by your computer, it's possible that Windows

Firewall or a third-party firewall is interfering. You may need to make a configuration change to let file and printer sharing work. However, in doing so, you must be *very careful* not to make your computer more accessible than absolutely necessary.

Use this checklist to enable file and printer sharing on both the computer that is sharing resources and the computer that is attempting to use them.

- On XP, be sure that you have run the Network Setup Wizard at least once. File and printer sharing are silently disabled until you do so.

- If the computer is running Vista or Windows XP Service Pack 2 or later, be sure that the Windows Firewall service is not blocking you. Open the Control Panel. On XP, open Security Center, and then Windows Firewall. On Vista, select Allow a Program Through Windows Firewall. Select the General tab. The Firewall should be On, and Don't Allow Exceptions should *not* be checked. On the Exceptions tab, be sure that File and Printer Sharing is checked.

- If you are using a third-party firewall service such as Norton Internet Security, be sure that this firewall is also configured to permit Windows File and Printer Sharing between computers on your subnet. The exact method for doing this varies from one product to another, but most have a fairly easy and explicit way to enable Windows file and printer sharing.

In general, you *cannot* safely share files and printers between computers that are not on the same network subnet—that is, directly connected on a network that is controlled by a single router.

Caution

If your computer is directly connected to the Internet, it is exceedingly dangerous to disable Windows Firewall or your third-party firewall package. Your computer may quickly become infected by viruses and Trojan horse programs that are constantly scouring the Internet looking for unprotected Windows computers.

Providing Shared Internet Access

Although you could give each computer its own dial-up modem or broadband modem, one of the principal advantages of installing a network is gaining Internet access for all your computers through a single connection. There are two simple ways to provide shared Internet access for a home or small office network:

- If you have cable or DSL broadband Internet service, get a hardware Internet connection-sharing router. It's easy to set up, costs little or nothing, provides a certain amount of added security to your network, lets you add on additional computers with no setup effort, and can let you use both wired and wireless connections at the same time.

- If you use standard dial-up Internet service (not AOL dial-up service), use the Windows Internet Connection Sharing service to share the connection with others through your network. This is an acceptable solution although the "sharing" computer must be turned on to use the Internet from your other computers.

Note

You cannot share an AOL dial-up connection, nor can you share connections to discount ISPs that require the use of their proprietary dial-up software.

Caution

For homes with more than one computer, some cable Internet providers may require you to connect your computers and cable modem to a hub, rather than to a router. However, this is dangerous—it exposes all your computers directly to the Internet. If you still have this sort of setup, I strongly recommend that you purchase a hardware cable/DSL connection-sharing router to place in between your cable modem and your computers. Otherwise, you *must not* enable File and Printer Sharing on your network.

Shared network connections provided by hardware routers and Windows Internet Connection Sharing (ICS) use a mechanism called *Network Address Translation* (NAT) to mediate between the computers on your network and the Internet via a single connection and single public IP address. The router or ICS computer has two connections, one to the Internet via a dial-up, cable, or DSL modem, and one to your LAN, as illustrated in the top part of Figure 6.16.

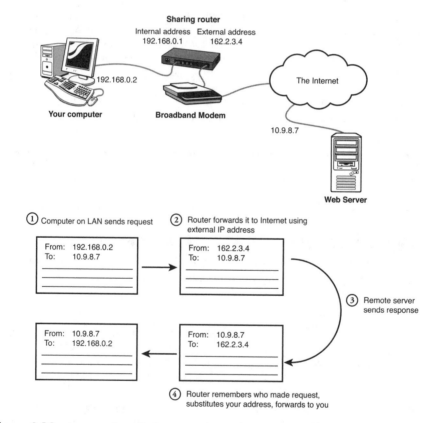

Figure 6.16   A connection-sharing router acts as an intermediary between your LAN and the Internet.

When one of your computers attempts to contact a website, it sends a data packet to the router or computer running ICS to be forwarded to the Internet, as illustrated in the bottom part of Figure 6.16. As it passes the outgoing network data packet to the Internet, the router replaces the packet's "from" address—the private IP address assigned to your computer—with the router's public address, so that the reply from the remote server will be returned through the Internet to the router. The router remembers from whom the request came, replaces the response's "to" network address with your computer's private address, and transmits it on its LAN connection.

This mechanism works quite well for communication initiated by computers on your network. When outside computers attempt to contact you, however, it's another story. If you have a web or email server on your network, for instance, the connection-sharing router or computer can be configured to send packets for particular network services to the correct computer; this is called *port forwarding*. Otherwise, incoming connection attempts are simply discarded. In this way NAT protects you against random probing by hackers, and it's very helpful to have this as a second level of protection in addition to Windows Firewall.

Adding a Connection-Sharing Router

Connection-sharing routers almost always have one 10Mbps Ethernet port that is used to connect to a cable or DSL modem, and have a second connection for your LAN. This LAN connection can take several forms:

- There may be a single 10/100Mbps Ethernet port.
- There may be four or more 10/100Mbps Ethernet ports, giving you a built-in switching hub.
- There may be a built-in wireless networking access point.
- There may be a combination of the preceding.

Because wireless devices and laptops are becoming so common, and because it's very nice to be able to offer wireless connectivity to friends and visitors even if you don't use it yourself, I recommend purchasing an 802.11g or 802.11n wireless router with a built-in four port switch. Routers without wireless can sometimes be found for $0 after rebate, but usually fall in the U.S. in the $10 to $40 range. If you shop carefully and look for a sale or rebate offer, wireless routers with four-port switches can also frequently be purchased for $10 to $40, so you're getting a lot of connectivity for no additional cost.

Note

If you are planning to use Voice over IP (VoIP) telephone service, contact your VoIP provider to see what sort of routers it supports.

You will need to ensure that your ISP provides you with a cable or DSL modem with an Ethernet port; USB or internal PCI adapters do not work with a router. Use a standard Ethernet patch cable to connect the modem to the Internet or WAN port on the router.

Then connect one of your computer's LAN adapters to one of the ports on the router, using another standard Ethernet patch cable.

Note

Even if you're going to use wireless connections, it's usually required, or at least easier, to use a wired connection to initially set up the router.

When you connect your computer's Ethernet port to the router, Windows automatically requests an IP address and configures the port's TCP/IP settings from default values provided by the router. You should then be able to open your web browser and view the router's setup web page, using the URL `//192.168.0.1` or `//192.168.1.1`, as instructed by your router's installation manual.

Your router establishes the connection to your ISP on your behalf, so you need the same information that you'd need to establish the connection directly through Windows. For a DSL connection, this often involves a username and password. For a cable connection, this often requires that you set the router's hostname to a specific name, or you may have to provide the router's MAC address (its Ethernet hardware address code) to your ISP; this number is usually printed in tiny letters on a label on the bottom of the router. Alternatively, if you've already used your cable Internet service by directly connecting your computer, you might be able to have the router *clone* your computer's MAC address—that is, copy your computer's address and use it on its Internet port so that your ISP doesn't have to make any changes.

Tip

If you previously had your computer connected directly to your cable or DSL modem, power the modem off and back on after you've connected it to the sharing router. This removes your computer's physical (MAC) address from the modem and from your ISP's end of the connection.

After installing the router, run the Network Setup Wizard on all your Windows XP computers. The wizard is described earlier in this chapter, under "Configuring a Workgroup Network." When asked to select a connection method, select This Computer Connects to the Internet Through Another Computer on My Network or Through a Residential Gateway.

On Windows Vista, you should not need to run any setup wizards—Vista automatically detects that you have an Internet connection on the network. However, if you've added a connection-sharing router to an existing network, you may need to adjust any fixed IP addresses you've manually assigned to computers on your network.

After Setting Up a Shared Connection

After the shared connection is set up, all your computers can use it automatically, through the network. The only problem you might run into is with Internet Explorer. If you previously used dial-up Internet, or if you previously had your broadband modem connected directly to your computer, and now Internet Explorer tries to establish a connection whenever you open it, perform the following steps:

1. Open Internet Explorer.

2. If the menu bar is not visible, press and release the Alt key. Select Tools, Internet Options.

3. Select the Connections tab. In the middle of the dialog, select Never Dial a Connection, and click OK.

This keeps Internet Explorer from attempting to make a direct Internet connection.

Using Windows Internet Connection Sharing

All Windows versions since Windows 98 Second Edition have a software version of NAT called Internet Connection Sharing (ICS). It does in software what a connection-sharing router does in hardware. If you have cable or DSL Internet service, I strongly recommend that you use a hardware router.

But, if you really want to, you can use the Windows ICS service to share a broadband connection. You may also want to use ICS if you have standard dial-up Internet service. Internet Connection Sharing can let you use dial-up Internet from two or more computers at once, without tying up additional phone lines—a neat trick. It does, however, require you to leave the computer that is set up to share its connection turned on all the time; at least, it must be on anytime anyone wants to use the Internet.

To set up ICS, select one of your computers to be the one that is to share its Internet connection. Set up and test its Internet connection first, before creating a LAN. For dial-up Internet, get the "sharing computer's" dial-up connection working first, before you connect your network. For broadband Internet, connect the "sharing computer's" network adapter to your cable or DSL modem, and get the Internet connection working first. Only then install a second network adapter that you'll use to hook up to your other computers.

Finally, configure the shared connection. The procedure depends on whether you're using XP or Vista.

Setting Up ICS on Windows XP

On XP, log on as a Computer Administrator. Run the Network Setup Wizard, covered earlier in the chapter, under "Configuring a Workgroup Network." The important points are as follows:

- When you're asked to selection a connection method, select the first choice, This Computer Connects Directly to the Internet. The Other Computers...Connect...Through This Computer.
- When asked to choose a connection, select the entry for the dial-up connection to your ISP.

Complete the rest of the Network Setup Wizard as described earlier in the chapter. If you had set up your LAN previously, be sure to enter the same workgroup name you used originally because the wizard wants to change the setting to MSHOME every time you run it.

When the wizard completes, go to the Network Connections window and locate the icon that represents your Internet connection. It should now say "Firewalled, Shared" and possibly "Disconnected." Right-click it and select Properties. View the Networking tab. In the list of components used by the connection, be sure that *only* Internet Protocol (TCP/IP) and QoS Packet Scheduler are checked. This prevents file sharing from being exposed to the Internet. The firewall does that, too, but it doesn't hurt to be extra safe.

Then restart your computer. Log on again, and try to view a web page (such as www.google.com). Your computer should automatically connect to your ISP, dialing or signing on if necessary. If the web page doesn't appear, you have to resolve the problem before continuing.

When the sharing computer can connect properly, run the Network Setup Wizard on your other Windows XP computers, except for one detail: When you run the wizard, select This Computer

Connects to the Internet Through Another Computer on My Network or Through a Residential Gateway.

Setting Up ICS on Windows Vista

To set up ICS on Vista, set up and test your Internet connection first. Be sure that it's working before you proceed. Then follow these steps on the "sharing" computer:

1. Click Start, Control Panel, Network and Internet, Network and Sharing Center. Under Tasks, select Manage Network Connections.

2. If you are using broadband Internet with a cable or DSL modem connected to your computer through its Ethernet adapter, locate the Local Area Connection icon for this connection, right-click it, and select Rename. Change the name from Local Area Connection to DSL Modem Connection or Cable Modem Connection or some other appropriate name. Confirm the User Account Control Prompt.

   Then right-click this icon and select Properties. Under This Connection Uses the Following Items, *uncheck* every item except QoS Packet Scheduler, Internet Protocol Version 4 (TCP/IPv4), and the two Link-Layer Topology Discovery items.

   You use a second network adapter to connect to the other computers on your network. If you haven't installed it yet, shut Windows down, unplug the computer, and install the adapter now. Power the computer back up, log on, and return to the Network Connections window.

3. If your Internet service is connection-based (standard dial-up, or DSL using a login name and password), right-click your Dial-up or Broadband Connection icon and select Connect so that your Internet connection will be up during the remaining steps. Then right-click it, select Properties, and confirm the User Account Control prompt.

   Otherwise, if you have always-on Internet service, such as that provided by most cable providers, right-click the Cable Modem Connection icon that you renamed earlier, right-click it, select Properties, and confirm the User Account Control prompt.

4. Select the Sharing tab, and check Allow Other Network Users to Connect Through This Computer's Internet Connection. If a drop-down list labeled Home Network Connection is visible, select the network connection that corresponds to the LAN adapter that connects to your other computers, *not* the connection that goes to your DSL or cable modem. Click OK.

5. When the process finishes, you may close the Properties dialog.

Now other users should be able to connect to the Internet through the shared connection. If your Internet service is connection-based, on their Network Connections windows they should see an icon representing the shared connection. They can right-click this icon to establish or disconnect the Internet connection if necessary.

For one last setup step, see "After Setting Up a Shared Connection" at the end of the previous section.

Setting Up Remote Access to Your Computer

Appendix C provides detailed instructions for setting up remote access to your computer. Appendix C is available on the CD-ROM that accompanies this book and online at www.informit.com/title/9780789736956.

Protecting and Securing Windows

It Takes More Than Just Software

Protecting and securing your computer is a major concern with the growing number of malicious software applications circulating on the Internet. The days of just applying the latest Windows security patches to your computer are over. New vulnerabilities or security holes are found almost daily and it usually takes Microsoft several days, if not weeks, to write and test a security patch to fix the hole. And it's not just Windows that you have to worry about. Where PC applications were once little worlds unto themselves, they're now deeply intertwined, so a bug in an MP3 player program can get exploited by a bug in a web browser, and a bug in a spreadsheet program can get exploited by a bug in an email program, and so on. The slow response by many software companies to fix these bugs, combined with the fact that most vulnerabilities are not widely known until they have already been used to attack thousands of computers are why it is now necessary to take an active approach to protecting your Windows computer.

Although security threats are an obvious concern to system administrators in enterprise-level networks, they are no less a problem for the at-home user. Taking the steps outlined in this chapter to protect your Windows PC is an essential part of protecting both its data and its operating stability.

Before we get into the details of using defensive software tools provided by Microsoft and by third-party vendors to secure your computer, though, I want to take a moment to talk about the bigger picture—that is, the strategies you should employ to keep your computer as safe as possible. You can't rely on software alone.

When I talk about computer security I'm talking about two main concerns:

- Preventing unauthorized people from using your computer, or obtaining the information you have in it, either by probing it physically, or by probing it with software through a network or the Internet.

- Preventing *malware* (bad and undesired software) from getting installed on your computer, software that will take advantage of you and your Internet connection to do things you don't want. Malware comes in many forms, including

  - *Spyware* that tracks what you type in hope of capturing information such as your passwords and credit card numbers.

  - *Adware* that displays advertisements for dubious products and services.

  - *Spamware* that uses your computer and your Internet connection to send massive quantities of spam email to others, under someone else's control.

  - *Botware* that lets someone harness your computer along with thousands of others to launch massive attacks against corporate, governmental, and military computers and networks.

  - Programs that delete your files or disable your computer. A relatively new variety is *ransomware*, which encrypts your files, and then offers to sell you the encryption key needed to recover them.

  - Programs that may not have malicious intent but which are installed without your knowledge or permission when you use legitimate software or media, and which end up causing problems on your computer. One example of this form of malware is a "copy protection" system that was secreted on some music CD titles produced by Sony BMG in 2005. If you played the CD on your computer, the Sony software installed itself without your consent or knowledge. It was designed to prevent you from making copies of your music CDs (even legal copies), but it also caused crashes, made it possible for viruses to attack your computer, and caused other problems. (After lawsuits were filed, Sony released a removal tool that caused *worse* problems.)

You may also see the terms *virus, Trojan horse*, and *rootkit*. These aren't so much forms of malware as methods for delivering it. A virus is a program that is programmed to attempt to transmit itself to other computers automatically. A Trojan horse is a program that relies on *you* to install it: It comes packaged along with some desirable software such as a "free Registry tune-up utility" or a "free music player," so that when you download and install the desirable program, you get the malware along with it. A rootkit is a piece of software that uses sketchy means to run with full administrator privileges, typically installs itself secretly, and hides its presence by burrowing so deeply into the operating system that it is virtually invisible to tools that track active processes, drivers, and services. Any of the forms of malware mentioned here could use rootkit techniques.

Let's go through some of easiest and most effective strategies you can use to address these concerns. In the rest of the chapter, I offer suggestions for applying them to protect your computer, your data, and your privacy.

Reduce Your Exposure

One of the most important things you can do to protect your computer against attack is to give criminals as little as possible to grab on to. If you're building a house in a rough neighborhood, would you put twenty doors on it? No, you'd put in just one or two big, thick massive doors with big locks, with maybe bars over them. That's what we want do to with your computer. Here are some ways you can limit the number of doors:

- Install only needed software and services. Because the interconnectedness of today's software means that any application could be a door through which criminals might come, it makes sense to install only the software and Windows services that you truly need.

- Uninstall unwanted software. Many new computers come with applications preinstalled, sometimes *lots* of applications. Many of these applications have a history of serious security vulnerabilities, especially media programs like "Mmmmm Jukebox" and "RrrrPlayer." I'm not naming names here. Just take this advice: If you don't intend to use it, uninstall it. It's hard enough keeping the software you actually use up to date, let alone all that buggy stuff you never asked for.

- Keep Windows Firewall (or a third-party firewall program) turned on at all times so that Windows file sharing and other network services on your computer can't be reached from the Internet.

- If you have high-speed Internet service such as cable or DSL, use a connection-sharing router (gateway) between your cable or DSL modem. Normally, you'd get one of these to share your Internet connection with several computers. But even if you have just one computer, one of these devices can act as a firewall to protect your computer from being probed over the Internet. (Before you go buy one of these, though, check to see if your DSL your cable modem has a router function built in.)

◄◄ For more information about connection sharing routers, **see** "Network Hardware," **p. 326**.

And finally, you should do the majority of your work using a user account that has the least privileges needed to get your job done. Specifically, if at all possible, don't use a Computer Administrator account for day-to-day use, even if you're the only person who uses your computer. When you're using a Computer Administrator account on XP, any program you run intentionally or *inadvertently* has complete access to your computer and Windows. Instead, on XP, use a Power User or Limited account, and use the Run As right-click option, or switch users to log on to an Administrator account when you have to perform maintenance or install new software. On Vista, create a Standard User *and* an Administrator account for yourself, with passwords on both accounts. When you're prompted by User Account Control, enter the username and password of an Administrator account. This ensures that most of the time, any bad program you accidentally run can do only limited damage.

Take Advantage of the Tools You Have

Windows was designed to help you control access to your computer. There are several tools that come free with Windows and can help you prevent accidents and purposeful damage and theft, including the following:

- Set up user accounts and passwords. If when your computer boots up it goes directly to the desktop display, you are not taking advantage of Windows' capability to maintain separate accounts for each user, and to limit what different people may do with the computer. Set up a separate user account for each person who uses each computer, be sure that each account requires a password, and be sure that Windows prompts for a password when it starts up.

- Be sure that kids and non-computer-savvy people have Standard or Limited user accounts, not Computer Administrator accounts.

- On Vista, use the Parental Controls feature to restrict the content that kids can view, limit their ability to install software, and if you want, monitor their activity to enforce your guidelines.

- Take advantage of the NTFS file system permission system to limit access to sensitive files containing payroll, financial, and personal information so that just your account or users you specify can access this information. Vista installs only on a disk formatted with NTFS, but XP worked with both FAT and NTFS. If you have XP installed on the FAT file system, have Windows convert it to NTFS.

- On Vista, *don't* disable the User Account Control system. It helps ensure that only programs that *you* explicitly authorize can make changes to Windows itself.

- If you have XP, upgrade Internet Explorer to version 7 to take advantage of its improved protection against unwanted incoming software.

Keep Abreast of Updates

Bugs are found in Windows and application programs all the time. There's nothing particularly surprising or bad about this; Windows is huge, and there are thousands of programs out there. We can't expect it all to be perfect. There is a constant race between software developers trying to find their bugs so they can fix them, and criminals looking for unfixed bugs so they can find ways to exploit them for nefarious purposes. Your job, as a spectator in this race, is to be sure to keep your software up to date so that you always have the latest fixes. Your goal is to have the necessary updates in place before some hacker tries to find out whether *your* computer has a known vulnerability that he or she can use.

Microsoft has the well known Windows Update service that automatically sends software updates to you when a fix to a serious security bug has been detected. You *really* should take advantage of this service. In addition, if you click Start, All Programs, Windows Update, you can upgrade (free) to the Microsoft Update service, which extends Windows Update and automatically delivers patches to other Microsoft products you have, such as Microsoft Office.

In addition, be sure to frequently visit the websites of the vendors of the software you have installed. If you can, register to receive email updates when new software versions are released.

Tip

The Secunia Personal Software Inspector, a free download, scans your installed software for many common applications and lets you know which ones are out of date. It can even help you download updates. Check out http://psi.secunia.com.

Finally, if your PC manufacturer included a service that checks for and notifies you of updates to all the software on your computer, by all means take advantage of it. (I expect that this type of monitoring and notification service will become a more common and valuable third-party offering in the future.)

Note

If you're running Windows XP, be sure to install the Internet Explorer 7 that was made available through Windows Update. It has significantly better protection against malware than IE6.

And of course, it should go without saying that you should *not* still be using Windows 3.1, 95, 98, or Me on any computer that's connected to the Internet. Microsoft stopped developing security fixes for these retired operating systems long ago, and they rely on the completely unsecurable FAT file system. Treat Windows 9x like the overripe, long-dead skunk it is—pick it up by the tip of its tail and drop it out the nearest window.

Be Skeptical

I don't want to insult you, but it has to be said: No matter how hard you work to keep your computer safe, *you* are the biggest security risk your computer has. In repairing dozens of compromised computers for friends and colleagues in recent years, most of the virus and malware infections I've found came from something the user did deliberately. This included following links to "fix your computer" pop-up ads, installing codec software to permit viewing of videos (yes, you guessed it: porn), installing "free" utility programs such as birthday reminders, and so on.

Computer security requires a lot of skepticism on your part. Treat software like a stranger who's knocking on your door in the middle of the night. Installing a program, after all, is about the same as giving it the key to your house. So, before you install *any* software on your computer, give it a good grilling. Check its references. Do a background check. If something is free, ask why it would be free—what is the vendor getting out of it? (This doesn't mean that all free software is bad, just that you need to give it a good hard look before giving it free run of your computer.) Here are some other things to consider:

- Never, *ever* buy anything that is advertised

    ...in a pop-up window that appears when you are visiting a website owned by someone other than the software manufacturer.

    ...in a spam email.

    ...with graphics that flash brightly, have chaser borders, and so on. If it has to be marketed in a way that would appeal to Homer Simpson, avoid it.

    ...with a graphic that mimics a Windows dialog box, or warns you that it has detected some situation on your computer.

- Avoid any program that purports to clean or optimize anything on your computer, except disk defragmenters. (There are several legitimate disk defragmenting programs, but most other optimizing programs are useless at best. Be especially wary of memory or Registry optimizers.)

- Don't open any email that purports to include a software fix. No legitimate vendor *ever* sends software updates by unsolicited email.

- Don't install software updates, patches, or "hacks" produced by anyone other than a program's original manufacturer.

- Before you download or purchase any Windows management or security software—or any software at all, for that matter—search for reviews of the product, giving greater credence to major publications. Chances are, if it hasn't been reviewed by a major computer magazine, it's not worth bothering with. Also, check www.stopbadware.org and www.wikipedia.org for warnings about the product.

- Be wary of emails or even phone calls that ask you for personal information or passwords that ask you to promptly sign in to some financial website, or that offer you a share of millions of dollars that are sitting in a foreign bank account.

Finally, the time to be the *most* skeptical is when something has gone wrong and you're desperate to get your computer fixed. There is an entire segment of the software industry oriented toward extracting money out of scared computer users. Don't be a victim. Be cautious, be careful, and research your cleanup options *from some other computer* before you do anything.

Keep Backups

This one is very simple: Software fails, and hard disks fail, so you need to make and keep backups. If you don't have an external hard disk drive or recordable DVD drive that you can use to back up your PC, *go get one*. They cost around $100. And then perform backups on a regular basis. Weekly should be fine; more often if you run your business on your computer.

There are no excuses. You just have to do this.

Apply Defense in Depth

Finally, you should use a security strategy that doesn't rely entirely on one mechanism to protect you because if that one defense is breached, you'll be entirely unprotected. Good antivirus programs, for example, often use several different ways to detect viruses. They try to match known program filenames and sizes, but they also watch for suspicious behavior such as installing unrecognized device drivers. This is a two-level defense: They filter out the viruses they can recognize up front, and then they watch what every program does to try to catch any newly created viruses that haven't yet been identified.

You can adopt defense-in-depth strategies yourself. On Vista, for example, if you use a non-Administrator account for your day-to-day work, install an antivirus program, let User Account Control work its magic, and use Internet Explorer in its default "safe" mode, you have five levels of protection working for you: the four I just listed, plus the file-access security mechanism of the NTFS file system on which Windows is installed. (Compare this to Windows 98, where the FAT file system was a security free-for-all, and you had to add an antivirus program to get just *one* level of protection.)

Here are some additional suggestions:

- Select an email provider that scans all email attachments for viruses before they ever get to your computer, as well as using an antivirus program on your own computer to scan all downloads and email attachments that you do download.
- Use a hardware Internet connection-sharing router on your Internet connection, as I mentioned previously under "Reduce Your Exposure." Along with Windows Firewall, this provides two levels of protection against hacking from the Internet.

Both these suggestions follow another important principle: Try to set up protection *outside* your computer. In general, it's a bad idea to have a computer try to protect itself because if something bad gets in, that "something bad" has direct access to the computer's defenses. It's better to have firewalls and virus protection both inside *and* outside of your computer so that if one line of defense goes down, the other can still stand.

So let's get to the practical details. The first essential strategy is to make sure all user accounts on your PC are password protected.

Windows Passwords

Passwords are your first line of defense for both local and remote attacks on your computer. However, the vast majority of home users simply do not use passwords for their Windows user accounts. For some it is too much of an inconvenience, whereas others just do not see why they need to use one because they trust everyone (family and friends) who has physical access to their computer. If your computer is never connected to any type of a network, including the Internet, this argument could be valid. But if you are like the majority of computer users and connect to the Internet, or if you have an unsecured wireless network, having accounts unsecured by passwords simply makes it too easy for someone who gains access to your computer to steal your information or install malware.

Setting Up a Password

So, first of all, you should set up a separate user account for each person who uses your computer. Even if you are the only person who uses your computer, I suggest that you create two accounts: an Administrator account for maintenance work, and a Standard (Vista) or Power User (XP) account for day-to-day work.

◄◄ To learn more about creating and managing user accounts, **see** "Managing Users" **p. 409**.

Then, if you do not already have passwords assigned to each of the accounts on your computer, it is very easy to set them up. Just open the Control Panel and click on User Accounts. Then click on the name of the account and click the Create Password button. To set a password for a user, right-click on the name of the account and select Set Password.

Tip

You can easily run the Local User and Group manager from either the command prompt or the Start Menu. On Windows XP and 2000, click Start, Run. On Vista, click Start. Then, type **lusrmgr.msc** and press Enter.

Keep in mind that a password is only as good as an attacker's ability to guess or crack it using any number of simple brute-force utilities. Here are my recommendations for a good password:

- The password contains at least one number and at least one special character such as ")(*&^%$#."
- The password contains both upper- and lowercase letters.
- Common words are not used.
- Personal information such as variation of name, address, and phone number is not used.
- Your password is at least eight characters long.
- You change your password at least twice a year.

Aside from these guidelines, I also recommend you use different passwords for each of your online accounts. Using the same one is like using the same key for your car, your home, your office, and your safety deposit box. If someone discovers your password, a lot of your personal information as well as any financial data could be at risk.

Tip

You can have Windows ensure that all the accounts on your computer have an adequately complex password. For instructions, see "Setting Local Security Policy" on page 432.

You should also encourage all users to create a Password Reset disk so that they can still log on if they forget their passwords. It's especially important to create and hide a Password Reset disk for a least one of your Computer Administrator accounts. If you can't remember the password to any of your computer's Administrator accounts, you'll really be stuck!

◀◀ To read about Password Reset disks, **see** "Local Accounts and Password Reset Disks," **p. 432**.

◀◀ If you or another user forgets his or her password, **see** "Dealing with a Lost Password," **p. 452**.

Improving Password Security

The early versions of Windows had a very different method of implementing passwords than the NT-based operating systems NT, 2000, XP, and Vista. In Windows 98/Me, passwords were weakly encrypted and then stored in a password file on the file system, available to anyone who wanted to play with it. This was extremely insecure; anyone could just delete the password file and then have full access to your computer.

Starting with Windows NT, passwords were handled much more securely. Today, in NT's descendants Windows 2000, XP, and Vista, user passwords are stored by what is called the Security Account Manager, commonly known as the SAM. The SAM stores encrypted password data in a restricted part of the system Registry that can be accessed by only the system account. This prevents a user, either locally or remotely, from loading up the Registry editor and retrieving password information. To add another level of security, the passwords are stored in a 128-bit one-way hash with an industry standard encryption method known as MD4 Message Digest. *Hash* means that is no way to go backward from the encrypted form to the original; given a password to validate, Windows has to encrypt it and compare it to the encrypted original. This makes the password very difficult to crack even if access is gained to the SAM database. (However, even this method is still vulnerable to a brute-force attack in which software simply cranks through millions of likely passwords over several hours, hoping for a match. This is why it's crucial that you use an obscure password with a variety of characters, so that it's unlikely to be guessed or be found in any dictionary.)

This seemed like a good plan. Unfortunately, there was a flaw—a gaping, Grand Canyon–sized flaw. The version of Microsoft's file sharing protocol used by DOS, OS/2, Windows 3.1, 9x, and Me didn't have the means to work with highly encrypted passwords. So, on Windows NT, 2000, and XP, to maintain networking compatibility with Windows 9x and earlier operating systems, Windows stores each password encrypted in two different ways: once in that very strongly encrypted, effectively irreversible form, and again in a very poorly protected form. This second format is called the LanMan hash and if present in the security section of the Registry, software does have a good chance at extracting the original passwords. In fact, tools such as RainbowCrack, L0phtCrack, and Cain can break (that is, guess) a password stored in the LanMan hash format in a few *seconds*.

The bottom line is that by default, Windows NT, 2000, and XP store passwords in the easily broken LanMan hash format, so that users of older operating systems can use their shared files "out of the box," and thus user accounts on these operating systems can be broken into by someone with physical access or network access to the computer. Vista, on the other hand, does *not* store passwords in the LanMan hash format by default, so it's not vulnerable to this particular assault.

You may want to change the default settings in the following circumstances:

- If you use Windows XP, 2000, or NT, and you don't need to share files or printers with computers running Windows Me, 98, 95, 3.1, DOS or OS/2, change Local Security Policy (or Group Policy, on a domain-type network) to prevent storage of passwords in LanMan hash format.

- If you use Windows Vista, and you *do* have to share files and printers with computers running Windows Me and earlier, you have two options: Either turn off Password Protected Sharing so that every network user can access your shared resources without a password, or change Local Security Policy to store passwords in the LanMan hash format—and don't assume that even encrypted files on your computer are safe if someone steals your computer.

To change the LanMan hash policy on Windows XP, log on as a Computer Administrator, click Start, Run, type **secpol.msc**, and press Enter. On Vista, click Start, type **secpol.msc**, and press Enter. In the left pane, select Local Policies, Security Options. In the right pane, locate Network Security: Do Not Store LAN Manager Hash Value on Next Password Change. Set to Enabled to prevent the LanMan hash from being stored, or Disabled to store it. *All users will have to reset their passwords after this policy change is made.*

Caution

If you have information in your computer that is sensitive enough that you feel the need to protect it with Windows' built-in file encryption, you *have* to take steps to ensure that nobody can break into your user account. On Windows 2000 and XP, you must set the Do Not Store LAN Manager Hash policy value as described in the previous paragraph. And on any operating system, you must use a long, complex password. If you don't take these steps, and someone can steal your computer and break your password, file encryption won't help you at all.

Note

I don't endorse the use of the password-cracking tools I mentioned earlier, but if you do acquire one to attempt to recover a lost password on your system, I would strongly urge you not to run it on your computer unprotected. Instead, install and boot a second copy of Windows, copy the SAM registry hive from the original installation to a removable disk, install yet another copy of Windows inside a virtual machine, and install and run the cracking software there. That way you won't infect your main computer with whatever might tag along with the cracking program.

User Account Control

Windows Vista includes a feature called User Account Control (UAC) that significantly improves Vista's capability to resist viruses and spyware. Although it seems to have gotten a lot of bad press, I think that the criticism is misguided. UAC not only makes Vista more secure than any previous Windows operating system, it can also make managing Windows *more* convenient, not less. During the first week or so of using a new Vista computer, when you're installing applications and tweaking things, yes, you may get prompted more than a few times. But this minor annoyance fades away quickly, and the protection that UAC provides remains.

UAC is actually a collection of several operating system features that work together to one purpose: to run every program with the lowest level of privilege possible for it to still get its job done. This is called the Principle of Least Privilege, and it's a standard concept in all areas of security. For example: Do you have the key to the CFO's office at your business? You shouldn't, unless you're the

CFO or her assistant. You have the key to the front door, and the key to your office, and *maybe* the supply room, and that's it—just what you need to get your job done. It just doesn't make sense to give employees access to more than they need, not just to protect the company from a bad-egg employee, but also in case a good employee's keys get stolen.

UAC applies this principle to Windows. It lets software installers and Windows management programs run with full permissions. These tend to run only for a short time and have limited capabilities. All other programs run with restricted permissions that don't let them modify files in the Windows folder, or data in the section of the Windows Registry that controls Windows itself, so they can't mess Windows up. And just as importantly, any additional programs that they fire up, accidentally or on purpose, can't do any damage either.

The way this works is that for each user account there is a specific list of privileges that the account may or may not have. These include the ability to

- Back up and restore other users' files
- Take ownership of others' files
- Modify files in the Windows folder and other system folders
- Debug and modify other running programs
- Install, start, and stop system services and device drivers

and so on. In previous versions of Windows, every program that a user ran was granted all the user's associated privileges. Thus, every program an Administrator ran had complete access to the entire operating system, even a game program that had no legitimate use for these privileges. With User Account Control, programs are normally run with a restricted or *filtered* list of the user's "potential" privileges; privileges that could compromise Windows are withheld. Only when a program is explicitly run with elevated permissions does the program receive the full complement of privileges. And, before a program is run this way, Windows prompts you to confirm that you indeed intended to run the particular program with full permissions. The hope is that if this occurs when a rogue software installer is activated, you'll notice the program's unusual name or lack of digital signature, and deny its request to run.

Note

This is the entire purpose of User Account Control: to enable *you* to evaluate every opportunity that comes along for a program to muck with Windows. If you get in the habit of automatically approving every UAC prompt that appears, or worse, if you disable UAC, it will all be for naught. This is why I said "Be Skeptical" earlier in this chapter. It's a bit of a pain to have to pay this much attention, but there's just no way for any computer to be secured without the personal cooperation and participation of its owner.

As a bit of background, you might be interested to know that User Account Control actually consists of the several major components:

- **Admin Approval Mode** and **Over-the-Shoulder Credentials**—This is the visible part of User Account Control. When you or any other application attempts to run a program that was designated by its developer as requiring Administrator privileges, Windows prompts you for confirmation before it is allowed to run. If your logon account is an Administrator-type account, you are asked to confirm or deny the request to run the program. If your logon account is not an Administrator-type account, Windows asks you to provide the password to an Administrator account. Thus, you never need to log off to perform administrative duties; you can just type a password to elevate management programs on an as-needed basis. And all normal software runs with the limited permissions of a Standard user account. What's not to love about this?! (Apple Macintosh fans will note that the Mac OS has had this feature for years.)

If it's really necessary, you can also run any regular, unmarked program with full privileges. For example, it's sometimes helpful to run a Command Prompt window with elevated privileges; it and any programs it runs all get full privileges.

- **Folder and Registry Virtualization**—On Vista, the \Program Files and \Windows\ System32 folders and the HKEY_LOCAL_MACHINE section of the Registry cannot be modified by standard users, only Administrative users, Windows Installer, or other system processes. This prevents spyware installers and Trojans run from standard user accounts from infecting Windows. However, thousands of older application programs were written expecting to be able to modify these locations. On Vista, if a legacy program attempts to save files or Registry data in a protected folder or under HKEY_LOCAL_MACHINE, and the user was not explicitly given access rights to the particular file, folder, or Registry key, Windows transparently and silently writes the data to locations in which the user *does* have permission to write. The application doesn't notice the difference; when it goes back to read the file or data later, Windows transparently passes it the information from the alternate location*.

  One downside to this is that information expected to be seen by all users of the system is not shared, and each user has his or her own private copy instead. Thus, for example, the stored highest score of a game may not reflect the scores of other players. (The workaround for this is to set explicit permissions on the relevant Registry key or file so that all users can read and write to it. The application's installer should do this, or you can do it manually.)

- **Windows Integrity Mechanism**—On Vista, all programs and files are given an integrity designation that reflects not just how trustworthy they are, but also how risky their environment is or their origins are. For example, programs such as Internet Explorer that connect to a network or the Internet are typically given low integrity designations because they *could* inadvertently be induced to run malware. Device drivers, on the other hand, usually get very high integrity rankings because it's assumed that they came from a reputable source and because their program files are stored in a well-secured location under the \Windows folder, where malware can't alter them.

  What makes this useful is that lower-integrity programs are not given the unrestricted capability to send information to higher-level programs. This prevents, for example, an ActiveX plug-in run by Internet Explorer from impersonating you by sending "key pressed" and "mouse clicked" messages to a management application. Likewise, files created by low integrity programs (for example, files downloaded by Windows Explorer) retain this designation.

- **User Interface Design**—Because privilege elevation is performed at the time that a program is started, Vista's management tools may seem awkward at first, compared to XP's. Programs that perform tasks that don't require administrator privileges, such as changing

*64-bit applications, services, and any modern application that indicates that it knows about User Account Control is not given this handholding treatment; these are expected to know not to attempt to write data in systemwide locations unless explicit permission has been granted, and attempts to do so just fail. When virtualization is used, files are redirected to folders under %userprofile%\AppData\Local\VirtualStore and attempts to modify Registry data in or under HKEY_LOCAL_MACHINE are redirected to HKEY_CURRENT_USER\ Software\Classes\VirtualStore\Machine.

the clock's time zone, have to be packaged separately from programs that do require privileges, such as configuring the Internet time server used to keep the system clock on track. Dialogs such as System Properties (the one you see when you right-click Computer and select Properties) had to be split into administrative and nonadministrative versions. As a result, when you click a button or setting that requires administrative privileges to change. Windows has to actually close the application whose button you pressed and start up a similar, administrative version. Microsoft labels all such buttons and settings with a four-color shield icon. Windows Explorer was also modified for User Account Control. Explorer normally runs without elevated permissions, so to perform file management operations in protected areas such as the root folder of the boot drive, it has to spawn small utility programs to do the actual work. These invoke the UAC consent dialogs when they are run. Many of the improvements in UAC in Vista Service Pack 1 involved tweaking these utility programs so that just one is needed to perform most tasks. Prior to SP1, some folder operations that felt like just one step to the user were performed internally in several steps, each by a separate program, resulting in several UAC prompts.

Several Local Computer or Group Policy settings can be changed to disable or strengthen User Account Control (for example, on the one hand, to run elevated programs without bothering to prompt Administrators, or on the other to disable Over-the-Shoulder Elevation by non-Administrators). In all but a very few exceptional cases, you should *not* disable User Account Control. If you find it annoying at first, my suggestion is to just wait a week or two. After your computer is more stable and you've gotten it set up the way you like it you'll find that you get fewer and fewer prompts, and the irritation will go away. Also, when UAC is disabled, Registry and folder virtualization is also disabled, so many older applications will no longer work correctly.

Windows Update

As I mentioned at the start of this chapter, new vulnerabilities are discovered in Windows all the time. Keeping your computer up to date and secure from newly discovered vulnerabilities is a big part of the game. Using free services such as Microsoft Windows Update enables you to easily make sure that your computer is always up to date. Additionally, Windows XP and Vista can be configured to automatically check for and install updates automatically, without your having to do anything.

Hotfixes, Updates, and Service Packs

When program flaws or security vulnerabilities are discovered by or reported to Microsoft, work begins on developing a patch to correct the problem. Fixes for bugs that have a limited impact are subject to somewhat limited testing, and are released as hotfixes on Microsoft's TechNet support site, with the view that only people affected by the particular problem will search for and install the fix. The idea is to get the fix out quickly, on a more or less "use at your own risk" basis.

Fixes for bugs that have severe security implications or impact large numbers of users are subject to more extensive testing on an accelerated schedule. These are distributed through Windows Update: the security fixes as Critical updates and the performance fixes as Recommended updates. To make it easier for corporate network managers to manage the distribution of updates to large numbers of users, Microsoft tends to release Windows Update patches in batches on a fixed monthly or weekly schedule. Corporate managers can also install server software to intercept and manage the flow of updates so that they can be tested between the time Microsoft releases them and employees receive them.

About every two years, give or take, Microsoft takes all the security patches and updates that have been developed since an operating system's initial release, throws in a small number of new features and enhancements, and calls the collection a Service Pack. One reason this is done is to make updating a PC that has never been updated much easier: You have to apply only one update, instead of dozens of individual patches and additional features. A Service Pack is also subject to very extensive testing, usually through a beta program that involves computer and peripheral manufacturers, and then corporate customers and then sometimes the public, to ensure that all the fixes work well together. It's eventually released to the public for downloading and through Windows Update.

In one instance (Windows XP Service Pack 2), Microsoft used a Service Pack to deliver significant changes to the operating system. Many components of Windows XP were rewritten to operate more securely, Windows Firewall was added, and network security was changed drastically. However, this was an exceptional instance; generally Service Packs don't introduce significant new features, just fixes, sometimes new versions of programs like Windows Media Player, and often small enhancements to existing features: new protocols, support for new devices, and the like.

The Windows Update service is a valuable tool that helps you keep on top of the monthly security patches that Microsoft releases (and the occasional Critical update). Using Windows Update ensures that your computer will get that update when it is released, minimizing the amount of time your computer is potentially vulnerable to security threats.

Using Windows Update

Windows Update is very easy to use. It can be accessed a number of ways within Windows. You can launch it by using the Windows Update shortcut found at the top of the All Programs menu in the Start menu; or by opening a copy of Internet Explorer and selecting Tools, Windows Update; or by navigating IE directly to www.windowsupdate.com.

If it's been a while since your last visit, or if you are visiting the website for the first time, you may be required to install a special control that detects which of the available updates your PC needs. This control is itself updated frequently, so over time you may have to permit its installation more than once.

Note

If you have other Microsoft products installed on your computer, such as Microsoft Office, you can follow the link on the Windows Update page to install Microsoft Update. This makes Windows Update look for and install patches to your other Microsoft Products as well as Windows itself—otherwise it's the same as Windows Update. I recommend using it. On Vista, you can also have Automatic Updates download updates for other Microsoft products, as I'll show shortly.

After the site has loaded and the control has initialized, you will have two options, Express and Custom, that enable you to manually update your computer with the latest security patches as well as bonus applications, as shown in Figure 7.1.

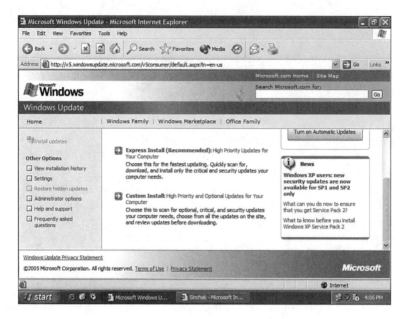

Figure 7.1   Windows Update options.

If you are in a rush and don't care about which updates are getting installed and why, select Express Install. Choosing Custom Install allows you to see exactly which updates are available for your system and gives you the option of which ones to install. I personally like the Custom Install because I like to see what updates are coming in.

After you select the method of updating your computer, Windows Update launches the update utility and checks your computer for available updates. If any updates are available, they are displayed. If you selected Express Install, just click the Install button to begin installing the updates if any are available. If you selected Custom Install, browse through the provided list of updates and click the Add button for any that you want downloaded and installed to your PC. When you're finished, click the Install button.

At this time the download utility is launched, which automatically downloads the updates and installs them one by one. If a restart is required, you are prompted with the option to restart immediately or restart later.

Occasionally an update available on the Windows Update service must be installed by itself, without any other of the available updates. If that is the case for an update you select, you will notice that any other updates that you had selected become unselected and you can't select any other updates. You should download and install the lone update and perform the required system reboot. After rebooting, restart the Windows Update service and select the remaining updates you want to install.

Configuring Automatic Updates

Automatic Updates are a great feature of Windows XP and Vista. Configuring your computer to automatically update itself is the best way to keep on top of the latest security patches, and doing so is very easy.

Note

If you have Windows XP installed but not Service Pack 2 or 3, you must install one of these Service Packs to get Automatic Updates. Use the Windows Update procedure described in the previous section to get SP2 or SP3. To find out what your current XP Service Pack level is, open Windows Explorer (My Computer will do), and then click Help, About Windows. The Service Pack level is displayed at the end of the line that lists the version number.

If you are not currently receiving automatic updates, you can turn the feature on by following this procedure:

1. Open up Control Panel by clicking Start, Control Panel.

2. On XP, select Security Center, and then at the bottom, select Automatic Updates.

   On Vista, select System and Maintenance, and then under Windows Update, select Turn Automatic Updating On or Off.

3. The Automatic Updates controls are shown in Figure 7.2, with the Vista version on the left and the XP version on the right. There are four different update options.

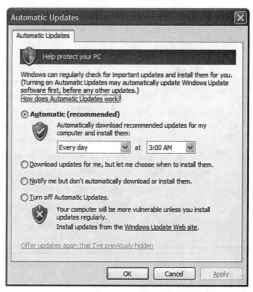

Figure 7.2   The Automatic Updates setup controls on Vista (left) and XP (right).

You can have Windows

- Fully automate downloading and installing the updates at a specific time
- Automate the downloading but have you confirm the installation
- Just notify you of new updates
- Disable automatic updates

I suggest that at the bare minimum you have Windows automatically download the latest updates and notify you when they are ready to be installed. Ideally, the best option is to have Windows handle both the downloading and the installation.

On Vista, you can elect to download Recommended (performance-related) as well as Critical (security-related) fixes, and to download updates for other Microsoft products you have installed, in addition to Windows. When enabled, these two options ensure that you always have the latest fixes installed, and I recommend using them.

4. After you have selected the update method, click OK.

Note

If you let Automatic Updates use the default setting of installing updates in the wee hours of the morning, but your computer is turned off at night, don't worry; it starts the process the next time the computer is turned on. Also, the download process doesn't interfere with your web surfing. The downloading mechanism tries pretty hard to stay out of your way by downloading only when your Internet connection is idle.

Updating all the software on your computer on top of the operating system is very important to securing your computer. Even if the operating system is secure, vulnerabilities in any software application that you run on top of your operating system could give an attacker another door into your computer.

Note

Automatic Updates occasionally installs an update that requires Windows to be restarted. In this case it pops up a warning giving you five minutes to save your work and close your applications before the restart occurs. If you're busy at the time, and don't want to stop working at this time, click the Restart Later button to postpone the restart an hour. If the Restart Later button is grayed out, switch users and log on using a Computer Administrator account. When the restart message appears, click Restart Later. Then switch back to your main account and finish your work. This can be irritating, but in my experience it happens less often than than once a month, and getting security updates automatically is worth the occasional annoyance.

On the other hand, if you have a computer that *must* not restart without warning (such as one that controls medical equipment, household lighting, and so on), be sure to configure Automatic Updates to download but not automatically install updates.

Firewalls

The moment that your computer connects to the Internet by any means, it becomes vulnerable to just about anyone else on the Internet. Anyone who knows the IP address of your computer, or is scanning blocks of IP addresses, could be looking for known and unknown vulnerabilities that they can use to compromise your Windows installation. Quite often your computer is scanned by viruses and Trojans that have infected other computers on the Internet and are trying to spread themselves to more systems.

Note

An IP address, which is short for Internet Protocol address, is a value assigned to your computer by your Internet service provider or network administrator to identify your computer on a local or wide area network (like the Internet).

Even if you think you have nothing valuable on your computer, you *do* have to secure your computer from outside attack. Some attackers are looking to see whether you have shared files that might contain information to help them commit identity theft or bank fraud—account numbers, personal identification information, telephone numbers, email addresses of friends, and so on. But many more of them aren't after information at all. They want to infect your computer with software that they can control remotely so that they can use your computer to send spam, launch attacks on other computers and networks, and otherwise use your computer and your Internet connection to commit crimes.

A lot of junk traffic on the Internet is caused by these viruses, Trojans, and attackers. Applications that filter out a lot of this junk and block it from ever getting to the core of your operating system are called *firewalls*. Originally, a firewall was installed and run on a separate, highly secured computer or router device that was placed in between the Internet and other computers. Today, the concept has been extended to include software installed inside the very machine that the firewall is trying to protect. I'll have more to say about that later.

Two different variations of firewalls are on the market: hardware firewalls and software firewalls. Software and hardware firewalls behave and work similarly; the difference is that hardware firewalls are separate physical machines that are located on a network and filter all network traffic going through them. Software firewalls are just special software applications that run on your computer on top of the operating system. The advantage of a hardware firewall is that it can protect a number of computers, whereas a software firewall can protect only the computer on which it is installed. Internet connection-sharing routers (gateways) are a form of hardware firewall, and I strongly encourage you to use one with any high-speed Internet connection for this reason. You can also purchase dedicated hardware firewall devices for prices ranging from a few hundred to a few thousand dollars, although their implementation is outside the scope of this book.

How Software Firewalls Protect Your PC from Attacks

Software firewalls all use a similar methodology. The firewall software monitors all data coming into and going out of your network adapter or Internet connection, and blocks any attempt to use protocols or network services that you don't want outsiders to see.

Every network service from music sharing to file sharing to the World Wide Web uses an identifiable port number to indicate the type of network service being performed. If an IP address is like a phone number, a port number is like a telephone extension; the IP address routes data to your computer, and the port number indicates what it's for. For example, file and printer sharing uses the TCP protocol, using port numbers 137 and/or 445. Firewall software thus blocks any data designated for ports 137 or 445 traveling to or from the Internet at large from passing through your computer's network connection so that outsiders can't see your shared files. Other computers on your home network have IP addresses that are mathematically related to yours, so firewall software lets data to and from them pass freely. Obviously, blocking *every* port on your system at all times is impractical. Completely closing off all traffic into your system would cause problems for any applications on your system that make use of the LAN or the Internet, including web browsers, instant messenger applications, or computer games. Generally, firewalls are set up to permit any data *you* transmit to freely pass out to the Internet, and to permit responses to your data to come back, but to block any other data that arrives unsolicited that is not clearly in response to a request you initiated. For example, when you view a web page, the flood of data that comes back from the remote web server is identifiably in response to a request you sent out; but other data arriving from random locations is rejected. If, for example, you were to run a web server such as Internet Information Services (IIS) on your computer, you would want the firewall to let in any incoming data addressed to port 80, which indicates HTTP requests. Setting up permission for this data to enter is called *opening* a port.

When a port is open so that legitimate requests and response can come in, hackers can also send in specially malformed data designed to trigger known flaws in Windows and other service programs, in the hope of being able to take over the computer. To fight that problem, most modern firewalls have a feature called *packet inspection*. Packet inspection looks at the content of the data coming in from the Internet, "eavesdropping," as it were, to look for known vulnerabilities. Some third-party firewall software can perform this level of inspection; Microsoft's Windows Firewall provided with XP and Vista does not.

Windows Firewall

Windows XP and Vista include a software firewall as an intrinsic part of the operating system. Prior to Windows XP Service Pack 2, it was not enabled by default. The versions supplied with Windows XP Service Pack 2 and Windows Vista are enabled by default, and do a pretty good job of isolating a computer from the Internet out of the box—that is, as initially installed, with no work on your part.

If you do not already have the Windows Firewall enabled on your computer and you want to do so, it is easy to enable. On XP, you must first log on as a Computer Administrator. On XP or Vista, open Control Panel, open the Security Center, and double-click the Windows Firewall icon. (In Classic view, just open the Windows Firewall icon.) On Vista, click Change Settings. Then select On and click OK.

Configuring the Windows Firewall is also very simple. To permit incoming data to reach a network-based application, select the Exceptions tab and click Add Program or Add Port, using the filename or port number provided by the application program's instructions.

To configure the firewall's more advanced options, open up the firewall settings again, using the icon in Control Panel, and select the Advanced tab. This is where you can specify which connections the firewall protects, individual port exceptions for each connection, and on XP, the ICMP settings and logging information.

Caution

If you use file and/or printer sharing at home or your office, Windows Firewall lists an exception labeled File and Printer Sharing. This lets other computers gain access to your computer's shared files and printers.

If you take your computer out of your home or office to a public location such as a Wi-Fi hotspot, an Internet café, a client's office, and so on, your shared resources are automatically reachable by others at that site, and this is a severe security risk.

On XP, before you connect to a "foreign" network, open the Windows Firewall and select Don't Allow Exceptions on the General tab. Don't uncheck this until you're back home. Vista is able to track the different networks to which you connect, and it prompts you to identify a new network as Public or Private (or Public, Home or Work). Use Public whenever you connect to a network that has computers or users that you don't trust. This automatically disables access to your shared files and printers.

Individual Connection Settings

Each of the network connections for which you have the firewall enabled can be configured separately to have different ports opened and closed. This enables you to run various services on your computer, such as an FTP or web server, and allow access to the data behind your software firewall by the outside world.

If you have more than one connection on your computer, such as a wired network connection and a wireless, you can configure each separately so that you need to open only the ports on the connection on which you use an application for greater security. For example, you may play games on your computer that require a specific port to be opened while you are at home using your wired network connection. Opening the port on your wireless connection as well is not needed in this situation and just poses a security risk.

To allow the outside world to access services, you need to open "holes" in the firewall so that it does not filter out traffic on that port. Opening holes in the Windows firewall is very simple. While on the Advanced tab of the Firewall Settings window, highlight the connection you want to edit from the list and click the Settings button. This displays the Advanced Settings window, as shown in Figure 7.3, listing some predefined services that you can check to make accessible through the firewall.

To open a service for access from the outside world, just check the box next to the service if it is already on the list. Otherwise, you need to click on the Add button to create a custom service.

If you need to create a custom service and have clicked the Add button, just enter the name of the application for which you are opening a port in the Description box. Then enter the port number that you need to open in the External and Internal port boxes and click OK (this port should be specific by the developer or publisher of the software).

ICMP Settings

ICMP is short for Internet Control Message Protocol, which is normally used by network administrators as a suite of commands that can be used to monitor and diagnose network issues. You have probably heard of the ping command-line program, which is widely used to check whether network connections are working. Ping relies on the ICMP Echo command. Unfortunately, ICMP messages can also be used to create excessive traffic on a user's connection and slow down networks. Because these commands can be used to abuse computers and networks, it is best to have the firewall enable only Incoming Echo Request (ping), and enable others temporarily only if you have a specific use for them.

On Windows XP, you can control whether Windows Firewall lets Windows receive ICMP messages from the Advanced tab on the Windows Firewall dialog. Click the ICMP button and check the names of the ICMP messages you want to accept, as shown in Figure 7.4. (If necessary, you can unblock ICMP messages on a per-connection basis from the ICMP tab of the connection settings dialog.)

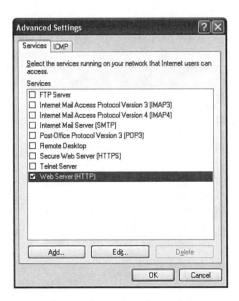

Figure 7.3   Windows Firewall service settings.

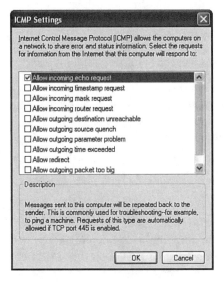

Figure 7.4   Windows Firewall ICMP settings (XP only).

On Windows Vista, ICMP messages are normally managed automatically through the Network Location feature, according to the type of network to which the computer is connected:

- On public networks, all incoming ICMP messages are blocked.
- On private (home) networks, ICMP Echo (ping) messages are allowed in when File and Printer Sharing is enabled. All other ICMP messages are blocked.
- On corporate (domain) networks, all ICMP messages are allowed in.

To manage ICMP filtering manually, you must use the Windows Firewall with Advanced Security management tool. This advanced configuration screen lets you configure outgoing as well as incoming network filtering, and rules can be created for home, public, and domain network connections.

To have Vista respond to ICMP Echo (ping) requests under *all* circumstances, follow these steps:

1. Click Start, All Programs, Administrative Tools, Windows Firewall with Advanced Security.

2. In the left pane, select Inbound Rules. Then, from the Action menu, select New Rule.

3. Select Custom, and click Next. Select All Programs and click Next.

4. For Protocol Type, select ICMPv4, and then click Customize.

5. Select Specific ICMP Types, check Echo Request, click OK, and then click Next.

6. Click Next twice to skip the IP address and connection security pages.

7. Be sure that Domain, Private, and Public are all checked, and then click Next.

8. For Name, enter `ICMP Echo under all circumstances` and click Finish.

You may then close the window.

I won't go into this tool in any more detail because, as I'll discuss in the next section, for home and small office users, it's far more important to prevent bad software from getting *into* your computer than to prevent bad data from getting *out*. Vista's advanced firewall configuration tool is meant for use on corporate networks where network managers have to block not just malware but legitimate network services that could compromise business policies.

Third-Party Firewalls

Besides the Windows Firewall that Microsoft provides with Windows XP and Vista, there is a wide variety of add-on software firewalls on the market. Most of them are not free, and all claim to offer a level of protection much higher than Windows Firewall. Some of the common features that add another level of protection provided by commercial third-party firewalls include

- **Intrusion detection systems**—These are advanced systems that do packet inspection looking for known signatures of "bad" data trying to get into your computer.

  Other forms of intrusion detection include monitoring software services for evidence of tampering or repeated unsuccessful login attempts—these can indicate attempts to break into your system via web services such as IIS and FTP, if you have them installed—but none of the personal firewalls I've seen perform this more valuable function.

- **Process communication monitoring**—PCM looks at the traffic that is sent between services running on your computer.

- **Outgoing data monitoring**—Firewalls with this feature look at all the outgoing data that is sent from your computer. Windows Firewall just blocks unwanted incoming data, but firewalls with outgoing filtering also can block data from going out. For example, this would be useful if your computer got infected with spyware. With outgoing filtering, the spyware might not be able to phone home with your personal information—*if* the spyware didn't disable the firewall software first.

The version of Windows Firewall on Vista *can* be set up to perform outgoing data filtering, but it's not interactive—that is, it doesn't monitor activity, notify you, and ask you what to do when a new program first tries to transmit data, as most third-party firewalls do. However, as I'll explain next, this ability is not as useful as you might think.

To be honest, I don't think that it's worth *spending money* on a software-based personal firewall program. As I discussed earlier, Windows XP and Vista come with an adequate firewall that blocks unexpected data arriving from your network or Internet connection. The people who sell firewall products will tell you that this does only half the job, that you need something to monitor and block outbound data too. But think about this for a moment: If there is bad network traffic on its way *out*, there is already bad software *in your computer*. The people who write this bad software aren't amateurs, they're professional high-tech criminals. The first thing they have it do is disable firewall and antivirus software. So, before your expensive firewall could find something it would want to block, it would most likely already have been shut off.

This is the fundamental problem with any type of protection software that runs inside the same computer that it's trying to protect—if it slips up even once, or if an attack arrives through some unanticipated means, the game is over. So preventing bad software from ever getting into your computer is your number one job. Having a firewall that blocks unwanted incoming data is a valuable tool in that defense, and Windows comes with an adequate one built in, free. Better still, as I've mentioned already, put an inexpensive hardware-based Internet connection sharing router (gateway) between your cable or DSL modem and your network or computer, even if you have only one computer. That way you have *two* lines of defense against malware arriving via networking software ports. Use an ISP that does virus scans on all email attachments, and install an antivirus program to help prevent malware getting in by other means, such as removable media, email attachments, and web browser exploits. This is defense in depth, and it will help you a lot more than having an outgoing-traffic firewall.

But, still if you really, *really* want to add a software-based firewall, it's not a *bad* idea (just not very useful). Several of them are free, after all. Most of them cause very little performance degradation. There are reports of problems with interactions between firewall products and certain games and copy protection schemes, but you can usually temporarily disable the firewall if this occurs (but *only* if you're also using a hardware connection-sharing router so that you have continuous protection).

Table 7.1 lists several add-on firewall programs that you can use with Windows XP and Vista. Most of the paid products have discounts for multiple-computer or multiple-year licenses. Several of the free products have paid versions that offer additional features. This information was current at the time this book went to press. I strongly recommend that you look up prices, compatibility issues, test results, and reviews of the *current* versions of these or any other protection products before you make a selection. Also, if you're going to install third-party firewall, antivirus, and antispyware software, see whether the manufacturer has a package that provides all the services you want for one price. There are often suites that combine several protection products for a lower total cost.

Table 7.1 Personal Firewall Products for XP and Vista

Product	Price	XP	x64 XP	Vista	x64 Vista	URL
AVG Internet Security [1]	$55 [3]	✓	✓	✓	✓	www.grisoft.com
CA Personal Firewall	$50 [3]	✓		✓		www.ca.com
Comodo Firewall Pro wall.	free	✓	✓	✓	✓	www.personalfire-comodo.com
Core Force [2]	free	✓				force.coresecurity.com
ESET Smart Security [1]	$60	✓	✓	✓	✓	www.eset.com
GhostWall	free	✓	✓			www.ghostsecurity.com
Jetico Personal Firewall v.2	$40	✓	✓	✓	✓	www.jetico.com
Kaspersky Internet Security [1]	$80 [3]	✓	✓	✓	✓	www.kaspersky.com
Lavasoft Personal Firewall [4]	$26	✓	✓	✓	✓	www.lavasoftusa.com
McAfee VirusScan Plus [1]	$40	✓		✓	✓	www.mcafee.com
Norman Personal Firewall [1]	$30	✓		✓		www.norman.com
Norton Internet Security [1]	$60	✓		✓	✓	www.symantec.com
Online Armor Personal Firewall	free	✓				www.tallemu.com
Outpost Firewall Pro	$40 [3]	✓	✓	✓	✓	www.agnitum.com
Panda Antivirus+Firewall	$50	✓	✓	✓	✓	www.pandasecurity.com
PC Tools Firewall Plus	free	✓		✓		www.pctools.com
Sophos Computer Security	$247 [5]	✓	✓	✓	✓	www.sophos.com
Trend Micro Internet Security [1]	$50 [3]	✓		✓	✓	www.trendmicro.com
Webroot Desktop Firewall	free	✓		✓		www.webroot.com
ZoneAlarm Free Firewall	free	✓		✓		www.zonealarm.com

[1] *Available only as part of a suite that includes other protection tools*

[2] *Also restricts access to files and the Registry on a per-program basis, an unusual feature*

[3] *License covers three computers*

[4] *This appears to be a rebranded version of Outpost Firewall Pro*

[5] *License covers five computers*

Antivirus and Antispyware Software—Which Do You Need?

You may be wondering what the difference is between spyware and viruses, and why there are separate antispyware and antivirus programs. The short answer to the first question is "not that much," and to the second question, "to get you to spend more money." But, you bought this book to get the long answers, so I'll try to expand on this a bit.

As I've mentioned, *spyware* refers to what the program does, whereas *virus* refers to how the program spreads itself around. So, there's overlap. A spyware application can be a virus, and a virus could act as spyware. Remember those Venn diagrams you drew in third grade? Here's one for spyware and viruses:

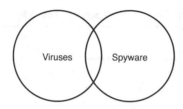

Given that the two types of programs overlap some, but not completely, you might think—or be fooled into thinking—that you need separate tools to protect yourself from them. But this isn't the case. There is no difference at all in the mechanisms that are used to detect, block, and remove the two categories of programs. Antispyware and antivirus programs both work exactly the same way—by scanning for program files known to be bad, by examining the known Registry locations that are used to fire up programs when Windows starts, and so on. The difference is that antispyware programs look for only spyware, whereas antivirus programs look for all forms of malware. Also, most antispyware programs monitor things much less aggressively, whereas antivirus programs typically thoroughly scan every file that's read or written and every program every time it's run. Thus, in Venn diagram terms,

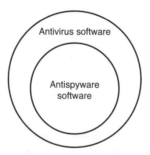

Any antivirus program worth its salt *should* do complete antispyware duties. Why the two types of program then? The main reason is that antivirus programs tend to be expensive, and have to be paid for every year, so most people don't bother with them. When spyware exploded onto the scene, some developers created free detection and removal programs to help clean up existing spyware infections. These evolved into real-time prevention systems, which, as added-value products, were good enough to charge a little money for. Antivirus manufacturers were perceived as being slow to add spyware to their databases*, so antispyware applications were able to get a foothold as a commercial concept. Thus, today there are markets for both types of products: Antivirus programs as the premium product, and antispyware programs as cheaper alternatives that address just the one type of threat (which, after all, comprises the bulk of computer infections).

They were wary of lawsuits from manufacturers angry about having what they considered their legitimate software labeled as spyware or as malicious. There are indeed some cases where it's a judgement call, as in the case of remote control software that's installed with a purchased application to let the manufacturer provide support assistance, or a web browser plug-in that measures your response to advertisements.

So, you should not *have* to purchase both an antispyware and an antivirus product. A good antivirus program should eliminate both threats. Any manufacturer that charges extra for antispyware protection on top of antivirus protection is not giving you a good deal. Which type should you get? If your Internet service provider scans all email attachments for viruses, and you rarely receive documents and files from other people, you're probably okay with just antispyware protection, and you get can it for free. If you have Windows Vista, you already have it, with Windows Defender. If you have XP, you can download Windows Defender, or one of the other free products listed in Table 7.1. Or, you *can* spend money on antispyware software if you want to.

You can even use more than one antispyware program if you want to be really thorough, or if you end up with a spyware infection that your first program missed. (It does happen.)

Antivirus programs definitely offer a better level of protection, although at greater cost in computer performance if not money. Before you opt for antivirus software, note that Microsoft delivers a program called the Malicious Software Removal Tool via Windows Update, and it's updated about once a month to take out the worst of the known viruses (about 110 of them, at the time this book was written). It removes only existing infections, however, and does nothing to prevent you from getting a virus in the first place. That might be enough for you. But certainly, even if it isn't completely necessary, it's never bad to add more protection.

Caution

Although having more protection is always good, there are still limits and with antivirus programs, one such program is the limit. Don't install two; they tend to interfere with each other, and you may end up with a nonbootable system.

Before deciding on any malware protection software, my advice is to check out current reviews of the most recent version of any product that interests you, to be sure that it's worth what (if anything) you're spending on it, that it has been tested and demonstrated to really block the majority of the bad stuff out there, and that it doesn't slow your computer down more than necessary.

Another important point to consider is how the protection software gets updated. New virus and spyware programs are created all the time, so your antivirus or antispyware program's "most wanted list" must be updated frequently. All the paid products are designed to automatically and frequently contact their manufacturer over the Internet to check for updates—some even do this hourly. This is a good thing. The free products vary: Some perform automatic updates, and some require you to manually initiate the update check. If you're the type of person who can remember to perform a manual update at least once a week, you should be okay with a free product that doesn't do automatic updates. Otherwise, buy one that updates itself without your help.

Note

Because antispyware programs tend not to hurt computer performance much, it's actually not a bad idea to have *two* antispyware applications on your computer. This can be an antivirus/antispyware combination plus an additional antispyware program, or just two antispyware programs. Having two sets of eyes watching out for you can be very helpful.

And finally, remember that you are by far the most important protection mechanism of all. Keep Windows and all your application software and especially media-playing programs (QuickTime Player, RealPlayer, WinAmp, and so on) up to date, and be *very* cautious about installing software from websites you visit.

Antivirus Software

Computer viruses are programs that do the same sorts of things that other forms of malware do: delete or encrypt files, extort money out of you, record your keystrokes in hopes of capturing your credit card numbers or passwords, and so on. What makes them "viral" is that they are programmed to try to spread themselves around. After they are installed on your computer, they set about trying to transmit themselves to other computers via your network connection by copying themselves onto removable disks that you insert, or by emailing copies of themselves to people in your email program's address book. (There are even a few benign computer viruses that replicate, but don't actually do any damage. But these are in the minority.)

Antivirus utilities typically scan all files that the computer attempts to read or execute as well as automatically block the methods most viruses use to spread themselves around. Most antivirus utilities detect viruses based on *signatures*, or recognizable patterns in the virus program's files. Antivirus signature or definition databases must constantly be updated to include the latest viruses. Furthermore, antivirus programs should block executable files attached to email messages, and might also block the running of various types of scripts embedded in emails and other documents. Some antivirus programs detect viruses by monitoring all program activity, and detect software attempting to install itself in unusual ways. These antivirus programs can protect you from potential viruses for which they do not yet have signature definitions.

As I mentioned earlier, a good antivirus program should scan for and remove *all* forms of malware, including all forms of spyware, not just viruses. You shouldn't be required to pay extra for an antispyware program. It doesn't *hurt* to install an additional antispyware program, though, if you want the additional protection.

Tip

If you are working on a computer that does not have any antivirus software installed and want to do a quick check for viruses, check out Trend Micro's Housecall website located at http://housecall.trendmicro.com for a free online virus scan. Then, get yourself a dedicated AV program that proactively protects your PC.

Third-Party Antivirus Programs

Table 7.2 lists several antivirus programs that you can use with Windows XP and Vista. (Products that don't include real-time scanning of files as they're accessed are not included.) Most of these programs also protect against spyware and rootkits. Most of the paid products have discounts for multiple-computer or multiple-year licenses. Several of the free products have paid versions that offer additional features. This information was current at the time this book went to press. I strongly recommend that you look up prices, compatibility issues, test results, and reviews of the *current* versions of these or any other protection products before you make a selection. Also, if you're going to install firewall, antivirus, and antispyware software, see whether the manufacturer has a package that provides all the services you want for one price. There are often suites that combine several protection products for a lower total cost.

To help you make a selection, check out computer reviews of current product versions (only), and independent lab tests. For some good independent testing results, check out www.icsalabs.com, www.virusbtn.com/vb100 and www.av-comparatives.org. If you have a subscription to *Consumer Reports*, its website has good reviews too. When evaluating an antivirus program, your main criteria should be a high detection percentage, and then speed and a low percentage of false positives (warnings about files that don't contain viruses).

Table 7.2   Antivirus Programs for Windows XP and Vista

Product	Price	XP	x64 XP	Vista	x64 Vista	URL
Ad-Aware Plus	$27	✓		✓	✓	www.lavasoft.com
avast!	free/$40 [1]	✓	✓	✓	✓	www.avast.com
AVG Anti-Virus Free Edition	free [2]	✓	✓	✓	✓	free.grisoft.com
Avira Antivir	free [1,2]	✓	✓	✓	✓	www.free-av.com
BitDefender	$25	✓	✓	✓	✓	www.bitdefender.com
CA Anti-Virus	$40 [3]	✓		✓		www.ca.com
Comodo AntiVirus	free	✓				www.comodo.com
ESET NOD32	$40	✓	✓	✓	✓	www.eset.com
F-Prot Antivirus	$30 [5]	✓	✓	✓	✓	www.f-prot.com
F-Secure Client Security	$66 [3]	✓		✓		www.f-secure.com
G DATA AntiVirus	€36	✓	✓	✓	✓	www.gdata.de/portal/US
Kaspersky Anti-Virus	$60	✓	✓	✓	✓	www.kaspersky.com
McAfee VirusScan Plus	$40	✓		✓	✓	www.mcafee.com
Norman Antivirus & Antispyware	$50	✓		✓		www.norman.com
Norton Antivirus	$40	✓		✓	✓	www.symantec.com
Panda Antivirus+Firewall	$50	✓	✓	✓	✓	www.pandasecurity.com
PC Tools AntiVirus	free [2]	✓		✓		www.pctools.com
Sophos Anti-Virus	$190 [5]	✓	✓	✓	✓	www.sophos.com
ThreatFire [4]	free	✓		✓		www.threatfire.com
Trend Micro AntiVirus plus AntiSpyware	$40	✓		✓	✓	www.trendmicro.com
Webroot Antivirus	$40	✓		✓		www.webroot.com
Windows Live OneCare	$40 [3]	✓		✓	✓	onecare.live.com

[1] Free only for personal, noncommercial, noninstitutional use.

[2] A paid version is available that provides additional features.

[3] License covers three computers.

[4] ThreatFire detects malware based solely on its behavior. It can be used in addition to a standard antivirus program that recognizes malware based on a database.

[5] License covers five computers.

Antispyware Software

Spyware has become the fastest growing concern among computer users today. Because of vulnerabilities discovered mostly in Internet Explorer and the bundling of spyware with some common applications, spyware is often secretly installed on a user's machine. The first time most users notice an indication of the presence of spyware on their system is when, out of nowhere, an advertisement pops up relevant to something they are or had been doing on their computer. In other instances, worse types of spyware may record details of what is happening on your computer, such as the websites you visit and passwords and account numbers you enter, and send this information to criminals through the Internet, never giving any clues to you that it is there. Other forms of spyware funnel your attempts to search Google or other search engines to other search sites, or sneakily redirect your web browser from legitimate banking sites to phony lookalikes that capture your logon name and password; then they empty your bank account.

Currently there are dozens of spyware-removing utilities. Ironically, some of them are actually spyware themselves. This is the reason for my suggestion earlier in the chapter never to buy software advertised through pop-up ads. Usually, these products cause an endless sequence of the very problems they purport to solve; their only real function is to extort more and more money from you.

Thankfully, there are a few utilities that are free and also happen to be among the best utilities to remove spyware from your computer and protect it from getting infected in the future.

As I mentioned earlier in the section titled "Antivirus and Antispyware Software—Which Do You Need?", spyware utilities detect spyware applications by their attempts to modify specific Registry entries and to hook into the Windows keyboard driver, as well as through a database of known spyware program files. Antispyware programs tend to be less aggressive than antivirus programs, and thus don't slow your computer down as much. Thus, whether or not you have an antivirus program that does antispyware duties, there's no reason not to install a antispyware tool. (It's not a bad idea to have two antispyware tools in place because sometimes one will catch things the other misses.) Windows Defender is free and is even preinstalled on Windows Vista. I'll discuss Windows Defender in detail in the next section because it's now a standard part of Windows. Following that, I'll list some third-party products. Later in the chapter, I'll describe what to do if you end up with a spyware or virus infection.

Windows Defender

Windows Defender (formerly called Microsoft Windows AntiSpyware) is Microsoft's entry in the pool of available antispyware software. Originally developed by Giant Software before Microsoft acquired the company in 2004, Windows Defender is a comprehensive package, offered free, that not only removes already-installed spyware, but actively protects against future infections.

When you are running Windows Defender and visit a web page that attempts to secretly install software, or if you run a software installer that changes settings that Defender suspects might indicate that you've loaded spyware, Defender will display a pop-up balloon notifying you that it has detected changes. Click on the balloon, and then click on the Review and Take Action link to see an analysis of the changes, as illustrated in Figure 7.5. The SpyNet user community's consensus of the program's risk will be displayed, if available, along with a listing of what the program has done.

Under Action, select Permit or Deny for each detected change, and then click Apply Changes. Denied changes are rolled back. (And if you joined the SpyNet community from the settings link in the Windows Defender window, your choice will be sent back to Microsoft as a vote in favor of or against the software. These votes, plus additional analysis, help Microsoft make recommendations to future users.)

Similar notifications are also given when any application on your computer attempts to modify the startup programs or modify other Internet-related settings.

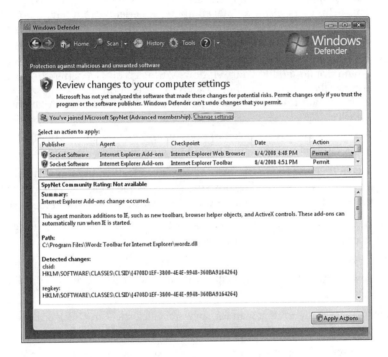

Figure 7.5 Windows Defender pop-up notification.

Windows Defender is installed by default on Vista. To install it on XP, log on using a Computer Administrator account, open Internet Explorer and visit www.microsoft.com, search for Windows Defender, and then download and install the software. After you have it installed, click on the desktop icon to start the utility and follow these steps:

1. The Setup Assistant guides you through the steps of configuring your spyware protection. Click Next to continue.

2. Step 1 of 3 asks you whether you want to enable AutoUpdate. AutoUpdate automatically downloads the latest spyware definitions for you on a regular basis, unlike the other utilities mentioned earlier. It is highly recommended that you enable this option and click Next.

3. The next step gives you an opportunity to enable or disable the real-time protection agents mentioned earlier that require a response from you before any Internet settings can be

changed. This is one of the best features of Windows Defender and should definitely be left enabled. Click Next to continue to the final step.

4. The final step gives you the opportunity to participate in something called SpyNet. SpyNet is basically a method that enables you to report the results of your personal spyware scans and the names of programs that you approve or block from installation back to Microsoft so it can use the information to update its definitions database. There are three choices:

   - **Basic membership**—You are notified when Defender detects known bad software, but software that has not been categorized is *not* removed and you are not warned. This helps users with minimal computer experience from having to make decisions that may end up disabling their legitimate software. When Defender detects bad software on your computer, it notifies Microsoft just for statistical purposes.

   - **Advanced membership**—You are notified if Defender detects unrecognized software attempting to modify your Windows settings. This is a better choice for users who feel comfortable evaluating whether a given application is expected and legitimate or not. Your decision is communicated to Microsoft to help categorize the newly detected software.

   - **No membership**—You can opt out of SpyNet. You are not notified if Defender detects uncategorized software, and nothing is communicated back to Microsoft.

   In general, it is best to use the Basic or Advanced feature, because it helps Microsoft improve the spyware database; however, some people concerned about their privacy may want to disable this feature. Either way, click Finish to close the Setup Assistant.

5. The next screen gives you the opportunity to run a full system scan. I suggest you click Run Scan Later and update the definitions first.

6. After the main interface loads, click on the File menu bar item and select Check for Updates. If any updates are available, they are automatically installed. Click on Close to continue.

7. Now you are ready to do a scan for spyware. Click the Run Quick Scan Now button to start the scan.

8. After the scan is over, if anything is found, a summary of the results is shown. Click View Report to view the details and to remove any spyware found.

9. On the Scan Results screen, you can see a list of every item found with a drop-down box for the recommended action to be taken (Ignore, Quarantine, Remove, or Always Ignore). By default, Windows Defender selects what it believes is the appropriate action for the severity of the spyware, based on its spyware database. However, you can always override that selection by selecting a new option in the drop-down menu for the item on the left. After you have all the items actions selected, click Continue and then Yes on the confirmation screen to execute the actions.

Tip

Windows Defender has some additional privacy protection features that you may want to investigate. Click on the Tools icon on the main program screen to explore the Settings and Tools items.

The Software Explorer tool lets you examine programs that Windows runs when it starts and when you log on. This is a useful feature, but the autoruns tool provides a much more comprehensive view of the various ways that programs can be started. Read more about it later in this chapter under "What to Do If the Automated Utilities Fail."

Third-Party Spyware Removal Programs

Most antivirus programs include antispyware features, so if you have or add antivirus protection, you should be covered for spyware as well. But antispyware programs tend not to degrade the performance of your computer, so it can't hurt to add an additional antispyware program, from another manufacturer with a different (and perhaps better) list of spyware definitions.

Table 7.3 lists several antispyware programs for Windows XP and Vista. Many of the antivirus programs listed in Table 7.2 root out all forms of spyware, so I won't repeat those products here. Table 7.3 lists only products that don't perform full antivirus duties.

Table 7.3   Antispyware Programs for Windows XP and Vista

Product	Price	XP	x64 XP	Vista	x64 Vista	URL
Ad-Aware Free [2]	free	✓		✓	✓	www.lavasoft.com
a-squared Anti-Malware Free [2]	free	✓	✓	✓	✓	www.emsisoft.com
AntiSpy	$18	✓	✓	✓	✓	www.omniquad.com
CounterSpy	$20	✓		✓	✓	www.sunbelt-software.com
ParetoLogic Anti-Spyware	$40	✓				www.paretologic.com
Spy Sweeper	$30	✓		✓		www.webroot.com
Spybot Search and Destroy	free	✓	✓	✓	✓	www.safer-networking.org
Spyware Blaster [3]	free	✓	✓	✓	✓	www.javacoolsoftware.com
Spyware Doctor Starter Edition [2]	free	✓		✓		www.pctools.com
SUPERAntiSpyware [1,2]	free	✓		✓		www.superantispyware.com
Windows Defender	free	✓	✓	✓	✓	www.microsoft.com
XoftSpy SE	$40	✓				www.paretologic.com
ZoneAlarm Anti-Spyware	$20	✓		✓		www.zonealarm.com

[1] *Free only for personal, noncommercial, noninstitutional use.*
[2] *A paid version is available that provides additional features.*
[3] *Attempts to block new infections but does not remove spyware.*

Most of the paid products have discounts for multiple-computer or multiple-year licenses. Several of the free products have paid versions that offer additional features. This information was current at the time this book went to press. I strongly recommend that you look up prices, compatibility issues, test results, and reviews of the *current* versions of these or any other protection products before you make a selection. Also, if you're going to install firewall, antivirus, and antispyware software, see whether the manufacturer has a package that provides all the services you want for one price. Suites often combine several protection products for a lower total cost.

Among the antispyware programs, most of the free ones require you to manually perform software updates and scans of your computer, whereas most of the paid ones do both of these functions automatically (Windows Defender, though, is free, and is completely automatic.) Consider this when you're evaluating a product. If you're good about remembering to perform updates and scans, a manually operated product may be fine for you, otherwise, lean toward an automatic one. Also, some free antispyware programs detect but do not remove spyware; only their paid counterparts perform removal.

Caution

There are a bunch of phony antispyware applications that do *not* actually detect or remove spyware infections, but only extort money from you. These products are often advertised with web browser pop-up ads that warn you that your computer is infected with some sort of malware. *Never* buy protection software that's advertised in a pop-up ad of any sort—no legitimate program is advertised this way. Before you purchase any antispyware program, check a reputable source to be sure that the program is legitimate. The Wikipedia.org website can be helpful, or check out a computer magazine website such as pcmag.com.

Cleaning an Infected Computer

You might suspect that your computer has a spyware or virus infection if you see any of the following symptoms:

- Advertisement boxes pop up for products that have *nothing* to do with the websites you're visiting. Typically the advertisements will be for online gambling, drugs, pornography, and spyware cleanup software.

- Toolbars, links, or favorites appear in your web browser that you didn't put there.

- When you attempt to use a standard search engine such as Yahoo! or Google, you are taken to some other search site. Similarly, when you type the name of a website in the Address bar, you are taken to a completely unrelated site.

- Your browser's home page is changed so that every time you open Internet Explorer or another web browser you are brought to a site that you don't want to use. Even if you try to change the default page to your preferred site (or "blank"), the undesired site still comes up.

- When you try to use a secured website (one whose name begins with https:) for banking or online purchases at a legitimate site, your web browser warns you that the site's certificate is incorrect or that the site is not secure.

- When you run the Task Manager and view the Processes tab, you see programs in the Image Name column that you know aren't normal, or whose filename consist of random letters, usually running under your username.

- Web browsing is much slower than you know it should be.

- Your computer starts crashing shortly after visiting a disreputable website.

If you have any of these symptoms, you need to check to see whether your computer has a spyware infection. Unfortunately, as much as malware removal technology has matured, so have the skills of the criminals who write malware, so detecting and removing it has become dishearteningly difficult. In the following section, I give you some tips for identifying and removing malware from your computer.

Identifying Spyware

There are several ways to examine the programs running on your computer to see whether any are spyware. Here are a few suggestions:

- Try using an online scanning/cleanup tool, such as Trend Micro HouseCall (housecall. trendmicro.com), F-Secure Online Virus Scanner (support.f-secure.com/env/home/ ols.shtml), or ESET Online Scanner (www.eset.com/onlinescan). On XP, be sure to run the scan from a Computer Administrator account.

- Open Internet Explorer. If the menu is not visible, press and release the Alt key. Select Tools, Manage Add-Ons, Enable or Disable Add-Ons. Inspect the list of enabled add-ons. Be suspicious of any that have no entry in the Name or Publisher column. (The one labeled Research is okay, though.)

- Press Ctrl+Alt+Del. On Vista, select Start Task Manager. Select the Processes tab. Look at the list of program filenames in the Image Name column. (Most spyware programs run under your username, but some run as services. On Vista, click Show Processes from All Users to see the full list, including services, or view the Services tab.)

- Download and run live.sysinternals.com/procexp.exe and live.sysinternals.com/ autoruns.exe. Right-click any entry and select Properties to view more information on the program. (I'll talk a bit more about these utilities in a later section.)

- Open Windows Defender, select the Tools icon, the Software Explorer, and wait for the Classification list to fill in. This column shows how Microsoft's SpyNet community has rated the program's risk level.

- Download and run HijackThis as described at the end of this chapter.

If you suspect that a program you see running in the Task Manager is spyware, use Google to search for the names of the programs you see running (in Program Manager, this is what's shown in the Image Name column). You'll find out pretty quickly whether any of them are spyware applications. If Google just displays a blank white screen when you search for a particular filename, you may have found a spyware program—some of them are programmed to block any attempt you make to search for their filenames. If this happens, try searching from another computer to confirm your suspicion.

Of course, an antispyware program does all this for you automatically. If you have one installed, run it (you may need to boot in Safe Mode, as described in the next section). If you don't have antispyware software installed, there are three online detection tools to try. Check out the Endpoint Assessment Test and Rootkit Detection test at www.sophos.com, BOClean at www.comodo.com, and the web browser–based scan at housecall.trendmicro.com. Better yet, download and run one or more of the free programs listed in Table 7.3.

Installing and Running Antispyware Software

If you suspect that your computer has been compromised with spyware, the first thing you'll do is to download and install an antispyware program. (Several were described earlier in this chapter in Table 7.3.) The second thing you'll do is to scratch your head wondering why you can't download the application, or install it, or get it to run. The reason is that a large number of spyware programs actively block any attempt you make to obtain or run antispyware tools. (It's pretty creepy to watch this happen.) So, here are some tips for getting an antispyware program up and running.

If you can't download the program at all—if, for example, the download progress bar never progresses—you have to download it on another computer, copy the downloaded file to a recordable CD or a USB flash drive, and install it from this media.

If you find that the program doesn't install, be sure you are logged on using a Computer Administrator account (this is particularly important on Windows XP; Vista should just prompt you via User Account Control). If that isn't the problem, restart your computer in Safe Mode and try again. To do this, click Start. On XP, click Shut Down, and then Restart. On Vista, click the triangular arrow at the bottom right corner of the Start menu and select Restart.

Windows shuts down, the screen goes black, your computer BIOS displays its text-based startup message, and the screen goes black again, as it always does just before the first Windows startup display appears. At this point start repeatedly pressing the F8 key. When the Advanced Startup Options menu appears, select Safe Mode. When Windows has started, log on using a Computer Administrator account, or the Administrator account itself, if it's available, and then install and run the antispyware program.

When Windows is running in Safe Mode, the antispyware program can't download program updates. Let it do a complete scan first anyway, and let it remove anything it can find. Then restart Windows normally, start the antispyware program, have it download and install updates, restart in Safe Mode again, and perform another full scan.

If these steps fail to remove the spyware infection, see "What To Do If the Automated Utilities Fail" after the next section.

Recovering from Browser Hijacks

Many spyware applications change your Internet Explorer home page as well as your default search page. As soon as you open Internet Explorer or attempt to do a search, you are bombarded with advertisements and bogus search results. This is called *browser hijacking*. Typically, the change to your home page and search page settings isn't the only problem—the change is usually made by software that remains in your computer, which is why it's often futile to simply block unwanted add-ons or reset your Internet Explorer settings. The malware just changes them back. So you should first perform a thorough spyware detection and removal. When you're sure your computer is clear, reset Internet Explorer to its default settings, and then tweak it back the way you want it.

If your web browser's settings are severely mangled after removal of the spyware, there is usually a way to completely reset them to all default settings. For Internet Explorer 7, follow these steps:

1. Close all open instances of Internet Explorer.

2. Open Internet Explorer. If the File menu is not visible, press and release the Alt key.

3. Click Tools, Internet Options. Select the Advanced tab.

4. Click Reset, and then Reset again.

5. Close Internet Explorer, and then reopen it. If the File menu is not visible, press and release the Alt key.

6. Select Tools, Manage Add-Ons, Enable or Disable Add-Ons. Enable the add-ons that you recognize as legitimate and that you want to continue to use (see Figure 7.6). Click OK to save your changes.

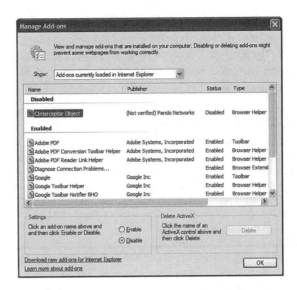

Figure 7.6 You can enable and disable individual browser add-ons.

7. Select View, Toolbars, and enable the toolbars that you recognize and want to use.

What to Do If the Automated Utilities Fail

Spyware is constantly evolving as its authors work to get ahead of the spyware removal utilities. One of the biggest problems with spyware removal tools is that they rely almost exclusively on matching definitions of known malware programs, and fixes for new malware can be created only after people have already been infected by it. You might be unlucky enough to be one of the people who gets hit by the new program before your antispyware program has the information it needs to find and remove it. Worse, some of the new spyware I've seen recently digs so deeply into Windows that common antispyware programs don't have the capacity to remove it even if they do find it.

If you have an existing infection that you're having trouble with, try a different spyware removal tool. What one misses another might catch. Try the free programs first, and any of the paid programs that offer a full-featured free trial period, before you consider paid products. I wouldn't pay for anything, though, before moving on to Google.

After antispyware programs, Google is the next tool to try. Search for any of the following:

- The program's filename
- The *exact* text of any messages it displays, surrounded by double quotes (")
- The name of or text from any website it forces you to view

and see whether this leads you to a removal procedure.

If you're willing to really get on your hands and knees to investigate what's gotten into your computer, there are some *very* useful programs available from Sysinternals.com, which is now owned by Microsoft. The following tools can give you a very good look at what's going on inside Windows. (If they don't run, the spyware may be blocking them. You may need to run them from Safe Mode to get anywhere.) The utilities are as follows:

- `live.sysinternals.com/procexp.exe`—Lists all running programs, and lets you examine information about each program file.

- `live.sysinternals.com/autoruns.exe`—Lists all programs that Windows starts automatically. This tool is far better than any other such program out there because it knows about printer monitors, browser and Windows Explorer plug-ins, and dozens of other ways that malware can get loaded by Windows. You'll probably find that a given spyware application is listed in several different places, so you should comb through autoruns' listings thoroughly. Autoruns can enable and disable any of the autostart programs it finds.

Tip

The first time you use AutoRuns, click Options, and check Hide Signed Microsoft Entries so that you'll be able to look at just the "foreign" programs. If you find an entry you'd like to remove, uncheck it to temporarily disable it, or right-click and select Delete to remove it entirely. Two other useful right-click options are Search Online, which performs a Google Search on the program's filename and Jump To, which displays the program Registry entry.

- `live.sysinternals.com/procmon.exe`—Lets you monitor all activity in all tasks, including Registry reading and writing, file activity, and so on. Procmon has filtering options that let you watch just for activity involving specific Registry entries or specific files so that you can see which application is creating, modifying, reading, or writing suspicious Registry entries or files (must be run with full Computer Administrator privileges).

Enter the appropriate utility URL into Internet Explorer and click Run, or save the downloaded file to your desktop and run it from there. For `procexp.exe` you need to save the file, right-click it, and select Run As on XP or Run as Administrator on Vista, to run the program as a Computer Administrator.

Finally, various websites have online forums where volunteers might be able to help you. Most of these sites use the popular diagnosis software called HijackThis to take a snapshot of all the programs running on your computer, various parts of the system configuration, and Internet Explorer settings. The software enables a user to save a copy of the results, which can then be posted on one of the various websites dedicated to this utility. Individuals who volunteer their time take a look at your log and help you figure out what entry is causing the problem.

To get started, visit www.trendmicro.com to search for and download the latest copy of HijackThis. Then, follow this procedure to generate your log:

1. After you have HijackThis downloaded, launch the application (it doesn't require an installation).

2. Click on the Scan button to reveal your log (see Figure 7.7).

Figure 7.7   Generating the HijackThis log.

3. Next, click the Save Log button to save a text file with the contents of the scan on your computer.

Now that you have your log generated, post it on one of these popular websites that are known for their dedicated HijackThis support:

- http://forum.tweaks.com/forum
- http://forums.spywareinfo.com
- http://forums.whatthetech.com

After you have posted your HijackThis log on one or more of the websites, you are likely to get a response within a day. When the culprit is identified, open up HijackThis again and check the box next to the line for the program file you want to remove and click Fix Checked. You are asked to confirm the delete and then the operation is completed. After a reboot, the problem *could* be solved. To be honest, though, I've found that this is an iffy proposition—the responses you get from the volunteers are sometimes hard to follow, incomplete, or inaccurate, and simply deleting files using HijackThis is not often sufficient to fix a real spyware infection. But, as they say, your mileage may vary.

Bootable Tools

As a last resort, if the spyware application is so deeply rooted within Windows that you cannot remove the offending programs while Windows is running even in Safe Mode, you may have to boot your computer using removable media—this way, your copy of Windows won't be running at all, and the spyware can't block your efforts. The Recovery Console on your Windows XP or Vista installation media can help you do this. Boot from the CD or DVD and follow the setup prompts to repair your Windows installation with the Recovery Console. A Command Prompt window opens and you can use the `cd`, `dir`, and `delete` commands to navigate through your Windows folder and delete the spyware program's files.

Another helpful bootable utility is at www.avast.com/eng/avast_bart_cd.html.

Managing Windows

Managing Users

Modern versions of Windows, the branch of the family tree that includes Windows NT, 2000, XP and Vista, incorporate the distinct concept of a "user." Given your username and password, besides applying your preferences for the desktop and applications, Windows can track which of several dozen privileges you should be allowed to exercise, including the right to install new software, change other users' passwords, access the computer remotely via a network, or—when your disk is formatted appropriately—access any given file. Here are the elements of the Windows environment that are or can be user-specific:

- Your User Profile, a folder in which your personal files are stored, including your [My] Documents folder, your Desktop folder, personal Start menu additions, the Outlook or Outlook Express mailbox and address book files, Favorites (bookmarks), temporary files, and the files that contain personal Registry entries. Your User Profile is usually stored in a folder under \Users on Windows Vista, and under \Documents and Settings on Windows XP, although a network administrator can instruct Windows to use an alternate location.

- Registry entries under the HKEY_CURRENT_USER branch and custom additions to HKEY_CLASSES_ROOT, which are used to store your software preferences.

- Environment variables such as PATH and TEMP, which control the behavior of many programs (the information for these are stored in the Registry, but are set through the System Properties control panel; Chapter 9, "Windows Commands and Scripting," discusses environment variables in more detail).

- File and folder access permissions for files stored on disks with NTFS formatting.

- Shared network printer, file, and folder mappings and access permissions.

- Windows management and configuration permissions, such as the ability to change the clock, install hardware, or back up the hard disk.

- On a corporate network with Active Directory, automatic installation of application software.

As you can see, this is a huge improvement over Windows 9x, where anyone could use the computer with or without a password, and do anything he wanted with it. And, although you certainly can (with some effort) configure Windows 2000, XP, or Vista to be just as indiscriminate, it's in your own best interest to take advantage of Windows' security features.

In this section I'll give you a bit of background on the Windows security system, and then we'll go over how to set up and manage user accounts. If you want to get right to it, skip ahead to "Adding and Deleting User Accounts from the Control Panel" later in this chapter.

Domain and Workgroup Environments

Windows was designed to work in both the home/small office environment and the corporate environment, and these two worlds have distinctly different security needs and management techniques. For home and small office use, convenience, minimal cost, and protection from Internet-related viruses are the key concerns. In the corporate world, centralized management, ability to delegate authority, and fine-grained control are essential requirements. I'll briefly describe how Windows addresses these two distinctly different sets of needs.

Windows uses two different security models, called the Workgroup model and the Domain model, respectively. The difference is illustrated in Figure 8.1.

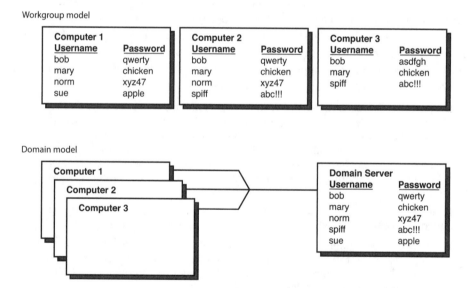

Figure 8.1 In the Workgroup model, user accounts are maintained separately on each computer. In the Domain model, user accounts are centralized.

In the Workgroup model, each computer maintains its own separate list of user accounts. You can see in the figure that user Mary has accounts on all three computers. Spiff has accounts on just two. Norm has accounts on all three, but on one computer, the password is different. This illustrates the important features of Workgroup security:

- User accounts and passwords, called *local accounts* in this model, have to be entered on each computer separately. This is fine if you have only a few computers, or if each person uses just one computer. If you want for a person to be able to use any of your computers, though, you have to create a user account on each one.

- If a user changes her password, the change has to be made at each computer separately. (This is discussed further in Chapter 7, "Networking Windows.")

- Although this form of security is a bit more difficult to administer, it's less expensive because you don't need an additional central server or expensive Windows Server operating system.

- Anyone knowing the password to a computer administrator account on a given computer can do anything at that computer: change user accounts, view files, or reconfigure anything.

- Additional entries, called *local groups*, can be created (although on the XP and Vista Home versions, it's not easy). These consist of lists of users. To simplify security management, you can grant file access privileges to groups, rather than having to specify individual users.

With the Domain model, each computer is connected to a network, and when a user attempts to sign on, the computer refers the logon request to a computer running one of the Windows Server versions to see whether the name and password are recognized. The important points are as follows:

- The centralized list of usernames and passwords ensures that nobody has to visit each and every computer to add or remove user accounts.

- A user has only one password to remember, and it's recognized by every computer in the organization.

- In a large organization, the added initial cost of a central server (or servers) and the more expensive Windows Server operating system, eventually, is more than offset by subsequent savings in management and maintenance labor costs.

- With Microsoft's Active Directory software, assignment of security privileges and delegation of management rights can be extremely well controlled. Although a master network manager can indeed do anything, the ability to add users and computers, control file security, or access files and folders can be delegated along the company's organizational lines at any level of detail. For instance, department managers might be given the ability to change just their direct subordinates' passwords, but not to make any changes in network configuration at all.

- Large organizations usually have more than one domain server as insurance against failure and for speedier access at distant worksites. Management updates (such as password changes) entered into any one server automatically propagate to the others.

- Accounts created in the domain server are called *global accounts* because they're recognized by every computer, and computers on the network are called *domain members*. Likewise, *global groups* can be created and used to manage security on files and folders.

- Users' profile folders can be stored on central servers so that each user's preferences, settings, and files are available no matter which computer is used.

- Computers on a domain network can also have local accounts and groups, which apply just to the one individual computer, just as on a standalone computer or a computer on a workgroup network. There is usually a local administrator account that can be used, for example, to install hardware drivers, but this local administrator logon can't manage the domain server.

And last but not least: If you use your computer on a corporate domain network, you probably can't make any changes to your computer's user accounts or security setup—not if your organization's network manager did his job correctly. You can skim this section, though, to get an idea of what is going on behind the scenes.

However, if you are setting up your own computer for your personal use, or for a small office, read on. You'll see how to use the workgroup model to create individual local accounts, and how to take best advantage of the limited but important security features available to you.

Tip

How do you tell whether your computer is set up for domain or workgroup-type security? On XP, click Start, right-click My Computer, select Properties, and select the Computer Name tab. Under Full Computer Name, the dialog will have the word *Workgroup* or *Domain*. On Vista, click Start, right-click Computer, and select Properties. Under Computer Name, Domain and Workgroup Settings, the word *Workgroup* or *Domain* appears on the line below Computer Description.

Note

Windows Vista Home Basic, Home Premium, and XP Home Edition can't be part of a domain network; these editions use the Workgroup model only.

Account Types

When you log on, Windows consults a database that it keeps hidden away on your hard disk (for local accounts) or on a networked domain server (for domain accounts). Along with your password, this database contains settings that determine exactly what you are allowed to do to with the computer, such as change other users' passwords. Some of these permission settings are associated directly with your account, but most are inherited through a system called *user groups*, which contain lists of one or more usernames. Permissions to read files and change Windows settings are usually assigned to groups, and you inherit any privileges assigned to the groups of which you're a member.

User accounts can be customized to some extent, but basically fall into one of four categories, which are, in increasing order of privilege the following:

- Guests
- Standard users (called *limited users* on XP)
- Power users
- Computer administrators

I'll briefly discuss each of these in turn.

Guest Accounts

Guest accounts have minimal access rights; they can run programs but cannot install them, and, in general, cannot make any changes to the system, nor read or save files in shared folders. As the name implies, this account type is designed to let someone use your computer to read email, print a file, and so on, but not see or modify anything of yours.

By default, a single guest-type account is set up when you install Windows Vista or XP. The account name is (big surprise) *Guest*. It has no password assigned, and it is also disabled by default so that it can't be used unless you take steps to enable it. I'll talk more about that later in this chapter.

Note

On a computer that's part of a Domain network (which we discussed in the previous section), a guest account's user profile is automatically deleted after the user logs off. Thus any documents saved in [My] Documents or other per-user folders disappear as soon as the guest logs off.

Computer Administrators

With a computer administrator account you can make any change, and read or write any file on the computer. While logged on with a computer administrator account on Windows 2000 or Vista, any software you run has full access to the computer, and if you find something that you don't have permission to view, you can *give* yourself permission. This is, of course, a good thing when you're installing a new device or a new application, but it's a terrible risk for day-to-day use, as any virus or other bad software that you might run inadvertently will also have full access to your computer.

To help mitigate this risk, Microsoft added the User Account Control (UAC) feature to Windows Vista. On Vista, by default, programs that a computer administrator runs *don't* get full administrator privileges, unless the program indicates to Windows that it requires administrative rights, *and* you have been shown a User Account Control prompt *and* you have instructed Windows to let the program run with full privileges. This requirement for interactive approval makes it much more difficult for a malicious program to stealthily take over your computer.

Caution

Although UAC has gotten some bad press and has been called an annoyance, I think it's the single most important and useful feature added to Windows in the last 10 years. Incredibly, some big-name writers feel as if the UAC prompt is saying to them "You ignorant boob, you don't really want to manage user accounts, do you? I don't think you can be trusted to do it, but if you click Continue, I'll go along... reluctantly." Nothing can be further from the truth. What a UAC prompt is saying is this: "I just got a request to manage user accounts. I'm pretty sure that it was you who made the request, but there's always a small chance that some nasty program is in there trying to impersonate you, and I know you wouldn't want to just let it run. Better safe than sorry, right, Bucky? So... it really was you who wanted to do this, right?" This is exactly what Windows has needed for about 10 years now, and it's a *big* step in the right direction. So, don't pay any attention to the goofs who tell you that you should disable User Account Control. And don't get into the habit of instantly approving all UAC dialogs. Whenever one appears, be sure that it appeared because *you* intended to run a program that requires administrative powers.

Also, be aware that User Account Control is disabled when you start Windows in Safe Mode.

Limited or Standard Users

Limited user accounts (as they're called on XP) or *standard user* accounts (as they're called on Vista) can log on, save files, and run most programs, but cannot install software, configure Windows, change security settings, or do much else that doesn't involve the user's own personal data. Limited user accounts are ideal for home systems, and are meant for kids, houseguests, relatives, and non-computer-literate employees—in short, anyone who needs to use your computer, but whom you're worried might accidentally cause a problem.

On Windows XP, limited user accounts are somewhat annoying because the users can't even change the screensaver or the Windows desktop setup. On Vista, they're not so inconvenient, and in fact, they're the account type Microsoft recommends for all users for day-to-day-use. Standard users can change basic preference settings such as the screen saver, and, if they attempt to change a significant system setting, they'll get the User Account Control prompt. So, if they know an administrator password, they can type it in and proceed, or an administrator can come by and type it in for them. Windows XP Home Edition and the Vista Home versions offer only the two account types just described: limited/standard and administrator accounts.

Power Users

A fourth account type, called *power user*, is available on Windows 2000 Professional, Windows XP Professional, and the Vista Business, Ultimate, and Enterprise versions. On Windows XP, power users can change some settings—for instance, power management and desktop settings—and can install minor application programs, as long as they don't replace any Windows components. Serious changes to Windows, such as networking configuration and device driver management, are not allowed. Thus, on XP, the power user's capabilities are a good compromise between the anything-goes nature of the administrator account and the annoying lockdown on the limited account type.

On Vista, however, by default the power users category has no more privileges than the standard user category. (You can read about the rationale for this by reading www.microsoft.com/technet/technetmag/issues/2007/06/ACL.) So, although some corporate network managers might choose to take advantage of the power users category for specific reasons, for the average Vista-based computer owner it offers no benefits.

Note

Remember, what defines these various account types is group membership. For example, a computer administrator user is one whose account is a member of the Administrators group. A standard user is one whose account is a member of the Users group but not Administrators. The accounts have different capabilities because of the different privileges assigned to the Users and Administrators groups.

Which Type of Account to Use?

With all of these possibilities, and with the differences between Vista and XP, which type of account should you use for your own day-to-day work? Table 8.1 lists our recommendations, based on the version of Windows you're using.

Table 8.1   Suggested User Account Types Based on Windows Version

Windows Version	Type of Account to Use
Vista Home Basic, Home Premium, Business, and Ultimate	Create an administrator account for yourself and perhaps for one or two other people that you trust will install *only* safe software and whom you *totally* trust to manage the computer. Create standard user accounts for anyone else: children, guests, and other users that you don't want to have making unsupervised changes to your computer. You may even want to set up a standard user account for yourself, for normal day-to-day work. You can always make administrative changes from these accounts by providing administrator account and password.
Vista Enterprise	Vista Enterprise is used only in large corporate environments, and network administrators manage user accounts and security remotely. If you do end up managing your own computer running Enterprise, see the preceding entry for suggestions.
XP Home Edition	Create a computer administrator account for yourself, and for other people only if you trust them *completely*. Create limited user accounts for anyone else, especially guests and children. From those accounts, you have to log on with one of the computer administrator accounts to make any significant changes. You can use Switch User to do this.
XP Professional	Create power user accounts for yourself and for other trusted users, using the Windows 2000 User Manager control panel that I'll describe shortly. Create limited user accounts for children, guests, and other nonadministrative users. Do not use the administrator account or other computer administrator accounts for day-to-day use. To perform administrative tasks, use Switch User to log on as administrator, or use the `runas` command, which we'll discuss shortly.

If you find that you or another user can't get his or her job done with the account type that you've selected, you can always change the account type later on. The new privileges take effect the next time the user logs on.

Now, before we cover the tools you'll use to manage user accounts, let's finish our rundown of the Windows user and group system by looking at the accounts and group names that come preinstalled with Windows.

Default Accounts and Groups

When you install Windows, several standard local user accounts and user groups are created as part of the installation process. Some of these are used for maintenance, and some Windows uses internally. You can, and should, add additional accounts for your own use. We'll cover that shortly. Here, though, are the default entries that you'll encounter when you go to add your own.

Table 8.2 lists the local user accounts installed with Windows. Some additional user accounts are created if you install Internet Information Services. In addition, several local groups are created, as listed in Table 8.3.

Table 8.2   Default Local Users

Username	Description
Administrator	System administrator, primary member of Administrators group, can make any change via the account's membership in the Administrators group.
	For the most part, Microsoft intends for you to create and use your own administrator-level accounts, and not use the built-in administrator account directly, except in dire emergencies. That is, there is a predefined account with the name Administrator, but you probably won't ever actually use it. Instead, you will use other accounts with administrator "powers." When procedures in this book say that you have to use a computer administrator account, it means that you should use one of these other accounts. However, the built-in Administrator account is still there for emergency use, and depending on which version of Windows you're using, it may be disabled except under certain exceptional conditions. I'll describe these conditions later in the chapter under "Logging On as Administrator."
ASPNET*	Account under which ASP.NET web server applications are run; it has just enough privilege and file access rights to perform the job but is restricted from accessing the rest of the computer.
Guest	Account that can be used to let unknown users log on with no password. Can be disabled for logon, but is used as the account whose permissions are checked for file access over the network when Simple File Sharing is enabled.
HelpAssistant§	This account is created when you issue a Remote Assistance request. It is the account used to control access by the person from whom you've requested assistance. (Not present on Vista, although it may still exist if you upgraded from XP.)
IUSR_*xxx**	On XP with IIS installed, this account is used for anonymous access via the IIS web server; *xxx* is the name of your computer. The general public is able to view only web pages that are readable by **IUSR_*xxx*** or Everyone.
	On Windows Vista, this function is assigned to a built-in security principal (a term that we'll discuss shortly) named IUSR. IUSR does not appear in the list of users shown in the Computer Management Local Users and Groups tool.
IWAM_*xxx**	This is account is used as the user associated with "out-of-process" (CGI and ASP) web applications run by the IIS web server.
SUPPORT_*nnnnnnnn*§	This is the logon account used by the Remote Assistance system; *nnnnnnnn* is an eight-digit hexadecimal number. (Not used on Vista, although it may still exist if you upgraded from XP).

Only on Windows 2000 Professional and Windows XP Professional with Internet Information Services installed.
§*Windows XP only, all versions*

Table 8.3   Default Local Groups

Group	Description
Administrators	Members of this group have computer administrator privileges, by virtue of the long list of User Rights Assignments granted to this group by default (see Table 8.6) .
Backup Operators	Members of this group have permission to back up and restore any file on the computer. (They can thus read and write any file as well as change file ownership and permissions.) This group is generally created also as a Domain group and used for access by remote network-based backup services.

Group	Description
Cryptographic Operators‡	Members of this group can install certificates and perform other cryptographic management functions.
Distributed COM Users‡	Members can launch and use Distributed COM objects.
Event Log Readers‡	Members can view and read data from the Windows event log.
Guests	By default, contains only the Guest user account, which is disabled by default, and which has an absolute minimum of privileges. Guest accounts were discussed earlier in the chapter.
HelpServicesGroup§	This group is used for special accounts associated with support applications such as Remote Assistance, and is not meant for normal user accounts. The group exists so that permissions and privileges can be assigned for all support applications collectively.
IIS_IUSRS‡	This group is used to assign permissions to files needed by Internet Information Services and to content files that it is to distribute to anonymous (unauthenticated) users.
Network Configuration Operators	Members of this group can change network TCP/IP settings, and force the release and renewal (repair) of DHCP addresses.
Performance Log Users‡	Members can set up and receive performance log events, schedules, and triggers.
Performance Monitor Users‡	Members can view performance counter data.
Power Users*	Power users have limited management ability; for example, they can configure the screensaver and install some software, but not modify Windows itself. On XP, power users can share printers and folders, and change some other settings, but not, for example, install new hardware. On Vista, by default the Power Users group has no additional privileges over those assigned to the Users group.
Remote Desktop Users†	Members of this group are allowed to log on via Remote Desktop. Membership can be edited directly or via the Remote tab on the System Properties dialog. (In addition, accounts must have a password set in order to connect via Remote Desktop.)
Replicator	The Replicator account is used on domain networks to copy files from a domain server to the local computer, automatically. This group should not be modified in any way.
TelnetClients*	Members of this group are allowed to log on via the Telnet service.
Users	By default, all local user accounts are listed in this group; it's meant to assign basic access rights for anyone who has a valid, normal logon account.

*Windows 2000 Professional and Windows XP Professional only
§Windows XP only, all versions
†Windows XP Professional Only
‡Windows Vista Only

Security Principals

User and group names can be used when you're assigning permissions to files and folders. There is an additional set of names called *security principals* that are like groups, in that you can specify them as having access to files, folders, or other objects. However, their "membership" is contextual. When Windows encounters one of these names in an access control list, it evaluates whether the current user or program has a designated characteristic. For example, if I designate that the SERVICE principal is to be granted access to a certain folder, any Windows service will be able to access the folder, no matter what user account the service is using. These principal names can also be used to deny access; for example, a Deny entry for entity NETWORK would mean that a given user might be able to access a file while logged on locally, but would not be able to access the file over the network. Table 8.4 lists the built-in security principals.

Table 8.4   Built-in Security Principals

Name	Associated With...
ANONYMOUS LOGON	Network access with no username or password supplied (used, for instance, to confirm that Windows can let an unknown network user see the list of shared folders, but not have access to any files).
Authenticated Users	Any user using a recognized account name and if required, password. Exception: The Guest account is never considered an Authenticated User.
BATCH	A program that is not attached to the keyboard and mouse; for example, a program run by the Task Scheduler.
CREATOR GROUP	In an access control list, represents the primary group of the owner.
CREATOR OWNER	The user who created and thus owns the object (for example, file or folder).
DIALUP	Users who are attempting file access via a dial-up modem or Virtual Private Network (VPN) connection.
Enterprise Domain Controllers	Access by a computer that is a domain controller.
Everyone	Any user using any means of connection, including Guests but not anonymous network connections.
INTERACTIVE	A user who is logged in via the keyboard and video display.
INTERNET°	A user who is accessing the computer over the network whose network location is public rather than private. The NETWORK principal also applies in this case. This principal can be used to deny access to files or resources when the remote user is not on a trusted network.
IUSR°	(Windows Vista only) An anonymous website visitor, used by Internet Information Services to access files and web applications. IUSR takes the place of the IUSR_xxxxx local user account used for this purpose on Windows 2000 and XP.
LOCAL SERVICE	A program that is running as a Windows service without authenticated access to the network.
NETWORK	A user who is accessing the computer over the network via file sharing. The network's location may be designated public or private.
NETWORK SERVICE	A program that is running as a Windows service with access to the network; this service *cannot* interact with the desktop.
OWNER RIGHTS	(Windows Vista only) Used to assign rights and restrictions that apply to an object's (for example, a file's) owner. When an OWNER RIGHTS entry is added to an object's access control list, the owner loses the *implicit* ability to manage the object's permissions. In this case such permission must be granted explicitly, if desired.
REMOTE INTERACTIVE LOGON	A user who has logged in via Remote Desktop.
Restricted	A program that is running in a domain-member computer under a restricted security context.

Name	Associated With...
Self	The user, security, or computer object in which this entry appears (in Active Directory only); used, for instance, in permission lists to let users change their own passwords.
SERVICE	Any program that is running as a Windows service.
SYSTEM	A part of the Windows operating system itself.
TERMINAL SERVER USER	A user who has logged in via Remote Desktop or, on Windows Server versions, a Terminal Services session.

‡*Windows Vista Only*

In addition, on Windows Vista, each service has an associated security principal. This makes it possible to individually control each service's capability to access files, folders, system resources, and functions. For instance, if you examine the security settings on most of the executable .exe and .dll files in the \windows\system32 folder, you'll see that TrustedInstaller is listed as the owner, and only TrustedInstaller has the capability to write and modify these files. TrustedInstaller is the principal name for the Windows Module Installer service also known as Windows Installer. This protects most system software from inadvertent or malicious modification: Only Windows Installer can modify these program files, and it verifies and informs you of the authenticity and trustworthiness of a program installation package before it installs it.

Account Permissions

Computer administrator users gain most of their powers by virtue of membership in the Administrators group, which is created by Windows, cannot be deleted, and is recognized by Windows as a special entity. Windows management software and the operating system itself check to see whether you are a member of the Administrators group before deciding whether to let you make certain changes; and at deeper levels, Windows knows to let administrators bypass the normal security mechanisms that protect files and folders. In addition, on Vista, the built-in account named Administrator is set up to bypass User Account Control. (For more information, see "Logging On as Administrator" later in the chapter.)

There are a number of u*ser rights*, such as the ability to change the system clock, that can be individually assigned to users or groups. They serve as the means by which Windows restricts or grants the ability for users or programs to change the way Windows works and, when necessary, to circumvent security features. Not surprisingly, the Administrators group is listed for nearly all of them. On Windows XP and Vista Home versions, these permission settings cannot be changed. However, on Windows Vista Business, Enterprise, and Ultimate, and on XP Professional, Windows 2000 and earlier versions of Windows NT, other accounts can be given these permissions as well.

For example, if you've set up Remote Desktop access to your computer, you know that you have to list the users who are able to log on remotely, using the Remote tab on the System Properties dialog. That dialog actually makes the listed user a member of the Remote Desktop Users group.

That group has the "Allow logon through Terminal Services" user right. Thus, the listed users can log on through Remote Desktop.

Although you probably don't want to change their assignment, the settings can be seen in the Local Security Policy management tool. To open this tool, follow these steps:

- On Vista, open the Control Panel, and then click System and Maintenance, Administrative Tools, Local Security Policy. You have to confirm the User Account Control prompt.

- On XP, open the Control Panel, click Performance and Maintenance, and then Administrative Tools. You must be logged on as a computer administrator.

- On either operating system, if you've customized your Start Menu to display the Administrative Tools menu, you can click Start, All Programs, Administrative Tools, Local Security Policy. On XP, if you're not logged on as a computer administrator, right-click the menu item and select Run As, and then select Administrator.

In the left pane, select Local Policies, User Rights Assignment. The Policy column lists the various user rights, and the Security Setting column lists the users and groups that are granted the rights, as shown in Figure 8.2.

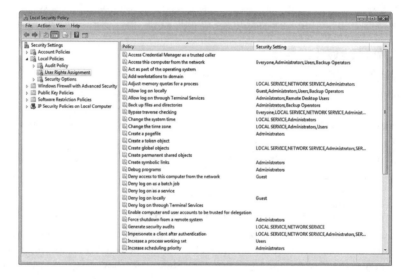

Figure 8.2   User Rights Assignments lists the accounts, groups, and security principals that are granted each privilege.

Table 8.5 lists the standard user rights used by Windows Vista, XP, and Windows Server 2003. In the description column, most entries refer to users. Here, *users* means any user who is either explicitly listed in the policy entry, is a member of a group that is listed, or has an associated security principal that is granted the associated right. When the description refers to the rights of programs, remember that programs are associated with a specific user, so the program's privileges are the same as the associated user's privileges.

Table 8.5   User Rights

Policy	Description
Access Credential Manager as a trusted caller°	Allows programs to access stored passwords and other credentials for all users. Do not assign this privilege to user accounts; it is for use only by the logon system and backup/restore systems.
Access this computer from the network	Allows user to access the computer via file and printer sharing.
Act as part of the operating system	Allows a program to impersonate any user, thus having access to any user's resources.
Add workstations to domain	Allows user to add a computer to the domain (domain controller only).
Adjust memory quotas for a process	Allows user to increase memory usage limits on another running program.
Allow log on locally°	(See Log on Locally. The policy name is different on Vista.)
Allow logon through Terminal Services	Allows user to log on via Terminal Services or Remote Desktop Connection.
Back up files and directories	Allows user to read any file, folder, or Registry entry in the context of performing a system backup.
Bypass traverse checking	Allows user to use a subdirectory (folder) to which he or she has permission, even though he or she does not have permission to read the parent folder. This is normally granted to Everyone and should *not* be disabled.
Change the system time	Allows user to set the clock and date.
Change the time zone°	Allows user to change the computer's time zone. Vista differentiates between the time and the time zone setting so that a standard user can change the time zone while traveling, whereas only an administrator can change the clock time itself.
Create a pagefile	Allows user to modify the virtual memory Page File settings.
Create a token object	Allows a program to create a security token, which could be given to other programs to grant them special access rights.
Create global objects	Allows a program running under a Terminal Service session to create Windows software objects such as semaphores and mutexes that are visible by other sessions.
Create permanent shared objects	Allows a program to create an Active Directory object, or a kernel-mode name object inside Windows.
Create symbolic links°	Allows the user to create symbol links in the file system. Symbolic links are directory (folder) entries that refer to other files or folders, and thus create multiple names for one physical file.
Debug programs	Allows a program to halt, start, breakpoint, or read the contents of other programs.
Deny access to this computer from the network	Any user who ends up with this policy, by virtue of direct listing, group membership, or security principals, is prohibited from accessing shared files and printers on the computer, as well as other network resources such as Remote Procedure Calls. This policy supercedes and negates "Access this computer from the network."
Deny logon as a batch job	In a similar fashion, this policy invalidates "Log on as a batch job."
Deny logon as a service	Invalidates "Log on as a service."
Deny logon locally	Invalidates "Log on locally."
Deny logon through Terminal Services	Invalidates "Allow logon through Terminal Services."

(continues)

Table 8.5   Continued

Policy	Description
Enable computer and user accounts to be trusted for delegation	Allows user to set the Trusted For Delegation setting on a user or computer Group Policy object.
Force shutdown from a remote system	Allows user to shut down or restart Windows remotely through network services.
Generate security audits	Allows a program to write audit entries to the security log.
Impersonate a client after authentication	Allows a program to impersonate a client using a token received from Windows, usually via networking, without explicitly having provided the username and password. Component Object Model (COM) servers often require this privilege and gain it by virtue of being assigned the SERVICE security principal, which is listed for this policy.
Increase a process working set	Allows a user to instruct Windows to increase the amount of physical memory allocated to the user's programs.
Increase scheduling priority	Allows a program to increase another program's execution priority. If a user has this right, for example, he can modify program permissions using the Task Manager.
Load and unload device drivers	Allows user to force Windows to load or unload device drivers.
Lock pages in memory	Allows program to force Windows to keep specific blocks of memory fixed in place; used by some device drivers.
Log on as a batch job	Allows a user to have programs started by the Task Scheduler, or, in some cases, by certain services.
Log on as a service	Allows user account to be used to run Windows services.
Log on locally	Allows user to log on directly using the keyboard and display. On domain servers, generally only administrators are given this privilege. (Called "Allow log on locally" on Vista.)
Manage auditing and security log	Allows user to enable auditing on specific files, folders, and other objects. Auditing as a whole must be enabled separately.
Modify an object label°	Allows a user to modify the "integrity" label on files, Registry keys, processes, and other objects owned by other users, and to raise the integrity label of owned objects. Integrity labels are used, for example, to mark downloaded programs as less trustworthy than programs on a CD, and to make Internet Explorer run with reduced privileges.
Modify firmware environment values	Allows user to set systemwide environment variables.
Perform volume maintenance tasks	Allows user to perform disk cleanup and defragmentation.
Profile single process	Allows user to use system tools to measure detailed behavior and performance of application programs.
Profile system performance	Allows user to use system tools to measure detailed behavior and performance of Windows itself.
Remove computer from docking station	Allows user to undock a laptop computer. (The policy can be disabled entirely to let anyone undock the computer without having to log on.)
Replace a process-level token	Allows a program to replace the default token (user identity) of another program that it has started itself.
Restore files and directories	Allows user to write to and change security settings of any file, folder, or Registry entry in the context of performing a system restore.

Policy	Description
Shut down the system	Allows user to shut down or restart Windows. On a domain controller, generally only administrators are granted this privilege.
Synchronize directory service data	Allows user to perform Active Directory synchronization.
Take ownership of files or other objects	Allows user to take over ownership of any file, folder, or other system object. Having taken ownership, the user can then change the object's access permissions at will.

°*Windows Vista only*

In the Local Security Settings tool, each policy is listed along with the groups or principals that are granted the associated privilege. Table 8.6 lists the default assignments for Windows Vista and XP Professional in a different way, showing all the privileges granted to each group and security principal. Remember that a given user will likely be a member of several of these groups or principals, so user gains the combined privileges from each. To maintain tighter security, on a server fewer rights are usually granted to interactive users. Usually only administrators are allowed to log on directly, and regular users access the computer only over the network.

Table 8.6   Default User Rights Assignments

User, Group, or Principal	Privilege
Administrators	Access this computer from the network Adjust memory quotas for a process Allow logon through Terminal Services Back up files and directories Bypass traverse checking Change the system time Change the time zone° Create a pagefile Create global objects Create symbolic links° Debug programs Force shutdown from a remote system Impersonate a client after authentication Increase scheduling priority Load and unload device drivers Log on as a batch job° (Allow) Log on locally Manage auditing and security log Modify firmware environment values Perform volume maintenance tasks Profile single process Profile system performance Remove computer from docking station Restore files and directories Shut down the system Take ownership of files or other objects
ASPNET	Access this computer from the network Deny logon locally Deny logon through Terminal Services Impersonate a client after authentication Log on as a batch job Log on as a service

(continues)

Table 8.6   Continued

User, Group, or Principal	Privilege
Backup Operators	Access this computer from the network Back up files and directories Bypass traverse checking Log on as a batch job° (Allow) Log on locally Restore files and directories Shut down the system
Everyone	Access this computer from the network Bypass traverse checking
Guest	Deny access to this computer from the network Deny logon locally *(when Guest is disabled from the Users control panel)* (Allow) Log on locally
INTERACTIVE	Create global objects‡
IUSR_xxx‡	Access this computer from the network Log on as a batch job Log on locally
IWAM_xxx‡	Access this computer from the network Adjust memory quotas for a process Log on as a batch job Replace a process-level token
LOCAL SERVICE	Adjust memory quotas for a process Bypass traverse checking° Change the system time° Change the time zone° Create global objects° Generate security audits Impersonate a client after authentication° Replace a process-level token
NETWORK SERVICE	Adjust memory quotas for a process Bypass traverse checking° Create global objects° Generate security audits Impersonate a client after authentication° Log on as a service‡ Replace a process-level token
Power Users	Access this computer from the network‡ Bypass traverse checking‡ Change the system time‡ Log on locally‡ Profile single process‡ Remove computer from docking station‡ Shut down the system‡
Remote Desktop Users	Allow logon through Terminal Services
SERVICE	Adjust memory quotas for a process‡ Create global objects‡ Generate security audits‡ Impersonate a client after authentication Log on as a service‡ Replace a process-level token‡ (on Vista, specific services may have some additional rights granted)

User, Group, or Principal	Privilege
SUPPORT_nnnnnnnn	Deny access to this computer from the network Deny logon locally Log on as a batch job
Users	Access this computer from the network Allow logon through Terminal Services‡ Bypass traverse checking Change the system time‡ Change the time zone° Increase a process working set° (Allow) Log on locally Profile single process‡ Remove computer from docking station Shut down the system

°*On Windows Vista but not XP*
‡*On XP but not on Windows Vista*

Although you can change these assignments, it's somewhat risky (you might find that you can no longer log on, use, or manage your own computer), so you should have a very good reason for doing so. One need for adding additional privileges occurs when you install and run a Windows service using a special user account. You will need to add that account to the "Log on as a service" policy entry.

As another example, I run an email server system that requires recipients to have a Windows user account, and the accounts must have the "Log on as a batch job" privilege. I don't want most of these email users to have access to the server computer, so I've rounded up the mail users into a group called Email Users, and have added that group to "Log on as a batch job." I also deleted most of them from the Users group because they *only* need to pick up mail, and never log on.

Caution

Do not disable the "Bypass traverse checking" privilege. It may *sound* like a risky privilege, but it's an essential one. It lets users and services reach below folders in which they have no read permission to get to subfolders that they do have permission to see. Many services and applications depend on this.

Adding and Deleting User Accounts from the Control Panel

Unless your computer is a member of a domain network, the most straightforward way to create and manage user accounts is with the User Accounts applet in the control panel. Here, you can create user accounts, change passwords (your own, and if you are a computer administrator, other peoples'), change the Welcome Screen picture associated with the account, and make a password reset disk to have on hand in case you forget your password.

Because the User control panel can vary depending on the version of Windows you're using and your network setup, use the following list to jump to the instructions for your situation:

- For Windows XP, skip ahead to the section titled "The User Control Panel on Windows XP."

- For Windows Vista on a corporate domain network, skip ahead to "Vista User Management on a Domain Network."

- Otherwise, to manage Windows Vista in a home or on a small office network, continue to the next section.

The User Control Panel on Windows Vista

To open the user control panel applet on Vista, click Start, Control Panel, Add or Remove User Accounts. After you respond to the User Account Control prompt, you should see something similar to Figure 8.3. (If you see a smaller dialog box instead, your computer is part of a domain network—in this case, please skip ahead to the section titled "Vista User Management on a Domain Network").

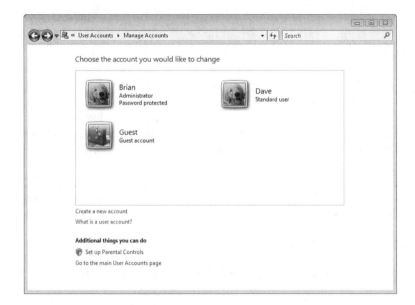

Figure 8.3   The User Accounts control panel applet lets you create and manage user accounts.

The control panel displays an icon for each local user account on this system. You can see details about each of the user accounts, including whether the user has administrative rights and whether the account is password protected. You might also notice in Figure 8.3 that the Guest account is disabled. By clicking on it here, you can change the enabled or disabled status of the Guest account.

If you click on a user account to manage it, a screen like the one shown in Figure 8.4 appears.

Figure 8.4   Modifying a user account with the User Accounts control panel applet.

In the User Accounts Control Panel applet, quick-click actions do the following:

- **Change the Name**—This option changes the user's "display" name that appears on the Welcome Screen and Start menu. (It does *not* change the actual account logon name; for that, you have to use the Management Console, described in "Managing Users from the Management Console.")

- **[Create | Change] a Password**—This option changes depending on whether an account already has an assigned password. If the password is blank, you have the option to create a password. If the password is not blank, you have the option to change it.

Caution

If you change another user's password, the user loses access to his or her encrypted files and stored passwords. If the user has forgotten his or her password and has encrypted any files, try the techniques in the section titled "Dealing with a Lost Password," later in this chapter, before resetting the user's password.

- **Remove the Password**—This option shows up only if a password is currently assigned to the account. If the account has no password, this action is not displayed.

- **Change the Picture**—This option changes the 48×48 pixel graphic associated with the user's account. You can select from a variety of included icons or browse to any other graphic. If the selected graphic is too large to fit in the 48×48 pixels, it is scaled down to fit. Full-sized, full-color, high-detail photos are, therefore, not recommended. Windows stores the default set of pictures in the \ProgramData\Microsoft\User Account Pictures\Default Pictures folder, and your selected image is in \Users*username*\AppData\Local\Temp\ *username*.bmp.

- **Change the Account Type**—This option enables you to change the account from a limited account to an administrative account or vice versa. This is equivalent to adding or removing the user account from the local Administrators group. To assign a user to additional groups, use the method that I'll describe in "Managing Users from the Management Console."

If you've customized an account's group membership, its type displays as "Unknown account type" in the User Accounts window.

- **Delete the Account**—This option deletes the account, including the user's profile folder. Don't delete an account unless you're sure you don't need the associated settings. It is safer to *disable* an account until you're sure you don't need it, using the management console interface described shortly.

In Figure 8.4, I am modifying the account with which I am logged in. This not only modifies the voice of the quick-click actions to the first person (for example, "Change *my* password" rather than "change *the* password"), but an additional action also appears:

- **Set Up My Account to Use a .NET Passport**—This option associates a Microsoft .NET Passport account to your local user account, relieving you from manually entering the Passport username and password for .NET services that require authentication through the Passport service. Clicking this option starts a wizard. If you do not currently have a passport, the wizard enables you to create one on the spot, although you must have an active connection to the Internet for this wizard to complete successfully.

Note

Carefully consider the privacy implications before you configure your account to use the .NET Passport feature. If you do, anyone using your account may automatically have access to any websites or services that use Passport as the logon mechanism. Essentially, you may be giving Windows and Microsoft permission to validate web transactions in your name.

Here is my recommendation for the best way to add new user accounts to your Windows Vista computer:

1. Make a list of the accounts you want to create, and the passwords you want to assign to each.

2. Log on as a computer administrator and open the User Accounts control panel.

3. Click Create a New Account. Enter a logon name for this user. I have a habit of using the person's first initial and last name, but you can choose any sort of naming scheme that you want to use.

4. Select the account type, standard user or administrator. See the section titled "Which Type of Account to Use?" earlier in the chapter to help choose the right type.

5. An icon appears for the new account, under Pick an Account to Change. Click on the new icon.

6. Click Create a Password, and enter the password twice as indicated. We recommend that you create passwords for all your user accounts, even if just you or your family uses the computer. This helps limit access to any personal information on your computer should it get stolen or should someone come snooping.

   You can also add a password hint, but remember that anyone can see this hint, so if security is an issue, it's best to leave this blank.

7. If you are creating an account for a child or an employee whose Internet usage you want to monitor and record, select Set Up Parental Controls and follow the configuration wizard.

8. If you want, change the user's picture.

9. If you need to create other new accounts, click Manage Another Account.

Before any of these users log on for the first time, you might also want to prepare a customized default user profile, as described later in this chapter in the section "Managing User Profiles."

Vista User Management on a Domain Network

If your Windows Vista computer is part of a Windows domain network, the Users control panel is limited because the intention is that most user accounts will be created and managed by on the domain server(s). And, as a member of a domain, the Users control panel applet no longer lets you create new local user accounts. You can still use it to change your own password and alter other personal account settings. To create or manage other local user accounts, use the Local Users and Groups management tool discussed later in this chapter.

The User Accounts Control Panel on Windows XP

To open the User Accounts control panel applet on Windows XP, click Start, Control Panel, User Accounts. You should see something similar to Figure 8.5.

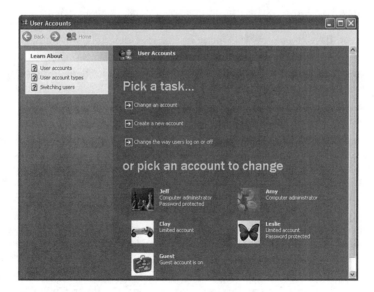

Figure 8.5 The XP User Accounts control panel applet.

The control panel displays an icon for each local user account on this system. You can see details about each of the user accounts, including whether the user has administrative rights and whether the account is password protected. You might also notice in Figure 8.5 that the Guest account is enabled. By clicking on it here, you can change the enabled or disabled status. Holding the mouse pointer over one of the accounts opens a pop-up with additional information about what you can change by going into the account. You must be logged on as a computer administrator to create or modify another user's account.

Tip

On XP, to run the User Accounts control panel as a computer administrator when you're not currently logged on as one, open a command prompt window and type

```
runas /user:Administrator "control nusrmgr.cpl"
```

On XP Home Edition, substitute the name of a computer administrator account for **Administrator**.

Note

Before we go further into this topic, it's important to know that if you are using Windows XP Professional, the one thing the control panel tool *won't* let you do is to put user accounts into the Power Users category. If you want to create power user accounts on XP, create new user accounts as limited users, using the User Accounts Control Panel, and then use the tool described later in this chapter under "The Windows 2000 User Manager, for Vista and XP, Too" to change the accounts to power users. If you have to make changes to the password, picture, and so on later on, you can still use the regular XP control panel tool to do that.

To manage an account, click on its icon. Then use the items in the Tasks list to do the following:

- **Change the Name**—This option changes the user's display name that appears on the Welcome screen and Start menu. (It does *not* change the actual account logon name; for that, you have to use the Management Console, described in "Managing Users from the Management Console.")

- **[Create | Change] a Password**—This option changes depending on whether an account already has an assigned password.

- **Remove the Password**—This option only shows up if a password is currently assigned to the account.

- **Change the Picture**—This option changes the 48×48 pixel graphic associated with the user's account. You can select from a variety of included icons or browse to any other graphic. If the selected graphic is too large to fit in the 48×48 pixels, it will be scaled down to fit. Windows stores these images in folder \Documents and Settings\All Users \Application Data\Microsoft\User Account Pictures.

- **Change the Account Type**—This option allows you to change the account from a Limited account to a computer administrator account or vice versa. This is equivalent to adding or removing the user account from the local Administrators group. To assign a user to other groups (Power Users, for instance), use the method that I'll describe in "Managing Users from the Management Console."

  If you've customized an account's group membership, its type will display as "Unknown account type" in the User Accounts window.

- **Delete the Account**—This option deletes the account, including the user's profile folder. Don't delete an account unless you're sure that you don't need the associated settings. It is safer to *disable* an account until you're sure you don't need it, using the management console interface described shortly.

If you are managing the account to which you are currently logged on, the titles of the Task list changes slightly. For example, one item might say "Change *my* password" rather than "Change *the* password." An additional action also appears:

- **Set Up My Account to Use a .NET Passport**—This option associates a Microsoft .NET Passport account to your local user account, relieving you from manually entering the Passport username and password for .NET services that require authentication through the Passport service. Clicking this option starts a wizard. If you do not currently have a passport, the wizard allows you to create one on the spot, although you must have an active connection to the Internet for this wizard to complete successfully.

Note

Carefully consider the privacy implications before you configure your account to use the Passport feature. If you do, then anyone using your account may automatically have access to any websites or services that use Passport as the logon mechanism. Essentially, you may be giving Windows and Microsoft permission to validate web transactions in your name.

Here is my recommendation for the best way to add new user accounts to your Windows XP computer:

1. Make a list of the accounts you want to create, and the passwords you want to assign to each.

2. Log on as a computer administrator and open the User Accounts control panel.

3. Click Create a New Account. Enter a logon name for this user. I have a habit of using the person's first initial and last name, but you can choose any sort of naming scheme that you want.

4. Select the account type, computer administrator or limited user. See "Which Account Type to Use?" earlier in this chapter if you need help deciding. On Windows XP Home Edition, you must have at least one computer administrator account (in addition to the main Administrator account that remains hidden until you log on in Safe mode).

5. Click on the icon for the new account below the Pick an Account to Change option.

6. Click Create a Password, and enter the password twice as indicated. We recommend that you do create passwords for all of your user accounts, even if just you or your family uses the computer. This helps limit access to any personal information on your computer should it get stolen or should someone come snooping.

   You can also add a password hint, but remember that anyone can see this hint, so if security is an issue, it's best to leave this blank.

7. If you want, change the user's picture.

8. If you need to create other new accounts, click Change Another Account under Related Tasks and repeat steps 3 through 7.

If you are using Windows XP Professional and you want to turn some of the accounts into power user accounts, see "The Windows 2000 User Manager, for Vista and XP, Too," later in this chapter for instructions. You can also use the Local Users and Groups tool, described in "Managing Users from the Management Console" to create new security groups to simplify the job of file security. (On XP Home Edition, you cannot create or use security groups.)

Finally, before any of these users log on for the first time, you might also want to prepare a customized default user profile, as described later in this chapter in the section "Managing User Profiles."

Setting Local Security Policy

In a business setting, you might want to set your computer's local security policy to require good passwords. To do this on Windows Vista, open the Control Panel, and then click System and Maintenance, Administrative Tools, Local Security Policy. You have to confirm the User Account Control prompt.

On XP, log on as a computer administrator and open the Administrative Tools control panel applet, which you'll find in the Control Panel's Performance and Maintenance category. Open the Local Security Policy item, or, if you're not logged on as a computer administrator, right-click Local Security Policy and select Run As.

Now, in the left pane, open Account Policies, and select Account Lockout Policy. In the right pane, double-click the following entries and make the following settings, in this order:

1. Account lockout threshold: 5 invalid logon attempts

2. Account lockout duration: 5 minutes

3. Reset account lockout counter after: 5 minutes

Then in the left pane, select Password Policy, and make the following settings:

> Minimum password length: 8 characters
>
> Password must meet complexity requirements: enabled

You may also want to enable the settings that require employees to change passwords every so many days.

Local Accounts and Password Reset Disks

Administrators can reset the password for any user account, meaning they could potentially change a password, log on as a user, and see all the user's preferences and files. In addition, before Windows XP, if a user could reset your password he would have carte blanche access to everything in the your profile, including stored passwords, encrypted files, and more. Windows XP and Vista handle this differently. If a local administrator forces a password change of a local user account, Windows erases all other passwords associated with the user account, including the security key required to decrypt files encrypted using the included Encrypting File System (EFS). This means that a local administrator can't see your encrypted files, but if you lose your password and need to have your password reset, *you'll lose your encrypted files, too.*

For local accounts, Windows XP and Vista provide a mechanism so that you can protect yourself from this consequence of a forgotten password by creating a *password reset disk*. This floppy disk or removable USB drive lets you log on to your user account without the password and without losing any other associated passwords or EFS keys. Think of it as a physical key to your computer account.

You can create a password disk for your own account only, by following these steps:

1. Insert a blank, formatted floppy into your A: drive, or plug in a removable USB drive.
2. Click Start, Control Panel.
3. On Vista, click User Accounts and Family Safety, and then User Accounts. In the left Tasks pane, click Create a Password Reset Disk.

   On XP, select the icon for your user account, and then click Prevent a Forgotten Password from the Related Tasks list.
4. Follow along with the wizard.
5. Store the completed password reset disk in a secure location.

Remember: Someone who gets hold of this disk has access to your account and all your files, so keep it somewhere safe and secure. Each user must create his or her own password reset disk. However, you will *not* need to re-create this disk if you change your password.

If you have forgotten your password, you can sign on from the Welcome screen using these steps:

1. Attempt to sign on using the Welcome Screen.
2. After the unsuccessful attempt, on XP, click the link marked Did You Forget Your Password? Then click Use Your Password Reset Disk.

   On Vista, click Reset Password.
3. Insert your password reset floppy disk or USB drive.
4. Follow the wizard to reset your password.

Then put the reset disk away in case you need it again in the future.

Note

If you are a domain network user, you can simply contact a domain user administrator to reset your password or unlock your account. On domain accounts, EFS keys are not destroyed when the account is reset, so the password reset disk mechanism is not needed.

Managing Users from the Management Console

On Windows Vista Ultimate, Enterprise, and Business editions, on XP Professional and on Windows 2000, there is an additional tool for user maintenance called the Local Users and Groups Management Console. You can get to it several ways, but these are the easiest:

- Right-click [My] Computer, select Manage, and then select Local Users and Groups.
- Type **start lusrmgr.msc** at the command prompt.

The display will look something like that shown in Figure 8.6.

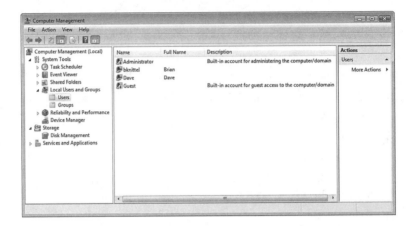

Figure 8.6 The Local Users and Groups Management Console gives you fine-grained control over security group membership.

When you're in the MMC, you can right-click on either the Users or Groups folders in the left pane to view and create new users and groups. You can double-click an individual user or group to manage properties related to that object, and you can right-click a user or group to rename or delete the object.

You can also use this tool to create new local security groups. If, for instance, you want only certain employees to have access to your accounting files, you might create a group named Accounting. Add the appropriate users to this new group. Then edit the file security settings for the folders that hold your accounting files and other sensitive financial files, and be sure that only the groups Accounting and Administrators have read and write access.

This will be easier to maintain than adding each individual user to several folders' access lists. In the future, to grant or deny someone access to the folders, you need only add or remove him from the Accounting group, rather than add or remove him from several different folders.

To create a new group, right-click Groups in the left pane, and select New Group. Type in a name for the group, such as "Accounting," and a short description. Click Create to save the new group.

To add users to a group, follow these steps:

1. In the Groups list, double-click the desired group name.

2. Click Add, and under Enter the Object Names to Select, enter the desired usernames separated by semicolons.

   Alternatively, you can click Advanced and Find Now to get a list of names. Right-click any you want to add, and then click OK.

3. Click OK, and then click OK again to save the changes.

Now, you can view the security properties for your sensitive folders or files, click Edit to edit the access permissions, and click Add to add your new group. Be sure to uncheck permissions you don't want to grant to the groups Users or Everyone, if you use this method.

Managing Users on Another Computer

If you want to connect to a different computer to manage local users and groups, simply right-click Computer Management (Local) in the left pane on the screen depicted in Figure 8.6, select Connect to Another Computer, and enter the computer name. Now all options in the Computer Management MMC reflect the configuration of the remote system, and you can manage the users and groups in the same way as on the local system; however, to do this, you must be currently logged on to your computer using a login name and password that is a valid computer administrator account on the remote computer.

The Windows 2000 User Manager, for Vista and XP, Too

If you are using Windows 2000 Professional, your Users control panel dialog looks like the one shown in Figure 8.7.

Figure 8.7 The Windows 2000 User Manager control panel applet.

Interestingly, it's also available on Windows XP and Vista, although you have to perform a little trick to bring it up. It has two very important uses: You can use it to make Windows log on automatically, and on XP Professional, you can use it to easily create power user accounts. To start it up, open a command prompt window with Start, All Programs, Accessories, Command Prompt, and type

```
control userpasswords2
```

If you are not currently logged on as a computer administrator, you will be prompted to enter an administrator account name and password, on both XP and Vista.

To change the security level of an existing account, select the name from the user list and click Properties. Select the Group Membership tab, and select one of the following categories:

- **Standard User**—Select this category to make the account a power user account. This is the best account type for day-to-day use on XP, although it's not especially useful on Vista, as discussed earlier in this chapter.

- **Restricted User**—This is what Windows XP calls a limited user and Vista calls a standard user. Select this account type for guests, kids, or other people that you want to let use your computer, but not make configuration changes.

- **Other**—To create an administrator account, check Others, and then select Administrators from the list.

Click OK to save your settings. If you modify your own account, the change won't take effect until you log off and back on again.

Caution

If you use this tool to change accounts from being administrators to lower levels, be *sure* to leave *at least* one other account as an administrator. If you inadvertently reduce the privilege of all accounts, on XP Home and on Vista, you may be able to gain access to the main administrator account by booting in Safe mode. Otherwise, you'll have to reinstall Windows to regain administrative control.

You can also use this tool to assign a password to the administrator account on Windows XP Home Edition. On Home Edition, there is an account with the name Administrator, which is only available when you boot Windows in Safe mode. By default, it has no password.

Microsoft did this so that even if you forget the password of the computer administrator account(s) you've set up yourself, you can still get into your computer. The downside is that *anyone* can boot your computer in Safe mode, select this administrator account, and gain access to every file on your computer. If this concerns you, select Administrator from the list of users, and click Reset Password.

Remember that if you forget the password to the administrator account, you may not be able to manage Windows.

Another important use for this dialog is to instruct Windows to log on automatically when it's turned on and started up. To set this up, uncheck Users Must Enter a User Name and Password to Use This Computer. Click Apply, and Windows will prompt you for a username and password. This account will sign on automatically when Windows starts up.

Note

If you enter the wrong password, all that happens is that the automatic logon fails and Windows stops at the Welcome screen during startup.

You must also disable the requirement that users have to type Ctrl+Alt+Del before logging on. To do this, see the section "Controlling How Users Log On and Off" later in the chapter.

Managing Users from the Command Prompt

You can manage user accounts from the Command Prompt as well as from the GUI. I tend to use this method when doing quick, simple changes to user accounts, or when creating a large number of accounts for, say, a classroom computer. Here are some commands that you might find handy:

To list all local users:

```
net user
```

To list all local security groups:

```
net localgroup
```

To show all members of a local group:

```
net localgroup groupname
```

To create a local user account (it's automatically added to the Users local group):

```
net user username password /add
```

To add a local user to a local group:

```
net localgroup groupname username /add
```

To modify an existing local user's password:

```
net user username newpassword
```

To delete a local user account (but not the user's profile folder):

```
net user username /del
```

Of course, the commands that create or modify accounts require administrator privileges. On Windows Vista, you must use an *elevated command prompt* window to issue them. On XP, you have to be logged on as a computer administrator to create or modify other users' accounts.

▶▶ To learn about elevated command prompts, **see** "User Account Control and the Command Line," **p. 548**.

Putting them together, you might use these commands to create a new power user account on XP:

```
net user bknittel secretpassword /add
net localgroup "Power Users" bknittel /add
```

Or use these commands to delete one:

```
net user bknittel /del
rd "c:\Users\bknittel*" /s
```

That last command is "iffy"—if a folder with your username already existed in the Users folder when you created the account, or if you log on to a Windows domain network, Windows sometimes adds .XXX to the user profile folder name, where XXX is the computer or domain name. Thus, you can't always be sure of the name of the folder to delete.

Automating User Management

When you have many user accounts to create or modify, you should look to Windows automation tools to help simplify the job and minimize errors due to typing mistakes. You can use the command-line tools I mentioned previously inside batch files as an excellent means of getting the job done. You can also use Windows Script Host (WSH). WSH is by far the more flexible of the two options. By tying in to the Active Directory Service Interfaces (ADSI), you can create, read, or modify any information or configuration options available for a user account.

Here's an example. A common task that help desk personnel often require is the ability to easily unlock user accounts after a user has entered too many incorrect passwords. The following script file named unlock.vbs prompts for an account name and unlocks the account. From the command line, unlock runs the script. The user who is running the script must have the rights to unlock the target account.

```
Set WshNetwork = WScript.CreateObject("Wscript.Network")

CurDomName = WshNetwork.UserDomain
DomainName = InputBox("Enter the Domain Name", "Domain", CurDomName)
UserName   = InputBox("Enter the account name to unlock", "User ID")

on error resume next

Set myUser = GetObject("WinNT://" & DomainName & "/" & UserName & "")

If myUser is Nothing Then
    msgbox "Unable to find user account " & DomainName & "\" & UserName
ElseIf myUser.IsAccountLocked Then
    myUser.IsAccountLocked = 0
    myUser.SetInfo
    If Err.Number then
        msgbox "Unable to unlock account, you may not have permission"
    Else
        msgbox UserName & " is now unlocked"
    End If
Else
    msgbox UserName & " is already unlocked"
End if
```

For more on this topic, you might consider some of these excellent references:

> *Windows Vista Guide to Scripting, Automation, and Command Line Tools* by Brian Knittel; ISBN 0789737280 (our favorite, of course!), due out in late 2008, or its predecessor, *Windows XP Under the Hood*

> *Windows NT/2000 ADSI Scripting for System Administrators* by Thomas Eck; ISBN 1578702194

> *Windows 2000 Windows Script Host* by Tim Hill; ISBN 1578701392

You'll also find some downloadable examples of administrative scripts at InformIT.com (www.informit.com) and the Microsoft Technet Script Center (www.microsoft.com/technet/scriptcenter). Microsoft has posted a page describing new scriptable management capabilities added to Windows Vista at www.microsoft.com/technet/scriptcenter/hubs/vista.mspx. I also recommend taking a look at Andrew Clinick's administrative scripts from the Microsoft TechEd 2000 conference. The "Script in Orlando" article and source code are available for download at msdn.microsoft.com/en-us/library/ms974582.aspx.

Managing User Profiles

A *user profile* is a folder that contains all of a user's personalized information: the Registry file that contains his customized settings, his `Desktop` and `[My] Documents` folders, and application data such as the Outlook Express address list and email database. By default, a user's profile is a folder with the same name as the user's login name, under `\Documents and Settings` on Windows XP and under `\Users` on Windows Vista.

The organization of the profile folders is very different on XP and Vista. The main difference is that on Vista, Microsoft has taken pains to provide separate data that belongs to users from data that belongs to the computer. Thanks to the Internet, we are moving toward a computing world where people are starting to expect their data, email, and documents to be available from any computer, anytime, anywhere. To make this possible, your data has to be stored in a centralized place, reachable from anywhere, or at least, a copy has to be sent to a centralized storage facility whenever you create or modify a document. The new Vista user profile organization makes this easier to achieve because "user data" (like email and documents) is stored in one set of folders, and "computer data" (like downloaded files, temporary files and cached Internet graphics) is stored in a separate set of folders. This distinction is important already on corporate domain networks that provide roaming user profiles, and it will become more important for everyone as new online services are developed. These same considerations apply to making backups more effective. Keeping useful data separate from "discardable" data makes backups faster and easier to perform, and that makes them more likely to be done on a regular basis.

On a standard Vista installation, assuming that Windows is installed on drive C:, the drive's directory structure looks like this:

```
C:\
    Windows
    Program Data
    Program Files
    Users
        myname          ...(one folder per user account, created
        yourname            after logging on for the first time)
        ...
        Default
        Public
```

Each of the folders under `\Users` is a user profile folder. For example, in the example just given, `\Users\myname` and `\Users\yourname` are profiles. Each user's data is stored in subfolders under the profile, according to the layout in Table 8.7.

Table 8.7   Subfolders in a Vista User Profile

Folder Name	Purpose
AppData (hidden folder)	Per-user application data. Subfolders Local, **LocalLow**, and **Roaming** are used to separate data that will never leave this computer from data that should be copied back to a central server if the account is on a corporate network with roaming profiles.
Contacts	Address book data.
Desktop	Files and shortcuts that appear on the desktop.
Documents	Personal documents. This folder was named **My Documents** in Windows XP.
Downloads	Files downloaded from the Internet.
Favorites	Favorites links for Internet Explorer.
Links	Shortcuts to important Windows folders.
Music	Personal folder for music files.
Pictures	Personal folder for images.
Saved Games	Data saved by games.
Searches	Saved search queries.
Videos	Personal folder for multimedia files.

Information that is meant to be shared by *all* users is stored under either the \ProgramData folder or the \Users\Public folder. The distinction between the two is that \Users\Public is meant to hold files that are of direct interest to humans (such as documents, pictures, video and so on), whereas \Program Data is meant to hold support data for applications (fonts, game data, and so on).

Table 8.8 shows the correspondence between the new Vista profile structure and the XP structure.

Table 8.8   Vista and XP User Profile Structures

Windows Vista Folders Under \Users	Windows XP Equivalent Folders Under \Documents and Settings
Username	*Username*
AppData	
Local	*Username*\Local Settings
Temp	*Username*\Local Settings\Temp
VirtualStore	
LocalLow	
Roaming	*Username*\Application Data
Microsoft	
Windows	
Cookies	*Username*\Cookies
Network Shortcuts	*Username*\NetHood
Printer Shortcuts	*Username*\PrintHood
Recent	*Username*\Recent

Windows Vista **Folders Under** \Users	**Windows XP Equivalent** **Folders Under** \Documents and Settings
SendTo	*Username*\SendTo
Start Menu	*Username*\Start Menu
Templates	*Username*\Templates
Themes	
Contacts	
Desktop	*Username*\Desktop
Documents	*Username*\My Documents[*]
Downloads	
Favorites	*Username*\Favorites
Links	
Music	*Username*\My Documents\My Music*
Pictures	*Username*\My Documents\My Pictures*
Saved Games	
Searches	
Videos	
Public	
Desktop°	All Users\Desktop
Documents	All Users\Documents⁺
Downloads	
Favorites	All Users\Favorites
Music	All Users\Documents\My Music
Pictures	All Users\Documents\My Pictures
Recorded TV	
Videos	All Users\Documents\My Videos
Default	Default User
(same subfolders as standard user)	(same subfolders as standard user)
Windows Vista **Folders Under** \ProgramData	**Windows XP Equivalent** **Folders Under** \Documents and Settings
Microsoft	All Users\Application Data
Windows	
Start Menu	All Users\Start Menu
Templates	All Users\Templates

*Displayed in Windows Explorer as **My Documents** or **Username's Documents** and so on.
+Displayed in Windows Explorer as **Shared Documents.**
° Displayed in Windows Explorer as Public Desktop, Public Documents, and so on

Windows Vista setup creates *junction points* and *symbolic links* on the Windows drive that provide a measure of compatibility with applications that were hard-wired to expect the Windows XP user profile structure. Junction points and symbolic links are special virtual folders that point to other, real folders. For example, if an application attempts to read from folder \Documents and

Settings, Vista will show it the contents of \Users. Table 8.9 lists the junction points and symbolic links that are installed in Windows Vista. Don't delete these unusual folder entries, and to the extent possible, just forget that they exist. They are hidden, system files by default, in fact, so you will only see them when you instruct Windows Explorer or the dir command line command to display hidden and system files.

Table 8.9   Compatibility Junction Points and Symbolic Links

Junction or Link	Target Folder
\Documents and Settings	\Users
\Users	
Username	
Application Data	\Users*username*\AppData\Roaming
Cookies	\Users*username*\AppData\Roaming\Microsoft\Windows\Cookies
Local Settings	\Users*username*\AppData\Local
My Documents	\Users*username*\Documents
NetHood	\Users*username*\AppData\Roaming\Microsoft\Windows\Network Shortcuts
PrintHood	\Users*username*\AppData\Roaming\Microsoft\Windows\Printer Shortcuts
Recent	\Users*username*\AppData\Roaming\Microsoft\Windows\Recent
SendTo	\Users*username*\AppData\Roaming\Microsoft\Windows\SendTo
Templates	\Users*username*\AppData\Roaming\Microsoft\Windows\Templates
All Users	\ProgramData
\ProgramData	
Application Data	\ProgramData
Desktop	\Users\Public\Desktop
Documents	\Users\Public\Documents
Favorites	\Users\Public\Favorites
Start Menu	\ProgramData\Microsoft\Windows\StartMenu
Templates	\ProgramData\Microsoft\Windows\Templates

Here is an example of how this set of junction points and links assists older applications. If an application attempts to access the contents of the folder \Documents and Settings\All Users\Start Menu, the following folder name transformation takes place:

1. \Documents and Settings is translated to \Users, so the path becomes \Users\All Users\Start Menu.

2. Next, \All Users is translated to \Program Data, so the path becomes \Program Data\Start Menu.

3. Finally, \ProgramData\StartMenu is translated to \ProgramData\Microsoft\Windows\StartMenu.

The application is shown the contents of this final folder name. Thus, it sees the Start menu items in the folder used by Vista, even though it used the pathname used by XP.

When you create a new user account, the user's profile folder is *not* created right away. Instead, it's created when the user logs on for the first time, and it's copied from the default user profile stored on XP in \Documents and Settings\Default User and on Vista in \Users\Default. I'll talk more about this in a moment.

Windows provides a means of managing user profiles. To bring it up on XP, right-click My Computer, select Properties, and then select the Advanced tab. On Vista, right-click Computer, select Properties, click Advanced System Settings, and approve the User Account Control prompt. Then, on either OS, click the Settings button in the User Profiles box. You should see something similar to Figure 8.8.

Figure 8.8   The User Profiles management dialog.

Notice the three buttons:

- **Change Type**—This configures whether the selected user will use the network-stored roaming profile folder (for domain networks only) or a locally stored profile folder.

- **Delete**—This permanently deletes the selected profile but not the user's account. If the user should log back on, a new profile folder will be created.

- **Copy To**—This copies the selected profile to another profile directory, overwriting the files and settings in the destination profile with those in the selected users' profile.

One important reason to know about user profiles is that you can customize the default profile used for new accounts on your computer.

Configuring a Default User Profile

If you aren't happy with the initial desktop and other settings created for each user at the time of logon, you can configure a profile and copy it into the default user profile. Subsequently, new users who log on to the system for the first time will get your desired settings, rather than the default profile provided out of the box. Here's how to do it:

1. Create a new user account (someone without an existing personal profile on the system) and log on to that account.

2. Make all the changes you want included in the default profile. For example, you can set a default screensaver configuration, add some default favorites, set up a default search provider for Internet Explorer, drop some shortcuts on the desktop, reorganize the shortcuts on the Start bar, set the desktop background, and so on. You can also delete the sample files in the Documents and Pictures folders, or create new files and folders.

3. Log off from this user account and log back in as with a computer administrator account. Note that you *must* log off from the new account in order to free the associated Registry files; doing a fast user switch does not work.

4. On Vista, click Start, Computer, and then press and release the Alt key. On XP, click Start, My Computer. Then, on either OS, select Tools, Folder Options, and go to the View tab. Check Show Hidden Files and Folders and click OK. Otherwise, you will not be able to see the Default User folder.

5. Open the User Profiles dialog box as described earlier in "Managing User Profiles."

6. Select the profile of the user you just configured, and click the Copy To button. (If the Copy To button is grayed out, restart Windows and try again. Sometimes Windows keeps the profile's Registry files locked for a while, and restarting is the quickest way around this.)

7. Click Browse. On XP, browse to \Documents and Settings\Default User on the drive on which Windows is installed (usually C:). On Vista, browse to \Users\Default. Then click OK. Click OK again to close the Copy To dialog. You have to confirm overwriting the default profile.

Now, when you log on as a user who has not previously logged on to this computer, the initial settings will come from the prepared default profile.

Roaming User Profiles

Roaming profiles are available on domain networks only. A roaming profile is a profile folder created by a domain administrator and stored on a network server. When you log on using a domain account that is configured with a roaming user profile, the profile folders are copied from the network to the computer you are using. When you log out, any changes to your documents or profile settings are copied back to the domain server, so those changes will be available on subsequent logins from different systems. It's a nifty idea—your preferences, desktop, and documents can literally follow you anywhere in the world.

Note

Some relatively unimportant folders are *not* copied back and forth between the domain server and a local computer to save time and network traffic. By default, these folders include `Local Settings`, `Temp`, `Temporary Internet Files`, and the `History` folder. The list of ignored folders is stored in the Registry under `HKEY_CURRENT_USER\Software\Microsoft\Windows NT\CurrentVersion\Winlogon\ExcludeProfileDirs`, which can be configured per-user. For example, on Vista, the `AppData\Local`, `AppData\LocalLow`, and `Recycle Bin` folders are excluded.

Controlling How Users Log On and Off

Although Windows 9x treated user authentication (logging on) as an option, user tracking is deeply ingrained in the Windows NT product line that led to Windows XP and Vista—a user must always log on before the Windows desktop can appear. Table 8.10 lists the various mechanisms available on various Windows configurations.

Table 8.10   Logon Options Available for Windows

Windows Version	Classic Logon Dialog	Welcome Screen	Vista Logon Screen	Automatic Logon
2000 Professional, any network	✓			✓
XP, standalone or workgroup	✓	✓		✓
XP Pro, domain member	✓			
Vista, standalone or workgroup		✓	✓	✓
Vista Business/Enterprise/ Ultimate, domain member			✓	

The logon methods are as follows:

- The **classic logon dialog** requires you to type in a username and password. On computers that are members of a domain network, you must also enter a Windows domain name. The username and domain name can be entered in the form *domainname\username* or *username@domain*. To use a local account, enter ***computername\username*** or ***username@computername***.

- The **Welcome screen** provides a list of cute icons, one for each available local account. On Windows XP, you can instruct Windows to show or not show specific accounts on the Welcome screen by using the Registry Editor, as described later in this chapter in "Showing and Hiding Accounts on the Welcome Screen." To log on to any hidden account, you must press Ctrl+Alt+Del twice to bring up the classic logon dialog. You can also entirely disable the Welcome screen on XP. The XP Welcome screen is automatically disabled when the computer is joined to a domain network. In these cases, Windows displays the classic logon dialog.

  On Vista, you cannot determine which accounts are shown or hidden on the Welcome screen.

- The **Vista Logon screen** replaces the classic logon dialog on Vista computers that are members of a domain network. It has flashy graphics like the Welcome screen, but it shows only the icon of the last user to log on. To use another account, you must click Switch User. You are then prompted to type in an account name, password, and domain name, as in the classic logon dialog. It's rather confusing to see "Switch User" because this seems to imply that the first account is still logged on, but it isn't necessarily so.

You can also tell Vista to use the Logon screen even if you are not a member of a domain network, on any version of Vista, by changing a security policy setting using these steps:

1. Click Start, type `secpol.msc` into the Search box, and press Enter.

2. In the left pane, open the Local Policies list, and select Security Options.

3. In the right pane, double-click Interactive Logon: Do Not Display Last User Name.

4. Select Enabled, click OK, and close the Local Security Policy window.

With this setting in effect, the Welcome Screen is disabled and the Vista Logon screen displays boxes into which you must type a username and password. There is no list of account names or icons.

■ On Windows 2000, and on XP and Vista computers that are not part of a domain network, you can instruct Windows to **automatically log on**, using a specified username and password upon startup. The logon process still takes place; it just doesn't require user interaction for the first logon after startup. We'll discuss this option later in the chapter.

Finally, you can also enable or disable the requirement that users must press Ctrl+Alt+Del before they can log on. It's safer to make this a requirement because it is then impossible for a rogue program to mimic the logon dialog or Welcome screen and fool you into giving up your password. When you press Ctrl+Alt+Del, the real Windows logon/security system takes over, and no program can intercept or interfere with this.

The following sections describe how to enable and disable these logon mechanisms on various versions of Windows.

Windows 2000 Professional

To configure logons on Windows 2000, log on as an administrator and run the Users and Passwords control panel. (Alternately, open a Command Prompt window and type `control userpasswords`).

To configure the Ctrl+Alt+Del requirement, select the Advanced tab, and check or uncheck Require Users to Press Ctrl+Alt+Delete.

To enable automatic logon, see the "Enabling Automatic Logon" section later in this chapter.

Windows XP, Standalone or Workgroup Network

To choose the logon method, log on as a computer administrator, open the User Accounts applet under the Control Panel, and select Change the Way Users Log On or Off. To use the Logon dialog, uncheck both Use Fast User Switching and Use the Welcome Screen. To use the Welcome screen, check both options.

To configure the Ctrl+Alt+Del requirement, open a Command Prompt window and type the command `control userpasswords2`. Select the Advanced tab and check or uncheck the box labeled

Require Users to Press Ctrl+Alt+Delete. When enabled, this option applies only to the Classic logon method, so it only makes sense to enable this when you have also disabled the Welcome screen or if the computer is a member of a domain network.

To enable automatic logon, see the section "Enabling Automatic Logon" later in this chapter.

Windows XP, Domain Network

The Welcome screen is not used on XP when the computer is a member of a domain network.

To configure the Ctrl+Alt+Del requirement, open a Command Prompt window and run the command `control userpasswords2`. Select the Advanced tab and check or uncheck the box labeled Require Users to Press Ctrl+Alt+Delete.

Windows Vista, Standalone or Workgroup Network

The Welcome screen cannot be disabled on Windows Vista in this configuration.

To configure the Ctrl+Alt+Del requirement, open a Command Prompt window and run the command `control userpasswords2`. Select the Advanced tab and check or uncheck the box labeled Require Users to Press Ctrl+Alt+Delete.

To enable automatic logon, see section "Enabling Automatic Logon" later in this chapter.

Windows Vista, Domain Network

To configure the Ctrl+Alt+Del requirement, open the Control Panel and select User Accounts. Select Give Other Users Access to This Computer. Select the Advanced tab and check or uncheck the box labeled Require Users to Press Ctrl+Alt+Delete.

Logging on as Administrator

The Welcome screen does not normally list the built-in local Administrator account. The Administrator account is enabled and appears on the Welcome screen only under circumstances that depend on the version of Windows you're using:

- On XP Pro, the account is enabled by default, but appears on the Welcome screen only if no other computer administrator user is defined. If you want, you can force it to be displayed even if another computer administrator account is defined, as I'll explain in the next section.

- On XP Home, the account is enabled only when the computer is booted in Safe mode. And even in Safe mode, Administrator appears on the welcome screen only if no other computer administrator is defined. On the various Home versions, by default, there is no password on the Administrator account.

- On all versions of Windows Vista, the Administrator account is enabled only if you upgraded your computer from XP Professional *and* Administrator was the only computer administrator account defined before the upgrade *and* the computer is not a member of a domain network. In this one case, the Administrator is always available, and User Account Control is enabled when it's in use.

  Otherwise, on all Vista versions, the Administrator account is disabled unless the computer is booted in Safe mode *and* no other computer administrator account is defined. This means that if you forget the password to your own Administrator account(s), you *cannot* fix things by booting up in Safe mode!

- Furthermore, on Vista computers that are joined to a Domain network, the built-in Administrator account is disabled under *all* circumstances. For administrative work, you must log on using an account that is a member of the Local Administrators or domain administrators groups. (If the computer is having problems, a Domain Administrator can log on using cached credentials, or may need to boot up in Safe Mode with Networking to gain access to the network.)

Although this explanation may seem needlessly complicated, Microsoft's intentions are sound: It's trying to balance the need to let you recover from disasters with the need to make computers more secure. It's no good if any bozo can just boot your computer up in Safe mode and gain access to all of your files.

Now, on XP, if you don't know the passwords to any of the computer Administrator accounts displayed on the Welcome screen, or if none of the displayed accounts have administrative privileges but you need to perform some administrative function, you can get around the problem this way:

- On XP Pro, press Ctrl+Alt+Del twice at the Welcome screen to display the classic logon dialog. Enter Administrator as the username, and enter the administrator password to log on.
- On XP Home, restart the computer in Safe mode. Select the Administrator account. You can then make one of your computer's user accounts a computer administrator.

On Vista, if you have somehow deleted or disabled the last Administrator-level account, boot the computer in Safe mode. Then

- If the Administrator account appears on the Welcome screen, select it, and use the Control Panel to create or enable an administrator-type account.
- If the Administrator account does *not* appear, you're in trouble. If your computer is a member of a domain network, a domain administrator can help you. Otherwise, it means that there is still an active Administrator-type account. If you've forgotten its password, you'll have to follow the instructions in "If You've Forgotten Your Password" later in this chapter.

Remember that on XP you can often save yourself the trouble of actually logging on as Administrator; you can right-click a shortcut and select Run As, or use the runas command at the command prompt, to run programs with administrator privileges. On Vista, User Account Control makes it easy to run administrative tools from any user account.

▶▶ For more information about the runas command, **see** "runas," **p. 553**.

Showing and Hiding Accounts on the Welcome Screen

The Welcome screen normally displays all regular and computer administrator user accounts except the built-in Administrator account. There are some exceptions to this that depend on the version of Windows you're running. This section explains these differences.

On Windows XP

On XP, by default, the Administrator account and system service accounts are not shown on the Welcome screen, except in the following circumstances:

- On XP Pro, the Administrator account is not normally shown unless there are no other computer administrator accounts. You can force it to be shown, as discussed shortly.
- On XP Home, the Administrator account is not shown unless there are no other computer administrator accounts *and* the computer was started in Safe mode.

You can instruct Windows XP to display the Administrator account or to show or remove specific user accounts by editing the Registry key `HKEY_LOCAL_MACHINE\SOFTWARE\Microsoft\Windows NT\CurrentVersion\Winlogon\SpecialAccounts\UserList`. (The Registry is discussed in Chapter 6, "Tweaking and Tuning Windows.") This key holds values that determine which accounts are omitted from the Welcome screen.

The `UserList` key contains values that name the accounts to be hidden, such as Administrator, HelpAssistant, and NetShowServices. The associated values determine how the account is displayed:

Value	Result
0	Account will not be shown.
1	Account will be shown.
0x00010000	Any account whose name starts with the same letters as the value name will not be shown.

To add the Administrator account to the XP Pro Welcome screen, log on as an administrator and run `regedit`. Open the key indicated earlier and change the `Administrator` value from `0` to `1`. To hide a user account, add a new DWORD value with the same name as the user's logon name, and enter the numeric value `0`.

You can log on to a hidden account by pressing Ctrl+Alt+Del twice at the Welcome screen to display the Logon dialog.

On Vista

On Windows Vista, account appearance on the Welcome Screen is based on membership in the Users security group, and these rules:

- Accounts that are members of the group Users appear on the Welcome screen, except…
- The Administrator account does not appear, unless there are no other Administrator-type accounts *and* the computer was started in Safe Mode.

If you want to hide a Vista account from the Welcome screen (for example, an account that you use only to run a scheduled task or service), you can hide it using the instructions for hiding an account on XP, as discussed in the previous section. Alternatively, you can remove the account from the Users group. In this case, however, you have to be sure that the account still has access to necessary files and programs through the Everyone entry or through explicitly granted access permissions.

Fast User Switching

Windows XP and Vista have a feature called Fast User Switching that lets you log on to other accounts without logging off from the first. You might compare this to having a big lazy susan on your desk—instead of cleaning off your desk so someone else can work at it, you just turn it around, leaving your original workspace intact, although out of reach. This is almost exactly what Fast User Switching does. When you switch users, you remain logged in and your programs even keep running; they're just not visible while someone else's desktop is displayed. Several different people can trade off use of the computer using this technique.

Fast User Switching is useful in several different scenarios:

- You can use it to temporarily log on as a computer administrator to install software, without having to log off from your primary account. (This is helpful on XP, but Vista User Account Control lets you do this without the trouble of switching users.)

- You can let someone else use your computer while your own applications run uninterrupted.

- You can leave your computer in a locked state, at the Welcome screen, while your applications continue to run. You can then come back later, or even connect from another location using Remote Desktop Connection, and in either case pick up exactly where you left off.

To Switch User on XP, click Start, Log Off, Switch User. On Vista, click Start, click the arrow at the bottom right of the Start menu, and select Switch User. Or, on either OS, you can just use the Windows+L keyboard shortcut.

This brings you back to the Welcome screen. From here, you can log back on to your original account to reconnect with your original session, or you can log on as another user.

Note

By default, you'll get kicked back to the Welcome screen if your screensaver has time to activate. If you don't like having to sign back on after clearing the screensaver, right-click the desktop, select Properties, view the Screen Saver tab, and uncheck On Resume, Display the Welcome Screen.

I recommend saving any open documents before switching users. If another user shuts Windows down or manages to crash the system, your data could be lost if you have not saved it.

And keep this in mind: You already know that running multiple applications requires more system resources. Running multiple applications for multiple concurrent users takes even more. Things will run more smoothly if you have a fast processor and a lot of RAM. Also, some applications may not work correctly in this new multiuser environment. If the application you are using was written to the Microsoft Windows XP or Vista Logo standards (see www.microsoft.com/winlogo for details), it should behave properly.

If you are using Windows XP and Fast User Switching doesn't seem to be available on your computer, you may have to make a trade-off. Several Windows XP features are mutually exclusive with Fast User Switching*:

- **Domain Networks**—If your computer is a member of a corporate domain network, Fast User Switching is not available, period. Bummer!

- **Login Dialog**—If you have disabled the Welcome screen and use the Login Dialog to log on, Fast User Switching is not available. You can get Fast User Switching by re-enabling the Welcome screen, as discussed previously.

- **Offline Files**—If you have enabled Offline File access (network caching), Fast User Switching is not available. You must choose between one and the other. To disable Offline Files, open Windows Explorer and select Tools, Folder Options. Use the Offline Files tab to make the change, and then enable Fast User Switching.

- **Serial Keys**—This accessibility feature is not useable with Fast User Switching and vice versa. Serial Keys provides support for alternative input devices such as puff and sip devices, switch-driven input devices, and other serial-based keyboard or mouse alternatives.

To enable Fast User Switching on Windows XP, log on as a computer administrator. Disable any competing features, and then open the User Accounts control panel applet. Select the task Change the Way Users Log On or Off, and then check Use Fast User Switching. If you want to disable it, follow the same steps but uncheck the option. Yours must be the only account currently logged on.

Note

You should know that Fast User Switching is closely related to the Remote Desktop service. You'll get kicked back to the Welcome screen if someone else logs on to your computer using Remote Desktop Connection while you're working. If the remote user logs on to a different account than you were using, they just get their usual desktop. If they log on to your account, they see your desktop and running applications—in essence they just take over your session.

Enabling Automatic Logon

You can't make Windows give up on the concept of user accounts, but you *can* tell Windows to log on to one specified account automatically when it boots up. You might want to do this in a kiosk environment, in an industrial control installation where the computer's job is simply to run some specialized software, or in a *very* trusting home or work environment with just one user.

Note

Automatic logon can't be enabled on a Windows XP or Vista computer that is a member of a domain network.

You must not enable the Require Users to Press Ctrl+Alt+Delete option if you want to enable automatic logon.

To bypass the Welcome screen or logon dialog, follow one of these procedures:

- On a standalone or workgroup Windows 2000 computer, log on as Administrator, and open the Users and Passwords control panel.

- On Windows XP, log on as a computer administrator. Open a command prompt window, type the command **control userpasswords2**, and press Enter.

- On Vista, open a command prompt window, type the command **control userpasswords2**, and then press Enter. Confirm the User Account Control prompt.

These restrictions don't apply to Windows Vista.

Select the Users tab. Uncheck Users Must Enter a User Name and Password to Use This Computer and click OK. You are prompted for a username and password. If the account has no password, leave the password fields blank.

Caution

When you set up automatic logon, the password is stored in the Registry in plain view of anyone who uses the computer. Clearly, this isn't as big a security risk as having a computer that makes itself available to any passerby, so that's not the problem. It *is* a problem if this username and password are valid on any other computer. Thus, if you do need to use automatic logon, be sure to set up and use an account and password used *only* for this one purpose.

The next time Windows boots up, it will automatically log on using this account information. You can use shortcuts placed in the Startup folder to automatically run applications. And you can use Local Security Policy to disable any features you don't want this unprotected computer to make available.

To prevent the automatic logon, hold down the Shift key while Windows starts up.

By default, the automatic logon occurs only when Windows first starts up. If necessary for your application, you can instruct Windows to immediately log back on to the specified account whenever a logoff occurs. To do this, create a REG_SZ registry value named ForceAutoLogon in HKEY_LOCAL_MACHINE\SOFTWARE\Microsoft\Windows NT\CurrentVersion\Winlogon, and set the value to 1. To suppress the automatic re-logon, press and hold the Shift key as you log off.

In any case, on Vista and XP, you can use Switch User to log on to another account whenever necessary.

To change Windows back so that it presents the Welcome screen or logon dialog, follow the procedure listed previously, but this time check Users Must Enter a User Name.

Dealing with a Lost Password

It will eventually happen that you or one of your users will forget his password, or worse, the Administrator password.

In this case, there are only a few things you can do. You should try them in the following order.

1. If the user created a Password Reset disk as discussed earlier, use it as described earlier in "Local Accounts and Password Reset Disks" to log on. The first thing that the user should do after that is to set a new password.

2. On a domain network, the network administrator can reset the password for any domain account. For standalone computers, workgroup computers, or local accounts, continue....

3. All the remaining options result in the user losing his or her encrypted files and stored passwords, if any. If there *are* any encrypted files, now is the time to stop and try to remember that password one more time.

4. On XP Home Edition, boot your computer in Safe mode. From the Welcome Screen, select the Administrator account, which by default has no password. Use the Users control panel applet to reset the password on the desired account.

5. If you have access to any computer administrator account, log on using that account, and use the User Accounts control panel to change the other account's password, or remove the password entirely. Then the user can log on and select a new password.

If it's the Administrator account password you're trying to reset, and Administrator doesn't appear in the User Accounts control panel, use the Local Users and Groups Management Console, described earlier. Open the Users list, right-click Administrator, and select Set Password.

6. If you get here, it means you have no way to log on as a computer administrator. Oh dear. Things get very dicey from here on down.

One way to reset the Administrator password is to use a special-purpose "cracking" tool developed just for this purpose. You can visit www.winternals.com and purchase ERD Commander or the entire Administrator's Pak package. Windows XP/2000/NT Key from LostPassword.com also works well. Both programs require you to boot up from a floppy disk or CD, which runs a program that clears out the Administrator password. I know of three other such programs, although I haven't personally tested them: NTAccess from www.sunbelt-software.com NTAccess (same name, different program) from www.mirider.com, and Emergency Boot CD from ebcd.pcministry.com.

7. If you have a second hard drive or disk partition on your hard drive with at least 2GB of free space, you can install a second copy of Windows into the alternative partition or drive, and boot it up. You can then copy files from the original installation, or reset the permissions on the original files so that any other user can read them. This doesn't fix the lost password problem but it does let you rescue your data.

8. Equivalently, you can remove your hard drive and install it in another computer running Windows XP or 2000, and copy or at least unsecure your files.

9. Finally, you can perform a clean install of Windows on your original disk partition. This will erase all of your existing user accounts and preferences, and you will have to reinstall your applications. But your files will be intact. When you re-create user accounts, Windows will create new profile folders with different names. Files in the previous installation's [My] Documents folders will be the original profile folders. You'll have to use Windows Explorer to dig into \Documents and Settings (on XP), or \Users (on Vista) to find them. You probably need to take ownership of the profile folders before you can edit their permissions to let you see into them.

Prevention is the best medicine in this case, so you might want to take a minute now to create a password reset disk for your personal account and your computer's Administrator account. If you manage many computers, it also can't hurt to get a copy of the Administrator Pak from winternals.com now, before you run into a crisis.

Note

This section's given you just the basics of user management. As you might guess, it's a large topic. If you want to get into more detail, I recommend you pick up a copy of *Special Edition Using Microsoft Windows Vista, Special Edition Using Microsoft XP Professional, 3rd Edition* (or the comparable XP Home version), all published by Que.

Managing Hardware

Over the past several years, Windows and hardware compatibility have improved immensely, mostly because a single operating system—Windows XP—has dominated the operating system market for more than 5 years, and thus device driver writers have had essentially just one big target to aim at. Also, modern plug-and-play PCI bus hardware has now entirely replaced the previous generation of manually configured ISA bus devices, so configuration errors are nearly impossible, resource conflicts are essentially a thing of the past, and contention for resources a nonissue because modern busses provide for many more interrupt and IO port options. (Windows Vista, by default, won't even try to use ISA devices.)

The end result is that I've found that I can summarize just about all you need to know about hardware management in just four bullet points:

- Always check the manufacturer's instructions *before* you install or plug in a new device. Sometimes you need to install the driver software package before Windows sees the device for the first time. This is especially true of USB-attached devices.

- If Windows crashes after you've installed the device, shut Windows down, remove the device, and replace any original hardware. That should get you back on the air. The device driver was almost certainly at fault, and the manufacturer will most likely have a new one on its website. Install the update.

- Driver problems are fairly rare, but are most common in display adapters. If you've made several changes, suspect the display adapter first.

- Cheap hardware devices always work. It's the expensive ones you have to watch out for.

There's a bit more to it than that, so I'll explain how to use the Windows Device Manager to update drivers and diagnose problems. But the first time you run into trouble, come back to this page and see whether the issue wasn't covered in those four bullet points.

Using Device Manager

To manage hardware devices, Windows uses a tool called—not surprisingly—Device Manager. This applet has remained pretty much the same since it was introduced in Windows 95. It can be accessed from the Computer Management application in the Administrative Tools menu folder, or, more commonly, from the Control Panel System applet's Hardware Properties page as shown in Figure 8.9.

On Vista, you'll get a User Account Control prompt when you start Device Manager. On XP, you must be logged on as a computer administrator to use the tool; if you're not, but you know the Administrator password, you can use the Run As method to start it up: Click Start, Administrative Tools, right-click Computer Management, and select Run As. Then check The Following User, select an Administrator account, and enter the password.

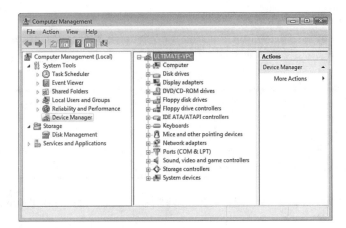

Figure 8.9   The Windows Device Manager.

Note

If Administrative Tools doesn't show up under your Start menu, you can add the link. Right-click the Start button, and then select Properties, Start Menu, Customize. On XP, select the Advanced tab. Then locate System Administrative Tools in the list, and select Display on the All Programs Menu and the Start Menu.

Note

You can also start Device Manager from a command prompt, by typing **start devmgmt.msc**. On XP, the command prompt window must be running from a Computer Administrator account. On Vista, you have to get past the User Account Control prompt.

If Device Manager is not running as an administrator, you can view, but not change, device settings.

Viewing Devices

As you can see in Figure 8.9, devices are categorized into types. Each type has a + next to it that can be expanded to show the devices contained within the type. (Windows Explorer uses the same sort of display.) If Windows knows of any problems with any hardware devices, those categories will be opened by default, and Windows will display a yellow exclamation point icon next to each of the problem devices.

You can also view devices in the following formats:

- **Devices by connection**—This view lists devices based on their connection to each other. It may be useful to determine how multiple devices are connected to an external bus (USB or PCMCIA), for example.

- **Resources by type**—This view, which is the default, lists devices by the type of resource— Direct Memory Access (DMA) channel, input/output ports, Interrupt Request (IRQ), or memory.

- **Resources by connection**—This view lists devices by the resource (Direct Memory Access [DMA] channel, input/output ports, Interrupt Request [IRQ], or Memory) and how they are connected.

Configuring Devices Manually

Sometimes, a device fails to function after the Windows PnP subsystem configures it. This is an extremely rare occurrence, but might occur if you are using a legacy ISA bus device on XP.

Note

Support for the ISA bus is rapidly disappearing. On Windows Vista, by default only a minimal ISA driver system is enabled, just enough to let Vista use the ubiquitous PS/2 keyboard and mouse interfaces. Full ISA/PnP support is present, but disabled. If you have ISA hardware that you absolutely must use on Vista, contact the hardware manufacturer and see whether they can provide updated drivers or installation instructions for Vista. (Good luck with that!) For more information, see www.microsoft.com/whdc/system/bus/PCI/ISA-bus.mspx.

Windows allows you to manually configure a device, as long as it is not configured as an ACPI-compliant device, by following these steps:

1. Open the Device Manager.

2. Right-click the device and choose Properties from the pop-up menu.

3. Select the Resources property page shown in Figure 8.10.

Figure 8.10 The Resources device properties page in the Device Manager.

4. Clear the Use Automatic Settings check box (if the box is grayed out, the device is managed by ACPI and you can't configure it manually).

5. Choose an alternative configuration in the Setting Based On list box. If no alternative configuration will work, you can then manually select a resource and click the Change Setting button to manually assign a resource. It's best to select resource settings that are not already in use by other devices. If in doubt, switch the Device Manager view to Resources by Type to see what DMA channels, interrupts, I/O addresses, and I/O ports are already in use.

6. Repeat step 5 for each resource in question.

7. Click the OK button to save your changes.

Forcing Detection and Reinstallation

If you've installed a new device and afterward discover that you should have installed its device drivers before the hardware, or if Windows for some reason fails to locate the correct driver for the device, or if you inadvertently misled it so it *can't* find the correct driver, you can force Windows to begin the detection and installation process again. Here are the steps:

1. In the Device Manager, locate the device, which will most likely have a yellow exclamation point icon next to it. Right-click it and select Uninstall.

2. If the manufacturer provided a device driver installer disk or if you have downloaded such an installer, run it now. This usually puts the drivers in your Windows folder along with files that help Windows locate the correct driver the next time it identifies the device.

3. If the device is an internal device and is not currently installed, shut down Windows and install it, and then restart Windows. For an external USB or FireWire device, just unplug and then plug the device back into a USB or FireWire port.

4. Go back to the Device Manager, right-click your computer's name at the top of the device list, and select Scan for Hardware Changes. This will start the detection process and pop up the New Hardware Wizard. You should be able to select all the "automatic" choices to let Windows locate and install the drivers itself.

Dealing with the Blue Screen of Death

When a regular application program crashes, Windows displays the familiar message "Such-and-such application has encountered a problem and needs to close," and then terminates the application. However, when a device driver or a part of the Windows kernel itself fails, Windows can't just carry on. It halts and displays an error message in white text on a blue screen, at which point all you can do is write down the cryptic message and cycle the power on your computer. This display is known as the *Blue Screen of Death*, and was so common with earlier versions of Windows that it was reduced to the acronym BSOD.

Note

Windows Vista, presumably, should experience fewer BSODs than previous versions of Windows because Vista has begun to use device drivers that run outside the Windows kernel, in the more restricted "user mode" processing environment. As user mode drivers are developed and distributed with newer hardware, driver bugs that used to bring down the entire system will simply bring up a notification that the particular driver failed and has been terminated. The driver should be restarted automatically and Windows should be able to resume normal operation.

BSODs have three main sources: failed disk drives, failed memory chips, and buggy device drivers. If you get a BSOD after installing a new device or updating a device driver, restart Windows in

Safe mode by pressing F8 immediately after your BIOS screen disappears. Then perform a device driver roll back, use System Restore to restore the most recent saved configuration, or use the Device Manager to delete the device. Restart Windows, and it should now boot up correctly. Get an updated driver from the device's manufacturer before attempting to reinstall it.

For detailed instructions about starting in Safe mode, how to deal with a BSOD, and using driver rollback, see Chapter 12, "Windows Troubleshooting."

▶▶ For instructions on performing a system restore, **see** "Restoring a Restore Point" **p. 503**.

Updating Device Drivers

If you suspect that a device driver is causing system problems, or if you find that a hardware vendor has released a newer version with additional features, you can use the Device Manager to perform a driver update.

Caution

Check the manufacturer's website for upgrade instructions because they may use a different procedure than the one I'll describe here. If the manufacturer does describe its own procedure, ignore my instructions and follow the instructions carefully.

In the absence of specific manufacturer instructions, here are the steps:

1. You will usually obtain a driver update as on a CD, or through a download from the manufacturer's website. The CD can be used as is. In the case of a download you will usually obtain either an `.exe` installer file or a `.zip` file.

   If you download an `.exe` file, run it while logged on as a computer administrator. It may update the drivers itself and exit. Or it may indicate that it wants to store extracted files in a directory. I usually direct such programs to store files in a folder named `c:\drivers\`*manufacturer* substituting the device manufacturer's name.

   If you get a `.zip` file, open it using WinZip, Windows Explorer, or another ZIP utility, and again, extract the files into `c:\drivers\`*manufacturer*.

   If you have the updated drivers on a CD, insert it now.

2. Open the Device Manager, right-click the device you want to update, and select Update Driver.

3. If you want, check the box to let Windows check Windows Update. Then click Next.

4. Select Install from a List or Specific Location (Advanced) and click Next.

5. If the driver is on a CD, check Search Removable Media. If the driver is in your hard disk, check Include This Location in the Search, click Browse, and locate the manufacturer-specific folder in which you expanded the driver files.

6. Click OK, and then follow the remaining prompts to complete the wizard. You may be asked to select the correct device from a list of devices supported by the same driver.

Windows will install the driver, and may or may not ask you to restart the computer.

Driver Certification and Signing

Device driver software is developed and distributed primarily by hardware manufacturers (also called Original Equipment Manufacturers or OEMs). Many manufacturers put their drivers through a series of tests and other requirements mandated by Microsoft to earn a Windows Vista or XP logo, which means that they can include the trademarked Windows logo on their packaging and advertising, and can represent their product as meeting Microsoft's standards. Manufacturers can additionally put drivers through a rigorous and expensive testing process at Microsoft's Windows Hardware Quality Laboratory (WHQL). Drivers that pass WHQL testing are eligible to be included on the Windows installation DVD or CD, and can be distributed through Windows Update. These drivers *should* be more reliable, and are definitely more convenient than drivers that don't have "logo" certification. However, lack of the certification doesn't necessarily mean that the driver failed testing. It's more likely that the manufacturer just didn't want to spend additional money on testing and licensing for a product that's near or past the end of its profit-making life.

Driver *signing* is another certification process that's frequently confused with a process of approval by Microsoft, but it's not that at all. Signing is simply the inclusion with software of a digital certificate or mathematical signature issued under the auspices of a recognized digital signature authority such as VeriSign Inc., Comodo, or other companies. Signing can be applied to scripts and application programs as well as device drivers. All that signing guarantees is that the origin of the software can be traced to the owner of the digital certificate, and that no viruses or other hacks have been added (at least, none that weren't there when the manufacturer released the software). Microsoft does not have to be involved in this process at all, and exercises no approval or control over it, although WHQL certification comes with special digital signature that guarantees the driver's WHQL status. There are, in fact, four levels of driver signing, in increasing order of trustworthiness:

- **Unsigned**—The driver has no digital signature. The driver might be okay, but it could include a keyboard logger and spambot under the control of a con artist in Elbonia.
- **Self-signed**—The driver has a digital signature, but the signature file was not issued by a recognized certificate authority, thus the provenance of the signature cannot be traced. This could be the case for software developed in-house at a small company that didn't want to spend $200 a year for a certificate.
- **Authenticode-signed**—The signature was issued by a digital certificate authority recognized by Microsoft, providing at least some assurance that the driver indeed did come from the company named in the certificate. The driver might not work, but at least it's not a forgery.
- **WHQL-signed**—The driver was validated in Microsoft's testing labs.

The trend is toward encouraging hardware manufacturers to add signatures for drivers that run inside the Windows kernel (kernel-mode drivers). Signing at least provides an audit trail that positively identifies the origin of a driver and thus introduces some measure of responsibility for its behavior and incentive to improve it. Many older drivers do not include signatures of any type, but for 64-bit versions of Windows Vista, Microsoft now *requires* that kernel-mode drivers be signed before they can be installed.

In all cases, WHQL-signed drivers are installed without question, automatically. In fact, on Vista, the New Hardware Wizard runs and installs a WHQL driver even when the current user is not an administrator. For drivers with less stellar credentials, Windows treatment of the driver can be adjusted through Local Security Policy (for standalone computers) or Group Policy (for domain computers). Administrators can eliminate the ability to use unsigned drivers, or can relax the policy, depending on their hardware and security needs. The various installation options are, in decreasing order of trust:

- Install silently, without question.

- Install only after warning about the driver's signed or unsigned status.

- Install after warning by administrator only. Nonadministrator users cannot install.

- Driver cannot be installed at all. (An exception is made for debugging versions of the driver when installed on a computer configured for debugging and testing kernel device drivers.)

2000, XP, Vista, and the Server versions all have different default policies. For example, the 64-bit versions of Vista simply don't allow you to use unsigned drivers at all, whereas Windows 2000 installs unsigned drivers with only a warning.

For a rundown of the policy defaults for each version of Windows, see www.microsoft.com/whdc/winlogo/drvsign/drvsign.mspx. For a detailed look at the mechanisms behind code signing, I recommend the "Code Signing Best Practices" white paper at www.microsoft.com/whdc/winlogo/drvsign/best_practices.mspx.

On a domain network, the policy is determined by domain administrators and delivered via Group Policy. To change the policy settings on a Windows 2000 or XP computer that is not a member of a domain network, log on as a computer administrator, click Start, Run, and type `secpol.msc`. Under Local Policies, Security Options, locate the entry titled Devices: Unsigned Driver Installation Behavior. The policy settings cannot be changed locally on Vista.

Selecting an Older Device Driver

In some rare cases you may find that your hardware device's manufacturer has not provided a driver for Windows Vista or XP, even on its website. This should happen only in cases of older devices no longer being sold or supported. In this case, on x86 versions of Windows, you *may* be able to install and use a Windows 2000 version of the driver, or a Windows Driver Model (WDM) driver. Windows Me drivers are WDM-compatible.

Before installing an older driver for your device, though, you should check for new versions. The very first place you should check is the Windows Update website. You can search the Windows Update website as part of the Device Manager Wizard. If you don't find a driver there, try the manufacturer website. If you don't know what the manufacturer website is, try one of the following websites:

> http://www.driversplanet.com/
> http://www.driverzone.com/
> http://www.driverguide.com/
> http://www.windrivers.com/

If you still can't find a newer certified Windows Vista or XP driver, you can try to install either a Windows Driver Model driver or a Windows 2000 driver. This usually requires a manual install using the following steps:

1. Select the device in Device Manager and click Properties.

2. Click the Update Driver button to start the Hardware Update Wizard.

3. Enable the Install from a List or Specified Location (Advanced) radio button and click Next.

4. Click Don't Search. It will choose the Driver to Install radio button. Click Next.

5. Click the Have Disk button, and then Browse.

6. Locate the disk and directory containing the driver's `.inf` file, and then click OK.

7. Select the appropriate device, click the Next button, and then click Finish.

Replacing Hardware

Sooner or later, everyone has to replace some hardware on his computer. It might be the replacement of a malfunctioning network card, a disk drive that is starting to fail, or just installing a faster video card. If your version of Windows is not part of an Open License or Enterprise purchase, you may find that when you have replaced a new piece of hardware, your installation will require that you reactivate Windows to continue to use it.

Microsoft created Windows Product Activation (WPA) to discourage casual copying of Microsoft products. For security reasons, Microsoft does not provide much information on exactly what type of hardware is used to create the hardware key contained in your Windows product ID, but we do know that the specific set of hardware devices in your computer factors into WPA's identification scheme. Nor is Microsoft providing information on exactly how many changes are allowed in a given time period before the product will be required to be reactivated. What is important to know is that if you change your hardware sufficiently, you may be required to reactivate Windows because it will think that it may have been illegally copied to another computer. We believe that as long as major hardware changes occur no more often than every six months, WPA will not get agitated. In any case, although it may be irritating and offensive, the worst that should happen is that you may have to make a toll-free call to Microsoft to get a verbal authorization code.

Note

For the curious, and technical minded, take a look at the Fully Licensed home page at http://www.licenturion.com/xp/. You'll find an in-depth discussion of the Installation ID and hardware key mechanism used on early releases of Windows XP, as well as an application to examine the Installation ID.

Using Driver Rollback

If after installing a device driver you find that the driver did not work, has caused a system instability, or caused another problem, you can easily replace it with the previous driver using driver rollback. You can accomplish this task by following the directions found on p. 723 ("Device Driver Rollback") of Chapter 12, "Windows Troubleshooting."

Disk Management

Windows comes with tools that let you easily set up a new hard disk through processes called *partitioning* and *formatting*. After they are in use, additional tools help you manage and reclaim free space, and keep the disk's contents organized for fast access through a process called *defragmentation*. This section covers these tools. First, you get a brief overview of the processes involved. If you're already familiar with these processes, you can skip ahead to the instructions.

All disk drives must be partitioned and formatted before Windows can use them. You can think of this as comparable to surveying a newly discovered land and staking out counties, cities, and homesites (but without the eviction of the indigenous inhabitants, which tends to get ugly). When you install Windows on a new computer, the Windows setup program partitions and formats at least one disk for you. However, if you later add additional internal or external hard disks to increase capacity, you'll need to handle this process yourself.

As we discuss in Chapter 10, "Windows File Systems," a partition or volume is a large chunk of a hard disk's available storage space. Usually, each partition is identified by a *drive letter*, such as C or D. The use of drive letters goes back to the day when each floppy or hard disk was always formatted in one allotment, so originally each physicially separate disk drive had one letter. Soon, however, manufacturers increased hard drive capacity to the point that MS-DOS's FAT file system couldn't cope with the amount of data they contained, so drives had to be *partitioned* into more managable chunks; thus many disks sprouted two, three, or more drive letters, each representing a separate portion of the disk's storage space. Today, Windows NTFS file system can handle individual disk drives up to 2TB (that's 2,000GB or 2,000,000MB) in size in a single partition, and you may decide to use your hard disks as whole units. However, there are still reasons that you might want to split a given physical disk into as several volumes:

- To make it possible to boot up your computer with your choice of different versions of Windows or other operating systems.

- So that you can put data files on a different volume than Windows. Thus, if you need to reformat the partition that contains Windows, your data will survive.

- So that you can put programs and data on separate drives, making backup easier.

- So that the data for a given application can be confined to one volume, and if too much data is generated, it doesn't fill up volumes used for other purposes, such as the one on which Windows is installed.

However you decide to divide up a new disk's storage space, partitioning is most easily done when a brand new disk is first installed, or in the case of an external FireWire or USB drive, when it is attached to the computer for the first time. After one or more partitions are in place and there is data on the disk, it's *very* difficult to change the sizes—although this can be done by third-party applications such as PartitionMagic, and Windows Vista can do it if the disk isn't too full. In any case, it's best to decide how you want a new disk to be partitioned before you start using it.

There are also some decisions to make about the type of partitioning to use:

- On Windows Vista and on 64-bit versions of Windows XP, you must select one of two possible ways of organizing the disk's first few data blocks, which contain the partitioning information. The two schemes are called Master Boot Record (MBR) or GUID Partition Table (GPT). GPT is sometimes used on computers with Itanium or non-Intel-compatible processors, and systems with external RAID disk arrays larger than 2TB. However, some third-party disk tools and most older operating systems—including 32-bit versions of Windows XP—can't use GPT-partitioned disks. Unless you know that you need to use GPT, when Windows prompts you, select MBR.

- On Windows 2000, XP Pro, and Vista Ultimate and Enterprise, you can tell Windows to set a hard disk up as a basic or dynamic disk. Dynamic disks have some advantages: For example, you can tell Windows to add additional space to a volume after it's full. However, older operating systems can't access dynamic disks, so if you need to multiboot your computer into Windows 98, for instance, *and* you want the older OS to be able to use the disk, it's not a viable option. Also, you can't protect a dynamic disk with Vista's BitLocker drive encryption mechanism.

- On basic disks, you can set up at most four partitions, which must be designed as either primary or extended partitions. Only one can be the Extended type. An extended partition can then be further subdivided into one or more logical drives, each of which gets its own drive letter. This scheme is an unfortunate historical legacy, but we have to live with it. Here's the bottom line:
  - If you want to divide a hard disk into four or fewer partitions, use primary partitions.
  - If you need to carve out five or more separate drive letters, create the first three partitions as primary partitions. Then make an extended partition with the remaining space and divide it up into drives four, five, and so on.

- After partitioning, you have to select a disk format. The options for hard disks are FAT16, used on MS-DOS; FAT32, which was used on Windows 95, 98, and Me; or NTFS, which is the format of choice for Windows NT, 2000, XP, and Vista. The NTFS format is less prone to losing track of data due to software crashes, but partitions formatted with NTFS can't be used by MS-DOS or Windows 95, 98, and Me. Even Linux has trouble with NTFS. If you don't run any of these operating systems on your computer, use NTFS. Otherwise, select FAT32. (By the way, other operating systems have still other formatting choices. If your hard disk has partitions with a format other than FAT or NTFS, the partitions aren't usable on Windows. Windows simply skips over them and doesn't assign them a drive letter.)

▶▶ For more information about disk formats and their options and functions, **see** "Disks, Partitions, and Volumes," **p. 597**.

▶▶ For more detail about dynamic disks, visit technet.microsoft.com and search for "What Are Dynamic Disks and Volumes."

Regardless of what file system or storage types you elect to use on your hard drives, all routine disk maintenance and configuration is done from one place: the Disk Management console.

Partitioning and Formatting with the Disk Management Console

The Disk Management console is shown in Figure 8.11.

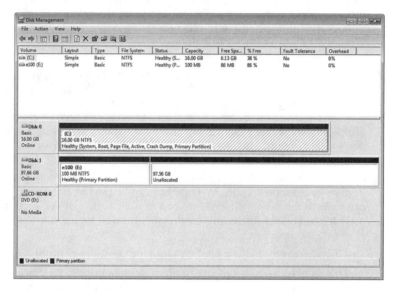

Figure 8.11   The Disk Management console.

You must be logged on as an administrator to use this tool on Windows XP. On Vista, you just have to be able to get past the User Account Control prompt. You can open the Disk Management console in several different ways, the easiest being as follows:

- Right-click on [My] Computer and choose Manage. Then from within the Computer Management console, expand the Storage item and select Disk Management.

- On XP, on the command line, type **diskmgmt.msc**.

- On Vista, type **diskmgmt .msc** on the command line or in the Start menu's search box.

The following are just some of the tasks that can be performed using the Disk Management console:

- Create new partitions and logical drives.

- Expand or shrink the size of existing partitions (Vista only).

- Create new volumes.

- Determine disk size, file system, disk health, and other pertinent information. This can easily be done by looking at each volume in the Disk Management console as shown in Figure 8.11.

- Format volumes and partitions.

- Assign drive letters or paths to hard drives and removable storage drives. This can be done by right-clicking on the volume of concern and selecting Change Drive Letter and Paths.

- Mount and unmount drives.
- Upgrade basic storage to dynamic storage.
- Extend the size of dynamic volumes.

Some of the more complex of these tasks are discussed in more detail in the following sections, but most can be explained in brief.

Note

In the following section, I'll show you how to manage disks from the GUI. You can also use the **diskpart** utility to manage disks from the command line. This tool is especially handy for helping mass-production setup of new computers. For more information, on XP you can search the Windows Help and Support Center for **diskpart**. There are two Overview articles named DiskPart; one is the diskpart program in the Recovery Console and the other is for the full version. You want to read the article that starts "DiskPart.exe is a text-mode command interpreter..." For the Vista version, which has capabilities the XP version doesn't, you have to go online for information. Go to technet.microsoft.com and under the list of TechCenters, click on Windows Vista. Then search for diskpart. You want the article titled "DiskPart Command-Line Options."

Adding a New Disk

After you've installed a new internal hard disk, or have plugged in a new external FireWire or USB hard drive, you need to set up one or more partitions and format them before you can use the new drive.

To create a new partition or logical drive, follow these steps:

1. Open the Disk Management console as discussed previously.

2. The very first time that Disk Management runs after a new disk has been attached, Windows may ask you to select a partitioning scheme. You are first shown a list of the newly detected disks. Confirm that there are check marks next to the disk(s) that you want to initialize, and then click Next.

3. The next set of choices depends on the version of Windows you are using. On Vista, you are asked to select the MBR or GPT partitioning scheme. In most cases you should select MBR, as discussed earlier in this chapter.

On XP Pro, Vista Enterprise, and Vista Ultimate, you are asked whether to format the disks as Basic or Dynamic. By default, the Dynamic option is unchecked. Check Dynamic only if you are sure the disks won't need to be used by other operating systems. Then click Next.

▶▶ For more information about disk formats and their options and functions, **see** "Disks, Partitions, and Volumes," **p. 597**.

Now, you can create and format partitions on the new disk, using the steps described in the following sections. The procedures vary slightly, depending on whether you're working with a basic or dynamic disk.

Creating New Partitions and Logical Drives on a Basic Disk

To create a new partition or logical drive on a basic disk, follow these steps:

1. Open the Disk Management console as discussed previously.

2. To create a new partition, right-click an unallocated region of a basic disk, and select New Partition. To create a logical drive, right-click in an extended partition, and select New Logical Drive.

3. Follow the onscreen prompts in the New Partition Wizard to enter the desired partition type and size and so on.

Then you can format the new partition, using the steps described shortly in "Formatting Disks and Volumes."

Creating New Simple Volumes on Dynamic Disks

To create a new simple volume from the Disk Management console, follow these steps:

1. Open the Disk Management console as discussed previously.

2. Right-click the unallocated space on the dynamic disk on which you want to create the simple volume, and then click New Volume.

3. In the New Volume Wizard, click Next and then click Simple. Follow the onscreen prompts to complete the process.

You can create other types of volumes on dynamic disks in much the same fashion. Dynamic disk volumes, however, can only be read by Windows 2000, XP Pro, Vista Enterprise, and Vista Ultimate, so you may not want to use them if you dual-boot your computer with other operating systems.

Formatting Disks and Volumes

Windows supports formatting numerous kinds of media, partly due to its excellent multimedia support. You can format hard drives, removable storage media (such as USB and Zip drives), and DVD-RAM disks to name a few of your options.

Note

Although you can format removable media from within the Disk Management console, unless you already have Disk Management open, it's probably easier to do it from Windows Explorer—just open [My] Computer, right-click the drive, and select Format. For hard disks, you do have to use Disk Management.

Windows is fairly intelligent and self-protective, and will not allow you to format the system or boot partitions. Those options will be grayed out. To begin the process of formatting a hard drive or removable media device, right-click the volume (or unallocated space) of interest from within the Disk Management console and select Format, which opens the window shown in Figure 8.12.

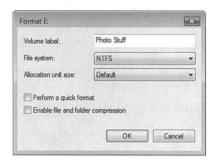

Figure 8.12   Formatting a new drive or partition.

Formatting removable media such as DVD-RAM, Flash, or ZIP disks follows the same process, except that you will usually not have the choice of file systems; in most cases removable media (other than floppies) are formatted with the FAT (which is really to say FAT16) file system. On Windows Vista with Service Pack 1 installed, you can also format Flash (USB or memory card) disks with the exFAT file system. ExFAT supports larger devices and file sizes than FAT and its format can be extended by media device manufacturers.

Note

At the time this was written, exFAT was supported only by Windows Vista with Service Pack 1 installed. Use the exFAT format on a Flash disk only if you know that it is supported by all the media devices and computers that you need to use with the disk.

The options available to you during a format operation are fairly simple, but deserve some mention.

- **Volume Label**—A descriptive name that you use to readily identify the volume. You should keep the label as short as possible and avoid using the following reserved characters: < > : " / \ | * ? + and . because they will cause problems when accessing volumes over the network. (Windows does not stop you from using these characters in a volume name—you just have to know not to use them.) If a disk is formatted with the FAT file system, the label can contain up to 11 characters. If the disk is formatted with the NTFS file system, the limit is 32 characters.

- **File System**—Depending on the size of the volume to be formatted, you can elect to format it as FAT (FAT16), FAT32, or NTFS. For hard disks, use NTFS formatting, unless you have to be able to read and write the disk volume from MS-DOS, Windows 9x, or Linux. To share the volume with MS-DOS, use FAT16. To share with Windows 9x or Linux, choose FAT32. On Vista SP1, for removable Flash disks, you can also select the exFAT format.

- **Allocation Unit Size**—If you will want to convert a basic disk to dynamic later on, select 512 bytes. Otherwise, leave the setting on Default.

- **Perform a Quick Format**—Check to perform a quick format that zaps the volume's directory structure, and thus removes all files from the disk, but does not scan the disk for bad sectors. Use this option only if the disk has been previously formatted and is known to not have any damage to it. Also, check this if you're running Windows under Virtual PC or another emulator, and the disk is a virtual disk.

■ **Enable File and Folder Compression**—This option enables file and folder compression on the new volume. Remember that this will prevent you from later using EFS encryption unless compression is removed. In most cases, compression is not necessary.

Of course, should you need to format drives from the command prompt, you still can. The `format` command has the following syntax:

```
format volume [/fs:filesystem] [/v:label] [/q] [/a:unitsize] [/c]
```

The parameters for the `format` command are outlined in Table 8.11.

Table 8.11   Parameters for the *format* Command

Parameter	Description
Volume	Specifies the mount point, volume name, or drive letter of the drive you want to format.
/fs:*filesystem*	Specifies the file system to use: FAT, FAT32, or NTFS. Floppy disks can use only the FAT file system.
/v:*label*	Specifies the volume label. If you omit the /v command-line option or use it without specifying a volume label, **format** prompts you for the volume label after the formatting is completed.
/q	Performs a quick format. Deletes the file table and the root directory of a previously formatted volume but does not perform a sector-by-sector scan for bad areas.
/a:*unitsize*	Specifies the cluster size, also known as *allocation unit* size, to use on FAT, FAT32, or NTFS volumes. If ***unitsize*** is not specified, it will be chosen based on volume size.
/c	NTFS only. Files created on the new volume will be compressed by default.

Creating Mounted Drives

Windows lets you join two separate NTFS-formatted drives or volumes into one larger, virtual volume. It's called *mounting*, and it works by making the entire contents of one volume appear in the place of a specified folder on another volume. For example, if I created a new empty folder named `c:\photos`, I could format a new hard disk, and mount it to `c:\photos`. The root folder of the new volume will appear as the contents of `c:\photos`, and subdirectories in the new volume will appear as subdirectories of `c:\photos`. One reason you might want to do this is if you needed to add space to an existing file system but don't want to change your directory structure. As long as you don't mind that the added space is only available in a specific set of folders, mounting a new drive is a nifty way to do it.

To create a mounted drive from the Disk Management console, follow these steps:

1. Open the Disk Management console as discussed previously.

2. Right-click the partition or volume you want to mount, and then click Change Drive Letter and Paths.

3. To mount a volume, click Add. Click Mount in the following empty NTFS folder and enter or browse to the empty folder. To unmount a volume, click it and then click Remove.

Note

I might add that this concept is fairly new to Windows, although the UNIX operating system has used this scheme since the 1970s. That's how UNIX gets by without drive letters—all disks are joined into a single file system "tree."

Converting Basic Disks to Dynamic Disks

Dynamic disks have a slightly different partition structure than the basic disks that we inherited from MS-DOS. Dynamic disks have some advantages: For starters, you can later extend them with noncontiguous blocks of unallocated space. They can't be read by older operating systems, however, so if you dual-boot your computer you probably don't want to use them. If you're running straight XP or Vista, and use NTFS-formatted disks already, you might consider it.

Note

Dynamic disks are available only on Windows 2000, XP Professional, Vista Enterprise, and Vista Ultimate. Windows 2000 and XP Professional don't let you make dynamic disks on laptops, or on FireWire or USB drives, although Vista does.

If you have Windows Vista Ultimate or Enterprise, and intend to use BitLocker drive encryption, don't convert your disk. You can't set up BitLocker on a dynamic disk.

To convert a basic disk to dynamic from the Disk Management console, follow these steps:

1. Open the Disk Management console as discussed previously.

2. Right-click the basic disk you want to convert and select Convert to Dynamic disk. Follow the onscreen prompts to complete the process. Looking at Figure 8.11, the area to click in is that area on the left side of each disk in the bottom frame.

Extending Dynamic Volumes

To extend a dynamic volume from the Disk Management console, follow these steps:

1. Open the Disk Management console as discussed previously.

2. Right-click the simple or spanned volume you want to extend and click Extend Volume. Follow the onscreen prompts to complete the process.

A few things to keep in mind when attempting to extend volumes:

- On Windows XP, you cannot extend a system volume or a boot volume. This means, in almost all cases, that drive C can't be extended without the use of third-party tools. However, Vista does let you extend any volume, provided there is space available.
- You cannot extend striped volumes.
- You cannot extend a dynamic volume that was upgraded from a basic volume to a dynamic volume in Windows 2000 if you've subsequently upgraded to Windows XP. (Got that?)
- If you extend a spanned volume, you cannot delete any portion of it without deleting the entire spanned volume.

Moving Dynamic Disks to Another Computer

Every dynamic disk contains a complete copy of the database that describes the volume configuration of *every* dynamic disk in the attached computer. Thus, if you move a dynamic disk from one computer to another, Windows has to reconcile the dynamic disk's volume table—which describes the setup on the original computer—with the new computer's volume layout, before you can use the disk.

Before you remove the disk from the original computer, open the Disk Manager and check to see whether the disk contains striped, mirrored, or spanned volumes. Unless you move all the relevant disk drives together, you have to break any mirrors, and copy off and then delete any spanned or striped volumes before removing the disk.

When you've installed the disk in the new computer, open the Disk Management console. On the menu, click Action, and then Rescan Disks. Right-click any disks marked Foreign, select Import Foreign Disk, and then follow the import wizard's instructions from there. This updates the disk's volume database and makes it available for use.

Resizing Partitions

If you run out of space in a volume on your hard disk and the disk has unallocated, free space available, you may be able to extend the overcrowded volume. Or, you may be able to take space away from one partition and give it to another. How you do this, and whether it's even possible, depends on whether your disk is set up as a Basic or Dynamic Disk.

Resizing on a Basic Disk

If you are using basic storage on your disk drive and you decide that you need to adjust your partition layout after it has been initially created, you have three or four possible means to this end: You can use the `diskpart` utility, you can delete and re-create partitions, or you can use a third-party utility such as Partition Magic. Finally, if you're using Windows Vista, the Disk Management console might be able to do the job for you by itself.

Using the `extend` command within the `diskpart` utility, you can add more space to existing primary partitions and logical drives as long as you meet the following requirements:

- The basic volume must be formatted with NTFS.
- You can extend a basic volume using space from the same physical hard disk only (unlike dynamic volumes). The basic volume must be followed by contiguous unallocated space. That is, on a basic disk, you can grow a volume out into only whatever empty space immediately follows it.
- You can extend a logical drive only within the contiguous free space that exists in the partition that contains the logical drive. That is, within an extended partition, again, you can grow the volume out into only whatever available space follows it.

If you meet all the aforementioned requirements, you can extend a basic disk as follows:

1. Open a command window: click Start, Run and enter **cmd** into the Run box. Press Enter.
2. Type **diskpart**.

3. Type **list volume**. Write down what volume you want to extend.

4. Type **select volume** *n*, where *n* is the volume you identified in the previous step.

5. Type **extend size=n**, where *n* is the extended size of the volume in MB.

If working from the command line is not your thing, and you are not ready to perform mass deletions (as required by the third method), you may want to consider using a third-party disk utility, such as Partition Magic from Symantec. Partition Magic allows you to redesign your partition table graphically within the Windows GUI and then on the subsequent restart performs the required actions to carry out your wishes.

Resizing on Vista

Windows Vista introduced "shrink" and "extend" capability in the Disk Management console. You can shrink a volume, creating unallocated space after it, subject to three conditions:

- The volume must be formatted with NTFS, not FAT.

- There must be no "fixed" files in the space that you want to deallocate from the end of the volume. Fixed files include the Windows page file (which may be fragmented into several pieces), file allocation table segments, and log/change files that are part of NTFS's journaling (transaction) system.

- There must be room in the part of the volume that is to remain to hold any data blocks that are stored in the part of the volume that is to be lopped off.

To deallocate space from an NTFS volume on Vista, select the volume in the Disk Manager screen, right-click, and select Shrink. Windows computes the maximum amount of space that can be removed (that is, how much space there is between the end of the last fixed file and the end of the volume, while still accounting for the capability to move data out of the end of the volume into free space at the beginning). You can free up this or a smaller amount.

Vista may likewise allow you to extend basic and dynamic NTFS-formatted volumes. You can extend an NTFS volume on a basic disk if there is unallocated space immediately following it. You can extend an NTFS volume on a dynamic disk if there is unallocated space anywhere on the physical disk. Right-click the volume and select Expand. The wizard walks you through expanding the volume. By default, it expands the volume by the maximum amount available.

Resizing the Brutally Hard Way

If you choose not to use either of the other methods presented, you can still resize your basic disks, with no out-of-pocket cost. It is quite laborious, however. You'll need to back up all pertinent data on the partition(s) in question, delete the partitions, and then re-create them sized to your liking. After formatting the new partitions, you have to then restore your data onto them. Yuck.

Resizing on a Dynamic Disk

If you are running with dynamic storage volumes on XP Professional, Vista Enterprise, or Vista Ultimate, resizing your volumes is an easy process. You simply right-click on the volume that you want to expand, and select Extend Volume. This will open the Extend Volume Wizard, which will allow you to enter the size by which you want to extend the volume. After the wizard has finished, which is a relatively quick process, you will have a volume that is now larger...all without a restart of the computer or the time-intensive process of copying and recopying all the files in that volume. It's quite a time saver.

On Windows XP, shrinking a volume to get space that you can give to another volume isn't possible, even on a dynamic disk; you have to use a third-party tool such as Partition Magic.

Converting FAT16/FAT32 File Systems to NTFS

Should you make the decision to upgrade your hard disk's file system from FAT16 or FAT32 to NTFS, you will need to perform the upgrade from the command line by using the convert command. The convert command has the following syntax:

```
convert [volume] /fs:ntfs [/v] [/cvtarea:FileName] [/nosecurity] [/x]
```

The parameters for the convert command are outlined in Table 8.12.

Table 8.12 Parameters for the *convert* Command

Parameter	Description
Volume	Specifies the drive letter (followed by a colon), mount point, or volume name to convert to NTFS.
/fs:ntfs	Required. Converts the volume to NTFS.
/v	Specifies verbose mode; that is, all messages will be displayed during conversion.
/cvtarea:FileName	Specifies that the Master File Table (MFT) and other NTFS metadata files be written to an existing, contiguous placeholder file. This file must be in the root directory of the file system to be converted. Use of the **/cvtarea** parameter can result in a less fragmented file system after conversion. For best results, the size of this file should be 1KB multiplied by the number of files and directories in the file system; however, the **convert** utility accepts files of any size.
	You must create the placeholder file using the **fsutil *file* createnew** command prior to running **convert**, which does not create this file for you. **convert** overwrites this file with NTFS metadata. After conversion, any unused space in this file is freed.
/nosecurity	Specifies that the converted files and directory security settings are accessible by everyone.
/x	Dismounts the volume, if necessary, before it is converted. Any open handles to the volume will no longer be valid.

To convert your C: drive and apply standard security restrictions, for example, the command is

```
convert c: /fs:ntfs
```

Only hard disks can be updated; NTFS isn't used on removable media such as floppies, flash disks and CD-RWs. You *can* format a USB or FireWire-attached hard drive with NTFS, however.

Caution

Converting your existing FAT or FAT32 volume to the NTFS file system will preclude you from reading these disks under Windows 9x or MS-DOS. Even Linux has problems with NTFS. This sort of limitation is one reason why people who deal with multiboot scenarios stick with FAT-based disks.

Note

Unknown to most people, the **convert** command on Windows 2000 produces a volume that does not have the default NTFS permissions settings that you would get after installing Windows itself. The version of **convert** that comes with Windows XP and Vista fixes this problem by automatically applying the correct default permissions to all folders. When used with the **/cvtarea** switch to create an unfragmented MFT, there is virtually no difference anymore between a volume converted to NTFS during setup of Windows or one converted later using the **convert** command.

Converting the NTFS File System to FAT16/FAT32

Reversion from NTFS to FAT16 or FAT32 is not supported by Windows; however, using a third-party disk utility such as Partition Magic will allow you to perform this task.

Hard Drive Cleaning

It may seem that after getting your hard drives set up and configured to your liking all of your work is done. No such luck! Over time Windows systems accumulate hundreds and possibly thousands of unnecessary (or at least, no longer necessary) files and folders on your hard drives. Not only do these files and folders waste valuable space, they can slowly degrade system performance. This section, shows you how to keep your hard drives slim and trim.

Cleaning Up Temporary Files

Temporary files are—drum roll, please—files that Windows or application programs need to create and for just a short time, and can live without afterward. Internet Explorer stores web page text and graphics in files on your hard disk, and these, in all likelihood, are used once and never again. Similarly, Microsoft Word creates temporary files while you're working on a document, and if it crashes before you save the document and exit Word, can leave these files hanging around.

Windows stores most temporary files in only a handful of places. That is not to say that some rogue program does not deposit some in a random folder; just that in most cases, you can find most of the dead wood by checking only a few locations. On Windows XP, these places are

- %USERPROFILE%\Local Settings\Temp—Here you will typically find temporary files that were not properly cleaned up by the application that created them.

- %USERPROFILE%\Local Settings\Temporary Internet Files—Here you find the cache used by applications such as Outlook and Internet Explorer. These folders and files are usually hidden, but they are there in droves.

- %SYSTEMROOT%\Temp—Another dumping ground that some applications like to use for their temporary files.

%USERPROFILE% is usually \Documents and Settings*YourAccountName* and %SYSTEMROOT% is usually \Windows. On Vista, different folders are used for these same purposes:

- %USERPROFILE%\AppData\Local\Temp—Application temporary files.
- %USERPROFILE%\Local Settings\Temporary Internet Files—Internet Explorer and Windows Mail cache files.
- %SYSTEMROOT%\Temp—On Vista, this folder typically holds only a few log files left over from Windows setup, and not much more.

%USERPROFILE% is usually \Users*YourAccountName*.

Using the Disk Cleanup Utility

The easiest way to help clear out unneeded files from your hard drives is to use the Disk Cleanup utility on a regular basis. The Disk Cleanup utility is launched by clicking Start, [All] Programs, Accessories, System Tools, Disk Cleanup. You can also launch it by right-clicking on a drive icon in any Explorer window and choosing Properties, Disk Cleanup.

There are two useful tricks to getting more out of Disk Cleanup. The first thing is to make use of two undocumented switches for the Disk Cleanup utility that can be accessed from the command line. The second is to schedule the Disk Cleanup utility to run automatically, using advanced settings of your choice, thus purging your hard disk of specific types of unwanted types of files on a regular basis.

Tip

If you run the Disk Cleanup tool from the command line rather than from the Start menu, using the command-line options I'll describe shortly, it lists some extra categories of files to clean up and can do a more thorough job.

To run Disk Cleanup with extra cleanup options, follow these steps:

1. Open a Command Prompt window and type

```
cleanmgr /d x /sageset:n
```

where *x* represents the drive letter you want to clean, and *n* is any number between 1 and 65535. The /sageset:*n* value provides a means for you to create multiple preconfigured Disk Cleanup instances, each with the specific drives and options selected that you desire. Which value you choose for the /sageset:*n* value doesn't matter; it is only used to store your settings in the Registry to allow you to run Disk Cleanup with these options again in the future.

2. On Vista, select whether to clean up temporary files in just your own user profile, or in all user profiles. You'll have to confirm a User Account Control prompt to clean up other users' files.

3. After you press Enter, the hard disk grinds a bit. Then up will pop the Disk Cleanup Settings dialog. The actual categories offered may be different on your computer. You can click on each option to read a description of it. Note that choosing to compress files that are not often used could take a long while, during which time the compression occurs.

Select the categories of files you want to delete, and then click OK to save these settings into the Registry.

4. Create a shortcut to `cleanmgr /sagerun:n`, where *n* is the number you chose previously in step 1.

5. Using the Scheduled Task Wizard (Start, Settings, Control Panel, Scheduled Tasks), create and configure a scheduled task to run daily or weekly using the shortcut you created in step 3.

On Vista, if you want the scheduled task to clean up files for all users, edit the scheduled task's properties and make the following changes:

- On the General tab, click Change User or Group, type the name SYSTEM, and then click OK.
- Check Run with Highest Privileges.

You will probably want to create a Disk Cleanup setting and shortcut for each drive on your system.

Note

On Vista, if you elect to clean up files for all users, and you have the option to delete restore points and shadow copies, think carefully before you check this option. This deletes all but the most recent restore point, and all of the saved previous versions of changed files. It may also delete all but the most recent complete PC bckup. I'd select this option only if I was *really* desperate to free up disk space, and my system had been running perfectly in its current configuration for several weeks.

Defragmenting for Greater Speed

Computers store information on their hard disks in a disorganized fashion, using whatever bits and pieces of free space they find, and as files are added and deleted, the unused space gets more and more spread out in tiny little bits. Imagine if you had to place 50 pieces of paper flat on your desk, without overlapping. You would line them up nicely, one next to the other, in order, although it might nearly cover your desk. Now take 20 pages away at random, and put a 20-page essay down in their place. They can't all get put down side by side now, so you'll have to put each page wherever you can, in any empty space you can find. Fine, but now try to pick them up, in order. Oops! They're all scattered all over the place, and to find page 1, and then page 2, and then page 3...you're going to be a this for a while.

That's fragmentation. And on your hard drive, there aren't just 50 places for pages to be scattered, but tens of millions. Over time, the slowdown from increasing fragmentation becomes significant. Consider this: Reading 4MB from a typical PC's hard disk takes about .05 seconds if the data is contiguous (laid out all in one stretch). Reading the same amount of data can take up to *8 full seconds* if the data is scattered in 100 fragments all over the disk—that's 160 times slower. (Have you ever sat drumming your fingers as Word took 8 seconds or more to open a document? Yes, I thought you have.)

Cleaning up your hard disk by collecting the scattered pieces of each of your files and moving them into consecutive spaces on the disk is called *defragmentation*, and Windows comes with a tool to do a fair job of it. To use the tool,

- From the menu: Click Start, All Programs, Accessories, System Tools, Disk Defragmenter. Or, you can get to it in the Computer Management console, under Storage.

  Or

- From the command line: type `dfrg.msc`.

On XP, you must be logged on as a computer administrator to run the Disk Defragmenter. On Vista, you just have to get past a User Account Control prompt.

The built-in Disk Defragmenter has been around in more or less the same form since Windows 95. On Vista, however, Microsoft made some interesting changes. First, it recognized the necessity of performing regular defragmentation runs, so Microsoft added it to the default set of Scheduled Tasks installed with Windows: It is set up to run every Wednesday at 1:00 a.m., or the next time you start your computer after that. Microsoft also removed the cool graphic display that shows how files are scattered all over your disk, and on which you could watch data move around. It was a bit like watching an ant farm. On Vista, you just get a dialog box that says "Defragmenting hard disks... This may take from a few minutes to a few hours." Not too informative, but it does the job adequately. The Vista defragmenter knows to suspend operations while you're actively working. It's also aware of the "volume shadow copy" service that we'll discuss later in this chapter, and tries to move data around without making the shadow copy service have to copy too much data. On XP, the display is a bit more interesting. To see whether defragmentation is severe (or more precisely, to see whether the Windows defragmenting tool is going to do anything about it), you can run an analysis on a volume by clicking the Analyze button. When the analysis is complete, you can click the Defragment button to start the process, which is shown in Figure 8.13.

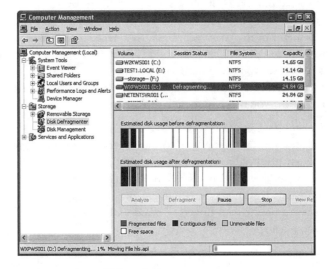

Figure 8.13   Defragmenting a volume (XP version).

Defragmenting a volume is an extremely CPU- and hard drive–intensive operation, and on XP it not only makes your computer sluggish while it's running, its work is severely hampered if you continue to work with the computer while it's working. In particular, saving documents or otherwise writing files to the disk can make the XP defragmenter have to start over from scratch.

As with the Disk Cleanup utility, the true power of the Disk Defragmenter comes if you use the Windows Task Scheduler to create a scheduled event for it and allow it run weekly during a low-usage time. As I mentioned, Vista does this by default. You can manually create a similar scheduled task on XP.

Tip

The defragmentation tool provided with Windows is a "lite" version of a commercial product called Diskeeper. You can also buy disk defragmenters that do a more thorough job, and which, for example, can also defragment the Windows page file. Check out PerfectDisk at www.raxco.com and Diskeeper at www.diskeeper.com (with one k) for two such products. If you use your computer for serious work, I'd *strongly* recommend that you get a good defragmenter, and set it up to run weekly to monthly. It's one of only a few types of add-on tool that can really pay you back with added productivity.

Although you can perform disk defragmentation with the GUI, you can also do it from the command line, which is helpful if you want to create a cleanup batch file or script. You can defragment a volume with the `defrag` command, which on Vista has the following syntax:

```
     defrag volume [-a] [-f] [-v]
or   defrag -c [-r | -w] [-f] [-v]
```

or on XP, the following syntax:

```
defrag volume [-a] [-f] [-v]
```

The parameters for the `defrag` command are outlined in Table 8.13.

Table 8.13   Parameters for the *defrag* Command

Parameter	Description
volume	The drive letter or a mount point of the volume to be defragmented.
-c	Defragments all volumes on the computer (Vista only).
-r	Partial defragment: leaves fragments over 64MB in size alone (Vista only).
-w	Full defragment: consolidates even large chunks (Vista only).
-a	Analyzes the volume and displays a summary of the analysis report.
-v	Displays the complete analysis and defragmentation reports.
-f	Forces defragmentation of the volume even if free disk space is low. This can considerably slow the process.

Without options -a or -f, defrag makes its own decision whether to defragment or not. And on Vista, without -r or -w, Vista assumes -r and performs a partial defragment. This isn't such a problem: 64MB is a large chunk of data to be able to read at once.

A few points should be kept in mind when attempting to perform disk defragmentation:

- A volume must have at least 15% free space to be defragmented. Defrag uses this space as a sorting area for file fragments. If a volume has less than 15% free space, defrag won't try unless you specify the -f option and even then will only partially defragment the volume.

- You cannot defragment volumes that the file system has marked as dirty. A volume could be marked as dirty if it is online and has outstanding changes that must be made at the next successful startup or if Windows previously crashed while it was saving changes to the disk. A volume that is marked as dirty may be in an inconsistent status, which requires that the CHKDSK utility be run to verify and repair the consistency of the volume. To solve this, restart Windows.

- You cannot run the defrag command and GUI Disk Defragmenter utility simultaneously. And you cannot defragment more than one volume at a time because the actual work is done by an underlying Windows service, and it works on just one volume at a time.

Backing Up Your Disk

I'm sure I don't need to warn you of the importance of backing up your hard drive. Computers are *so* much more reliable today than they were even a decade ago, but they do still fail, and you can be sure that one day when you turn on your computer you'll see nothing on the screen but "Hard Drive Failure." All those photographs, songs, job leads, love letters, all that work…all gone. It's a sickening feeling. And it could happen tomorrow. So: You have to back up.

The good news is that it's not expensive, and it's not difficult. You can get a high-capacity tape drive, but these days, I find it's just as easy to use a 250 or 500GB FireWire or USB-2 portable hard drive. These currently cost less than $200—sometimes *much* less if you can find a sale or rebate promotion, and the security they give you is well worth the cost. (If it makes you feel better, when the first hard drive came out in 1956, that much disk space would have cost $13.6 billion in today's dollars.) My own backups are about 40GB in size, so I can do one every week and easily fit four on a single portable drive.

Microsoft does provide some sort of backup tool with every version of Windows, although the tools' serviceability varies from version to version, as outlined in Table 8.14.

Table 8.14   Backup Programs Provided with Windows

Windows Version	Backup Program
2000 Professional	The **NTBackup** program provided with Windows 2000 does a decent job of backing up to tape or disk drives. You can buy better programs, but this one is adequate for home and small business use.
XP Professional	**NTBackup** is also provided with XP Pro, and it works better than Windows 2000's version, thanks to the Volume Shadow Copy service (VSS) that we discuss shortly.
	Automated System Recovery is XP's replacement for Windows 2000's Emergency System Recovery and Windows 9x's Emergency Startup Disks.

Windows Version	Backup Program
XP Home Edition	**NTBackup** is on the Windows XP Home setup CD-ROM, but is not installed by default. (Perhaps Microsoft thought that it was too complex for home users?) To install it, insert your Windows XP setup CD-ROM, use Windows Explorer to browse to \VALUEADD\MSFT\NTBACKUP, and double-click ntbackup.msi. If you're not a computer administrator, right-click ntbackup.msi, select Run As, and use an Administrator account. Automated System Recovery is not available.
Vista	Windows Vista does not provide NTBackup, nor Automated System Recovery. (Although, if you need to restore backup sets created by NTBackup, you can download a tool from Microsoft's website.) Instead, Vista versions come with one or more new backup tools: **File and Folder Backup, Complete PC Backup,** and **Previous Versions**. The tools provided with the various Vista versions vary:
Home Basic	Vista Home Basic provides only the File and Folder backup option. You can back up to CD/DVD media and removable disks, but not to a network folder. Backups cannot be scheduled automatically. You can back up user files and documents, but not applications or Windows itself. For adequate coverage, we recommend using a third-party backup program.
Home Premium	See the preceding notes for Home Basic. The only additions are that backups to network shared folders are supported, and backups may be scheduled with the Task Scheduler.
Business, Enterprise, Ultimate	All three Vista backup options are available.

For Vista, it appears that Microsoft decided to provide only fall-down-easy backup systems in the hope that more people would actually use them. So, for more sophisticated backups, you'll have to look to a third-party vendor.

Note

If you have backup sets created by **ntbackup** that have files you need to restore onto a computer running Vista, you can download a utility from Microsoft's website to do the job. Go to www.microsoft.com, search the downloads section for Windows NT Backup—Restore Utility.

Note

In a business environment, if you have more than three or four computers, you should seriously think about acquiring an enterprise backup solution, such as Backup Exec or NetBackup. These systems can reach through the network and back up each computer onto one central tape or disk library. This not only saves time and labor, but the automation helps ensure that backups get done regularly rather than sporadically-if-ever.

Backup Integrity

Backup programs on Windows 2000 were frequently unable to back up the Registry data for logged-on users and services, and in many cases, in-use data files. The result was that full disk backups omitted some key files, and if you had to restore Windows after a complete failure, these files and user settings were missing. Or, files that were actively being updated during the backup could be saved in an inconsistent state, with different parts of the file saved before, during, and after changes were made. The Volume Shadow Copy Service (VSS) built into Windows XP and Vista solves both of these problems.

Volume Shadow Copy

The Volume Shadow Copy Service, also called the Volume Snapshot Service, is provided with Windows XP and Vista. The service provides a way to take a "snapshot," also called a *shadow copy*, of an entire disk volume frozen at a moment in time. This system is used to support several types of backup mechanisms on Windows. Here's one way that it's used: A backup program can request that Windows make a shadow copy of a disk drive, and it's this copy that actually gets backed up. Applications and services can continue to modify, create, and delete files, but Windows saves a copy of the original version of every subsequently changed data block on the disk in a file called a *shadow archive*. As the backup program reads through the disk volume, Windows feeds it unchanged data blocks directly from the disk, and original copies of any changed data blocks from the shadow archive. Thus, the backup program sees a view of the hard disk in the exact form it was in at the moment the snapshot was taken, whereas every other application sees ongoing, changing data from moment to moment. When the backup has completed, the shadow copy can be deleted, and Windows releases the frozen copies of the changed data, so overall there is no cost to the file system.

Note

You may read statements in some books and on some websites—even some Microsoft websites—that state or imply that the Shadow service is not provided with Vista Home versions, but that's not the case. The reason for the confusion is that Vista's Previous Versions feature is frequently called the Shadow Copies feature. The Home versions of Vista lack this feature as well as Complete PC backup. But the underlying Volume Shadow Copy Service *is* provided with all versions of Windows Vista and XP, and it definitely helps to create more consistent and complete backups on Vista Home Basic and Premium.

Volume snapshots on XP are meant to be temporary, and definitely don't survive a reboot. On Vista, however, besides helping to provide better backups, the Volume Shadow Copy service can provide persistent shadow copies—disk volume snapshots that are kept and used more or less indefinitely. This new capability was used to completely redesign the System Restore feature on Vista, and to construct the Previous Versions features available on Vista Business, Enterprise, and Ultimate. Both these features are based on this new VSS capability.

Here's how they work: Vista uses the Volume Shadow Copy mechanism to take a snapshot of every hard disk that is protected by System Protection (System Restore) every so often—usually daily, at or after 4:00 a.m., or whenever something causes Windows to save a System Restore Point, like installing a new device driver. As discussed earlier, the Volume Shadow Copy service monitors all changes to the hard disk from this point on, and sequesters a copy of the original version of every disk block that gets changed. Unlike the temporary snapshots created just for the duration of a disk backup operation, these shadow copies are kept more or less permanently (that is, until the original-data archive takes up 15–30% of your disk space, or until 64 snapshots have accumulated—then older snapshots are deleted). These daily snapshots in effect are a set of instantly available "backup copies" of the hard disk stretching backward in time. These copies serve as the restore points from which Windows can extract and restore essential Windows files, and, for Vista Ultimate, Business, and Enterprise, provide a historical view of file changes, made available as previous versions.

Now, when you first start thinking about this, you may be alarmed. Doesn't having this feature mean that, if Windows is keeping, say, 20 days worth of snapshots, whenever you write to the disk Windows has to also store copies of the original data 20 times? And as you add files to your computer over time, won't shadow copies of the disk's *older* contents end up using most of your disk space? No, it's not nearly as bad as it might seem at first.

First of all, shadow copies consume extra disk space and cause a disk performance penalty only when existing data is *changed* for the *first time* after a snapshot is taken—only then, and just once, does the original data have to be preserved. For example, if you copy, say, 1GB of digital photographs onto your hard disk, these newly added files don't affect the snapshots—they weren't there when the snapshots were taken, and the Shadow service knows not to make backup copies of disk blocks that were previously unused. The only disk blocks that have to be preserved in this case are the ones that hold the lists of filenames in the folder to which you added the photographs, and only the original empty version has to be preserved. And folders don't take up much space.

Suppose that you then drag the photographs from one folder to another. Again: no penalty. When you move or rename files, only the folder entries are changed; the bulk of the data is untouched. The only thing that will make you lose disk space to shadow copies is if you later edit and overwrite files after a subsequent volume snapshot is taken. Or, you delete them *and* empty the Recycle Bin. Then the Volume Shadow Copy service has to read the original data blocks and write them into the shadow archive before writing the changed data to the files. Because *most* files don't change over time, volume shadowing just doesn't consume that much extra space.

Furthermore, the shadowing process has been highly optimized on Windows Vista. Even if there are 20 separate active shadow copies of a hard disk (that is, 20 days worth of snapshots), the architecture of the Shadow service ensures that only *one* copy of each original data block has to be saved to maintain all the shadows. Even the built-in disk defragmenting service was redesigned with its impact on the Shadow service in mind because when the defragmenter shuffles data around, the Shadow service has to back up all data moved from its original location.

Finally, the amount of disk space that can be used to hold shadow copy data is limited usually to 15% of the hard disk space, or up to 30% for disks that are used to hold complete PC backups, which we discuss shortly. If the amount of disk space needed by shadow copies starts to exceed this limit, Windows automatically deletes older shadows. Also, regardless of disk space, no more than 64 shadow copies are kept.

The Darker Side of Shadows

Volume shadowing is performed at the volume level, which sees a disk as just a huge array of data blocks, one after another. It's up to the higher-level NTFS file system driver to interpret these disk blocks as folders, file data, free space, and so on. If it was being pure about this approach, VSS wouldn't know anything about what's inside the disk blocks that it's copying. However, for performance reasons, this isn't exactly true.

First of all, it would be a waste of shadow space if VSS had to keep a copy of the previously unused disk blocks when a brand new file was saved—the data in these blocks wasn't part of a file, and will never need to be recovered. Furthermore, the copies of changed disk blocks—the shadow data itself—are stored in files *on the protected disk itself*, and VSS would end up spinning in circles if it tried to archive data in the shadow archive files, which change as a result of its own activity. Finally, there is no need to back up the page file, hibernation file, or other enormous disk files whose contents have only transient significance. Thus, for practical reasons, VSS isn't "pure," and gets some information about the files to which the blocks it monitors belong.

Besides empty space, the files that VSS omits shadows are listed in the registry under **HKEY_LOCAL_MACHINE\ SYSTEM\CurrentControlSet\Control\BackupRestore\FilesNotToSnapshot**, and applications (including Windows itself) can tell the Shadow service to exclude additional files. Presumably this is how the page file is excluded. If you're worried about the security of data archived by VSS, you should know that exclusion is not guaranteed. VSS is allowed to *try* to bypass files listed in **FilesNotToSnapshot**, but data in these files could still end up copied into the shadow files stored in **\System Volume Information**.

Note

For more information about the VSS, Previous Versions, and System Restore on Vista, check out the video at channel9.msdn.com/ShowPost.aspx?PostID=287219. It's a 50-minute interview with some of the features' primary developers.

Backup Files and Folders on Vista

All versions of Windows Vista include the Backup Files and Folders system, which can copy user files (but not Windows itself, nor applications) to alternative disk drives, recordable media, or network shares. For marketing reasons, different versions of Vista have more or less capable versions of this facility.

Note

This is the only backup tool provided for free with Vista Home Basic and Home Premium. Backup Files and Folders gives you a very easy way to protect and, if necessary, recover your personal data files. Vista Ultimate, Business, and Enterprise editions offer this tool along with two additional backup and restore mechanisms: Previous Versions and Complete PC Backup. Previous Versions provides one-stop-shopping recovery of files and folders backed up several different ways. Complete PC Backup helps you recover from a total system or disk failure. We'll talk about these additional tools later in this section.

To back up or restore files your files, or all users' files, click Start, All Programs, System Tools, Backup Status and Configuration. This brings up a panel with the major category icons on the left: Back Up Files, Restore Files, and (on Vista Business, Enterprise and Ultimate) Complete PC

Backup, as shown in Figure 8.14. If you click on one of the icons, two or more action items appear, which themselves may have additional choices, as follows:

Back Up Files choices:

- Set Up Automatic File Backup (not on Home Basic)
- Backup Now
- Change Backup Settings
- Turn On/Turn Off Automatic Backup (not on Home Basic)

Restore Files choices:

- Restore Files (restores only your own files)

    Files from the latest backup

    Files from an older backup
- Advanced Restore (restores files for all users)

    Files from the latest back up made on this computer

    Files from an older backup made on this computer

    Files from a backup made on a different computer (this choice also lets you restore a backup that no longer appears in the backup catalog, for example, after you have performed a Complete PC Restore)

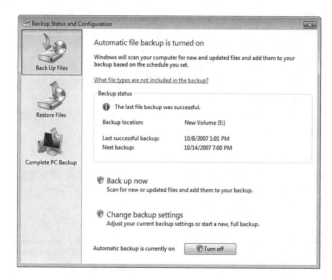

Figure 8.14 The Backup Status and Configuration tools on Vista.

Backups may be saved to and restored from an attached hard disk, recordable DVD or CD media, a magnetic tape drive (if available), or a network shared folder. The network options is not available on Home Basic.

What Gets Backed Up

Microsoft doesn't state clearly what Backup Files and Folders actually backs up, other than to say that you can elect to back up files in these categories: pictures, music, videos, email, documents, TV shows, compressed files, and "additional files."

Just what qualifies a file as a "document" is not specified, which is disturbing, to say the least. As far as I've been able to determine, the categories such as documents, music, and so on are determined from the file extensions. "Additional files" covers all file extensions not part of the other categories, *except* file types that Windows does not back up at all.

The types of files not backed up are again not explicitly documented, but Microsoft states that it *doesn't* back up files stored on hard disks formatted with the FAT file system, system files (.sys and .drv files), program files (.exe and .dll files), the recycle bin, temporary files, and user profile settings. Also, it does not back up email that's stored on a web-based email service such as Gmail or Hotmail, nor presumably data for email programs other than Outlook or Windows Mail.

Caution

Files that have been encrypted using Encrypting File System (EFS), which is available on Vista Business, Enterprise, and Ultimate editions *are* backed up if you have Vista Service Pack 1 or later, but are *not* backed up by the original release of Vista.

Backups are stored in the target drive or media in a folder named *computername*\Backup Set YYYY-MM-DD HHMMSS, where *computername* is the name of your computer and YYYY-MM-DD HHMMSS is the date and time of the last full backup in UTC (Greenwich Mean Time). The first backup and several subsequent backups are stored within this in subfolders named Backup Files YYYY-MM-DD HHMMSS. One subfolder corresponds to the initial backup date and time, and the others correspond to subsequent backups, which are incremental backups containing only files changed or added since the original. As the number of new and changed files increases over time, Windows will eventually suggest that you create a new full backup folder and set, or you can create a new full backup manually from the user interface.

Within the backup folders is a folder named Catalogs, which contains a database listing the backed-up files, and one or more Zip files containing the saved files, in Zip-compressed format. Each of these files is under 200MB in size to make it easier for Windows to split the backup contents across multiple media if need be.

Tip

If you want to quickly pull out just a single backed-up file, you can explore into these Zip files. Be aware, though, that files larger than 200MB or files that have alternate data streams are split during backup into multiple files in possibly more than one Zip file, so you should use the regular Restore function, which I'll describe shortly, to extract these.

The remainder of the section tells you how to create backups and restore data from them if necessary.

Scheduling Regular Backups

On Windows Home Premium, Business, Enterprise, and Ultimate editions, Windows requires to you to schedule automatic period backups before you can begin to use the Backup Files and Folder system. To do this, click Start, All Programs, System Tools, Backup Status and Configuration. Click Set Up Automatic File Backup, and select a backup schedule and destination target. However, remember, that

- If you want the backups to be saved to a network folder, the computer or server that is sharing the folder must be up and running when your computer performs its backups.

- If you save the backups to an external hard drive, the drive must be attached when your computer is scheduled to perform backups.

- If you save to recordable CD or DVD media, you should leave blank media in the drive before the scheduled backup. If blank media are not present when the scheduled backup starts, Windows prompts you to start the backup when you return to your computer or the next time you log on. If the backup requires more than one disc, Windows likewise stops when the first has been filled up, and prompts you to insert another the next time you log on.

You select the backup location on a screen labeled Where Do You Want to Save Your Backup. Here, you can select any available *extra* hard disks (but not the one on which Windows is installed), and any attached recordable CD or DVD drives, and on all but Home Basic, a network location in the form *computername**sharename* or *computername**sharename*\subfolder.

On Vista Home Basic, there is no built-in mechanism to schedule automatic backups, but you can work around this by using the Task Scheduler and the command-line version of the backup program, which we discuss shortly.

Performing a One-Time Backup

On Vista Home Premium, Ultimate, and the business versions of Vista, if you want to suppress the automatically scheduled backups and want to create backups only on your own terms, follow these steps:

1. Let the program walk you through setting up automatic backups. You have to do this. Pick any schedule you like.

2. Let the program perform the first full backup.

3. Click Turn Off to disable subsequent automatic backups.

Whether you are using manual or scheduled backups, you can perform a backup at any desired time by using the Backup Status and Configuration tool.

- To perform an incremental backup, select the Back Up Files button and click Back Up Now.

- To force Windows to perform a full backup, click Change Backup Settings, change the destination if desired and click Next, change the file types if desired and click Next, check Create a New Full Backup Now, then click Save Settings and Start Backup.

This starts the full backup.

Restoring Files and Folders on Vista

If you are using Vista Business, Enterprise, or Ultimate, the easiest way to restore files is to use the Previous Versions mechanism. To restore a file or folder (and its contents) to a saved version, right-click the file or folder in Explorer and select Restore Previous Version. Select the desired saved version from the list and click Restore. To recover a deleted file or folder, right-click the folder containing it, find an appropriate previous version, and click Open. Locate the desired file and drag it to a new location on your desktop or disk.

Tip

Shadow copies (listed in the Location column) are the fastest to restore. Shadow backups are created daily or more often, and also whenever Backup Files and Folders backups are made, and they stick around for a while, so use one of the Shadow copies if you can. Backups stored on external disks, network shares, DVD media, CD media, and tapes are progressively slower to use.

On any version of Vista, you can restore your own files from the Backup program. Click Start, All Programs, System Tools, Backup Status and Configuration. Click the Restore Files button. Then select Files from the Latest Backup or Files from an Older Backup.

To restore files for other users, or all users, or to restore files from a backup made on another Vista computer, select Advanced Restore from the Restore Files panel. The wizard walks you through selecting files as just mentioned. If you elect to restore files from a backup made on a different computer, you have to browse to the folder that contains the computer's backup.

Tip

You can also use the Different Computer option if you want to restore files from a backup, but the backup doesn't appear in the list of older backup files. This could happen if Windows loses its backup catalog because of a data error or a complete PC restore. Windows doesn't remember any of the backups made after the date of the complete PC backup that was used to do a complete restore.

When you have selected a backup to restore, click Add Files to restore individual files, Add Folders to restore entire folders (and their contents), or Search to locate files and folders by name. You are shown a dialog that looks like the standard Open File dialog, except that here you can browse only for files that are stored in the backup. Locate a file or folder that you want to restore and click Add, as shown in Figure 8.15.

When you have selected all the files and/or folders you want to recover, click Next.

Then select In the Original Location to restore the files in their original location, overwriting any existing copies of the files that might be there now. Select In the Following Location to restore the files into an alternative location. Finally, click Start Restore to begin the recovery process. Windows may prompt you to insert CD, DVD, or tape media, if necessary.

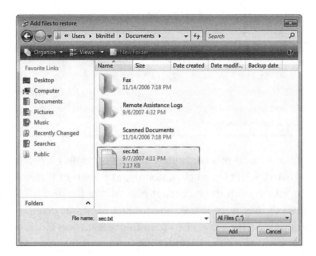

Figure 8.15   The Add Files to Restore dialog lets you browse for backed-up files.

Previous Versions

On Windows Vista Business, Enterprise, and Ultimate, Windows uses the automatic Shadow Copy archive—discussed earlier in this section—to let you see back in time into folders and files as they were at the times shadow snapshots were taken. The Previous Versions mechanism also keeps track of files that were backed up by File and Folder Backup to alternative hard disks, network shares, and removable media such as disks, recordable CDs and DVDs, or magnetic tape. These backup sources are merged into one list of available versions of every file and folder on every protected drive.

The Previous Versions mechanism can be very helpful, but it has some significant limitations that you need to be aware of:

- Unless you also perform backups to external disks or tape, Previous Versions *does not* protect you against a hard disk failure because shadow copies are kept on the same hard disk as the original files.

- Shadow copies are made only of files on disks that are protected by System Protection (System Restore). Unless you enable it for other drives, by default, only your boot drive is protected.

- Shadow copies can be purged automatically if Windows runs low on disk space and as the shadows age. You can't count on having access to previous copies indefinitely.

- If you create a file and then delete it before Windows has had a chance to take a snapshot, there is no previous version to recover.

- Likewise, if you make several changes to a document in one day, you can't recover each saved version—you can recover only the copies made when snapshots are taken, usually around 4:00 a.m. every day, or the first time the computer is running and left sitting idle after that. (Snapshots are also taken when you install software or update drivers.)

Caution

If you dual-boot your computer with Windows XP, every time you boot XP, Vista loses all shadow copy versions and restore points, and all but the most recent complete PC backup as well. There are steps you can take to prevent this, by preventing XP from seeing your Vista hard disk, but they are very cumbersome. The same applies to dual-booting with Window Server 2003. For more information, see bertk.mvps.org/html/dualboot.html. If you need to dual-boot XP and Vista, and you need keep your Vista restore points (and Previous Versions), your best bet is to use the BootItNG tool from www.terabyteunlimited.com.

To recover a previous version of a file, right-click the file, select Restore Previous Version, and if a desired version is listed, select it and click Restore, as shown in Figure 8.16. You can also reach the Previous Versions tab from the Properties page of any file or folder. Previous Versions of folders show the folders as they were at the time the snapshot was taken. But remember that the Date Modified timestamp is the time that the file or folder itself was last modified before the backup or snapshot was made; it is *not* the backup time.

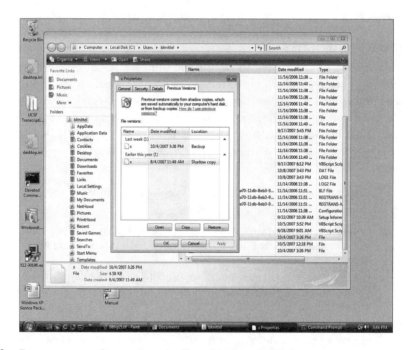

Figure 8.16   To recover an earlier version of a file, select it and click Restore.

To recover a previous version of a file or folder you have renamed or deleted, locate the folder that *contained* the deleted file or folder, right-click it, and select Restore Previous Versions. Select a snapshot, and click Open. Now, drill down to find the file or folder you want to restore. Drag it out of the window in which it appears (the window whose title shows the snapshot or backup date), and drag it to the desired location.

A file or folder might have no previous versions listed for several reasons:

■ The file may not have changed since it was created. To see whether Previous Versions is working, save a backup copy of the file, and then change it. You should then be able to see a previous version.

■ A snapshot may not have been taken before the file was last modified.

■ If the file is stored on a drive that is not protected by System Protection, shadow copies are not available. To enable protection, see the section titled "System Restore" later in this chapter.

■ If your computer is running XP or a Vista Home version, Previous Versions are not available.

■ You may have renamed the file. View older versions of the folder that contains the file, and look for the file under its original name.

■ If your computer is a member of a domain network, your network administrator may have disabled the feature through Group Policy.

■ The file might be excluded from shadow copies by the Registry key `HKEY_LOCAL_MACHINE\ SYSTEM\CurrentControlSet\Control\BackupRestore\FilesNotToSnapshot`. Although the shadow service works at the disk block level, and it shouldn't really know about the contents of the disk it's shadowing, it does actually have the *option* of peering into the disk's contents to optimize performance, and it *can* exclude the listed files from shadowing. This is done mostly only for files that are large, change frequently, and don't need to be backed up. By default, this key excludes Windows Update downloads, Performance and Reliability monitoring logs, and Outlook offline-mailbox copies. Applications and Windows itself can tell the shadow service to exclude additional files not listed under that Registry key.

■ If your computer does not have a network adapter, if your adapter is disabled, or if you have unchecked File and Printer Sharing for Microsoft Networks on the adapter's properties page, Previous Versions is not listed, even if they are present. (Yes, this is very strange, but Previous Versions was originally a Windows Server facility, and it's still intimately tied into networking.)

By the way, even though the Previous Versions feature isn't available on Vista Home versions, the volume shadowing system *is* there and it's fully functional. Thus, previous versions of your files are there on your hard disk, in the "virtual" shadow volumes. I'd say there's a nice opportunity here for a clever software developer to write a handy utility to browse and recover files for Vista Home users.

Complete PC Backup on Vista

Complete PC Backup is a backup/restore option available on Windows Vista Business, Enterprise, and Ultimate editions only. This backup tool creates a complete image of your computer's hard disks onto an alternate hard disk, recordable DVD media, or network folder. You can also back up to a network folder if you perform the backup from the command line.

Inside Complete PC Backup

Internally, Complete PC Backup (CPCB) is a *very* clever system that uses the Volume Shadow Copy Service and technology borrowed from Microsoft Virtual PC. What CPCB does is create a virtual hard disk, whose contents are stored in a single file on the destination disk. If you're familiar with Virtual PC, the Complete PC Backup is just a VHD file containing the exact contents of your hard disk. The CPCB program uses the Volume Shadow Copy service to take a snapshot of your hard disk, opens the virtual disk, and copies your hard disk to it, block by block. The resulting VHD file is not compressed, but it is compact; unused disk blocks are not copied. (And in case you are getting ideas, don't bother trying to mount and boot this VHD file inside Virtual PC—it doesn't work. You *can* mount the VHD file as a secondary disk in a virtual machine, and grab files out of it, or you can use the **vhdmount** utility to mount the VHD file as a virtual disk right in XP or Vista—do a Google search for vhdmount for more information.)

Every time you perform a subsequent complete PC backup, Windows additionally asks VSS to create a permanent shadow copy of the drive holding the VHD (virtual disk) file, and then updates the VHD file with the current contents of your hard drive. Thus, the VHD file gets the most recent data, and the shadow copy(ies) enable the Complete PC Restore program to offer to restore files from the shadow (older) versions of the VHD file, at least until the shadow data on the backup disk hits 30% of the disk's capacity, and older shadow copies are purged. This system is *very* clever; the Shadow service does all the work of tracking multiple versions of the VHD image of your hard disk.

This also explains why, if there is damage to the System Volume Information folder or if you purge restore points and previous versions using the Disk Cleanup Wizard, Complete PC Backup can restore only the most current complete PC backup. It will have the VHD file, which contains the most up-to-date disk image, but not the shadow copies that hold changed blocks from the older versions.

To start the tool, click Start, All Programs, Accessories, System Tools, Backup Status and Configuration.

Tip

Before you run your first complete PC backup, perform a Disk Defragmentation. When you make subsequent complete backups, less will have moved around, so the (shadow) copies of earlier backups will take less space and thus will stick around longer.

Caution

If your hard disk is encrypted with BitLocker, you should know that the data on a complete PC backup is *not* also encrypted. You should be sure to secure the backup media. You can also protect sensitive files and folders with the Encrypted File System. This data *will* still be encrypted on the backup media.

Complete PC Backup to a Network Folder

The Complete PC Backup GUI doesn't offer you the choice, but you can save a complete PC backup to a network shared folder if you run the backup from the command line.

First, you must open an elevated command prompt. To do this, click Start, All Programs, Accessories, and right-click Command Prompt. Select Run As Administrator, and then approve the User Account Control prompt.

Then type the command

```
wbadmin start backup -backuptarget:destination -include:volumelist
```

where *destination* is a drive and path to a mapped network folder, or a UNC-format network path of the form \\servername\sharename[\subfolder], and *volumelist* is a comma-delimited list of drive letters. For example, to back up drives C and D, the command might be

```
wbadmin start backup -backuptarget:\\myserver\cpcbackups -include:c:,d:
```

Add -quiet to the command line to prevent wbadmin from prompting you to confirm starting the backup. You'd want to do this if you run the backup as a scheduled task or from a batch file or script.

When the backup is complete, the target folder will contain a folder named WindowsImageBackup, containing a folder with the same name as the backed-up computer, containing a folder named Backup *YYYY-MM-DD HHMMSS*, where *YYYY-MM-DD HH MM SS* is the backup time in UTC (Greenwich Mean Time, several hours ahead of time in the Americas). Within that folder is one VHD file for every backed-up disk drive, and ancillary files that are used by the restore utility. If you perform a second backup to the same folder, the Backup *YYYY...* folder is renamed.

Recall that if you perform complete PC backups to a network destination, only the most current version of the VHD file is kept, and on network shares, there may be no Volume Shadow copy made on the *remote* volume, so older versions of the Complete PC backup may not be available. Furthermore, a network backup does not appear in the Previous Versions list, although a shadow copy on your *local* disk, from which the complete PC backup is made, will be present for some time.

Restoring a Complete PC Backup

You can restore a complete PC backup using a GUI tool or the command line. The GUI tool restores your entire computer to a previous state, including *all* files on *all* hard drives. This is a drastic operation: It essentially erases your all your hard disks and restores them to their state at a previous time. *All* changes made since the selected backup are lost, including any files you added in the meantime.

If you are sure that you want to restore the entire complete PC backup, follow these steps:

1. You need to have a running version of Windows Vista, so if you've had to replace your computer or hard disks, you need to install Vista before restoring the complete PC backup. Don't bother configuring anything!

The PC must have at least the same number of hard disks as the original PC, and these disks must be at least as large as the originals.

You also need the backup data, which is stored on a hard drive or DVD/R media. If you backed up to a network folder, you have to copy the WindowsImageBackup folder onto a drive that is accessible to the Windows setup program such as a secondary internal hard disk.

2. Restart Windows, and during startup press F8 repeatedly. In the Advanced Boot Options menu, select Repair Your Computer. On the System Recovery Options menu, select Windows Complete PC Restore. If Windows can't get to the Advanced Boot Options menu, boot from your Windows setup DVD and select Repair Your Computer.

When the restore operation is complete, Windows restarts.

3. If you restored Windows onto larger hard disks than you started with, you'll find that after restoring, the new disks only have as much usable space as your original disks. If your disks are formatted with NTFS, you can use the Disk Management console, which is described earlier in this chapter, to expand your disk's volumes to incorporate the unallocated space. See the instructions in"Resizing on Vista" for more information. Some people have reported that the Disk Manager GUI doesn't permit them to expand partitions after a complete PC restore. In this case, the diskpart command may be able to do the job.

Tip

After you've performed the restore, you might want to then restore files from Windows file and folder backups (discussed later in this chapter) made after the complete PC Backup. However, you'll find that the later backups don't appear in the list of available backups because when you performed the restore, you reverted to the earlier version of the backup catalog. You can get around by this problem by using the Restore from a Backup Made on a Different Computer option. You'll have to manually browse for the later backup sets.

Restoring Individual Files or Folders from a Complete Backup

Because Complete PC Backup saves full image copies of your hard disks, it stands to reason that you should be able to extract individual files from these backups. But, for whatever reason, Microsoft chose not to make it easy. So, before you try, see whether the desired file or folder is available through Previous Versions. Windows keeps the shadow copy from which the Complete PC Backup was made for some time, so you might be able to recover what you need that way.

The command-line program wbadmin has a restore option that *should* let you recover individual files or folders from a backup. However, it refuses to perform this task on Windows Vista. The only option on Vista is to dig into the VHD file and extract the desired files manually. You can do this in one of two ways.

First, if you have Microsoft Virtual PC and are running Windows XP or Vista in it, you can mount the VHD file as a second or third drive on a virtual machine, and access the files that way. To mount the VHD file in Virtual PC, before you boot the virtual machine, open its Settings dialog, select Hard Disk 2 or 3, click Browse, and locate the VHD File in the Complete PC Backup destination drive under the WindowsImageBackup folder. Then boot up the virtual machine and look inside the mounted drive, which will be labeled E or F. If you have the Virtual Machine Additions involved, you can use Windows Explorer to drag files out of the virtual drive onto your real desktop or another folder. (And, as I mentioned earlier, the VHD disk image is not bootable, so you can't run your imaged copy of Vista under Virtual PC.)

You might also try to obtain a copy of the program vhdmount, which lets you see into the VHD file as though it were a disk drive attached to your computer. To read more about this option, do a Google search for the words *download vhdmount*.

Automated System Recovery on XP

Automated System Recovery (ASR) is an advanced restoration option of the Backup utility available on Windows XP Professional, but not on XP Home Edition, nor any version of Vista. ASR can be used to restore your system if other disaster recovery methods fail or are not available for use. Using ASR, you can restore the operating system back to a previous state, which will allow you to start Window XP Professional. You should always consider ASR your last resort for recovery, after Safe mode, the Recovery Console, and Last Known Good Configuration, which are detailed in Chapter 12, "Windows Troubleshooting." You should make a point to keep your ASR media up to date as you make configuration changes to your computer in order to minimize the amount of recovery required should you ever need to use ASR. To use the ASR Wizard to create a set of ASR media, you only need to click on the Automated System Recovery Wizard button on the main page of the Backup tool, as shown in Figure 8.17.

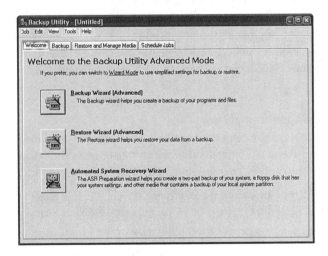

Figure 8.17 Start the Automated System Recovery Disk Wizard from the main page of the Backup utility.

Using NTBackup Backup on XP

Using the Windows XP NTBackup utility consists of three distinct processes: creating one or more backup configurations, scheduling backups to occur automatically, and performing restorations.

There are five types of backups you can perform:

- **Normal backup**—Copies all selected files and marks each file as having been backed up (the archive bit—the "changed since last backup" file attribute—is cleared). Only the most recent backup set is required to perform restoration. This is also called a *full backup*.

- **Incremental backup**—Copies only those files created or changed since the last normal or incremental backup; the archive attribute is then cleared. Using normal and incremental backups, you will require the last normal backup and *all* intervening incremental backups in order to perform restoration.

- **Differential backup**—Copies files created or changed since the last normal backup; the archive bit is left alone. Differential backup set will get larger over time, as more and more files are changed since the last normal backup. Eventually a new normal backup has to be performed. The benefit is that only two backup sets are needed to restore all files: the last normal backup, and the most recent differential backup.

- **Copy backup**—Copies all selected files but does not mark each file as having been backed up (the archive attribute is not cleared). Copy backups have no effect on any other type of backup operation.

- **Daily backup**—Copies all selected files that have been modified the day the daily backup is performed. The archive attribute is not cleared in this case. This is a risky procedure as files modified right around midnight could be left behind, and missing a day leaves files unprotected.

In addition to your system's drives, you will see that NTBackup has a choice to back up something called *System State*. This is a collection of Registry data, device drivers, and system programs. When you back up your entire hard drive, this stuff is included, so you don't need to specify it in that case. It's mainly an option you can use to back up Windows XP itself before installing a new driver or application. The new System Restore feature does just as good a job of this, so System State is less necessary now than in the past. System Restore is discussed later in this chapter.

Creating the Backup Configurations

The Windows XP NTBackup utility makes it extremely simple to create a backup configuration. The basic steps to create the configuration are outlined here, although your options and decisions will vary depending on how your system and backup media devices are configured.

1. Log on as a computer administrator user. Start the Backup Wizard by clicking Start, All Programs, Accessories, System Tools, Backup; or, at the command prompt, type `ntbackup`.

2. Start the Backup Wizard by clicking the Backup Wizard (Advanced) button.

3. Click Next to dismiss the opening page of the wizard. From the What to Back Up page, select the scope of the backup: everything, selected files, or System State, which includes the Registry and Windows' protected files. Click Next.

   If you chose to back up selected files and folders, proceed to step 4, otherwise skip to step 5.

4. From the Items to Back Up page, choose the files and folders to back up, as shown in Figure 8.18, and then click Next. If you have mapped network drives to drive letters, you can also back up these folders even though they are stored on other computers.

5. From the Backup type... page, choose the backup filename and location and click Next. In the case of a removable hard drive, enter the drive letter for the drive, followed by a filename that identifies your backup. You can also store the backup on another computer, using a network drive. For the filename, you might want to use names that incorporate the name of the computer and the date and type of the backup. For example, I might name a full backup of my computer named JAVA on July 4 as `java_full_0704.bkf`.

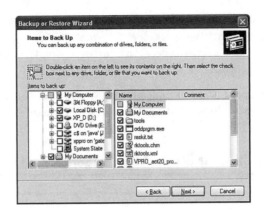

Figure 8.18   Selecting files to back up. In this example, both the C: and D: drives will be backed up.

6. To configure advanced options, including scheduling and disabling volume shadow copy, click Advanced and proceed to step 7. If you want to perform this backup immediately, click Finish.

7. From the Type of Backup page, select the type of backup you want (the default is Normal) and click Next. I personally perform normal backups monthly, and differential backups weekly or more often, but you can use a different schedule; certainly do it no less often than I do!

8. From the How to Back Up page, select your preferences as they relate to verification and volume shadow copy and select Next. It's generally not necessary to verify backups written to a disk. If you're backing up to tape, you may want to verify.

9. From the Backup Options page, select whether to append or overwrite existing data and select Next. For backups to a disk, select overwrite rather than append.

10. From the When to Back Up page, select when you want to perform this backup and click Next. If you selected Now, click Finish to start the backup.

11. If you selected Later, you will be able to configure scheduling options. When you have completed setting all scheduling options, click Next. Enter the username and password information of a computer administrator account when requested (to ensure that this user has permissions to perform backups). Click Finish to complete the procedure.

Additionally, you can choose to create a backup configuration manually, however you will still make all of the same decisions as when using the Backup Wizard.

Excluding Files from Backups

If you watch the backup procedure in action, you may see it copying large files that you know aren't valuable, and which you would just as soon not have backed up at all. Although you could manually locate and uncheck these files in the list of files to back up, you can also make settings in NTBackup to exclude them automatically.

NTBackup ignores all files listed under Registry key `HKEY_LOCAL_MACHINE\system\CurrentControlSet\Control\BackupRestore\FilesNotToBackUp` (exclusions for all users), and under `HKEY_CURRENT_USER\system\CurrentControlSet\Control\BackupRestore\FilesNotToBackUp` (exclusions for the user running NTBackup).

The `FilesNotToBackUp` list is also excluded by the System Restore feature, discussed in Chapter 12. Many file types are excluded by default. The default list of files types designated for exclusion are listed in Table 8.15.

Table 8.15 Default *FilesNotToBackUp* Categories

File Categories
Automated System Recovery Error File
Automated System Recover Log File
Background Transfer (Automatic Updates) metadata
Catalog Database
Client Side Cache (offline files)
Digital Rights Management
Internet Explorer cache index
Memory Page File
Microsoft Writer (Bootable State)
MS Distributed Transaction Coordinator database
Netlogon
Files manually listed for exclusion in NTBackup
Hibernation file
Registry Writer data
SUS (Software Update) Client
System Restore index data
Task Scheduler log
Temporary files (TEMP environment variable)
Winlogon debugging information

You can add exclude additional files by following these steps:

1. Start NTBackup, and select the link for Advanced mode.

2. Select Tools, Options, and view the Exclude Files tab.

3. Click one of the Add New buttons, under All Users or under your user account name.

4. Select a listed file extension (file type), such as .xyz to eliminate all .xyz files, or enter a file-matching pattern such as DATA*.Z*, to match files based on name as well as extension, as shown in Figure 8.19.

Figure 8.19   Listing files or file types for exclusion.

5. Select or type a path, and check or uncheck Applies to All Subfolders.

6. Click OK, and either add more entries, or click OK again to save the updated list.

Scheduling Backups on XP

Managing a backup schedule is very easy in Windows XP. Simply switch to the Schedule Jobs tab from the Backup utility advanced view. Each day on the calendar will show what type of backup is scheduled for that day. Holding the cursor over a backup will display the backup name. You can edit the backup properties, including rescheduling the backup, by clicking it. You can also create new backup configurations by clicking the Add Job button.

After a Disaster: Performing the Restoration on XP

Should the day actually come that you need to put your backup system to the test, the actual process of performing the restoration is a relatively easy task in Windows XP Professional—as long as you are ready for the task. The basic steps to perform a restoration are outlined here, although your options and decisions will vary depending on how your system and backup media devices are configured.

1. You will need a working copy of Windows XP. If your original installation of Windows is working, and you just need to recover a few files, this isn't a concern. But if you lost your entire hard drive, you'll need to install a fresh copy of Windows XP. You'll be replacing this installation with the version saved on your backup, so don't spend any time configuring it, just get it to the point of being able to run ntbackup and read the saved backup files.

If Windows won't boot normally, try Safe mode.

2. Log on as a computer administrator user. If you have an antivirus program installed, disable it. (You don't need to do this if you started Windows in Safe mode.) Then start the Backup Wizard by clicking Start, Programs, Accessories, System Tools, Backup, or click Start, Run and enter **ntbackup**.

3. Start the Backup Wizard by clicking the Restore Wizard (Advanced) button from the main page of the Backup utility.

4. Click Next to dismiss the opening page of the wizard.

5. From the What to Restore page, select the backup set and the files you want to restore (all, or just some). If your desired backup set is not listed, click the Browse button to locate it. You will need to browse to the disk files that you stored on the removable disk or on a network folder. After making your selections, click Next.

6. To configure advanced options, such as changing the restoration location, click Advanced and proceed to step 7. Otherwise, click Finish to start the restoration.

7. From the Where to Restore page, select the restoration location for the files and click Next. Generally you will want to restore files to their original location, unless you want to be able to compare the files you have on your disk now with the files in the backup set; in that case, you must restore them to a different folder.

8. From the How to Restore page, select your option in regards to overwriting existing files and click Next. In most cases, you will want to replace all files in all circumstances; this will get you back to the original version you had in the backup set. If you are just recovering files you accidentally deleted, you do not want the restore operation to overwrite newer files.

9. From the Advanced Restore Options page, select the options you want, and click Next.

10. Click Finish to start the restoration.

Note

Before performing a restore that includes the Registry, NTBackup examines Registry value `HKEY_LOCAL_MACHINE\system\CurrentControlSet\Control\BackupRestore\KeysNotToRestore`. Keys listed here are not restored. If a key name ends with \, the key's subkeys are also not restored. If a key name ends with *, the subkeys are merged based on Start values. This helps when restoring Windows onto a computer with a different hardware setup. For more information see support.microsoft.com/default.aspx?kbid=249694.

The following list provides some additional help when deciding which advanced restore options to choose.

- **Restore Security**—Restores security settings for each file and folder. You usually want this enabled.

- **Restore Junction Points, and Restore File and Folder Data Under Junction Points to the Original Location**—Restores junction points on your hard disk as well as the data that the junction points point to. If you are restoring a mounted drive, and you want to restore the data that is on the mounted drive, you must select this check box. If you do not select this check box, you will only restore the folder containing the mounted drive. This applies to very few users, so if you don't know what a junction point is, you don't need to worry about it.

- **Preserve Existing Volume Mount Points**—Prevents the restore operation from writing over any volume mount points you have created on the partition or volume you are restoring data to. Again, if you haven't created mount points, leave the default setting alone.

- **Restore Removable Storage Database**—Restores the Removable Storage database and deletes the existing Removable Storage database. If you are not using the Removable Storage manager to manage storage media (tapes, for instance), you do not need to select this option.

Note

After restoring a full system, restart Windows. You may find that some of your hardware doesn't work when Windows comes back up. To fix this, open the Device Manager, right-click each of the nonfunctioning devices in turn, and select Uninstall. Restart Windows again. Log back on as a computer administrator, and the Found New Hardware Wizard should pop up. Let it locate device drivers automatically. This *ought* to get everything working again.

If you really do need to restore the Registry and Windows itself, however, you might be better off using the System Restore feature that's built into Windows. It does require that your hard disk is intact, but it's a more sophisticated system that's better for recovering from serious configuration goof-ups.

Third-Party Backup Solutions

Windows XP and Vista come with possibly adequate backup systems, but for effective, reliable, complete backups, you're best off using an add-on program purchased from a reputable vendor.

We recommend that you investigate the following backup systems:

- Norton Ghost (www.symantec.com)
- Norton Go-Back (www.symantec.com)
- Acronis True Image Home (www.acronis.com)
- Backup4All (www.backup4all.com)

and many more...the list grows daily. I'd recommend checking out recent reviews at www.pcmag.com, or another reputable magazine's website. (Watch out for bogus sites with names like backup-software-reviews-online.com and such.)

There are also now many online backup services, which have the tremendous appeal of storing your data somewhere far, far away, safe from theft or destruction at your home or office. These products include the following:

- **@Backup** (www.backup.com)—Prices start at $49.50 per year for 2GB of storage. (Actually you get quite a bit more storage at this price because the service saves *90 days* worth of daily backups.)

- **Carbonite Online Backup** (www.carbonite.com)—$49.95 per year for unlimited storage (but it doesn't back up application files or Windows itself).

- **Iron Mountain Connected Backup for PC** (backup.ironmountain.com)—Prices start at $80 per year for 250MB of storage.

- **IBackup** (www.ibackup.com)—Prices start at $99.50 per year for 5GB.

I've been using @Backup for several years, and now I don't think that I would ever go without having an automatic, daily offsite backup.

System Restore

Sometimes, installing a device driver causes such severe instability that you need to restore your system to a previously known good state. In the old days, the only way to do this was to restore your system from a backup. Today, however, Windows Vista and XP have a System Restore application that can be used to restore a previous configuration of Windows. Windows keeps a list of *restore points*, backup files containing critical system information and driver files, that you can use to take a step back in time.

What Restore Points Actually Restore

Although they look and work the same from the user's point of view, under the hood, the mechanism behind Restore Points on XP and Vista are very different. On XP, when you create a restore point, Windows saves a copy of a few critical driver files and databases, such as Registry hives, Windows Management Instrumentation configuration, the Internet Information Services metabase (if IIS is installed), and the COM registration database. It subsequently monitors all accesses to files on protected drives, and the first time an attempt is made to delete or modify any of a long list of protected file types, Windows first squirrels away a backup copy of the file. Restore points on XP are contained in compressed folders that contain selected driver files and Registry and configuration data . Over time, they also accrue the original versions of files that have subsequently been changed or deleted.

On Vista, the Volume Shadow Copy Service is used, as described earlier in this chapter. No data is copied right away, but from the moment of the snapshot onward, all changes to the hard disk are monitored, and changed data blocks are collected and saved. The entire hard disk, rather than individual files, is covered this way. Later, if you perform a System Restore, the selected file types are pulled out of the snapshot image and copied to their proper places.

Regardless of the mechanism used, restore points protect and can restore the following file types:

- The Registry, including all the per-user Registry sections from the user profiles but excluding the security (SAM) sections that contain user passwords.
- The COM+ database.
- File system configuration data.
- The Windows File Protection .dll cache.
- The WMI database.
- On Windows XP, the IIS Metabase (if IIS 6 is installed), and all files with extensions in the enormous Monitored File Extensions list, which is found in file \windows\system32\restore\Filelist.xml.

Restore points do *not* include

- Files listed under the Registry keys FilesNotToBackUp, and Registry keys listed in under the key KeysNotToRestore, both under HKEY_LOCAL_MACHINE\System\CurrentControlSet\ Control\BackupRestore.

- On Windows XP, files listed in the <Exclude> sections of \windows\system32\restore\ Filelist.xml are not backed up.

- Internet Explorer cookies, favorites, history, and cached files.

- The [My] Documents folder and subfolders in all user profiles.

- Digital Rights Management settings.

- SAM Registry hives. (System Restore does *not* restore passwords, so it can't help you if you changed your password and now can't remember the new one, but on the plus side, it also won't overwrite your current password with some old one that you've since forgotten.)

- Windows Product Activation data.

On XP, these files are not put into the restore point's .cab file. On Vista, they're present in the volume snapshot, but are not restored by System Restore. In addition, network files—that is, the contents of network folders and roaming user profiles—are neither saved nor restored.

All system and user-specific Registry keys are backed up as well. During a restore operation, Registry keys that describe the current hardware environment are *not* restored, as they are re-created every time Windows boots, nor is the SAM security database.

On XP, by default, all hard drives are protected by System Restore. If you have extra disk drives that that don't contain Windows components or application programs, you can disable System Restore on those drives to save disk space.

To do this on XP, follow these steps:

1. Log on as a computer administrator.

2. Click Start and right-click My Computer. Select Properties.

3. Select the System Restore tab.

4. Select a drive from the Available Drives list and click Settings.

5. Check Turn Off System Restore on This Drive, or lower the amount of disk space that System Restore is allowed to use for its backups.

On Vista, by default, only the boot volume is protected. You can disable this if you want, or you can enable protection for other volumes, using the following steps:

1. Click Start, right-click Computer, and select Properties.

2. Select Advanced System Settings, and confirm the User Account Control prompt.

3. Select the System Protection tab.

4. Check or uncheck drives to enable or disable protection. You cannot specify the amount of disk space available for restore points if you're using the GUI on Vista. By default, the size is set when the first restore point is created, to 30% of free space or 15% of the size of the volume, whichever is less. On a volume used as the destination disk for Complete PC Backup, the maximum allocation is set to 30% of the disk size.

   You can manually adjust the maximum amount of space available for all Volume Shadow storage, which includes System Restore and Previous Versions. To view the current amount of allocated space, open an elevated command prompt window and type the command `vssadmin list shadowstorage`. To adjust the maximum amount of space to use, type `vssadmin resize shadowstorage /for=x: /on=x: /maxsize=nGB`, where x is a drive letter, and n is the maximum space to use in GB.

Note

Recall that on Vista Business, Ultimate, and Enterprise, the Previous Versions feature relies on the same shadow mechanism as System Restore. If you want to have Windows provide Previous Versions protection on volumes other than your boot volume, you have to enable it using the preceding instructions.

The restore data (`.cab` files on XP, shadow data on Vista) are stored in the `\System Volume Information` folder on each monitored drive, and are kept for some length of time, depending on the amount of free disk space and the maximum disk space that System Restore is permitted to use. On XP, restore points are kept up to 90 days, disk space permitting. On Vista, up to 64 points are kept, space permitting.

By default, on an NTFS-formatted disk, this folder is not accessible by any user, not even Administrator, although you can make it readable by typing these commands at the command prompt:

```
cd \
cacls "System Volume Information" /E /G Administrator:R
```

On Vista and XP Home Edition you must substitute another computer administrator user's name for Administrator. Enable the display of Hidden and System files in Windows Explorer using Tools, Folder Options, View, and then you can browse the folder.

Caution

Do *not* delete or modify any files in a System Volume Information folder under any circumstances. To save space, unmodified files are not saved in successive **.cab** files, so Windows could conceivably need *all* the files to perform a successful system restore. If you need to recover the space used by restore points and shadow backups, use the Disk Cleanup wizard to delete them.

When you are finished poking around, be sure to type the command

```
cacls "System Volume Information" /E /R Administrator
```

to restore the folder's security settings.

Creating Restore Points

Windows XP and Vista automatically create a restore point when any of the following occurs:

- You start Windows for the first time after its initial installation and setup
- You install an application that uses the Microsoft Installer or a modern installation program like InstallShield as its setup program
- Windows is about to install updates received via Automatic Updates or Windows Update

- You have restored files using Microsoft Backup (described earlier in this chapter)
- 24 hours have elapsed since the last restore point was created, whether your computer was turned on or not

If you're concerned that something you're about to do might cause damage, you can also manually create a restore point.

Note

It's worth noting that System Restore does *not* back up documents or user files, only system files. The Previous Versions mechanism on Vista Business, Enterprise, and Ultimate *can* back up and restore documents, though, using the same mechanism that's behind System Restore.

To manually create a restore point on XP, follow these steps:

1. Open the System Restore application from the System Tools folder located in the Accessories folder on the All Programs menu. If you're not logged on as a Computer Administrator, right-click the System Restore menu item, select Run As, and run it as Administrator.
2. Select the Create a Restore Point radio button and click the Next button.
3. Specify a description for the restore point in the restore point description field; for example, "Just before installing Dangerously Buggy Program."
4. Click the Create button.
5. The restore point will be created. When finished, click the Close button to close the application.

On Vista, follow this procedure:

1. Click Start, right-click Computer, and select Properties.
2. Select Advanced System Settings, and confirm the User Account Control prompt.
3. Select the System Protection tab and click the Create button.
4. Specify a description for the restore point in the restore point description field; for example, "Just before installing Dangerously Buggy Program." Then click the Create button.

Restoring a Restore Point

Assuming your computer will boot into Normal mode or Safe mode, and you either manually created a system restore point, or Windows created one for you when you installed your now-deprecated device driver or acrimonious application, you can restore a previous configuration.

Caution

System Restore protects a huge number of files, and this can include *your* files, not just Windows' applications and drivers. If you have created important files since the restore point was made, you might want to back them up before performing a system restore.

First, you need to get Windows up and running. Often you can use Safe mode; reboot your computer and start tapping the F8 key down as soon as the system BIOS startup message appears. When Windows Advanced Startup Options menu appears, select Safe Mode and press Enter.

Note

I suggest that you use Safe mode to perform a System Restore, even if Windows can boot normally. If you do attempt to restore without using Safe mode, and you have an antivirus program installed, be sure to disable the antivirus program while you're performing System Restore. If you can't get Windows started, use the Startup Repair function on your Windows Vista setup DVD. See "Startup Repair" in Chapter 12 for more help.

After Windows XP is running, follow these steps to restore the system to its previous state:

1. Be sure that all users are logged off, and then log on as a computer administrator. Click Start, All Programs, Accessories, System Tools, System Restore.

2. Select the Restore My Computer to an Earlier Time and click the Next button.

3. Select the desired restore point, and then click the Next button.

4. Confirm that you do want to continue with the restore, and click Next to begin the restore procedure.

On Vista, the procedure is slightly different:

1. Be sure that all other users are logged off. Then click Start, All Programs, Accessories, System Tools, System Restore, and confirm the User Account Control prompt.

2. If the default restore point is acceptable, click Next. Alternatively, select Choose a Different Restore Point and click Next. Check Show Restore Points Older Than 5 Days. Select a restore point, and click Next.

3. Confirm that you do want to continue with the restore, and click Next to begin the restore procedure.

If you had added or removed hardware, shut Windows down and restore your original hardware setup before turning the computer back on. Otherwise, just restart Windows. When Windows is up and running again, find out what went wrong before reinstalling the troublesome hardware. You may need to download and install updated device drivers.

If you are unable to boot your system to Windows or if Windows, once booted, is too unstable to activate System Restore, see "Using the System Restore Tool" in Chapter 12. This section explains how to use System Restore from Safe mode, a command prompt, or your Vista setup DVD.

Note

As I mentioned earlier, this chapter has a lot to cover, more than we can fit here. If you want more detail, we have books that dish it out in spades…check out *Special Edition Using Microsoft Windows XP Professional, 3rd Edition,* or the *Home Edition* edition, *3rd Edition* (good grief!), or perhaps *Special Edition Using Windows Vista, 2nd Edition,* all published by Que.

Windows Commands and Scripting

The Windows Command Prompt

The Windows GUI is fine for the casual user, but for tasks that you have to perform over and over every day, the Command Prompt window just might be your best friend. Visualize the difference between a hunt-and-peck typist and a Mavis Beacon *summa cum laude* graduate. That's the difference between someone who uses only the GUI, and someone who knows how and when to take advantage of Windows' command-line interface. After you've learned how to use command-line tools and memorized the basics, you'll find that you can type a command *much* more quickly than you can take your hands off the keyboard, grab the mouse, and navigate through endless menus.

If you don't believe me, do an experiment: See how long it takes to get to the Windows Firewall control panel using the GUI, versus typing **start firewall.cpl** followed by the Enter key. The command line is also less distracting: You can type the command you want without having to read and scroll through all the commands you *don't* want to use.

Speed-typing aside, there are several other important reasons to know how to use the command line, batch files, and Windows Script Host:

- There are some commands and management tools available through the command line that aren't available through the GUI.

- You can put often-used sequences of commands into a batch file or script, and repeat complex tasks (or even simple tasks) with just a few keystrokes.

- Batch files and scripts serve as a form of documentation. Not only do they perform a job, they are themselves a description of a procedure, step by step, with nothing left out.

- Batch files and scripts encapsulate skill and knowledge. If you write one to perform a complex task, it will be much easier to teach someone else how to use the batch file than it would be to show him how to perform all the individual steps inside.

To open a Command Prompt window you can use any of the following methods:

- Click Start, All Programs, Accessories, Command Prompt.
- On Windows XP, click Start, Run. Type **cmd** and press Enter.
- On Windows Vista, click Start (or press the Windows key), type **cmd** into the Search box, and press Enter.
- For convenience, you can drag a copy of the Command Prompt shortcut in the Accessories menu into your Quick Launch bar, and run it from there.
- On Windows Vista, hold down the Shift key when you right-click any folder on the desktop or in any Explorer window, and then select Open Command Window Here.

The Windows Command Prompt window looks and behaves a lot like the screen you may remember from the pre-Windows days of MS-DOS. But, the Command Prompt window is a gateway to a full 32-bit environment closer to UNIX than MS-DOS. Command prompt programs (technically, they're called *console applications*) are actually full-fledged Windows programs; the only difference is that their window displays text output with no graphics and accepts typed text input; it's like using a very powerful electric typewriter.

Note

The next few sections describe how the Command Prompt environment works in some detail. If you want to skip ahead to the "how to" information, jump down to "Editing Command Lines" on p. 521.

What the Command Prompt Really Does

When you use the Start menu to open a Command Prompt window, what's actually happening is that you're running a program named cmd.exe, the Windows command shell. Cmd is defined as a console application, as opposed to a GUI application, so as the program is started up, Windows opens a blank, black window. Cmd prints a *prompt*, a bit of text to indicate that it's waiting for you to type something. On Windows Vista, it might look like this:

```
C:\Users\bknittel>
```

On Windows XP, it might look like this:

```
C:\Documents and Settings\bknittel>
```

When you respond to the prompt by typing a command and pressing Enter, cmd looks at the first word in the line of text you typed. It interprets this as the name of the program you want to run. It searches for an executable program file with this name, and if it finds one, starts up the program. Any other text on the line you typed is provided to the program for it to interpret, according to its own conventions, telling it what you want it to do.

For example, if I type the command

```
ping www.mycompany.com
```

cmd will search several standard folders for a program named ping. It will find ping.exe, which is a network-testing utility, in \windows\system32. Cmd will instruct Windows to run ping.exe and provide it with the additional text I typed, www.mycompany.com. Ping interprets this additional text as the name of another computer whose network connection I'd like to test. It will perform the network test and print a few lines into the Command Prompt window. When the ping program exits (finishes), `cmd.exe` prints another prompt, and the cycle starts over.

Note

You can also run Windows graphical applications by name from a Command Prompt window. On Windows XP and all earlier versions, the next prompt appears as soon as the GUI application has started. On Windows Vista, the next prompt doesn't appear until you close the application. You can get around this on Vista by preceding the program name with the word **start**, as discussed later in this chapter.

Environment Variables

Where exactly does cmd look for these program files? The list of locations is defined by a setting called the *PATH environment variable*. The environment is a set of text values that Windows makes available to all programs. Each one consists of a name like PATH or USERNAME, followed by an equal sign and additional text. You can see them by opening a command prompt window and typing **set** followed by the Enter key; the output will look something like this:

```
ALLUSERSPROFILE=C:\ProgramData
APPDATA=C:\Users\bknittel\AppData\Roaming
CommonProgramFiles=C:\Program Files\Common Files
COMPUTERNAME=JAVA
ComSpec=C:\WINDOWS\system32\cmd.exe
HOMEDRIVE=C:
HOMEPATH=\Users\bknittel
LOCALAPPDATA=C:\Users\bknittel\AppData\Local
LOGONSERVER=\\JAVA
NUMBER_OF_PROCESSORS=1
OS=Windows_NT
Path=C:\Windows\system32;C:\Windows;C:\Windows\System32\Wbem;c:\bin
PATHEXT=.COM;.EXE;.BAT;.CMD;.VBS;.VBE;.JS;.JSE;.WSF;.WSH;.MSC
    ⋮
```

Each of these lines shows the name of an environment variable and its value. Windows defines most of these variables and values for you, although you can define environment variables for your own use in batch file programming. Of the predefined variables, Windows uses PATH and PATHEXT to locate programs that you want to run.

Note

Actually, Windows uses the **PATH** to locate *any* program it's told to run, whether it's from the command line, a line in a batch file, the Start menu's Run dialog, the Windows Vista search box, a shortcut, or from inside another program. It also uses the **PATH** to locate the Dynamic Link Libraries (DLLs) used by most Windows programs. When a program needs to use a DLL, Windows first looks in the folder that contains the calling program's **.EXE** file, and then it searches through the folders in the **PATH**.

Of course, if a command or DLL file is specified using a full pathname, the **PATH** list isn't used.

When you type a command on the command line, cmd first checks to see whether the command is one of the *built-in* commands that it handles directly, by itself, without any program file at all. Built-in commands include dir and several others, which are discussed later in this chapter.

If the command isn't recognized as a built-in command, cmd looks at the PATH environment variable and interprets it as a list of folders to search for a program file. The folder names are separated by semicolons, so for the PATH in the environment variable list you saw earlier, cmd will look at the following folders, in this order:

```
C:\WINDOWS\system32
C:\WINDOWS
C:\WINDOWS\system32\WBEM
c:\bin
```

The first three folders were put into the PATH list by Windows so that cmd can find the standard programs provided with Windows: Notepad, ping, and so on. I added the last folder myself so that cmd can find some additional programs and batch files that I wrote. I'll tell you how to do this later in this chapter.

As it scans through these folders, Windows looks for a file whose name matches the name you typed on the command line, and whose extension (file type) is any one of those listed in the PATHEXT environment variable. Table 9.1 lists the most common file extensions used on executable files, batch files and scripts.

Table 9.1 Common Program File Extensions

Extension	Type of Program
.COM	MS-DOS executable file, absolute binary format
.EXE	Standard MS-DOS, Windows, OS/2, or other application
.BAT	Batch file, written for **cmd.exe** or MS-DOS **command.com**
.CMD	Batch file, written for **cmd.exe**
.VBS	Windows Script Host script, written in VBScript
.VBE	Encrypted VBScript script
.JS	Windows Script Host script, written in JScript
.JSE	Encrypted JScript script
.WSF	Windows Script Host script, in XML format
.WSH	Windows Script Host settings file
.MSC	Microsoft Management Console (MMC) plug-in

To continue with our sample command,

```
ping www.mycompany.com
```

because ping isn't one of the built-in commands, cmd looks in the first folder listed in the PATH environment variable for a file named ping.com. If a file with this name is present, cmd instructs Windows to run the program. If ping.com isn't found, cmd checks for ping.exe, then ping.bat, and so on, through the PATHEXT list. If no file is found in the first PATH folder, cmd goes to the second folder in the PATH and repeats the process. If a file can't be found in any of the folders, cmd prints an error message and gives up.

Of course, if you type a specific file extension as part of your command line, for example, if you type

```
ping.exe www.mycompany.com
```

Windows will look through the PATH folders only for a file with the specified extension, and will not use the PATHEXT list. Likewise, if you specify the command using a specific path, as in

```
c:\windows\system32\ping www.mycompany.com
```

Windows will not search through the PATH list.

Tip

If the same program or batch file is in more than one folder in your search path, and the first one that cmd finds is not the one you want, type the full pathname before the command to eliminate any ambiguity about which copy of the program you want to use. For example

```
c:\windows\system32\ping
```

tells cmd exactly where to find the ping program.

In any case, when Windows has located a program file that matches the command name you typed, it uses the file's extension to see what type of program it is to run. The extension .COM indicates a very old-style MS-DOS application. .BAT and .CMD files contain commands that cmd.exe is to interpret one line at a time just as if you were typing them at the command prompt. .EXE files are executable program files that could be MS-DOS programs, 16-, 32-, or 64-bit Windows applications, console applications, or they could be programs that are associated with other add-on program environments such Interix (POSIX UNIX). Windows has to examine the contents of the file to see exactly what it is.

Executable Program Types

When Windows is instructed to run an .EXE file, Windows has to examine the file to determine what type of program it represents.

All MS-DOS and Windows executable files start with a block of data in the standard format that has been used by all versions of Windows and MS-DOS versions 2.0 and later. The file starts with the ASCII characters "MZ", followed by values that describe the location within the file of the executable instructions.

In the case of a true MS-DOS application, this header data describes the actual MS-DOS program. For Windows and console applications, the header fields point to a tiny MS-DOS program contained within the file that simply prints "This program cannot be run in DOS mode" and exits. This is called the *MS-DOS stub*, and it ensures that if you attempt to run the application under MS-DOS, it will not crash the older operating system. Windows knows to look past the stub for a second descriptive data block called a New Executable (NE) or Portable Executable (PE) header, farther in the file.

The second header describes where within the file to find the program's executable code, its resources (dialog and text data), debugging information, and other file sections, and also indicates the CPU type and Windows subsystem to which the program belongs. The CPU type indicates the instruction set for which the program is designed, and can specify the x86 (32-bit), x64 (64-bit), Itanium (64-bit), Alpha, or MIPS instruction sets. The subsystems include the following:

- 16-bit Windows GUI application
- 32-bit Windows GUI application
- 64-bit Windows GUI application
- 32-bit Windows console application
- 64-bit Windows console application
- OS/2 1.x console application
- POSIX (Interix or UNIX) console application
- Other types including device driver, DLL, and so on

Note

The Alpha and MIPS processors and the OS/2 subsystem, alas, are no longer supported.

Thus, between the file extension and, for .EXE files, the two header structures, Windows can determine whether it's being asked to run a script or batch file, an MS-DOS program, a Windows program, or a program designed for another supported operating system; and whether the application uses a GUI or the console window's character-oriented interface.

Program Subsystems

In addition to standard Windows GUI applications, Windows supports several sorts of console-mode applications. Windows console programs are actually full-fledged Windows programs that can use the standard Windows application programming interface (API); they just don't have graphical windows of their own. Instead, they interact through the text window of the Command Prompt window that started them.

Windows can also run programs based on other operating system standards. It does this using additional software, installed with Windows, that provides the system functions these other programs expect. This is called *emulation*, where Windows makes itself look and act like another operating system. Any of several emulation environments may be available, depending on your version of Windows, as listed in Table 9.2.

Table 9.2   Windows Emulation Subsystems

Subsystem	Description
MS-DOS	MS-DOS applications (.COM and .EXE files) are run inside of an emulation program named **NTVDM.EXE** ("NT Virtual DOS Machine"), which emulates standard PC hardware, and provides the DOS and BIOS system call support expected by MS-DOS applications. The Virtual DOS Machine is described later in this chapter. (Not available on 64-bit versions of Windows.)
Interix (POSIX)	A POSIX-compliant (UNIX-like) environment is provided as part of the Subsystem for UNIX-Based Applications (SUA), a free download available for Windows Vista Ultimate and Enterprise and Windows Server 2003. A comparable package called Services for UNIX (SFU) is available for Windows 2000 Professional, XP Professional, and earlier Windows Server versions. SUA and SFU are described in Appendix A, "Windows Tool Reference."

Subsystem	Description
16-bit Windows	16-bit Windows applications are supported by the WinOldAp system, which translates 16-bit Windows function requests into the appropriate 32-bit requests. Emulation is provided by **ntvdm.exe** (NT Virtual DOS Machine) and **wowexec.exe** (Windows on Windows); 16-bit Windows programs run inside a virtual Windows 3.1 environment provided by these programs. (Not available on 64-bit versions of Windows.)
32-bit Windows	X64 versions of Windows Vista and XP can run 32-bit x86 Windows applications through an emulation subsystem called WOW64. This subsystem provides not only support for running the 32-bit programs on a 64-bit processor, but it also manages access to the Registry so that 32-bit and 64-bit programs "see" settings appropriate to their environment. For an interesting, non-Microsoft article on WOW64, see developer.amd.com/articlex.jsp?id=65.
OS/2 1.x	Windows NT 3.51, NT 4.0, 2000 Professional, and 2000 Server include a subsystem that runs IBM OS/2 version 1.x (character mode) applications. The OS/2 subsystem is not included in Windows XP or Vista.

Note

The 64-bit versions of Windows do not support 16-bit Windows (Windows 3.1) applications nor MS-DOS applications; The necessary emulation environments are not and will not be provided as an integral part of 64-bit Windows. If you need to use these older applications under 64-bit Windows, you must install a full-scale emulator program like VMWare or Microsoft Virtual PC, install a 16-bit or 32-bit operating system in an emulated PC, and run the old applications there. This seems roundabout, but it works very well. There is also an open-source emulator system called Bochs (bochs.sourceforge.net) that has a strong focus on providing good support for MS-DOS games.

The goal of the subsystem mechanism is that any supported program should run exactly as it would under its native operating system, yet to you, the user, it should appear and act like any other Windows console-mode application. It's a nice theory, although I've found that in practice, 16-bit and even some older 32-bit Windows applications work better under their "real" preferred operating systems running inside a virtual computer such as VMWare or Virtual PC than they do under current versions of Windows. This is usually the case even though a number of Windows subsystems and application compatibility mechanisms are supposed to automatically smooth over the differences between the various versions of Windows. For example, I have found that the old 32-bit desktop publishing program Interleaf doesn't run at all on Windows XP, but it runs fine on Windows Me running inside Virtual PC.

MS-DOS Emulation

MS-DOS applications performed disk, printer, keyboard, and mouse input/output operations through support routines provided by MS-DOS. The application would store a code number corresponding to a desired system service in a CPU hardware register, and then execute a CPU interrupt instruction, which would transfer control to DOS or the Basic Input/Output System (BIOS) routines in the lower range of system memory. These services provided a way for an application program to display text output on the screen, read characters from the keyboard and coordinates from the mouse, and to create, read, and write disk files, without the program's having to contain the code to handle the details of these operations.

However, instead of using interrupt instructions, Windows applications read and write files by calling functions in Dynamic Link Libraries provided into Windows. An interrupt instruction would simply make Windows display the message "Your program has performed an illegal operation" and terminate the program. Therefore, MS-DOS applications are run inside a "container" program called `ntvdm.exe` that provides code to simulate the DOS functions. `Ntvdm.exe` intercepts CPU interrupt instructions, and calls the appropriate Windows library functions on the program's behalf. It also contains code to mimic the MS-DOS segmented memory structure. When you attempt to run an MS-DOS application, Windows actually runs `ntvdm.exe`; it reads the desired MS-DOS program into its own address space and lets it run. At this point, the MS-DOS application cannot tell it is not running on an old-fashioned PC over MS-DOS*.

To achieve better performance, MS-DOS programs frequently bypassed MS-DOS's limited input/output support and took direct control of some hardware devices, including graphics adapters, parallel ports (LPT ports), and serial ports (COM ports). This was necessary because there was no standardized way of addressing graphics adapters, and on the slower computers of that era, it was not possible to process thousands of characters per second for a high-speed modem or printer when there were several layers of software involved. Windows NT, 2000, and XP do not allow any user program to have direct access to hardware devices. So, `ntvdm.exe` emulates the graphics adapter and COM1, COM2, LPT1, LPT2, and LPT3 hardware as well; that is, it intercepts attempts by an MS-DOS application to directly manipulate these hardware devices, and uses the appropriate Windows system functions to get the intended results.

Ultimately, the MS-DOS environment provides support for the following MS-DOS services and emulates standard hardware devices through code built into `ntvdm.exe`:

- All standard BIOS and DOS function interrupts.
- Mouse support (MOUSE.COM) interrupts.
- Display and keyboard hardware.
- PC-standard timers, programmable interrupt controllers, and the speaker interface.
- SoundBlaster-compatible sound adapter hardware. (No matter what sort of sound hardware your computer has, MS-DOS applications "see" a standard, low-end SoundBlaster adapter.)
- Intel 386 memory management hardware.
- Up to 16MB of memory, which the MS-DOS application thinks is the entirety of system memory, but which is simply a standard block of memory in ntvdm's address space.

Ntvdm's emulation works pretty well for graphics and LPT printer devices, but the serial (COM) port simulation is iffy, and network printing support is sometimes troublesome. I've run into these sorts of problems:

- DOS programs that use network printers, such as the old DOS FoxPro database program, don't always eject a page after printing, or sometimes eject too many pages.
- DOS modem software doesn't work perfectly. Data is lost between the software and the modem, resulting in slow communications and even modem hang-ups.

Ntvdm.exe is a descendant of SoftPC, an early 1990s PC emulator that let people run DOS and Windows 95 on Apple Macintosh computers. The original Insignia Solutions, Ltd copyright is still tucked away inside ntvdm.exe, as is the cryptic comment "NtVdm : Using Yoda on an x86 may be hazardous to your systems' health."

- Games that attempt to use ntvdm's SoundBlaster emulation may generate hideous screeching sounds or may crash entirely.

Unfortunately, when problems like these do occur, there is little or nothing you can do about it. I keep an old laptop with Windows 95 on hand for the rare occasion that I really have to run an MS-DOS communications program that fails under a more modern version of Windows. Or, as I mentioned earlier, you might try a more industrial-strength emulator program such as VMWare, Virtual PC, or Bochs.

Special versions of some standard MS-DOS device drivers are provided with Windows. These are true MS-DOS drivers that "think" they're running inside MS-DOS, although they are specially coded to work in this emulation environment. They are loaded into the MS-DOS environment when `ntvdm.exe` starts up through configuration files `config.nt` and `autoexec.nt`, which are discussed later in this chapter. The additional standard services are

- High memory access service, provided by `himem.sys`.
- CD-ROM extensions, provided by `mscdexnt.exe` (this is a special version of `mscdex.exe` that doesn't expect to connect to a DOS-mode CD-ROM device driver, but which relies instead on the CD-ROM devices under Windows' control).
- Networking support (access to shared files and printers), provided by `redir.exe`. If you have installed a Novell NetWare client, a partial implementation of the NetWare interface is provided to DOS programs by `nw16.exe` and `vwipxspx.exe`.
- DOS Protected Mode Interface (memory support) provided by `dosx.exe`, which replaces DOS's `emm386.exe`.

Additional support for ANSI screen output and national language support can be loaded as well; see "Configuring the MS-DOS Command Environment" (this chapter) for more information.

Interpreting Command-Line Syntax

Commands entered at the command prompt start with the name of the command to run, but there may be more. Any additional text items on the command line after the program name are called *arguments*, and they are given to the program to interpret. For example, the command

```
ping mycompany.com
```

runs the program `ping.exe`, and the extra text `mycompany.com` is given to `ping.exe` to interpret. Each program interprets its command-line arguments in its own way, according to the design of the programmer who created it.

Most programs expect to see some fundamental information like the name of a file to process or the name of a website to test. Some programs require more than one argument like this, for example, an input filename and an output filename. (The order in which they're entered usually matters! For example, the first name might always be interpreted as the name of the input file, and the second name as the name of the output file.)

Then, many programs can be made to adjust their behavior by specifying additional arguments variously called *options*, *switches*, or *flags*. For example

```
ping www.mycompany.com
```

tests the network connection to a given Internet host by sending four test data packets. You can tell ping to send eight test data packets by adding the -n option:

```
ping -n 8 www.mycompany.com
```

Things get decidedly hairier at this point, for there is little consistency in how these options are specified. Some programs don't want a space between an option and value; for example, the author of ping might just as well have required you to type

```
ping -n8 www.mycompany.com
```

Other programs, mostly those that were originally written by Microsoft or borrowed from the earlier CP/M operating system, use options that start with a slash rather than the UNIX tradition of using a dash; for example,

```
dir /b
```

There's simply no way to know what options are available, or how to format them, other than to look at the documentation. What you need to know is the program's *command-line syntax*, which is a formal way of saying "what it expects to see."

There are several possible ways to get a description of a program's command-line syntax. For a given program, which for the sake of example let's call xxx, you can try these things:

- Type **xxx /?** Some programs recognize /? as a plea for help and print out a description of the command-line syntax.
- Type **help xxx**, which invokes the Windows command-line help system.
- Click Start, Help and Support and search for xxx. This is more likely to be helpful on Windows XP than Vista. Microsoft stripped much of the built-in help for command-line programs out of Vista.
- On Windows XP: Search Help and Support for the string command line reference, and click the link to Command Line Reference A-Z.
- On Windows Vista: Search Help and Support for the string command-line reference. Click the link to Command Line Reference for IT Pros and scroll down to the Technical Reference section. (The links in that section all lead to the Microsoft website, so you'll need a working Internet connection.)
- Perform an Internet search for xxx.

There's no way to tell beforehand which of these methods will work; you may want to try all of them.

Command-line syntax is usually described in a way that indicates what parts you *have* to type, what parts are optional, and what parts have to contain names or other information particular to your situation. The documentation will usually define its particular conventions somewhere, but this is a very common format:

- **boldface** indicates text that you have to type literally.
- *italics* indicate something that's just representative; you don't type this literally, but replace it with your own information. In some Microsoft documentation, angle brackets < > are used for this purpose also.

- Square brackets [ ] enclose optional parts. You don't type the brackets themselves. They must mean that you can type what's inside them or leave it out.

- Ellipses (…) indicate that you can type more, or repeat the previous items as many times as desired.

- The vertical bar I separates a series of choices; you are to enter just one of the listed options. Sometimes, alternate choices of long sequences of options are printed on separate lines.

For example, the command to create directories (folders) can be typed as mkdir or md, and this is how Microsoft describes its syntax:

mkdir [*drive:*]*path*

md [*drive:*]*path*

The two lines indicate two alternate choices. The boldface mkdir or md is something that is to be typed literally. You don't type the word *path* literally; *path* just shows where you are to type the name of the folder you want to create. *Drive* and its following colon are optional; they can be typed or omitted. You do have to read the description of the command to know that *drive* is supposed to be a single letter representing a disk drive; the syntax description can't provide that information symbolically.

This stuff may be confusing at first, but you'll soon get the hang of it, and you'll find that a glance at syntax description will convey a lot of information about what a program can and can't do.

Environment Variable Substitution

Environment variables are named text strings that Windows uses to communicate information to programs, batch files, and scripts. Batch files also frequently use environment variables to hold and modify data. As it examines command lines that you've typed or that it has read from a batch file, cmd replaces strings of the form %*name*% with the value of the named environment variable. For example, the command

    echo %path%

is interpreted as if you had typed the command

    echo c:\windows\system32;C:\WINDOWS;C:\WINDOWS\System32\Wbem

Echo prints out whatever is on its command line, thus, the command echo %path% displays the value of the path variable. Environment variable substitution can be used anyplace on any command line, as long as the resulting text is a valid command.

Note

Environment variable names are not case sensitive. To cmd, **%path%**, **%Path%**, and **%PATH%** are all the same.

Input and Output Redirection

Console programs read interactive input from the keyboard and display it on the screen. They do this through a mechanism called *standard input/output streams*. Each console program has available to it a stream or source of input called the *standard input*, and two output streams, *standard output* and *standard error*. By default, keyboard input to the console window is fed to the application's standard input, and anything the application prints on the standard output or standard error streams appears in the console window, as illustrated in Figure 9.1. As you might guess, the standard output stream is used for the program's principal output, whereas the standard error stream is used for error messages and warnings.

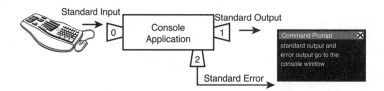

Figure 9.1   Console applications have three standard input/output streams.

Note

The concept of redirectable standard I/O has a long history. It started in the Multics operating system developed at MIT in the late 1960s. In the 1970s, the developers of the UNIX operating system adopted the idea and added the < and > syntax. The 8-bit CP/M operating system "borrowed" it from UNIX, MS-DOS took it from CP/M, and Windows inherited it from MS-DOS. This reminds me of the Tom Lehrer song "I Got It From Agnes," but maybe we shouldn't go there.

You can think of console applications as having a sort of "plumbing." The standard I/O streams act like pipes through which information flows, and they can easily be *redirected*, or connected, to files or other console applications. For example, the standard output stream, which usually appears in the console window, can be directed to a file using the > character on the command line. Placing >output.txt on the command line redirects what would have appeared in the console window into the file named output.txt. Similarly, the < character redirects the standard input. Placing <input.txt on the command line connects file input.txt to the standard input, so the application will read from that file instead of the keyboard. For example, the command

```
sort <input.txt >output.txt
```

runs the sort console application; when it reads from the standard input, it reads file input.txt, and whatever it writes to the standard output stream goes into file output.txt, as illustrated in Figure 9.2. Of course, you can specify any filenames that you want to use; it doesn't have to be input.txt or output.txt. Also, the files input.txt and output.txt will be read from and written to in the current directory, but you can control this by specifying a path as part of the redirection command; for example:

```
sort <c:\myproject\rawdata\input.txt >c:\myproject\results\output.txt
```

Notice that in this command the standard error stream is not redirected. If the sort command runs into any sort of problem and prints an error message on the standard error stream, the message will appear in the console window where you can see it.

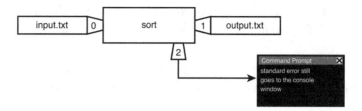

Figure 9.2 The standard I/O streams can be redirected to files.

However, if you want to, you *can* redirect the standard error to a file. You might want to do this in a batch file that will be run when nobody is logged on, to collect any error messages in a log file so they can be printed or viewed later. To redirect the standard error stream, put 2>*filename* on the command line. For example, if you typed the command

```
sort <input.txt >output.txt 2>error.txt
```

and sort printed any error messages, they would appear in file error.txt rather than in the console window.

What's this business with the number 2? If you look back at Figures 9.1 and 9.2, you'll see that the little pipe fittings for the standard I/O streams have numbers attached to them. The standard output is designated as stream #1, and the standard error as stream #2. A number before > redirects a specific stream. So, 2>error.txt indicates that the program's standard error output stream is to be redirected into file error.txt.

You can also instruct Windows to write both the standard output and standard error streams to the same file. This will produce one file with the output of both streams mixed together. The syntax for this is 2>&1, as in the command

```
sort <input.txt >output.txt 2>&1
```

It means "Stream 2 goes to the same place as stream 1." It's peculiar, but it's a very handy thing when you need it.

Finally, you should know that if the filename you specify when redirecting data output exists before you run the command, the > redirection feature erases that file. That is, after you type these three commands:

```
dir >file.txt
ping mycompany.com >file.txt
echo This is the third command >file.txt
```

file.txt will contain only one line of text, reading "This is the third command." The first command puts the output of the dir command into file.txt, and then ping overwrites that with its output, and then echo replaces that.

To get around this problem you can use the append operator >>. When you add >>*filename* to a command line, the standard output is *added to* the file if it already exists; if the file didn't exist, it is created. The commands

```
dir >file.txt
ping mycompany.com >>file.txt
echo This is the third command >>file.txt
```

will create a file named `file.txt` that contains the output of all three commands: first the `dir` listing, followed by the output of the `ping` command, followed by the line `This is the third command`.

Table 9.3 has a complete listing of all the redirection variations. You can use any name in the place of *filename*, and you can enter a plain filename or a path and filename.

Table 9.3   Input/Output Redirection Functions

Syntax	Result
`<filename`	Standard input is read from *filename*
`>filename`	Standard output is written to *filename*
`1>filename`	(Equivalent to `>filename`)
`2>filename`	Standard error is written to *filename*
`>>filename`	Standard output is appended to *filename*
`1>>filename`	(Equivalent to `>>filename`)
`2>>filename`	Standard error is appended to *filename*
`>filename 2>&1`	Standard output and standard error are both written to *filename*
`>>filename 2>&1`	Standard output and standard error are both appended to *filename*

Tip

You can add a space between the > or >> and the filename; it works with or without the space. You might want to get into the habit of adding a space because it will help you if you want to use the name completion feature that is discussed later in the chapter.

Tip

If the file that you want to create has a space in its name, put quotes around the name. You can put the > or >> inside or outside of the quotes; `">filename with space"` and `> "filename with space"` work equally well. But again, it's probably better to get in the habit of putting the > outside the quotes so that you can use name completion.

By the way, the older `COMMAND.COM` shell used by MS-DOS, Windows 9x, and Me does not support any of the numeric variations of output redirection, such as 2>&1 and 2>. These are part of the enhancements made to `cmd.exe`, and are available on Windows NT, 2000, XP, and Vista only, as well as the Windows Server versions.

Finally, if you are familiar with the UNIX operating system and shell script programming, you should know that the << input redirection mechanism is *not* available in the Windows command shell.

Command Pipelines

You can direct the output of one command to the input of another using the *pipeline* operator |. The concept is illustrated in Figure 9.3. The command

```
tasklist | findstr "winword"
```

runs the `tasklist` program, which writes a listing of all running programs to the standard output. (This program is provided with XP Professional and all versions of Vista.) The pipeline operator | redirects this output to the input of the `findstr` command, which writes to *its* standard output only lines containing the text string `winword`. This combined command thus prints a listing of just information about running instances of Microsoft Word.

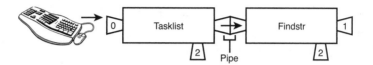

Figure 9.3 The pipeline operator | connects the output of one program to the input of another.

You could accomplish the same thing by redirecting the output of the first command to a file, and then running the second command with input from the same file, like this:

```
tasklist >filex
findstr "winword" <filex
delete filex
```

but the pipeline mechanism actually runs the two programs simultaneously, and doesn't store the intermediate output in a disk file; the pipeline is more efficient because it all takes place in the computer's main RAM.

Pipelines aren't limited to two commands; if you need to, you can hook up several commands in sequence. For example,

```
dir /b /s c:\ | findstr "net" | more
```

uses `dir` to list the entire contents of the C drive; its output is passed to `findstr`, which filters out only those lines containing the string `net`, and *that* output is passed to `more`, which displays one screen of text at a time and waits for you to press the spacebar before displaying the next screen.

Command Separators

You can type several commands on one input line using the special *command separator* delimiters that `cmd.exe` recognizes. The delimiters are described in Table 9.4.

Table 9.4   Command Separators

Syntax	Description
command1 & command2	Runs **command1**, and then **command2**. Example:
	`dir >listing.txt & notepad listing.txt`
command1 && command2	Runs **command1**, and only if it is successful (that is, if **command1** sets its error status value to 0), runs **command2**. If the **command1** indicates an error, the remainder of the command line is discarded. Example:
	`copy file.dat a: && copy second.dat a:`
command1 || command2	Runs **command1**, and only if it fails (that is, if **command1** sets its error status value to something other than 0), runs **command2**. Example:
	`copy file.dat a: || goto copyfailed`

In addition, parentheses can be used to group multiple commands. We'll talk about that later in the chapter when we cover batch file programming.

Command-Line Quoting

When a command-line program requires you to specify information such as the name of a file to process or an option to use, you usually type this information after the command name, with the items separated by spaces. For example, the `delete` command erases the file or files named on its command line:

```
delete somefile.txt anotherfile.txt
```

Unfortunately, because Windows filenames can contain spaces in the middle of the name, a command like

```
delete C:\Documents and Settings\bknittel\My Documents\a.txt
```

will attempt to delete four files: `C:\Documents`, `and`, `Settings\bknittel\My`, and `Documents\a.txt`. To solve this problem, cmd interprets quotation marks (`" "`) to mean that the text enclosed is to be treated as part of one single argument. For example, the command

```
delete "C:\Documents and Settings\bknittel\My Documents\a.txt"
```

deletes the one indicated file. The quotation marks are not seen as part of the filename; they just keep it all together.

Note

You can also separate command-line arguments with the semicolon (`;`) or comma (`,`), but not all programs accept them. I recommend that you don't use these characters to separate arguments—use spaces. But, some programs do see them as separators, so, as with spaces, if you have a filename with a comma or semicolon in the name you'll have to put quotes around the name.

Escaping Special Characters

As you've already seen, the following characters have special meaning to cmd:

```
< > ( ) & | , ; "
```

If you need to use any of these characters as part of a command-line argument to be given to a program (for example, to have the `find` command search for the character >), you need to *escape* the character by placing a caret (^) symbol before it. This indicates that the character is to be treated like any other character and removes its special meaning. To pass a ^ character as an argument, type `^^`.

For example, the `echo` command types its arguments in the Command Prompt window. The command

```
echo <hello>
```

would cause a problem because cmd would think that you want to redirect input from a file named `hello` and that you want to redirect output to...well, there is no filename after >, so cmd would print an error message. However, the command

```
echo ^<hello^>
```

prints <hello>.

Because the characters ( ) < > & | and ; have special meaning to cmd.exe (they are the command separators and redirection operators), if you want to specify one of these characters as part of an argument to a command-line program, you have to tell cmd to ignore its special meaning. To do this, you have to precede the character with a caret (^) character. This is called *escaping* it. For example, if you wanted to use the findstr command to search a file named listing.txt for lines containing &, you would have to type the command this way:

```
findstr ^& listing.txt
```

Without the ^, cmd would treat the & as a command separator and would see the line as two separate commands.

To pass the ^ character itself as part of a command-line argument, you have to escape it in the same way, as in the command

```
findstr ^^ listing.txt
```

The first ^ means, "take the following character literally and ignore its special meaning." The second ^ is passed to findstr.

Editing Command Lines

One big area of improvement in cmd.exe over the old MS-DOS command.com shell is its command-line editing feature. I don't know about you, but although I'm a fast typist, my error rate is about 20%. A few letters forward, a backspace, a few more forward, another backspace. Luckily, it's very easy to edit the input to console windows. If you used the DOSKEY utility under MS-DOS, you'll find some of this familiar, but cmd.exe's editing features are even further improved. The Backspace, Delete, and Left and Right Arrow keys work as you would expect. Table 9.5 lists additional keys you can use to edit command lines.

Table 9.5   Command Line Editing Keys

Key	Effect
Esc	Erases the current input line and returns the cursor to the left margin.
Ctrl+Left Arrow	Moves the cursor one word to the left.
Ctrl+Right Arrow	Moves the cursor one word to the right.
Home	Moves the cursor to the beginning of the current input line.
End	Moves the cursor to the end of the current input line.
Ins	Toggles between overwrite and insert mode. In overwrite mode, keystrokes replace previously entered characters. In insert mode, keystrokes insert new characters at the cursor position sliding previous text to the right. The initial setting—Insert or Overwrite—can be set in the console window's Properties page.
F1	Copies one character from the previous command into the current command line.
F2 *x*	F2 followed by any character (for example, *x*) retypes text from the previous command line up to and but not including the character *x*.
F3	Retypes the remainder of the previously entered command line, from the cursor point forward to its end.
F4 *x*	F4 followed by any character (for example, *x*) deletes characters in the current line from the cursor point up to but not including the character *x*.
F5	Retypes the entire text of the previous input line into the current input line.

(continues)

Table 9.5   Continued

Key	Effect
F6	Types Ctrl+Z; not really useful in Windows 2000 or XP.
F7	Displays a pop-up box containing the previously entered input lines. You can scroll through them with the arrow keys and press Enter to retype the selected line, or Esc to cancel.
Alt+F7	Deletes the command history.
xxx F8	F8 typed after any text will recall the most recent command from the history list whose first characters match the characters typed. Repeated presses of F8 will search back for the next most recent matching command.
F9	Prompts you for a number *n*, and then retypes the *n*th command back in the history list.
Up Arrow	Recalls the previously entered line; repeated use scrolls through the last 20 or so input lines.
Down Arrow	Used after the Up Arrow key, scrolls back down through the last few input lines.
PgUp	Recalls the oldest command in the history list.
PgDn	Recalls the most recently typed command.
Alt+Space, E	Displays the Edit menu, from which you can choose Mark, Paste, Find, or Scroll.

Paste takes whatever text is in the clipboard and "types" it into the console window.

Mark lets you select a rectangular block of text with the mouse or cursor keys; press Enter to copy the marked text to the clipboard.

We'll go into this in more detail in the next section.

The ability to use the up and down arrow keys to recall previously entered lines is especially useful because you can quickly fix incorrectly entered commands, or simply save yourself typing when entering a series of similar commands.

Command-line editing works not only when typing commands at the command prompt itself, but also when typing text input to most console programs. However, the history list (the list of input lines that you can scroll through with the Up and Down Arrow keys) is maintained separately for the input to the command prompt and for each program you run.

Name Completion

When you are typing command lines to cmd, you'll often need to type file and folder names. Name completion makes this easier—you can type just the first few letters of a file or folder name, press a control key, and cmd will finish typing the name for you. This is called *pathname completion* or *filename completion*, a nifty but not widely known feature that, like most of the other fun new features in cmd, Microsoft has borrowed from the UNIX operating system.

By default, the Tab key is used for both filename and pathname completion. That is, if you type a partial filename or pathname and press the Tab key, cmd will automatically add on the remainder of the first filename or folder name that matches what you've typed up to that point. If this is the correct name, you can just continue typing on the command line. This is a great timesaver!

If the name that cmd types is not the one you were looking for, you can press the Tab key again to see the next matching name. Pressing Tab repeatedly cycles through all matching names. What's more, you can hold the Shift key down while pressing Tab to cycle backward.

If cmd finds no matching file or folder name, it beeps and does nothing.

Tip

If you have to type a long pathname such as \Program Files\Internet Explorer\MUI, you can use name completion for each part of the name. For this example, you could type the following:

`dir \pr` (Tab) `\i` (Tab) `\m` (Tab)

Try this on your own computer. It's pretty slick—cmd adds the required quotation marks and moves them into the correct positions automatically.

Cmd is smart enough to know that certain commands expect only a folder name. For example, if you've typed cd or rd on the command line, name completion will match only directory names and will ignore filenames. It's clever (if a bit spooky) but this mechanism kicks in only for the few commands that are "obviously" directory-only commands.

If you want to take explicit control of whether cmd should match file or folder names, you can use the TweakUI Power Toy for Windows XP or the shareware tool TweakVI for Windows Vista (both discussed in Chapter 5, "Tweaking and Tuning Windows") to specify different control keys for filename and pathname completion. For example, you can set the filename completion character to Ctrl+F and the pathname character to Ctrl+D. When you press Ctrl+F ,cmd will match only to filenames, and will ignore any potential matching subdirectory names. Likewise, Ctrl+D will match only folder names.

There are other ways to make these settings, but the TweakUI and TweakVI tools are the easiest. For more information about TweakUI for XP, see Microsoft Knowledge Base article number 310530.

Copy and Paste in Command Prompt Windows

Although console programs don't have the display windows and menus of ordinary Windows programs, you can still use the mouse to copy and paste text to and from Command Prompt windows.

The usual Ctrl+C shortcut doesn't work to copy text from a Command Prompt window. To copy text to the Clipboard, you have to extract a rectangular block of text—you can't select text line by line as you're used to. Position the mouse at the upper-left corner of the block of text you want, drag it down to the bottom-right corner, and then press Enter. While you're selecting text, the word *Select* appears in the window's title. Figure 9.4 shows how a Command Prompt window looks when selecting text.

You can also select text using the window's System menu. Click the upper-left corner of the window or press Alt+space and then select Edit, Mark. Use the arrow keys to move the cursor to the upper-left corner of the desired area; then hold the Shift key down while moving the cursor to the lower-right corner. Press Enter to copy the selected text.

Also, in a Command Prompt window, the usual Ctrl+V shortcut doesn't perform a paste operation. You *can* paste text into a Command Prompt window using the System menu: Press Alt+space and then select Edit, Paste. The program running in the window has to be expecting input; otherwise it's just ignored.

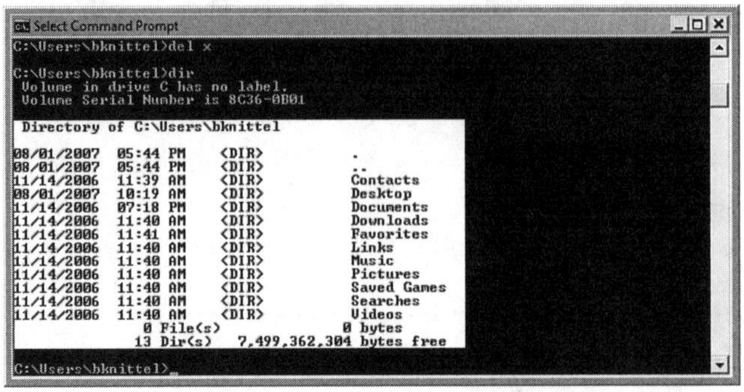

Figure 9.4 To copy text to the Clipboard, select a block of text with the mouse and press Enter.

Tip

The keyboard shortcut for Paste is worth memorizing: Alt+space, E, P.

By the way, "cut" isn't available—once something is typed in a Command Prompt window, it can't be removed.

If you need to run a mouse-aware MS-DOS program in a Command Prompt window, you'll want to disable the Select feature so that mouse movements will be sent to the program rather than being interpreted by the console program window. To disable the use of the mouse for copying text, select the window's Properties dialog box and uncheck Quick Edit mode, as shown in Figure 9.5.

Figure 9.5 A Command Prompt window's Properties dialog box lets you select the QuickEdit mode, screen mode, scroll length, editing properties, and screen colors.

DOSKEY Macros

DOSKEY is a command-line helper program that originated in MS-DOS, where it provided the up-and-down arrow key command recall feature that's now a standard part of the 32-bit Windows command window. A modified version of DOSKEY is also provided with Windows Vista, XP, and 2000. You don't need to run DOSKEY to get the command-line editing features, but you can use it to print out the command history, and more importantly, to define *macros*, which are keyboard shortcuts. For example, I use the command

```
doskey n=notepad
```

to define n as a command macro, and henceforth I can edit a text file by typing a command line like

```
n myfile.bat
```

instead of having to type

```
notepad myfile.bat
```

Once the macro is defined, n is seen as the word notepad whenever it's typed as the first word on a command prompt line. In the long run, this really does save time and frustration—you can't imagine how many times I've typed ntoepad instead of notepad!

By default, DOSKEY macros affect only text read by cmd.exe—that is, commands typed at the command prompt itself. You can define macros that will affect the input of specific command-line programs using the /EXENAME option. For example, the command

```
doskey /exename=ftp.exe anon=anonymous
```

defines anon as a macro that turns into the word anonymous when it's typed as the input to ftp.exe, the command-line File Transfer Protocol client.

Table 9.6 lists symbols that have special meaning inside a DOSKEY macro. You can use these symbols to construct macros complex enough to handle jobs that you would otherwise have to write small batch files to accomplish. With these symbols, upper/lowercase does not matter; $g and $G are treated the same.

Table 9.6   Special Symbols in DOSKEY Macros

Symbol	Function
$G	Works like > on the command line; lets you perform output redirection when the macro is run. Use GG to put >> in the macro to append output.
$L	Works like < on the command line; lets you perform input redirection when the macro is run.
$B	Works like | on the command line; lets you create a pipeline when the macro is run.
$T	Works like & on the command line; lets you specify several commands that are to be run in sequence when the macro is encountered.
$n	Where n is a single digit, is replaced by the nth argument on the macro's command line.
$*	$* is replaced by all the arguments on the macro's command line.
$$	Appears as a single $ when the command is run.

For example, after the macro definition

```
doskey fs=findstr /i /c:"$1" $2.log $B more
```

the command

```
fs index ww3svc
```

will be treated like the command

```
findstr /i /c:"index" ww3svc.log | more
```

which will search for a specified string in a specified log file and page the results through more.

It's important to know that unless you use $*, $1, $2, or the other $n symbols to explicitly tell DOSKEY to copy command-line arguments from your typed command line to the replacement line, they will be discarded. For example, with the definition

```
doskey n=notepad
```

the command

```
n myfile.txt
```

will open Notepad but the filename will not be seen. You have to define the macro this way

```
doskey n=notepad $*
```

to ensure that any arguments on the command line after n are passed along to notepad.

The command doskey /macros:all will list all defined macros.

To load your favorite DOSKEY macros every time you open a Command Prompt window, it won't help to put the DOSKEY command in autoexec.bat (which is ignored) or \windows\system32\autoexec.nt (which is used only by the MS-DOS emulation system). Instead, you have to put the desired macro definitions into a text file (one macro per line with the format name=replacement) and make an entry in the Registry to tell cmd.exe to load these settings every time it starts up.

You can define DOSKEY macros for all users by setting a Registry value named AutoRun under key HKEY_LOCAL_MACHINE\Software\Microsoft\Command Processor, or just for yourself by setting value AutoRun under HKEY_CURRENT_USER\Software\Microsoft\Command Processor. The entry should be a String (REG_SZ) or Expandable String (REG_EXPAND_SZ) with the name AutoRun and the value

```
doskey /macrofile="full path to macro definition file"
```

A helpful shortcut here is to define the value as an Expandable String (REG_EXPAND_SZ) under HKEY_CURRENT_USER... with the text

```
doskey /macrofile="%userprofile%\doskey.macros"
```

You can then create the file doskey.macros in your own profile folder (for example, this might be C:\Users\bknittel on Windows Vista, or C:\Documents and Settings\bknittel on Windows XP). My own doskey.macros file contains the following entries:

```
n=notepad $*
e=explorer .
```

```
home=cd /d %userprofile%
desktop=cd /d %userprofile%\Desktop
macdef=start /wait "" notepad "%userprofile%\doskey.macros" $T doskey /reinstall $T
    ➥ doskey /macrofile="%userprofile%\doskey.macros"
u=cd /d d:\project
```

Here's what they do:

- Macro n lets me run Notepad with one character.

- Macro e pops open a Windows Explorer window in the current directory.

- Home sets the current directory to my Windows profile folder and desktop sets the current directory to my Desktop folder.

- Macdef (whose definition is displayed on two lines here but is actually typed all on one line in doskey.macros) lets me modify my macro definitions and have the changes take effect without having to close the Command Prompt window and open a new one. It opens the macro definition file for editing, clears the defined macros, and then reloads the definitions. Start /wait is used here so that DOSKEY doesn't run until after Notepad exits.

- The last macro, u, is a quick shortcut to a commonly used folder. I add and delete macros like this all the time, as my work projects come and go. They save a lot of typing.

Note

The version of DOSKEY (**doskey.exe**) provided with Windows 2000 and XP works only in the 32-bit command prompt environment, not the 16-bit emulated MS-DOS environment. Running DOSKEY inside **autoexec.nt** or after running **command.com** has no effect. This means that the Up and Down Arrow keys will not recall commands in the 16-bit command shell.

The version of DOSKEY provided with Windows 98 and Me (**doskey.com**) is the original 16-bit version that works inside the **command.com** shell. On Windows 98 or Me, it's most effectively loaded in **autoexec.bat**, before Windows is loaded.

If you frequently use the MS-DOS environment on Windows XP or Vista, and if you can get a copy of **doskey.com** from Windows 98 or Me, and put it into your \windows\system32 folder, you can load it **DOSKEY.COM** in **autoexec.nt** and get the arrow-key recall feature.

For a full description of all of DOSKEY's features, type

```
help doskey | more
```

at the command prompt.

Command Extensions

Under Windows 2000 and XP, lines in a Command Prompt window or listed in a batch file are processed by cmd.exe, which is known as the command shell or command-line processor. It performs the same function that command.com did under DOS and earlier versions of Windows, but it has been expanded and includes many additional features. If you haven't used the command-line environment since the days of MS-DOS, and especially if you write batch files, you need to know about cmd's important and useful enhancements. Table 9.7 lists some of the ways that cmd handles commands differently than command.com. For more information, search Windows Help for "cmd."

Table 9.7 Command Extensions provided by *cmd.exe*

Command	Enhancement
Cd	The **cd** (Change Directory) command can change the current drive letter as well as the current directory. For example, `cd /d w:\serverfolder` changes the drive letter to **W:** as well as changing the current directory to **\serverfolder**. This is especially useful in batch files where you may have an environment variable that contains a drive letter and path, as in **cd /d %userprofile%**.
pushd *path* popd	**Pushd** is a new command that also changes the current directory (or drive and directory), but also "remembers" the previous drive and directory. **Popd** returns to the previous drive and directory. **Pushd** and **popd** commands can be nested—three **pushd**s followed by three **popd**s get you back to where you started. **Pushd** can take a network path name as its argument, for example, **pushd \\server\docfiles**. This will automatically map a drive letter to the network path, starting with drive z: and working backwards.
for	The **for** command has been extensively enhanced and now has the capability to scan directories, scan directories recursively, iterate through number ranges, scan the lines of a file or the output of a command-line program, and more. Special substitution operators let you extract specific parts of the matched filenames or tokens. For more information type the command **help for	more**.
set	The **set** command, which lets you define environment variables, has been enhanced to let you perform mathematical calculations on environment variables, extract substrings, and prompt for user input. For more details, type **help set	more**.
call	The batch file command **call** can now call subroutines defined within the same batch file, using the syntax **call :***label* [*arguments…*].
goto	The batch file command **goto** can now jump directly to the end of the file, to terminate the batch procedure or return from the batch subroutine, with the syntax **goto :EOF**.
setlocal endlocal	In a batch file, **setlocal** saves a copy of the environment variables, and subsequent changes or additions to the environment do not persist after the batch file exits. An **endlocal** command inside the batch file restores all environment variables to their value at the time of **setlocal**. **Setlocal** can also be used to enable and disable all these command extensions, and to enable or disable delayed expansion, a complex but important feature that comes into play when you write complex batch files. Delayed expansion is disabled by default, and must be enabled in a batch file with the command **setlocal enabledelayedexpansion**. Delayed expansion is described in more detail shortly.

In addition, input and output redirection operators have been enhanced, as described earlier in this chapter under "Input and Output Redirection." Multiple commands can be typed on one command line, using the separators discussed earlier under "Command Separators. "

Printing in the Command-Line Environment

Windows applications generate printed output through calls to the Windows programming interface. Output is page oriented; that is, applications generate output by describing to Windows what to draw on successive whole pages of paper. Output is graphical in nature; lines, images, and text are all drawn pixel by pixel. The application doesn't know how to tell the printer how to draw these things; it simply tells Windows what it wants drawn, and Windows communicates this to a printer driver that sends the appropriate manufacturer-specific commands to the printer.

Console applications are distinctly different. Windows console applications have no concept of formatting; they simply spit text out character by character, line after line. The output from these programs is plain text, with no font, pagination or formatting information whatsoever. If you used MS-DOS you may be familiar with the technique of directing output to the lpt1 device, as in the command

```
dir >lpt1
```

On Windows, this does direct the directory listing to device LPT1, your computer's parallel port device, but there are several reasons this might not produce the listing you intended:

- If you are using a laser or inkjet printer, this inherently page-oriented device will not "kick out" the printout until it receives a form-feed instruction. Most likely, nothing will come out until you try to print the next document. And then the page margins and default font will likely be unsatisfactory.

- If your printer is connected to a USB port, this won't work at all unless you share the printer on your network, and then use the net command to redirect LPT1 output to the printer via the network share.

- Many cheap inkjet and laser printers cannot interpret ASCII text directly and will generate no output at all. PostScript printers will likely simply generate an error page. Only dot-matrix printers and page printers with a built-in page-description language (for example, printers with Hewlett-Packard PCL support) will generate valid text.

The best way to get printed output from Windows console applications is to redirect their output to a file on your hard disk, and then open and print the file with Notepad or your favorite word processor.

For example, to get a printed listing of the files in your My Documents folder, you might open a command prompt window and issue these commands:

```
cd My Documents
dir >listing.txt
notepad listing.txt
```

You can then print this listing from within Notepad. To get printed output from a batch file, you can use this command line:

```
notepad /p listing.txt
```

which makes Notepad open the file, print it, and then immediately exit, without any manual interaction. The printout will use Notepad's default font and margins, which you should set beforehand.

MS-DOS applications like WordPerfect take full responsibility for communicating with the printer, and want to send specific formatting codes to the printer. The MS-DOS emulation subsystem simply passes these codes directly to the printer, so you must configure the MS-DOS program to tell it what make and model printer you are using. The issues I discussed previously still apply: USB printers and inexpensive page printers will likely not work at all.

Some MS-DOS applications can use printers shared on your network, as long as the share names of the devices are 8 characters or fewer in length, and the names of the computers are 15 characters or fewer in length. For example, WordPerfect 5.1 can be told to use network printers given the printer's network share name, which will look something like \\mycomputer\laserjet.

If your MS-DOS application doesn't know explicitly how to use networked printers, you may also be able to let it use a network printer by redirecting an MS-DOS LPT printer port to a network printer. You must use an LPT port number for which there is no physical LPT port on your computer. Because most computers do have an LPT1 parallel printer port, you must use LPT2, LPT3, up to LPT9. (Some MS-DOS programs can only use printers up to LPT3.) The command

```
net use lpt2: \\mycomputer\laserjet
```

makes the MS-DOS LPT2 device point to the shared printer named laserjet on the computer named mycomputer. Once this is done, you can configure your MS-DOS application to print to LPT2.

You can also use this technique to let MS-DOS applications print to USB printers attached to your own computer. Set up sharing on your USB printer, and then issue the net use command using the name of your own computer on the command line. Again, remember that this will work only if the USB printer can accept raw text, or if it uses a page description language (formatting code set) that your MS-DOS application knows how to use.

To stop redirecting an LPT port to a network printer, issue the command

```
net use lpt2: /d
```

substituting lpt3 for lpt2 if that's what you were using.

Print Screen

On Windows, the MS-DOS Print Screen function does not work as it did in the real MS-DOS. When an MS-DOS program is running in window mode, the PrtScr key works just as it normally does in Windows: It copies a bitmap picture of the screen or current window to the Clipboard. You have to paste the bitmap into a document (in, say, Word or WordPad), and then print that document.

When an MS-DOS program is running in full-screen mode, the PrtScr key still doesn't send the screen to the printer. Instead, it copies the screen's *text* to the Clipboard. To print it, again, you'll need to paste the text into a document and print it as a separate step.

Stopping Runaway Programs

Occasionally you'll type a command that starts spewing page after page of text to the screen, or one that displays some sort of ominous warning about making a change to Windows that can't be undone, and you'll want to stop it—pronto.

Most command-line programs will quit if you press Ctrl+C. If that doesn't work, Ctrl+Break often works. As a last resort, you can simply close the Command Prompt window by clicking its close box in the upper-right corner. This will kill the program in at most a few seconds.

On Windows Vista and XP Professional, you may also find the tasklist and taskkill command-line programs useful. Type **tasklist** to get a list of active programs. This will display something like this:

```
Image Name                    PID Session Name      Session#    Mem Usage
========================== ====== ================ ======== ============
System Idle Process             0 Services                0        16 K
System                          4 Services                0       216 K
smss.exe                      368 Services                0       372 K
csrss.exe                     444 Services                0     3,320 K
wininit.exe                   488 Services                0     2,628 K
winlogon.exe                  532 Services                0     5,584 K
setiathome.exe               1072 Services                0    20,252 K
...
winword.exe                  2756 Console                 1    22,784 K
cmd.exe                      1904 Console                 1     4,320 K
tasklist.exe                 2772 Console                 1     4,148 K
```

The PID column contains the Process Identification number (PID) of each running program. You can kill a program with the command

```
taskkill /force /pid nnn
```

with the PID number of the program you want to stop in place of *nnn*.

Configuring the Command-Line Environment

In this section, I'll tell you a bit about how cmd may be adjusted to better meet your own needs. Some of these settings change how the Command Prompt window appears, whereas others change the software environment itself. If you were used to the MS-DOS environment, some of the software settings will be familiar, although the method of changing them is quite different.

Console Window Properties

You can make several changes to the appearance of console program windows. For better visibility, or to make a program look more like it's running under MS-DOS, you can press Alt+Enter to run the program in *full-screen* mode. If you run a DOS graphics program, this will happen automatically. In this mode, the program takes over the whole screen and all other Windows features disappear. You can always press Alt+Enter to bring back the Windows desktop.

You can set the screen mode and the number of lines that the window can scroll using the window's Properties dialog box, as shown earlier in Figure 9.5. You can also set the window's colors and font. Usually, you won't need to adjust the font. It's best to simply resize the window in the normal way and Windows will size the characters accordingly.

Changing the Search Path

By default, Windows sets the PATH environment variable to a standard list of Windows folders. If you plan on writing your own programs, batch files, Windows Script Host scripts, or other application programs, it's a good idea to place them in a folder of their own and then add that folder to the path.

You can change the search path in any of three ways.

First, you can set a new value for the PATH environment variable using the set command, as in this example:

```
set path=c:\bat;%path%
```

This makes the folder `c:\bat` the first folder in the path. The `;%path%` ensures that the prior `PATH` folders are retained in the path list, otherwise you wouldn't be able to run programs not in `c:\bat`.

Second, you can use the `path` command, which is a shortcut version of `set path`:

```
path c:\bat;%path%
```

These commands have the same effect: They set the environment variable `PATH` to `c:\bat`, followed by the previous `PATH` definition.

Note

If the folder you're adding to the path has spaces in its name, put quotes around the name.

You could also add a new folder to the *end* of the search path with a statement like this:

```
set path=%path%;"c:\bat"
```

The ordering matters only if there are versions of the same command in more than one folder in the path; the version in the first folder to be searched will be the one that Windows runs.

Tip

If you mess up the path and cmd stops working, just close the Command Prompt window and open another. You'll be back in action.

Putting your own folders ahead of the Windows folders in the list can be a blessing or a curse. If you create a program or batch file with the same name as a standard Windows program, yours will run instead of the standard program. If this is what you want, great, but if not…the result can be very confusing.

The path and set commands change environment variables only for the current instance of the cmd program. If you close the Command Prompt window and open a new one, you'll be back to the initial default `PATH`.

The third way of changing the `PATH` makes the change appear in all future cmd prompt windows. To do this, you'll need to make the change on the System Properties dialog box, as I'll discuss shortly under "Setting Default Environment Variables."

Predefined and Virtual Environment Variables

Environment variables can be set in any of six places. If a given variable name is set in more than one place, the last definition encountered is used. The sources are processed in the following order:

1. Predefined, built-in system variables (for example, `APPDATA`).

2. Systemwide variables defined in the System Properties dialog box.

3. User-specific variables defined in the System Properties dialog box. However, a user-specific `PATH` definition does *not* replace the systemwide definition. Instead, it's *added* to the beginning of the systemwide definition.

4. Variables defined in logon scripts (batch or WSH-type).

These first four sources are processed when a user logs on, and they form the user's default environment; the remaining sources are processed each time a new cmd process is started, and any changes are lost when cmd is closed.

5. Variables defined in AUTOEXEC.NT, when *and* only when a DOS program is run.

6. Variables defined on the command line, in batch files, or in Windows Script Host scripts through WshShell.Environment("Process").

The following variables are defined by default for all users (systemwide):

Variable Name	Usual Value on Windows Vista
ALLUSERSPROFILE	C:\ProgramData
APPDATA	C:\Users*username*\AppData\Roaming
CommonProgramFiles	C:\Program Files\Common Files
COMPUTERNAME	*computername*
ComSpec	C:\WINDOWS\system32\cmd.exe
HOMEDRIVE	C:
HOMEPATH	\Documents and Settings*username*
LOCALAPPDATA	C:\Users*username*\AppData\Local
LOGONSERVER	(Varies)
NUMBER_OF_PROCESSORS	(Varies)
OS	Windows_NT
Path	C:\WINDOWS\system32;C:\WINDOWS;C:\WINDOWS\System32\Wbem (this entry varies depending on the location of Windows)
PATHEXT	.COM;.EXE;.BAT;.CMD;.VBS;.VBE;.JS;.JSE;.WSF;.WSH;.MSC
PROCESSOR_ARCHITECTURE	(Varies)
PROCESSOR_IDENTIFIER	(Varies)
PROCESSOR_LEVEL	(Varies)
PROCESSOR_REVISION	(Varies)
ProgramData	C:\ProgramData
ProgramFiles	C:\Program Files
PROMPT	PG
PUBLIC	C:\Users\Public
SESSIONNAME	(Varies)
SystemDrive	C:
SystemRoot	C:\WINDOWS
TEMP	C:\Users*username*\AppData\Local\Temp
TMP	C:\Users*username*\AppData\Local\Temp

(continues)

Variable Name	Usual Value on Windows Vista
USERDOMAIN	*computername* or *domainname*
USERNAME	*username*
USERPROFILE	C:\Users *username*
windir	C:\Windows

When you need to copy files to or from a user's personal folder (such as the Desktop or My Documents folder), or to a system folder such as Program Files, you should use these environment variables to specify the folder's location, rather than assume that the folder is on the C drive in the default location. Sometimes Windows gets installed on other drives, and sometimes network managers change the locations of the profile folders. So, for example, to copy a shortcut named My Progarm.lnk from the current directory onto everyone's desktop, use a command like this:

```
copy "My Program.lnk" %ALLUSERSPROFILE%\Desktop
```

rather than

```
copy "My Program.lnk" c:\Documents and Settings\All Users\Desktop
```

which assumes specific locations and even then works only on Windows XP, not Vista.

This is especially important if you are writing batch files (or scripts) that have to run on both Windows Vista and XP, and perhaps earlier versions of Windows. The user profile folder structure was changed significantly for Windows Vista. Several of the predefined variables have different standard values on Windows XP:

Variable Name	Usual Value on Windows XP
ALLUSERSPROFILE	C:\Documents and Settings\All Users
APPDATA	C:\Documents and Settings*username*\Application Data
HOMEPATH	\Documents and Settings*username*
PATHEXT	.COM;.EXE;.BAT;.CMD;.VBS;.VBE;.JS
TEMP	C:\DOCUME~1*username*\LOCALS~1\Temp
TMP	C:\DOCUME~1\username\LOCALS~1\Temp
USERPROFILE	C:\Documents and Settings*username*

If you use the variables rather than the fixed location names, your batch file should work correctly no matter on what version of Windows it runs.

In addition to the predefined environment variables, when cmd's command extensions are enabled, several virtual environment variables are available. The following environment variable names are computed dynamically *each time they're used* on a command line or in a batch file:

Name	Value
CD	The current directory drive and path
DATE	The current date, formatted as by the DATE command
TIME	The current time, formatted as by the TIME command
RANDOM	A random number between 0 and 32,767
ERRORLEVEL	The exit status of the previous program
CMDEXTVERSION	The version number of command extensions
CMDCMDLINE	The command line used to start cmd itself

These entries don't really exist in the environment; cmd just fakes it by substituting the appropriate value when it runs into, for example, %date%.

Note

If you define an environment variable with one of these names, your fixed defined value will always supercede the dynamic value.

The maximum size for an individual environment variable (name, equal sign, and value) is 8,192 bytes. The total size of all environment variables must be less than 65,536KB.

Setting Default Environment Variables

To define environment variables permanently so that they are defined whenever you log on, use one of the following procedures.

- On Windows Vista, if you are a Computer Administrator, click Start, right-click Computer, and select Properties. In the Tasks pane click Advanced System Settings. Accept the User Account Control prompt. Then, when the System Properties dialog appears, click the Environment Variables button.

- On Windows Vista, if you are not a Computer Administrator and don't know the Administrator password, open the Control Panel and click User Accounts and Family Safety. At the top of the window, click User Accounts. In the Tasks pane at the left, click Change My Environment Variables.

- On Windows XP, click Start, right-click My Computer and select Properties. Next, view the Advanced tab and click Environment Variables.

Regardless of the method, Windows displays the dialog box shown in Figure 9.6.

The top part of the dialog box lets you define the default variables for your own account. You can click New to add a new variable, or you can click Edit or Delete to modify an existing entry.

The lower part of the dialog box edits the default variables provided to *all* user accounts. These settings can only be edited by an Administrator, and the settings may be overridden by user-specific entries.

Figure 9.6 The Environment Variables dialog box lets you edit default environment variables for your account or for all users.

An interesting feature of this dialog is that in *most* cases, if a variable is defined in the User Variables list, the user version overrides the System version. However, in the case of the PATH variable, the User version is *prepended* to the System version. This helps prevent users from accidentally ending up with a PATH that is missing all the standard Windows program folders. Here's an example. If the System PATH in the lower list is defined as

```
C:\WINDOWS\system32;C:\WINDOWS;C:\WINDOWS\system32\WBEM
```

and the User PATH in the upper list is defined as

```
c:\bat;"c:\program files\my special stuff"
```

then the user's actual PATH environment variable will be set to

```
C:\WINDOWS\system32;C:\WINDOWS;C:\WINDOWS\system32\WBEM;c:\bat;
    ➥ "c:\program files\my special stuff"
```

at logon.

On Vista, or on Windows XP with the Support Tools package installed from your XP setup CD, you can use setx command to set default Registry entries from the command line—this is perhaps the easiest way of all to do it. Setx works in a way similar to set, except that it modifies your *default* environment values rather than the current values. The command

```
setx variablename "value"
```

sets the default value for just your account, whereas the command

```
setx variablename "value" /m
```

sets it for all users (systemwide). For example, the command

```
setx prompt "%computername% $p$g"
```

sets your default command-line prompt to include the computer name. After executing this command, you must open a new Command Prompt window to see the effect. (Setx can do some very sophisticated things, including extracting values from the Registry and from files. Type the command setx /? for more information.)

Note

If you're familiar with Windows Script Host, you can also modify the default personal and systemwide environment variables with WSH scripts by modifying the WshShell.Environment("system") and WshShell.Environment("user") collections, respectively.

I recommend that you create a folder to contain your own personal batch files and scripts, perhaps named c:\bat, and add it to your user PATH as discussed here. This way, your scripts and batch files can be run from any command prompt you own, without worrying about where they're stored.

AutoRun

Normally, when it first starts, cmd examines the Registry for a value named AutoRun under the keys

    HKLM\Software\Microsoft\Command Processor

and

    HKCU\Software\Microsoft\Command Processor

Note

HKLM and HKCU are short for HKEY_LOCAL_MACHINE and HKEY_CURRENT_USER, respectively.

AutoRun values with type REG_SZ (string) or REG_EXPAND_SZ (string with environment variables to be expanded) are taken as commands to be run when an instance of cmd first starts up; first the HKEY_LOCAL_MACHINE value is examined, and if defined, run, and then the HKEY_CURRENT_USER value is checked.

AutoRun settings can be used to perform some of the functions that used to be provided by the AUTOEXEC.BAT file in DOS. In particular, you can use it to run DOSKEY to set macros via an AutoRun command (we'll discuss this later in the chapter).

If you want to run more than one command with the AutoRun feature, create a batch file, and have the AutoRun value specify this batch file's name.

If necessary, you can disable AutoRun commands by starting cmd with /D on its command line, as I'll discuss later in this chapter.

Note

This "autorun" setting is not related to the Autorun feature that launches applications or plays media when you insert a CD or DVD.

Configuring the MS-DOS Command Environment

As mentioned earlier, versions of Windows based on Windows NT (NT, 2000, XP, and Vista) use a command prompt shell program named `cmd.exe`. As it turns out, to maintain maximum compatibility with old MS-DOS programs and old batch files, the original MS-DOS `command.com` shell is actually still available on the 32-bit flavors of these versions of Windows XP as part of the 16-bit compatibility subsystem. Here's how it works: If you run an MS-DOS program in a Command Prompt window, cmd assumes that you're going to work in the 16-bit world for a while. So, when the DOS program finishes, the window switches to the `command.com` shell. You'll notice several differences:

- The current directory name is changed to its old-style 8.3 equivalent. For example, if your current directory had been `C:\Documents and Settings\naleks`, when the DOS program exits, the directory will be displayed as `C:\DOCUME~1\NALEKS`.

- Environment variable names change to all uppercase letters.

- The extended versions of the built-in commands will be unavailable.

- If you've run `command.com` explicitly, you cannot close the window by clicking its Close button—`command.com` doesn't get the message to quit. You'll have to type **exit** to close the window.

These changes make it more likely that old programs and batch files will be able to run. However, if you want, you can keep `cmd.exe` as your command shell even when using MS-DOS programs, by configuring the MS-DOS environment.

To maintain compatibility with as many old DOS programs as possible, ntvdm can be configured to mimic an older environment. You can configure ntvdm's memory and window options through a properties dialog box, and you can configure the virtual DOS environment itself through configuration files that mimic the old `CONFIG.SYS` and `AUTOEXEC.BAT` files. Here is how the default configuration works:

- By default, ntvdm gives an MS-DOS program as much regular and DOS Protected Mode Interface (DPMI) memory as it asks for. No Extended (XMS) or Expanded (EMS) memory is available.

- Ntvdm reads configuration options from `\windows\system32\config.nt` and executes the batch file `\windows\system32\autoexec.nt` before running the program. These files are installed along with Windows and contain important default settings that permit the use of high memory, networking, and emulated SoundBlaster sound hardware.

These settings should work for most MS-DOS programs. You can modify these files to make changes that will apply to all MS-DOS programs, or you can create customized versions for specific applications; we'll discuss this in the next section.

If you need specially tuned DOS environments for special applications, you may want to configure Windows shortcuts for these applications, or at least create shortcuts that open custom-configured Command Prompt windows. To create a customized MS-DOS environment, right-click the name of the MS-DOS program you want to run and select Properties. If you change any of the default properties and save the settings, Windows will create a file with the same name as the program file, but with extension `.PIF`. This `.PIF` file holds the customized settings. It is listed in

Explorer as a "Shortcut to MS-DOS Program." Use this shortcut to run the program. If you need to run a batch file before running the program, follow this same procedure, but create a shortcut to the batch files instead of the program itself.

Note

You must use the shortcut to start the MS-DOS program in order to take advantage of any configuration changes you've made. If you run the .EXE file directly, Windows will not know to look at the .PIF (shortcut) file.

Window and Memory Options

The Properties dialog box for an MS-DOS application shortcut (.PIF file) lets you set the virtual MS-DOS environment's memory display and mouse properties. To customize these properties, right-click the MS-DOS application file itself, or if you've already created customized properties, you can right-click the MS-DOS Application Shortcut icon, and then select Properties.

Here are the most common settings to change:

- The working folder on the Program page
- The Extended Memory and Initial Environment options on the Memory page
- The Always Suspend option on the Misc page

In the next sections, I'll describe all the property pages in more detail so that you can see what configuration options are available. The General, Security, Summary, and Backup pages (if they appear on your system) are the same as for any other Windows file, so I won't describe them here.

Program Settings

The Program tab displays a typical Shortcut property page and has the following settings (see Figure 9.7):

- **Cmd Line**—The path to the MS-DOS program file or batch file, and any additional command-line arguments you need. If you enter **?** on the command line, Windows will prompt you for command-line arguments when you run the shortcut. Whatever you type will be used in place of ?.

- **Working**—The drive and folder to use as the initial working directory for the program. If you leave this field blank, the initial directory will be the one containing the MS-DOS program. If the shortcut will be used by several people, you may want to use environment variables in this path. For example, "%userprofile%\My Documents" will specify each user's own My Documents folder regardless of its actual location.

- **Batch File**—Ostensibly, the name of a batch file to run before starting the program. As far as I can tell, however, this feature does not work.

- **Shortcut Key**—Optional. Specifies a hotkey that is supposed to start the program. However, this feature does not appear to work either.

- **Run**—Selects the initial window size: Normal, Maximized, or Minimized (icon). Full Screen is different; see the screen settings.

- **Close on Exit**—If this option is checked, the window will close when the program exits. If this option is unchecked, the window will remain open but inactive, and the title will include the word *Inactive*. You will want to leave this checked in most cases.

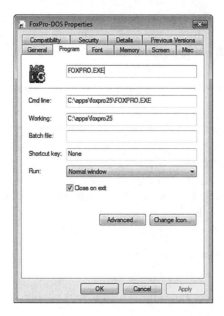

Figure 9.7   The MS-DOS Shortcut Program tab. The Advanced button lets you specify a custom `config.nt` or `autoexec.nt` file.

Tip

If a DOS program fails to run, uncheck this box and try to run the program again. You'll then have time to read any error messages that appear.

The Program tab also lets you specify alternate configuration and startup batch files to use instead of `CONFIG.NT` and `AUTOEXEC.NT`. To change the configuration files associated with a shortcut, click the Advanced button and enter the paths and names of the desired files. The default values are `%SystemRoot%\SYSTEM32\CONFIG.NT` and `%SystemRoot%\SYSTEM32\AUTOEXEC.NT`. I will describe the settings in these files shortly.

Tip

If your MS-DOS program has timing or speed problems, it may be that it expects to be able to change the settings of the PC's timer chips. If you click the Advanced button and check the Compatible Timer Hardware Emulation option, the problem may go away.

Font Settings

The Font tab lets you select the font used when the program is running in a window. The default setting, Auto, lets Windows resize the font as you resize the window, but you can specify a fixed size. If you do, the window will not be resizable.

Tip

If you want to switch to a fixed font size, you can do it while the program is running. Right-click the upper-left corner of the program's window, select Properties, and view the Font tab. Make any desired changes and then choose Save Properties for Future Windows with the Same Title when Windows offers you this option.

Memory Settings

The Memory tab, shown in Figure 9.8, lets you specify the type and amount of memory to make available to the MS-DOS program. The plethora of memory types came about as different ways of coping with the original PC's limited memory hardware options. Some programs can use any type of memory, but others specifically require access to XMS or EMS memory—your program's installation instructions will tell you what type of memory it requires or can take advantage of. Here's a list of the settings:

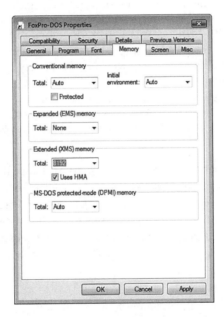

Figure 9.8 The Memory tab lets you make various memory formats available to the DOS program.

- **Conventional Memory, Total**—The amount of memory between 0 and 640KB. The Auto setting provides up to 640KB. You will probably never need to alter this setting.

- **Initial Environment**—The number of bytes to set aside for environment variables. Auto directs ntvdm to use the amount specified in the SHELL setting in CONFIG.NT. If you use complex batch files, you may want to increase this setting to 2000 bytes or more.

- **Protected**—If checked, this option prevents the program from altering memory in the range occupied by the simulated MS-DOS system components. Check this box only if you experience unexplained crashes.

- **Expanded (EMS) Memory**—If your program requires EMS (paged) memory, set this to Auto or a fixed number. (Your program's installation instructions will tell you if it needs EMS memory.)

- **Extended (XMS) Memory**—If your program can use XMS expanded memory, set this to Auto or a fixed number.

- **Uses HMA**—This option normally has no effect because the High Memory Area is used by the simulated MS-DOS program.

- **MS-DOS Protected-Mode (DPMI) Memory**—By default, this option is set to Auto. You can disable or permit a fixed amount of DPMI memory, if necessary.

Screen Settings

The screen settings let you determine whether the program has direct access to the whole screen at startup. These settings include the following:

- **Usage**—Lets you select between full-screen and window as the initial display mode. In full-screen mode, the MS-DOS program takes over the primary display and can display graphics.

- **Restore Settings at Startup**—If this option is checked, the last-used window size and font will be reused the next time you start the program. If you want to provide a consistent environment for multiple users, uncheck this box, make the appropriate initial settings, and then make the PIF file nonwritable by other users using file security settings.

- **Fast ROM Emulation**—When this option is checked, the Virtual DOS Machine emulates the graphics functions normally provided by the display adapter's built-in (read-only memory) BIOS program.

- **Dynamic Memory Allocation**—When this option is checked, Windows releases memory assigned to the virtual graphics display when the program switches from graphics to text display. If you get a blank screen when the program switches back, try unchecking this box.

When the MS-DOS program is running and attempts to change the display from text-based to graphical, Windows will automatically switch to full-screen mode. You can manually switch back and forth between full-screen and window mode by pressing Alt+Enter. If the program is using a text display, you can continue using it in window mode. If it is displaying graphics, however, the program will be suspended (frozen) and minimized unless it's in full-screen mode. Windows, unfortunately, can't display a little windowed version of the DOS graphical display.

Miscellaneous Settings

The miscellaneous settings tab determines how the program behaves when it's running in a window. Most of the settings are self-explanatory. The tab is shown in Figure 9.9. Here are the less obvious settings:

- **Always Suspend**—If this option is checked, the MS-DOS program will be frozen when it's not the active window. Because MS-DOS programs didn't anticipate multitasking, they tend to burn lots of CPU time even when idle. Suspending the program when you're not using it makes your system more responsive. However, if you are running a communications or database program that needs to run while you do other things, uncheck this box.

Figure 9.9 The miscellaneous settings tab lets you control the program's use of the mouse and keyboard.

- **Idle Sensitivity**—This is also related to the idle CPU issue. Windows tries to guess when the DOS program is just spinning its gears doing nothing and gives it a lower priority when it thinks this is the case. A high Idle Sensitivity setting means that Windows will lean toward thinking the program is idle, resulting in snappier performance for other applications. A lower Idle Sensitivity setting will make Windows give the DOS application more time. The DOS application will be better able to perform background (noninteractive) processing, while making your Windows applications more sluggish. Raise this setting if your DOS program makes everything else too slow, or lower it if your DOS program can't get its job done. In the latter case, also uncheck Always Suspend.

- **Exclusive Mode**—Dedicates the mouse to the DOS program.

- **Fast Pasting**—Determines how quickly Windows will stuff simulated keystrokes into the MS-DOS programs when you paste in text from the Windows clipboard using Alt+space, Edit, Paste. If characters are lost when pasting, uncheck this option.

- **Windows Shortcut Keys**—These check boxes let you determine which special keystrokes should be passed to Windows rather than to the MS-DOS programs. If your MS-DOS program needs key combinations such as Alt+Tab and Alt+Enter, you will need to uncheck the relevant boxes on this page. The DOS program will get these keystrokes in full-screen mode or when its window is active, so be prepared to lose the corresponding Windows shortcut.

It's especially tricky if you uncheck Alt+Enter and the program switches to full-screen mode. You will have to type Ctrl+Alt+Del to open the Task Manager if you want to switch back to the Windows desktop before the program exits.

Compatibility Settings

Windows compatibility settings let you limit the capabilities of the virtual display adapter seen by the MS-DOS program. The relevant settings are Run in 256 Colors, Run in 640×480 Screen Resolution, Disable Desktop Composition, and Disable Display Scaling on High DPI Settings. If your MS-DOS program has problems displaying graphics screens, try checking these boxes.

CONFIG.NT

Just as MS-DOS used CONFIG.SYS to make initial memory allocations and to load device drivers, ntvdm uses CONFIG.NT to configure the virtual DOS environment.

The default CONFIG.NT file as installed by Windows is located in \windows\system32 and contains several pages of comment text, which you may want to read. Here are the default settings in this file:

```
dos=high,umb
device=%systemroot%\system32\himem.sys
files=40
```

You can edit CONFIG.NT to modify the defaults for all MS-DOS applications, or you can create alternate files using a different name for use with specific applications. In the latter case, use the Advanced button on the Program Settings properties page for the program's shortcut to enter the alternate filename. I'll use the name CONFIG.NT in the discussion that follows to refer to any config file.

Note

For starters, if you use MS-DOS database applications, you will probably want to increase the **FILES=** setting in **CONFIG.NT** to **100** or more. You may also want to add the ANSI cursor control module with the line

```
device=%systemroot%\system32\ansi.sys
```

Other than these two adjustments, it's unlikely that you'll need to make any other changes.

The full set of options for CONFIG.NT is listed in the rest of this section.

COUNTRY=*xxx*[,[*yyy*][,[[*path*]]*filename*]]

tells MS-DOS to use an alternate character set and date/time format. *xxx* is a country/region code, *yyy* is an optional code page designator, and *filename* designates an optional driver containing country code information. If you use the virtual MS-DOS environment outside the U.S., view the Help and Support Center and search for "country."

DEVICE=[*path*\]*filename* [*parameters*]

loads a device driver. Hardware device drivers will almost certainly *not* work in Windows XP, but certain software services implemented as drivers will. Examples include himem.sys, which is required to let MS-DOS programs access memory above 640KB, and ansi.sys, which interprets character sequences that some DOS programs use to control the cursor. These drivers are located in folder %systemroot%\system32.

DEVICEHIGH=[*path*\]*filename* [*parameters*]

or

DEVICEHIGH [SIZE=*xx***]** [*path*]*filename* [*parameters*]

similar to *device* but attempts to load the device driver into upper memory blocks, leaving more conventional memory for MS-DOS applications. If there is insufficient room in upper memory or if the device himem.sys has not been loaded, the driver will be loaded into conventional memory. The alternate size=*xx* format lets you specify the number of bytes of high memory that must be free; *xx* must be specified in hexadecimal.

DOS=[HIGH|LOW][, UMB|NOUMB]

DOS=HIGH specifies that MS-DOS should move parts of itself into the high memory area (the first 64KB past 1MB). The default is LOW, where DOS resides entirely in conventional memory. The optional keyword UMB indicates that DOS should make upper memory area blocks (the memory beyond 1MB+64KB) available for DOS, devices, and programs.

DOSONLY

If this keyword is present in CONFIG.NT, COMMAND.COM will be permitted to run only MS-DOS programs. Normally, if you typed the name of a Windows program at its command prompt or in a batch file, it would run the Windows program in a separate environment. This may disrupt some DOS terminate-and-stay-resident (TSR) programs, so the DOSONLY option lets you prevent this from happening.

ECHOCONFIG

If the command ECHOCONFIG appears, CONFIG.NT commands echo to the Command Prompt window while ntvdm is initializing. The default is for the commands not to be displayed.

FCBS=*n*

File Control Blocks (FCB) is an archaic structure used by DOS version 1.0 programs to manage files. Few, if any, surviving MS-DOS programs require FCB, but if you have one, you can use the FCBS statement to instruct ntvdm to allocate space for *n* of them. (At this late date, if you do need them, you'll already know it because you'll have had to deal with this on every prior version of DOS and Windows.)

FILES=*n*

sets the maximum number of concurrently open files available to MS-DOS applications. The default value is 20. You may want to increase this number to 100 or more if you use database applications such as MS-DOS FoxPro.

INSTALL=[path\]*filename* [*parameters*]

loads a TSR into memory prior to running AUTOEXEC.NT.

One program that you may need to install in AUTOEXEC.NT is setver.exe. Setver intercepts programs' requests to find out what version of DOS is running, and it lies to them. Its purpose is to let you run programs that would otherwise be unhappy to find that they're running on DOS version 5.0, which is what ntvdm would tell them. If your MS-DOS application complains about the DOS version number, open the Help and Support Center and search for "setver."

NTCMDPROMPT

By default, when an MS-DOS program is run from the command line or a batch file and exits, cmd runs `command.com` to handle all further commands. This makes it possible to run old MS-DOS batch files. If you specify `NTCMDPROMPT` in `CONFIG.NT`, cmd will not run `command.com`, but will remain in control between MS-DOS programs. This lets you write modern batch files to use with MS-DOS programs.

SHELL=[*path*]*filename* [*parameters*]

specifies an alternate shell program to use if you do not want to use `command.com` as the MS-DOS shell. You can also use this command to specify `command.com` with startup options. For example, the entry

```
shell=%systemroot%\system32\command.com /E:2048/P
```

requests 2048 bytes for environment variables. The `/P` option is required to prevent `command.com` from exiting after processing one command.

STACKS=*n*,*s*

When a hardware interrupt occurs, ntvdm needs memory stack space to temporarily store information for the interrupt handler. The `stacks` option lets you instruct ntvdm to allocate separate stack space for interrupt handlers. The numbers *n* and *s* instruct ntvdm to allocate *n* blocks of *s* bytes each. *n* can be 0 or 8 through 64. *s* can be 0 or 32 to 512. The default values are 9 and 128, respectively. If necessary, you can save memory for program use by specifying `stacks=0,0`; this may or may not cause a program crash. You can specify `stacks=8,512` to allocate plenty of stack space if you suspect that interrupt handlers are causing DOS crashes.

SWITCHES=/K

makes MS-DOS programs treat the keyboard as a conventional 96-key keyboard even if it uses the extended 102+ key layout. If you use this switch and also load `ansi.sys`, specify `/k` after `ansi.sys` as well.

The following items are permitted in `CONFIG.NT` for compatibility with historical `CONFIG.SYS` settings but have no effect in Windows XP:

- `buffers`
- `driveparm`
- `lastdrive` (`lastdrive` is always Z)

AUTOEXEC.NT

`AUTOEXEC.NT` serves the same purpose `AUTOEXEC.BAT` did on MS-DOS systems: It is a batch file that lets you run programs that set up the command environment before you begin working. The default version of AUTOEXEC.NT installed with Windows is located in \windows\system32 and contains the following commands:

```
lh %SystemRoot%\system32\mscdexnt.exe
lh %SystemRoot%\system32\redir
lh %SystemRoot%\system32\dosx
SET BLASTER=A220 I5 D1 P330 T3
```

MSCDEXNT provides support for CD-ROM drives, REDIR is the network interface, DOSX provides upper-memory support (it serves the same purpose EMM386.EXE did on MS-DOS), and the SET command provides DOS programs with information about the simulated SoundBlaster sound hardware. No matter what kind of sound system your computer has, MS-DOS programs "see" a SoundBlaster–compatible card (although the emulation is less than perfect).

In addition, if you've installed the Client for Novell Networks, AUTOEXEC.NT will also run nw16.exe and vwipxspx.exe, which give DOS applications access to the Novell application programming interface (API).

You can load other programs and set environment variables in AUTOEXEC.NT, but remember that they will be loaded every time you run an MS-DOS program. If you need particular terminate-and-stay-resident programs only for some MS-DOS applications, set up a customized AUTOEXEC file just for those applications.

Tip

One program that's handy to add to **AUTOEXEC.NT** is **doskey**, which gives **command.com** the same editing commands as those provided by **cmd.exe**, and in addition, lets you define abbreviated commands called *aliases*. To read about this program, start the Help and Support Center and search for "doskey."

MS-DOS Environment Variables

In MS-DOS, memory is a limited resource, and MS-DOS is particularly stingy with environment variable space. If you need to define more than a dozen or so environment variables in any MS-DOS–style batch files, you'll probably need to extend the amount of space allocated to environment variables either on the Properties dialog box of an associated shortcut or in a shell= command in a CONFIG.NT file. These techniques were described earlier in this chapter.

When you first start an MS-DOS program or command.com, ntvdm inherits the default Windows environment, but with the following changes:

- All variable names are changed to uppercase. MS-DOS programs do not expect to find lowercase letters in environment variable names.
- The COMSPEC variable is added, which contains the path and filename of the command shell, usually command.com.
- The TEMP and TMP variables are reset to the system default, rather than the user-specific setting.
- Pathnames in all environment variables are changed to use DOS-compatible 8.3-character names.

User Account Control and the Command Line

Windows Vista introduced the User Account Control (UAC) feature, which restricts the capability of programs to modify system files and settings unless they are explicitly given elevated permissions by the user. What this means in practical terms is that when User Account Control is in effect, programs run as if they were being run by a non-Administrator user, and they cannot modify files in the Windows folder, the Program Files folder, or make changes to systemwide settings in the Registry*. But when a GUI program is marked by its developer as requiring Administrator privileges, whenever you attempt to run it, Windows displays a User Account Control dialog so that you can either

- Run the program with full access privileges, if your account has Computer Administrator privileges

- Run the program in the context of a Computer Administrator user's account, if your account doesn't have Administrator privileges, but you can supply an Administrator account password

However, User Account Control treats console applications (command-line programs) differently. Windows doesn't pop up a User Account Control dialog for a command-line program, and thus a command-line program can't run with elevated privileges unless it's started up from the Windows GUI, or it's started by a program or Command Prompt window that itself has elevated privileges. Either way, at some point, you have to start with the GUI.

What this means in practical terms is that if you want to use command-line programs or batch files to manage Windows settings or to modify files in the protected Windows and Program Files folders, you have to take the extra step of instructing Windows to start the process with elevated privileges. There are (of course) several ways to do this:

- **Perform a one-time elevation**—Locate the desired batch file or command-line program in Windows Explorer, the Start menu, or on the desktop, right-click it, and select Run as Administrator. Windows pops up a UAC dialog before it runs the program.

- **Start the program in elevated mode from the Search window**—If the program or batch file is in the PATH, type its name into the Windows search box on the Start menu, and then press Ctrl+Shift+Enter. This instructs Windows to start the program in Elevated mode, and you get the UAC prompt.

- **Edit the program's shortcut to indicate that elevation is required**—Create or locate a shortcut to the batch file or command-line program, right-click it, and select Properties. View the Shortcut tab, click Advanced, and check Run as Administrator. Now, whenever the shortcut is used, Windows pops up a UAC dialog.

- **Start a Command Prompt window with elevated privileges**—After you do so, execute the command from there: Right-click any Command Prompt window menu item or shortcut and select Run as administrator. After confirming the User Account Control

---

To maintain some level of backward compatibility, older programs—those that don't have a "manifest" file—are led to believe that they can change system Registry settings and files in protected folders, through a mechanism called Registry and File Virtualization. Instead of saving the changes in the real system Registry sections and folders, Windows actually saves the settings in alternate locations in the user's Registry section and in the user's profile folder. For more information about virtualization, see "User Account Control" in Chapter 7 (p. 379).

pop-up, the Command Prompt window and *any* program that you run from within it runs with elevated privileges. Even GUI programs that you start from within it are run with elevated privileges and no further UAC prompts. Windows reminds you of this by changing the title of the window to "Administrator: Command Prompt."

Opening an Elevated Command Prompt

If you find yourself frequently needing to use elevated command-line programs, you can combine two of the preceding techniques: create a shortcut that opens an elevated Command Prompt window by following these steps:

1. Right-click the desktop and select New, Shortcut.
2. Type **cmd.exe** and press Enter.
3. Type **Elevated Command Prompt** and press Enter.
4. Right-click the new shortcut icon and select Properties.
5. Click the Advanced button, check Run as Administrator, and click OK.
6. If you want a visual reminder that the resulting Command Prompt window runs programs with elevated privileges, select the Colors tab. From the row of color samples, click the brick-red color, or set the Screen Background color values to Red = 128, Green = 0, Blue = 0.
7. Click OK.

Now, whenever your use this shortcut, Windows displays the User Account Control dialog. The resulting Command Prompt window includes the phrase Elevated Command Prompt in its title, and if you changed the background color, its red shade also serves to warn you that whatever programs you run from this window have free rein to modify any file or setting.

Tip

If you're a real keyboard fanatic, you can even open an elevated Command Prompt window without touching the mouse. Just hit the Windows key, and then type this sequence: **c m d** Ctrl+Shift+Enter Alt+C.

Note

You can't run Explorer or any window derived from Explorer—for example, Printers or Network Connections—from an elevated Command Prompt window unless you first change a setting, following these steps:

1. Log on to the Computer Administrator account that you will be using through User Account Control, if you are not already logged on to this account.
2. Open Windows Explorer, and select Tools, Folder Options.
3. On the View tab, check Launch Folder Windows in a Separate Process, and then click OK.
4. Log off.

Now, you can issue commands such as **explorer .** or **control netconnections** from within the elevated Command Prompt window. Without this setting, Explorer windows started from the privileged Command Prompt window may not open, or may not actually have the desired elevated privileges.

◀◀ To learn more about User Account Control, **see** "User Account Control," **p. 379**.

Useful and Important Commands

There are several commands that you should become very familiar with...these are some of the command-line tools that you'll use nearly every day once you've become a master of command line-fu.

Note

There are, of course, hundreds of others. Appendix B, "Windows Command Reference," contains a listing of all standard Windows programs, and the ones marked **CMD** are command-line programs. You might want to scan through that listing to see the range of programs that is available. For some tips about getting usage instructions for programs that interest you, see "Interpreting Command-Line Syntax" earlier in this chapter. Appendix A lists hundreds more add-on tools that you can obtain.

cd

Each Command Prompt window has the concept of a *current drive* and *current directory* (also called the *default directory* or *default folder*), which is its starting place when looking for files. Although Windows Explorer displays its current directory in its status and address bars, it's most common for the Command Prompt window to show the current directory name in its prompt; the indicator it prints to tell you it's ready to accept another command. For example, the prompt

```
C:\Users\bknittel>
```

indicates that the current drive is `C:` and the current directory is `\Users\bknittel`.

You can change the current drive by typing a command line that consists of only a drive letter and colon, for example

```
d:
```

You can change the current directory by typing the `cd` or equivalently the `chdir` command, followed by a pathname:

```
cd \Users\public
```

Note

For the **cd** command (only), quotes around a pathname that contains spaces are optional.

Each drive letter has its own default directory, so the commands

```
cd c:\program files
cd d:\setup
cd e:\temp
```

set the default directory on `c:`, `d:`, and `e:` drives without changing the default drive letter.

You can specify full or relative paths. If the path doesn't start with a `\` character, it's interpreted relative to the current directory. For example, if the current directory is `\Users`, the commands `cd \Users\bknittel` and `cd bknittel` are equivalent. The command

```
cd \
```

returns to you the current drive's root (top level) directory.

The special directory name .. is interpreted as "the directory above," or the *parent* directory, so if the current directory is C:\Users\bknittel, the command cd .. changes to C:\Users, and cd ..\scott changes to C:\Users\scott.

You can make the cd command change the drive and directory by adding /D to the command line, as in

```
cd /D d:\setup\english
```

This is especially useful in batch files, where you might want to change to a specific drive and directory whose name is specified in an environment variable, as in

```
cd /d %userprofile%\My Documents
```

which changes to your My Documents folder no matter the drive on which it's located.

Tip

On Windows Vista, you can start a Command Prompt window with a desired folder preselected as the current directory. From any Windows Explorer view, hold down the Shift key, right-click the desired folder, and select Start Command Window Here. On XP you can get the same handy functionality by downloading the Windows XP Powertoy "Open Command Window Here" from www.microsoft.com/windowsxp/downloads/powertoys/default.mspx.

pushd and *popd*

The command pushd *path* changes the current directory to the specified *path*. The previous current drive and directory are remembered, and the command popd restores the previous path. Pushd saves as many directory changes as you care to make, and each popd returns to the directory in use before the corresponding pushd.

If the path specified to pushd contains a drive letter, the current drive is changed as well.

When command extensions are enabled (which they are, by default), you can specify a network path, for example, \\server\sharename\path, and pushd will automatically map a drive letter to the network path, starting with the letter *Z* and working backward. Popd automatically deletes the temporary drive mappings.

Note

If you search your hard drive for **cd.exe**, **pushd.exe**, or **popd.exe**, you'll find that they don't exist. There are no executable files corresponding to these commands. They are built-in commands handled directly by **cmd.exe**.

dir

The dir command lists the contents of directories (folders). It's handy enough to know that the command dir by itself lists the contents of the current directory; with this and cd, you can explore the entire hard disk.

Dir has dozens of options. I won't list them all here; you can see the entire list by typing `dir /?` at the command prompt. Here are a few of the most useful variations:

Command	Description
dir /p	Prints a listing, pausing when the screen fills with text. Press Enter to continue the listing. You can use /p with any of the command variations.
dir *filename*	Lists just files matching *filename*. You can use wildcard characters in the *filename*: * matches anything; ? matches exactly one character. For example, dir *.exe lists all files ending with .exe, and dir print*.* lists all files whose names start with print.
	Put the *filename* in quotes if the name contains spaces. You can also specify a drive letter and/or path to search a particular drive or directory.
dir ... /od	Sorts the files from youngest to oldest.
dir ... /oen	Lists files sorted by extension (.*xxx*), and then by name.
dir ... /ah	Lists hidden files.
dir ... /s	Lists the current or specified directory and its subdirectories as well; for example, dir /s "c:\program files*.exe" lists all .EXE files in c:\program files and all of its subdirectories.
dir ... /b	Removes the file date, size and other information. Prints just the names of matched or located files.

The last variation I've found especially useful when I'm creating a batch file that is to perform some operation on a list of files. I use a command line

```
dir /b *.txt >mybatch.bat
```

which puts all the names into file `mybatch.bat`. Then I can edit `mybatch.bat` and put commands before each of the filenames.

more

Many command-line programs print out more text than fits in the console window. In most cases, you can resize the window or scroll the window contents up to read it all, but there's another way. The utility `more` displays text a screen at a time, letting you press a key when you're ready to move on to the next screen.

There are two easy ways to use more: You can view a file with the command

```
more filename
```

but most often, you'll use `more` to page through the output of another program. With no file-name argument, `more` reads the standard input, so you can pipe text to it like this:

```
dir /s | more
```

Because the command `dir /s` lists the contents of the current directory and all subdirectories, its output is often quite long. Piping the output through `more` pauses it after each screen. When `more` has halted, it will display -- More -- at the bottom of the screen. Press the spacebar or Enter key to move on to the next screen.

There are some command-line options and other functions available as well. To read about the type more /? or rather,

```
more /? | more
```

Tip

Sometimes you may find it more convenient to redirect command output into a file and then view the file in Notepad so that you can search for text and can scroll backward as well as forward. To view a program's output in Notepad, issue the command this way:

```
some command line here >out.txt && notepad out.txt && del out.txt
```

runas

Runas lets you run a program using the credentials of another user. The program appears in your Command Prompt window (or, if it's a GUI program, on your desktop), but it has the rights and privileges of another user. On Windows XP, it's especially handy when you want to quickly run an administrative program as Administrator without logging on using that privileged account.

Runas lets you do on the command line what the right-click option Run as Administrator does in Windows Explorer. On Windows Vista, runas is not terribly useful because it can't run programs with elevated privileges unless it itself is run in an elevated mode. If you are going to have to open an elevated Command Prompt window to run runas, you can just run the desired program directly. Still, if you have to maintain Windows XP systems, runas can be very useful. I find that I frequently use it to start cmd.exe, creating an administrator's Command Prompt window from which I can run other commands. The full syntax of the runas command is

```
runas [/noprofile] [/env] [/netonly] [/smartcard]
      [/user:username] command line
```

The command line options are

Option	Description
/noprofile	Specifies that the user's profile (Registry settings) should not be loaded. This causes the application to load more quickly, but can make some applications malfunction.
/env	Uses the current environment variables instead of the user's default variables.
/netonly	The credentials specified are for remote access only, not local file access.
/smartcard	Uses the credentials on a smart card. If this option is used, the /user option may be omitted.
/user	Specifies the user account to use to run the program. Can be a local account (for example, Administrator), or a domain account in the format user@domain or domain\user.
command line	The command to run, and any additional arguments

As I mentioned, I've found that I use `runas` frequently on Windows XP, but for the most part only in these three ways:

- `runas /user:Administrator mmc` opens the Microsoft Management Console. From there, you can click File, Add/Remove Snap In to open management tools.

- `runas /user:Administrator control` *panelname*`.cpl`, where *panelname* is the name of a Control Panel applet file. I'll talk about this more in the next section.

- `runas /user:Adminstrator cmd` opens a Command Prompt window with Administrator privileges. The new window will run under the Administrator logon name, and any programs you run from this command prompt will also have Administrator privileges.

Note

You can't run Explorer or any window derived from Explorer—for example, Printers and Faxes—from this Command Prompt window unless you first change a setting, following these steps:

1. Log on to the Computer Administrator account that you want to use.

2. Open Windows Explorer, and select Tools, Folder Options.

3. On the View tab, check Launch Folder Windows in a Separate Process, and then click OK.

4. Log off.

Now, when you issue a command such as **explorer .** or **control netconnections** from within a Command Prompt window that was started with **runas**, Explorer windows work. Without this setting, Explorer windows started from the privileged Command Prompt window simply do not open.

start

The `Start` command has several useful functions. First off, it lets you open a file in its associated application directly from the command line. For example, the command

```
start myspreadsheet.xls
```

opens the named spreadsheet file in the associated program, usually Excel. If the filename has spaces in it, you have to type the command this way:

```
start "" "my spread sheet.xls"
```

Note

Even with quotes around the name, this form of the **start** command requires you to specify an initial argument whose value is not actually used. The pair of quote marks after the word **start** signifies an argument with no characters. This satisfies **start**'s need to take the filename from the *second* argument.

The second use for `start` is to launch an application from a batch file so that the program runs in its own separate window, and the batch file immediately continues on to its next command. If the command is a batch file or command-line program, that initial argument I mentioned previously is used as the window's title. Here's how it's used:

```
dir *.* >list.txt
start notepad list.txt
… more commands
```

Start is also useful in this same way in the Windows Vista Command Prompt window. In all previous versions of Windows, when you started a Windows application by typing its name, the program started and the next command prompt immediately appeared. On Vista, the next prompt doesn't appear until the Windows application is closed. You can, however, precede your command with start to make the prompt return immediately.

control

You can run Control Panel applets from the command line using the control command. There are three reasons you might want do to this:

- To more quickly open a control panel. If you already have a command prompt window open, it's faster to type control firewall.cpl than to poke your way through the Start menu, open the Control Panel, and then open the Windows Firewall window.

- To run a control panel applet as a Computer Administrator. Again, it's much faster to type runas /user:Administrator "control firewall.cpl" than to log off and back on, or to switch users. However, this type of usage isn't as necessary on Vista as it was on Windows XP, which didn't have the User Account Control system that makes it possible for regular users to run privileged programs.

- To run a control panel applet that is not listed in the Control Panel window. For example, to configure Windows to log on automatically at startup, you have to type control userpasswords2, or if you're not logged on as a Computer Administrator, runas /user:Administrator "control userpasswords2"

The syntax for the control command has three variations:

control *filename*.**cpl**	Opens the primary control panel applet contained in the file *filename*.cpl stored in \ windows\system32 or elsewhere in the PATH.
control *filename*.**cpl** *appletname*	Opens an alternate applet contained in a .CPL file; some .CPL files contain code for more than one control panel applet.
control *specialname*	Opens a control panel applet or system configuration window corresponding to a special name recognized by control.exe, or listed in the Registry under HKEY_LOCAL_MACHINE\SOFTWARE\Microsoft\ Windows\CurrentVersion\Control Panel\Cpls or HKEY_CURRENT_USER\SOFTWARE\Microsoft\Windows\ CurrentVersion\Control Panel\Cpls.

Table 9.8 lists the various control panel applets and system windows you can open from the command line. Not all versions or installations of Windows will have all these control panels.

To run the control panel with Administrator privileges, on Windows Vista you can simply type the command and Vista displays a User Account Control dialog. Alternately, you can issue the commands from an elevated Prompt window (See "Opening an Elevated Command Prompt," earlier in this chapter.) On Windows XP, you can use runas, with the control command enclosed in quotes, as in

```
runas /user:Administrator "control appwiz.cpl"
```

Table 9.8   Control Panels Applets from the Command Line

Argument(s) After *control*	Vista	XP	Applet Title
access.cpl	✓	✓	Ease of Access Center/Accessibility Options
Admintools	✓	✓	Admintrative Tools*
appwiz.cpl	✓	✓	Add/Remove Programs
bthprops.cpl	✓	✓	Bluetooth Properties
Color		✓	Display Appearance Properties
collab.cpl	✓		People Near Me settings
cttune.cpl		✓	ClearType Tuning (source: PowerToys for Windows XP download)
date/time	✓	✓	Date and Time Properties
desk.cpl	✓	✓	Display Settings
desktop	✓		Personalization
desktop	✓	✓	Display Properties, Themes tab
fax.cpl			Fax Properties (Windows 2000 only)
firewall.cpl	✓	✓	Windows Firewall
folders	✓	✓	Folder Options
fonts		✓	Fonts*
hdwwiz.cpl	✓	✓	Add Hardware
inetcpl.cpl	✓	✓	Internet Options
infrared	✓	✓	Wireless Connection (IRDA infrared)
international		✓	Regional and Language Options
intl.cpl	✓	✓	Regional and Language Options
irprops.cpl	✓	✓	Wireless Link (IRDA infrared)
joy.cpl	✓	✓	Game Controllers
main.cpl mouse	✓	✓	Mouse Properties
main.cpl keyboard	✓	✓	Keyboard Properties
main.cpl pc card (PCMCIA)	✓	✓	PCMCIA or Removable Hardware
mmsys.cpl	✓	✓	Sounds and Audio Devices
modem.cpl	✓	✓	Modem Properties
mouse		✓	Mouse Properties
msmq.cpl		✓	Microsoft Message Queuing Service
ncpa.cpl	✓	✓	Network Connections*
netconnections		✓	Network Connections*

Argument(s) After *control*	Vista	XP	Applet Title
netsetup.cpl	✓	✓	Network Setup Wizard
NetWare		✓	Client Services for NetWare
nusrmgr.cpl	✓	✓	User Accounts
nwc.cpl		✓	Client Services for NetWare
odbccp32.cpl	✓	✓	ODBC Data Source Administrator
ports	✓	✓	System Properties, Computer Name tab
powercfg.cpl	✓	✓	Power Options
printers	✓	✓	Printers [and Faxes, on XP]*
sapi.cpl		✓	Speech Properties
scannercamera	✓	✓	Scanners and Cameras*
schedtasks	✓	✓	Scheduled Tasks*
speech	✓	✓	Speech Properties
sticpl.cpl	✓	✓	Scanners and Cameras
sysdm.cpl	✓	✓	System Properties
sysdm.cpl add new hardware		✓	Add New Hardware Wizard
tabletpc.cpl	✓		Pen and Input Devices
telephon.cpl	✓	✓	Phone and Modem options
telephony	✓	✓	Phone and Modem options
timedate.cpl	✓	✓	Date and Time Properties
tweakui.cpl			Tweak UI (Windows 98, ME, and 2000 version only; Windows XP version is a Start menu item)
ups.cpl	✓	✓	UPS properties or Power Management
userpasswords	✓	✓	User Accounts
userpasswords2	✓	✓	On Windows Vista and XP, displays Windows 2000 version of User Accounts. Allows setting of automatic logon account. Prompts for Administrator password if necessary, no need to use **runas**.
wscui.cpl	✓	✓	Security Center
wuaucpl.cpl	✓	✓	Windows Update/Automatic Updates

This control panel does not work when started by runas unless you have set the administrator account to run Explorer windows in separate processes, as described earlier in this chapter under "User Account Control and the Command Line."

net

The net command is a universe of its own; it performs 22 different functions involving networking and (strangely enough) Windows service management. The net command by itself lists these functions. These are very handy commands to know if you spend a lot of time working with networked computers. The functions available under Windows 2000, XP, and Vista are listed in Table 9.9.

Table 9.9   *net* **Subcommands**

net Subcommand Function	
net accounts	Adjusts the password requirements settings for local accounts on this computer
net computer	Adds or deletes computers from a domain network
net config	Displays or sets parameters for the server (file sharing server) or workstation (file sharing client) Microsoft networking components
net continue	Reactivates a paused service
net file	Lists your files that are being used by others, and optionally can disconnect the file and clear its "locked" status
net group	Lists, adds, or modifies global user groups on the local computer or domain
net help	Displays help information for these subcommands
net helpmsg	Prints a text description of a network error code number
net localgroup	Lists, adds, or modifies local user groups on the local computer or domain server
net name	Lists the names or aliases for the Windows Message service (this is not the same as Windows Messenger; it's a rarely used notification service); not available on Windows Vista
net pause	Pauses a Windows service on the local computer
net print	Lists and manages print jobs queued on the local computer or another networked computer
net send	Sends a message to another user or computer (again, this service is rarely used and is not available on Windows Vista, and is likely disabled on XP)
net session	Lists network files in use by the local computer or another networked computer; can also disconnect open files
net share	Lists, adds, or removes shared folders
net start	Starts a Windows service
net statistics	Prints network data transfer statistics
net stop	Stops a Windows service
net time	Synchronizes the computer's clock with another computer or time server
net use	Maps a drive letter to a shared folder, or a printer LPT port to a shared printer
net user	Lists, adds, or manages local user accounts
net view	Lists computers in a network workgroup or domain, and can also list folders and printers shared by a specific computer

You can get help for any of these commands by typing

```
net help subcommand
```

on the command line. The most important uses are listed in the following sections. These are especially useful in batch files that have to access shared folders; the batch file can create drive mappings on demand.

net view

The net view subcommand has several useful variations:

Command	Description
net view	Lists all the computers in the current domain or workgroup
net view /domain	Lists all of the domains on the network
net view /domain:*xxx*	Lists all of the computers in the specified domain *xxx*
net view /network:nw	Lists all available Novell NetWare servers
net view *computername*	Lists all of the printers and folders shared by the specific computer

net use

The net use subcommand lets you map networked files and folders to drive letters or printer devices on your computer. There are several variations:

Command	Description
net use *x:* *computer**sharename*	Maps drive letter *x*: to shared folder *sharename* on computer named *computer*.
net use *x:* *computer**sharename*\ *subfolder*\...	Maps drive letter *x*: to a subfolder of the shared folder *sharename* on computer *computer*. The apparent "root" directory of the mapped drive will be the subfolder.
net use *x:* *computer**sharename* / /user:*username*	Maps drive letter *x*: to shared folder *sharename* on computer *computer* using an alternate user's credentials. net use will prompt for a password if necessary.
net use *x:* *computer**sharename* / /user:*username password*	As in the preceding command, but the password is specified on the command line. This is a security risk but may be your only option when mapping drives using an alternate username from a batch file.
net use lpt*n*: *computer**printername*	Maps a specified LPT printer port (for example, LPT2) to a network shared printer, for use by MS-DOS applications. Note: You cannot map an LPT port that corresponds to a physical printer port in your computer.
net use ... /persistent:yes|no	On a net use command line, /persistent: yes stores the current and subsequent drive mapping in your profile so that the mapping is restored the next time you log on. /persistent:no makes the current and subsequent mapping appear in the current logon session only.
net use *x:* /d	Unmaps drive letter *x*:, that is, disconnects it from a shared folder.
net use lpt*n*: /d	Disconnects the specified LPT port from a network shared printer.

net share

The `net share` command shares an existing folder on your computer to the network, or cancels file sharing. The most important variations are

Command	Description
net share *sharename drive:path*	Shares the specified folder under the specified share name
net share *sharename* /delete	Cancels the specified share

Additional options can specify how files are cached if a remote user requests offline access to the shared folder; type **net help share** for details.

net start *and* net stop

`net start` and `net stop` have nothing to do with networking. Instead, they can start and stop Windows services on your computer. The argument after `start` or `stop` is the "short" name of the service.

Note

Each Windows service has a short name (also called the *service name*) and a long name (also called the *display name*). The Services management window lists only the display names. To see the short names of the services on your computer, type the command **sc query**. The `sc` command is a more comprehensive command-line service manager, which is also worth learning about; see "Managing Services from the Command Line" in Chapter 6 for more information.

I've found this command to be most helpful on Windows Server computers, where it's easier to type

```
net stop dns
net start dns
```

at a command prompt than to use Computer Management to restart the service when it's gone haywire.

findstr

`findstr` searches text files and folders for strings, optionally using a powerful pattern matching scheme called *regular expressions*. (If you're familiar with UNIX or Linux, `findstr` is a lot like `grep`.) Findstr has a slew of options. You can see the whole list by opening a Command Prompt window and typing **help findstr**, which prints the following:

```
FINDSTR [/B] [/E] [/L] [/R] [/S] [/I] [/X] [/V] [/N] [/M] [/O] [/P] [/F:file]
        [/C:string] [/G:file] [/D:dir list] [/A:color attributes] [/OFF[LINE]]
        strings [[drive:][path]filename[ ...]]
  /B          Matches pattern if at the beginning of a line.
  /E          Matches pattern if at the end of a line.
  /L          Uses search strings literally.
  /R          Uses search strings as regular expressions.
  /S          Searches for matching files in the current directory and all
              subdirectories.
```

```
/I         Specifies that the search is not to be case sensitive.
/X         Prints lines that match exactly.
/V         Prints only lines that do not contain a match.
/N         Prints the line number before each line that matches.
/M         Prints only the filename if a file contains a match.
/O         Prints character offset before each matching line.
/P         Skip files with non-printable characters.
/OFF[LINE] Do not skip files with offline attribute set.
/A:attr    Specifies color attribute with two hex digits. See "color /?"
/F:file    Reads file list from the specified file(/ stands for console).
/C:string  Uses specified string as a literal search string.
/G:file    Gets search strings from the specified file(/ stands for console).
/D:dir     Search a semicolon delimited list of directories
strings    Text to be searched for.
[drive:][path]filename
           Specifies a file or files to search.
```
Use spaces to separate multiple search strings unless the argument is prefixed
with /C. For example, 'FINDSTR "hello there" x.y' searches for "hello" or
"there" in file x.y. 'FINDSTR /C:"hello there" x.y' searches for
"hello there" in file x.y.

You can specify the options in either uppercase or lowercase. For example, \I and \i are equally acceptable.

In the form

  findstr /c:"*whatever string you want to find*" filename…

findstr scans through every file named on the command line (you can use wildcards), and prints out each line that contains the exact string. Some of the more useful options that you can put on the command line between findstr and /c are

/b	Matches the string only if occurs at the beginning of the text line. findstr /b /c:"mouse" will match the line "mouse ate my cheese" but not "my house has a mouse."
/e	Like /b, but makes findstr print lines only if the search text is found at the end of the input line.
/i	Ignores case; lines with mouse, MOUSE, or Mouse will match /c:"mouse".
/s	Searches for files in the current directory and all subdirectories. This is especially useful if you specify the filenames with wildcards, for example: findstr /s /i /c:"mouse" *.txt

findstr can also search for complex patterns using a pattern matching formula called a *regular expression*. Regular expressions are complex and beyond our scope here, but if you need to pull information out of or rearrange text files, they're an *extremely* powerful tool. You can find lots of information about them on the Net. The regular expressions used by findstr can use any of the following elements:

Pattern Item	Matches...
.	Any one character
*	Zero, one, or more occurrences of the item immediately before *
^	Beginning of the line; ^abc matches abc only if it occurs at the beginning of a line
$	End of the line; abc$ matches abc only if it occurs at the end of a line
[xyz]	Any one character listed in the set of characters between the brackets (you *do* type the brackets in this case)
[^xyz]	Any one character not in the set of characters listed between the brackets
[x-y]	Any one character in the range from *x* to *y*
\<	The beginning of a word (that is, printing text preceded by whitespace or a line break)
\>	The end of a word (that is, whitespace following printing characters or a line break)
x	The character *x*
\x	The character *x*, where *x* would otherwise have special meaning, that is, . * ^ $ [ ] or \

For full information on `findstr` regular expressions refer to the online Command Reference.

Other Programs

If you write batch files to manage Windows, which is the topic of the next section, you may want to investigate some additional commands that provide some powerful abilities:

- `reg`—Reads and writes Registry settings.
- `regini`—Loads bulk Registry values, helpful when installing applications or configuring workstations in bulk.
- `sc`—Manages Windows services and device drivers.
- `setx`—Sets per-user or system default environment variables. Can extract information from the Registry or parse it out of text files, if desired.
- `winrm`—Manages Windows remotely through the WS-Management web service protocol (Vista only). `winrm` is going to play an increasingly significant role as the basis for Microsoft's remote management strategy in the coming years.

For more help type the command name followed by /?.

In addition, scan through Appendixes A and B for additional programs that are either included with Windows or can be installed as add-ons. There are hundreds and hundreds of command-line tools available to you, and who knows—one of them might be just the thing you need to save yourself hours and hours of work.

Batch Files

Batch files are, in essence, command-line commands typed into a text file rather than typed directly at the command prompt. You can tell the command shell to read this text file and interpret its commands as if you were typing them. This serves several purposes:

- It can save you a lot of typing because you only need to type the batch file commands once, but you can have Windows run the commands as many times as you want. This is really important with long sequences of commands, but I even more frequently write what I call "tiny handy batch files," with single letter names, and perhaps only one command inside, to do things like change the current directory to a commonly used folder. These batch files can save you quite a bit of time and trouble.

- You can write the batch file in such a way that it records *steps* of a particular job without storing the *particulars*; you can then provide the particulars when you use the batch file. For example, if you repeatedly have to extract and print information from different data files, you might write a batch file that performs these steps but doesn't contain the name of the actual data file to be processed. You can supply that name when you use the batch file. This, again, can save you time and mental energy: After the batch file is written, you don't have to think about what's inside the batch file. It's just a new Windows command that you can use whenever you need.

- The contents of the batch file serve as a form of documentation, which lists the steps necessary to perform a particular job. A year after you've completed some project, you might have forgotten the steps involved in processing your data files, but you can always read the batch file yourself to refresh your memory.

Batch files can also use primitive programming commands to handle varying situations: "if a particular situation arises, do this, otherwise, do that" or "repeat this step for every file in a certain folder."

Note

On Windows Vista, batch files that perform administrative actions or modify files in protected system folders will work only if you run them with elevated permissions. See "User Account Control and the Command Line" earlier in this chapter for details.

Creating and Editing Batch Files

You can place batch files in any folder you want. You can place them on your own hard drive, or you may want to place your batch files on a shared network folder so they can be used from any computer. I place my personal batch files in a folder named c:\bat and put this folder in the PATH so that I can run them by name from any command prompt.

Regardless of their folder location, batch files should be given the extension .CMD or .BAT. Either is fine. The .BAT extension is more traditional, whereas .CMD makes it clear that the batch file is written for Windows NT, 2000, XP, or Vista because DOS and Windows 9x will not recognize such files as batch files.

To create a sample batch file, open a Command Prompt window or use the one opened earlier in this section. Type the command

```
notepad test.bat
```

and then click Yes when Notepad asks, Do you want to create a new file? In the empty Notepad window, type the following lines:

```
@echo off
cls
echo The command line argument is %1
pause
```

Save the file and at the command line type:

```
test xxx
```

The Command Prompt window should clear, and you should see the following:

```
The command line argument is xxx
Press any key to continue . . .
```

Press Enter, and the command prompt should return. You can use this same procedure to create any number of batch files.

Later, if you want to edit the files, you can use the name notepad command to open and modify the files and make changes.

One batch file you may want to create right now is named bat.bat, with this one line inside:

```
pushd c:\bat
```

With this file in place, if you type bat at any command prompt, your current directory will be instantly changed to c:\bat so that you can edit or create new batch files. Type popd to go back to whatever directory you were using beforehand.

Of course, you could just type pushd c:\bat directly. It may seem silly to create a batch file just to save nine keystrokes, but when you're actively developing batch files, you'll quickly find that this really does make life easier.

I have about a dozen batch files like this that I use on a daily basis to move into directories for specific projects. For projects that use special command-line programs, the batch file has a second line that adds the program directory to the beginning of the search path, using a command such as this:

```
path c:\some\new\folder;%path%
```

If you find yourself frequently working with command-line programs, you will want to make "tiny handy batch files" for your projects as well.

Batch File Programming

The following sections discuss programming techniques that take advantage of the extended commands provided by the cmd shell. The commands that are most useful in batch files are listed in Table 9.10.

Table 9.10   Batch File Commands

Command	Use
call	Calls a batch file subroutine.
echo	Displays text to the user.
setlocal/endlocal	Saves/restores environment variables.
exit	Terminates batch file.
for	Iterates over files, folders, or numbers.

Command	Use
goto	Used for flow control.
if/else	Executes commands conditionally.
pause	Lets the user read a message.
pushd/popd	Saves/restores the current directory.
rem	Used for comments and documentation. Windows ignores any lines that start with the word **rem** or **remark**.
set	Sets environment variables, performs calculations, and prompts for user input.
shift	Scans through command-line arguments.
start	Launches a program in a different window.

If you've written batch files for DOS, Windows 9x, and Windows NT, you'll find that most of these commands have been significantly enhanced, so even if you are familiar with these commands, you should read the discussions in this chapter, and check out the online Command Line Reference in Windows Help and Support.

Argument Substitution

Many times you'll find that the repetitive tasks you encounter use the same programs and steps, but operate on different files each time. In this case, you can use command-line arguments to give information to the batch file when you run it. When you start a batch file from the command line with a command such as

```
batchname xxx yyy zzz
```

any strings after the name of the batch file are made available to the batch program as arguments. The symbols %1, %2, %3, and so on are replaced with the corresponding arguments. In this example, anywhere that %1 appears in the batch file, cmd replaces it with xxx. Then, %2 is replaced with yyy, and so on.

Argument substitution lets you write batch files like this:

```
@echo off
notepad %1.vbs
cscript %1.vbs
```

This batch file lets you edit and then run a Windows Script Host program. If you name the batch file ws.bat, you can edit and test a script program named, say, test.vbs just by typing this:

```
ws test
```

In this case, cmd treats the batch file as if it contained the following:

```
@echo off
notepad test.vbs
cscript test.vbs
```

This kind of batch file can save you many keystrokes during the process of developing and debugging a script.

Note

The command **@echo off** at the top of a batch file keeps cmd from printing out each of the program steps as it encounters them. This reduces "clutter" in the Command Prompt window. If your batch file is behaving in some way you don't understand, you can temporarily change this to **@echo on**, to see the steps as they are run.

Besides the standard command-line arguments %1, %2, and so on, you should know about two special argument replacements: %0 and %*. %0 is replaced with the name of the batch file, as it was typed on the command line. %* is replaced with *all* the command-line arguments as they were typed, with quotes and everything left intact.

If I have a batch file named test.bat with the contents

```
@echo off
echo The command name is %0
echo The arguments are: %*
```

then the command test a b c will print the following:

```
The command name is test
The arguments are: a b c
```

%0 is handy when a batch file has detected some problem with the command-line arguments the user has typed and you want it to display a "usage" message. Here's an example:

```
if "%1" == "" (
    rem - no arguments were specified. Print the usage information
    echo Usage: %0 [-v] [-a] filename ...
    exit /b
)
```

If the batch file is named test.bat, typing test would print out the following message:

```
Usage: test [-v] [-a] filename ...
```

The advantage of using %0 is that it will always be correct, even if you rename the batch file at a later date and forget to change the "usage" remarks inside.

Argument Editing

cmd lets you modify arguments as they're replaced on the command line. Most of the modifications assume that the argument is a filename and let you extract or fill in various parts of the name. You might want to use this feature when, say, a batch file argument specifies a Microsoft Word file with the .DOC extension, and you want the batch file to construct a new filename with the same root name but a different extension.

When command extensions are enabled, cmd can insert edited versions of the arguments by placing a tilde (~) and some additional characters after the % sign. The editing functions let you manipulate filenames passed as arguments. Table 9.11 lists the edit options, using argument number 1 as an example.

Table 9.11   Argument Editing Expressions

Expression	Result
%~1	Removes surrounding quotes (").
%~f1	Fully qualified pathname.
%~d1	Drive letter only.
%~p1	Path only.
%~n1	Filename only.
%~x1	File extension only.
%~s1	Short DOS 8.3 file and path.
%~a1	File attributes.
%~t1	Modification date/time of file.
%~z1	Length of file in bytes.
%~$PATH:1	Fully qualified name of the first matching file when searching **PATH**. If no file is found, the result is a zero-length string. The filename must include the proper extension; **PATHEXT** is not used.

For example, if I ran a batch file with the argument `"under the hood.doc"`, the results might be as follows:

Expression	Result
%~1	`under the hood.doc`
%~f1	`C:\book\ch11\under the hood.doc`
%~d1	`C:`
%~p1	`\book\ch11`
%~n1	`under the hood`
%~x1	`.doc`
%~s1	`C:\book\ch11\UNDERT~1.DOC`
%~a1	`--a------`
%~t1	`04/20/2002 12:42 PM`
%~z1	`45323`
%~$PATH:1	

Here's how these features might be used: Suppose that I have a series of files that I need to sort. The input files could come from any folder, but I want to store the sorted files in `C:\sorted` and give them the extension `.TAB` regardless of what the original extension was. I can write a batch file named `sortput.bat` to do this:

```
@echo off
sort <%1 >c:\sorted\%~n1.tab
```

The `sort` command will read the file as I've specified it on the command line, but the output file will use only the base part of the input file's name. If I run the command

```
sortput "c:\work files\input.txt"
```

the substituted command will be

```
sort <"c:\work files\input.txt" >c:\sorted\input.tab
```

Conditional Processing with *if*

One of the most important capabilities of any programming language is the ability to choose from among different instructions based on conditions the program finds as it runs. For this purpose, the batch file language has the `if` command.

The Basic *if* Command

In its most basic form, `if` compares two strings and executes a command if the strings are equivalent:

```
if string1 == string2 command
```

This is used in combination with command-line variable or environment variable substitution, as in this example:

```
if "%1" == "ERASE" delete somefile.dat
```

If and only if the batch file's first argument is the word ERASE, this command will delete the file `somefile.dat`.

The quotation marks in this command aren't absolutely required. If they are omitted and the command is written as

```
if %1 == ERASE delete somefile.dat
```

the command will still work as long as some command-line argument is given when the batch file is run. However, if the batch file is started with no arguments, `%1` would be replaced with nothing, and the command would turn into this:

```
if == ERASE delete somefile.dat
```

This is an invalid command. cmd expects to see something before the `==` part of the command and will bark if it doesn't. Therefore, it's a common practice to surround the items to be tested with some character—any character. Even `$` will work, as shown here:

```
if $%0$ == $ERASE$ delete somefile.dat
```

If the items being tested are identical, they will still be identical when surrounded by the extra characters. If they are different or blank, you'll still have a valid command.

The `if` command also lets you reverse the sense of the test with the `not` option:

```
if not "%1" == "ERASE" then goto no_erase
```

Checking for Files and Folders

The `exist` option lets you determine whether a particular file exists in the current directory:

```
if exist input.dat goto process_it
    echo The file input.dat does not exist
```

```
        pause
        exit /b
:process_it
```

Of course, you can specify a full path for the filename if that's appropriate, and you can use environment variables and % arguments to construct the name. If the filename has spaces in it, you'll need to surround it with quotes.

The not modifier can be used with exist as well.

Tip

The **exist** test checks only for files, not folders. However, the special file **nul** appears to exist in every folder. You can perform the test

```
if exist c:\foldername\nul command
```

to see whether the folder *c:\foldername* exists.

Checking the Success of a Program

When a command line or even a Windows program exits, it leaves behind a number called its *exit status* or *error status* value. This is a number that the program uses to indicate whether it thinks it did its job successfully. An exit status of zero means no problems; larger numbers indicate trouble. There is no predetermined meaning for any specific values. The documentation for some programs may list specific error values and give their interpretations, which means that your batch files can use these values to take appropriate action. How? Through the errorlevel variation of the if command.

After running a command in a batch file, an if statement of the form

```
if errorlevel number command
```

will execute the command if the previous program's exit status value is the listed number or *higher*. For example, the net use command returns 0 if it is able to map a drive letter to a shared folder, and it will return a nonzero number if it can't. A batch file can take advantage of this as follows:

```
@echo off

net use f: \\bali\corpfiles
if errorlevel 1 goto failed
    echo Copying network data...
    if not exist c:\corpfiles\nul mkdir c:\corpfiles
    copy f:\*.xls c:\corpfiles
    exit /b
:failed
    echo Unable to access network share \\bali\corpfiles
    pause
```

You can also use not with this version of the if command. In this case, the command is executed if the error status is *less* than the listed number. The error testing in the previous example can be rewritten this way:

```
if not errorlevel 1 goto success
    echo Unable to access network share \\bali\corpfiles
    pause
    exit /b
:success
    echo Copying network data...
    if not exist c:\corpfiles\nul mkdir c:\corpfiles
    copy f:\*.xls c:\corpfiles
```

In this version, the flow of the batch file is a bit easier to follow. However, even this can be improved upon, as you'll see next.

Grouping Commands with Parentheses

Often, you'll want to execute several commands if some condition is true. In the old days, before the extended cmd shell came along, you would have to use a goto command to transfer control to another part of the batch file, as in the if exist example given in the previous section. With the extended version of if, this is no longer necessary.

The extended if command lets you put more than one statement after an if command, by grouping them with parentheses. For example, you can place multiple commands on one line, as shown here:

```
if not errorlevel 1 (echo The network share was not available & exit /b)
```

Or you can put them on multiple lines:

```
if not errorlevel 1 (
    echo The network share was not available
    pause
    exit /b
)
```

I recommend the second version, because it's easier to read. Look how much clearer the network file copying example becomes when parentheses are used instead of goto:

```
@echo off

net use f: \\bali\corpfiles
if errorlevel 1 (
    echo Unable to access network share \\bali\corpfiles
    pause
    exit /b
)
echo Copying network data...
if not exist c:\corpfiles\nul mkdir c:\corpfiles
copy f:\*.xls c:\corpfiles
```

You can also execute one set of commands if the if test is true and another if the test is false by using the else option, as in this example:

```
if exist input.dat echo input.dat exists else echo input.dat does not exist
```

You can use else with parentheses, but you must take care to place the else command on the same line as if, or on the same line as the closing parenthesis after if. You should write a multiple-line if...else command using the same format as this example:

```
if exist input.dat (
    echo Sorting input.txt...
    sort <input.txt >source.data
) else (
    echo Input.txt does not exist. Creating an empty data file...
    echo. >source.data
)
```

Extended Testing

The extended if command lets you perform a larger variety of tests when comparing strings, and it can also compare arguments and variables as numbers. The extended comparisons are listed in Table 9.12.

Table 9.12   Comparison Operators Allowed by the *if* Command

Variation	Comparison
if *string1* **EQU** *string2*	Exactly equal
if *string1* **NEQ** *string2*	Not equal
if *string1* **LSS** *string2*	Less than
if *string1* **LEQ** *string2*	Less than or equal to
if *string1* **GTR** *string2*	Greater than
if string1 **GEQ** string2	Greater than or equal to
if **/i** (comparison)	Not case sensitive
if **defined** *name*	True if there is an environment variable *name*
if **cmdextversion** *number*	True if the cmd extensions are version *number* or higher

As a bonus, if the strings being compared contain only digits, cmd compares them numerically. For example, you could test for a specific exit status from a program with a statement like this:

```
some program
if %errorlevel% equ 3 (
    echo The program returned an exit status of 3 which
    echo means that the network printer is offline.
)
```

Processing Multiple Arguments

When you have many files to process, you may get tired of typing the same batch file commands over and over, like this:

```
somebatch file1.dat
somebatch file2.dat
somebatch file3.dat
...
```

It's possible to write batch files to handle any number of arguments on the command line. The tool to use is the `shift` command, which deletes a given command-line argument and slides the remaining ones down. Here's what I mean: Suppose that I started a batch file with the command line

```
batchname xxx yyy zzz
```

Inside the batch file, the following argument replacements would be in effect before and after a shift command:

Before Shift	After Shift
%0 = *batchname*	%0 = *xxx*
%1 = xxx	%1 = yyy
%2 = yyy	%2 = zzz
%3 = zzz	%3 = (blank)
%4 = (blank)	%4 = (blank)

This lets a batch file repeatedly process the item named by %1 and shift until %1 is blank. To process a variable number of command-line arguments, use the `shift` command to delete arguments until they're all gone, as in this example:

```
@echo off
if "%1" == "" (
    rem if %1 is blank there were no arguments. Show how to use this batch
    echo Usage: %0 filename ...
    exit /b
)

:again
rem if %1 is blank, we are finished
if not "%1" == "" (
    echo Processing file %1...

    rem ... do something with file %1 here
    rem - shift the arguments and examine %1 again
    shift
    goto again
)
```

If you want to have the program process a default file if none is specified on the command line, you can use this variation of the pattern:

```
@echo off

if "%1" == "" (
    rem - no file was specified - process the default file "test.for"
    call :process test.for
) else (
    rem - process each of the named files
:again
    rem if %1 is blank, we are finished
    if not "%1" == "" (
        call :process %1
```

```
        rem - shift the arguments and examine %1 again
        shift
        goto again
    )
)
exit /b

:process
echo Processing file %1...
    .
    .
    .
```

In this version, if no arguments are specified on the command line, the script will process a default file—in this case `test.for`. Otherwise, it will process all files named on the command line. This version of the pattern uses batch file subroutines, which are discussed later in this chapter under "Using Batch Files Subroutines."

The extended version of the `shift` command, `shift /n`, lets you start shifting at argument number *n*, leaving the lower-numbered arguments alone. The following illustrates what `shift /2` does in a batch file run with the command "`batchname xxx yyy zzz`":

Before Shift	**After Shift**
%0 = *batchname*	%0 = *batchname*
%1 = xxx	%1 = xxx
%2 = yyy	%2 = zzz
%3 = zzz	%3 = (blank)
%4 = (blank)	%4 = (blank)

In actual use, you might want to use this feature if you need to have the batch file's name (`%0`) available throughout the batch file. In this case, you can use `shift /1` to shift all the remaining arguments, but keep `%0` intact. You may also want to write batch files that take a command line of the form

```
batchname outputfile inputfile inputfile ...
```

with an output filename followed by one or more input files. In this case, you could keep the output filename `%1` intact but loop through the input files with `shift /2`, using commands like this:

```
@echo off

rem be sure they gave at least two arguments
if "%2" == "" (
    echo Usage: %0 outfile infile ...
    exit /b
)

rem collect all input files into SORT.TMP

if exist sort.tmp del sort.tmp
```

```
:again
if not "%2" == "" (
    echo ...Collecting data from %2
    type %2 >>sort.tmp
    shift /2
    goto again
)

rem sort SORT.TMP into first file named on command line

echo ...Sorting to create %1
sort sort.tmp /O %1
del sort.tmp
```

Working with Environment Variables

Although environment variables were initially designed to hold system-configuration information such as the search path, they are also the "working" variables for batch files. You can use them to store filenames, option settings, user input from prompts, or any other information you need to store in a batch program. The set command is used to set and modify environment variables.

However, you should know that, by default, changes to environment variables made in a batch file persist when the batch file finishes because the variables "belong" to the copy of cmd that manages the Command Prompt window and any batch files in it. This is great when you want to use a batch file to modify the search path so that you can run programs from some nonstandard directory. However, it's a real problem if your batch file assumes that any variables it uses are undefined (empty) before the batch file starts. Here's a disaster waiting to happen:

```
@echo off
set /p answer=Do you want to erase the input files at the end (Y/N)?
if /i "%answer:~,1%" EQU "Y" set cleanup=YES
... more commands here
... then, at the end,
if "%cleanup%" == "YES" (
    rem they wanted the input files to be erased
    del c:\input\*.dat
)
```

If you respond to the prompt with Y, the environment variable cleanup will be set to YES, and the files will be erased. However, the next time you run the batch file, cleanup will *still* be set to YES, and the files will be erased no matter how you answer the question. Of course, the problem can be solved by adding the statement

```
set cleanup=
```

at the beginning of the batch file. In fact, good programming practice requires you to do so in any case (you should always initialize variables before using them), but the point is still important: Environment variables are "sticky."

In the old DOS days, a batch file program would usually add set statements to the end of batch files to delete any environment variables used by the program. However, cmd provides an easier method of cleaning up.

If you plan on using environment variables as working variables for a batch file, you can use the setlocal command to make any changes to the variables "local" to the batch file. At the end of the batch file, or if you use an endlocal command, the environment will be restored to its original state at the time of the setlocal command. It would be prudent to put setlocal at the beginning of any batch file that does not require its environment changes to persist outside the batch file itself.

Environment Variable Editing

As with the old command.com, in any command, strings of the form %var% are replaced with the value of the environment variable named var. One of cmd's extensions is to let you modify the environment variable content as it is being extracted. Whereas the edits for command-line arguments are focused around filename manipulation, the edits for environment variables are designed to let you extract substrings.

The following types of expressions can be used:

Expression	Result
%name:~n%	Skips the first n letters and returns the rest
%name:~n,m%	Skips n letters and returns the next m
%name:~,m%	First (leftmost) m letters
%name:~-m%	Last (rightmost) m letters

Using the environment variable var=ABCDEFG, here are some examples:

Command	Prints
echo %var%	ABCDEFG
echo %var:~2%	CDEFG
echo %var:~2,3%	CDE
echo %var:~,3%	ABC
echo %var:~-3%	EFG

Expressions of the form %name:str1=str2% replace every occurrence of the string str1 with str2. str2 can be blank to delete all occurrences of str1. You can start str1 with an asterisk (*), which makes cmd replace all characters up to and including str1.

Using the environment variable var=ABC;DEF;GHI, here are some examples:

Command	Prints
echo %var:;= %	ABC DEF GHI
echo %var:;=%	ABCDEFGHI
echo %var:*DEF=123%	123;GHI

The first example listed is particularly useful if you want to use the PATH list in a for loop; for wants to see file or folder names separated by spaces, whereas PATH separates them with semicolons. I'll discuss this in more detail later on.

◄◄ For more details on working with environment variables, **see** "Environment Variables," **p. 507**.

Processing Multiple Items with the *for* Command

You'll often want to write batch files that process "all" of a certain type of file. Command-line programs can deal with filename wildcards: For example, you can type `delete *.dat` to delete all files whose names end with `.dat`. In batch files, you can accomplish this sort of thing with the `for` loop.

Note

If you have a UNIX background, the need for special statements to deal with wildcards may seem confusing at first. On UNIX and Linux systems, the command shell expands all command-line arguments with wildcards into a list of names before it starts up the command, so to the command it appears that the user typed out all the names. This is called *globbing*. On DOS and Windows, the shell doesn't do this. When command-line arguments contain wildcard characters, it's up to the command or batch file to expand the name into a list of filenames.

The basic version of the `for` command scans through a set or list of names and runs a command once for each. The format for batch files is

```
for %%x in (set of names) do command
```

where `set of names` is a list of words separated by spaces. The `for` command executes `command` once for each item it finds in the set. At each iteration, variable x contains the current name, and any occurrences of `%%x` in the command are replaced by the current value of x. You can choose any alphabetic letter for the variable name. Also, upper- and lowercase matters, meaning *a* and *A* are different to the `for` command.

Note

When you type a **for** command directly at the command prompt, you use only single percent signs. In a batch file, you must double them up. Otherwise, they confuse cmd because they look sort of like command-line arguments. cmd could have been written to know the difference, but it wasn't, so we're stuck with this.

For example, the command

```
for %%x in (a b c d) do echo %%x
```

prints four lines: a, b, c, and d. What makes `for` especially useful is that if any item in the set contains the wildcard characters ? or *, `for` will assume that the item is a filename and will replace the item with any matching filenames. The command

```
for %%x in (*.tmp *.out *.dbg) do delete %%x
```

will delete any occurrences of files ending with `.tmp`, `.out`, or `.dbg` in the current directory. If no such files exist, the command will turn into

```
for %%x in () do delete %%x
```

which is fine...it does nothing. To get the same "silent" result when specifying the wildcards directly in the `delete` command, you would have to enter

```
if exist *.tmp delete *tmp
if exist *.out delete *.out
if exist *.dbg delete *.dbg
```

because delete complains if it can't find any files to erase.

As another example, the command

```
for %%F in ("%ALLUSERSPROFILE%\Documents\
    ➥My Faxes\Received Faxes\*.tif") do echo %%~nF: received %%~tF
```

prints a list of all faxes received from the Windows XP Fax service and the time they were received*.

Note

If you use variable substitution edits, choose as your **for** variable a letter that you don't need to use as one of the editing letters. **for** stops looking at the editing expression when it hits the **for** variable letter. For instance, in the example, if I had needed to use the **~f** editing function, I would have had to choose another variable letter for the **for** loop.

The extended for command lets you scan for directories, recurse into subdirectories, and several other useful things that you can't do any other way.

Using Multiple Commands in a for Loop

cmd lets you use multiple command lines after a for loop. This makes the Windows XP for command much more powerful than the old DOS version. In cases where you would have had to call a batch file subroutine in the past, you can now use parentheses to perform complex operations.

For example, this batch file examines a directory full of Windows bitmap (BMP) files and makes sure that there is a corresponding GIF file in another directory; if the GIF file doesn't exist, it uses an image-conversion utility to create one:

```
@echo off
setlocal
echo Searching for new .BMP files...

for %%F in (c:\incoming\*.bmp) do (
    rem output file is input file name with extension .GIF
    set outfile=c:\outgoing\%%~nF.gif
    if not exist %outfile% (
        echo ...Creating %outfile%
        imgcnv -gif %%F %outfile%
    )
)
```

Therefore, every time you run this batch file, it makes sure there is a converted GIF file in the \outgoing folder for every BMP file in the \incoming folder. This sample script uses several of the techniques we've discussed in this chapter:

- A setlocal statement keeps environment variable changes in the batch file from persisting after the batch is finished.

On Vista, the path would be "%ALLUSERSPROFILE%\Microsoft\Windows NT\MSFax\Inbox.tif".

- The `for` loop and `if` command use parentheses to group several statements.
- The environment variable `outfile` is used as a "working" variable.
- The batch file uses `echo` statements to let you know what it's doing as it works.

A batch file like this can make short work of maintaining large sets of files. You might accidentally overlook a new file if you were trying to manage something like this manually, but the batch file won't.

As a final example, the following handy batch file tells you what file is actually used when you type a command by name. I call this program `which.bat`, and when I want to know what program is run by, say, the `ping` command, I type the following:

```
which ping
```

The batch file searches the current folder, and then every folder in the PATH list. In each folder, it looks for a specific file, if you typed a specific extension with the command name, or it tries all the extensions in the PATHEXT list, which contains .EXE, .COM, .BAT, and the other usual suspects:

```
@echo off

if "%1" == "" (
    echo Usage: which command
    echo Locates the file run when you type 'command'.
    exit /b
)

for %%d in (. %path%) do (
    if "%~x1" == "" (
        rem the user didn't type an extension so use the PATHEXT list
        for %%e in (%pathext%) do (
            if exist %%d\%1%%e (
                echo %%d\%1%%e
                exit /b
            )
        )
    ) else (
        rem the user typed a specific extension, so look only for that
        if exist %%d\%1 (
            echo %%d\%1
            exit /b
        )
    )
)
echo No file for %1 was found
```

As you can see, the `for` command lets you write powerful, useful programs that can save you time and prevent errors, and the syntax is cryptic enough to please even a Perl programmer.

Delayed Expansion

Environment variables and command-line arguments marked with `%` are replaced with their corresponding values when cmd reads each command line. However, when you're writing `for` loops and compound `if` statements, this can cause some unexpected results.

For example, you might want to run a secondary batch file repeatedly with several files, with the first file handled differently, like this:

```
call anotherbatch firstfile.txt FIRST
call anotherbatch secondfile.txt MORE
call anotherbatch xfiles.txt MORE
```

You might want to do this so that the first call will create a new output file, whereas each subsequent call will add on to the existing file.

You might be tempted to automate this process with the for command, using commands like this:

```
set isfirst=FIRST
for %%f in (*.txt) do (
    call anotherbatch %%f %isfirst%
    set isfirst=MORE
)
```

The idea here is that the second argument to anotherbatch will be FIRST for the first file and MORE for all subsequent files. However, this will not work. cmd will replace %isfirst% with its definition MORE when it first encounters the for statement. When cmd has finished processing % signs, the command will look like this:

```
set isfirst=FIRST
for %%f in (*.txt) do (
    call anotherbatch %%f FIRST
    set isfirst=MORE
)
```

Because FIRST is substituted before the for loop starts running, anotherbatch will not see the value of isfirst change, and the result will be

```
call anotherbatch firstfile.txt FIRST
call anotherbatch secondfile.txt FIRST
call anotherbatch xfiles.txt FIRST
```

which is not at all what you wanted.

There is a way to fix this: Delayed expansion lets you specify environment variables with exclamation points rather than percent signs, as an indication that they are to be expanded only when cmd actually intends to really execute the command. Because ! has not traditionally been a special character, this feature is disabled by default. To enable delayed expansion, specify /V:ON on the cmd command line or use SETLOCAL to enable this feature inside the batch file. The statements

```
setlocal enabledelayedexpansion
set isfirst=FIRST
for %%f in (*.txt) do (
    call anotherbatch %%f !isfirst!
    set isfirst=MORE
)
```

will work correctly.

Although delayed expansion is disabled by default in Windows XP, you can change the default setting through the Registry key HKLM\Software\Microsoft\Command Processor\ EnableExtensions. If this DWORD value is present and set to 0, command extensions are disabled by default. Any nonzero value for EnableExtensions enables them.

Another place delayed expansion is useful is to collect information into an environment variable in a for list. The following batch file adds c:\mystuff and every folder under it to an environment variable named dirs:

```
setlocal ENABLEDELAYEDEXPANSION
set dirs=
for /R c:\mystuff %%d in (.) do set dirs=!dirs!;%%d
```

The for statement recursively visits every folder, starting in c:\mystuff, and %%d takes on the name of each folder in turn. The set statement adds each directory name to the end of the dirs variable.

Using Batch File Subroutines

The cmd shell lets you write batch file subroutines using the call command. Although the new capability to group statements with parentheses makes batch file subroutines somewhat less necessary than they were in the past, the subroutine is still an important tool in batch file programming.

For example, in a task that involves processing a whole list of files, you might write a batch file subroutine to perform all the steps necessary to process one file. Then, you can call this subroutine once for each file you need to process.

In the old days of command.com, batch file subroutines had to be placed in separate .BAT files. You can still do this, but with cmd, you can also place subroutines in the same file as the main batch file program. The structure looks like this:

```
@echo off

rem MAIN BATCH FILE PROGRAM -----------------------

rem call subroutine "onefile" for each file to be processed:
cd \input
for %%f in (*.dat) do call :onefile %%f    ← subroutine called here

rem main program must end with exit /b or goto :EOF
exit /b

rem SUBROUTINE "ONEFILE" ---------------------------
:onefile
echo Processing file %1...
echo ... commands go here ...
exit /b
```

The call command followed by a colon and a label name tells cmd to continue processing at the label. Any items placed on the call command after the label are arguments passed to the subroutine, which can access them with %1, %2, and so on. The original command-line arguments to the batch file are hidden while the call is in effect.

Processing returns to the command after the call when the subroutine encounters any of these conditions:

- The end of the file is reached.
- The subroutine deliberately jumps to the end of the file with the command goto :EOF.
- The subroutine executes the command exit /b.

Normally, any of these conditions would indicate the end of the batch file, and cmd would return to the command prompt. After call, however, these conditions just end the subroutine, and the batch file continues.

Caution

You must be sure to make the main part of the batch file stop before it runs into the first subroutine. In other scripting languages such as VBScript, the end of the "main program" is unmistakable, but in the batch file language it is not. You must use **goto :EOF** or **exit /B** before the first subroutine's label; otherwise, cmd will plow through and run the subroutine's commands again.

Tip

When I have a bunch of files that I have to process in some way, I often don't like to use the **for** command. Instead I use the command **dir /b >filename.bat** to create the beginnings of the batch file. I edit the batch file with Notepad and put **call :process** before each filename. I put **@echo off** at the top. At the bottom, I put the lines

```
     goto :EOF
:process
     echo Processing file %s...
     ...
     (commands go here)
```

The reason I go to this trouble is that I can manually delete from the list any files that I want to skip—you can't do that with **for**!. And if I have to interrupt the procedure before it finishes, I can delete the **call** lines for any files that had already been processed, or use a **goto** to skip over them, before running the batch file again.

Prompting for Input

If your batch file has to print a message you definitely don't want the users to miss, use the pause statement to make the batch file sit and wait until they've read the message and acknowledged it. Here's an example:

```
echo The blatfizz command failed. This means that the world as
echo we know it is about to end, or, that your input file needs to
echo be corrected.
pause
exit /b
```

If you want to ask a user whether to proceed after a mishap, or if you want the batch file to prompt for input filenames or other data, you can use the new extended set /p command. set

/p reads a user's response into an environment variable, where it can be tested or used as a command argument. Here's an example:

```
:again
    echo The input file INPUT.DAT does not exist
    set /p answer=Do you want to create it now (Y/N)?
    if /i "%answer:~,1%" EQU "Y" goto editit
    if /i "%answer:~,1%" EQU "N" exit /b
    echo Please type Y for Yes or N for No
    goto again
```

These commands ask the user to type a response, examine the leftmost letter with %answer:,1%, and take the appropriate action only if the user types a valid response. To prompt a user for a yes/no answer, use a series of commands following this pattern:

```
:again
    echo If the question is long or requires an explanation,
    echo use echo commands to display text before the question.
    set /p answer=Ask the question here (Y/N)?
    if /i "%answer:~,1%" EQU "Y" command to execute for Yes
    if /i "%answer:~,1%" EQU "N" command to execute for No
    echo Please type Y for Yes or N for No
    goto again
```

Put a single space after the question mark on the set /p command. If you use this pattern more than once in the same batch file, be sure to use a different label for each one. I used again in this version, but you can use any word as the label.

If the work that has to be done given either the Yes or No answer is more than a few commands (placed in parentheses), you can use be a goto :label command to continue execution in another part of the batch file.

You can modify this pattern to create a menu. In the following example, the batch file prompts the user to type a letter corresponding to a desired action:

```
@echo off
:getmenu
    echo.
    echo Options: [A]dd, [D]elete, [P]rint, [Q]uit, [H]elp
    set /p answer=Enter selection:
    if /i "%answer%" == "A" goto do_add
    if /i "%answer%" == "D" goto do_del
    if /i "%answer%" == "P" goto do_print
    if /i "%answer%" == "Q" exit /b
    rem use pressed H or an unrecognized letter. Offer help.
    echo.
    echo Press A to add a new entry, D to delete the
    echo current entry, P to print a phone list, or Q
    echo to quit this batch file.
    goto getmenu
:do_add
    rem add a new entry…
```

Notice that if the user types **H** (for Help) or any unrecognized letter, the program prints a list of instructions, and then goes back and prompts again. Otherwise, the batch file jumps to the label do_add, do_del, or do_print to do the requested work.

This was a very basic introduction to batch file construction, but I hope that gave you an overview of what is possible. The best way to learn more is to try to automate some task that you find *yourself* doing over and over...the effort will be well worth it!

The next section gives an overview of scripting, in which you can construct programs even more powerful than batch files.

Running GUI Applications from a Batch File

If you want to start a GUI program from within a batch file, you should know the batch file doesn't continue to the next command until the GUI program is closed. This may be what you want. If, however, you want the batch file to proceed immediately to the next command, you must use the start command to run the GUI application. As an example, the following batch file displays the contents of a folder. A directory listing is written to a text file in the user's temporary file folder, and then displayed in Notepad.

```
@echo off
dir >%TEMP%\dir_listing.txt
start notepad %TEMP%\dir_listing.txt
```

Caution

You might be tempted to "clean up" by deleting **dir_listing.txt** immediately after the **start** command, but it's not a good idea. Windows might resume processing the batch file before Notepad has had a chance to read the contents of **dir_listing.txt**. Unfortunately there is no built-in command that could be used to make the batch file delay for a second or so before continuing, so it's best to just leave the temporary file there until the Disk Cleanup Wizard gets rid of it.

Note

When you start a GUI program from the command prompt on Windows XP and all earlier versions of Windows, the command prompt reappears as soon as the GUI program has been started. On Windows Vista, the command prompt *doesn't* return until the GUI program exits, just as in a batch file. Why Microsoft changed this behavior, I don't know. You can use the **start** command at the Vista command prompt, just as I described for use in batch files, to work around this annoyance.

Scripting with Windows Script Host

As you saw in the previous sections, batch files give you a means to automatically run programs. There is some limited programming capability; that is, you have the means to take different actions depending on the conditions encountered, but for the most part, as helpful as they are, batch files just let you push data into and pull data out of existing programs.

Scripts, on the other hand, give you access to full-scale programming languages that can more easily manipulate data, and from which you can not only run existing command-line programs, but can also

- Use the features of many Windows programs such as Word and Excel to create documents or perform calculations.

- Gain access to Windows files, folders, network settings, the Registry, disk configuration, and just about every other part of Windows.

- Write your own programs from scratch, to manage data, manage Windows, send email, or... well, just about anything else.

The range of what you can do with scripting is pretty much limited only to your imagination and your skill as a programmer. And that's the rub because it does take some training and practice to build up that skill. Scripting is a complex subject that could easily fill several books of this size, so here we'll just be able to scratch its surface. I'll give you an overview. And, I hope that you'll be intrigued enough to learn more through other books and resources. I'll give you some suggestions for follow-up reading at the end of this chapter.

Script Languages

Windows scripting is managed through a program called *Windows Script Host* or WSH. The word *host* here is significant. It refers to the fact that Windows Script Host is a "framework" program that provides support for scripting without being tied to a specific script programming language. Out of the box, Windows comes with the VBScript and JScript languages, so you can use whichever of these two programming languages you prefer. Or, if you're already more familiar with one of the other script programming languages available from third-party vendors, you can download and install one of these other languages, usually at no cost. Table 9.13 lists several widely used languages for which WSH versions are available.

Note

Windows Script Host is installed by default with Windows Vista, XP, and 2000. For Windows 98 and Me it was available as a free download, but it is no longer available from Microsoft because Windows 98 and Me are no longer supported.

Table 9.13 Windows Script Host Languages*

Language	Description
VBScript	VBScript is a version of Microsoft Visual Basic used in Windows Script Host, Internet Explorer, and Internet Information Services. It's *very* similar to Visual Basic for Applications (VBA), which is used as the scripting or macro language for Microsoft desktop products such as Word and Excel. If you know how to write macros for Word and Excel, you know VBScript. VBScript is installed by default with Windows Script Host.
JScript	JScript is a programming language modeled after Netscape's JavaScript language. Microsoft made its own version just to keep things interesting and incompatible. If you've written client-side web page scripts, you're probably already familiar with JScript; now you can use it to manage and manipulate Windows. JScript is installed by default with Windows Script Host.
Perl	Perl was developed in 1987 by developers in the UNIX community. From the very start, Perl was an "open" language—its writing, debugging, and subsequent development were carried out by the public, for no charge. It's a very popular, powerful language that's especially well suited for manipulating text. It has powerful string-handling and pattern-matching capabilities, and huge repositories of free Perl scripts are available on the Internet. As a programming language, though, it's on the strange side, and may not be a good choice if you're new to programming. A free version for Windows called ActivePerl can be downloaded from www.activestate.com.

Language	Description
Python	Python is another very popular scripting/programming language from the UNIX world. It originated at the National Research Institute for Mathematics and Computer Science (CWI) in Amsterdam. It's a portable object-oriented language and is much less cryptic than Perl. A free Windows Script Host plug-in called ActivePython is available at www.activestate.com.
Object REXX	REXX is a language that originated in 1979 as a scripting language for IBM mainframes. Since then, IBM has made it available for IBM Linux, AIX, OS/2, and Windows as well as its mainframe operating systems. Object REXX began as an IBM product but is now a free, open-source project. For information, visit www.rexxla.org.
Ruby	Ruby is a fairly new language that originated in Japan. It's currently more popular in Europe and Japan than in the U.S., but it's picking up steam. A port of Ruby to the Windows Script Host environment is available at http://arton.hp.infoseek.co.jp/.*

UNIX and Linux enthusiasts loudly sing the praises of Perl and Python, and in fact each of the languages has its disciples, but for a first-time programmer, VBScript is probably the easiest of these languages to learn. If you use Microsoft desktop applications, VBScript is definitely an important language to know because it's used inside Word, Excel, Access—in fact *most* Microsoft products—as the built-in macro language. You'll get a double payoff for learning VBScript because experience you gain writing scripts will help you write macros, and vice versa.

With this in mind, for this chapter, I'll provide the examples in VBScript.

Creating and Editing Scripts

Scripts are plain text files with a special file extension that tells Windows Script Host what language the script is written in; the most common extensions are listed in Table 9.1. The two most common are .VBS for a VBScript script, or .JS for a JScript script.

As stated previously, I suggest that you create a special folder to hold your scripts and batch files, for example c:\bat, so that you can put this folder into the search path and thus have access to them from any Command Prompt. For instructions, see "Creating and Editing Batch Files" earlier in this chapter. When you've done this, open a Command Prompt window and type the command **bat** to change to your batch file directory.

It's easy to create and edit scripts using the Notepad accessory. Let's create a simple script to display your logon (user) name. In the Command Prompt window you just opened, type **notepad myname.vbs** and press Enter. When Notepad asks whether you want to create a new file, click Yes. Then, type the following lines into the Notepad window:

```
set wnet = CreateObject("WScript.Network")
uname = wnet.UserName
wscript.echo "Your user name is " & uname
```

Save the file by clicking File, Save, or equivalently, by pressing Alt+F, and then Alt+S.

---

* You might also search the Web for "ActiveScriptRuby." A few other language plug-ins have been made by independent developers, but they appear to be partial implementations and so are not listed here. For a survey, see www.mvps.org/scripting/languages.

Now, type the following line in the Command Prompt window:

```
cscript myname.vbs
```

This will run your script as a console (command line) application, and the result will print out in the console window. In my case, it prints:

```
Your user name is bknittel
```

Now, type the command

```
wscript myname.vbs
```

This runs your script as a Windowed (GUI) application. Instead of printing text at the command prompt, a dialog box pops up, as shown in Figure 9.10.

Figure 9.10   The WScript command runs scripts as GUI applications, and text output is displayed in dialog boxes.

In most cases, it's easier to run script applications using the command-line interface. You can set cscript to be the default so that it is used to automatically run a script when you enter only its name. To do this, enter this command at the command prompt:

```
cscript //nologo //h:cscript //s
```

being sure to double-up the slashes as shown. You only need to do this once; this setting will "stick" permanently.

Now, you can run a script simply by typing its name. Type the command myname and press Enter. Recall that .VBS is in the PATHEXT list of executable file types, so when Windows looks for a program named myname it finds myname.vbs, and uses cscript to run it.

Note

If you have Windows Defender or another antivirus or antispam package installed, running a script by name may trigger a security warning. Click the appropriate button to allow the script to run. You may need to retype the command to get the script run. You should only have to go through this once for each new script you write.

Security Issues

When you run a script (or batch file, or any other program, for that matter), the script can do anything that your user account's permissions let it do. If you are using a Computer Administrator account, this means the script can do *anything*, including deleting Windows entirely.

You should take a moment to consider what might happen if some other user was able to modify your script file to do something other than what you intended. The next time you run the script, it will run with your account's permissions. Another user could use this technique to have you inadvertently give him or her Administrator privileges, cause damage, or, well...the mind boggles.

Here's what you can do to prevent this from happening:

- Be sure that your scripts are stored on a disk formatted with the NTFS file system. The FAT file system offers no user-level security whatsoever. Another user could modify your scripts to do whatever they wanted, and if you ran the modified script, it would run with your account's permissions.

- On Windows XP Home Edition or Windows XP Professional with Simple File Sharing enabled, open a Command Prompt window and, assuming that the batch file folder is c:\bat, type this command:

```
cacls c:\bat /T /G "%username%":F Users:R
```

  This replaces the permissions on this folder and its contents to give you (and only you) read/write privileges, and gives all other users read-only access.

- On Windows Vista, Windows XP Professional with Simple File Sharing turned off, or on Windows 2000 Professional, you can use the preceding method, or if you want to do it the hard way, you can use the GUI: Open Windows Explorer and locate the folder that contains your scripts. Right-click the folder and select the Security tab. Add your user account to the list of names, and click Full Control. For the Users or Power Users entries, uncheck everything but Read & Execute. If you can't change these entries, log on as a (or contact your) system administrator, or click the Advanced button, uncheck the Inherit from Parent setting. Click OK, and then make the changes. Then, click Advanced again, check Replace Permission Entries..., and click OK to close the dialogs. (I told you it could be easier to use the command line to manage Windows!)

Running Scripts

As I mentioned in the previous section, if the folder that contains your scripts is listed in the PATH environment variable, and if you've set cscript (the command line version of Windows Script Host) to be the default script processor, you can run your scripts just as you would any other Windows command, by typing its name.

If your script contains a programming error, Windows Script Host may either refuse to run it, or may stop in the middle of running it. Let's demonstrate this. Open a Command Prompt window and switch to your scripts directory (type **bat**, if you're using the method I suggested). Edit the sample script by typing **notepad myname.vbs**, and add on to the third line so that it reads

```
wscript.echo "Your user name is " & uname & " no closing quote here
```

Save the file, and run it again by typing **myname** at the command prompt. This time you will see this message:

```
C:\Users \bknittel\myname.vbs(3, 68) Microsoft VBScript
compilation error: Unterminated string constant
```

This message tells us three things:

- VBScript found an error in the script program.

- The error occurred on the third line in the file; the (3, 68) part tells you this. The 3 is the number of the line in the file with the error, and the 68 is a number that tells what sort of problem VBScript found. You don't need to know what 68 means because its meaning is written in plain English.

- The message `Compilation error: Unterminated string constant` means that a text message was missing the second quotation mark (") that should have been there to indicate its end.

When errors like this occur, you'll need to determine what's wrong with the script before you can continue. The description of the message will often help you figure out what's wrong; you may have this sort of syntax error, that is, there may be a missing keyword, quotation mark, or other typographical error, or the program might be attempting to work with invalid data.

Tip

To view and edit the script line that caused the error, open the script with Notepad. Turn line wrapping off by clicking Format and unchecking Word Wrap. (You just need to do this once; it will still be unchecked the next time you run Notepad.) Now, press Ctrl+G. Windows will pop up the Goto Line dialog. Type the line number reported by Windows Script Host (3, in the example you just saw), and press Enter. This will move the cursor right to the offending line.

Scripting and COM Objects

Although the programming languages that you can use with Windows Script Host are powerful programming tools by themselves, most of their usefulness comes from their capability to work with external software components called *Component Object Model (COM) objects*.

In the most general sense, objects are little program packages that manipulate and communicate information. They're a software representation of something tangible, such as a file, a folder, a network connection, an email message, or an Excel document. You interact with objects through their properties and methods. *Properties* are data values that describe the attributes of the thing the object represents. For example, a file or folder object might have a `name` property that represents the associated file or folder's name. *Methods* are actions—program subroutines—you can use to alter or manipulate whatever the object represents. For example, a file object might have a `delete` method that, if activated, would delete the associated file.

Most importantly, objects extend the capabilities of the language from which they're used. Although VBScript doesn't know how to manage network printers, it does know how to let you use a COM object that *can* manage network printers.

Hundreds of different COM objects are available in Windows, representing things like network connections, files and folders, printers, user accounts, email messages, and Active Directory information. In addition, many application programs such as Word and Excel are totally accessible as COM objects themselves, so if you have Microsoft Office or another desktop suite installed, your scripts can create documents, spreadsheets, and charts.

In VBScript, the statement used to create an instance of a particular object is

```
set variable = CreateObject("objectname")
```

where *variable* is the name of the variable you want to use to refer to the object reference, and *objectname* is the type of object you want to create.

Once an object has been created, you refer to its properties and methods as *variable.name*, where *variable* is an object variable, and *name* is the name of a method or property. Let's look again at the sample script you created at the beginning of this section on scripting:

```
set wnet = CreateObject("WScript.Network")
uname = wnet.UserName
wscript.echo "Your user name is " & uname
```

The first line creates a WScript.Network object, and stores it in variable wnet. WScript.Network objects provide properties and methods for working with—you guessed it—Windows networking.

The second line sets a normal VBScript variable with the value of the object's UserName property, which is the name of the currently logged on user: you.

The third line uses the built-in WScript object, an object that is automatically provided by Windows Script Host. Its echo method prints whatever text is provided on the program line into the console window or a dialog box (depending on whether the script is being run as a console program with cscript or a GUI program with wscript).

The point I want to make here is that VBScript itself doesn't know how to determine your user-name, but Windows comes with a component called the WScript.Network object that does. And there are thousands of object types provided with Windows.

Some of the most important objects used for management scripting in Windows Script Host are listed in Table 9.14.

Table 9.14   Some Windows Management COM Objects

Object Name	Representations
Scripting.FileSystemObject	Drives, files, folders, text file contents
WScript	Command-line arguments, script input and output streams
DOMDocument	XML and HTML files
WScript.Shell	Windows desktop, special folders, the Registry, command-line programs
WSHShortcut	Desktop shortcuts
WSHEnvironment	Environment settings (current and default)
WHSNetwork	Network printer icons, network drive mappings, current computer name, and username
CDO.Message	Email message (outgoing) with optional attachments
SWbemServices	Windows Management Instrumentation (WMI); provides access to services, device drivers, running tasks, network configuration, user accounts, and more than 100 other aspects of Windows configuration
IADs	Active Directory users, groups, containers, domains, computers, and all other AD objects

In addition, applications such as Microsoft Word and Excel provide objects such as `Word.Document` and `Excel.Sheet`. You can create and manipulate these objects as well; so, for instance, a script could easily create a telephone directory Word document by pulling information out of Active Directory.

Sample Scripts

Here are a few practical scripts that demonstrate the kinds of things you can accomplish with scripting in Windows. They range from information gathering to workflow management.

Listing Network Printer Connections

The following script, `listprinters.vbs`, lists the computer's printer mappings:

```
set wshNetwork = CreateObject("WScript.Network")

set maps = wshNetwork.EnumPrinterConnections
for i = 0 to maps.Length-2 step 2
    WScript.echo "Port:", maps.item(i), "  Name:", maps.item(i+1)
next
```

The output on my computer looks like this:

```
Port: USB002    Name: Samsung ML-1710 Series
Port: Microsoft Document Imaging Writer Port:   Name: Microsoft Office Document
     ➥ Image Writer
Port: HPLaserJet4V    Name: HP LaserJet 4V JetDirect
Port: SHRFAX:    Name: Fax
Port: C:\Documents and Settings\All Users.WINDOWS\Desktop\*.pdf    Name: Acrobat
     ➥ Distiller
```

Reading and Writing Registry Values

The following script, `countme.vbs`, shows how a script may read and write Registry values. This demonstration script just prints a running count of how many times it has been run.

```
set shell = CreateObject("WScript.Shell")
nruns = shell.RegRead("HKCU\Software\MyScripts\countme\number of runs")
nruns = nruns+1
wscript.echo "Number of runs:", nruns

Shell.RegWrite "HKCU\Software\MyScripts\countme\number of runs", nruns,
"REG_DWORD"
```

If you create this script and type

```
countme
countme
countme
```

at the command prompt, you'll see the count increase by one each time. In addition, if you use `regedit` to view key HKEY_CURRENT_USER\Software\MyScripts\countme, you'll see that the program indeed saves a value in the Registry (click View, Refresh after running `countme` to see that the value changes).

Sending Email from a Shortcut

Finally, here is a long-ish but practical script meant for someone who regularly has to email files to a colleague as part of their day-to-day job. With this script, you can simply drag files on the Desktop and drop them onto a shortcut icon, and they'll be mailed without your having to do anything else.

The script takes any files named on its command line and sends them to a specific person as email attachments. To use this script, you would first edit it to use the correct email addresses, and you'll need to add the name of your organization's SMTP mail server (the server for outgoing mail). Then, create a shortcut to the script on your desktop.

When you drop files on a shortcut, Windows runs the associated program with the names of the dropped files as command-line arguments. In our case, the program is the following script. It uses the Collaboration Data Objects (CDO) tool provided with Windows Vista, XP, and 2000.

```
if WScript.arguments.count <= 0 then   ' no files were specified
    MsgBox "Usage: mailfiles filename..., or drag files onto shortcut"
    WScript.quit 0
end if
const cdoSendUsingPort = 2             ' standard CDO constants
const cdoAnonymous     = 0

sender    = "brian@mycompany.com"      ' sender of message
recipient = "sheila@mycompany.com"     ' recipient of this message
subject   = "Attached: sales lead form"
mailservername = "mail.mycompany.com"  ' name of SMTP (outgoing mail) server

set msg  = CreateObject("CDO.Message") ' create objects
set conf = CreateObject("CDO.Configuration")
set msg.configuration = conf

With msg                               ' build the message
    .to        = recipient
    .from      = sender
    .subject   = subject
    .textBody  = "Attached to this message are files for you."

    nfiles = 0                         ' count of files attached
    for each arg in WScript.arguments  ' treat each argument as a
        .AddAttachment arg             ' file to be attached
        nfiles = nfiles+1
    next
End With
prefix = "http://schemas.microsoft.com/cdo/configuration/"
With conf.fields                       ' set delivery options
    .item(prefix & "sendusing")        = cdoSendUsingPort
    .item(prefix & "smtpserver")       = mailservername
    .item(prefix & "smtpauthenticate") = cdoAnonymous
.update                                ' commit changes
End With
on error resume next        ' do not stop on errors
msg.send                    ' deliver the message
on error goto 0             ' restore normal error handling
```

```
if err then                    ' if something went wrong...
    MsgBox "Error sending message"
else
    if nfiles = 1 then plural = "" else plural = "s"
    MsgBox "Sent " & nfiles & " file" & plural & " to " & recipient
end if
```

Note

The files named on the command line used to run this script must fully specify the drive letter and path to the file, otherwise the CDO object is likely to issue the cryptic error message, **The specified protocol is unknown.** When you drag one or more files onto the script's shortcut, Windows does pass the full path and filename. You encounter this peculiarity only if you run the script from the command line.

Learning More About Scripting

Useful scripting is at first a complex undertaking because you have to learn about programming *and* about Windows management scripting tools at the same time. It's far too much to cover in a single chapter of single book; I've just tried to give you a taste.

For more in-depth coverage of the command line, batch files, and scripting, check out Brian's book *Windows Vista Guide to Scripting, Automation, and Command Line Tools*, or its predecessor *Windows XP Under the Hood*, both published by Que, which have tutorials as well as a handy desk reference.

For a detailed reference to all VBScript statements, functions, objects, and constants, see the online or downloaded version of the VBScript Language Reference, which you can get at msdn.microsoft.com/scripting.

Finally, I've found that some of the Microsoft public newsgroups can be a great source of information for everyone from beginners to old hands. The newsgroups microsoft.public. scripting.vbscript and microsoft.public.scripting.wsh are particularly valuable. You can learn a lot by reading the discussions, and unlike most newsgroups I've tried, in these you have a reasonably good chance of getting a useful answer if you post a concise, realistic question. Although some of the conversation on these newsgroups concerns the use of VBScript in web server and web browser applications, most of the discussion is applicable to scripting as well.

Windows PowerShell

Microsoft has developed a new scripting environment called Windows PowerShell. It's meant not so much to replace Windows Script Host, but to provide a "next generation" framework for software developers to create new command-line and script-based management tools for Windows, applications, and services. And indeed, it has some very interesting capabilities. It's not included in any standard Windows or Windows Server installation, but is available as a free download from www.microsoft.com/downloads. It runs on Windows Vista, XP with Service Pack 2 (or later), and Windows Server 2003 SP1 and later. It also requires you to have installed Windows .NET Framework version 2.0 or later.

Windows PowerShell is not your father's scripting language. To quote Bruce Payette, one of PowerShell's developers and the author of *Windows PowerShell in Action* (Manning Press, 2007), "We are developing a new class of object-based languages. And we've been told more than a few times that we were crazy."

So there you have it: it's a programming language designed by crazy people.

Its syntax, structure, and programming techniques are quite unlike anything you're likely to be familiar with—it definitely requires some patience and detailed tutorials to get the hang of it. I don't have room in this book to do this, but I can give you enough an idea of its flavor to perhaps pique your interest, and can point you toward resources that can get you on your way to PowerShell expertise.

PowerShell Concepts

To give you an idea of what Windows PowerShell is about—and let's call it WPS from here on—WPS prompts for and processes command lines just as `cmd.exe` does. You can type in commands such as `cd` (change directory) and `dir` (list the contents of the current directory), just as in `cmd.exe`. However, each PowerShell command line is actually being interpreted as a step of a program, like a line in a Windows Script Host script. You can thus set and modify variables, and call functions and procedures that perform complex tasks. You can develop and test bits of WPS scripts interactively, line by line, experimenting as you go, and moving bits of tested code into a script file as you've gotten them to work correctly.

The WPS programming language looks and works a lot like other programming languages, perhaps a bit like C or Java. One programming language is pretty much like any other on that score, so suffice it to say that WPS has all the mechanisms that you expect, including variables, if-then-else and looping structures, subroutines and functions, and so on.

In addition to running GUI and standard command-line programs such as Notepad and ping, WPS has over a hundred additional built-in commands called "cmdlets," small bits of Microsoft .NET programming code built into WPS that are executed when you type their names. Each cmdlet can be given arguments, like the command-line programs you're used to. The flags or switches that specify options to WPS commands tend to be longer and spelled out. A WPS command might look like this:

```
Get-ChildItem c:\windows\*.* | Sort-Object length -descending
```

Cmdlets draw on the .NET programming interface, and they have standard input and standard output streams like console programs, so that the output of one cmdlet can be piped to the input of another. This sounds very familiar, right? No! Here is where things take a left turn: When a WPS pipeline connects one cmdlet to another, instead of text flowing from one program to the next, WPS passes *objects* (specifically, .NET objects). WPS cmdlets generate, manipulate, filter, and describe objects, which themselves represent files, folders, network connections, devices, and so on—and many of the cmdlets work on objects in a generic way without even knowing what the objects represent. Text is generated only when a stream of objects reaches the console window.

This isn't just a very unusual programming mechanism. It's downright peculiar. However, after you wrap your mind around it, it becomes *very* powerful. Here is an example. The `get-process` cmdlet generates a stream of objects that represent the programs, services, and other tasks running on your computer. Issued alone on a command line like this:

```
get-process
```

it generates a nice listing of processes, like this:

Handles	NPM(K)	PM(K)	WS(K)	VM(M)	CPU(s)	Id	ProcessName
105	3	11144	7156	45		1060	audiodg
439	5	1588	1716	87		444	csrss
228	5	2948	4904	57		496	csrss
89	3	1392	688	36	0.36	3544	dwm
814	33	40912	21568	194	48.89	3580	explorer
0	0	0	16	0		0	Idle
590	11	3124	744	48		588	lsass
…							

Windows PowerShell knows that for human-readable output, it should display a table of important properties for each of the objects—process objects in this case—that reach the command window. However, you can just as easily instruct WPS to pass each of these objects to another cmdlet, where they can be manipulated in some way. For example, the `get-member` cmdlet displays a list of the properties and methods for a given stream of objects it receives, so the WPS command line

```
get-process | get-member
```

doesn't display a list of processes, but a list of the properties and methods that are available for the "process" object:

```
TypeName: System.Diagnostics.Process
```

Name	MemberType	Definition
Handles	AliasProperty	Handles = Handlecount
Name	AliasProperty	Name = ProcessName
…		
Close	Method	System.Void Close()
CloseMainWindow	Method	System.Boolean CloseMainWindow()
…		
BasePriority	Property	System.Int32 BasePriority {get;}
ExitCode	Property	System.Int32 ExitCode {get;}
…		

This cmdlet pipeline lists all processes, and then selects and displays only those that have accumulated more than 10 total minutes of CPU time:

```
get-process | where-object { $_.cpu -gt 10*60}
```

What's interesting, and powerful, is that the `where-object` doesn't know anything about process object specifically—it just passes through any object that has a property named `cpu` whose value is greater than 600.

Other cmdlets let you call object methods and change object properties, so you could use Windows PowerShell to view, interact with, and manage all the intricate details of Windows processes, or just as easily, files, folders, Registry settings, network settings, device settings; in fact, just about any component of Windows. You can add your own cmdlets to manage any other object that the .NET framework can create or use.

And we haven't even gotten to variables or other programming tools. PowerShell comes with over 100 built-in cmdlets that represent a wide range of programming constructs such as strings and text files, and Windows management objects and properties such files, folders, processes, and more.

Downloading and Installing Windows PowerShell

To obtain and install Windows PowerShell, follow these steps:

1. Check to see whether your computer has Microsoft's .NET Framework version 2.0 or later installed. Windows Vista has it by default, but on XP you need to check the Add and Remove Programs control panel to see whether it's present. If not, use Windows Update to get it, or visit www.microsoft.com/downloads.

2. Browse to www.microsoft.com/downloads. Search for Windows PowerShell. Select the appropriate download package for your computer and version of Windows. There are packages for x86 and x64 processors, and for Vista, XP, and Windows Server 2003. Download and install the program.

3. Run Windows Update (or Microsoft Update, if that's what your version of Windows calls it) to get any available critical security fixes for .NET Framework and/or Windows PowerShell.

(At the time this was written, a Windows PowerShell 2.0 was in beta testing, and it includes a GUI-based script-editing environment was under development. This tool might be ready by the time you read this—it's worth checking to see if it is.)

When the program has been installed, your Start menu will have a new entry for Windows PowerShell. One menu item opens the Windows PowerShell command prompt window, and the others lead to some helpful introductory documents. You can use these documents and some of the other resources listed in the next section to begin your exploration.

Tip

At some point you will want to start writing your own WPS script files. By default, WPS runs only scripts that have been digitally signed. To let it run scripts that you develop yourself, you have to relax PowerShell's security policy a bit. One way to do this is to issue the command

```
set-executionpolicy remotesigned
```

This retains the requirement that scripts executed from remote network locations must be signed, but relaxes security enough to run scripts in files stored on your own computer. You must also specify the full pathname to any script you want to run; WPS does not run scripts in the current folder with no path specification. This is, again, for security reasons.

Learning More About Windows PowerShell

The number of web and print resources for Windows PowerShell is smaller than that for Windows Script Host, but it's growing. Here are some places to start looking for introductions, tips, and examples:

- Usenet newsgroup microsoft.public.windows.powershell

- The Microsoft WPS team blog at http://blogs.msdn.com/powershell

- Samples and Tutorials: www.microsoft.com/technet/scriptcenter/hubs/msh.mspx
www.microsoft.com/technet/scriptcenter/topics/winpsh/convert/default.mspx

- Books: *Windows PowerShell Unleashed*, Tyson Kopczynski, Sams (2007)
Windows PowerShell in Action, Bruce Payette, Manning Press (2007)
Windows PowerShell: The Definitive Guide, Lee Holmes, O'Reilly (2007)

Windows File Systems

The file system is the structure used by the OS to name, store, organize, secure, and of course locate files on the various storage devices that can be connected to a computer. The primary goal of a file system is to allow the efficient storage and retrieval of data in the form of files, to control access to those files, as well as to keep them safe and secure. Good file systems store not only the file itself, but also *metadata* for the file. Metadata literally translates as "data about data," and is used by the file system to help categorize, organize, control, manipulate, secure, and protect the files. Simple examples of file metadata include the date and timestamp that a file was created, file attributes, pointers to the location of the file on the media, and more. More sophisticated file systems such as NTFS store additional metadata, giving greater control and integrity to the files. This chapter covers the various file systems and related structures that are used by Windows to manage drives, volumes, directories (folders), and files.

Disks, Partitions, and Volumes

In order to understand the structures and concepts in this chapter, some basic terminology must be defined and understood.

The file system is part of a hierarchical storage system, which means that the system has successive nested levels or layers. Physically it begins with a disk drive, such as a hard disk. A physical hard disk drive is divided into one or more *partitions*, which are physical areas of the disk. Windows normally uses two types of partitions, called *primary* and *extended*. Primary partitions are assigned drive letters directly by the operating system, and after they are formatted are also called *volumes*, and volumes are also called *logical drives*. Think of the partition as the raw physical space on the disk used by the volume, and think of a volume as the space after it is formatted with a file system, after which it appears to the OS as a drive letter. Extended partitions can contain one or more logical drives or volumes. Each volume must be *formatted* before it can be used, a process that writes the file system to the volume. The file system then manages the directories (also called folders) and files stored on the volume.

Basic Disks and Volumes

A disk set up with the standard system of using primary and extended partitions is referred to as a *basic disk*, and the volumes on a basic disk are also called *basic volumes*. Basic disks and volumes are accessible by virtually all operating systems, and represent the default setup used on most drives.

Basic disks can have up to four primary partitions, or up to three primary and one extended partitions. Each primary partition is a basic volume, and the extended partition can contain an unlimited number of logical drives, which are also basic volumes. Each basic volume must use contiguous physical space on the disk, and can be extended in size only if there is unallocated (nonpartitioned) space immediately following the end of the volume. Aftermarket utilities can be used to extend a volume if there is available space before the volume as well.

Dynamic Disks and Volumes

Many Windows 2000 and later versions can create and use a special partitioning scheme called a *dynamic disk*, which contains *dynamic volumes*. Dynamic disks use a special hidden database in the last megabyte of the disk to manage information about the dynamic volumes on the disk, as well as any other dynamic volumes on other dynamic disks in the system. Once a new dynamic disk is created or imported into a system, the hidden database for the new disk is added to the database on all dynamic disks in the system. Because each dynamic disk contains the same database, if the database on one is corrupted, Windows can rebuild it from the database on any of the other dynamic disks.

Dynamic volumes support several features not possible with basic volumes, such as

- A dynamic volume can be extended to include non-contiguous unallocated space on a single drive.
- A dynamic volume can be extended to span multiple (up to 32) drives.
- A dynamic volume can be striped (written distributively across multiple drives) for greater performance.

Windows 2000 and later Server editions also support these additional features:

- A dynamic volume can be mirrored (identical data written to two drives) for fault tolerance.
- A dynamic volume can be RAID-5, which divides the volume among three or more physical drives and stripes data and error correcting (parity) information for performance and fault tolerance.

There are unfortunately many limitations to the use of dynamic disks and volumes:

- Dynamic disks and volumes are supported only by Windows 2000, XP Professional, and Vista Business, Enterprise, and Ultimate editions.
- Dynamic disks and volumes are *not* supported by Windows XP Home, Vista Home Basic, or Vista Home Premium, nor are they supported by NT 4.0, Me/9x, or earlier versions.
- Portable (that is, laptop) systems do not support dynamic disks, even on internal drives.
- All volumes on a physical disk must be either basic or dynamic.

- Spanned dynamic volumes cannot be striped.
- Striped dynamic volumes cannot be extended or spanned.
- Removable media disks (floppy, optical, SuperDisk, Jazz, Zip) cannot be dynamic.
- USB or FireWire disks cannot be dynamic.
- Mirrored or RAID-5 dynamic volumes are internally disabled in non-Server versions of Windows 2000 and later, however some unauthorized patches are available (search for "XP RAID") to enable the hidden RAID functionality.

Because of the features, differences, and limitations of working with dynamic disks and volumes, they are mostly suited for server systems and not standard desktop or laptop PCs. As such, all further discussion of disks and volumes in this chapter will be about standard basic disks and volumes.

Creating Partitions

Partitioning a hard disk is the act of defining areas of the physical disk for an operating system to use as a logical volume. A volume is a formatted area of storage that has a drive letter assigned to it.

When you partition a disk for the first time, the partitioning software writes a master partition boot sector at cylinder 0, head 0, sector 1—the first sector on the hard disk. This sector contains data that describes the partitions by their starting and ending cylinder, head, and sector locations. When a system starts up, the motherboard ROM BIOS reads the partition table to determine which of the primary partitions is *active* (bootable) and, therefore, where to look for an operating system to load.

The standard disk partitioning tools provided in Windows vary according to the Windows version. Windows 9x/Me and earlier include the FDISK program, while the Windows NT family (2000/XP and Vista) includes both the DISKPART program and the much easier to use Disk Management tool (called Disk Administrator in Windows NT). The FDISK program is a text-based menu-driven utility that is run from a command prompt, while DISKPART is a text-based command-line utility (not menu driven), and Disk Management is a tool that runs under the Windows graphical user interface (GUI) environment. In most cases you would use FDISK if partitioning under Windows 9x/Me or earlier, or the Disk Management tool if partitioning under Windows NT/2000/XP or Vista. The command-driven DISKPART utility is somewhat difficult to use interactively because it is entirely command driven; however, it is very useful if you want to write scripts that automate its operation.

No matter which tool you use, the primary and extended partitions are created the same way, and as such are compatible across OS boundaries. For example, I can use the Disk Management tool in Windows XP to partition a drive that will later be installed in a system running Windows 98. Likewise, I can use the FDISK tool from Windows 98 to partition a drive that will later be installed on a system running Vista.

The partitioning rules for a single drive are as follows:

- There can be up to four total partitions on a drive.
- There are two main types of partitions, primary and extended.

- There can be only one extended partition on a drive.
- A primary partition, when formatted, is a single volume (drive letter).
- An extended partition is not formatted as a volume, but instead may contain one or more logical drives, each of which when formatted is a volume (drive letter).
- Only primary partitions can be marked active (bootable).
- Only one primary partition on a drive can be *active* at any given time.

If you combine these rules, you see that a single drive can have up to four primary partitions (with no extended partition), or up to three primary partitions along with a single extended partition. It is also possible to create only an extended partition containing one or more logical drives, but because only primary partitions can be bootable, that would not be suitable for a hard disk on which you want to load a bootable OS.

The limit of four partitions per drive dates all the way back to March 1983, when IBM and Microsoft released DOS 2.0 along with a ROM BIOS designed to boot from a hard disk. Together the updated BIOS and DOS defined the structure of the Master Boot Record (MBR), which contained a partition table with entries for up to four partitions. Originally this limited a single drive to supporting up to only four volumes (drive letters). But in 1987, IBM and Microsoft released DOS 3.3, which first included the extended partition with logical drives. Think of the logical drives as sub-partitions inside a single extended partition, thus allowing a single drive to be divided into more than four volumes. Using an extended partition, the number of total volumes on a drive is technically limited only by the size of the drive, but the OS can only handle up to a total of 24 drive letters (C: through Z:) at a time. In addition to the standard partitioning tools, the Windows SETUP program in Windows 95 and later can also partition (and format) drives during the start of the Windows installation process. In other words, you don't have to partition and format volumes in advance; if the drive is blank, you will be prompted at the start of the Windows installation process to partition and format the drive.

Note

Because FDISK, DISKPART, SETUP, and the Disk Management tool all depend on the BIOS setup information about the hard disk to determine the size and drive geometry of the hard disk, having correct drive settings saved in the BIOS setup is vital to the correct operation of these programs. If a 100GB hard drive is defined in the BIOS as a 100MB hard drive, for example, all these programs will see is 100MB. Fortunately most BIOS setup programs feature auto-detect capabilities that automatically identify drives properly. However, problems can arise if somebody uses manual settings and enters them incorrectly.

Don't get hung up on the fact that FDISK calls partitions primary or extended "DOS" partitions or logical "DOS" drives. This is true even though the operating system you are running or installing is a version of Windows. Primary partitions, extended partitions, and logical drives are essentially the same no matter what tool you use or OS you are running.

However, it is also true that older versions of Windows may be limited in the size of partitions that are supported as well as the different types of file systems supported on those partitions. For example, the original release of Windows 95 and all MS-DOS versions 6.x and earlier support only the FAT16 file system, which allows a single volume size of no more than 2GiB. Thus, a 20GiB hard disk prepared with the original Windows 95 (called 95a) or MS-DOS 6.x and earlier must have a minimum of 10 volumes (drive letters) to allocate all the space on the drive. Fortunately Windows 95B and later versions support single volumes of up to 2TiB or more, which is larger than any currently available drive, meaning that separating a single drive into multiple partitions is more of an option or personal preference instead of a necessity.

Even though you can partition and format even the largest drives as a single volume today, many people prefer to divide their drives into multiple volumes for organizational or data security reasons. For example, many people suggest a two-volume partitioning scheme that looks like this:

> C: for the operating system and applications
>
> D: for user data only

In this example, you could create two primary partitions or a primary partition along with an extended partition containing a single logical drive.

This two-volume arrangement makes backing up the data easier; just set the backup program to back up all of D:.

If a catastrophic failure in the file system wipes out or corrupts the C: volume, drive D:—which contains the data—may still be intact. Note however that multiple volumes like this will not protect against hardware failures. Because both volumes are on the same physical drive, if the drive fails, files on both volumes will be lost.

Note

Although external USB and FireWire (IEEE 1394) drives normally come pre-partitioned and formatted as a single FAT32 volume to allow immediate use on the widest variety of systems, you can use FDISK, DISKPART, or the Disk Management tool to delete and re-create the partitioning and file systems used on external drives to suit your specific needs. If you are using Windows 2000 or later and have no need for cross-compatibility with older Windows or Mac systems, I recommend reformatting external drives with NTFS.

Assigning Drive Letters to Volumes

When assigning drive letters to volumes, Windows normally assigns drive letters to primary partitions before assigning drive letters to logical drives in extended partitions. Because of this, using extended partitions with logical drives can often result in confusion over drive letter assignments.

As an example, let's say we have a system with a single 75GiB primary master ATA drive (physical disk 0) that we want to partition into three equal-sized (25GiB) volumes, with the first one bootable. This can be done several different ways. One method would be to simply create three 25GiB primary partitions, with the first one set active (bootable). Another would be to create a single 25GiB primary partition (set active) along with a 50GiB extended partition, and then further divide the extended partition into two 25GiB logical drives. Using three primary partitions, Windows would assign default drive letters as in Table 10.1.

Table 10.1   Drive Letter Allocations by Drive, Partition Order, and Type

Physical Disk	Partition Order	Partition Type	Drive Letter
0	1st	Primary (active)	C:
0	2nd	Primary	D:
0	3rd	Primary	E:

Using one primary partition plus an extended partition with two logical drives, Windows would assign default drive letters as in Table 10.2.

Table 10.2   Drive Letter Allocations by Drive, Partition Order, and Type

Physical Disk	Partition Order	Partition Type	Drive Letter
0	1st	Primary (active)	C:
0	2nd	Extended/1st logical drive	D:
0	2nd	Extended/2nd logical drive	E:

So far these different partitioning methods produce pretty much the same results as far as drive letters being assigned to physical parts of the disk. However if we add another drive to the system, the default drive letter assignments for volumes on the new drive will vary. As an example, let's add a second physical drive to the system (ATA Primary Slave, physical disk 1) and create a single primary partition on it. What drive letter will the new partition on the new drive assume? That depends on how your first drive was partitioned. If disk 0 was partitioned using three primary partitions, the default drive letter assignments would be as in Table 10.3.

Table 10.3   Drive Letter Allocations by Drive, Partition Order, and Type

Physical Disk	Partition Order	Partition Type	Drive Letter
0	1st	Primary (active)	C:
0	2nd	Primary	D:
0	3rd	Primary	E:
1	1st	Primary	F:

That seems perfectly normal; the partition on the new drive is assigned the next available letter F:. However if disk 0 had been partitioned using a primary partition plus an extended partition with logical drives, the default drive letter assignments would be as in Table 10.4.

Table 10.4   Drive Letter Allocations by Drive, Partition Order, and Type

Physical Disk	Partition Order	Partition Type	Drive Letter
0	1st	Primary (active)	C:
0	2nd	Extended/1st logical drive	E:
0	2nd	Extended/2nd logical drive	F:
1	1st	Primary	D:

This can be really confusing, as the primary partition on the new drive would be assigned as D:, and the existing logical drives in the extended partition on the first drive would change from D: to E: and from E: to F:. This not only confuses many users, but it can also confuse any previously installed applications as well. Fortunately Windows NT/2000/XP and Vista can easily change drive letter assignments for all except the boot volume using the Disk Management tool, but unfortunately such drive letter changes are not possible for Windows 9x/Me or earlier. If the second drive also has an extended partition with logical drives, it can get even more confusing, as shown in Table 10.5.

Table 10.5   Drive Letter Allocations by Drive, Partition Order, and Type

Physical Disk	Partition Order	Partition Type	Drive Letter
0	1st	Primary (active)	C:
0	2nd	Extended/1st logical drive	E:
0	2nd	Extended/2nd logical drive	F:
1	1st	Primary	D:
1	2nd	Extended/1st logical drive	G:
1	2nd	Extended/2nd logical drive	H:

The basic rule is that all primary partitions on any internal (ATA, SATA, or SCSI) drives are assigned letters before any logical drives in extended partitions on those same drives. To keep things simple as far as future drive assignments no matter what version of Windows you are using, I recommend creating only primary partitions on all drives, which will limit you to a maximum of four volumes per drive.

If you set up both drives using only primary partitions, the default drive assignments would be as shown in Table 10.6.

Table 10.6   Drive Letter Allocations by Drive, Partition Order, and Type

Physical Disk	Partition Order	Partition Type	Drive Letter
0	1st	Primary (active)	C:
0	2nd	Primary	D:
0	3rd	Primary	E:
1	1st	Primary	F:
1	2nd	Primary	G:
1	3rd	Primary	H:

This is obviously much simpler and more straightforward, and would be the recommended setup if you were using Windows NT/2000/XP or Vista. Unfortunately due to an artificially imposed limitation, such a setup is not possible with the FDISK program included with Windows 9x/Me or earlier.

Another alternative that is possible using the standard FDISK program is to create a single extended partition only on all drives except the first drive, and then divide the partition into one or more logical drives. For example, let's take the second physical drive (physical disk 1) in the previous example and set it up as a single extended partition with three logical drives. In that case, the drive letters for the new volumes would always be F:, G:, and H:, as shown in Table 10.7.

Table 10.7   Drive Letter Allocations by Drive, Partition Order, and Type

Physical Disk	Partition	Type	Drive Letter
0	1st	Primary (active)	C:
0	2nd	Extended/1st logical drive	D:
0	2nd	Extended/2nd logical drive	E:
1	1st	Extended/1st logical drive	F:
1	1st	Extended/2nd logical drive	G:
1	1st	Extended/3rd logical drive	H:

This would be true no matter whether the first drive was partitioned as three primary partitions or as a single primary and an extended with two logical drives. Also, in either case, the drive letter assignments would remain the same both before and after the second drive was added.

Tip

When partitioning a drive, I recommend creating only primary partitions, and avoid using extended partitions with logical volumes entirely. Primary partitions are defined solely by their entry in the MBR, whereas the entries defining logical volumes in extended partitions are stored in extended boot records that are scattered throughout the drive and linked together by a chain of pointers. Should one sector or entry in this chain be damaged or broken, you lose access to all the volumes after the broken link. In addition, many operating systems assign primary partitions drive letters before they assign letters to logical volumes in extended partitions, resulting in unexpected non sequential letter assignments. Using primary partitions exclusively keeps the disk structure much simpler, less confusing, easier to manage, and perhaps most importantly, much easier to recover in case of a disaster.

My personal preference is to keep things as simple as possible by avoiding extended partitions entirely, and instead create only primary partitions on all drives. This does limit the total number of volumes on a single drive to four or fewer, but I would rarely need to divide a single drive into five or more volumes anyway. The only problem with this recommendation is that if you are using Windows 9x/Me or earlier, the standard FDISK program included with those operating systems is artificially limited to create only a single primary partition on a drive. This means that if you want to divide a drive into two or more volumes, you are forced to use an extended partition with one or more logical drives. Fortunately this limitation is only in the FDISK program, and not in the actual operating systems. Windows 9x/Me and even DOS will support up to four primary partitions on a single drive, if you use a utility program other than the standard FDISK to create them.

Because the DISKPART utility and Disk Management tool included with Windows NT/2000/XP or Vista are not limited to creating only one primary partition per drive, you could temporarily boot those operating systems from a CD or a set of startup floppies in order to use DISKPART to partition a drive, or you could temporarily connect a drive to a system currently running Windows NT/2000/XP or Vista in order to partition it. But probably the easiest solution would be to simply use a third-party partitioning program to partition the drive as you like. One program I recommend as a replacement for FDISK is the Free FDISK program (the official FDISK of the FreeDOS Project), which is available from (www.freedos.org). Free FDISK can be copied to a Windows 9x/Me startup floppy in place of the standard FDISK program and will allow you to create up to four primary partitions on a single drive with no artificial limitations.

Running FDISK

If you run the Windows 95B (Win95 OSR 2.x) or later (Windows 9x/Me) version of FDISK with a hard drive greater than 512MB, FDISK offers to enable large disk support by prompting you with the following question:

```
Your computer has a disk larger than 512MB. This version of Windows
includes improved support for large disks, resulting in more efficient
use of disk space on large drives, and allowing disks over 2GB to be
formatted as a single drive.

IMPORTANT: If you enable large disk support and create any new drives on this
disk, you will not be able to access the new drive(s) using other operating
systems, including some versions of Windows 95 and Windows NT, as well as
earlier versions of Windows and MS-DOS. In addition, disk utilities that
were not designed explicitly for the FAT32 file system will not be able
to work with this disk. If you need to access this disk with other operating
systems or older disk utilities, do not enable large drive support.

Do you wish to enable large disk support (Y/N)...........? [Y]
```

If you answer Yes to this question, FDISK creates FAT32 volumes for all volumes larger than 512MiB. Answering No to this question forces FDISK to create only FAT16 volumes. Choosing to enable large disk (meaning FAT32) support provides several benefits:

- You can use a large hard disk (greater than 2GiB) as a single drive letter. In fact, your drive can be as large as 2TiB and still be identified by a single drive letter. This is because of the FAT32 file system, which allows for many more files per drive than FAT16.

- Because of the more efficient storage methods of FAT32, your files will use less hard disk space overall.

However, keep in mind that FAT32 volumes will be recognized only by operating systems with FAT32 support (Windows 95B or later, but not including Windows NT). If booting old MS-DOS games or applications via an MS-DOS 6.x or earlier startup floppy or CD, you won't be able to access a FAT32 hard disk volume unless you replace the MS-DOS 6.x or earlier version on the disk with the MS-DOS 7 or later versions included with Windows 95B or 98. This normally can be done by using the SYS A: command from the \Windows\Command folder. Another option is to use the Windows Startup menu in Win95B or Win98 (press F8 as Windows starts to load) and select

Command Prompt to get to a FAT32-capable DOS. On the other hand, you can select Start, Shutdown, Restart the Computer in MS-DOS Mode from the Windows desktop.

After answering the large disk support question, FDISK shows a menu similar to the following:

```
Current fixed disk drive: 1

    Choose one of the following:

    1. Create DOS partition or Logical DOS Drive
    2. Set active partition
    3. Delete partition or Logical DOS Drive
    4. Display partition information
    5. Change current fixed disk drive

    Enter choice: [1]
```

Option 5 is shown only if FDISK detects more than one drive on your system (if more than one is entered via your BIOS setup). In that case, FDISK defaults to the first drive, and via option 5 you can cause FDISK to work with any of the other hard disks on the system.

To create partitions or logical drives in extended partitions, select option 1. You can use option 4 to display the current partition layout of the drive.

After selecting option 1, the menu changes to enable you to create primary or extended partitions on a drive as follows:

```
Create DOS Partition or Logical DOS Drive

    Current fixed disk drive: 1

    Choose one of the following:

    1. Create Primary DOS Partition
    2. Create Extended DOS Partition
    3. Create Logical DOS Drive(s) in the Extended DOS Partition

    Enter choice: [1]
```

FDISK forces you to create a primary partition first on the boot drive, but on a secondary or non-boot drive, you can create only an extended partition if you choose. So, if you are partitioning the first drive in a system and it will be bootable, you would choose option 1.

At this point, you are prompted to decide whether you want to use the maximum available size for a primary DOS partition. If you say yes and you've enabled large disk support (FAT32), the primary partition will use the entire drive. Conversely, if you say yes and you did not enable large drive support (meaning you are using FAT16), the partition uses the entire drive or up to 2GiB of the drive, whichever is smaller.

Normally, I recommend making the primary partition the full size of the drive, keeping the entire drive as one letter. But there are various reasons you might want to split the drive into multiple partitions, such as for different operating systems, different file systems, applications, and so on.

However, if you decide to create a primary partition that is not the full drive, once that is done, you should then go back through the menus and create an extended partition using the rest of the drive, and then further divide it into logical drives. Or better yet, if you are using the Free FDISK program I mentioned earlier, you do not have to create an extended partition with logical drives, and instead you can simply create additional primary partitions to use the remaining space, up to a total of four per drive.

After all the partitions are created, the final operation is to make one of them active (bootable), which is option 2 from the main FDISK menu. Only primary partitions can be active. After that is done, all FDISK operations are complete, and you can exit the program.

When exiting FDISK after making partition changes, the system must be rebooted before these changes will be recognized. After rebooting, you must then format each of the volumes with the operating system FORMAT command, which creates the file system that allows the operating system to mange files on the volumes.

The C: volume usually must be formatted with the system files, although when you install Windows via the Windows Setup command, it detects whether the system files are present, and if not will install them for you.

Drive Partitioning and Formatting with Disk Management

Even though Windows 2000/XP and Vista have a very powerful command-line tool called DISKPART that can be used to partition and provides some FDISK-like capabilities, along with additional options useful for working with advanced disk structures such as RAID arrays and dynamic disks, most people should utilize the GUI-based Disk Management tool to perform hard disk partitioning and formatting when installing a new hard disk on an existing system.

Unfortunately DISKPART is a command-line program that is not really designed to be used interactively. It is definitely not a user-oriented tool, and has very little in the way of safety precautions to prevent one from setting up a disk improperly, or from destroying existing data on a disk. As such, it is highly recommended under Windows NT/2000/XP or Vista to use the Disk Management (also called Disk Administrator) tool instead.

Note

Note that DISKPART.exe is automatically installed in Windows XP and Vista as part of the base OS installation. It is not automatically installed with Windows 2000; however, DISKPART is included in the Windows 2000 Windows Recovery Console, which is on the Windows 2000 install CD. The Windows 2000 Recovery Console can also be installed to the hard drive, if desired, using the information in the following article:

Description of the Windows 2000 Recovery Console

http://support.microsoft.com/kb/229716

But perhaps the easiest way to get DISKPART for Windows 2000 is to simply download it for free from Microsoft. The following article contains links to download the Windows 2000 Resource kit tools (including DISKPART):

http://support.microsoft.com/kb/927229

The following list shows the major differences between FDISK and the Disk Management tool:

- **Disk Management is a true GUI-based utility**—Color-coded indicators for partition type and drive condition let you easily see which tasks you've performed with a drive. Wizards enable you to both partition and format a drive under the guidance of the tool.

- **Disk Management supports more file systems than FDISK**—Whereas FDISK is limited to FAT16 or FAT32, Disk Management also supports NTFS.

- **Disk Management partitions and formats hard disks with a simple process**—Unlike FDISK, which requires you to restart the system before a new volume can be formatted and uses a separate FORMAT program to finish the job, Disk Management can perform both tasks without the need to restart the computer.

- **Disk Management uses drive letters not already in use for hard disk or optical drives, regardless of the partition type**—Unlike FDISK, which can scramble existing drive letter assignments if you prepare a new hard disk with a primary partition, Disk Management assigns a drive letter to the new hard drive that follows those already in use. And, if installing a new drive causes conflicts with removable-media drives such as USB keychain or flash memory card readers you use occasionally, you can use Disk Management to select a different drive letter for the new hard disk or for existing hard disks or optical drives.

The Disk Management tool in Windows Vista has been further improved by the addition of capability to both expand and shrink existing partitions while preserving the contents. This can eliminate the need for third-party partitioning programs: Resizing partitions was perhaps the main reason to use after market tools in Windows XP and previous versions. Unfortunately the shrink feature is limited in many ways, and often fails to allow a shrink because of immovable system files or other problems.

To use Disk Management to partition a new hard disk

1. Open the Start menu, right-click [My] Computer, and select Manage from the context menu.

2. From the Computer Management screen, click Disk Management in the left window. The current hard disk drive letter is displayed in the upper-right window, and physical hard disks are displayed in the bottom-right window (see Figure 10.1). A newly installed drive is shown as unallocated space.

3. Select the new hard disk, right-click it, and select New Partition from the right-click menu to start the partitioning process.

4. Click Next at the opening screen of the New Partition Wizard.

5. Select Primary or Extended partition. Generally, you should choose an extended partition unless you want to create a primary partition that you can use to start the computer. Click Next to continue.

6. If you want to leave part of the hard disk unallocated, change the partition size. Otherwise, click Next to continue.

7. The New Partition Wizard displays the changes it's about to make to the new drive (see Figure 10.2). Click Finish to complete the partitioning process.

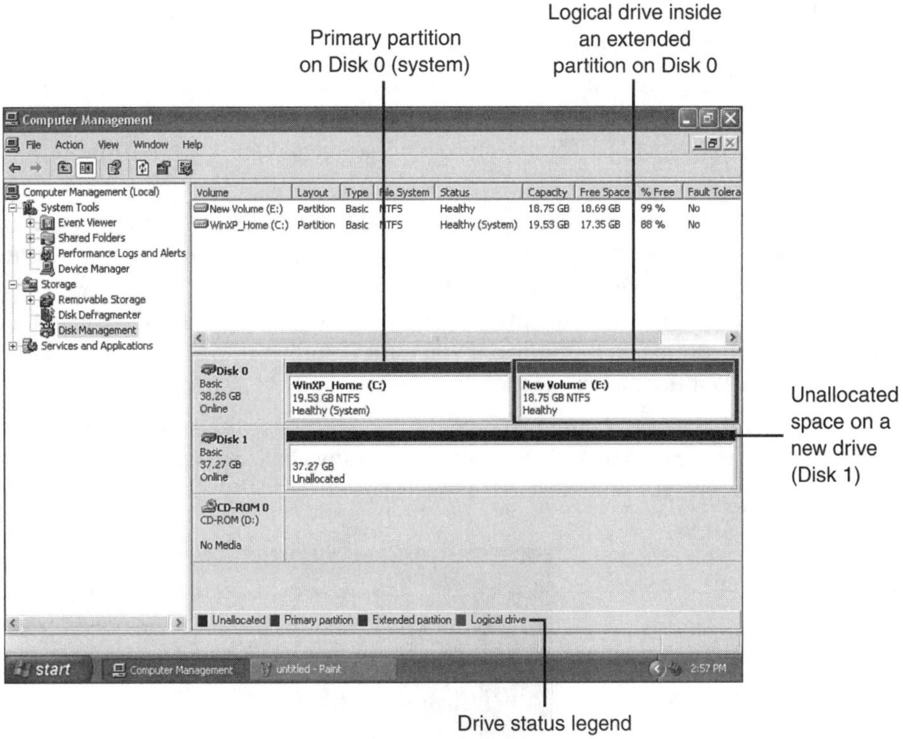

Primary partition
on Disk 0 (system)

Logical drive inside
an extended
partition on Disk 0

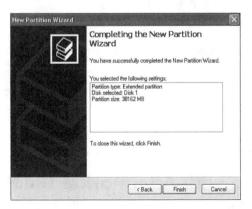

Unallocated
space on a
new drive
(Disk 1)

Drive status legend

Figure 10.1 The Computer Management view of a system with a newly installed hard disk (Disk 1). Because New Volume (E:) was prepared after the CD-ROM drive (D:) was installed, it has a higher drive letter.

Figure 10.2 The New Partition Wizard prepares to create an extended partition from Disk 1.

8. After the wizard finishes, the Computer Management view displays the newly partitioned hard disk as free space. Right-click the partition, and select New Logical Drive to continue.

9. Click Next to continue with the wizard. Click Next again to select a logical drive.

10. To create more than one logical drive, change the maximum size of the partition size. To create a single logical drive, click Next.

11. Select the drive letter to assign. By default, the next available drive letter is displayed, but you can choose any unused drive letter. If you prefer, you can mount the new logical drive into an empty NTFS folder, or even not assign a drive letter or path. Click Next to continue.

12. Select the format options. By default, the new logical drive is formatted with NTFS, but you can choose FAT32 if the logical drive is 34.36GB (32GiB) or less. If the logical drive is larger than 32GiB, Windows can only format the drive using NTFS. You can also specify the volume label, select a particular allocation unit (cluster) size, enable file/folder compression, and perform a quick format. If you want to format the drive later, select Do Not Format This Partition. Click Next to continue.

13. Again, the New Partition Wizard displays a list of changes to be made. Click Back to return to a particular menu if you need to make any changes, or click Finish to format the logical drive with the options selected (see Figure 10.3).

Figure 10.3 The New Partition Wizard prepares to format a logical drive on Disk 1 with the options shown.

14. Repeat steps 10–14 if you didn't use all the free space as a logical drive and want to prepare additional logical drives.

No rebooting is necessary, and the color-coded legend at the bottom of the Disk Management display helps you track the status of the disk preparation process.

Drive Partitioning with Aftermarket Utilities

Often there are excellent free programs that are available to get around the limitations in the existing standard utilities. For example, previously in this chapter I recommended the Free FDISK program available from (www.freedos.org) because it can create multiple primary partitions on a single drive. This is useful because the standard FDISK is limited to creating only a single primary partition, forcing the use of an extended partition with logical drives in order to create multiple volumes on a single physical drive.

One might think that the Disk Management tool included with Windows NT/2000/XP and Vista would be free from artificial limitations, but unfortunately that is not the case. One major limitation with Disk Management is the artificially imposed inability to format a FAT32 volume larger than 32GiB. For example, if you have a 100GiB external USB drive that you would like to share between systems running Windows 9x/Me and/or Apple Macintosh systems as well as systems running Windows 2000/XP or Vista, using FAT32 would allow the drive to be both read and written by *all* of those systems. Unfortunately the Disk Management tool (as well as DISKPART and FORMAT) will only allow you to format a volume larger than 32GiB as NTFS, which will render it unreadable by most systems except those running Windows NT/2000/XP or Vista. One solution would be to connect the drive to a Windows 9x/Me system where you could use the standard FDISK and FORMAT programs there to format the entire drive (up to 2TiB) as FAT32. However if you don't have access to such a system, or don't want to try to create a bootable floppy or CD with USB support, I recommend using the free SwissKnife utility, which can be downloaded from CompuApps (www.compuapps.com). The SwissKnife utility is a graphical program that runs under all versions of Windows 95B and higher, and for example will allow you to partition and format a FAT32 volume more than 32GiB on Windows NT/2000/XP or Vista as well.

These free tools are useful for creating new partitions and volumes that the standard utilities cannot; however, there are even more powerful tools available commercially that can modify existing partitions. Alternative partitioning programs such as PartitionMagic by Symantec and Partition Commander by V-Com enable you to take an existing hard drive and perform the following changes to it without loss of data:

- Create, resize, split, move, and merge partitions on the fly without losing data.

- Convert between file systems without losing data—conversions include FAT16 to FAT32 and NTFS; FAT32 to FAT16; NTFS to FAT16 and FAT32; primary to logical and vice versa; and FAT32 to NTFS under Windows 2000/XP and Vista. It also includes support for Ext2 and Linux SWAP file systems.

- Move applications between partitions and automatically update the drive-letter references after partitioning with the DriveMapper utility.

- Undelete FAT16, FAT32, Linux Ext2, and NTFS partitions that have been deleted. You can restore partitions that have been deleted on disk as long as the space has not been reallocated or written over.

- Copy or move a partition to another partition or drive.

Note

I still recommend standard utilities such as FDISK, DISKPART, Disk Management, or Windows SETUP be used for initial partitioning and setup of most drives (these utilities destroy existing data), but these aftermarket utilities can be very useful for reconfiguring a system that is already partitioned.

Before doing any modifications to a partition containing important data, a backup is highly recommended as insurance.

High-Level (Operating System) Formatting

As you learned in the previous section, Windows 2000/XP and Vista can automatically perform high-level formatting with the New Partition Wizard as part of the Disk Management tool. When using FDISK or DISKPART, a separate FORMAT utility must be used to format the volume once it is partitioned. The operating system format is called a *high-level format* to distinguish it from physical or *low-level format* that is sometimes used to initialize drives before they are partitioned. The primary function of the high-level format is to create the NTFS or FAT file system structures on the disk so that the operating system can manage files. You must first partition a drive using FDISK, DISKPART, or Disk Management (or some third-party utility) before formatting a drive. Each volume (primary partition or logical drive in an extended partition) must be formatted before it can be used for data storage.

Usually, you perform the high-level format with the FORMAT.COM program or the formatting utility in Windows Explorer. FORMAT.COM uses the following syntax and optional parameters under Windows 2000/XP and Vista:

```
FORMAT volume [/FS:file-system] [/V:label] [/Q] [/A:size] [/C] [/X]
FORMAT volume [/V:label] [/Q] [/F:size]
FORMAT volume [/V:label] [/Q] [/T:tracks /N:sectors]
FORMAT volume [/V:label] [/Q]
FORMAT volume [/Q]
```

```
  volume          Specifies the drive letter (followed by a colon),
                  mount point, or volume name.
  /FS:filesystem  Specifies the type of the file system (FAT, FAT32, or NTFS).
  /V:label        Specifies the volume label.
  /Q              Performs a quick format.
  /C              NTFS only: Files created on the new volume will be compressed
                  by default.
  /X              Forces the volume to dismount first if necessary.  All opened
                  handles to the volume would no longer be valid.
  /A:size         Overrides the default allocation unit size. Default settings
                  are strongly recommended for general use.
                  NTFS supports 512, 1024, 2048, 4096, 8192, 16K, 32K, 64K.
                  FAT supports 512, 1024, 2048, 4096, 8192, 16K, 32K, 64K,
                  (128K, 256K for sector size > 512 bytes).
                  FAT32 supports 512, 1024, 2048, 4096, 8192, 16K, 32K, 64K,
                  (128K, 256K for sector size > 512 bytes).

                  Note that the FAT and FAT32 files systems impose the
                  following restrictions on the number of clusters on a volume:

                  FAT: Number of clusters <= 65526
                  FAT32: 65526 < Number of clusters < 4177918

                  Format will immediately stop processing if it decides that
                  the above requirements cannot be met using the specified
                  cluster size.

                  NTFS compression is not supported for allocation unit sizes
                  above 4096.
```

```
/F:size        Specifies the size of the floppy disk to format (1.44)
/T:tracks      Specifies the number of tracks per disk side.
/N:sectors     Specifies the number of sectors per track.
```

FORMAT.COM uses the following syntax with somewhat different optional parameters under Windows 9x/Me:

```
FORMAT drive: [/V[:label]] [/Q] [/F:size] [/B | /S] [/C]
FORMAT drive: [/V[:label]] [/Q] [/T:tracks /N:sectors] [/B | /S] [/C]
FORMAT drive: [/V[:label]] [/Q] [/1] [/4] [/B | /S] [/C]
FORMAT drive: [/Q] [/1] [/4] [/8] [/B | /S] [/C]
```

```
/V[:label]     Specifies the volume label.
/Q             Performs a quick format.
/F:size        Specifies the size of the floppy disk to format (such
               as 160, 180, 320, 360, 720, 1.2, 1.44, 2.88).
/B             Allocates space on the formatted disk for system files.
/S             Copies system files to the formatted disk.
/T:tracks      Specifies the number of tracks per disk side.
/N:sectors     Specifies the number of sectors per track.
/1             Formats a single side of a floppy disk.
/4             Formats a 5.25-inch 360K floppy disk in a high-density drive.
/8             Formats eight sectors per track.
/C             Tests clusters that are currently marked "bad."
```

Normally, the Windows FORMAT utility determines the cluster size used when you format the volume, based on the volume's size and the file system used. However, you can override the default using the /A:size parameter in the Windows NT/2000/XP/Vista FORMAT command, or a similar but undocumented switch /Z:size for the Windows 9x/Me FORMAT utility. Using the /A:size or /Z:size parameters, you can format the volume with cluster sizes that are larger or smaller than the defaults for the file system.

Caution

In general it is not recommended to override the default cluster sizes using the /A:size or /Z:size switches. Modifying the cluster size can increase or decrease the amount of slack on the partition, but it also can have a pronounced effect on the performance of the drive, and some disk utilities might not work with nonstandard cluster sizes.

Once a volume is formatted, the operating system can use the volume for storing and retrieving files.

During the high-level format, the program performs a defect scan. Defects marked by the drive manufacturer or low-level format (LLF) program as well as any newly unreadable sectors will show up during this scan as being unreadable tracks or sectors. When the high-level format encounters one of these areas, it automatically performs up to five retries to read these tracks or sectors. If the unreadable area was actually marked as such by the LLF, the read fails on all attempts.

After five retries, the FORMAT program gives up on this track or sector and moves to the next one. If an area remains unreadable after the initial read and five retries, it is marked in the FAT or MFT as a bad cluster.

Note

Because the high-level format doesn't overwrite data areas not actually used by the file system, in some cases it is possible to use programs such as Norton Utilities to unformat a hard disk that was accidentally formatted. Unformatting can be performed in some cases because the data from the drive's previous use might still be present.

File System Tool Limitations

The biggest problem with removing or creating a partition using a standard tool such as FDISK, DISKPART, or Disk Management is that the procedure is destructive. If you create a set of partitions but then change your mind about the disk structure, in most cases you must back up any data on those partitions, delete the partitions, and start over again. The standard tools have virtually no ability to move or change an existing partition while preserving data. That alone is cause for using these tools with care, but here are other limitations you should keep in mind:

- FDISK and DISKPART require a manual FORMAT before the volume is ready for use.

- FORMAT must normally check an entire volume for defects before writing the file system. Its defect management is rudimentary and can waste a lot of disk space with older drives that have disk errors.

- FDISK, DISKPART, and Disk Management offer no standard procedure for migrating data to a new drive.

- FDISK forces the use of extended partitions with logical drives when multiple volumes are desired, often causing confusion with drive letter assignments.

Although Disk Management in Windows NT/2000/XP and Vista does a significantly better job than FDISK, it's still a destructive process if you need to change your disk partitions, and there is no provision for migrating data. One exception is that the Disk Management tool in Vista has been enhanced with the capability to expand and shrink partitions while preserving data. This powerful new capability means that in many cases, after market utilities won't be needed for those tasks.

Many drive vendors offer some type of automatic disk installation software with their hard drives. These routines can make the task of disk installation and migration a fast, easy, and reliable operation.

Typical features of automatic disk installation programs include the following:

- **Replacement for FDISK/DISKPART and FORMAT**—A single program performs both functions more quickly than FDISK/DISKPART and FORMAT separately.

- **Database of drive jumpers for major brands and models**

- **Drive copy function**—Copies contents of an old drive to the new drive, retaining full OS and file system functionality.

- **CD-ROM drive letter relocation utility**—Moves existing CD/DVD drives to new drive letters (in order to make room for new hard drive letters) and resets the Windows Registry and INI file references to the new drive letters so that software works without reinstallation.

- Menu-driven or wizard-driven process for installing new hard drive
- Optional override of existing BIOS limitations for installation of large hard drives (>528MB, 8.4GB, 137GB, and so on)

Table 10.8 provides a basic overview of the most popular disk-installation programs. Most of these are available only in OEM versions that are included for free with drives sold retail. In some cases, the OEM versions can be downloaded from the drive manufacturer's website as well.

Table 10.8   Overview of Automatic Disk-Installation Programs

Vendor	Software	OEM	Retail
Ontrack	Disk Manager	Yes	Yes
Phoenix	DriveGuide	Yes	No
Western Digital	Data Lifeguard	Yes	No
Seagate	DiscWizard	Yes	No
Maxtor	MaxBlast	Yes	No

Note: Maxtor is owned by Seagate

Note that while many of these utilities can override BIOS limitations on older systems, normally I recommend upgrading the motherboard BIOS instead to overcome such limitations.

Drive Capacity Limitations

There have been two main barriers in Windows maximum drive capacities: 8.4GB and 137GB. Using a drive larger than 8.4GB requires support for LBA (logical block addressing) in both the BIOS and Windows, where drives of 8.4GB or less use CHS (cylinder head sector) addressing instead. Motherboard BIOSes added LBA support during 1998, so most systems dated from 1998 or newer should have it. Windows added LBA support in Windows 95B and later versions as well. An interesting quirk to allow backward compatibility,when you boot an older version of Windows that doesn't support LBA mode addressing (Windows 95A or earlier), drives larger than 8.4GB report as if they have 16,383 cylinders, 16 heads, and 63 sectors per track, which is 8.4GB. For example, this enables a 120GB drive to be seen as an 8.4GB drive by Windows 95A or earlier. That sounds strange, but I guess having a 120GB drive being recognized as an 8.4GB is better than not having it work at all. If you did want to install a drive larger than 8.4GB into a system with a BIOS dated before 1998, the recommended solution is either a motherboard BIOS upgrade or an add-on BIOS card with LBA support, and to install Windows 95B or later as well.

The 137GB drive capacity barrier has proven a bit more complicated than previous barriers because, in addition to BIOS and operating system issues, drive interface issues were also a problem. By 2001, the 137GB barrier had become a problem because 3 1/2" hard drives were poised to breach that capacity level. Supporting drives larger than this would require changes at the drive interface, the BIOS, and OS level. The drive interface solution came in the form of ATA-6, which was being developed during that year. To enable the addressing of drives of greater capacity, ATA-6 upgraded the LBA functions from using 28-bit numbers to using larger 48-bit numbers.

The ATA interface was originally designed using only 28-bit sector addressing (allowing up to 2^{28} sectors) at the interface level. This limited an ATA drive to 268,435,456 sectors, which was a capacity of 137,438,953,472 bytes, or 137.44GB. Thus, a barrier remained at 137GB because of the 28-bit LBA addressing used in the ATA interface. The numbers work out as follows:

```
                       Max. Values
--------------------------------
Total Sectors          268,435,456
--------------------------------
Total Bytes        137,438,953,472
Megabytes (MB)             137,439
Mebibytes (MiB)            131,072
Gigabytes (GB)              137.44
Gibibytes (GiB)             128.00
```

The ATA-6 and later specifications extended the LBA sector numbering to allow 48-bit addressing. This meant that the maximum capacity was increased to 2^{48} (281,474,976,710,656) total sectors. Because each sector stores 512 bytes, this results in a maximum drive capacity of

```
                         Max. Values
----------------------------------------
Total Sectors        281,474,976,710,656
----------------------------------------
Total Bytes      144,115,188,075,855,872
Megabytes (MB)           144,115,188,076
Mebibytes (MiB)          137,438,953,472
Gigabytes (GB)               144,115,188
Gibibytes (GiB)              134,217,728
Terabytes (TB)                  144,115
Tebibytes (TiB)                 131,072
Petabytes (PB)                   144.12
Pebibytes (PiB)                  128.00
```

As you can see, the 48-bit LBA in ATA-6 and later allows a maximum capacity of just over 144PB (petabytes = quadrillion bytes)! This applies to both ATA and SATA internal drives. Note that external USB or FireWire interfaces did not have any interface problems with respect to large drives; however, inside every external USB or FireWire drive enclosure is a standard ATA or SATA drive.

To take advantage of this, internal ATA and SATA drives larger than 137GB require 48-bit LBA support not only in the drive interface, but also in the OS as well as the motherboard BIOS.

To have 48-bit LBA support in the OS requires either

- Windows Vista.
- Windows XP with Service Pack 1 (SP1) or later.
- Windows 2000 with Service Pack 4 (SP4) or later.
- Windows 98/98SE/Me or NT 4.0 with the Intel Application Accelerator (IAA) loaded. This solution works only if your motherboard has an IAA-supported chipset. See www.intel.com/support/chipsets/iaa for more information.

To have 48-bit LBA support in the BIOS requires either

- A motherboard BIOS with 48-bit LBA support (usually dated September 2002 or later)
- An ATA or SATA host adapter card with onboard BIOS that includes 48-bit LBA support

If your motherboard BIOS does not have 48-bit LBA support, and an update is not available from your motherboard manufacturer, then you can use a card with an on board BIOS. Several companies offer PCI cards that offer 48-bit LBA support:

- **ACARD Technology**—http://www.acard.com
- **HighPoint Technologies**—http://www.highpoint-tech.com
- **Promise Technology, Inc.**—http://www.promise.com
- **SIIG, Inc.**— http://www.siig.com

If you have both BIOS and OS support as well, you can simply install and use a drive over 137GB just like any other. If you have BIOS support, but you do have OS support, portions of the drive past 137GB will not be recognized or accessible.

This can cause problems when installing Windows. For example, if you are installing Windows XP to a blank hard drive larger than 137GB, and you are booting from an original Windows XP CD (without Service Pack 1 or later integrated), then Windows will see only the first 137GB of the drive. During the installation you will only be able to create partitions using only the first 137GB of the drive. Once Windows XP was installed, you could apply Service Pack 1 or later, which would enable Windows to "see" the rest of the drive up to its full capacity. In other words, after installing the Service Pack update, the rest of the drive will be available. However it won't automatically be used; it will simply be available as new unpartitioned space.

At that point you can either add one or more additional partitions to use the unpartitioned space with the standard partitioning software such as the Disk Management tool, or use a third-party partitioning program such as Partition Magic from Symantec or Partition Commander from V-Com to resize or extend the first partition to use the remainder of the drive. If you are booting from a Windows XP CD with Service Pack 1 or later fully integrated (or slip-streamed), Windows will allow you to partition the full capacity of the drive (even over 137GB) during the Windows installation.

Operating system limitations with respect to large drives are shown in Table 10.9.

Table 10.9   Operating System Limitations

Operating System	Limitations for Hard Drive Size
Windows Vista	Windows Vista supports drives greater than 137GB.
Windows 2000/XP	Windows 2000/XP supports drives greater than 8.4GB; however, to support drives greater than 137GB requires Windows XP with Service Pack 1 (SP1) or later, or Windows 2000 with Service Pack 4 (SP4) or later.

(continues)

Table 10.9   Continued

Operating System	Limitations for Hard Drive Size
Windows 9x/Me	Windows 95A (original version) does support the INT13h extensions, which means it does support drives over 8.4GB; however, because of limitations of the FAT16 file system, the maximum individual partition size is limited to 2GB. Windows 95B/OSR2 or later (including Windows 98/Me) supports the INT13h extensions, which allows drives of more than 8.4GB, and also supports FAT32, which allows partition sizes up to the maximum capacity of the drive. However, Windows 95 doesn't support hard drives larger than 32GB because of limitations in its design. Windows 98 requires an update to FDISK to partition drives larger than 64GB.
Windows NT	Windows NT 3.5x does not support drives greater than 8.4GB. Windows NT 4.0 does support drives greater than 8.4GB; however, when a drive larger than 8.4GB is being used as the primary bootable device, Windows NT does not recognize more than 8.4GB. Microsoft has released Service Pack 4, which corrects this problem.
DOS/Windows 3x	DOS 6.22 or lower can't support drives greater than 8.4GB. DOS 7.0 or higher (included with Windows 95 or later) is required to recognize a drive larger than 8.4GB.
OS/2 Warp	Some versions of OS/2 are limited to a boot partition size of 3.1GB or 4.3GB. IBM has a Device Driver Pack upgrade that enables the boot partition to be as large as 8.4GB. The HPFS file system in OS/2 supports drives up to 64GB.
Novell	NetWare 5.0 or later supports drives greater than 8.4GB.

In some cases, the file system you select for a partition or volume may limit the capacity of an individual volume or even files on the volume. Table 10.10 shows the minimum and maximum volume size and file size limitations of the various Windows operating systems.

Table 10.10   Operating System Volume/File Size Limitations by File System

OS Limitations by File System	FAT16	FAT32	NTFS
Min. Volume Size (9x/Me)	2.092MB	33.554MB	—
Max. Volume Size (95)	2.147GB	33.554MB	—
Max. Volume Size (98)	2.147GB	136.902GB	—
Max. Volume Size (Me)	2.147GB	8.796TB	—
Min. Volume Size (NT-Vista)	2.092MB	33.554MB	1.000MB
Max. Volume Size (NT-Vista)	4.294GB	8.796GB	281.475TB
Max. File Size (all)	4.294GB	4.294GB	16.384TB

— = not applicable
MB = megabyte = 1,000,000 bytes
GB = gigabyte = 1,000,000,000 bytes
TB = terabyte = 1,000,000,000,000 bytes

As noted previously in this section, the original versions of Windows XP, Windows 2000/NT, and Windows 95/98/Me do not provide native support for ATA hard drives larger than 137GB.

However, as indicated earlier, that can easily be solved by loading the appropriate Service Packs or Intel Application Accelerator. Finally, note that the 137GB barrier affects internal ATA and SATA drives, and does not affect drives connected via USB, FireWire, SCSI, or other external interfaces.

Boot Sectors

To manage a disk and enable all applications to see a consistent interface to the file system no matter what type of storage hardware is being used, the operating system creates several structures on the disk. The most important of these are the boot sectors (also called boot records), of which there are two main types, called *Master Boot Records*, or *MBRs*, and *Volume Boot Records*, or *VBRs*.

There is only one MBR on a physical disk, and it is always found at the beginning of the disk. A single disk can contain multiple partitions (also called volumes), and there is a VBR at the start of each volume. The structure of the MBR is consistent among different operating systems and file systems, however the VBR structure depends mainly on the type of file system used on the volume. The following section looks into the structure and design of both MBRs and VBRs.

Figure 10.4 is a simple diagram showing the relative locations of the MBR and VBR on an 8.4GB disk with a single FAT partition.

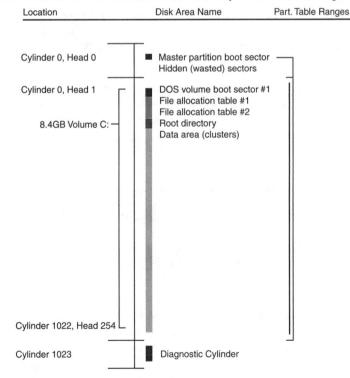

8.4GB Disk with LBA-assist Translation–16383/16/63 Physical to 1024/255/63 Logical Cylinders/Heads/Sectors

Figure 10.4   FAT16 file-management structures on a typical 8.4GB drive.

Note

Some removable cartridge drives, such as the SuperDisk (LS-120 and LS-240) and Iomega Zip drives, function like high-capacity floppy drives. They lack a master boot record (MBR) and can't be partitioned like hard disk drives. Other higher-capacity removable drives, such as the legacy Iomega Jaz or Castlewood Orb, function like hard drives and must be partitioned.

All PC hard drives using the FAT16 file system are similar.

Each disk area has a purpose and function. If one of these special areas is damaged, serious consequences can result. Damage to one of these sensitive structures usually causes a domino effect, limiting access to other areas of the disk or causing further problems in using the disk. For example, the OS normally can't access a drive at all if the MBR is corrupted. Therefore, you should understand these data structures well enough to be able to repair them when necessary. Rebuilding these special tables and areas of the disk is essential to the art of data recovery, which is covered in more detail in Chapter 11.

Master Boot Record

The first PC OS to support hard disks, DOS 2.0 (released on March 8, 1983), was also the first to introduce the capability to partition a drive. Partitioning assigns the available space on the drive to one or more volumes (drive letters). A common misunderstanding among newer users is to think that partitioning is necessary only if multiple volumes are desired, but the truth is that all drives that *can* be partitioned *must* be partitioned; in other words you have to partition a drive even if you are going to assign all the space to a single volume.

Although the primary use for partitioning today is to divide a single drive into one or more volumes for use by a single OS, originally it was intended to allow multiple different operating systems, each with different file systems, to coexist on a single drive. This multi-OS capability still exists today; however, after market utilities are often used to manage and boot multiple operating systems on a single machine.

Tip

If you want to dual-boot or multi-boot different Windows versions on a single partition without purchasing after market boot manager software, merely install the older versions such as Windows 95, 98, or Me first and then install newer versions such as Windows NT/2000/XP or Vista in succession, with the newest OS last. Each OS must be installed in a separate volume (drive letter) to prevent conflicts with shared folders and files. One rule is that you can only install one instance of Windows 95, 98/98SE, or Me because those operating systems share the same system files.

Another solution is to create multiple (up to four per drive) primary partitions, and install a different OS in each one. To do this you would create a new primary partition, set it as active (bootable) using FDISK/DISKPART or Disk Management, and then reboot and install the OS. You can create up to four primary partitions on a single drive, each with a different OS installed. To change the OS from which you boot, merely use the partitioning tools in the currently running OS to change which partition is active (bootable), and restart the system. Once restarted, it automatically boots the active partition.

A third solution (which I prefer) is to use a virtual machine (VM) program such as Microsoft Virtual PC (www.microsoft.com/virtualpc) or VMware (www.vmware.com) to create multiple virtual machines, each capable of managing and loading a separate OS. This software allows you to run multiple instances of the same or different operating systems on a single machine without repartitioning or reformatting any drives. Although there are some performance limitations with running multiple OS in virtual machines, depending on the type and number of processor cores and the amount of installed RAM, modern systems with multi-core processors that have hardware virtualization support and 2GB or more RAM can generally handle virtual machines.

To use a hard disk with different operating systems, you can create partitions to logically divide the disk. You can, for example, create one or more partitions for use with Windows and leave the rest of the disk storage area for use by another non-Windows OS, such as Linux. Each of the partitions appears as a separate drive letter to an OS that supports it. For example, Windows 9x/Me ignores any non-FAT partitions, whereas Windows 2000/XP and Vista sees both FAT and NTFS partitions but ignores others such as Linux and OS/2 HPFS partitions.

Even though Windows NT/2000/XP and Vista have an optional command-line disk partitioning program called DISKPART, disk partitions are usually prepared with the GUI-based Disk Management tool (also called Disk Administrator in some versions).

Information about each of the partitions on the disk is stored in a partition (or volume) boot record at the beginning of each partition. Additionally, a main table lists the partitions embedded in the master boot record.

The MBR, which is also sometimes called the master boot sector, is always located in the first physical sector of a disk (cylinder 0, head 0, sector 1) and consists of the following structures:

- **Bootstrap code**—The instructions used to locate and load the VBR from the active (bootable) partition.

- **Master partition table**—A table consisting of four 16-byte entries for up to four primary partitions, or three primary partitions and one extended partition. Each primary partition defines a logical drive, and an extended partition can be further partitioned into multiple logical drives. A given partition entry indicates which type of partition it is, whether it is bootable, where it is located physically on the disk, and how many sectors it occupies.

- **Signature bytes**—A 2-byte signature (55 AAh) used by the motherboard ROM and other code to validate the sector.

Primary and Extended Partitions

Most operating systems are designed to support up to 24 volumes on a single hard disk drive (represented by the drive letters C:–Z:), but the partition table in the MBR can have a maximum of only four entries. These entries can be for various types of partitions; however, Windows will normally recognize only primary and extended partitions.

An *extended* partition is listed in the master partition table the same as a primary partition, but it differs in that you can use its disk space to create multiple logical partitions, or *volumes*. You can create only one extended partition on a single drive, meaning that in many cases there will never be more than two entries in the master partition table, one primary and one extended.

The logical volumes you create in the extended partition appear as separate drive letters to the operating system, but they are not listed in the master partition table. Volumes in the extended partition are not normally bootable. You can create up to 23 volumes out of a single extended partition (assuming that you have already created a primary partition, which brings the total number of volumes to 24).

Each of the subpartitions in an extended partition includes an extended partition table located in the first sector of the subpartition. The first sector of the extended partition contains an extended partition table that points to the first subpartition and, optionally, another extended partition. The first sector of that extended partition has another extended partition table that can reference another volume as well as an additional extended partition. This chain of references continues, linking all the volumes in the extended partition to the master partition table. It is important to note that if the entry for the extended partition in the MBR is lost or damaged, the chain will be broken at the start and all volumes contained within will be inaccessible—essentially meaning that they will disappear.

Few people have any reason to create 24 partitions on a single disk drive, but the extended partition can create a chain of linked partitions on the disk that makes it possible to exceed the four-entry limitation of the master partition table.

Because the master boot record contains the first program loaded from disk that the system executes when you boot a PC, it has been a frequent target for creators of computer viruses or other malicious software. A program that infects or destroys the MBR can make it impossible for the BIOS to find the active partition, thus preventing the operating system from loading. Because the MBR contains the first program executed by the system, a virus stored there loads before any antivirus code can be loaded to detect it. To remove an MBR virus, you must first boot the system from a clean, uninfected disk, such as a floppy, bootable CD/DVD, or USB drive, and then run an antivirus program to test and possibly repair or restore the MBR.

Each volume on a disk contains a volume boot record starting in the first sector. With FDISK, DISKPART, or Disk Management tools, you can designate a primary partition as active (or bootable). The master boot record bootstrap code causes the VBR from the active primary partition to receive control whenever the system is started.

Although FAT12, FAT16, FAT32, or NTFS partitions are mainly used when running Windows, you can also create additional disk partitions for Linux, Novell NetWare, OS/2's HPFS, AIX (UNIX), XENIX, or other file systems or operating systems, using disk utilities provided with the alternative OS or in some cases a third-party disk partitioning tool such as PartitionMagic from Symantec. A partition that is not recognized by a particular operating system is simply ignored. If you install multiple operating systems on a single drive, a boot manager program (which might be included with the operating systems or installed separately) can be used to allow you to select which partition to make active each time you boot the system. As another alternative, you could install different operating systems in multiple different primary partitions and then use FDISK, DISKPART, Disk Management, or some other partitioning program to change the one you want to boot as active.

Table 10.11 shows the format of the master boot record and the included partition tables. The table lists the fields in each of the master partition table's four entries, the location on the disk where each field begins (the offset), and its length.

Table 10.11   Master Boot Record Format

Master Boot Program Code

Offset (Hex)	Offset (Dec)	Name	Length	Description
000h	0	Boot Code	440 bytes	Bootstrap code; loads the VBR from the active partition.
1B8h	440	Disk Signature	4 bytes	Random **dword** value representing the disk signature/NT drive serial number.
1BCh	444	-	2 bytes	Unused.

Partition Table Entry #1

Offset (Hex)	Offset (Dec)	Name	Length	Description
1BEh	446	Boot Indicator	1 byte	Boot status; 80h = active (bootable). Otherwise, it's 00h.
1BFh	447	Starting Head	1 byte	Starting head (or side) of partition in CHS mode.
1C0h	448	Starting Cylinder/Sector	16 bits	Starting cylinder (10 bits) and sector (6 bits) in CHS mode.
1C2h	450	System Indicator	1 byte	Partition type/file system.
1C3h	451	Ending Head	1 byte	Ending head (or side) of partition in CHS mode.
1C4h	452	Ending Cylinder/Sector	16 bits	Ending cylinder (10 bits) and sector (6 bits) in CHS mode.
1C6h	454	Relative Sector	4 bytes	Count of sectors before partition, which is the starting sector of partition in LBA mode.
1CAh	458	Total Sectors	4 bytes	Total number of partition sectors in LBA mode.

Partition Table Entry #2

Offset (Hex)	Offset (Dec)	Description	Length	Description
1CEh	462	Boot Indicator	1 byte	Boot status; 80h = active (bootable). Otherwise, it's 00h.
1CFh	463	Starting Head	1 byte	Starting head (or side) of partition in CHS mode.
1D0h	464	Starting Cylinder/Sector	16 bits	Starting cylinder (10 bits) and sector (6 bits) in CHS mode.
1D2h	466	System Indicator	1 byte	Partition type/file system.
1D3h	467	Ending Head	1 byte	Ending head (or side) of partition in CHS mode.
1D4h	468	Ending Cylinder/Sector	16 bits	Ending cylinder (10 bits) and sector (6 bits) in CHS mode.

(continues)

Table 10.11   Continued

Partition Table Entry #2

Offset (Hex)	Offset (Dec)	Description	Length	Description
1D6h	470	Relative Sector	4 bytes	Count of sectors before partition, which is the starting sector of the partition in LBA mode.
1DAh	474	Total Sectors	4 bytes	Total number of partition sectors in LBA mode.

Partition Table Entry #3

Offset (Hex)	Offset (Dec)	Description	Length	Description
1DEh	478	Boot Indicator	1 byte	Boot status; 80h = active (bootable). Otherwise, it's 00h.
1DFh	479	Starting Head	1 byte	Starting head (or side) of partition in CHS mode.
1E0h	480	Starting Cylinder/Sector	16 bits	Starting cylinder (10 bits) and sector (6 bits) in CHS mode.
1E2h	482	System Indicator	1 byte	Partition type/file system.
1E3h	483	Ending Head	1 byte	Ending head (or side) of partition in CHS mode.
1E4h	484	Ending Cylinder/Sector	16 bits	Ending cylinder (10 bits) and sector (6 bits) in CHS mode.
1E6h	486	Relative Sector	4 bytes	Count of sectors before partition, which is the starting sector of partition in LBA mode.
1EAh	490	Total Sectors	4 bytes	Total number of partition sectors in LBA mode.

Partition Table Entry #4

Offset (Hex)	Offset (Dec)	Description	Length	Description
1EEh	494	Boot Indicator	1 byte	Boot status; 80h = active (bootable). Otherwise, it's 00h.
1EFh	495	Starting Head	1 byte	Starting head (or side) of partition in CHS mode.
1F0h	496	Starting Cylinder/Sector	16 bits	Starting cylinder (10 bits) and sector (6 bits) in CHS mode.
1F2h	498	System Indicator	1 byte	Partition type/file system.
1F3h	499	Ending Head	1 byte	Ending head (or side) of partition in CHS mode.
1F4h	500	Ending Cylinder/Sector	16 bits	Ending cylinder (10 bits) and sector (6 bits) in CHS mode.
1F6h	502	Relative Sector	4 bytes	Count of sectors before partition, which is the starting sector of partition in LBA mode.
1FAh	506	Total Sectors	4 bytes	Total number of partition sectors in LBA mode.

Signature Bytes

Offset (Hex)	Offset (Dec)	Description	Length	Description
1FEh	510	Signature	2 bytes	Boot sector signature; must be 55AAh.

CHS = cylinder head sector
LBA = logical block address

The data in the partition table entries tells the system where each partition starts and ends on the drive, how big it is, whether it is bootable, and which type of file system is contained in the partition. The starting cylinder, head, and sector values are used only by systems running in CHS mode, which is standard for all drives of 8.4GB or less. CHS values do not work past 8.4GB and therefore cannot represent partitions on drives larger than that. Drives larger than 8.4GB can be fully addressed only in LBA mode. In that case, the starting cylinder, head, and sector values in the table are ignored, and only the Relative Sector and Total Sectors fields are used. The Relative Sector field indicates the precise LBA where the partition begins, and the Total Sectors field indicates the length, which is always contiguous. Thus, from those two values the system can know exactly where a partition is physically located on a disk.

Note

The processors on which the PC is based have an interesting design characteristic that is important to know for anybody editing or interpreting boot sectors. Numbers larger than 1 byte are actually read backward! This is called *little endian format* (as in reading the number from the little end first) or *reverse-byte ordering*. People typically read numbers in *big endian format*, which means from left to right, from the big end first. However, because PC processors read in little endian format, most numeric values larger than 1 byte are stored so that the least significant byte appears first and the most significant byte appears last. For example, the value for the Relative Sector field in the MBR for the first partition is usually 63, which is 3Fh in hex, or 0000003Fh (4 bytes long) in standard big endian hexadecimal format. However, the same number stored in little endian format would appear as 3F000000h. As another example, if a partition had 23,567,292 total sectors (about 12GB), which is 01679BBCh in hexadecimal, the number would be stored in the MBR partition table Total Sectors field in reverse-byte/little endian format as BC9B6701h.

As an aside, the use of reverse-byte order numbers stems from the way processors evolved from 8-bit (1 byte) designs to 16-bit (2 byte), 32-bit (4 byte), 64-bit (8-byte) designs, and beyond. The way the internal registers are organized and implemented dictates how a processor deals with numbers. Many processors, such as the Motorola PowerPC chips used in older Macintosh systems, read numbers in big endian format. Intel and AMD processors, on the other hand, are based on Intel x86 processor designs dating back to the original Intel 8088 processor used in the first IBM PC. Of course, how a particular processor reads numbers doesn't make any difference to those using a system. In the PC, the only people who have to deal with reverse-byte order or little endian numbers directly are machine or assembly language programmers—and of course those who also want to edit, modify, repair, or simply interpret raw boot sectors!

Each partition table entry contains a system indicator byte that identifies the type of partition and file system used in the partition referenced by that entry. Table 10.12 shows the standard values and meanings of the system indicator bytes for Microsoft operating systems, and Table 10.13 lists the values used by other systems.

Table 10.12 Standard System Indicator Byte Values

Value	Partition Type	Address Mode	Partition Size
00h	None	—	—
01h	Primary FAT12	CHS	0–16MiB
04h	Primary FAT16	CHS	16MiB–32MiB
05h	Extended	CHS	0–2GiB
06h	Primary FAT16	CHS	32MiB–2GiB
07h	NTFS/HPFS	Any	Any
0Bh	Primary FAT32	CHS	512MiB–2TiB
0Ch	Primary FAT32	LBA	512MiB–2TiB
0Eh	Primary FAT16	LBA	32MiB–2GiB
0Fh	Extended	LBA	2GiB–2TiB
42h	Dynamic	Any	Any

CHS = Cylinder head sector
LBA = Logical block address

Table 10.13 Nonstandard System Indicator Byte Values

Value	Partition Type	Value	Partition Type
02h	MS-XENIX root	80h	Minix v.1.1–v1.4a
03h	MS-XENIX usr	81h	Minix v1.4b-up or Linux
08h	AIX file system boot	82h	Linux swap file
09h	AIX data	83h	Linux Ext native file system
0Ah	OS/2 Bootmanager	83h	Suspend to Disk (S2D)
12h	HP/Compaq EISA configuration	93h	Amoeba file system
40h	ENIX 80286	94h	Amoeba bad block table
50h	Ontrack Disk Manager read-only DOS	B7h	BSDI file system (secondary swap)
51h	Ontrack Disk Manager read/write DOS	B8h	BSDI file system (secondary file system)
52h	CP/M or Microport System V/386	DBh	DR Concurrent DOS/CPM-86/CTOS
54h	Ontrack Disk Manager non-DOS	DEh	Dell OEM (hidden—system recovery/diagnostic)
55h	Micro House EZ-Drive non-DOS	E1h	SpeedStor 12-bit FAT extended
56h	Golden Bow Vfeature Deluxe	E4h	SpeedStor 16-bit FAT extended
61h	Storage Dimensions SpeedStor	F2h	DOS 3.3+secondary
63h	IBM 386/ix or UNIX System V/386	F4h	SpeedStor primary
64h	Novell NetWare 286	FEh	IBM OEM (hidden—system recovery/diagnostic)
65h	Novell NetWare 386	FFh	UNIX/XENIX Bad Block Table Partition
75h	IBM PC/IX		

These values can be useful for somebody trying to manually repair a partition table using a disk editor such as the Disk Probe utility (dskprobe.exe) included with the free Windows Support Tools on the Windows NT/2000/XP or Vista install disc, the Disk Edit program included with

Norton Utilities (now part of Norton SystemWorks), or WinHex from X-Ways Software (www.winhex.com).

Windows Disk Probe

Disk Probe is a free sector editor utility available from Microsoft that enables users with Administrator rights to directly edit, save, and copy sectors on a physical hard drive.

Disk Probe can read any physical or logical sector on a drive, and has special features for decoding and editing the MBR, partition tables, and volume boot sectors. Because some of these structures are literally outside of the file system on a drive, they are not accessible through most other applications. With this tool, a knowledgeable user can restore these important data structures if they are damaged, for example, by a boot sector virus. Using Disk Probe, data structures such as the MBR, partition tables, and VBRs can be edited directly.

In addition to editing, you can use Disk Probe for preventive maintenance by making backups of these critical sectors as files, which can be stored on another removable disk or media (such as a floppy, CD, flash drive, and so on). Once saved, they can be later restored in the event that these sectors are corrupted on your hard drive.

Disk Probe is one of the more powerful and interesting programs included in the Windows Support Tools packages available for several versions of Windows. You can find the Windows Support Tools on some of the Windows NT/2000/XP installation CDs (look in the \SUPPORT\TOOLS folder), and whether they are on the CD or not, they can also be downloaded for free from Microsoft. In fact, you are better off downloading them anyway because the versions included on the original Windows installation CDs have been superseded by later versions. To run Disk Probe, first download the Windows Support Tools from Microsoft (to find them, visit www.microsoft.com and search for "Windows Support Tools Download") or locate the tools on the Windows installation CD (they are normally in the \SUPPORT\TOOLS folder on the CD) and install them.

The latest versions of the Windows Support Tools for Windows NT and later are as follows:

- **For Windows NT**—Windows NT 4.0 SP4 Support Tools
- **For Windows 2000**—Windows 2000 SP4 Support Tools
- **For Windows XP**—Windows XP SP2 Support Tools

After the tools are installed, select Start, Windows Support Tools, and Command Prompt. At the prompt, enter **Dskprobe**. The program then launches in a window. Optionally you can run the program by opening Windows Explorer and navigating to the \Program Files\Support Tools folder, and then click on Dskprobe. The documentation for the program is available via the Help command on the menu bar.

Note

Unfortunately Microsoft has not produced a version of the support tools for Windows Vista, and the Windows XP version does not install on that operating system. However, Disk Probe from the Windows XP Support Tools does indeed run under Vista. To work around the installation problem you can download the XP version, use an extraction utility such as 7-zip (http://www.7-zip.org) to extract the dskprobe files from the installation, and then run the extracted **dskprobe.exe** file directly. Note, for Disk Probe to work properly under Vista, you must either disable UAC (User Account Control) or right-click the file and select Run as Administrator.

Figure 10.5 shows Disk Probe editing the MBR on one of my systems:

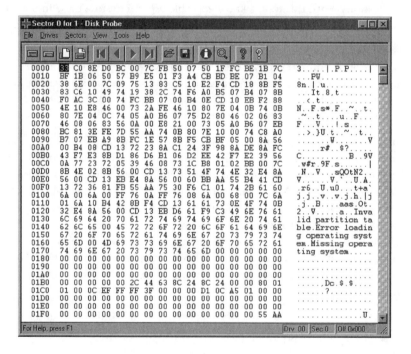

Figure 10.5   Editing an MBR with Disk Probe.

Note that editing critical sectors such as the MBR is like performing open-heart surgery on your system. Disk Probe and other sector editors such as Norton DiskEdit function at a level below the Windows file system, which means that the standard safety protocols are not in effect. Disk Probe gives you access to every byte on the physical disk without regard to normal security or access privileges, which makes it possible to damage or overwrite critical areas of the disk. If you change so much as a single byte inappropriately, you could render your system non-bootable, and possibly render the drive unrecognizable even if the system is booted from a floppy or CD. Fortunately the Disk Probe program defaults to read-only mode, which means you can run the program to view sectors without worrying about accidentally making changes. Before you do make any changes with a low-level tool such as Disk Probe, make sure you have a backup of any important data.

I have specialized in data recovery for many years, and in that line of work I regularly use sector editors such as Disk Probe to repair or restore critical boot sectors on hard drives that had otherwise been inaccessible by Windows. In a recent example, a client of mine was editing some rather large video files on an external FireWire drive. While working with the video-editing program, the program crashed, and the system suddenly stopped recognizing the drive. Upon disconnecting and reconnecting the drive, Windows saw the drive as a new unformatted drive and offered to format it! Hundreds of hours of shooting and editing video seemed lost forever.

To solve the problem, I took the drive out of the FireWire enclosure and connected it internally as a standard ATA slave drive to one of my test systems running Windows XP. I then started up the test system, loaded Disk Probe, and did a manual inspection of the MBR and VBRs. As is the case with most external USB or FireWire drives, the drive had been formatted with the FAT32 file system, and I very quickly discovered that somehow the first sector of the three-sector-long FAT32 volume boot record, which was at Logical Block Address (LBA) 63, had been overwritten with zeros! I knew from experience that FAT32 keeps a backup copy of the three-sector-long VBR at LBAs 66 through 68. So I used Disk Probe to copy sector 66 and paste it over sector 63, thereby restoring sector 63 and instantly solving the problem. I then powered the system off, removed the drive from my test system, reinstalled it into the FireWire enclosure, and reconnected it to the client's system, whereupon the drive was instantly recognized and all data was fully accessible.

Total elapsed time from "zero" to "hero" was less than 10 minutes after I received the drive; needless to say the client was ecstatic. Even a relatively simple job like this would cost hundreds to possibly thousands of dollars if sent to a professional data recovery service. Now you see why most people who *know* data recovery don't like to *teach* it (except me, of course).

FixMBR

Windows NT and later include special recovery tools designed to rebuild a corrupt MBR. The tools include the `FixMBR` (NT through XP) and `Bootrec /FixMBR` (Vista) commands. These commands overwrite only the master boot sector program code, leaving the existing partition table entries intact. This means that if the problem is in the boot code, these commands solve it by replacing the code; however, if the problem is instead with the actual partition tables, these commands do not resolve the problem.

Caution

If your system uses non standard MBR code, beware that the `FixMBR` or `Bootrec /FixMBR` commands replace it with standard MBR code, meaning that whatever functionality was being provided by the non standard code (such as a third-party multi boot loader or BIOS overlay) may be lost. Even more importantly, if you are using BIOS overlay software to override BIOS drive-size limitations (something I do *not* recommend), replacing the MBR code in this manner may result in your system becoming unbootable and losing access to any or all of the drives! Also, certain MBR virus programs (such as the infamous Monkey virus) relocate and encrypt the original MBR code before replacing it with virus code. If the MBR is rewritten by these tools, you lose access to the original MBR containing the partition tables. This means that unless you are able to re-create the partition table data manually using a sector editor you will lose access to all the partitions on the drive. In that case a data recovery specialist should be able to rebuild the partition tables and recover the data if no further writing is done to the drive.

In Windows NT through XP you can use the following steps to start the Recovery Console and use FixMBR to rewrite the MBR program code:

1. The Windows NT through XP setup disc is normally a bootable CD; however it is possible to burn a copy on a bootable DVD as well. Ensure that your system is capable of booting from the type of optical disc you are using (CD or DVD), and that the optical drive precedes the hard disk in the boot sequence. Hint: You may need to change your BIOS setup to inspect or change the startup boot sequence.

2. Insert the Windows Setup disc into the optical drive, and restart the system.

3. If prompted to press a key to start the computer from CD or DVD, press any key (such as the spacebar) to continue and start from the optical disc.

4. When the text-based part of Windows Setup begins, follow the prompts until the Welcome to Setup screen appears, and then press the R key to Repair Windows, which also means to start the Recovery Console.

5. If you are repairing a system that has more than one operating system installed, from the Recovery Console, choose the Windows installation that you need to access or repair.

6. When you are prompted, type the Administrator password. If the Administrator password is blank, just press Enter. If a password has been set but you do not have the correct password, or if the security database for the installation of Windows you are attempting to access is corrupted, Recovery Console will not allow access to the disks.

7. To replace the MBR program code, at the Recovery Console command prompt, type

   `FixMBR`

8. Press the Y key to proceed, or press the N key to cancel. If you press Y, the MBR program code will be replaced.

9. Finally, remove the disc and restart the system.

In Windows Vista, the former Recovery Console is now called the Recovery Environment. To rewrite the MBR program code in Vista, use the following procedure:

1. Ensure that your system is capable of booting from a DVD, and that the optical drive precedes the hard disk in the boot sequence. Hint: You may need to change your BIOS setup to inspect or change the startup boot sequence.

2. Insert the Windows Vista Setup disc into the optical drive and restart the system.

3. If prompted to press a key to start the computer from CD or DVD, press any key (such as the spacebar) to continue and start from the optical disc.

4. When the Install Windows dialog box appears, select a language, a time, a currency, a keyboard or an input method, and then click Next. Then press the R key to repair your computer, which also means that you are starting the Recovery Environment.

5. When the System Recovery Options dialog box appears, choose the Windows Vista installation that you need to access or repair. Note that only Vista operating systems are listed and can be repaired.

6. When you are prompted to Choose a Recovery Tool, select the Command Prompt.

7. To replace the MBR program code, at the Recovery Environment command prompt, type **Bootrec /FixMBR**.

8. Finally, remove the disc and restart the system.

If you are using Windows 9x/Me or an older version of Windows or DOS, you can perform the same task by using an undocumented feature in FDISK found in all versions of FDISK from MS-DOS 5.x to Windows Me. The undocumented FDISK feature can also be used on Windows NT and later systems by simply booting from a Windows 9x/Me startup floppy or installation CD, and running the command from the floppy or CD.

Undocumented *FDISK*

In DOS 5 and later versions, including Windows 9x/Me, FDISK gained some additional capabilities that were not originally documented by Microsoft. There are several undocumented FDISK parameters, but the one I am speaking about here is the /MBR (master boot record) parameter, which causes FDISK to rewrite the master boot record code, leaving the partition table area intact. This performs exactly the same function as the FixMBR command included in Windows NT/2000/XP and Vista versions.

As with FixMBR, the FDISK /MBR command is tailor-made for eliminating boot sector virus programs that infect the master boot record (located at cylinder 0, head 0, sector 1) of a hard disk. To use this feature, enter the following at a command prompt:

    FDISK /MBR

FDISK then rewrites the boot record code, leaving the partition tables intact. This should not cause any problems on a normally functioning system, but just in case, I recommend backing up the partition table information to floppy disk before trying it. You can do this by using a third-party product such as Norton Utilities.

The FDISK /MBR command rewrites the MBR on only the first (disk 0) drive by using BIOS calls. To rewrite the MBR of other drives, instead of /MBR you can use the /CMBR <drive number> switch, where <drive number> represents the drive on which you wish to rewrite the MBR. To determine the drive number, run the FDISK /STATUS command.

Normally when using FDISK to rewrite the MBR, only the program code portion is rewritten, leaving the existing partition tables intact. However, if the two signature bytes at the end of the sector (55 AAh) are damaged, these commands also overwrite the partition tables. This situation is highly unlikely because if the signature bytes are damaged, the system does not boot and acts as though there were no partitions at all. In that case, your system might be infected with a boot sector virus. You should scan for viruses with an up-to-date antivirus program and use it to guide repair.

Caution

FDISK /MBR or /CMBR <drive number> should be used only on systems using the normal master boot record structure. As with the **FixMBR** and **Bootrec /FixMBR** commands, if a BIOS overlay program such as Disk Manager, Disc Wizard, EZ-Drive, MaxBlast, Data Lifeguard Tools, or similar has installed a modified MBR to allow your system to access the drive's full capacity, using **FDISK** to rewrite the MBR wipes out the changes the program made to your MBR and could make your data inaccessible.

Volume Boot Records

The VBR starts in the first sector on any area of a drive addressed as a volume, including primary partitions or logical volumes inside an extended partition. On a floppy disk or removable cartridge (such as a Zip disk), for example, the volume boot record starts at the physical beginning of the disk because the disk is recognized as a volume without the need for partitioning. On a hard disk, the volume boot record is located as the first sectors within any disk area allocated as a primary partition, or as a logical drive (volume) inside an extended partition. Refer to Figure 10.4 for an idea of the physical relationship between this volume boot record and the other data structures on a disk. The specific length and content of the VBR varies according to the specific file system, but all of them have certain similar features. The volume boot record loosely resembles the master boot record in that it contains several similar elements such as program code, disk-specific data, and signature bytes. The specific elements in the volume boot record include

- **Jump Instruction to Boot Code**—A 3-byte Intel x86 unconditional branch (or jump) instruction that jumps to the start of the operating system bootstrap code within the sector.

- **BIOS Parameter Block**—Contains specific information about the volume, such as its size, the number of disk sectors it uses, the size of its clusters, and the volume label name. Used by the file system driver to determine the type and status of the media. Varies according to the type of file system on the media.

- **Boot Code**—The instructions used to locate and load the initial operating system kernel or startup file, usually either IO.SYS or NTLDR (depending on the Windows version).

- **Signature Byte**—A two-byte signature (55 AAh) used by the motherboard ROM and other code to validate the boot sector.

Either the motherboard ROM or the master boot record on a hard disk loads the volume boot record of the active partition on a disk. The program code in the volume boot record is given control of the system; it performs some tests and then attempts to load the first operating system file (in DOS/Windows 9x/Me the file is IO.SYS, in Windows NT/2000/XP the file is NTLDR, and in Vista the file is bootmgr). The volume boot record, similar to the master boot record, is transparent to the running system; it is outside the data area of the disk on which files are stored.

Note

Many of today's systems are capable of booting from drives other than standard floppy disk and hard disk drives. In these cases, the system BIOS must specifically support the boot drive. For example, some BIOS products enable you to select an ATAPI CD-ROM (or DVD) as a boot device, in addition to the floppy and hard disk drives. Many can also boot from drives connected to USB ports, adding even more flexibility to the system.

Other types of removable media, such as Zip cartridges and LS-120 disks, can also be made bootable. When the BIOS properly supports it, an LS-120 drive can replace the existing floppy disk drive as drive A:. Check the setup screens in your system BIOS to determine which types of drives can be used to start your system.

The VBR is typically created on a volume when the volume is high-level formatted. This can be done with the FORMAT command included with DOS and Windows, or you can also use Windows NT's Disk Administrator and Windows 2000/XP and Vista's Disk Management programs to perform this task after partitioning the disk. All volumes have a VBR starting in the first sector of the volume.

The VBR contains both program code and data. The single data table in this sector is called the *media parameter block* or *disk parameter block*. The operating system needs the information this table contains to verify the capacity of the disk volume as well as the location of important structures, such as the FATs on FAT volumes or the Master File Table on NTFS volumes. The format of this data is very specific.

Although all VBRs contain boot code in addition to the BIOS parameter block (BPB) and other structures, only the boot code from the VBR in the bootable volume is executed. The others are read by the operating system during startup to determine the volume parameters.

The VBR on FAT12 and FAT16 volumes is one sector long and contains the jump instruction, the main BPB, bootstrap code, and signature bytes. Table 10.14 shows the format and layout of the FAT12/16 VBR.

Table 10.14   FAT12/16 Volume Boot Record Format

Offset (Hex)	Offset (Dec)	Name	Length (Bytes)	Description
000h	0	BS_jmpBoot	3	Jump instruction to boot code, usually EB3C90h.
003h	3	BS_OEMName	8	OEM ID. Indicates which system formatted the volume. Typically, it's **MSWIN4.1**. Not used by the OS after formatting.
00Bh	11	BPB_BytsPerSec	2	Bytes per sector; normally 512.
00Dh	13	BPB_SecPerClus	1	Sectors per cluster. It must be a power of 2 greater than 0; typically 1, 2, 4, 8, 16, 32, or 64.
00Eh	14	BPB_RsvdSecCnt	2	Number of sectors reserved for the boot record(s); it should be 1 on FAT12/16 volumes.
010h	16	BPB_NumFATs	1	Count of FAT structures on the volume; usually 2.
011h	17	BPB_RootEntCnt	2	Count of 32-byte folder entries in the root folder of FAT12 and FAT16 volumes; it should be 512 on FAT12/16 volumes.
013h	19	BPB_TotSec16	2	16-bit total count of sectors on volumes with fewer than 65,536 sectors. If 0, BPB_TotSec32 contains the count.
015h	21	BPB_Media	1	Media descriptor byte; normally F8h on all nonremovable media, and F0h on most removable media.
016h	22	BPB_FATSz16	2	FAT12/16 16-bit count of sectors occupied by one FAT.
018h	24	BPB_SecPerTrk	2	Sectors per track geometry value for interrupt 13h; it's usually 63 on hard disks.
01Ah	26	BPB_NumHeads	2	Number of heads for interrupt 13h; it's usually 255 on hard disks.
01Ch	28	BPB_HiddSec	4	Count of hidden sectors preceding the partition that contains this volume; it's usually 63 for the first volume.
020h	32	BPB_TotSec32	4	32-bit total count of sectors on volumes with 65,536 or more sectors. If 0, BPB_TotSec16 contains the count.
024h	36	BS_DrvNum	1	Int 13h drive number; it's usually 00h for floppy disks or 80h for hard disks.
025h	37	BS_Reserved1	1	Reserved (used by Windows NT); it should be 0.

(continues)

Table 10.14 Continued

Offset (Hex)	Offset (Dec)	Name	Length (Bytes)	Description
026h	38	BS_BootSig	1	Extended boot signature; it should be 29h if the following three fields are present. Otherwise, it's 00h.
027h	39	BS_VolID	4	Volume serial number; used with BS_VolLab to support volume tracking on removable media. Normally generated using the date and time as a seed when the volume is formatted.
02Bh	43	BS_VolLab	11	Volume label. Matches the 11-byte volume label recorded in the root folder; it should be set to **NO NAME** if there is no volume label.
036h	54	BS_FilSysType	8	Should be **FAT12**, **FAT16**, or **FAT**. Not used by the OS after formatting.
03Eh	62	BS_BootCode	448	Bootstrap program code.
1FEh	510	BS_Signature	2	Signature bytes; should be 55 AAh.

The VBR on a FAT32 volume is 3 sectors long, although 32 sectors are reserved at the beginning of the volume for the default and backup VBRs. The default VBR is in sectors 0, 1, and 2, and the backup VBR is in sectors 6, 7, and 8. These are all created at the time the volume is formatted and do not change during normal use. The first sector contains a jump instruction, the BPB, initial bootstrap code, and signature bytes. The second sector is called the FSInfo (file system information) sector and contains signature bytes and information used to assist the file system software; the third sector contains only additional bootstrap code and signature bytes. Table 10.15 shows the format and layout of the first sector of the three-sector-long FAT32 VBR.

Table 10.15 FAT32 VBR Format, BPB Sector 0

Offset (Hex)	Offset (Dec)	Name	Length (Bytes)	Description
000h	0	BS_jmpBoot	3	Jump instruction to boot code; it's usually EB5890h.
003h	3	BS_OEMName	8	OEM ID; indicates which system formatted the volume. It's typically **MSWIN4.1**. Not used by the OS after formatting.
00Bh	11	BPB_BytsPerSec	2	Bytes per sector; normally 512.
00Dh	13	BPB_SecPerClus	1	Sectors per cluster; it must be a power of 2 greater than 0. It's normally 1, 2, 4, 8, 16, 32, or 64.
00Eh	14	BPB_RsvdSecCnt	2	Number of sectors reserved for the boot record(s); it should be 32 on FAT32 volumes.
010h	16	BPB_NumFATs	1	Count of FAT structures on the volume; usually 2.
011h	17	BPB_RootEntCnt	2	Count of 32-byte folder entries in the root folder of FAT12 and FAT16 volumes; should be 0 on FAT32 volumes.
013h	19	BPB_TotSec16	2	16-bit total count of sectors on volumes with fewer than 65,536 sectors. If 0, BPB_TotSec32 contains the count. Must be 0 for FAT32 volumes.
015h	21	BPB_Media	1	Media descriptor byte, normally F8h on all non removable media, F0h on most removable media.

Offset (Hex)	Offset (Dec)	Name	Length (Bytes)	Description
016h	22	BPB_FATSz16	2	FAT12/16 16-bit count of sectors occupied by one FAT; it should be 0 on FAT32 volumes, and BPB_FATSz32 contains the FAT size count.
018h	24	BPB_SecPerTrk	2	Sectors per track geometry value for interrupt 13h; usually 63 on hard disks.
01Ah	26	BPB_NumHeads	2	Number of heads for interrupt 13h; usually 255 on hard disks.
01Ch	28	BPB_HiddSec	4	Count of hidden sectors preceding the partition that contains this volume; usually 63 for the first volume.
020h	32	BPB_TotSec32	4	32-bit total count of sectors on volumes with 65,536 or more sectors. If 0, BPB_TotSec16 contains the count. Must be non zero on FAT32 volumes.
024h	36	BPB_FATSz32	4	FAT32 32-bit count of sectors occupied by one FAT. BPB_FATSz16 must be 0.
028h	40	BPB_ExtFlags	2	FAT32 only:
				Bits 0–3. Zero-based number of active FAT. Valid only if mirroring is disabled (bit 7 = 1).
				Bits 4–6. Reserved.
				Bit 7. 0 indicates FAT is mirrored; 1 indicates only the FAT referenced in bits 0–3 is active.
				Bits 8–15. Reserved.
02Ah	42	BPB_FSVer	2	Version number of the FAT32 volume. A high byte is a major revision number; a low byte is a minor revision number. It should be 00h:00h.
02Ch	44	BPB_RootClus	4	Cluster number of the first cluster of the root folder; usually 2.
030h	48	BPB_FSInfo	2	Sector number of extended FSInfo boot sector structure in the reserved area of the FAT32 volume; usually 1.
032h	50	BPB_BkBootSec	2	Sector number of the backup copy of the boot record; it's usually 6.
034h	52	BPB_Reserved	12	Reserved; should be 0.
040h	64	BS_DrvNum	1	Int 13h drive number; it's usually 00h for floppy disks or 80h for hard disks.
041h	65	BS_Reserved1	1	Reserved (used by Windows NT); it should be 0.
042h	66	BS_BootSig	1	Extended boot signature; it should be 29h if the following three fields are present. Otherwise, it's 00h.
043h	67	BS_VolID	4	Volume serial number; used with BS_VolLab to support volume tracking on removable media. Normally generated using the date and time as a seed when the volume is formatted.
047h	71	BS_VolLab	11	Volume label. Matches the 11-byte volume label recorded in the root folder, should be **NO NAME** if there is no volume label.
052h	82	BS_FilSysType	8	Should be **FAT32**. Not used by the OS after formatting.
05Ah	90	BS_BootCode	420	Bootstrap program code.
1FEh	510	BS_Signature	2	Signature bytes; it should be 55 AAh.

Table 10.16 shows the format and layout of the FAT32 FSInfo sector, which is the second sector of the three-sector-long FAT32 volume boot record.

Table 10.16   FAT32 VBR Format, FSInfo Sector 1

Offset (Hex)	Offset (Dec)	Name	Length (Bytes)	Description
000h	0	FSI_LeadSig	4	Lead signature, validates sector; it should be 52526141h.
004h	4	FSI_Reserved1	480	Reserved; it should be 0.
1E4h	484	FSI_StrucSig	4	Structure signature; it validates sector and should be 72724161h.
1E8h	488	FSI_Free_Count	4	Last known free cluster count on the volume. If FFFFFFFFh, the free count is unknown and must be recalculated by the OS.
1ECh	492	FSI_Nxt_Free	4	Next free cluster; it indicates where the system should start looking for free clusters. Usually set to the last cluster number allocated. If the value is FFFFFFFFh, the system should start looking at cluster 2.
1F0h	496	FSI_Reserved2	12	Reserved; it should be 0.
1FCh	508	FSI_TrailSig	4	Trailing signature; it should be 00 00 55 AAh.

Table 10.17 shows the format and layout of the FAT32 Boot Code sector, which is the third and final sector of the three-sector-long FAT32 volume boot record.

Table 10.17   FAT32 VBR Format, Boot Code Sector 2

Offset (Hex)	Offset (Dec)	Name	Length (Bytes)	Description
000h	0	BS_BootCode	510	Boot program code
1FEh	510	BS_Signature	2	Signature bytes; should be 55 AAh

It is interesting to note that this third sector has no system-specific information in it, which means the contents are the same from system to system. Thus, if this sector (and its backup at LBA 8) were damaged on one system, you could obtain a copy of this sector from any other FAT32 volume and use it to restore the damaged sector.

The VBR on NTFS volumes is 7 sectors long, although 16 sectors are reserved at the beginning of the disk for the VBR. A backup of the 16 sector VBR area is reserved at the end of the volume, which contains a backup VBR. The first sector of the 7 is the BPB sector, and it contains a jump instruction, the BPB, and signature bytes. Sectors 2–7 contain only additional boot code, with no signature bytes or any other structures. Because the boot code is not system specific, all but the first VBR sector should be the same on any NTFS volume. Table 10.18 shows the format and layout of the first sector of the 7-sector-long NTFS VBR.

Table 10.18   NTFS VBR Format, BPB Sector 0

Offset (Hex)	Offset (Dec)	Name	Length (Bytes)	Description
000h	0	BS_jmpBoot	3	Jump instruction to boot code; it's usually EB5290h.
003h	3	BS_OEMName	8	OEM ID; indicates which system formatted the volume. Typically, it's NTFS. Not used by the OS after formatting.
00Bh	11	BPB_BytsPerSec	2	Bytes per sector; it's usually 512.
00Dh	13	BPB_SecPerClus	1	Sectors per cluster; must be a power of 2 greater than 0. It's normally 1, 2, 4, or 8.
00Eh	14	BPB_RsvdSecCnt	2	Reserved sectors before the VBR; the value must be 0 or NTFS fails to mount the volume.
010h	16	BPB_Reserved	3	Value must be 0 or NTFS fails to mount the volume.
013h	19	BPB_Reserved	2	Value must be 0 or NTFS fails to mount the volume.
015h	21	BPB_Media	1	Media descriptor byte; it's normally F8h on all nonremovable media and F0h on most removable media.
016h	22	BPB_Reserved	2	Value must be 0 or NTFS fails to mount the volume.
018h	24	BPB_SecPerTrk	2	Sectors per track geometry value for interrupt 13h; usually 63 on hard disks.
01Ah	26	BPB_NumHeads	2	Number of heads for interrupt 13h; usually 255 on hard disks.
01Ch	28	BPB_HiddSec	4	Count of hidden sectors preceding the partition that contains this volume; normally 63 for the first volume.
020h	32	BPB_Reserved	4	Value must be 0 or NTFS fails to mount the volume.
024h	36	Reserved	4	Not used or checked by NTFS; it's normally 80008000h.
028h	40	BPB_TotSec64	8	Total count of sectors on the volume.
030h	48	BPB_MftClus	8	Logical cluster number for the start of the $MFT file.
038h	56	BPB_MirClus	8	Logical cluster number for the start of the $MFTMirr file.
040h	64	BPB_ClusPerMft	1	Clusters per MFT file/folder record. If this number is positive (00h–7Fh), it represents clusters per MFT record. If the number is negative (80h–FFh), the size of the record is 2 raised to the absolute value of this number.
041h	65	Reserved	3	Not used by NTFS.
044h	68	BPB_ClusPerIndx	1	Clusters per index buffer; it's used to allocate space for folders. If this number is positive (00h–7Fh), it represents clusters per MFT record. If the number is negative (80h–FFh), the size of the record is 2 raised to the absolute value of this number.
045h	69	Reserved	3	Not used by NTFS.
048h	72	BS_VolID	8	Volume serial number; used to support volume tracking on removable media. Normally generated using the date and time as a seed when the volume is formatted.
050h	80	Reserved	4	Not used by NTFS.
054h	84	BS_BootCode	426	Bootstrap program code.
1FEh	510	BS_Signature	2	Signature bytes; should be 55 AAh.

The Data Area

The data area of a partition is the place after the VBR where the actual files are stored. It is the area of the disk that is divided into clusters and managed by the file system. The specific content here varies based on what file system is used, the order in which the files are stored, the level of fragmentation of the files, and so forth. As such, it is not possible to show a specific structure here because the structures are dynamic—that is, changing with the changing files and data on the drive.

Diagnostic Read-and-Write Cylinder

On older systems without LBA support, partitioning programs such as FDISK normally reserve the last cylinder of a hard disk for use as a special diagnostic test cylinder. Because this cylinder is reserved, FDISK might report fewer total cylinders than the drive manufacturer states are available. If present, operating systems do not use this cylinder for any normal purpose because it lies outside the partitioned area of the disk.

On systems using a Host Protected Area (HPA), the system can reserve space on the end of a drive for system recovery or restoration software, diagnostics, and other utilities. This situation can account for additional discrepancies between the total capacity reported by FDISK and the drive manufacturer's reported capacity.

The diagnostics area enables software such as a manufacturer-supplied diagnostics disk to perform read-and-write tests on a hard disk without corrupting any user data. Many of these programs also swap spare cylinders for damaged cylinders if damaged cylinders are detected during testing.

File Systems

Physically, the hard disks and other media provide the basic technology for storing data. Logically, however, the file system provides the structure of volumes and folders in which you store individual files and the organizational model that enables the system to locate data anywhere on a given disk or drive. File systems typically are an integrated part of an OS, and in general the newer versions of Windows provide support for several file systems from which you can choose.

Normally a file system is chosen for a volume when that volume is created or formatted. In some cases there are utility programs that can change a file system from one type to another on an existing partition. Depending on the version(s) of Windows you are running, several file systems are available from which to choose. Each file system has specific limitations, advantages, and disadvantages, and which ones you use can also be limited by the operating system you choose.

The primary file systems to choose from today include

- File allocation table (FAT), which includes FAT12, FAT16, and FAT32
- New Technology File System (NTFS)

Note that only Windows 2000/XP and Vista support all of these file systems; older or less capable versions of Windows generally support only some of these file systems. Table 10.19 lists the file systems supported by various Microsoft operating systems including various versions of DOS and Windows.

Table 10.19   Microsoft OS File Systems Support

Operating System	FAT12	FAT16	FAT32	NTFS
MS-DOS 1.x-2.x	X			
MS-DOS 3.x-6.x	X	X		
MS-DOS 7.x-8.x	X	X	X	
Windows 3.1	X	X		
Windows 95	X	X		
Windows 95B	X	X	X	
Windows 98/98SE	X	X	X	
Windows Me	X	X	X	
Windows NT	X	X		X
Windows 2000	X	X	X	X
Windows XP	X	X	X	X
Windows Vista	X	X	X	X

Windows Vista supports reading and writing to FAT volumes; however, Vista can be installed only on NTFS volumes.

Although other operating systems may support other file systems, such as the Ext2FS supported by Linux or the HPFS (High Performance File System) supported by OS/2, this chapter focuses on the FAT and NTFS systems as supported by Windows.

Clusters (Allocation Units)

File systems store data in *clusters,* which are often called *allocation units.* The term *allocation unit* is appropriate because a single cluster is the smallest unit of the disk that the operating system can handle when it writes or reads a file. A cluster is equal to one or more 512-byte sectors, in powers of 2. Although a cluster can be a single disk sector, it is usually more than one. Having more than one sector per cluster reduces the size and processing overhead and enables the operating system to run faster because it has fewer individual units to manage. The trade-off is in wasted disk space. Because operating systems manage space only in full-cluster units, every file consumes space on the disk in increments of one cluster.

Because the operating system can allocate only whole clusters, a certain amount of wasted storage space inevitably results. File sizes rarely fall on cluster boundaries, so the last cluster allocated to a particular file is rarely filled completely. The extra space left over between the actual end of the file and the end of the cluster is called *slack.* A partition with large clusters has more slack space, whereas smaller clusters generate less slack.

The effect of larger cluster sizes on disk utilization can be substantial. A 2GiB partition containing about 5,000 files, with average slack of one-half of the last 32KiB cluster used for each file, wastes more than 78MiB (5000×(.5×32KiB)) of file space. When files of less than 32KiB in size are stored on a drive with a 32KiB allocation unit, waste (slack) factors can approach 40% of the drive's capacity. Newer file systems such as FAT32 and NTFS allow the use of smaller clusters, which use space on the disk more efficiently. For example, the same 2GiB partition with 5,000 files on it mentioned earlier would use 4KiB clusters with either NTFS or FAT32 instead of the 32KiB clusters used with FAT16. Assuming the same amount of slack for each file, the smaller cluster size reduces the average amount of wasted space on that partition from more than 78MiB to less than 10MiB.

Note

How much space does your current cluster size waste? To find out, you can download a free Windows utility called Karen's Disk Slack Checker from Karen Kenworthy's website. To find this and other useful utilities written by Karen, go to http://www.karenware.com/powertools.asp.

File Allocation Table

Until the release of Windows XP, the most commonly used file systems were based on a file allocation table, which keeps track of the data stored in each cluster on a disk. FAT is still the most universally understood file system, meaning it is recognized by virtually every operating system that runs on PCs, and even non-PCs. For example, FAT is even recognizable on Apple Mac systems. For this reason, although NTFS (covered later in this chapter in the section "NTFS") is usually recommended with Windows XP, for greater compatibility across systems and platforms, most external hard disks and removable-media drives still use FAT as their native file systems. Also, if you want to dual-boot Windows XP and Windows 9x/Me, you need to use FAT-based file systems even on your main drives.

Three main varieties of the FAT system exist, called FAT12, FAT16, and FAT32—all of which are differentiated by the number of digits used in the allocation table numbers. In other words, FAT16 uses 16-bit numbers to keep track of data clusters, FAT32 uses 32-bit numbers, and so on. The various FAT systems are used as follows:

- **FAT12**— Used on all volumes smaller than 16MiB (for example, floppy disks).

- **FAT16**— Used on volumes from 16MiB through 2GiB by MS-DOS 3.0 and most versions of Windows. Windows NT, Windows 2000, and Windows XP support FAT16 volumes as large as 4GiB. However, FAT16 volumes larger than 2GiB cannot be used by MS-DOS or Windows 9x/Me.

- **FAT32**— Optionally used on volumes from 512MiB through 2GiB, and required on all FAT volumes over 2GiB, starting with Windows 95B (OSR 2.x) and subsequent versions.

FAT12 and FAT16 are the file systems originally used by DOS and Windows and are supported by every other PC operating system from past to present. An add-on to the FAT file systems called VFAT is found in Windows 95 and newer. VFAT is a driver in Windows that adds the capability to use long filenames on existing FAT systems. When running Windows 95 or newer, VFAT is automatically enabled for all FAT volumes.

Although all PC operating systems support FAT12 and FAT16, Windows 2000/XP and Vista also have support for FAT32 as well as non-FAT file systems such as NTFS.

FAT12

FAT12 was the first file system used in the PC when it was released on August 12, 1981, and because it is so efficient on small volumes, it is still used today on all floppy disks as well as hard disks and other removable storage media FAT volumes less than 16MiB. FAT12 uses a table of 12-bit numbers to manage the clusters (also called *allocation units*) on a disk. A *cluster* is the storage unit in the data area of the disk where files are stored. Each file uses a minimum of one cluster, and files that are larger than one cluster use additional space in cluster increments. FAT12 cluster sizes are shown in Table 10.20.

Table 10.20   FAT12 Cluster Sizes

Media Type	Volume Size	Sectors per Cluster	Cluster Size
5 1/4" DD floppy disk	360K	2	1KiB
3 1/2" DD floppy disk	720K	2	1KiB
5 1/4" HD floppy disk	1.2MB	1	0.5KiB
3 1/2" HD floppy disk	1.44MB	1	0.5KiB
3 1/2" ED floppy disk	2.88MB	2	1KiB
Other media	0–15.9MiB	8	4KiB

DD = double density
HD = high density
ED = extra-high density
KiB = kibibyte = 1,024 bytes
MiB = mebibyte = 1,048,576 bytes

Each cluster on a FAT12 volume is typically eight sectors in size, except on floppy disks, where the size varies according to the particular floppy type. 12-bit cluster numbers range from 000h to FFFh (hexadecimal), which is 0–4,095 in decimal. This theoretically allows 4,096 total clusters; however, 11 of the cluster numbers are reserved and cannot be assigned to actual clusters on a disk. Cluster numbers start at 2 (0 and 1 are reserved), number FF7h is reserved to indicate a bad cluster, and numbers FF8h–FFFh indicate an end-of-chain in the FAT, leaving 4,085 clusters (4,096 – 11 = 4,085). Microsoft subtracts 1 from this to eliminate boundary problems, allowing up to exactly 4,084 clusters maximum in a FAT12 volume.

FAT12 volumes include 1 sector for the boot record and BPB (BIOS parameter block), two copies of the FAT (up to 12 sectors long each), up to 32 sectors for the root folder (less only on floppy disk media), and a data area with up to 4,084 clusters. Because each FAT12 cluster is 8 sectors (except on floppy disks), FAT12 volumes are limited to a maximum size of 32,729 sectors (1 sector for the boot record + 12 sectors per FAT × 2 FATs + 32 sectors for the root folder + 4,084 clusters × 8 sectors per cluster). This equals 16.76MB or 15.98MiB. FAT12 volume limits are detailed in Table 10.21.

Table 10.21   FAT12 Volume Limits

Volume Limit	Clusters	Sectors per Cluster	Total Volume Sectors	Volume Size (Decimal)	Volume Size (Binary)
Maximum size	4,084	8	32,729	16.76MB	15.98MiB

MB = megabyte = 1,000,000 bytes
MiB = mebibyte = 1,048,576 bytes

PC/MS-DOS 1.x and 2.x use FAT12 exclusively, and all later versions of DOS and all Windows versions automatically create a FAT12 file system on any disks or partitions that are 32,729 sectors or less (16.76MB) in size. Anything larger than that is automatically formatted as FAT16, FAT32, or NTFS. Characteristics of FAT12 include the following:

- Is used on all floppy disks
- Has a default format on FAT volumes of 16.76MB (15.98MiB) or less
- Is supported by all versions of DOS and Windows
- Is supported by all operating systems capable of reading PC disks

FAT12 is still used in PCs today on very small media because the 12-bit tables are smaller than those for FAT16 and FAT32, which preserves the most space for data.

FAT16

FAT16 is similar to FAT12 except it uses 16-bit numbers to manage the clusters on a disk. FAT16 was introduced on August 14, 1984, along with PC/MS-DOS 3.0, with the intention of supporting larger hard drives. FAT16 picked up where FAT12 left off and was used on media or partitions of more than 32,729 sectors (15.98MiB or 16.76MB). FAT16 could theoretically support drives of up to 2GiB or 4GiB. However, even with FAT16, DOS 3.3 and earlier were still limited to a maximum partition size of 32MiB (33.55MB) because DOS 3.3 and earlier used only 16-bit sector addressing internally and in the BPB (BIOS parameter block, stored in the volume boot sector, which is the first logical sector in a FAT partition). The use of 16-bit sector values limited DOS 3.3 and earlier to supporting drives of up to 65,535 sectors of 512 bytes, which is 32MiB (33.55MB).

As a temporary way to address drives larger than 32MiB, PC/MS-DOS 3.3 (released on April 2, 1987) introduced the extended partition, which could internally support up to 23 subpartitions (logical drives) of up to 32MiB each. Combined with the primary partition on a disk, this allowed for a total of 24 partitions of up to 32MiB each, which would be seen by the operating system as logical drives C–Z.

To take full advantage of FAT16 and allow for larger drives and partition sizes, Microsoft collaborated with Compaq, which introduced Compaq DOS 3.31 in November 1987. It was the first OS to use 32-bit sector addressing internally and in the BPB. Then the rest of the PC world followed suit on July 19, 1988, when Microsoft and IBM released PC/MS-DOS 4.0. This enabled FAT16 to handle partition sizes up to 2GiB using 64 sectors per cluster.

Each cluster in a FAT16 volume is up to 64 sectors in size. 16-bit cluster numbers range from 0000h to FFFFh, which is 0–65,535 in decimal. This theoretically allows 65,536 total clusters.

However, 11 of the cluster numbers are reserved and cannot be assigned to actual clusters on a disk. Cluster numbers start at 2 (0 and 1 are reserved), number FFF7h is reserved to indicate a bad cluster, and numbers FFF8h–FFFFh indicate an end of chain in the FAT, leaving 65,525 clusters (65,536 – 11 = 65,525). Microsoft subtracts 1 from this to eliminate boundary problems, allowing up to 65,524 clusters maximum in a FAT16 volume. FAT16 cluster sizes are shown in Table 10.22.

Table 10.22   FAT16 Cluster Sizes

Volume Size	Sectors per Cluster	Cluster Size
4.1MiB–15.96MiB[1]	2	1KiB
>15.96MiB–128MiB	4	2KiB
>128MiB–256MiB	8	4KiB
>256MiB–512MiB	16	8KiB
>512MiB–1GiB	32	16KiB
>1GiB–2GiB	64	32KiB
>2GiB–4GiB[2]	128	64KiB

1. Volumes smaller than 16MiB default to FAT12; however, FAT32 can be forced by altering the format parameters.
2. Volumes larger than 2GiB are supported only by Windows NT/2000/XP or Vista and are not recommended.
MB = megabyte = 1,000,000 bytes
KiB = kibibyte = 1,024 bytes
MiB = mebibyte = 1,024KiB = 1,048,576 bytes
GiB = gibibyte = 1,024MiB = 1,073,741,824 bytes

FAT16 volumes include 1 sector for the boot record and BPB, two copies of the FAT (default and backup) up to 256 sectors long each, 32 sectors for the root folder, and a data area with up to 65,524 clusters. Each FAT16 cluster can be up to 64 sectors (32KiB) in size, meaning FAT16 volumes are limited to a maximum size of 4,194,081 sectors (1 sector for the boot record + 256 sectors per FAT × 2 FATs + 32 sectors for the root folder + 65,524 clusters × 64 sectors per cluster). This equals a maximum capacity of 2.15GB or 2GiB. FAT16 volume limits are shown in Table 10.23.

Note

Windows NT/2000/XP can optionally create FAT16 volumes that use 128 sectors per cluster (64KiB) in size, bringing the maximum volume size to 4.29GB or 4GiB. However any volumes formatted in that manner are not readable in virtually any other OS. Additionally, 64KiB clusters cause many disk utilities to fail. For maximum compatibility, FAT16 volumes should be limited to 32KiB clusters and 2.15GB/2GiB in size.

Table 10.23   FAT16 Volume Limits

Volume Limit	Clusters	Sectors per Cluster	Total Volume Sectors	Volume Size (Decimal)	Volume Size (Binary)
Minimum size	4,167	2	8,401	4.3MB	4.1MiB
DOS 3.0–3.3 max.	16,343	4	65,533	33.55MB	32MiB
Win9x/Me max.	65,524	64	4,194,081	2.15GB	2GiB
NT-Vista max.	65,524	128	8,387,617	4.29GB	4GiB

MB = megabyte = 1,000,000 bytes
GB = gigabyte = 1,000
MB = 1,000,000,000 bytes
MiB = mebibyte = 1,048,576 bytes
GiB = gibibyte = 1,024MiB = 1,073,741,824 bytes

Some notable characteristics and features of FAT16 include

- FAT16 is fully supported by MS-DOS 3.31 and higher, all versions of Windows, and some UNIX operating systems.

- FAT16 is fast and efficient on volumes smaller than 256MiB but relatively inefficient on larger volumes because the cluster size becomes much larger than with FAT32 and NTFS.

- The boot sector information is not automatically backed up, and if damaged or destroyed, access to the volume is lost.

- In case of a problem, you can boot the system using any MS-DOS bootable floppy to troubleshoot the problem and if necessary, repair the volume. Many third-party software tools can repair or recover data from FAT16 volumes.

- The root directory (folder) can handle up to a maximum of 512 entries, which is further reduced if any root entries use long filenames.

- FAT16 has no built-in security, encryption, or compression capability.

- File sizes on a FAT16 volume are limited only by the size of the volume. Because each file takes a minimum of one cluster, FAT16 volumes cannot have more than 65,524 total files.

VFAT and Long Filenames

The original Windows 95 release introduced what is essentially the same FAT16 file system as was used in MS-DOS 6.x and earlier, except for a few important enhancements. Like much of the rest of Windows 95, the operating system support for the FAT file system was rewritten using 32-bit code and called *VFAT (virtual file allocation table)*. VFAT works in combination with the 32-bit protected mode VCACHE (which replaces the 16-bit real mode SMARTDrive cache used in DOS and Windows 3.1) to provide better file system performance. However, the most obvious improvement in VFAT is its support for long filenames. DOS and Windows 3.1 had been encumbered by the standard 8.3 file-naming convention for many years, and adding long filename support was a high priority in Windows 95—particularly in light of the fact that Macintosh and OS/2 users had long enjoyed this capability.

The problem for the Windows 95 designers, as is often the case in the PC industry, was backward compatibility. It is no great feat to make long filenames possible when you are designing a new file system from scratch, as Microsoft did years before with Windows NT's NTFS. However, the Windows 95 developers wanted to add long filenames to the existing FAT file system and still make it possible to store those names on existing DOS volumes and for previous versions of DOS and Windows to access the files.

VFAT provides the capability to assign file and folder names that are up to 255 characters in length (including the length of the path). The three-character extension is maintained because, like previous Windows versions, Windows 9x relies on the extensions to associate file types with specific applications. VFAT's long filenames can also include spaces, as well as the following characters, which standard DOS 8.3 names can't: +,;=[ ].

The first problem when implementing the long filenames was how to make them usable to previous versions of DOS as well as older 16-bit Windows applications that supported only 8.3 names. The resolution to this problem was to give each file two names: a long filename and an alias that uses the traditional 8.3 naming convention. When you create a file with a long filename in Windows 9x/Me, VFAT uses the following process to create an equivalent 8.3 alias name:

1. The first three characters after the last dot in the long filename become the extension of the alias.

2. The first six characters of the long filename (excluding spaces, which are ignored) are converted into uppercase and become the first six characters of the alias filename. If any of these six characters are illegal under the standard 8.3 naming rules (that is, +,;=[ ]), VFAT converts those characters into underscores.

3. VFAT adds the two characters ~1 as the seventh and eighth characters of the alias filename, unless this will result in a name conflict, in which case it uses ~2, ~3, and so on, as necessary.

Aliasing in Windows NT/2000/XP and Vista

Note that Windows NT/2000/XP and Vista creates aliases differently than Windows 9x/Me (as shown later).

NT/2000/XP and Vista begins by taking the first six legal characters in the LFN and following them with a tilde and number. If the first six characters are unique, a number 1 follows the tilde.

If the first six characters aren't unique, a number 2 is added. NT/2000/XP and Vista use the first three legal characters following the last period in the LFN for a file extension.

At the fifth iteration of this process, NT/2000/XP and Vista takes only the first two legal characters, performs a hash on the filename to produce four hexadecimal characters, places the four hex characters after the first two legal characters, and appends a ~5. The ~5 remains for all subsequent aliases; only the hex numbers change.

For example, I created six files using long names under Windows XP, and the automatically generated alias (short names) were as follows:

Long Filename (LFN)	Alias (Created by Windows)
New Text Document.txt	NEWTEX~1.TXT
New Text Document (2).txt	NEWTEX~2.TXT
New Text Document (3).txt	NEWTEX~3.TXT
New Text Document (4).txt	NEWTEX~4.TXT
New Text Document (5).txt	NE5A0A~1.TXT
New Text Document (6).txt	NE5A04~1.TXT

Note how the algorithm changes after the fifth file.

Tip

You can modify the behavior of the VFAT filename truncation mechanism to make it use the first eight characters of the long filename instead of the first six characters plus ~1. To do this, you must add a new binary value to the `HKEY_LOCAL_MACHINE\System\CurrentControlSet\control\FileSystem` Registry key called `NameNumericTail`, with a value of `0`. Changing the value to `1` returns the truncation process to its original state.

Although this Registry change creates more "friendly" looking alias names, it causes many programs working with alias names to fail and is not recommended.

VFAT stores this alias filename in the standard name field of the file's folder entry. Any version of DOS or 16-bit Windows can therefore access the file using the alias name. The big problem that still remains, however, is where to store the long filenames. Clearly, storing a 255-character filename in a 32-byte folder entry is impossible (because each character requires 1 byte). However, modifying the structure of the folder entry would make the files unusable by previous DOS versions.

The developers of VFAT resolved this problem by using additional folder entries to store the long filenames. Each of the folder entries is still 32 bytes long, so up to 8 might be required for each long name, depending on its length. To ensure that these additional folder entries are not misinterpreted by earlier DOS versions, VFAT flags them with a combination of attributes that is not possible for a normal file: read-only, hidden, system, and volume label. These attributes cause DOS to ignore the long filename entries, and prevent them from being mistakenly overwritten.

Caution

When using long filenames on a standard FAT12 or FAT16 partition, you should avoid storing them in the root folder. Files with long names that take up multiple folder entries can more easily use up the limited number of entries allotted to the root folder than files with 8.3 names. On FAT32 drives, this is not a problem because the root folder has an unlimited number of entries.

In an experiment, I created a small (1KiB) text file on a floppy disk and gave it a 135-character long filename using Windows 98. I copied the file and pasted it repeatedly into the root folder of a floppy disk using Windows Explorer. Before I could make 20 copies of the file, the system displayed a `File copying` error. The disk could not accept any more files because the multiple copies of the extremely long filename had used up all the root folder entries.

This solution for implementing backward-compatible long filenames in Windows 9x is ingenious, but it is not without its problems. Most of these problems stem from the use of applications that can access only the 8.3 alias names assigned to files. In some cases, if you open a file with a long name using one of these programs and save it again, the connection to the additional folder entries containing the long name is severed and the long name is lost.

This is especially true for older versions of disk utilities, such as Norton Disk Doctor for MS-DOS, that are not designed to support VFAT. Most older applications ignore the additional folder entries because of the combination of attributes assigned to them, but disk repair utilities usually are designed to detect and "correct" discrepancies of this type. The result is that running an old version of Norton Disk Doctor on a partition with long filenames results in the loss of all the long names. In the same way, backup utilities not designed for use with VFAT can strip off the long filenames from a partition.

Note

When using VFAT's long filename capabilities, you definitely should use disk and backup utilities that are intended to support VFAT. Windows 9x includes VFAT-compatible disk repair, defragmentation, and backup programs. If, however, you are for some reason inclined to use an older program that does not support VFAT, Windows 9x includes a clumsy, but effective, solution.

A program called LFNBK.EXE is included on the Windows 9x CD-ROM . It doesn't install with the operating system, but you can use it to strip the long filenames from a VFAT volume and store them in a text file called **LFNBK.DAT**. You can then work with the files on the volume as though they were standard 8.3 FAT files. Afterward, you can use LFNBK.EXE to restore the long filenames to their original places (assuming that the file and folder structure has not changed). This is not a convenient solution, nor is it recommended for use in anything but extraordinary circumstances, but the capability is there if needed. Some backup programs designed for disaster recovery (which enable you to reconstruct the contents of the hard drive without reloading Windows first) have used this feature to enable restoration of a Windows drive with long filenames from a DOS prompt (where only 8.3 alias names usually are supported).

Another problem with VFAT's long filenames involves the process by which the file system creates the 8.3 alias names. VFAT creates a new alias every time you create or copy a file into a new folder; therefore, the alias can change. For example, you might have a file called Expenses-January-Travel.doc stored in a folder with the alias EXPENS~1.DOC. If you use Windows 9x Explorer to copy this file to a folder that already contains a file called Expenses-December-Travel.doc, you are likely to find that this existing file is already using the alias EXPENS~1.DOC. In this case, VFAT assigns EXPENS~2.DOC as the alias of the newly copied file, with no warning to the user. This is not a problem for applications that support VFAT because the long filenames are unchanged, but a user running an older application might open the EXPENS~1.DOC file expecting to find the list of January travel expenses and see the December travel expenses list instead.

FAT32

FAT32 is an enhanced version of the FAT file system first supported by Windows 95B (also known as OEM Service Release 2, released in August 1996). FAT32 is also supported in Windows 98/Me, Windows 2000/XP, and Vista. FAT32 is not supported in MS-DOS 6.xx or earlier, the original release of Windows 95, or in any release of Windows NT.

FAT32 works just like FAT16; the only difference is that it uses numbers with more digits, so it can manage more clusters on a disk. Unlike VFAT, which is a Windows innovation that used existing FAT12/16 file system structures to handle long filenames, FAT32 is an enhancement of the entire FAT file system. FAT32 was first included in the Windows 95 OEM Service Release 2 (OSR2, also known as Windows 95B) and is also part of Windows 98/Me, Windows 2000/XP, and Vista.

One of the main reasons for creating FAT32 was to use disk space more efficiently. FAT32 uses smaller clusters (4KiB clusters for drives up to 8GiB in size), resulting in a 10%–15% more efficient use of disk space relative to large FAT16 drives. FAT32 also supports partitions of up to 2TiB in size, much larger than the 2GiB limit of FAT16. FAT32 cluster sizes are shown in Table 10.24.

Table 10.24   FAT32 Cluster Sizes

Volume Size	Sectors per Cluster	Cluster Size
32.52MiB–260MiB[1]	1	0.5KiB
>260MiB–8GiB	8	4KiB
>8GiB–16GiB	16	8KiB
>16GiB–32GiB	32	16KiB
>32GiB–2TiB[2]	64	32KiB

1. Volumes smaller than 512MiB will default to FAT16, although FAT32 can be forced by altering the format parameters.
2. Windows 2000/XP and Vista format FAT32 volumes only up to 32GiB; however, they support existing FAT32 volumes up to 2TiB.
MB = megabyte = 1,000,000 bytes
GB = gigabyte = 1,000MB = 1,000,000,000 bytes
TB = terabyte = 1,000GB = 1,000,000,000,000 bytes
KiB = kibibyte = 1,024 bytes
MiB = mebibyte = 1,024KiB = 1,048,576 bytes
GiB = gibibyte = 1,024MiB = 1,073,741,824 bytes
TiB = tebibyte = 1,024GiB = 1,099,511,627,776 bytes

Although the name implies that FAT32 uses 32-bit numbers to manage clusters (allocation units) on a disk, FAT32 actually uses only the first 28 bits of each 32-bit entry, leaving the high 4 bits reserved. The only time the high 4 bits are changed is when the volume is formatted, at which time the whole 32-bit entry is zeroed (including the high 4 bits). The high 4 bits are subsequently ignored when reading or writing FAT32 cluster entries; therefore, if those bits are non zero, they are preserved. Microsoft has never indicated any purpose for them other than simply being reserved.

So, although the FAT32 entries are technically 32-bit numbers, FAT32 really uses 28-bit numbers to manage the clusters on a disk. Each cluster on a FAT32 volume is from 1 sector (512 bytes) to 64 sectors (32KiB) in size. 28-bit cluster numbers range from 0000000h to FFFFFFFh, which is 0–268,435,455 in decimal. This theoretically allows for 268,435,456 total clusters. However, 11 of the numbers are reserved and cannot be assigned to actual clusters on a disk. Cluster numbers start at 2 (0 and 1 are reserved), the number FFFFFF7h is reserved to indicate a bad cluster, and numbers FFFFFF8h–FFFFFFFh indicate an end of chain in the FAT, leaving exactly 268,435,445 clusters maximum (268,435,456 – 11 = 268,435,445).

FAT32 volumes reserve the first 32 sectors for the boot record, which includes both the default boot record (3 sectors long, starting at logical sector 0) and a backup boot record (also 3 sectors long, but starting at logical sector 6). The remaining sectors in that area are reserved and filled with 0s. Following the 32 reserved sectors are two FATs (default and backup) that can be anywhere from 512 sectors to 2,097,152 sectors in length, with a data area 65,525–268,435,445 clusters.

Each FAT32 cluster is up to 64 sectors (32KiB) in size, so FAT32 disks or partitions could theoretically be up to 17,184,062,816 sectors (32 sectors for the boot record + 2,097,152 sectors per FAT × 2 FATs + 268,435,445 clusters × 64 sectors per cluster), which equals a capacity of 8.8TB or 8TiB. This capacity is theoretical because the 32-bit sector numbering scheme used in the partition tables located in the MBR limits a disk to no more than 4,294,967,295 ($2^{32}-1$) sectors, which is 2.2TB or 2TiB. Therefore, although FAT32 can in theory handle a volume of up to 8.8TB (terabytes or trillions of bytes), the reality is that we are currently limited by the 32-bit sector numbering in the partition table format of the MBR to only 2.2TB. In the future, this limitation will be addressed by both BIOS and OS updates that allow the use of a new type of partition table format called GUID (Globally Unique Identifier) Partition Table, or GPT.

Individual files can be up to 1 byte less than 4GiB in size and are limited by the size field in the folder entry, which is 4 bytes long. Because the clusters are numbered using 32-bit values instead of 16-bit ones, the format of the folder entries on a FAT32 partition must be changed slightly. The 2-byte Link to Start Cluster field is increased to 4 bytes, using 2 of the 10 bytes (bytes 12–21) in the folder entry that were reserved for future use.

Note

If you attempt to format a FAT32 volume larger than 32GiB on a system running Windows 2000/XP or Vista, the format fails near the end of the process with the following error:

```
Logical Disk Manager: Volume size too big.
```

This is by design. The format tools included with Windows 2000/XP and Vista will not format a volume larger than 32GiB using the FAT32 file system. Only the format tools are restricted as such; any preexisting volumes up to 2TiB are otherwise fully supported. The limitation is entirely voluntary; Microsoft is basically trying to force you to use NTFS on any newly created volumes larger than 32GiB. Unfortunately this means that if you are formatting an external USB or FireWire drive that will be moved between various systems, some of which include Windows 9x/Me or even Apple Mac systems, you must either format the drive on a Windows 98 or Me system, or use a third-party utility such as the SwissKnife program (available for free from www.compuapps.com) to partition and format the drive.

Windows 95 OSR2 and Windows 98 have additional limitations with FAT32. The ScanDisk tool included with those operating systems is a 16-bit program that has a maximum allocation size for a single memory block of 16MB minus 64KB. This means that ScanDisk cannot process volumes using the FAT32 file system that have a FAT larger than 16MB minus 64KB in size. Each FAT32 entry uses 4 bytes, so ScanDisk cannot process the FAT on a volume using the FAT32 file system that defines more than 4,177,920 clusters, which after subtracting the two reserved clusters leaves 4,177,918 actual clusters. At 32KiB per cluster—including the boot sector reserved area and the FATs themselves—this results in a maximum volume size of 136.94GB or 127.53GiB. The ScanDisk versions included with Windows Me and later do not have this limitation.

Table 10.25 lists the volume limits for a FAT32 file system.

Table 10.25   FAT32 Volume Limits

Volume Limit	Clusters	Sectors per Cluster	Total Volume Sectors	Volume Size (Decimal)	Volume Size (Binary)
Minimum size	65,535	1	66,601	34.1MB	32.52MiB
MBR max.	67,092,481	64	4,294,967,266	2.2TB	2TiB
Theoretical max.	268,435,445	64	17,184,062,816	8.8TB	8TiB

MB = megabyte = 1,000,000 bytes
GB = gigabyte = 1,000MB = 1,000,000,000 bytes
TB = terabyte = 1,000GB = 1,000,000,000,000 bytes
KiB = kibibytes = 1,024 bytes
MiB = mebibyte = 1,024KiB = 1,048,576 bytes
GiB = gibibyte = 1,024MiB = 1,073,741,824 bytes
TiB = tebibytes = 1,024GiB = 1,099,511,627,776 bytes

FAT32 is more robust than FAT12 or FAT16. FAT12/16 uses the first sector of a volume for the volume boot record, which is a critical structure. If the boot sector is damaged or destroyed, access to the entire volume is lost. FAT32 improves on this by creating both a default and a backup volume boot record in the first 32 sectors of the volume, which are reserved for this purpose. Each FAT32 volume boot record is three sectors long. The default boot record is in logical sectors 0–2 (the first three sectors) in the partition, and the backup is in sectors 6–8. This feature has saved me on several occasions when the default boot record was damaged and access to the entire volume was lost. In these situations, I was still able to recover the entire volume by manually restoring the volume boot record from the backup by using a sector editor such as Norton Diskedit (included with Norton SystemWorks by Symantec). Because FAT12 and FAT16 do not create a backup boot sector, if the boot sector is destroyed on those volumes, it must be re-created manually from scratch—a much more difficult proposition.

Another important difference in FAT32 partitions is the nature of the root folder. In a FAT32 partition, the root folder does not occupy a fixed position on the disk as in a FAT16 partition. Instead, it can be located anywhere in the partition and expand to any size. This eliminates the preset limit on root folder entries and provides the infrastructure necessary to make FAT32 partitions dynamically resizable. Unfortunately, Microsoft never implemented that feature in Windows, but third-party products such as PartitionMagic from Symantec can take advantage of this capability.

As with FAT12/16, FAT32 also maintains two copies of the FAT and automatically switches to the backup FAT if a sector in the default FAT becomes unreadable. The root directory (folder) in a FAT16 system is exactly 32 sectors long and immediately follows the two FAT copies; however, in FAT32, the root folder is actually created as a subdirectory (folder) that is stored as a file, relocatable to anywhere in the partition, and extendable in length. Therefore, a 512-file limit no longer exists in the root folder for FAT32 as it did with FAT12/16.

The main drawback of FAT32 is that it is not compatible with previous versions of DOS and Windows 95. You can't boot to a previous version of DOS or (pre-OSR2) Windows 95 from a

FAT32 drive, nor can a system started with an old DOS or Windows 95 boot disk see FAT32 partitions. Most recent distributions of Linux now support FAT32, and even Mac OS 8.1 and later can read and write FAT32 volumes. For all but the oldest of equipment, FAT32 is the most universally understandable format that supports larger volumes.

Some notable characteristics and features of FAT32 include the following:

- FAT32 is fully supported by Windows 95B (OSR2), 98, Me, 2000, XP, and Vista versions; however, Vista cannot be *installed* on a FAT32 volume.

- MS-DOS 6.22 and earlier, Windows 95a, and Windows NT do not support FAT32 and cannot read or write FAT32 volumes.

- Mac OS 8.1 and later support FAT32 drives.

- FAT32 is the ideal format for large, external USB or FireWire drives that will be moved between various PC and Mac systems.

- The root directory (folder) is stored as a subfolder file that can be located anywhere on the volume. Subdirectories (folders) including the root can handle up to 65,534 entries, which is further reduced if any entries use long filenames.

- FAT32 uses smaller clusters (4KiB for volumes up to 8GiB), so space is allocated much more efficiently than FAT16.

- The critical boot sector is backed up at logical sector 6 on the volume.

- Windows 2000/XP and Vista format FAT32 volumes only up to 32GiB. To format FAT32 volumes larger than 32GiB, you must format the volume on a Windows 98/Me system.

- In case of a boot problem, you must start the system using a bootable disk created using Windows 95B (OSR2), 98, Me, 2000, or XP. A limited number of third-party software tools can repair or recover data from FAT32 volumes.

- FAT32 has no built-in security, encryption, or compression capability.

- File sizes on FAT32 volumes are limited to 4,294,967,295 bytes ($2^{32} - 1$), which is 1 byte less than 4GiB in size.

FAT Mirroring

FAT32 also takes greater advantage of the two copies of the FAT stored on a disk partition. On a FAT16 partition, the first copy of the FAT is always the primary copy and replicates its data to the secondary FAT, sometimes corrupting it in the process. On a FAT32 partition, when the system detects a problem with the primary copy of the FAT, it can switch to the other copy, which then becomes the primary. The system can also disable the FAT-mirroring process to prevent the viable FAT from being corrupted by the other copy. This provides a greater degree of fault tolerance to FAT32 partitions, often enabling you to repair a damaged FAT without an immediate system interruption or a loss of table data.

Converting FAT16 to FAT32

If you want to convert an existing FAT16 partition to FAT32, Windows 98 and Me include a FAT32 Conversion Wizard that enables you to migrate existing partitions in place.

The wizard gathers the information needed to perform the conversion, informs you of the consequences of implementing FAT32, and attempts to prevent data loss and other problems. After you have selected the drive you want to convert, the wizard performs a scan for applications (such as disk utilities) that might not function properly on the converted partition. The wizard gives you the opportunity to remove these and warns you to back up the data on the partition before proceeding with the conversion. Even if you don't use the Microsoft Backup utility the wizard offers, backing up your data is a strongly recommended precaution.

Because the conversion must deal with the existing partition data in addition to creating new volume boot record information, FATs, and clusters, the process can take far longer than partitioning and formatting an empty drive. Depending on the amount of data involved and the new cluster size, the conversion can take several hours to complete.

After you convert a FAT16 partition to FAT32, you can't convert it back with Windows tools, except by destroying the partition and using FDISK to create a new one. After market partitioning utilities are available that can convert FAT32 back to FAT16 if you want. You should take precautions before beginning the conversion process, such as connecting the system to a UPS. A power failure during the conversion could result in a loss of data.

Third-Party Partitioning Utilities

Windows includes only basic tools for creating FAT32 partitions, but programs such as Partition Commander from VCOM (www.v-com.com) and PartitionMagic from Symantec (www.symantec.com) provide many other partition manipulation features. These programs can easily convert partitions back and forth between FAT16, FAT32, NTFS, and other file systems, as well as resize, move, and copy partitions without destroying the data they contain. They also allow changes in cluster sizes beyond what the standard Windows tools create.

File Allocation Table Tutorial

You can think of the FAT as a type of spreadsheet that tracks the allocation of the disk's clusters. Each cell in the spreadsheet corresponds to a single cluster on the disk. The number stored in that cell is a code indicating whether a file uses the cluster and, if so, where the next cluster of the file is located. Thus, to determine which clusters a particular file is using, you would start by looking at the first FAT reference in the file's folder entry. When you look up the referenced cluster in the FAT, the table contains a reference to the file's next cluster. Each FAT reference, therefore, points to the next cluster in what is called a FAT *chain* until you reach the cluster containing the end of the file. Numbers stored in the FAT are hexadecimal numbers that are either 12 or 16 bits long. The 16-bit FAT numbers are easy to follow in a disk sector editor because they take an even 2 bytes of space. The 12-bit numbers are 1 1/2 bytes long, which presents a problem because most disk sector editors show data in byte units. To edit a 12-bit FAT, you must do some hex/binary math to convert the displayed byte units to FAT numbers. Fortunately (unless you are using the DOS DEBUG program), most of the available tools and utility programs have a FAT-editing mode that automatically converts the numbers for you. Most of them also show the FAT numbers in decimal form, which most people find easier to handle.

With FAT16, the cluster numbers are stored as 16-bit entries, from 0000h to FFFFh. The largest value possible is FFFFh, which corresponds to 65,535 in decimal, but several numbers at the beginning and end are reserved for special use. The actual cluster numbers allowed in a FAT16 system range from 0002h to FFF6h, which is 2–65,526 in decimal. All files must be stored in cluster numbers within that range. That leaves only 65,524 valid clusters to use for storing files (cluster numbers below 2 and above 65,526 are reserved), meaning a partition must be broken up into that many clusters or less. A typical file entry under FAT16 might look like Table 10.26.

Table 10.26 FAT16 File Entries

Folder

Name	Starting Cluster	Size
USCONST.TXT	1000	4

FAT16 File Allocation Table

FAT Cluster #	Value	Meaning
00002	0	First cluster available
...	...	...
00999	0	Cluster available
01000	1001	In use, points to next cluster
01001	1002	In use, points to next cluster
01002	1003	In use, points to next cluster
01003	FFFFh	End of file
01004	0	Cluster available
...	...	...
65526	0	Last cluster available

In this example, the folder entry states that the file starts in cluster number 1000. In the FAT, that cluster has a nonzero value, which indicates it is in use; the specific value indicates where the file using it would continue. In this case, the entry for cluster 1000 is 1001, which means the file continues in cluster 1001. The entry in 1001 points to 1002, and from 1002 the entry points to 1003. The entry for 1003 is FFFFh, which is an indication that the cluster is in use but that the file ends here and uses no additional clusters.

The use of the FAT becomes clearer when you see that files can be fragmented. Let's say that before the USCONST.TXT file was written, another file already occupied clusters 1002 and 1003. If USCONST.TXT was written starting at 1000, it would not have been capable of being completely written before running into the other file. As such, the operating system would skip over the used clusters and continue the file in the next available cluster. The end result is shown in Table 10.27.

Table 10.27 Folder and FAT Relationship (Fragmented File)

Folder

Name	Starting Cluster	Size
PLEDGE.TXT	1002	2
USCONST.TXT	1000	4

FAT16 File Allocation Table

FAT Cluster #	Value	Meaning
00002	0	First cluster available
...	...	...
00999	0	Cluster available
01000	1001	In use, points to next cluster
01001	1004	In use, points to next cluster
01002	1003	In use, points to next cluster
01003	FFFFh	End of file
01004	1005	In use, points to next cluster
01005	FFFFh	End of file
...	...	...
65526	0	Last cluster available

In this example, the PLEDGE.TXT file that was previously written interrupted USCONST.TXT, so those clusters are skipped over, and the pointers in the FAT reflect that. Note that the defrag programs included with DOS and Windows take an example like this and move the files so that they are contiguous, one after the other, and update the FAT to indicate the change in cluster use.

The first two entries in the FAT are reserved and contain information about the table itself. All remaining entries correspond to specific clusters on the disk. Most FAT entries consist of a reference to another cluster containing the next part of a particular file. However, some FAT entries contain hexadecimal values with special meanings, as follows:

■ **0000h**—Indicates that the cluster is not in use by a file

■ **FFF7h**—Indicates that at least one sector in the cluster is damaged and that it should not be used to store data

■ **FFF8h–FFFFh**— Indicates that the cluster contains the end of a file and that no reference to another cluster is necessary

To compare FAT16 and FAT32, you can look at how a file would be stored on each. With FAT32, the cluster numbers range from 00000000h to 0FFFFFFFh, which is 0–268,435,455 in decimal. Again, some values at the low and high ends are reserved, and only values between 00000002h and 0FFFFFF6h are valid, which means values 2–268,435,446 are valid. This leaves 268,435,445 valid entries, so the drive must be split into that many clusters or fewer. Because a drive can be split into so many more clusters, the clusters can be smaller, which conserves disk space. The same file as shown earlier could be stored on a FAT32 system as illustrated in Table 10.28.

Table 10.28   FAT32 File Entries

Folder

Name	Starting Cluster	Size
USCONST.TXT	1000	8

FAT32 File Allocation Table

FAT Cluster #	Value	Meaning
0000000002	0	First cluster available
...	...	...
0000000999	0	Cluster available
0000001000	1001	In use, points to next cluster
0000001001	1002	In use, points to next cluster
0000001002	1003	In use, points to next cluster
0000001003	1004	In use, points to next cluster
0000001004	1005	In use, points to next cluster
0000001005	1006	In use, points to next cluster
0000001006	1007	In use, points to next cluster
0000001007	0FFFFFFFh	End of file
0000001008	0	Cluster available
...	...	...
268,435,446	0	Last cluster available

Because the FAT32 system enables many more clusters to be allocated, the cluster size is usually smaller. So, although files overall use more individual clusters, less wasted space results because the last cluster is, on average, only half filled.

Some additional limitations exist on FAT32 volumes. Volumes less than 512MiB default to FAT16, but FAT32 partitions as small as 32.52MiB can be forced using the proper utilities or commands. Anything smaller than that, however, must be either FAT16 or FAT12.

Using smaller clusters results in many more clusters and more entries in the FAT. A 2GiB partition using FAT32 requires up to 524,288 FAT entries, whereas the same drive needs only 65,536 entries using FAT16. Thus, the size of one copy of the FAT16 table is 128KiB (65,536 entries×16 bits = 1,048,576 bits/8 = 131,072 bytes/1,024 = 128KiB), whereas the FAT32 table is 2MiB in size.

The size of the FAT has a definite impact on the performance of the file system. Windows 9x/Me uses VCACHE to keep the FAT in memory at all times to improve file system performance. The use of 4KiB clusters for drives up to 8GiB in size is, therefore, a reasonable compromise for the average PC's memory capacity. If the file system were to use clusters equal to one disk sector (1 sector = 512KiB) in an attempt to minimize slack as much as possible, the FAT table for a 2GiB drive would contain 4,194,304 entries and be 16MB in size.

This would monopolize a substantial portion of the memory in the average system, probably resulting in noticeably degraded performance. Although at first it might seem as though even a

2MB FAT is quite large when compared to 128KiB, keep in mind that hard disk drives are a great deal faster now than they were when the FAT file system was originally designed. In practice, FAT32 typically results in a minor (less than 5%) improvement in file system performance. However, systems that perform a great many sequential disk writes might see an equally minor degradation in performance.

The partitioning program generally determines whether a 12-bit, 16-bit, or 32-bit FAT is placed on a disk, even though the FAT isn't written until you perform a high-level format (using the FORMAT utility). On today's systems, usually only floppy disks use 12-bit FATs, but FDISK also creates a 12-bit FAT if you create a hard disk volume that is smaller than 16MiB. On hard disk volumes of more than 16MiB, FDISK creates a 16-bit FAT. On drives larger than 512MiB, the FDISK program included in Windows 95 OSR2, and Windows 98/Me enables you to create 32-bit FATs when you answer yes to the question Enable Large Disk Support? when you start FDISK. You can also select FAT32 when you prepare a drive with the Windows 2000 or Windows XP Disk Management program (Windows NT doesn't support FAT32).

FAT volumes normally have two copies of the FAT. Each one occupies contiguous sectors on the disk, and the second FAT copy immediately follows the first. Unfortunately, the operating system uses the second FAT copy only if sectors in the first FAT copy become unreadable. If the first FAT copy is corrupted, which is a much more common problem, the operating system does not use the second FAT copy. Even the CHKDSK command does not check or verify the second FAT copy. Moreover, whenever the OS updates the first FAT, it automatically copies large portions of the first FAT to the second FAT. If the first copy was corrupted and subsequently updated by the OS, a large portion of the first FAT is copied over to the second FAT copy, damaging it in the process. After the update, the second copy is usually a mirror image of the first one, complete with any corruption. Two FATs rarely stay out of sync for very long. When they are out of sync and the OS writes to the disk, it updates the first FAT and overwrites the second FAT with the first. This is why disk repair and recovery utilities warn you to stop working as soon as you detect a FAT problem. Programs such as Norton Disk Doctor (included with the Norton Utilities which are a part of Norton SystemWorks) use the second copy of the FAT as a reference to repair the first one, but if the OS has already updated the second FAT, repair might be impossible.

Directories (Folders)

A *directory* is a simple database containing information about the files stored on a FAT partition. Directories are also called *folders* in Windows.

Each record in a folder is 32 bytes long, with no delimiters or separating characters between the fields or records. A folder stores almost all the information that the operating system knows about a file, including the following:

- **Filename and extension**—The eight-character name and three-character extension of the file. The dot between the name and the extension is implied but not included in the entry.

Note

To see how Windows extends filenames to allow 255 characters within the 8.3 folder structure, see the section "VFAT and Long Filenames," in this chapter.

- **File attribute byte**—The byte containing the flags representing the standard DOS file attributes, using the format shown in Table 10.32.

- **Date/time of last change**—The date and time that the file was created or last modified.

- **File size**—The size of the file, in bytes.

- **Link to start cluster**—The number of the cluster in the partition where the beginning of the file is stored. To learn more about clusters, see the section "Clusters (Allocation Units)," in this chapter.

Other information exists that a folder does not contain about a file. This includes where the rest of its clusters in the partition are located and whether the file is contiguous or fragmented. This information is contained in the FAT.

Two basic types of directories exist: the root directory (also called the root folder) and subdirectories (also called folders). Any given volume can have only one root folder. The root folder is always stored on a disk in a fixed location immediately following the two copies of the FAT. Root folders vary in size because of the different types and capacities of disks, but the root folder of a given disk is fixed. Using the FORMAT command creates a root folder that has a fixed length and can't be extended to hold more entries. The root folder entry limits are shown in Table 10.29. Subfolders are stored as files in the data area of the disk and can grow in size dynamically; therefore, they have no fixed length limits.

Table 10.29   Root Folder Entry Limits

Drive Type	Maximum Root Folder Entries
Hard disk	512
1.44MB floppy disk	224
2.88MB floppy disk	448
Jaz and Zip	512
LS-120 and LS-240	512

Every folder, whether it is the root folder or a subfolder, is organized in the same way. Entries in the folder database store important information about individual files and how files are named on the disk. The folder information is linked to the FAT by the starting cluster entry. In fact, if no file on a disk were longer than one single cluster, the FAT would be unnecessary. The folder stores all the information needed by DOS to manage the file, with the exception of the list of clusters the file occupies other than the first one. The FAT stores the remaining information about the other clusters the file occupies.

To trace a file on a disk, use a disk editor, such as the Disk Edit program that comes with the Norton Utilities. Start by looking up the folder entry to get the information about the starting cluster of the file and its size. Then, using the appropriate editor commands, go to the FAT where you can follow the chain of clusters the file occupies until you reach the end of the file. By using the folder and FAT in this manner, you can visit all the clusters on the disk that are occupied by the file. This type of technique can be useful when these entries are corrupted and when you are trying to find missing parts of a file.

FAT folder entries are 32 bytes long and are in the format shown in Table 10.30, which shows the location (or offset) of each field within the entry (in both hexadecimal and decimal form) and the length of each field.

Table 10.30   FAT Folder Format

Offset (Hex)	Offset (Dec)	Field Length	Description
00h	0	8 bytes	Filename
08h	8	3 bytes	File extension
0Bh	11	1 byte	File attributes
0Ch	12	10 bytes	Reserved (00h)
16h	22	1 word	Time of creation
18h	24	1 word	Date of creation
1Ah	26	1 word	Starting cluster
1Ch	28	1 dword	Size in bytes

Filenames and extensions are left-justified and padded with spaces (which are represented as ASCII 32h bytes). In other words, if your filename is "AL", it is really stored as "AL------", where the hyphens are spaces. The first byte of the filename indicates the file status for that folder entry, shown in Table 10.31.

Table 10.31   Folder Entry Status Byte (First Byte)

Hex	File Status
00h	Entry never used; entries past this point not searched.
05h	Indicates that the first character of the filename is actually E5h.
E5h	s (lowercase sigma). Indicates that the file has been erased.
2Eh	. (period). Indicates that this entry is a folder. If the second byte is also 2Eh, the cluster field contains the cluster number of the parent folder (0000h, if the parent is the root).

A word is 2 bytes read in reverse order, and a dword is two words read in reverse order.

Table 10.32 describes the FAT folder file attribute byte. Attributes are 1-bit flags that control specific properties of a file, such as whether it is hidden or designated as read-only. Each flag is individually activated (1) or deactivated (0) by changing the bit value. The combination of the eight bit values can be expressed as a single hexadecimal byte value; for example, 07h translates to 00000111, and the 1 bits in positions 2, 1, and 0 indicate the file is system, hidden, and read-only.

Table 10.32   FAT Folder File Attribute Byte

Bit Positions 7 6 5 4 3 2 1 0	Hex Value	Description
0 0 0 0 0 0 0 1	01h	Read-only file
0 0 0 0 0 0 1 0	02h	Hidden file
0 0 0 0 0 1 0 0	04h	System file
0 0 0 0 1 0 0 0	08h	Volume label
0 0 0 1 0 0 0 0	10h	Subfolder
0 0 1 0 0 0 0 0	20h	Archive (updated since backup)
0 1 0 0 0 0 0 0	40h	Reserved
1 0 0 0 0 0 0 0	80h	Reserved
Examples		
0 0 0 0 0 1 1 1	07h	System, hidden, read-only
0 0 1 0 0 0 0 1	21h	Read-only, archive
0 0 1 1 0 0 1 0	32h	Hidden, subfolder, archive
0 0 1 0 0 1 1 1	27h	Read-only, hidden, system, archive

Note

The **ATTRIB** command can be used to change file attributes. In the Windows GUI, you can also use the properties sheet for a file or folder to change the attributes. The archive bit changes automatically when a file is backed up or changed.

FAT File System Errors

File system errors can, of course, occur because of hardware problems, but you are more likely to see them result from software crashes and improper system handling. Turning off a system without shutting down Windows properly, for example, can result in errors that cause clusters to be incorrectly listed as in use when they are not. Some of the most common file system errors that occur on FAT partitions are described in the following sections.

Lost Clusters

Probably the most common file system error, *lost* clusters are clusters the FAT designates as being in use when they actually are not. Most often caused by an interruption of a file system process due to an application crash or a system shutdown, for example, the FAT entry of a lost cluster might contain a reference to a subsequent cluster. However, the FAT chain stemming from the folder entry has been broken somewhere along the line.

Lost clusters appear in the file structure as shown in Table 10.33.

Table 10.33   Lost Clusters in a File Structure

Folder

Name	Starting Cluster	Size
(no entry)	0	0

FAT16 File Allocation Table

FAT Cluster #	Value	Meaning
00002	0	First cluster available
...	...	...
00999	0	Cluster available
01000	1001	In use, points to next cluster
01001	1002	In use, points to next cluster
01002	1003	In use, points to next cluster
01003	FFFFh	End of file
01004	0	Cluster available
...	...	...
65526	0	Last cluster available

The operating system sees a valid chain of clusters in the FAT but no corresponding folder entry to back it up. Programs that are terminated before they can close their open files typically cause this. The operating system usually modifies the FAT chain as the file is written, and the final step when closing is to create a matching folder entry. If the system is interrupted before the file is closed (such as by shutting down the system improperly), lost clusters are the result. Disk repair programs check for lost clusters by tracing the FAT chain for each file and subfolder in the partition and building a facsimile of the FAT in memory. After compiling a list of all the FAT entries that indicate properly allocated clusters, the program compares this facsimile with the actual FAT. Any entries denoting allocated clusters in the real FAT that do not appear in the facsimile are lost clusters because they are not part of a valid FAT chain.

The utility typically gives you the opportunity to save the data in the lost clusters as a file before it changes the FAT entries to show them as unallocated clusters. If your system crashed or lost power while you were working with a word processor data file, for example, you might be able to retrieve text from the lost clusters in this way. When left unrepaired, lost clusters are unavailable for use by the system, reducing the storage capacity of your drive.

The typical choices you have for correcting lost clusters are to assign them a made-up name or zero out the FAT entries. If you assign them a name, you can at least look at the entries as a valid file and then delete the file if you find it useless. The CHKDSK and SCANDISK programs are designed to fix lost clusters by assigning them names starting with FILE0001.CHK. If more than one lost chain exists, sequential numbers following the first one are used. The lost clusters shown earlier could be corrected by CHKDSK or SCANDISK as shown in Table 10.34.

Table 10.34   Finding Lost Clusters

Folder		
Name	**Starting Cluster**	**Size**
FILE0001.CHK	1000	4

FAT16 File Allocation Table

FAT Cluster #	Value	Meaning
00002	0	First cluster available
…	…	…
00999	0	Cluster available
01000	1001	In use, points to next cluster
01001	1002	In use, points to next cluster
01002	1003	In use, points to next cluster
01003	FFFFh	End of file
01004	0	Cluster available
…	…	…
65526	0	Last cluster available

As you can see, a new entry was created to match the FAT entries. The name is made up because there is no way for the repair utility to know what the original name of the file might have been.

Cross-Linked Files

Cross-linked files occur when two folder entries improperly reference the same cluster in their Link to Start Cluster fields. The result is that each file uses the same FAT chain. Because the clusters can store data from only one file, working with one of the two files can inadvertently overwrite the other file's data.

Cross-linked files would appear in the file structure as shown in Table 10.35.

Table 10.35   Cross-Linked Files

Folder		
Name	**Starting Cluster**	**Size**
USCONST.TXT	1000	4
PLEDGE.TXT	1002	2

FAT16 File Allocation Table

FAT Cluster #	Value	Meaning
00002	0	First cluster available
…	…	…
00999	0	Cluster available
01000	1001	In use, points to next cluster

(continues)

Table 10.35   Continued

FAT16 File Allocation Table		
FAT Cluster #	**Value**	**Meaning**
01001	1002	In use, points to next cluster
01002	1003	In use, points to next cluster
01003	FFFFh	End of file
01004	0	Cluster available
...	...	...
65526	0	Last cluster available

In this case, two files claim ownership of clusters 1002 and 1003, so these files are said to be cross-linked on 1002. When a situation such as this arises, one of the files typically is valid and the other is corrupt, being that only one actual given set of data can occupy a given cluster. The normal repair is to copy both files involved to new names, which duplicates their data separately in another area of the disk, and then delete *all* the cross-linked files. Deleting them all is important because by deleting only one of them, the FAT chain is zeroed, which further damages the other entries. Then, you can examine the files you copied to determine which one is good and which is corrupt.

Detecting cross-linked files is a relatively easy task for a disk repair utility because it must examine only the partition's folder entries and not the file clusters themselves. However, by the time the utility detects the error, the data from one of the two files is probably already lost—although you might be able to recover parts of it from lost clusters.

Invalid Files or Folders

Sometimes the information in a folder entry for a file or subfolder can be corrupted to the point at which the entry is not just erroneous (as in cross-linked files) but invalid. The entry might have a cluster or date reference that is invalid, or it might violate the rules for the entry format in some other way. In most cases, disk repair software can correct these problems, permitting access to the file.

FAT Errors

As discussed earlier, accessing its duplicate copy can sometimes repair a corrupted FAT. Disk repair utilities typically rely on this technique to restore a damaged FAT to its original state, as long as the mirroring process has not corrupted the copy. FAT32 tables are more likely to be repairable because their more advanced mirroring capabilities make the copy less likely to be corrupted.

An example of a damaged FAT might appear to the operating system as shown in Table 10.36.

Table 10.36   Damaged FAT

Folder

Name	Starting Cluster	Size
USCONST.TXT	1000	4

FAT16 File Allocation Table

FAT Cluster #	Value	Meaning
00002	0	First cluster available
...	...	...
00999	0	Cluster available
01000	1001	In use, points to next cluster
01001	0	Cluster available
01002	1003	In use, points to next cluster
01003	FFFFh	End of file
01004	0	Cluster available
...	...	...
65526	0	Last cluster available

This single error would cause multiple problems to appear. The file USCONST.TXT would now come up as having an allocation error—in which the size in the folder no longer matches the number of clusters in the FAT chain. The file would end after cluster 1001 in this example, and the rest of the data would be missing if you loaded this file for viewing. Also, two lost clusters would exist; that is, 1002 and 1003 appear to have no folder entry that owns them. When multiple problems such as these appear, a single incident of damage is often the cause. The repair in this case could involve copying the data from the backup FAT back to the primary FAT, but in most cases, the backup is similarly damaged. Normal utilities would truncate the file and create an entry for a second file out of the lost clusters. You would have to figure out yourself that they really belong together. This is where having knowledge in data recovery can help over using automated utilities that can't think for themselves.

NTFS

Windows NT 3.1 (the first version of NT despite the 3.1 designation) was released in August 1993 and introduced the New Technology File System (NTFS), which is unique to NT-based operating systems (including Windows 2000 and Windows XP) and is not supported by Windows 9x/Me. NTFS includes many advanced features not found in the FAT file systems.

NTFS is the native file system of Windows NT through XP and Vista. Newer versions of Windows use enhanced versions of NTFS called NTFS 3.0 (Windows 2000) and NTFS 3.1 (Windows XP/Vista). Microsoft has also referred to NTFS 3.0 as NTFS 5 or NTFS 2000. Although NTFS is generally backward compatible, Windows NT 4.0 must have Service Pack 4 or above installed to be capable of accessing an NTFS 3.0/3.1 disk. Although NT/2000/XP and Vista support FAT partitions (and Windows 2000/XP and Vista support FAT32), NTFS provides many advantages over FAT, including long filenames, support for larger files and partitions, extended attributes, and increased security. NTFS, like all of Windows NT, was newly designed from the ground up. Backward compatibility with previous Microsoft operating systems was not a concern because the developers were intent on creating an entirely new 32-bit platform. As a result, few operating systems other than Windows NT through Vista can natively read NTFS partitions. More recently that has been changing; for example Apple included the ability to read (but not write) NTFS volumes in Mac OS X 10.3 (Panther) and later versions. Also NTFS drivers have become available for Linux, MS-DOS, and other OSs as well. Unfortunately most of these solutions have had to be reverse engineered because Microsoft has kept the internal technical details of NTFS mostly private.

NTFS supports filenames of up to 255 characters, using spaces, multiple periods, and any other standard characters except the following: *?/\;<>|. Since Windows NT 3.51, NTFS has also supported compression on a file-by-file (or folder-by-folder) basis through each file or folder's properties sheet. No third-party program, such as WinZip or PKZip, is needed to compress or decompress files stored on an NTFS drive. NTFS 5 also supports encryption on a file-by-file or folder-by-folder properties sheet.

Tip

To access advanced file attributes under NTFS such as compression, encryption, and indexing, right-click the file or folder, select Properties, and click the Advanced button to bring up the Advanced properties dialog box.

NTFS supports larger volumes (up to 16TiB), larger files, and more files per volume than FAT. NTFS also uses smaller cluster sizes than even FAT32, resulting in more efficient use of a volume. For example, a 30GiB NTFS volume uses 4KiB clusters, whereas the same size volume formatted with FAT32 uses 16KiB clusters. Smaller clusters reduce wasted space on the volume. NTFS cluster sizes are shown in Table 10.37.

Table 10.37   NTFS Cluster Sizes

Volume Size	Sectors per Cluster	Cluster Size
16MiB–512MiB	1	0.5KiB
>512MiB–1GiB	2	1KiB
>1GiB–2GiB	4	2KiB
>2GiB–2TiB[1]	8	4KiB

1. Larger cluster sizes can be forced by altering the format parameters; however, file compression is disabled if clusters larger than 8 sectors (4KiB) are selected.
MB = megabyte = 1,000,000 bytes
GB = gigabyte = 1,000MB = 1,000,000,000 bytes
TB = terabyte = 1,000GB = 1,000,000,000,000 bytes
KiB = kibibytes = 1,024 bytes
MiB = mebibyte = 1,024KiB = 1,048,576 bytes
GiB = gibibyte = 1,024MiB = 1,073,741,824 bytes
TiB = tebibytes = 1,024GiB = 1,099,511,627,776 bytes

NTFS uses a special file structure called a master file table (MFT) and metadata files. The MFT is basically a relational database that consists of rows of file records and columns of file attributes. It contains at least one entry for every file on an NTFS volume. NTFS creates file and folder records for each file and folder created on an NTFS volume. These are stored in the MFT and consume 1KiB each. Each file record contains information about the position of the file record in the MFT, as well as file attributes and any other information about the file.

NTFS was designed to manage clusters using up to 64-bit numbers, which is an astronomical amount, but the current implementations use 32-bit numbers instead. Using 32-bit numbers allows for addressing up to 4,294,967,295 clusters, each of which is typically up to 4KiB.

NTFS reserves a total of 32 sectors for a 16-sector-long default volume boot sector and a backup boot sector. The default boot sector is located at the beginning (logical sector 0) of the volume, whereas the backup boot sector is written at the logical center of the volume (if it was formatted using NT 3.51 and earlier) or at the end of the volume (if it was formatted with NT 4.0 or later, including 2000/XP and Vista).

An NTFS volume can therefore contain up to 34,359,738,392 total sectors (32 sectors reserved for the default and backup boot sectors, plus 4,294,967,295 clusters × 8 sectors), which is 17.59TB or 16.00TiB. The 32-bit sector-numbering scheme used in the partition tables located in the MBR limits a single disk to no more than 4,294,967,295 ($2^{32}-1$) sectors, which is 2.2TB or 2TiB.

Some Windows 2000 and later versions, including XP Pro and Vista Business/Enterprise and Ultimate, can get around this on nonbootable drives by using a *dynamic disk*. These versions of Windows offer two types of storage: basic disks and dynamic disks. *Basic disks* use the same structures as before, with an MBR on the disk containing a partition table limited to four primary partitions per disk, or three primary partitions and one extended partition with unlimited logical drives. Primary partitions and logical drives on basic disks are known as *basic volumes*.

Dynamic disks were first introduced in Windows 2000 and provide the capability to create dynamic volumes that can be simple (using only one drive), spanned (using multiple drives), or striped (using multiple drives simultaneously for increased performance). Dynamic disks use a hidden database (contained in the last megabyte of the disk) to track information about dynamic volumes on the disk and about other dynamic disks in the computer. Because each dynamic disk in a computer stores a replica of the dynamic disk database, a corrupted database on one dynamic disk can be repaired using the database on another. By spanning or striping multiple drives using dynamic disk formats, you can exceed the 2TiB limit of a single MBR-based partition. Note, however, that dynamic disks and volumes are intended for use on servers and not standard desktop PCs. As such this book won't be going into much more detail on dynamic disks and volumes, and in general you should not create them on standard desktop or mobile systems.

Although the 32-bit sector numbering in the partition tables on MBR disks limits NTFS basic disks to 2TiB volumes, you can use dynamic volumes to create NTFS volumes larger than 2TiB by spanning or striping multiple basic disks to create a larger dynamic disk. Because the dynamic volumes are managed in the hidden database, they are not affected by the 2TiB limit imposed by the partition tables in the MBR. In essence, dynamic disks enable Windows to create NTFS volumes as large as 16TiB. The volume limits for NTFS are listed in Table 10.38.

Table 10.38   NTFS Volume Limits

Volume Limit	Clusters	Sectors per Cluster	Total Volume Sectors	Volume Size (Decimal)	Volume Size (Binary)
Minimum size	32,698	1	32,730	16.76MB	15.98MiB
Basic disk max.	536,870,908	8	4,294,967,295	2.2TB	2TiB
Dynamic disk max.	4,294,967,295	8	34,359,738,392	17.59TB	16TiB

MB = megabyte = 1,000,000 bytes
GB = gigabyte = 1,000MB = 1,000,000,000 bytes
TB = terabyte = 1,000GB = 1,000,000,000,000 bytes
KiB = kibibytes = 1,024 bytes
MiB = mebibyte = 1,024KiB = 1,048,576 bytes
GiB = gibibyte = 1,024MiB = 1,073,741,824 bytes
TiB = tebibytes = 1,024GiB = 1,099,511,627,776 bytes

Some notable characteristics and features of NTFS include

- **Files are limited in size to 16TiB less 64KiB or by the size of the volume, whichever is lower**—NTFS supports up to 4,294,967,295 (2^{32}–1) files on a volume.

- **NTFS is not normally used on removable media because NTFS does not flush data to the disk immediately**—In addition, removing NTFS-formatted media without using the Safe Removal application can result in data loss. For removable media that can be ejected unexpectedly, you should use FAT12, FAT16, or FAT32 instead.

- **NTFS incorporates transaction logging and recovery techniques**—In the event of a failure, upon reboot NTFS uses its log file and checkpoint information to restore the consistency of the file system.

- **NTFS dynamically remaps clusters found to contain bad sectors and then marks the defective cluster as bad so that it will no longer be used.**

- **NTFS has built-in security features**—These enable you to set permissions on a file or folder.

- **NTFS has a built-in Encrypting File System (EFS)**—This performs dynamic encryption and decryption as you work with encrypted files or folders, while preventing others from doing so.

- **It enables the setting of disk quotas**—You can track and control space usage for NTFS volumes among various users.

- **NTFS has built-in dynamic compression, which compresses and decompresses files as you use them.**

NTFS Architecture—The MFT

Although NTFS partitions are very different from FAT partitions internally, they do comply with the extra-partitional disk structures described earlier in this chapter. NTFS partitions are listed in the master partition table of a disk drive's master boot record, just like FAT partitions, and they have a volume boot record as well, although it is formatted somewhat differently.

When a volume is formatted with NTFS, system files are created in the root folder of the NTFS volume. These system files can be stored at any physical location on the NTFS volume. This means that damage to any specific location on the disk will probably not render the entire partition inaccessible.

Typically, 12 NTFS system files (often referred to as *metadata* files) are created when you format an NTFS volume. Table 10.39 shows the names and descriptions for these files.

Table 10.39   NTFS System Files

Filename	Meaning	Description
$mft	Master file table (MFT)	Contains a record for every file on the NTFS volume in its **Data** attribute
$mftmirr	Master file table2 (MFT2)	Mirror of the MFT used for recoverability purposes; contains the first four records in **$mft** or the first cluster of **$mft**, whichever is larger
$badclus	Bad cluster file	Contains all the bad clusters on the volume
$bitmap	Cluster allocation bitmap	Contains the bitmap for the entire volume, showing which clusters are used
$boot	Boot file	Contains the volume's bootstrap if the volume is bootable
$attrdef	Attribute definitions table	Contains the definition of all system- and user-defined attributes on the volume
$logfile	Log file	Logs file transactions; used for recoverability purposes
$quota	Quota table	Table used to indicate disk quota usage for each user on a volume; used in NTFS 5
$upcase	Upcase table	Table used for converting uppercase and lowercase characters to the matching uppercase Unicode characters
$volume	Volume	Contains volume information, such as volume name and version
$extend	NTFS extension file	Stores optional extensions, such as quotas, object identifiers, and reparse point data
(no name)	Root filename index	The root folder (directory)

An NTFS partition is based on a structure called the master file table. The MFT concept expands on that of the FAT. Instead of using a table of cluster references, the MFT contains much more detailed information about the files and folders in the partition. In some cases, it even contains the files and folders themselves.

The first record in the MFT is called the *descriptor*, which contains information about the MFT itself. The volume boot record for an NTFS partition contains a reference that points to the location of this descriptor record. The second record in the MFT is a mirror copy of the descriptor, which provides fault tolerance, should the first copy be damaged.

The third record is the log file record. All NTFS transactions are logged to a file that can be used to restore data in the event of a disk problem. The bulk of the MFT consists of records for the files and folders stored on the partition. NTFS files take the form of objects that have both user- and system-defined attributes. Attributes on NTFS partitions are more comprehensive than the few simple flags used on FAT partitions. All the information on an NTFS file is stored as attributes of that file. In fact, even the file data itself is an attribute. Unlike FAT files, the attributes of NTFS files are part of the file itself; they are not listed separately in a folder entry. Folders exist as MFT records as well, but they consist mainly of indexes listing the files in the folder—they do not contain the size, date, time, and other information about the individual files.

Thus, an NTFS drive's MFT is much more than a cluster list, like a FAT; it is actually the primary data storage structure on the partition. If a file or folder is relatively small (less than approximately 1,500 bytes), the entire file or folder might even be stored in the MFT. For larger amounts of storage, the MFT record for a file or folder contains pointers to external clusters in the partition. These external clusters are called *extents*. All the records in the MFT, including the descriptors and the log file, are capable of using extents for storage of additional attributes. The attributes of a file that are part of the MFT record are called *resident* attributes, whereas those stored in extents are called *nonresident* attributes.

NTFS 3.0/3.1

Along with Windows 2000 came a new variation of NTFS called NTFS 3.0 (also sometimes referred to as NTFS 5 or 2000). NTFS was further updated to NTFS 3.1 in Windows XP. These updates of the NT file system include several new features that are exploited and even required by Windows 2000 and Windows XP. Because of this, when you install Windows 2000 or Windows XP, any existing NTFS volumes automatically are upgraded to NTFS 3.0 or 3.1 (there is no way to override this option). If you also run Windows NT versions earlier than Windows NT 4 Service Pack 4 (SP4), NT 4 is no longer capable of accessing the NTFS 3.x volumes. If you want to run both NT 4 and Windows 2000 or Windows XP on the same system (as in a dual-boot configuration), you must upgrade NT 4 by installing Service Pack 4 or later. An updated NTFS.SYS driver in Service Pack 4 enables NT 4 to read from and write to NTFS 3.x volumes.

New features of the NTFS 3.x file system include

- **Disk quotas**—System administrators can limit the amount of disk space users can consume on a per-volume basis. The three quota levels are Off, Tracking, and Enforced.

- **Encryption**—NTFS 3.x can automatically encrypt and decrypt files as they are read from and written to the disk (not available in Windows XP Home Edition).

- **Reparse points**—Programs can trap open operations against objects in the file system and run their own code before returning file data. This can be used to extend file system features such as mount points, which you can use to redirect data read and written from a folder to another volume or physical disk.

- **Sparse files**—This feature enables programs to create very large files as placeholders but to consume disk space by adding to the files only as necessary.

- **USN (Update Sequence Number) Journal**—Provides a log of all changes made to files on the volume.

- **Mounted drives**—You can attach volumes including drives and folders to an empty folder stored on an NTFS drive. For example, you can create a folder on one drive that allows you to access content stored on another drive.

Because these features—especially the USN Journal—are required for Windows 2000 to run, a Windows 2000/Server 2003 domain controller must use an NTFS 3.x partition as the system volume.

NTFS Changes in Windows XP

The location of the MFT has changed in NTFS 3.1 as used by Windows XP and Vista versus Windows 2000 and Windows NT. In Windows 2000 and Windows NT, the MFT is typically located at the start of the disk space used by the NTFS file system. In Windows XP and Vista, the `$logfile` and `$bitmap` metadata files are located 3GB from the start of the disk space used by NTFS. As a result, system performance has been increased by 5%–8% in Windows XP and Vista over Windows 2000 or Windows NT.

Another improvement is the amount of MFT information read into memory. During bootup, Windows XP and Vista read only a few hundred kilobytes of MFT information if all drives are formatted with NTFS. However, if some of or all the drives are formatted with FAT32, many megabytes of information (the amount varies by the number of drives and the size of the drives) must be read during bootup. Thus, using only NTFS-formatted drives enables Windows to utilize system memory more efficiently.

NTFS Changes in Windows Vista

There are several new additions to the functionality of NTFS in Windows Vista:

- **Transactional NTFS (TxF)**—Adds full transactional support to any file system operation or set of operations. TxF allows changes to be rolled back if they are not fully completed, preserving the integrity of both local and remote (server based) files, the file system, and the Registry.

- **Self-healing functionality**—Detects and repairs file system corruption automatically. This works like running CHKDSK, except that it is automatic and runs in the background. When in operation, a dedicated self-healing worker thread is triggered when corruption is detected. Unlike when running CHKDSK (which locks the entire volume), when self-healing only the individual corrupted files/folder are inaccessible. This feature also enables authorized users to administer and monitor repair operations.

- **Symbolic links**—A transparent redirection mechanism that works on both local and remote (server-based) files and folders. By default only elevated administrators can create symbolic links, which can be used, for example, to enable migrations from a UNIX or Linux environment to Windows.

- **Large sectors**—Vista supports drives with larger sector sizes. Traditionally, disk sectors have been 512 bytes in size. To continue making improvements in capacity, performance, and reliability, hard disk drive manufacturers are considering the production of drives with larger sectors (1024, 2048, or 4096 bytes). Because of issues with performance and backward compatibility, large sectors will first appear in Enterprise class (SAS, SCSI, and Fibre Channel) drives.

With the exception of large sectors, these changes are backward compatible, meaning that they are in effect only when running Vista, and do not affect Windows XP and earlier OS capability to access the same files, folders, or the file system in general.

NTFS Compatibility

Although NTFS partitions are not directly accessible by DOS and other operating systems, Windows is designed for network use, so other operating systems are expected to be capable of accessing NTFS files via the network. For this reason, NTFS continues to support the standard DOS file attributes and the 8.3 FAT naming convention.

One of the main reasons for using NTFS is the security it provides for files and folders. NTFS security attributes are called *permissions* and are designed to enable system administrators to control access to files and folders by granting specific rights to users and groups. This is a much more granular approach than the FAT file system attributes, which apply to all users.

However, you can still set the FAT-style attributes on NTFS files using the standard Windows file management tools, including Windows Explorer and even the command-prompt ATTRIB command. When you copy FAT files to an NTFS drive over the network, the FAT-style attributes remain in place until you explicitly remove them. This can be an important consideration because the FAT-style attributes take precedence over the NTFS permissions. A file on an NTFS drive that is flagged with the FAT read-only attribute, for example, can't be deleted by a Windows user, even if that user has NTFS permissions that grant full access.

To enable DOS and 16-bit Windows systems to access files on NTFS partitions over a network, the file system maintains an 8.3 alias name for every file and folder on the partition. The algorithm for deriving the alias from the long filename is the same as that used by Windows 95's VFAT. Windows NT and later also provides its FAT partitions with the same type of long filename support used by VFAT, allocating additional folder entries to store the long filenames as necessary.

Creating NTFS Drives

NTFS is designed for use primarily on hard disk drives, and not removable storage. You can't create an NTFS floppy disk, although you can format some removable media (any that use an MBR and partitions), such as Iomega Zip and Jaz cartridges, to use NTFS. Three basic ways to create an NTFS disk partition are as follows:

- Create a new NTFS volume out of unpartitioned disk space during the Windows installation process or after the installation with the Disk Administrator utility.
- Format an existing partition to NTFS (destroying its data in the process), using the Windows Format dialog box (accessible from Windows Explorer or Disk Administrator) or the FORMAT command (with the /fs:ntfs switch) from the command prompt.
- Convert an existing FAT partition to NTFS (preserving its data) during the Windows installation process or after the installation with the command-line CONVERT utility.

NTFS Tools

Because NTFS uses a fundamentally different architecture, virtually none of the troubleshooting techniques outlined for FAT are applicable when dealing with NTFS partitions, nor can the disk utilities intended for use on FAT partitions address them. Windows NT and later have a rudimentary capability to check a disk for file system errors and bad sectors with its own version of CHKDSK, but apart from that, the operating system contains no other disk repair or defragmentation utilities. Windows 2000 and later include both a command-line and GUI version of CHKDSK and also include a defragmenting tool that is run from Windows Explorer. Windows XP Professional also includes Disk Probe (DSKPROBE.exe), a direct disk sector editor, in its Windows

Support Tools (the Windows 2000 Resource Kit also contains Disk Probe). Vista doesn't include DiskProbe; you can run the version intended for Windows XP, however.

One difference between Windows 2000/XP and Vista's CHKDSK and Windows 9x/Me's SCANDISK is that CHKDSK cannot fix file system errors if it is run within the Windows GUI. If you run CHKDSK and select the Automatically Fix File System Errors option, you must schedule CHKDSK to run at the next system startup. You can run CHKDSK without this option to find file system problems; you can also run CHKDSK within the Windows GUI to look for and attempt to fix bad sectors.

Tip

You can use the **FSUTIL** command-line program in Windows XP and Vista to learn more about a particular drive's file system, including whether you need to run **CHKDSK** or a third-party disk repair tool. For example, to determine whether drive D: is *dirty* (has file system errors requiring repair), you would open a command prompt and enter this command:

FSUTIL DIRTY QUERY D:

For more examples of **FSUTIL** commands and syntax, enter **FSUTIL** with no options at a command prompt. Note that **FSUTIL** is not included with Windows 2000 or earlier versions.

The NTFS file system, however, does have its own automatic disk repair capabilities. In addition to Windows NT/2000/XP and Vista's fault-tolerance features, such as disk mirroring (maintaining the same data on two separate drives) and disk striping with parity (splitting data across several drives with parity information for data reconstruction), the OS has two features to help improve reliability:

- Transaction management
- Cluster remapping

NTFS can roll back any *transaction* (its term for a change to a file stored on an NTFS volume) if it isn't completed properly due to disk errors, running out of memory, or errors such as removing media or disconnecting a device before the transaction process is complete. Each transaction has five steps:

1. NTFS creates a log file of the metadata operations of the transaction (file updates, erasure, and so on) and caches the file in system memory.
2. NTFS stores the actual metadata operations in memory.
3. NTFS marks the transaction record in the log file as committed.
4. NTFS saves the log file to disk after the transaction is complete.
5. NTFS saves the actual metadata operations to disk after the transaction is complete.

This process is designed to prevent random data (lost clusters) on NTFS drives.

With cluster remapping, when Windows (NT–Vista) detects a bad sector on an NTFS partition, it automatically remaps the data in that cluster to another cluster. If the drive is part of a fault-tolerant drive array, any lost data is reconstructed from the duplicate data on the other drives.

Despite these features, however, there is still a real need for third-party disk repair and defragmentation utilities for Windows NT through Vista. These were scarce when Windows NT was first released, but third-party utilities that can repair and defragment NTFS drives are now widely available. One I recommend is Golden Bow's Vopt (www.vopt.com), which is a longtime favorite because of its incredible speed and efficiency.

File System Utilities

The CHKDSK, RECOVER, and SCANDISK commands are the core of the Windows damaged-disk recovery team. These commands are somewhat crude, and their actions sometimes are drastic, but at times they are all that is available or necessary. RECOVER is best known for its function as a data recovery program, and CHKDSK typically is used for inspection of the file structure. Many users are unaware that CHKDSK can implement repairs to a damaged file structure. DEBUG, a crude, manually controlled program, can also help in the case of a disk disaster—but only if you know exactly what you are doing.

SCANDISK is a safer, more automated, more powerful replacement for CHKDSK and RECOVER in Windows 9x/Me. Windows 2000/XP and Vista do not include SCANDISK and instead have beefed up CHKDSK designed to handle NTFS.

CHKDSK Operation

CHKDSK reports problems found in a disk volume's file system with one of several descriptive messages that vary to fit the specific error. Sometimes the messages are cryptic or misleading. CHKDSK does not specify how an error should be handled. It does not tell you whether CHKDSK can repair the problem, whether you must use some other utility, or what the consequences of the error and the repair will be. Neither does CHKDSK tell you what caused the problem nor how to avoid repeating the problem.

The primary function of CHKDSK is to compare the folder and FAT or NTFS MFT to determine whether they agree with each other—that is, whether all the data in the folder entries for the files (such as the starting cluster and size information) corresponds to what is in the FAT (such as chains of clusters with end-of-chain indicators). CHKDSK also checks subfolder file entries, as well as the special "dot" (.) and "double dot" (..) entries that tie the subfolder system together.

The second function of CHKDSK is to implement repairs to the disk structure. CHKDSK patches the disk so that the folder and FAT or MFT are in alignment and agreement. From a repair standpoint, understanding CHKDSK is relatively easy. On FAT volumes, CHKDSK almost always modifies the folders on a disk to correspond to what it finds in the FAT. There are only a few special cases in which CHKDSK modifies the FAT. When it does, the FAT modifications are always the same type of simple change.

Think of CHKDSK's repair capability as a folder patcher. Because CHKDSK cannot repair most types of FAT damage effectively, it simply modifies the disk folders to match whatever problems it finds in the FAT. On NTFS volumes, CHKDSK is very effective at correcting problems with the MFT.

Caution

You should never run **CHKDSK** with the **/F** parameter without first running it in read-only mode (without the **/F** parameter) to determine whether and to what extent damage exists.

Only after carefully examining the disk damage and determining how CHKDSK would fix the problems should you run CHKDSK with the /F parameter. If you do not specify the /F parameter when you run CHKDSK, the program does not make corrections to the disk. Rather, it performs repairs in a mock fashion. This limitation is a safety feature because you do not want CHKDSK to take action until you have examined the problem. After deciding whether CHKDSK will make the correct assumptions about the damage, you might want to run it with the /F parameter.

Problems reported by CHKDSK are usually problems with the software and not the hardware. You rarely see a case in which lost clusters, allocation errors, or cross-linked files reported by CHKDSK were caused directly by a hardware fault, although it is certainly possible. The cause is usually a defective program or a program that was stopped before it could close files or purge buffers. A hardware fault certainly can stop a program before it can close files, but many people think that these error messages signify fault with the disk hardware, which is almost never the case.

The *RECOVER* Command

The RECOVER command is designed to mark clusters as bad when the clusters contain unreadable sectors, and rewrite the entries for the file in the FAT or MFT in order to be able to read the remainder of the file past the unreadable sector. When the system can't read a file because of a problem with a sector on the disk going bad, the RECOVER command can essentially jump the pointers to the file data in the FAT or MFT so that the rest of the file can be read, as well as to mark the file system so another file does not use those clusters. When used improperly, this program can be dangerous. The RECOVER utility that was included in DOS 5.x and earlier was not supplied in Windows 9x/Me because its functionality has been replaced by SCANDISK. It was, however, re-introduced in Windows NT/2000/XP and Vista because SCANDISK had been replaced by an improved version of CHKDSK.

Caution

Be very careful when you use older versions of **RECOVER**. Used improperly, it can do severe damage to your files. If you enter the old DOS version of **RECOVER** command without a filename for it to work on, the program assumes that you want every file on the disk recovered and operates on every file and subfolder on the disk. It converts all subfolders to files, places all filenames in the root folder, and gives them new names (**FILE0000.REC**, **FILE0001.REC**, and so on). This process essentially wipes out the file system on the entire disk.

Fortunately the newer version of **RECOVER** included with Windows NT/2000/XP and Vista will not accept wildcards, and will work only on the single specific filename you enter with the command.

An improved version of RECOVER that recovers data from a specified file is only one of the command-line programs provided with Windows NT, 2000, and XP. To use this version of RECOVER, which works with both FAT and NTFS file systems, open a command prompt and enter the command as shown here:

```
RECOVER (drive\folder\filename)
```

For example, to recover all readable sectors from a file called Mynovel.txt stored in C:\My Documents\Writings, you would enter the following command:

```
RECOVER C:\My Documents\Writings\Mynovel.txt
```

Because the NT/2000/XP and Vista version of RECOVER requires you to specify a filename and path, it cannot destroy a file system the way the old DOS RECOVER command could.

SCANDISK

You should regularly check your FAT partitions under Windows 9x/Me for the problems discussed in this chapter and any other difficulties that might arise. By far the easiest and most effective solution for disk diagnosis and repair under Windows 9x/Me is the SCANDISK utility, included with DOS 6 and higher versions, as well as with Windows 9x/Me. This program is more thorough and comprehensive than CHKDSK or RECOVER under those operating systems and can perform the functions of both of them—and a great deal more.

SCANDISK is similar to a scaled-down version of third-party disk repair programs such as Norton Disk Doctor, and it can verify both file structure and disk sector integrity. If SCANDISK finds problems, it can repair folders and FATs. If the program finds bad sectors in the middle of a file, it marks the clusters (allocation units) containing the bad sectors as bad in the FAT and attempts to read the file data by rerouting around the defect.

Windows 9x includes both DOS and Windows versions of SCANDISK, which are named SCANDISK.EXE and SCANDSKW.EXE, respectively. Windows scans your drives at the beginning of the operating system installation process and automatically loads the DOS version of SCANDISK whenever you restart your system after turning it off without completing the proper shutdown procedure. You can also launch SCANDISK.EXE from a DOS prompt or from a batch file using the following syntax:

```
Scandisk x: [/a] [/n] [/p] [dblspace.nnn/drvspace.nnn]
x: - designator of the drive that you want to scan
/a - scans all local fixed hard disks
/n - noninteractive mode; requires no user input
/p - scans only, without correcting errors
/custom - runs Scandisk with the options configured in the
➥[CUSTOM] section of the Scandisk.ini file
dblspace.nnn or drvspace.nnn - scans a compressed volume file,
➥where nnn is replaced by the file extension (such as 001)
```

The SCANDISK.INI file, located in the C:\WINDOWS\COMMAND folder on a Windows system by default, contains extensive and well-documented parameters you can use to control the behavior of SCANDISK.EXE. Note that the options in the SCANDISK.INI file are applied only to the DOS version of the utility and have no effect on the Windows GUI version.

You also can run the GUI version of the utility by opening the Start menu and selecting Programs, Accessories, System Tools. Both versions scan and repair the FAT and the folder and file structures, repair problems with long filenames, and scan volumes that have been compressed with DriveSpace or DoubleSpace.

SCANDISK provides two basic testing options: Standard and Thorough. The difference between the two is that the Thorough option causes the program to scan the entire surface of the disk for errors in addition to the items just mentioned. You also can select whether to run the program interactively or let it automatically repair any errors it finds.

The DOS and Windows versions of SCANDISK also test the FAT in different ways. The DOS version scans and, if necessary, repairs the primary copy of the file allocation table. After this, it copies the repaired version of the primary to the backup copy. The Windows version, however, scans both copies of the FAT. If the program finds discrepancies between the two copies, it uses the data from the copy that it judges to be correct and reassembles the primary FAT using the best data from both copies. If the FAT information is not reconstructed correctly, some or all of your data might become inaccessible.

SCANDISK also has an Advanced Options dialog box that enables you to set the following parameters:

- Whether the program should display a summary of its findings
- Whether the program should log its findings
- How the program should repair cross-linked files (two folder entries pointing to the same cluster)
- How the program should repair lost file fragments
- Whether to check files for invalid names, dates, and times

Although SCANDISK is good, and is certainly a vast improvement over CHKDSK (but not the CHKDSK included in Windows NT/2000/XP and Vista, which was greatly improved), I recommend using one of the commercial packages, such as the Norton Utilities (included with Norton SystemWorks), for any major disk problems. These utilities go far beyond what is included in DOS or Windows.

Disk Defragmentation

The entire premise of a file system is based on the storage of data in clusters that can be located anywhere on the disk. This enables the computer to store a file of nearly any size at any time. The process of following a chain to locate all the clusters holding the data for a particular file can force the hard disk drive to access many locations on the disk. Because of the physical work involved in moving the disk drive heads, reading a file that is heavily fragmented in this way is slower than reading one that is stored on consecutive clusters.

As you regularly add, move, and delete files on a disk over a period of time, the files become increasingly fragmented, which can slow down disk performance. You can relieve this problem by periodically running a disk defragmentation utility on your drives, such as the one included with Windows. When you run the Disk Defragmenter, the program reads the pointers to all the clusters to all the files on the drive, in order to determine which files are fragmented.

The program then writes any fragmented files to contiguous clusters and deletes the originals. By progressively reading, writing, and erasing files, the defragmenting program eventually leaves the disk in a state where all files exist on contiguous clusters. As a result, the drive is capable of reading any file on the disk with a minimum of head movement, thus providing what is often a noticeable performance increase.

The Windows Defragmentation utility provides this basic defragmenting function. It also enables you to select whether you want to arrange the files on the disk to consolidate the empty clusters into one contiguous free space (which takes longer). The Windows 98/Me version adds a feature that examines the files on the disk and arranges them with the most frequently used program files grouped together at the front of the disk, which can make programs load more quickly. Such a function is not necessary under Windows NT through Vista because those newer versions of Windows use a prefetch function to more quickly locate frequently accessed files. Vista takes the prefetch feature a step further with an enhanced drive cache called SuperFetch, which monitors which applications you use the most and preloads them into memory for faster access.

To show how defragmenting works, see the example of a fragmented file shown in Table 10.40.

Table 10.40   Fragmented File

Folder		
Name	**Starting Cluster**	**Size**
PLEDGE.TXT	1002	2
USCONST.TXT	1000	4

FAT16 File Allocation Table		
FAT Cluster #	**Value**	**Meaning**
00002	0	First cluster available
...	...	...
00999	0	Cluster available
01000	1001	In use, points to next cluster
01001	1004	In use, points to next cluster
01002	1003	In use, points to next cluster
01003	FFFFh	End of file
01004	1005	In use, points to next cluster
01005	FFFFh	End of file
...	...	...
65526	0	Last cluster available

In the preceding example, the file USCONST.TXT is fragmented in two pieces. If you ran a defragmenting program, the files would be read off the disk and rewritten in a contiguous fashion. One possible outcome is shown in Table 10.41.

Table 10.41   Defragmented File

Folder

Name	Starting Cluster	Size
PLEDGE.TXT	1004	2
USCONST.TXT	1000	4

FAT16 File Allocation Table

FAT Cluster #	Value	Meaning
00002	0	First cluster available
…	…	…
00999	0	Cluster available
01000	1001	In use, points to next cluster
01001	1002	In use, points to next cluster
01002	1003	In use, points to next cluster
01003	FFFFh	End of file
01004	1005	In use, points to next cluster
01005	FFFFh	End of file
…	…	…
65526	0	Last cluster available

Although it doesn't look like much was changed, you can see that now both files are in one piece, stored one right after the other. Because defragmenting involves reading and rewriting a possibly large number of files on your drive, it can take a long time, especially if you have a large drive with a lot of fragmented files and not very much free working space on the drive.

Third-party defragmentation utilities, such as the Speed Disk program included in Norton Utilities, provide additional features, such as the capability to select specific files that should be moved to the front of the disk. Speed Disk also can defragment the Windows swap file and files that are flagged with the system and hidden attributes, which Disk Defragmenter will not touch.

Caution

Although the disk-defragmentation utilities included with Windows and third-party products are usually quite safe, you should always be aware that defragmenting a disk is an inherently dangerous procedure. The program reads, erases, and rewrites every file on the disk and has the potential to cause damage to your data when interrupted improperly. Although I have never seen a problem result from the process, an unforeseen event—such as a power failure—during a defragmentation procedure can conceivably be disastrous. I strongly recommend that you always run a disk-repair utility, such as **CHKDSK** (Windows NT/2000/XP or Vista) or **SCANDISK** (Windows 9x/Me), on your drives before defragmenting them and have a current backup ready.

Windows NT 4.0 does not include a defragmentation utility, but Windows 2000, XP, and Vista do. Note that third-party defragmentation utilities available for recent and current versions of Windows, such as Golden Bow Systems' VoptXP (www.vopt.com), are often faster and offer more features than Windows's own defragmentation programs.

Third-Party Programs

When you have a problem reading a file or portions of a drive, the best course of action might be to use one of the more powerful third-party disk-repair utilities on the market. Norton Utilities by Symantec (also included in Norton SystemWorks) stands as one of the more popular data recovery programs on the market today. This program is comprehensive and automatically repairs most types of disk problems.

Norton SystemWorks

Programs such as Norton Utilities Disk Doctor can perform much more detailed repairs with a greater amount of safety. Disk Doctor preserves as much of the data in the file as possible and can mark the FAT so the bad sectors or clusters of the disk are not used again. These programs also save Undo information, enabling you to reverse any data recovery operation.

Norton Utilities Disk Doctor is part of Symantec's Norton SystemWorks package, which includes a great many other useful tools. For example, Norton Utilities has an excellent sector editor (Norton Disk Editor) that enables you to view and edit any part of a disk, including the master and volume boot records, FATs, and other areas that fall outside the disk's normal data area. A sector editor can enable the professional PC troubleshooter or repairperson to work directly with any sector on the disk, but this does require extensive knowledge of sector formats and disk structures.

Note

Data recovery is a lucrative service that the more advanced technician can provide. People are willing to pay much more to get their data back than to replace a hard drive.

You also can create a rescue disk for restarting your system and testing the drive in case of emergencies, unerase accidentally deleted files (even if the Recycle Bin was bypassed), and unformat accidentally formatted drives.

Most Norton Utilities programs are designed to be run from within the Windows GUI, and several of the utilities include both Windows and command-prompt versions. Norton SystemWorks 2008 or later is required to support Vista, and you should be careful not to use older versions of Norton Utilities, such as version 8.0 (designed for Windows 3.1 and MS-DOS), with 32-bit versions of Windows because of the possibility of data loss due to a lack of support for long filenames and large drives.

File Systems and Third-Party Disk Utilities

The most important consideration when you purchase third-party disk utilities is to choose products that support your file system. For example, Norton Utilities supports both FAT (including FAT32) and NTFS files systems, as does SpinRite 6. Beware of older utilities that don't support NTFS, for example. Never use a disk utility not designed for your file system, and never use an out-of-date disk utility (designed for an earlier operating system) on your disk. In both cases, you could cause irreparable damage to the data on your drive.

Windows Data Recovery

Recovering lost data can be as simple as opening the Windows Recycle Bin, or it might require spending hundreds of dollars on specialized data recovery software or services. In the worst-case scenario, you might even need to send your drive to a data recovery center and potentially spend thousands of dollars to get your data back, if recovery is even possible at all. Several factors affect the degree of difficulty you might encounter in recovering your data, including

- How the data was lost or deleted
- What file system was used by the volume on which the data was stored
- Whether the physical drive uses magnetic, optical, magneto-optical, or flash memory technology to store data
- Which version of Windows or other OS you use
- Whether you already have data-protection software installed on your system
- Whether the drive has suffered physical damage to the heads, platters (media), actuators (motors), or logic board

The Windows Recycle Bin and File Deletion

The simplest data recovery of all involves retrieving files from the Windows Recycle Bin (a standard part of Windows since Windows 95). During normal operation, pressing the Delete key or clicking the Delete button when you have a file or group of files highlighted in Windows Explorer sends files to the Recycle Bin. Although a file sent to the Recycle Bin is no longer listed in its normal location by Windows Explorer, the file is actually not fully deleted, and is even protected from being overwritten.

By default, all versions of Windows except Vista reserve a maximum of 10% or 3.99GB (whichever is smaller) of the disk space on each hard disk volume for the Recycle Bin (removable-media drives don't have a Recycle Bin). Note that even though you can increase the slider beyond 10%, doing so has no effect, and the 3.99GB maximum size remains in effect. For Vista, the Recycle Bin can be at most 10% of the drive's capacity for drives of 40GB or less (basically the same as XP and earlier versions); however for larger drives the maximum is 4GB plus 5% of the capacity above 40GB. Thus, for a 500GiB drive, under XP the Recycle Bin is limited to 3.99GB, whereas under Vista the Recycle Bin is limited to 4GiB plus 5% of 460GB (23GB) or a total of 27GB. Note that these maximums can be reduced via the slider control in the Recycle Bin properties. After the Recycle Bin is full, Windows allows the oldest files to be overwritten. Thus, the quicker you realize that a file has mistakenly been deleted (sent to the Recycle Bin), the more likely it is you can retrieve it.

To retrieve a file from the Recycle Bin, open the Recycle Bin, select the file, right-click it, and select Restore. Windows then restores the file to its original location, removing it from the Recycle Bin in the process.

Note that if you hold down the Shift key when you select Delete or press the Delete key, the Recycle Bin is bypassed and the files are immediately deleted. The Recycle Bin is also automatically bypassed when you delete files at a command prompt. Retrieving files that have been fully deleted (that is, not in the Recycle Bin) requires third-party data recovery software.

The files in the Recycle Bin are stored in folders that are marked with both Hidden and System attributes. The Recycle Bin folder varies according to the OS and file system used:

- Windows 9x/Me or NT/2000/XP disks using FAT/FAT32: \RECYCLED
- Windows NT/2000/XP disks using NTFS: \RECYCLER
- Windows Vista (all disks): \$RECYCLE.BIN

Because these folders are marked with Hidden and System attributes, they are not normally displayed in Windows Explorer unless you have opted in the Tools menu, Folder Options, View settings to show hidden files and folders, as well as not to hide protected operating system files.

To undelete files stored in the Recycle Bin, first double-click the Recycle Bin icon on the Desktop. This launches the Recycle Bin explorer window, which includes a list of deleted files. If the list is long, it can be helpful to sort the list by clicking the column headings such as Name, Original Location, Date Deleted, Type, and Size. After you have found a file you want to recover, right-click the filename and select Restore, which moves the saved copy back to its original location.

Note that the Recycle Bin has many limitations concerning whether and when it actually saves files. For example, the Recycle Bin does not save files under the following circumstances:

- Files deleted from removable media such as floppy disks or flash drives.
- Files deleted at a command prompt.
- Files automatically deleted by an application or script.
- Files deleted from a remote (shared) drive, even on the remote system.
- Files overwritten with another file of the same name.

In all those cases, the deleted files bypass the Recycle Bin. It may still be possible to recover them later by using programs specifically designed to find deleted files and undelete them.

Recovering Files That Are Not in the Recycle Bin

The Recycle Bin is a useful first line of defense against data loss, but it is quite limited. As you learned in the previous section, it can be bypassed when you select files for deletion, and files stored in the Recycle Bin are eventually kicked out by newer deleted files. Also, the Recycle Bin isn't used for files deleted from a command prompt or when an older version of a file is replaced by a newer version.

Third-party file unerase/delete programs are necessary if you want to retrieve files not in the Recycle Bin. However, the effectiveness of these programs can vary depending on how long it's been since the file was deleted, how much the disk has been written to since, how fragmented the file was, what type of file system is used on the volume containing the file, and the size of the file.

In addition to the Recycle Bin, Vista Business, Enterprise, and Ultimate editions include a *Previous Versions* mechanism (also called *Volume Shadow Copy*), which takes periodic snapshots of files that are changed, creating historical copies as you work. This feature allows you to easily recover not only files that were accidentally deleted, but those that have been overwritten as well.

Undeleting Files Under NTFS

Because the file structure of NTFS is much more complex than any FAT file system version and some files might be compressed with NTFS's built-in compression, you should use an NTFS-specific file undeletion program to attempt to recover deleted files from an NTFS drive.

If you need to recover deleted files and have not already installed a program with delete protection such as Norton UnErase, you should consider a standalone file unerase/undelete program, such as

- **Avira UnErase Personal**—http://www.free-av.com
- **PC INSPECTOR File Recovery**—http://www.PCInspector.de
- **Undelete Plus**—http://www.Undelete-Plus.com

These programs are not only free for personal use, they are also fully functional and highly recommended.

Tip

Some file-undelete products for NTFS can undelete only files created by the currently logged in user, whereas others require the administrator to be logged in. Check the documentation for details, particularly if you are trying to undelete files from a system with more than one user.

Norton UnErase and Norton Protected Recycle Bin

Using Norton Utilities makes recovering deleted files fairly easy. Symantec has included a somewhat unique undelete tool called Norton UnErase in Norton SystemWorks 2002 and later versions, which are compatible with NTFS. The main difference between this tool and conventional undelete programs is a feature called Norton Protection, which creates and maintains an auxiliary type of recycle bin that stores more instances of deleted files for a specified period of time before purging them from the system. This Norton Protection works with the Norton UnErase program, giving it enhanced capabilities for recovering deleted files.

Caution

Do *not* install data-recovery software to a drive you are attempting to retrieve data from because you might overwrite the data you are attempting to retrieve. If you are trying to recover data from your Windows startup drive, install another hard disk into your system, configure it as a boot drive in the system BIOS, install a working copy of Windows on it, boot from that drive, and install your data recovery software to that drive. If possible, install a drive large enough so that you have several GB of free space on it for storing recovered data.

If you have already installed Norton Utilities, you probably have the Norton Protected Recycle Bin on your desktop in place of the regular Recycle Bin. Compared to the Windows standard-model Recycle Bin, the Norton Protected Recycle Bin protects files that have been replaced with newer versions and files that were deleted from a command prompt.

With the Norton Protected Recycle Bin installed, you can still restore files from the standard Windows Recycle Bin as you normally would, the only difference is that to open the standard Recycle Bin explorer you right-click the Norton Protected Recycle Bin and select either Open or Explore. To start the more advanced and more capable Norton UnErase Wizard, either double-click the Norton Protected Recycle Bin icon or right-click it and select UnErase Wizard. There you will see a listing of all protected files, including those in the standard Recycle Bin as well as the Norton Protected Recycle Bin. By selecting the Back button, you can also expand the listing by searching for all deleted files, including those that were not stored in either Recycle Bin. When you select the last option, you can narrow down the search with wildcards or file types and specify which drives to search. You must supply the first letter of the filename for files that were not stored in the Recycle Bin; you can also see which files were deleted by a particular program. To undelete a file with the Unerase Wizard, select the file, provide the first letter of the filename if necessary, click Quick View to view the file (if your file viewer supports the file format), and click Recover to restore the file to its original location.

The Norton Protected Recycle Bin stores files in a \RECYCLED\NPROTECT folder on FAT volumes, or a \RECYCLER\NPROTECT folder on NTFS volumes. The 2006 and earlier versions of the software completely hid these folders from the Windows FindFirst/FindNext APIs (Application Program Interfaces), which meant that they were invisible to disk scans or even Windows Explorer. This was originally intended to keep the protected files away from user mischief. However, after determining that malicious programs could also hide files there, Symantec released an update that would unhide the folder. The update is supposed to be distributed via the LiveUpdate (Symantec's automatic updates) feature; however I have found that in older versions (for example, NSW 2003) this does not work, and the folder remains completely hidden. To expose the folder without using LiveUpdate, visit the following site for instructions on how to update the Symevent files: http://tinyurl.com/ey7jl

Retrieving Data from Partitioned and Formatted Drives

When a hard disk, floppy disk, or removable-media drive containing files is formatted, the links and pointers to the clusters occupied by the existing files are lost. If a hard drive has been reparti-tioned or reformatted, the original file system and partition information are lost as well.

In such cases, more powerful data-recovery tools must be used to retrieve data. To retrieve data from an accidentally partitioned or formatted drive, you have a few options:

- Use a program that can unformat or unpartition the drive.
- Use a program that can bypass the newly created file system and read disk sectors directly to discover and retrieve data.

To retrieve data from a drive that has been partitioned, you must use a program that can read disk sectors directly.

Norton Unformat and Its Limitations

Norton Utilities and Norton SystemWorks offer Norton Unformat, which can be launched from the bootable CD to unformat an accidentally formatted FAT drive. However, Norton Unformat has significant limitations with today's file systems and drive types, including the following:

- *Norton Unformat doesn't support NTFS drives.* This means many Windows 2000—and XP–based systems can't use it for data recovery.
- *Norton Unformat cannot be used with drives that require device drivers to function, such as removable-media drives.*
- *Norton Unformat works best if the Norton Image program has been used to create a copy of the FATs and root directory.* If the image file is out-of-date, Unformat might fail; if the image file is not present, Unformat cannot restore the root directory and the actual names of folders in the root directory will be replaced by sequentially numbered folder names.
- *Norton Unformat cannot copy restored files to another drive or folder.* It restores data back to the same drive and partition. If Unformat uses an out-of-date file created by Norton Image to determine where data is located, it could overwrite valid data on the drive being unformatted.

For these reasons, Norton Unformat is not the most desirable method for unformatting a drive. You can use the powerful, but completely manual, Norton DiskEdit (DISKEDIT) to unformat a drive or retrieve data from a formatted drive, but other alternatives are simpler.

Recovering Lost Partitions and Files

Many products on the market can retrieve lost data to another drive, even if the data loss was due to accidental formatting or disk partitioning. One of the best and most comprehensive products is the EasyRecovery product line from Ontrack DataRecovery Services, a division of Kroll Ontrack, Inc. The EasyRecovery product line includes the following products:

- **EasyRecovery Lite**—Recovers data in more than 250 file types from accidentally deleted hard, floppy, and removable-media drives and repairs damaged or corrupted Zip files. Economical version limited to 25 files per session and 5 drives total.
- **EasyRecovery DataRecovery**—Same as EasyRecovery Lite except limited to any number of files on up to 20 drives total.
- **EasyRecovery FileRepair**—Repairs damaged or corrupted Zip and Microsoft Office (Word, Excel, Access, PowerPoint, and Outlook) files.
- **EasyRecovery EmailRepair**—Repairs damaged or corrupted Outlook and Outlook Express files.

■ **EasyRecovery Professional**—Combines the features of DataRecovery, FileRepair, EmailRepair, and FileRecovery, and adds the capability (called RawRecovery) to bypass the file system and recover more than 290 file types from accidentally partitioned or formatted drives. Limited to any number of files on 20 drives total.

A free trial version of EasyRecovery Professional displays files that can be recovered (and repairs and recovers Zip files at no charge); it can be downloaded from the Ontrack website (http://www.ontrack.com).

Which options are best for data recovery? Table 11.1 shows the results of various data-loss scenarios and recovery options when EasyRecovery Professional was used to recover data from a 19GB logical drive formatted with the NTFS file system under Windows XP.

Table 11.1   Data Recovery Options and Results with EasyRecovery Professional

Type of Data Loss	Data Recovery Method	Data Recoverable?	Details	Notes
Deleted folder	DeletedRecovery	Yes	All files recovered.	All long file and folder names preserved.
Formatted drive (full format)	FormatRecovery	Yes	All files recovered.	New folders created to store recovered files; long filenames preserved for files and folders beneath root folder level.
Logical drive deleted with Disk Management	AdvancedRecovery	Yes	All files and folders recovered.	All long file and folder names preserved.
Formatted drive with new data copied to it	FormatRecovery	Partial	Files and folders that were not overwritten were recovered.	Long filenames and folders preserved.
Formatted, repartitioned drive reformatted as FAT32 (117MB Disk 1)	AdvancedRecovery	No	Could not locate any files to recover.	
	RawRecovery	Partial	Nonfragmented files recovered.	Original directory structure and filenames lost; each file type stored in a separate folder and files numbered sequentially.

Type of Data Loss	Data Recovery Method	Data Recoverable?	Details	Notes
Formatted, repartitioned drive formatted as NTFS (18.8GB Disk 2)	AdvancedRecovery	No	Could not locate any files to recover.	
	RawRecovery	Partial	Nonfragmented files recovered.	Original directory structure and filenames lost; each file type stored in a separate folder and files numbered sequentially.

As Table 11.1 makes clear, as long as the data areas of a drive are not overwritten, complete data recovery is usually possible—even if the drive has been formatted or repartitioned. Thus, it's critical that you react quickly if you suspect you have partitioned or formatted a drive containing valuable data. The longer you wait to recover data, the less data will be available for recovery. In addition, if you must use a sector-by-sector search for data (a process called RawRecovery by Ontrack), your original folder structure and long filenames will not be saved. You will therefore need to re-create the desired directory structure and rename files after you recover them—a very tedious process.

Tip

If you use EasyRecovery Professional or EasyRecovery DataRecovery to repair damaged Zip or Microsoft Office files, use the Properties menu to select a location for repaired files (the original location or another drive or folder). By default, repaired Outlook files are copied to a different folder, whereas other file types are repaired in place unless you specify a different location.

As you can see from this example, dedicated data-recovery programs such as Ontrack EasyRecovery Professional are very powerful. However, they are also very expensive. Fortunately there are free data recovery programs that can do a similar job.

If you have lost or damaged the partition table, you essentially lose access to the entire disk and all the partitions and volumes it contains. In that case you can use software to scan the disk for existing partitions, identify their types and locations, and use that information to re-create the original partition table on the disk. One of the best programs for this purpose is the TestDisk program by CG Security: http://www.cgsecurity.org.

TestDisk is designed to recover lost partitions and make non-booting disks bootable again. It also includes a powerful program called PhotoRec, which works like the RawRecovery capability from Ontrack in that it is specifically designed to work around or under the file system (or even if no file system exists) and recover more than 80 different types of image and document files from accidentally formatted or deleted disks. Despite the incredible power and capability of these programs, both TestDisk and PhotoRec are free and highly recommended.

Using a Disk Editor

In my PC Hardware (Upgrading and Repairing) and Data Recovery/Computer Forensics seminars, I frequently use disk editor software to explore, modify, or copy sectors, clusters, and files on various drives. A disk editor is basically a tool that, at a minimum, lets you edit raw sectors on a disk. More powerful examples include support for interpreting file systems such as FAT and NTFS, as well as templates or decoders for interpreting special sectors such as the MBRs (Master Boot Records), EBRs (Extended Boot Records), VBRs (Volume Boot Records), directories (folders), and even specific file types.

I also use disk editors to retrieve lost data. Because a disk editor is a manual tool, it can sometimes be useful even when friendlier automatic programs don't work correctly or are unavailable. For example, in a physical sector mode, a disk editor can be used with any drive regardless of what file system was used, since at that level it is working underneath the OS and accessing the sectors of the drive directly. Additionally, because some of the more powerful disk editors can display the structure of your drives in a way other programs don't, they are great for learning more about disk drive structures as well as recovering lost data.

Types of Disk Editors

Several types of disk editors are available, from simple editors that display only raw disk sectors to those that offer very powerful boot sector and file system decoders and analyzers. There are both freeware and commercial sector editors as well, and some of the free ones are surprisingly powerful and well designed. I have used and recommended the following disk editors over the years:

Freeware disk editors:

- **Microsoft DSKPROBE (Disk Probe)**—http://tinyurl.com/yja7vw
- **HexEdit**—http://www.mitec.cz
- **HxD**—http://www.mh-nexus.de
- **SectEdit**—http://www.roadkil.net
- **Tiny Hexer**—http://www.mirkes.de

Commercial disk editors:

- **DiskEdit (Norton SystemWorks)**—http://www.symantec.com
- **WinHex**—http://winhex.com

All these programs are extremely useful, but I probably use Disk Probe, WinHex, and DiskEdit the most. Disk Probe is a Windows-based editor included with the Windows NT through XP Support Tools, which can be found in the \SUPPORT\TOOLS folder on most Windows installation discs, and/or can be downloaded from the Microsoft website. Windows Vista unfortunately does not include the support tools; however you can download the Windows XP support tools from Microsoft, extract the DSKPROBE.* files, and subsequently use the DSKPROBE.EXE program under Vista.

The WinHex program from X-Ways Software, shown in Figure 11.1, is one of the most powerful Windows-based disk editors I know of, and is available in a free downloadable trial version as well as full-blown commercial and even forensics versions.

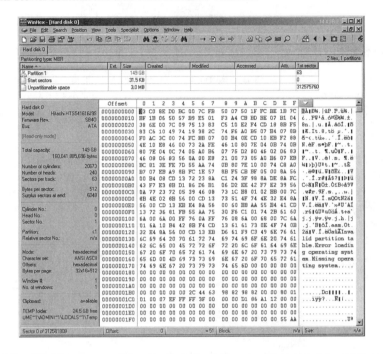

Figure 11.1 WinHex shown editing the first physical sector of a hard disk, which contains the MBR (Master Boot Record).

The DiskEdit program included with the Symantec Norton SystemWorks (NSW) suite is the most powerful DOS-based disk editor I know of, and is extremely useful for bare-bones disk editing purposes, especially when booting corrupted systems from a floppy disk.

The following sections show how to use various disk editors to perform several data recovery tasks.

Using a Disk Editor to Recover an NTFS Volume Boot Sector

I've seen problems with lost or corrupted VBRs (Volume Boot Records) on many occasions. The key that tells you the VBR is corrupt is that the drive appears in Windows as having a drive letter, but Windows thinks that the drive has not been formatted. An error message appears as shown in Figure 11.2.

If this message appears and you do have data on the drive, make sure you select **No** to prevent formatting the drive, or the problem will become much more severe!

Figure 11.2 `Disk is not formatted` error message due to corrupted VBR.

One of the best tools for repairing a damaged VBR is the Disk Probe (`DSKPROBE.EXE`) disk editor, available for free from Microsoft. Earlier I told you where to get Disk Probe; after you have the `DSKPROBE.*` files on your system, you can run the program by clicking on the `DSKPROBE.EXE` file.

To repair a corrupt VBR using Disk Probe, use the following steps:

1. Run Disk Probe, and then select Drives, Physical Drive. Under Available Physical Drives, select PhysicalDrive*X*, where X = the ordinal number of the disk you want to edit. If you aren't sure which is which, use Disk Management to find what the ordinal is of the disk in question (see Figure 11.3).

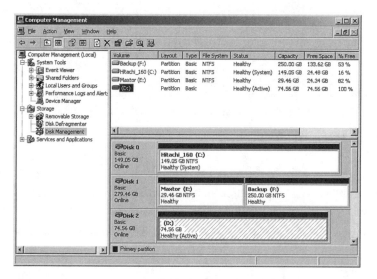

Figure 11.3 Using Disk Management to determine the ordinal of a drive (drive D: = Disk 2 in this case) with a corrupt VBR.

Note that the drive letter may not logically match the ordinal number. In this example, I have an internal drive on my system that has a single partition, along with two external USB drives, one with a single partition and another with two partitions. They are configured and seen by Windows Explorer, Disk Management, and Disk Probe as

Windows Explorer	Disk Management	Disk Probe
C:	Disk 0	PhysicalDrive0
D:	Disk 2	PhysicalDrive2
E:	Disk 1	PhysicalDrive1
F:	Disk 1	PhysicalDrive1

Because the error message indicated that drive D: was not formatted, that would correspond to Disk 2 or PhysicalDrive2 in this example. Note in the Disk Management display where Disk 2 (drive D:) does not list a file system (the other drives show NTFS), and that it says that the drive space is 100% free. (In actuality the drive used in this example has many files and is only 17% free.)

2. Double-click the PhysicalDriveX you want to edit. In the box below, uncheck Read Only and press the Set Active button. You will then notice that the Active Handle has been set to PhysicalDriveX; select OK (see Figure 11.4).

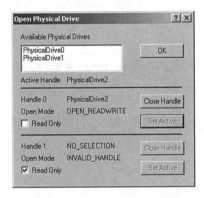

Figure 11.4   Selecting a physical drive, making it active and enabling write access in Disk Probe.

3. Open the Sectors Menu, and then select Read. Enter 0 for Starting Sectors and 1 for Number of Sectors (those should be the default settings), and then click the Read button. The sector data should appear as shown in Figure 11.5.

4. You are now looking at sector 0, which is the Master Boot Record (MBR) of your physical disk. You can verify this by checking the ASCII text on the right side in the bottom half of the sector, which reads, "Invalid partition table," "Error loading operating system," and "Missing operating system." The partition table data can be seen in the 64 bytes starting at offset 0x1BE. To interpret the partition table data intelligently, open the View menu, and then select Partition Table. The first partition in the table is selected by default. To select one of the three other partitions, from the box labeled Partition Table Index, you can use the scrollbar to select the partition you want and double-click on that partition. This drive has only a single partition (1) (see Figure 11.6).

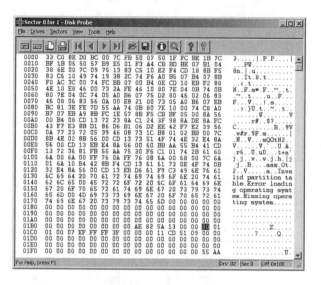

Figure 11.5 Disk Probe with data from Sector 0 (the MBR) loaded.

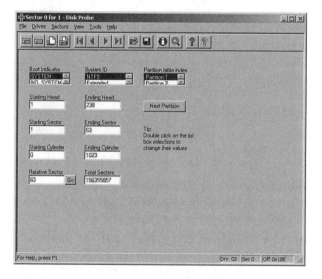

Figure 11.6 Disk Probe showing partition table data for partition 1.

5. When you have selected the partition containing the VBR you want to repair, note the data shown for Relative Sector and Total Sectors. The Relative Sector figure is the sector number of the first sector in the partition, which is the sector containing the VBR. The Total Sectors figure indicates the total number of sectors in the partition. The Total Sectors figure also indirectly tells us the number of the last sector in the partition, which contains the backup VBR if the partition is a primary partition that was formatted by Windows NT 4.0 or later, using NTFS. To calculate the sector number of the last sector in the partition, add the

Relative Sector and Total Sectors figures, then subtract 1. In this example the math works out as $63 + 156{,}355{,}857 - 1 = 156{,}355{,}919$. This means that the last sector in the partition is sector number 156,355,919 and that sector should also contain the backup VBR.

6. Now that you know both the starting and ending sectors for the partition, you can go to the starting sector by clicking on the Go button next to the Relative Sector box. In this example it takes you to sector 63. To see the raw sector data you can change the view by opening the View menu and selecting Bytes. At this point you should be looking at the VBR data, but in this example the VBR has been completely overwritten with zeros, as shown in Figure 11.7.

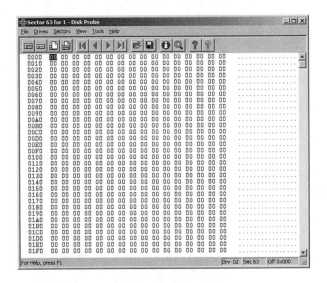

Figure 11.7   Disk Probe showing overwritten VBR data.

7. Now let's go to the backup VBR, which is contained in the last sector in a primary partition. To navigate there, open the Sectors menu, select Read, and then type the sector number you previously calculated for the last sector in the Starting Sector box, leaving the Number of Sectors to read as set to 1. Then click the Read button to read the sector. You should now see the backup copy of the VBR, which you can identify by noting ASCII strings such as "NTFS" near the beginning of the sector, and error messages such as A disk read error occurred, NTLDR is missing, NTLDR is compressed, and Press Ctrl+Alt+Del to restart near the end of the sector. The display should show the backup VBR as shown in Figure 11.8.

8. Now you are ready to write the good backup VBR over the corrupted original VBR, thus repairing the drive. To do this, open the Sectors menu and select Write. Make absolutely *sure* the dialog box shows the correct Handle and PhysicalDrive. In the Starting sector to Write Data box, type in the starting sector of the partition, which is the same as the Relative Sector number you noted in step 5. Figure 11.9 shows how this should look in my example. When you are sure everything is entered correctly, click on the Write it button to actually write the data. You are given a very strong last warning (and chance to back out); select Yes to continue.

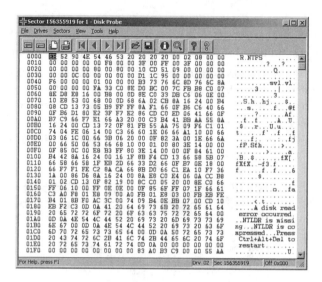

Figure 11.8 Disk Probe showing the backup VBR, which is also the last sector in a primary partition.

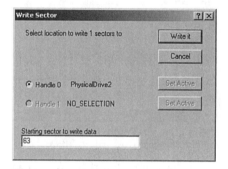

Figure 11.9 Disk Probe showing the Write Sector dialog for writing the backup VBR over the corrupted original VBR at sector 63.

9. Now you can confirm that the original VBR has been restored. To do this, open the Sectors menu and type in the Relative Sector number from step 5 (63 in this example) and leave the Number of Sectors set at 1, and then click the Read button. Verify that the correct boot sector data is visible, and that you are positioned at the proper sector (63). The display should appear like Figure 11.10.

10. To finish the job, close Disk Probe and reboot the system. The drive will now appear formatted and any files in the volume should be accessible. Open Disk Management to view the drive (see Figure 11.11).

Now you see that drive D: (Disk 2) shows up as having an NTFS file system, and that only 17% of the drive is free. All the files on the drive that were "lost" before are now fully accessible.

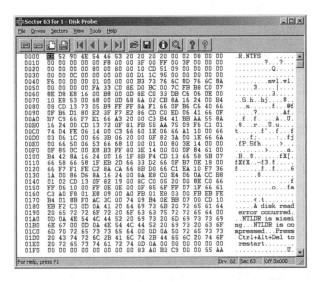

Figure 11.10   Disk Probe showing the restored VBR data at sector 63.

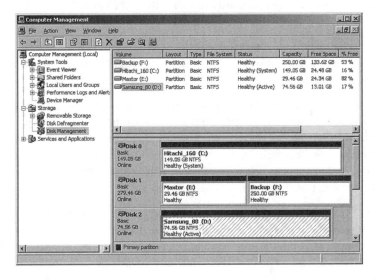

Figure 11.11   Using Disk Management to show that the file system (NTFS) is now visible, and data is present where it wasn't being shown before.

As you can see, using a disk editor such as Disk Probe can be very helpful in correcting what might otherwise be a disk disaster!

Using a Disk Editor to Undelete Files

This section discusses two of the simpler procedures you can perform with a disk editor:

■ Undeleting a file on a floppy disk

■ Copying a deleted file on a hard disk to a different drive

In these examples I am using the Norton DiskEdit program (an old favorite); however, note that most of the other disk editors I listed previously (including the freeware ones) could be used just as well. When using a different editor, the concepts and techniques remain the same; only the screens and commands differ.

If you have Norton SystemWorks, SystemWorks Professional, or Norton Utilities for Windows, you have Norton DiskEdit. To determine whether it is installed on your system, look in the Norton Utilities folder under the Program Files folder for the following files: `DISKEDIT.EXE` and `DISKEDIT.HLP`.

If you don't find these files on your hard disk (they aren't automatically installed in newer versions of NSW), you can find them on the installation CD. If you have SystemWorks or SystemWorks Professional, look for the CD folder called `\NU` to locate the files. In NSW 2006 and newer versions, the `DiskEdit.*` files are buried in a .cab (compressed cabinet) file. To extract the `DiskEdit.*` files you can use a program such as 7-zip (www.7-zip.com).

DiskEdit is a command prompt program designed primarily to access FAT-based file systems such as FAT12 (floppy disks), FAT16 (MS-DOS and early Windows 95 hard disks), and FAT32 (Windows 95B/Windows 98/Me hard disks). You can use DiskEdit with Windows NT, Windows 2000, and Windows XP if you prepared the hard disks with the FAT16 or FAT32 file systems. DiskEdit will also work on NTFS volumes; however, in that case it can only be used in physical sector mode.

I strongly recommend that you first use DiskEdit with floppy disks you have prepared with non-critical files before you use it with a hard disk or vital files. Because DiskEdit is a completely manual program, the opportunities for error are high.

The DiskEdit files can easily fit on a floppy disk, but if you are new to the program, you might want to put them on a different drive from one you will be examining or repairing. *Never* copy DiskEdit files (or any other data recovery program) to a drive that contains data you are trying to recover because the files might overwrite the data area and destroy the files you want to retrieve. For example, if you are planning to examine or repair floppy disks, create a folder on your hard disk called `DiskEdit` and copy the files to that folder.

You can use DiskEdit without a mouse by using keyboard commands, but if you want to use it with a mouse, you can do so if your mouse attaches to the serial or PS/2 mouse ports (USB mice generally don't work from the command prompt, but if your USB mouse has a PS/2 mouse port adapter, you can use it by plugging the mouse and adapter into the PS/2 port). You must load an MS-DOS mouse driver (usually `MOUSE.COM`) for your mouse before you start DiskEdit. If you have a Logitech mouse, you can download an MS-DOS mouse driver from the Logitech website. If you have a Microsoft mouse, Microsoft doesn't provide MS-DOS drivers you can download, but you can get them from the website http://www.bootdisk.com/readme.htm#mouse.

For other mice, try the Microsoft or Logitech drivers, or contact the vendor for drivers. Keep in mind that scroll wheels and other buttons won't work with an MS-DOS driver. I recommend you copy your mouse driver to the same folder in which DiskEdit is located.

Using DiskEdit to Examine a Drive

To start DiskEdit:

1. Boot the computer to a command prompt (not Windows); DiskEdit needs exclusive access to the drives you plan to examine. If you use Windows 9x, press F8 or Ctrl to bring up the startup menu and select Safe Mode Command Prompt, or use the Windows 9x/Me Emergency Startup disk (make one with Add/Remove Programs). If you use Windows 2000 or XP, insert a blank floppy disk into drive A:, right-click drive A: in My Computer, and select Format. Select the Create an MS-DOS Startup Disk option and use this disk to start your computer.

2. Change to the folder containing your mouse driver and DiskEdit.

3. Type **MOUSE** (if your mouse driver is called `MOUSE.COM` or `MOUSE.EXE`; otherwise, substitute the correct name if it's called something else). Then press Enter to load the mouse driver.

4. Type **DISKEDIT** and press Enter to start the program. If you don't specify a drive, DiskEdit scans the drive on which it's installed. If you are using it to work with a floppy disk, enter the command **DISKEDIT A:** to direct it to scan your floppy disk. DiskEdit scans your drive to determine the location of files and folders on the disk.

5. The first time you run DiskEdit, a prompt appears to remind you that DiskEdit runs in read-only mode until you change its configuration through the Tools menu. Click OK to continue.

After DiskEdit has started, you can switch to the drive you want to examine or recover data from. To change to a different drive, follow these steps:

1. Press Alt+O to open the Object menu.

2. Select Drive.

3. Select the drive you want to examine from the Logical Disks menu.

4. The disk structure is scanned and displayed in the DiskEdit window.

DiskEdit normally starts in Directory mode, but you can change it to other modes with the View menu. When you view a drive containing data in Directory mode, you will see a listing similar to the one shown in Figure 11.12.

The Name column lists the names of the directory entries, and the `.EXT` column lists the file/folder extensions (if any). The ID column lists the type of directory entry, including

- Dir—A directory (folder).
- **File**—A data file.
- **LFN**—A portion of a Windows long filename. Windows stores the start of the LFN before the actual filename. If the LFN is longer than 13 characters, one or more additional directory entries is used to store the rest of the LFN. The next three columns list the file size, date, and time.

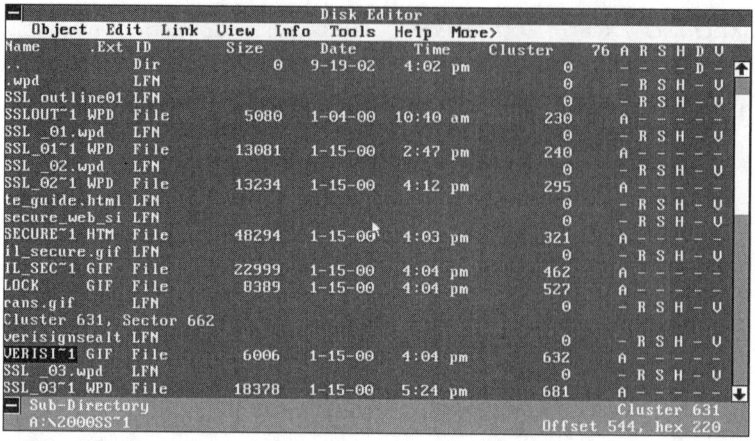

Figure 11.12 The Norton DiskEdit directory view of a typical floppy disk.

The Cluster column indicates the cluster in which the first portion of the file is located. Drives are divided into clusters or allocation units when they are formatted, and a *cluster* (allocation unit) is the smallest unit that can be used to store a file. Cluster sizes vary with the size of the drive and the file system used to format the drive.

The letters *A*, *R*, *S*, *H*, *D*, and *V* refer to attributes for each directory entry. *A* (archive) means the file hasn't been backed up since it was last modified. *R* is used to indicate that the directory entry is read-only, and *S* indicates that the directory entry has the System attribute. *H* indicates that the directory entry has the Hidden attribute, whereas *D* indicates that the entry is a directory. Finally, *V* is the attribute for an LFN entry.

The file VERISI~1.GIF (highlighted in black near the bottom of Figure 11.12) is interesting for several reasons. The tilde (~) and number at the end of the filename indicates that the file was created with a 32-bit version of Windows. 32-bit versions of Windows (Windows 9x/Me, 2000, and XP) allow the user to save a file with a long (more than eight characters) filename (plus the three-character file extension such as .EXE, .BMP, or .GIF). In addition, long filenames can have spaces and other characters not allowed by earlier versions of Windows and MS-DOS. The process used by various versions of Windows to create LFN entries is discussed in Chapter 10, in the section called "VFAT and Long Filenames."

When you view the file in Windows Explorer or My Computer, you see the long filename. To see the DOS alias name within the Windows GUI, right-click the file and select Properties from My Computer or Windows Explorer. Or, you can use the DIR command in a command-prompt window. The LFN is stored as one or more separate directory entries just before the DOS alias name. Because the actual long name for VERISI~1.GIF (Verisignsealtrans.gif) is 21 characters, two additional directory entries are required to store the long filename (each directory entry can store up to 13 characters of an LFN), as seen in Figure 11.12.

Determining the Number of Clusters Used by a File

As discussed earlier in this chapter, an area of the disk called the file allocation table stores the starting location of the file and each additional cluster used to store the file. VERISI~1.GIF starts at cluster 632. Clusters are the smallest disk structures used to store files, and they vary in size depending on the file system used to create the disk on which the files are stored and on the size of the drive. In this case, the file is stored on a 1.44MB floppy disk, which has a cluster size of 512 bytes (one sector). The cluster size of the drive is very important to know if you want to retrieve data using DiskEdit.

To determine the cluster size of a drive, you can open a command-prompt window and run CHKDSK C: to display the allocation unit size (cluster size) and other statistics about the specified drive.

To determine how many clusters are used to store a file, look at the size of the file and compare it to the cluster size of the drive on which it's stored. The file VERISI~1.GIF contains 6,006 bytes. Because this file is stored on a floppy disk that has a cluster size of 512 bytes, the file must occupy several clusters. How many clusters does it occupy? To determine this, divide the file size by the number of clusters and round the result up to the next whole number. The math is shown in Table 11.2.

Table 11.2   Determining the Number of Clusters Used by a File

File Size (FS) of VERISI~1.GIF	Cluster Size (CS)	Result of (FS) Divided by (CS) Equals (CR)	(CR) Rounded Up to Next Whole Number
6,006	512	11.73046875	12

From these calculations, you can see that VERISI~1.GIF uses 12 clusters on the floppy disk; it would use fewer clusters on a FAT16 or FAT32 hard disk (the exact number depends on the file system and size of the hard disk). The more clusters a file contains, the greater the risk is that some of its data area could be overwritten by newer data if the file is deleted. Consequently, if you need to undelete a file that was not sent to the Windows Recycle Bin or was deleted from a removable-media drive or floppy drive (these types of drives don't support the Recycle Bin), the sooner you attempt to undelete the file, the more likely it is that you can retrieve the data.

The normal directory display in Norton DiskEdit shows the starting cluster (632) for VERISI~1.GIF. If a file is stored on a drive with a lot of empty space, the remainder of the clusters will probably immediately follow the first two—a badly fragmented drive might use noncontiguous clusters to store the rest of the file. Because performing data recovery when the clusters are contiguous is much easier, I strongly recommend that you defragment your drives frequently.

To see the remainder of the clusters used by a file, move the cursor to the file, press Alt+L or click the Link menu, and select Cluster Chain (FAT); you can also press Ctrl+T to go directly to this view. The screen changes to show the clusters as listed in the FAT for this file, as shown in Figure 11.13. The clusters used by the file are highlighted in red, and the filename is shown at the bottom of the screen. The symbol <EOF> stands for *end of file*, indicating the last cluster in the file.

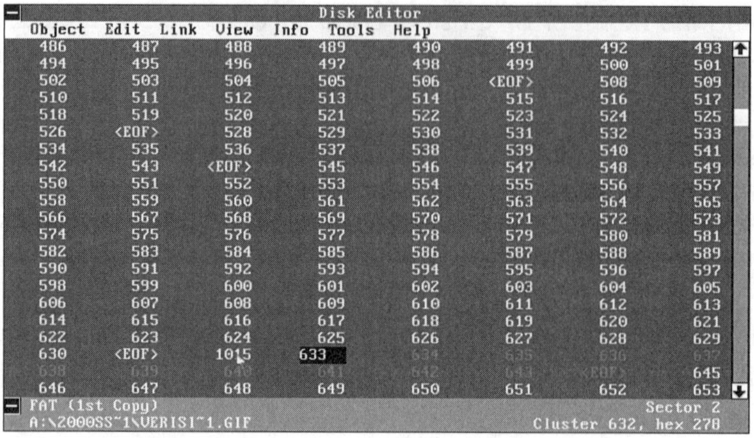

```
                              Disk Editor
   Object  Edit  Link  View  Info  Tools  Help
    486     487      488      489      490      491      492      493
    494     495      496      497      498      499      500      501
    502     503      504      505      506    <EOF>      508      509
    510     511      512      513      514      515      516      517
    518     519      520      521      522      523      524      525
    526    <EOF>     528      529      530      531      532      533
    534     535      536      537      538      539      540      541
    542     543    <EOF>      545      546      547      548      549
    550     551      552      553      554      555      556      557
    558     559      560      561      562      563      564      565
    566     567      568      569      570      571      572      573
    574     575      576      577      578      579      580      581
    582     583      584      585      586      587      588      589
    590     591      592      593      594      595      596      597
    598     599      600      601      602      603      604      605
    606     607      608      609      610      611      612      613
    614     615      616      617      618      619      620      621
    622     623      624      625      626      627      628      629
    630    <EOF>    1015     633
                                                                645
    646     647      648      649      650      651      652      653
   FAT (1st Copy)                                          Sector 2
   A:\2000SS~1\VERISI~1.GIF                      Cluster 632, hex 278
```

Figure 11.13   The FAT view of VERISI~1.GIF. All its clusters are contiguous.

How the Operating System Marks a File When It Is Deleted

If a file (VERISI~1.GIF, in this example) is deleted, the following changes happen to the disk where the file is stored, as shown in Figure 11.14:

- The default directory view shows that the first character of the filename (V) has been replaced with a σ (lowercase sigma) character.

- There are now two new types of entries in the ID column for this file and its associated LFN:

  - **Erased**—An erased file
  - **Del LFN**—An LFN belonging to an erased file

Note also that the beginning cluster (632) is still shown in the Cluster column.

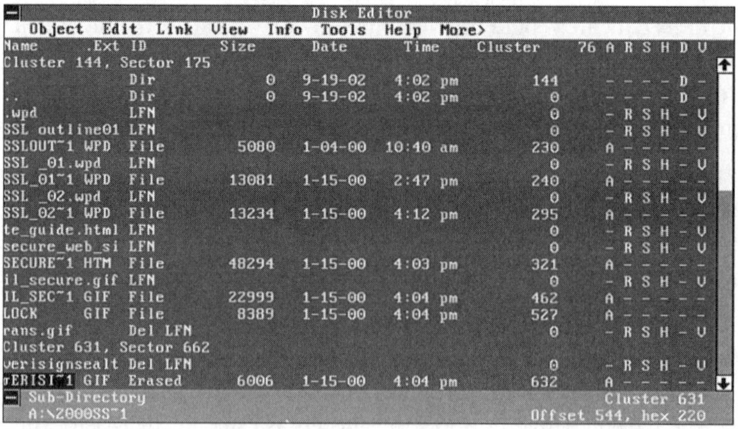

```
                              Disk Editor
   Object  Edit  Link  View  Info  Tools  Help  More>
Name      .Ext ID     Size      Date      Time    Cluster    76 A R S H D V
Cluster 144, Sector 175
.               Dir       0    9-19-02   4:02 pm      144      - - - - D -
..              Dir       0    9-19-02   4:02 pm        0      - - - - D -
.wpd            LFN                                     0      - R S H - V
SSL outline01 LFN                                       0      - R S H - V
SSLOUT~1 WPD  File     5080    1-04-00  10:40 am      230      A - - - - -
SSL _01.wpd   LFN                                       0      - R S H - V
SSL_01~1 WPD  File    13081    1-15-00   2:47 pm      240      A - - - - -
SSL _02.wpd   LFN                                       0      - R S H - V
SSL_02~1 WPD  File    13234    1-15-00   4:12 pm      295      A - - - - -
te_guide.html LFN                                       0      - R S H - V
secure_web_si LFN                                       0      - R S H - V
SECURE~1 HTM  File    48294    1-15-00   4:03 pm      321      A - - - - -
il_secure.gif LFN                                       0      - R S H - V
IL_SEC~1 GIF  File    22999    1-15-00   4:04 pm      462      A - - - - -
LOCK     GIF  File     8389    1-15-00   4:04 pm      527      A - - - - -
rans.gif      Del LFN                                   0      - R S H - V
Cluster 631, Sector 662
verisignsealt Del LFN                                   0      - R S H - V
σERISI~1 GIF  Erased   6006    1-15-00   4:04 pm      632      A - - - - -
   Sub-Directory                                          Cluster 631
   A:\2000SS~1                                      Offset 544, hex 220
```

Figure 11.14   The Directory view after VERISI~1.GIF has been deleted.

Zeroes have also replaced the entries for the cluster locations after the beginning cluster in the FAT. This indicates to the operating system that these clusters are now available for reuse. Thus, if an undelete process is not started immediately, some or all of the clusters could be overwritten by new data. Because the file in question is a GIF graphics file, the loss of even one cluster will destroy the file.

As you can see from analyzing the file-deletion process, the undelete process involves four steps:

- Restoring the original filename
- Locating the clusters used by the file
- Re-creating the FAT entries for the file
- Relinking the LFN entries for the file to the file

Of these four, the most critical are locating the clusters used by the file and re-creating the FAT entries for the file. However, if the file is a program file, restoring the original name is a must for proper program operation (assuming the program can't be reloaded), and restoring the LFN entries enables a Windows user accustomed to long filenames to more easily use the file.

If you want to make these changes to the original disk, DiskEdit must be configured to work in Read-Write mode.

To change to Read-Write mode, follow these steps:

1. Press Alt+T to open the Tools menu.

2. Press N to open the Configuration dialog box.

3. Press the spacebar to clear the check mark in the Read Only option box.

4. Press the Tab key until the Save box is highlighted.

5. Press Enter to save the changes and return to the main display.

Caution

As a precaution, I recommend that you use DISKCOPY to make an exact sector-by-sector copy of a floppy disk before you perform data recovery on it, and you should work with the copy of the disk, not the original. By working with a copy, you keep the original safe from any problems you might have; plus, you can make another copy if you need to.

After you change to Read-Write mode, DiskEdit stays in this mode and uses Read-Write mode every time you use it. To change back to Read-Only mode, repeat the previously listed steps but check the Read-Only box. If you are using DiskEdit in Read-Write mode, you will see the message Drive x is Locked when you scan a drive.

Undeleting an Erased File

After you have configured DiskEdit to work in Read-Write mode, you can use it to undelete a file.

To recover an erased file, follow this procedure:

1. To change to the folder containing the erased file, highlight the folder containing the erased file and press Enter. In this example, you will recover the erased file VERISI~1.GIF.

2. Place the cursor under the lowercase sigma symbol and enter a letter to rename the file.

3. If the keyboard is in Insert mode, the lowercase sigma will move to the right; press the Delete key to delete this symbol.

4. This restores the filename, but even though the ID changes from Erased to File, this does *not* complete the file-retrieval process. You must now find the rest of the clusters used by the file. To the right of the filename, the first cluster used by the file is listed.

5. To go to the next cluster used by the file, press Ctrl+T to open the Cluster Chain command. Because you changed the name of the file, you are prompted to write the changes to the disk before you can continue. Press W or click Write to save the changes and continue.

6. DiskEdit moves to the first cluster used by the deleted file. Instead of cluster numbers, as seen earlier in Figure 11.13, each cluster contains a zero (0). Because this file uses 12 clusters, there should be 12 contiguous clusters that have been zeroed out if the file is unfragmented.

7. To determine whether these are the correct clusters for the file, press Alt+O or click Object to open the Object menu. Press C to open the Cluster dialog box (or press Alt+C to go to the Cluster dialog box). Enter the starting cluster number (**632** in this example) and the ending cluster number (**644** in this example). Click OK to display these clusters.

DiskEdit automatically switches to the best view for the specified object, and in this case, the best view is the Hex view (see Figure 11.15). Note that the first entry in cluster 632 is GIF89a (as shown in the right column). Because the deleted file is a GIF file, this is what we expected. Also, a GIF file is a binary graphics file, so the rest of the information in the specified sectors should not be human-readable. Note that the end of the file is indicated by a series of 0s in several disk sectors before another file starts.

Because the area occupied by the empty clusters (632–644) contains binary data starting with GIF89a, you can feel confident that these clusters contain the data you need.

8. To return to the FAT to fill in the cluster numbers for the file, open the Object menu and select Directory. The current directory is selected, so click OK.

9. Move the cursor down to the entry for VERISI~1.GIF, open the Link menu, and click Cluster Chain (FAT). The Cluster Chain refers to the clusters after the initial cluster (632); enter **633** in the first empty field, and continue until you enter **643** and place the cursor in the last empty field. This field needs to have the <EOF> marker placed in it to indicate the end of the file. Press Alt+E to open the Edit menu and select Mark (or press Ctrl+B). Open the Edit menu again and select Fill. Then, select End of File from the menu and click OK. Refer to Figure 11.13 to see how the FAT looks after these changes have been made.

Start of file

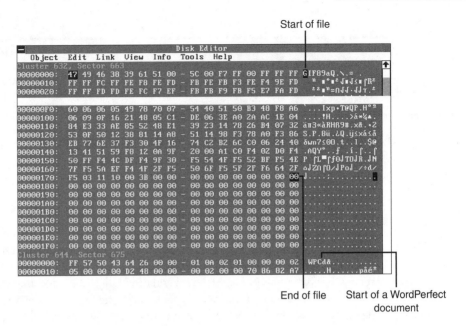

End of file   Start of a WordPerfect document

Figure 11.15 The start and end of the file VERISI~1.GIF.

10. To save the changes to the FAT, open the Edit menu again and select Write. When prompted to save the changes, click Write; then click Rescan the Disk.

11. To return to Directory view, open the Object menu and select Directory. Click OK.

12. The LFN entries directly above the VERISI~1.GIF file are still listed as Del LFN. To reconnect them to VERISI~1.GIF, select the first one (verisignsealt), open the Tools menu (press Alt+T), and select Attach LFN. Click Yes when prompted. Repeat the process for rans.gif.

13. To verify that the file has been undeleted successfully, exit DiskEdit and open the file in a compatible program. If you have correctly located the clusters and linked them, the file will open.

As you can see, this is a long process, but it is essentially the same process that a program such as Norton UnErase performs automatically. However, DiskEdit can perform these tasks on all types of disks that use FAT file systems, including those that use non-DOS operating systems; it's a favorite of advanced Linux users.

Retrieving a Deleted File from a Disk

What should you do if you need to retrieve an erased file from a disk? It's safer to write the retrieved file to another disk (preferably a floppy disk if the file is small enough) or to a different drive letter on the hard disk. You can also perform this task with DiskEdit.

Tip

If you want to recover data from a hard disk and copy the data to another location, set DiskEdit back to its default Read-Only mode to avoid making any accidental changes to the hard disk. If you use DiskEdit in a multitasking environment such as Windows, it defaults to Read-Only mode.

The process of locating the file is the same as that described earlier:

1. Determine the cluster (allocation unit) size of the drive on which the file is located.

2. Run DiskEdit to view the name of the erased file and determine which clusters contain the file data.

However, you don't need to restore the filename because you will be copying the file to another drive.

The clusters will be copied to another file, so it's helpful to use the Object menu to look at the clusters and ensure that they contain the necessary data. To view the data stored in the cluster range, open the Object menu, select Cluster, and enter the range of clusters that the cluster chain command indicates should contain the data. In some cases, the first cluster of a particular file indicates the file type. For example, a GIF file has GIF89a at the start of the file, whereas a WordPerfect document has WPC at the start of the file.

Tip

Use Norton DiskEdit to view the starting and ending clusters of various types of files you create before you try to recover those types of files. This is particularly important if you want to recover files from formatted media. You might consider creating a database of the hex characters found at the beginning and ending of the major file types you want to recover.

If you are trying to recover a file that contains text, such as a Microsoft Word or WordPerfect file, you can switch DiskEdit into different view modes. To see text, press F3 to switch to Text view. However, to determine where a file starts or ends, use Hex mode (press F2 to switch to this mode). Figure 11.16 shows the start of a Microsoft Word file in Text format and the end of the file in hex format.

To copy the contents of these clusters to a file safely, you should specify the sectors that contain the file. The top of the DiskEdit display shows the sector number as well as the cluster number. For example, the file shown in Figure 11.5 starts at cluster 75207, which is also sector 608470. The end of the file is located in sector 608503.

Start of file (text mode) End of file (hex mode)

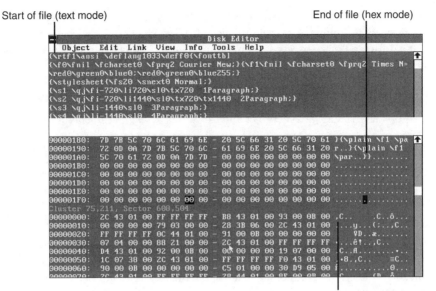

Junk data in cluster after end of file (hex mode)

Figure 11.16 Scrolling through an erased file with DiskEdit.

To write these sectors to a new file, do the following:

1. Open the Object menu.

2. Select Sector.

3. Specify the starting and ending sectors.

4. Click OK.

5. Scroll through the sectors to verify that they contain the correct data.

6. Open the Tools menu.

7. Click Write Object To.

8. Click To a File.

9. Click the drive on which you want to write the data.

10. Specify a DOS-type filename (eight characters plus a three-character extension); you can rename the file to a long filename after you exit DiskEdit.

11. Click OK, and then click Yes to write the file. A status bar appears as the sectors are copied to the file.

12. Exit DiskEdit and open the file in a compatible program. If the file contains the correct data, you're finished. If not, you might have specified incorrect sectors or the file might be fragmented.

Disk editors are powerful tools you can use to explore drives and retrieve lost data. However, your best data recovery technique is to avoid the need for data recovery. Think before you delete files or format a drive, and make backups of important files. That way, you won't need to recover lost data very often.

Data Recovery from Flash Memory Devices

Flash memory devices such as USB drives and cards used in digital cameras and digital music players present a unique challenge to data recovery programs. Although, from a user standpoint, these devices emulate conventional disk drives, have file allocation tables similar to those found on floppy disks, and can usually be formatted through the Windows Explorer, many data recovery programs that work well with conventional drives cannot be used to recover data from flash memory devices—especially when the device has been formatted.

Under several conditions, data loss can occur with a flash memory device. Some of them, such as formatting of the media or deletion of one or more photos or files, can occur when the device is connected to the computer through a card reader or when the flash memory device is inserted into a digital camera. When photos are deleted, the file locations and name listings in the file allocation tables are changed in the same way as when files are deleted from magnetic media: The first character of the filename is changed to a lowercase sigma, indicating the file has been erased. Just as with magnetic media, undelete programs that support removable-media drives and/or disk editors can be used to retrieve deleted files on flash memory devices in the same way that they retrieve deleted files from magnetic media. Data files can also be damaged if the flash memory card is removed from a device before the data-writing process is complete.

However, retrieving data from a formatted flash memory device, whether it has been formatted by a digital camera or through Windows, is much more difficult. Unformat programs such as the command-line Norton Unformat program provided with Norton Utilities and Norton SystemWorks can't be used because flash memory devices are accessible only from within the Windows environment, and most command-line programs are designed to work with BIOS-compatible devices such as hard and floppy drives.

In addition, traditional undelete programs that rely exclusively on the file system, such as Ontrack EasyRecovery Lite and DataRecovery, do not work if the flash memory device has been reformatted because in that case the previous file system is destroyed.

Note

When a digital camera formats a flash memory card, it usually creates a folder in which photos are stored. Some cameras might also create another folder for storing drivers or other information.

If you need to recover data from a formatted flash memory device, the following programs work extremely well:

- **Ontrack EasyRecovery Professional**—Free evaluation and more information are available from http://www.ontrack.com.
- **PhotoRec**—Powerful freeware program available from http://www.cgsecurity.org.
- **PC INSPECTOR Smart Recovery**—Freeware available from http://www.PCInspector.de.

To recover data from a formatted flash memory card with EasyRecovery Professional, the RawRecovery option (which recovers data on a sector-by-sector basis) must be used. This option bypasses the file system and can be used on all supported media types. A built-in file viewer enables you to determine whether the recovered data is readable.

PhotoRec works with more than 80 standard photo image and other file formats and also bypasses the file system, enabling it to recover data from severely damaged or reformatted drives. PC-Inspector Smart Recovery also bypasses the file system and can recover several types of files as well.

With these products, you might recover data from not just the most recent use before format, but also leftover data from previous uses. As long as the data area used by a particular file hasn't been overwritten, the data can be recovered—even if the device has been formatted more than once. In cases where you can't seem to get everything back, you might try using several programs because one may find what another might miss.

FAT File System Troubleshooting

Here are some general procedures to follow for troubleshooting drive access, file system, or boot problems:

1. Start the system using a Windows startup disk, or any bootable MS-DOS disk that contains FDISK.EXE, FORMAT.COM, SYS.COM, and SCANDISK.EXE (Windows 95B or later versions preferred).

2. If your system can't boot from the floppy, you might have more serious problems with your hardware. Check the floppy drive and the motherboard for proper installation and configuration. On some systems, the BIOS configuration doesn't list the floppy as a boot device or puts it after the hard disk. Reset the BIOS configuration to make the floppy disk the first boot device if necessary and restart your computer.

3. Run FDISK from the Windows startup disk. Select option 4 (Display partition information).

4. If the partitions are listed, make sure that the bootable partition (usually the primary partition) is defined as active (look for an uppercase *A* in the Status column).

5. If no partitions are listed and you do not want to recover any of the data existing on the drive now, use FDISK to create new partitions, and then use FORMAT to format the partitions. This overwrites any previously existing data on the drive.

6. If you want to recover the data on the drive and no partitions are being shown, you must use a data recovery program, such as the Norton Utilities or Lost and Found, to recover the data.

7. If all the partitions appear in FDISK.EXE and one is defined as active, run the SYS command as follows to restore the system files to the hard disk:

    SYS C:

8. For this to work properly, it is important that the disk you boot from be a startup disk from the same operating system (or version of Windows) you have on your hard disk.

9. You should receive the message System Transferred if the command works properly. Remove the disk from drive A: and restart the system. If you still have the same error after you restart your computer, your drive might be improperly configured or damaged.

10. Run SCANDISK from the Windows startup disk or an aftermarket data-recovery utility, such as the Norton Utilities, to check for problems with the hard disk.

11. Using SCANDISK, perform a surface scan. If SCANDISK reports any physically damaged sectors on the hard disk, the drive might need to be replaced.

NTFS File System Troubleshooting

The process for file system troubleshooting with Windows 2000 and later is similar to that used for Windows 9x. The major difference is the use of the Recovery Console in Windows NT through XP or the Recovery Environment in Vista.

In Windows NT through XP you can use the following steps to start the Recovery Console:

1. The Windows NT through XP setup disc is normally a bootable CD, however it is possible to burn a copy on a bootable DVD as well. Ensure that your system is capable of booting from the type of optical disc you are using (CD or DVD), and that the optical drive precedes the hard disk in the boot sequence. Hint: You may need to change your BIOS setup to inspect or change the startup boot sequence.

2. Insert the Windows Setup disc into the optical drive and restart the system.

3. If prompted to press a key to start the computer from CD or DVD, press any key (such as the spacebar) to continue, and start from the optical disc.

4. When the text-based part of Windows Setup begins, follow the prompts until the Welcome to Setup screen appears, and then press the R key to Repair Windows, which also means to start the Recovery Console.

5. If you are repairing a system that has more than one operating system installed, choose the Windows installation that you need to access or repair from the Recovery Console.

6. When you are prompted, type the Administrator password. If the Administrator password is blank, just press Enter. If a password has been set but you do not have the correct password, or if the security database for the installation of Windows you are attempting to access is corrupted, Recovery Console does not allow access to the disks.

After you start the Recovery Console you can do the following:

1. Type **HELP** for a list of Recovery Console commands and assistance.

2. Run DISKPART to examine your disk partitions.

3. If the partitions are listed, make sure that the bootable partition (usually the primary partition) is defined as active.

4. If no partitions are listed and you do not want to recover any of the data existing on the drive now, use CREATE to create new partitions, and then use FORMAT to format the partitions. Note that previously existing data on the drive is lost.

5. If no partitions are listed and you do want to recover any of the data existing on the drive, you can use a partition recovery program such as TestDisk (www.cgsecurity.org) to recover any previously existing partitions on the disk.

6. If all the partitions appear in DISKPART and one is defined as active, you can run the FIXBOOT command as follows to restore the volume boot record to the system partition on the hard disk:

    FIXBOOT

7. Type **EXIT** to restart your system.

8. If you still have the same error after you restart your computer, your drive or file system might be improperly configured or damaged.

9. To repair the file system, restart the Recovery Console and run CHKDSK /F to check for and repair file system problems.

In Windows Vista the former Recovery Console is now called the Recovery Environment. To start the Recovery Environment in Vista, use the following procedure:

1. Ensure that your system is capable of booting from a DVD, and that the optical drive precedes the hard disk in the boot sequence. Hint: You may need to change your BIOS setup to inspect or change the startup boot sequence.

2. Insert the Windows Vista Setup disc into the optical drive and restart the system.

3. If prompted to press a key to start the computer from CD or DVD, press any key (such as the spacebar) to continue and start from the optical disc.

4. When the Install Windows dialog box appears, select a language, a time, a currency, a keyboard or an input method, and then click Next. Then press the R key to Repair Your Computer, which also means to start the Recovery Environment.

5. When the System Recovery Options dialog box appears, choose the Windows Vista installation that you need to access or repair. Note that only Vista operating systems are listed and can be repaired.

6. When you are prompted to Choose a Recovery Tool, select the Command Prompt.

After you start the Recovery Environment you can do the following:

1. Run DISKPART to examine your disk partitions.

2. If the partitions are listed, make sure that the bootable partition (usually the primary partition) is defined as active.

3. If no partitions are listed and you do not want to recover any of the data existing on the drive now, use CREATE to create new partitions, and then use FORMAT to format the partitions. Note that previously existing data on the drive will be lost.

4. If no partitions are being listed and you do want to recover any of the data existing on the drive, you can use a partition recovery program such as TestDisk (www.cgsecurity.org) to recover any previously existing partitions on the disk.

5. If all the partitions appear in DISKPART and one is defined as active, you can run the BootRec /FixBoot command as follows to restore the volume boot record to the system partition on the hard disk:

```
BootRec /FixBoot
```

6. Type **EXIT** to restart your system.

7. If you still have the same error after you restart your computer, your drive or file system might be improperly configured or damaged.

8. To repair the file system, restart the Recovery Console and run CHKDSK /F to check for and repair file system problems.

Windows Troubleshooting

Troubleshooting Basics

Most experienced computer technicians will tell you that troubleshooting is a combination of skill and art. Troubleshooting is a skill, in that it can be learned as a process. It is an art, in that it also requires intuition, imagination, and even plain old dumb luck. Regardless of those factors, however, the more experience you gain, the better your troubleshooting ability becomes.

Troubleshooting can be a frustrating, anxiety-filled process, particularly if you are working on a mission-critical system, or if it is your personal machine that is malfunctioning. However, it is important to remain patient and objective when trying to resolve an issue and don't forget that the cause may not be related to Windows at all, but rather your hardware. Although I offer some basic guidelines here, I cover hardware problems in much more detail in *Upgrading and Repairing PCs* and *Upgrading and Repairing Laptops*.

Regardless of the source of your problems, it is crucial that you follow an organized method of troubleshooting rather than fiddling with things at random, hoping to get lucky. To troubleshoot a problem with Windows, you need to follow a deductive process. You are like Sherlock Holmes, eliminating the impossible until all that is left, however improbable, must be the cause of the problem. As you gain more experience troubleshooting Windows, you will begin to recognize problems that you have encountered before, which enables you to go straight to the root cause and apply a solution.

In this chapter, you will look at some of the more common errors encountered with Windows, and examine the tools that the Windows operating system provides to help solve these problems. Before we dive into these topics, here are some general tips for improving and refining your basic troubleshooting skills.

- **Always check the physical first**—Before you start drilling into the core of the operating system, always check the physical components of a malfunctioning machine first. For example, if you are troubleshooting a machine that is freezing during Windows startup, check to see whether all internal hard drive cable connections are secure.

It is astonishing how many errors occur due to a simple physical fault, and how many times these faults are overlooked by troubleshooters. Don't assume that just because a machine worked the last time you used it that nothing has changed. Hard drive cables can vibrate loose from their connectors; RAM modules can thermal-creep out of their sockets if the socket clasps are faulty or have come undone due to vibration; likewise power surges, overmatched power supplies, and poor-quality AC power can cause any number of obscure errors.

- **Never assume anything**—Faulty assumptions will absolutely kill a troubleshooting session. Don't take anything for granted when working on a problem. Verify your assumptions about the hardware and software status of a system before moving forward.

- **Determine if system changes have recently taken place**—Changes to onboard or external hardware, application updates, or operating system updates could cause problems with a system. Longtime *Byte* magazine author Jerry Pournelle's classic troubleshooting question, "What changed since the last time it worked?" continues to be a useful part of troubleshooting. Check system logs, Windows Update logs, and System Restore points to help determine what changes have taken place.

- **Document everything**—Before you begin to make changes to a malfunctioning system, you should record as much information about the problem as possible. Write down word for word any error messages that are being displayed. Sometimes, you see an error message only once, and chances are you won't remember exactly what it said if you don't write it down. A digital camera that can shoot close-up photos is a valuable troubleshooting tool.

Write notes detailing all the symptoms of the problem. If troubleshooting an error that occurs repeatedly over a certain time interval, take note of the times when it occurs. If you are able to access Windows Event Viewer, copy down any pertinent error messages that appear in the logs.

And, perhaps most important, create an ongoing record of any changes you make to the hardware and software while you are trying to solve the problem. It may seem absurd to think that you would forget a step you took during your troubleshooting process, but it happens more often than most technicians would care to admit.

- **If a change made to the system doesn't solve the problem, reverse it**—If you change a Windows setting to try to solve a problem, and making the change doesn't work, remember to change the setting back. If you don't do this while working on a system, you introduce an increasing amount of changing variables that will make it extremely difficult to isolate the source of a problem.

- **Create a summary once the problem is solved**—Once you have solved a problem, write down the details of the problem, the steps you took to solve the problem, and the appropriate dates and times. Don't leave these details solely dependent on your memory; a permanent record is much more reliable.

- **Know when to walk away**—When any of us experiences a problem with a computer, especially if it is our personal system, we always want to get the problem resolved as quickly as possible. However, there comes a time when it's best to walk away from a malfunctioning system for a little while, and come back to it fresh after a break.

Very few people can maintain peak concentration for hours at a time. Taking a break isn't "giving up"; it's a necessary part of the troubleshooting process that keeps you from becoming part of the problem. If it's the end of the day, pack it up and get a good night's sleep. That's likely to do far more for your ability to identify and fix a problem than bouncing off the walls all night long.

- **You don't have to know everything in order to be a good troubleshooter**—Part of being a top-class troubleshooter is being able to effectively use external information resources. Remember that it is not only acceptable, but also often required to draw upon the experience of others to help you to solve a problem. This experience can be found in books, web resources, knowledgeable friends and family members, and especially representatives of the technical support departments of hardware and software manufacturers.

Finally, if you ever get so frustrated that you want to take a sledgehammer to your PC, here's one last piece of troubleshooting advice from Confucius: "Do not use a cannon to kill a mosquito."

What You'll Find in This Chapter

In this chapter, you will look at a variety of different Windows problems and solutions. Specifically, you will split these problems into three categories:

- Problems encountered during Windows installation
- Problems encountered during Windows startup
- Problems encountered while Windows is running

You'll also look at additional tools and resources that can be used to find solutions to problems, such as the Microsoft Knowledge Base (MSKB) and the Windows Support Tools located on the Windows XP installation CD. Although the Windows Vista DVD doesn't include Windows Support Tools, you can install the Windows Server 2003 Support Tools on a Windows Vista system and use them on Windows Vista. They are located in the Support\Tools folder on the Windows Server 2003 CD.

Note

This chapter deals specifically with troubleshooting problems with the Windows XP and Windows Vista operating systems. If you are looking for more detailed information on PC hardware, check out *Upgrading and Repairing PCs* (ISBN 0-7897-3697-7) or *Upgrading and Repairing Laptops* (0-7897-3376-5) from Que Publishing. These are the definitive guides to everything that can be plugged into a tower case or crammed into a portable PC. For a no-holds barred troubleshooting book for Windows XP, check out *Leo Laporte's PC Help Desk*, (0-7897-3394-3); for Windows Vista, check out *Microsoft Windows Vista Help Desk* (0-7897-3587-3), also from Que.

A Word About Viruses and Spyware

If the top cardinal rule of troubleshooting is *check the physical first*, the next cardinal rule is *check for viruses or spyware second*.

There are two key reasons for this. The first is that both viruses and spyware can introduce several different behavioral variables into a Windows-based PC. Plainly speaking, viruses and spyware can cause more than one kind of problem behavior to appear. This can be incredibly misleading when you are trying to isolate the cause of the problem. More often than not, if you try to troubleshoot a malfunctioning Windows PC without first checking whether there is a virus or spyware present, you will end up chasing your tail.

The second reason is that if you make repairs to a malfunctioning Windows installation where the problem is attributable to a virus or spyware, you are treating only the symptom, not the disease. In fact, there is a good chance that the virus or spyware will undo the repairs you have made as soon as you restart the system, which will send you running down another false trail.

Note

Viruses and spyware can also hide in System Restore restore point files. Some antivirus vendors such as Symantec (makers of Norton Antivirus) recommend that you discard existing restore points after you detect and remove a virus. By doing so, you assure that the virus cannot reappear if you restore your system to an earlier time.

After you have verified that there are no physical problems with a sick computer, your second step should always be to scan the system for viruses and spyware. There are a number of free and commercially available programs you can use to find and eliminate viruses and spyware. Ideally, you should have two variations of such programs: one version that is used on a system while Windows is up and running, and another version that is "bootable"; that is, that you can use from system startup to scan the machine before Windows is loaded. You'll find more information an antivirus and antispyware programs in Chapter 7, "Protecting and Securing Windows."

Windows "Sickbed" Symptoms

Generally speaking, Windows XP and Windows Vista will exhibit one of five major symptoms when it encounters a problem that causes a core component of the operating system to malfunction:

1. Windows will cease functioning, and the system will display a STOP Error screen, also known in more colorful terms as the Blue Screen of Death.

2. Windows will terminate an open application and display a dialog box informing you of this action, and (if configured to do so) will offer you the opportunity to send an error report to Microsoft.

Note

Windows Vista tracks problems that cause system lockups (as well as less serious problems you might not even notice) with its new Problem Reports and Solutions feature in Control Panel. Problem Reports and Solutions also provides solutions for reported problems, so be sure to check it after you have a system problem.

3. Windows will stop and restart the EXPLORER.EXE service, also known as Windows Explorer. A dialog box (essentially the same dialog box that is displayed with symptom #2) informs the user of this event.

4. The computer will suddenly reboot while it is in operation.

5. The system will lock up entirely, and can be unlocked only by pressing the reset button on the computer.

These five symptoms can occur during different stages of Windows operation, including during installation, during startup, and during normal operation. Table 12.1 lists when each symptom may occur:

Table 12.1 Windows Error Symptoms

Windows Status	Symptoms That Can Occur
During installation	1, 4, 5
During startup	1, 4, 5
During normal operation	1, 2, 3, 4, 5

If any of these symptoms occur, they indicate that there is a hardware or software problem that is interfering with the normal functioning of Windows. The troubleshooting methods and tools you use to discover and correct the problem will often be determined by what stage Windows is in when symptom occurs.

Windows Installation Troubleshooting

If you encounter a problem while trying to install Windows XP or Windows Vista, there are a few specific things you should look at to try to fix the problem and perform a successful installation.

Legacy/Unsupported Hardware Devices

A large number of problems encountered when installing Windows are due to incompatible hardware. This doesn't mean that the hardware device in question is defective, only that the Windows OS does not support it. Although Windows supports an impressive number of hardware devices, it would be impractical (if not impossible) to support every third-party PC hardware product that exists (or has ever existed) on the market.

Legacy/unsupported hardware can cause Windows Setup to fail, resulting in a STOP error screen, a frozen computer, or a computer that continually reboots at the same point during the installation process.

Before beginning an installation of Windows XP or Windows Vista, you should compile a list of your computer's hardware components and check this list against Microsoft's Windows Hardware Compatibility List (HCL). As of this writing, the Windows HCL is presented on the Microsoft website as a selection of catalogs. You can check hardware components against the appropriate Windows catalog to see whehter the device is supported by the operating system. Microsoft is constantly updating these catalogs to include new components as they are tested and approved for Windows XP and Windows Vista.

The Windows HCL catalogs are located at

> http://www.microsoft.com/whdc/hcl/default.mspx

The Windows Vista Hardware Compatibility List is used for both Windows XP and Windows Vista. Other catalogs are used for server products (Windows 2000 Professional/Server and Windows Server 2003) and for legacy products.

Also, if you are unsure of the compatibility of a hardware device, you should check the support website of the company that produced it. Hardware manufacturers will often release updated driver software and/or information concerning their products' compatibility with Windows XP or Windows Vista on their support sites. Finally, I recommend that you remove nonessential hardware from your system before performing a Windows XP or Windows Vista installation. This will minimize the chances of encountering an incompatible hardware device during setup, allowing you to later search for and install functional third-party drivers once the Windows installation is complete.

Windows XP Upgrade Advisor

If you are performing an upgrade installation of Windows XP (that is, installing it on a system that already has a previous version of Windows on it), there may be software programs or device drivers present on the system that are incompatible with Windows XP. These programs and drivers can cause the Windows upgrade procedure to fail, or can result in nonfunctioning devices or programs once Windows XP is installed. This is why I recommend that most users install Windows XP from scratch rather than perform an upgrade installation. However, should you need to perform an upgrade installation, Windows XP provides some help.

To check the existing files and devices on a machine before you upgrade it to Windows XP, you can use the Windows XP Upgrade Advisor. This program is located on the Windows XP installation CD. To run this program, log on to the system you intend to upgrade, and place the installation CD into the CD-ROM drive. When the CD startup menu appears, select Check System Compatibility, and then select Check My System Automatically.

Note

You can also download the Windows XP Upgrade Advisor at http://www.microsoft.com/windowsxp/pro/upgrading/advisor.mspx.

The Upgrade Advisor will scan your system, and then create a report that lists all potential software compatibility issues. It will also perform a scan of your hardware devices, and inform you of any possible upgrade issues with them. Use the created report as a guideline and a resource to check into possible problems before you perform an upgrade installation of Windows XP.

For more information on performing an upgrade installation of Windows XP refer to Chapter 4, "Upgrading Windows."

Windows Vista Upgrade Advisor

The Windows Vista Upgrade Advisor can be used on systems running 32-bit versions of Windows XP (as well as those running 32-bit versions of Windows Vista). The advisor requires a working Internet connection during operation. It recommends what edition(s) of Windows Vista are most suitable for the computer being tested, determines what upgrades would be necessary to enable a system to run a different Windows Vista edition, informs you of programs that must be updated after installation, removed before installation and reinstalled, or programs that are not compatible with Windows Vista, as well as driver and hardware issues that may exist.

Note

The Windows Vista Upgrade Advisor is available from http://www.microsoft.com/windows/products/windowsvista/buyorupgrade/upgradeadvisor.mspx.

Before running the advisor, be sure that all plug-and-play (PnP) devices such as USB and FireWire (IEEE-1394) devices you use with the computer are plugged in and turned on. Devices that are not plugged in and turned on cannot be detected.

The Windows Vista Upgrade Advisor uses Internet Explorer to report its results, using a multi-tabbed interface. It is an excellent tool for evaluating individual computers or a small number of client PCs on a home office/small office network. However, if you need to plan for large-scale deployment of Windows Vista in a corporate network environment, you should use the Windows Vista Hardware Assessment Tool as the first step in evaluating your systems, followed by version 5 or later of the Application Compatibility Toolkit, as discussed in the following sections.

Note

If you are primarily concerned about the 3D graphics performance of a Windows XP or Windows Vista system, you should also use the System Requirements Lab analyzer, a free web-based evaluation tool.

Users with ATI graphics hardware should run the ATI version, available at http://ati.amd.com/technology/ WindowsVista/AreYouVistaReady.html. Users of NVIDIA graphics hardware should run the NVIDIA version, available from http://www.nzone.com/content/nzone/srl/nzone_srl.asp?gameid=3596. Users with other graphics hardware can run either version.

Both versions provide Good-Better-Best evaluations of graphics card memory and performance, hard disk capacity, optical drive type, processor type and speed, and other major features.

◄◄ For more information on performing an upgrade installation of Windows Vista refer to Chapter 4, "Upgrading Windows."

Note

If you are unable to locate native device drivers for some devices under Windows XP, keep in mind that you might be able to use Windows 2000 device drivers. Similarly, if you are unable to locate native device drivers for some devices under Windows Vista, you might be able to use Windows XP device drivers. Use these fallback drivers only if you are unable to find suitable native device drivers.

Updating Computer Firmware

One commonly overlooked aspect of a computer's internal makeup that can cause a Windows installation to fail is outdated firmware. As I discuss extensively in *Upgrading and Repairing PCs*, firmware is software that is written onto read-only memory (ROM) chips, which are then integrated into a piece of hardware. Every motherboard has a ROM chip that contains the basic input/output system, also known as the ROM BIOS. The ROM BIOS chip holds the startup programs and drivers that are used to get the computer running before the operating system is loaded. Think of the ROM BIOS as the starter engine for your PC; it gets your system firing so that it can start up the big engine—the operating system.

There are a number of different BIOS manufacturers. Companies that build motherboards collaborate with BIOS manufacturers to create a customized version of BIOS for specific models of motherboards. Currently, the most popular BIOS manufacturers are Phoenix Technologies (which also owns the former Award Software) and American Megatrends, Inc. (commonly abbreviated as AMI).

Most modern motherboards store the BIOS on a type of chip known as a *flash ROM*. The flash ROM gets its name from its capability to be erased and reprogrammed with a flash BIOS upgrade utility program. This procedure is known as *flashing the BIOS*. When BIOS manufacturers make improvements to their software, they release these updates as flash ROM upgrades. Motherboard manufacturers usually offer these upgrades as downloadable files from their websites. BIOS upgrades are primarily used to add functionality to your system's motherboard, or to fix a bug that was in the earlier version of the BIOS.

Before doing a new installation of Windows XP or Windows Vista, you should check the version of the BIOS firmware on your motherboard. The BIOS version information is normally displayed when you first power on your computer. On most systems, you can press the Pause key on your keyboard to freeze the screen when the BIOS version is being shown so that you have time to write down the information. After you have the information recorded, press any key to resume startup. If this method doesn't work on your computer, enter the BIOS setup and locate the BIOS version in the setup screen. This is done by pressing a certain key (usually the Delete key) after you have switched the power on.

To check whether you have the most recent version of your system BIOS, contact the tech support of the manufacturer of your motherboard, or look up the make and model of your motherboard on the manufacturer's website. Many motherboard companies have lists or tables that match up motherboard models with the most recent firmware version available for them. If necessary, update to the latest version of the firmware before installing Windows XP or Windows Vista.

You should also note that the motherboard is not the only system hardware component that has a flash ROM. Video cards, sound cards, and optical drives also have flash ROMs integrated into them, and manufacturers of these components often create and release firmware upgrades for these devices. As with BIOS firmware, check for new versions by visiting the manufacturer's website.

Other Common Windows Installation Issues

If your system hardware is compatible with Windows XP or Windows Vista, but the installation process cannot be completed successfully, there is a good chance that there is a fault with either a system component, or with the installation media itself.

Here are some of the more common causes of Windows Setup failures (that aren't related to hardware device incompatibilities):

- **Faulty RAM modules**—A malfunctioning RAM module will create havoc with Windows Setup. RAM chips can malfunction because they are defective, or if you have overclocked your PC's processor in the system BIOS, causing it to run faster than its design specifications. There are third-party memory diagnostic programs available that will run from a bootable floppy or CD that you can use to test the integrity of the system's RAM. Microsoft has a free program called the Windows Memory Diagnostic, which you can download at http://oca.microsoft.com/en/windiag.asp. The Windows Memory Diagnostic is also included on the Windows Vista installation DVD. To run it, boot your computer with the Windows Vista installation DVD, select Repair Your Computer, and select Windows Memory Diagnostics Tool from the System Recovery Options menu. For more information, see "Memory Diagnostic," p. 786.

- **Defective hard drive**—If the system hard drive has errors on it, it's possible that Windows Setup will be unable to copy critical operating system files to it in order to complete the installation. Again, there are a number of utilities you can use to test a hard drive's integrity; the website of the manufacturer of the drive is a good starting point to look for such a utility.

- **Overheating system**—One common environmental issue that will cause a system to either freeze up or to reboot repeatedly is if the inside of the system is not being adequately cooled. This is of particular concern if you have overclocked any of your system's components (the CPU and GPU in particular). An overheated processor, RAM module, or hard drive can all lead to a locked up system or one that spontaneously reboots. Ensure that all case fans and the CPU cooling fan are installed correctly and are operational.

- **Defective installation media**—Installation problems can be caused by something as simple as a damaged or otherwise defective Windows installation CD or DVD. Check the surface of the CD or DVD for scratches and other marks. You can clean and polish the surface with products such as Digital Innovations' SkipDr and others.

- **Improper power supply load**—If your system hardware requires more power than the power supply is rated to provide, it can cause instability both during and after the installation process. The best short-term solution is to remove any unnecessary hardware from your PC, thus easing the load on the power supply. From there it's time to get yourself a more powerful, high-quality power supply unit, like those available from PC Power and Cooling.

Note

The Windows installation process will sometimes result in the creation of a STOP error screen, or Blue Screen of Death. You will take a look at how to interpret STOP errors later in this chapter.

Pre-Windows Startup Troubleshooting

Possibly the most frustrating situation to troubleshoot is when you are unable to successfully start Windows. If something is malfunctioning while Windows is up and running, you can use the tools provided by the operating system to try and solve the problem. But, how do you troubleshoot a Windows problem when you can't even get into Windows? Thankfully, there are also a number of methods and tools available for you to fix a non-starting Windows installation. Some of these options are accessed by using a scaled-down startup version of Windows known as *Safe mode*. Although, before you try to boot Windows in Safe mode, I do recommend that you try to use the Last Known Good Configuration option discussed later in this section.

Before you begin to familiarize yourself with Windows-specific troubleshooting tools and methods, however, you need to be able to recognize and fix errors that can occur before the Windows operating system begins to load.

Common Boot Error Messages and Solutions

The chain of events that takes place when a computer is turned on is known as the *boot process*. There are a number of steps that take place during the boot process that are entirely independent of the operating system installed on the computer. If an error occurs on a Windows-based PC during any of these steps, the boot process freezes and Windows does not begin to load.

The first step in troubleshooting a non–Windows-related boot error message is to determine which software component is responsible for generating the error message. There are four primary software components that come into play during the boot process:

- **Motherboard ROM BIOS**—The motherboard ROM BIOS is the initial software program that runs upon powering up the computer. It is responsible for testing your system's hardware components, and then initiating the chain of events that leads to the loading of an operating system, such as Windows.

- **Adapter Card ROM BIOS Extensions**—Adapter card ROM BIOS extensions are ROM BIOS chips integrated into hardware components such as video cards and SCSI disk controllers. The motherboard ROM BIOS scans for adapter card ROM BIOS extensions, and initializes these devices accordingly.

- **Master Boot Record (MBR)**—The Master Boot Record (MBR), as discussed in Chapter 10, "Windows File Systems," is a small program located in the very first physical sector of a hard disk (cylinder 0, head 0, sector 1). The MBR contains the master partition table, which lists all the partitions on a hard disk. Each partition entry in the master partition table includes information on what type of partition it is (primary or extended), whether the partition is bootable or not, where the partition physically exists on the hard disk, and how many sectors it takes up. In addition to the master partition table, the MBR also contains the instructions used to discover and load the volume boot record from the active (bootable) partition, and a two-byte signature (55AAh) used by the motherboard ROM BIOS to validate the sector occupied by the MBR.

- **Volume Boot Record**—The Volume Boot Record is located in the first sector of the bootable partition on a hard disk. The Volume Boot Record contains information about the volume it resides on, as well as instructions that are used to locate and load the operating system (with Windows XP, the Volume Boot Record is used to find and load the NTLDR file). The Volume Boot Record also contains a two-byte signature (55AAh), similar to the MBR, that is used to validate the sector it occupies.

With this information in mind, here are some common boot error messages and solutions.

Missing Operating System

During the boot process, the Volume Boot Record on the hard disk is tested for a specific two-byte signature (55AAh). If this signature is not found, the error message `Missing Operating System` is shown, and the boot process freezes.

This error is commonly caused by invalid BIOS settings, usually attributable to a dead or dying CMOS battery. CMOS stands for *complimentary metal oxide semiconductor*, and refers to a type of RAM chip that is located on the motherboard. The system BIOS reads and writes settings to and from the onboard CMOS chip, which is powered by a small battery so that the settings aren't wiped out when the computer is powered down. One of the settings that the system BIOS reads from the CMOS chip on startup is the hard disk configuration data.

If the CMOS battery is dead or dying, the hard disk settings in the CMOS chip can become corrupted or disappear entirely. Subsequently, when the system BIOS queries the CMOS chip on startup, it receives invalid hard disk settings, which causes the boot process to fail.

Tip

One dead giveaway that you have a failing CMOS battery is if the date and time information in the BIOS setup screen is constantly resetting itself when you power down your computer.

CMOS batteries can usually be replaced. Many computer and electronics stores carry CMOS batteries; you can also check with the manufacturer of your motherboard to see whether they sell them. The most common battery in recent systems is the CR2032 lithium watch and vehicle remote control battery (available in most jewelry and automotive departments).

NO ROM BASIC – SYSTEM HALTED

If the two-byte signature of the Master Boot Record is not 55AAh, the motherboard BIOS displays an error message. These error messages differ between various BIOS manufacturers. For example, the NO ROM BASIC – SYSTEM HALTED error message is displayed by BIOS ROMs created by American Megatrends, Inc. (AMI).

This error message can be caused by missing boot files, a corrupt boot record, a hard disk failure, or a virus. To repair this issue with Windows XP, boot the system from the Windows XP installation CD, choose to open the Recovery Console, and run the `fixmbr` command. This will rebuild the Master Boot Record. After completing the operation, eject the Windows XP installation CD and reboot the system.

◀◀ For more information concerning the Windows XP Recovery Console, **see** "Using the Recovery Console," **p. 731**.

If this solution doesn't work, the problem may be attributable to a boot-sector virus. A boot-sector virus copies code onto the partition table of a hard disk. The virus is loaded into memory on startup, which means that to attempt to remove it, you need to use a bootable antivirus program disk. If the program successfully locates and removes the virus, you should restore the MBR using the `fixmbr` command in Windows XP Recovery Console and reboot the system.

With Windows Vista, boot the system with the Windows Vista installation DVD or Recovery Environment disc, click Next at the opening dialog, and then click Repair Your Computer. After the system identifies your installation, click Next, and then select Startup Repair from the System Recovery Options dialog. The system identifies the problem, performs repairs, and provides you with the option to see the repairs it performed. Click Finish, and the system restarts.

If the system does not start properly, reboot the system and repeat the process. You can run Startup Repair up to five times before you need to try manual repair options with the Command Prompt. The Windows Vista Command Prompt in System Recovery Options offers access to all Windows Vista commands, not just a few as with the Windows XP Recovery Console.

◀◀ For more information concerning the Windows Vista Recovery Environment, **see** "Windows Recovery Environment," **p. 780**.

Boot Error Press F1 to Retry

This error message is generated by the Phoenix BIOS when the Master Boot Record is corrupt or missing, or if the system is unable to access the boot drive. This message is the same as the NO ROM BASIC - SYSTEM HALTED message generated by AMI BIOS. See the previous section for details on how to fix this problem.

Invalid Drive Specification

This error is most commonly caused by trying to access a hard disk that hasn't been properly partitioned and formatted yet, or if the master partition table located in the Master Boot Record has been damaged. If you are certain that the hard disk is properly formatted and partitioned, try to restore the MBR using the fixmbr command from the Recovery Console (Windows XP), or use the Startup Repair dialog (Windows Vista).

Invalid Media Type

This message is generated if the volume boot sector, directory, or file allocation tables are damaged or not yet initialized. One likely cause of this error is if you attempt to access a hard disk that hasn't been formatted yet. Formatting is what creates the Volume Boot Record, file allocation tables, and directories on the hard disk.

If there is data on the disk that you don't want destroyed, use a data recovery tool that can bypass the file system and copy any recovered data to a different known-working drive, such as Ontrack Easy Recovery DataRecovery, available from www.ontrack.com.

Hard Disk Controller Failure

This message indicates that the hard disk controller has failed, or that the controller is unable to communicate with the attached hard disk. Check the drive cables to see if they are properly connected. Also, check if the hard disk is receiving power, and is spinning up when the system is powered on. If these factors are all accounted for, there may be physical damage to the hard disk, the controller, or the data and/or power cables. Try replacing the data cable first, and if that doesn't solve the problem, try replacing the hard disk. If the error still occurs, it's likely that the disk controller on the motherboard is defective.

Boot Configuration Data Error Messages

Windows Vista uses the Boot Configuration Data store (BCD store) file to store boot configuration, replacing Windows XP's Boot.ini. If the BCD store is missing information or is damaged, Windows Vista cannot start. The Windows Vista Startup Repair option, part of Windows RE, can be used to repair some BCD problems. The Windows Vista command prompt, also part of Windows RE, provides access to the Bootrec.exe and Bcdedit.exe tools for repairing BCD stores. See Microsoft Knowledge Base article 927391 for details, available from http://support.microsoft.com.

Windows Startup Troubleshooting

This section deals with errors that occur after the non-Windows portion of the boot process is complete, and the Windows startup process begins. Windows XP and Vista offer several tools you can use to identify and solve startup problems. Before digging too deep into how to solve problems with Windows startup, it's important that you have a basic understanding of the steps that a Windows XP or Windows Vista –based PC follows during startup. This information can be found in Chapter 2, "Windows Startup."

The method you use to solve a Windows startup problem is generally based on one of three criteria:

- If the problem occurs immediately after you have installed a new device driver, updated an existing driver, or installed a new software application
- Whether or not you are able to start Windows in Safe mode
- How valuable the data is on your system

The third bullet point should not be dismissed lightly. Of course, everything you have on your computer's hard disk counts as valuable data. However, in my experience, there comes a time during an extended troubleshooting session where I ask myself, "Is it worth it to continue working on this problem, or would it be better to just wipe the hard disk clean and reinstall everything?"

If you have reliable backups of your critical data, you should not reject the idea of repartitioning, reformatting, and reinstalling Windows just because it seems like too much work, or because it seems like the coward's way out. Rebuilding a nonfunctioning Windows PC is often the best, most time-effective way to bring a system back to a working condition.

Note

The Microsoft System Configuration Utility is a troubleshooting tool that can be used to configure a number of Windows startup options. You will find more information on this utility in the section "Windows XP and Windows Vista Troubleshooting Tools" later in this chapter.

Before proceeding, it's worth noting that many of the tools discussed here, the Recovery Console and System Restore in particular, have applications to troubleshooting Windows that go above and beyond pure startup problems.

Windows Advanced Options Menu

If you are unable to start Windows normally, you need to access the Windows Advanced Options menu. As discussed in Chapter 4, this menu is accessed by pressing the F8 key on your keyboard once the POST is completed, and before the Windows splash screen appears.

Once the Windows Advanced Options menu opens, you can choose from the following actions in both Windows XP and Windows Vista:

> Safe Mode
>
> Safe Mode with Networking
>
> Safe Mode with Command Prompt
>
> Last Known Good Configuration
>
> Start Windows Normally

Last Known Good Configuration

Last Known Good Configuration is not the first option listed in the Windows Advanced Options menu, but it is usually the first method you should use to try to repair a Windows startup problem. Specifically, Last Known Good Configuration should be used as the first method of repair if the Windows startup problem began immediately after

- A new device driver was installed
- An update to an existing driver was made
- A new software program was installed

The Last Known Good Configuration option causes Windows to reverse all driver and Registry changes made since the last time you successfully logged on to Windows. This means that if the problem is related to a newly installed driver or program (and you haven't successfully logged on to Windows since the driver or program was installed), you can use Last Known Good Configuration to revert to the original driver or remove the offending program's entries from the Windows Registry.

To initiate Last Known Good Configuration, access the Windows Advanced Options menu, use the arrow keys on your keyboard to scroll down to the Last Known Good Configuration menu item, and press the Enter key. If you are running more than one operating system on your computer, you will need to select the appropriate Windows installation from the menu that appears next. Windows will then attempt to revert to the previous settings, and will automatically restart.

Using Last Known Good Configuration will reverse every driver and Registry change made since your last successful logon. If you installed more than one driver or program in the last session before Windows startup failed, all of these changes will be wiped out. In this situation, you may end up with software programs that appear in the Start menu that will not run properly because their Registry entries have been removed. To correct this, manually uninstall the program by deleting the appropriate folder(s) in the Program Files directory, and delete the program shortcut located in the `<systemdrive:>\Documents and Settings\<username>\Start Menu\Programs` folder. Then, reinstall the program.

Tip

If you are positive that you know which driver or program is causing Windows startup to fail, you may want to bypass the Last Known Good Configuration and go straight to trying to start Windows in Safe mode. That way, you can deal with the specific piece of offending software using Device Manager, or through Add/Remove Programs (Windows XP) or Programs and Features (Windows Vista) in Control Panel. This allows you to deal directly with the rogue driver or software, instead of reversing all the driver and Registry changes made since your last logon.

Starting Windows in Safe Mode

If using Last Known Good Configuration does not solve the Windows startup issue, you should try starting Windows in Safe mode. Using Safe mode gives you the ability to load Windows with only the minimal drivers required to start the core operating system. Starting Windows in Safe mode is sometimes the only way to gain access to a system when the problem is related to a software driver or program.

Note

Microsoft recommends that you try using Last Known Good Configuration before you try booting into Safe mode. However, starting Windows in Safe mode does not overwrite the Last Known Good Configuration information; this means that you can still go back and try Last Known Good Configuration even after you have started Windows in Safe mode.

To start Windows in Safe mode, restart the computer and press and hold the F8 key on the keyboard. This will open the Windows Advanced Options menu. From this menu, you can choose to start Windows in Safe mode, with three different options:

- *Safe mode* is the standard mode for starting Windows with only the necessary drivers. This is usually the option to choose when you want to start Windows in Safe mode.

- *Safe Mode with Networking* starts Windows in Safe mode, but includes the drivers necessary for Windows to load its networking components. This can be useful if you want to access online help, but don't have access to another Internet-enabled computer.

- *Safe Mode with Command Prompt* loads the minimum driver set, and then takes you directly to a command prompt rather than loading the Windows GUI interface.

Starting Windows in Safe mode circumvents a number of drivers and settings. For instance, audio drivers aren't loaded, so you will not have sound when in Safe mode. Also, you will usually not be able to access USB or FireWire devices such as external hard drives. However, you can use USB-based keyboards and mice as long as your computer's firmware supports these devices. For more information about using Safe mode, refer to Chapter 2.

If you are able to start Windows in Safe mode, there are a number of tools you can use to diagnose and solve the problem that is preventing Windows from starting normally.

Device Driver Roll Back

If the Windows startup problem is related to a new or updated device driver (and you are aware of which driver is causing the problem), you can use the Device Driver Roll Back option to revert to the previous version of the driver.

Every time you install an updated driver, Windows XP and Vista store a copy of the previous driver on your system. When you use the Driver Roll Back function, it looks for the previous version of the driver, and replaces the new driver with the last-used version.

After you have started Windows in Safe mode, open the Control Panel. If you do not have Control Panel configured to appear in Classic view, choose this option in the left sidebar menu, and then double-click on the System applet. Select the Hardware tab and click on the Device Manager button. Expand the hardware category that the device with the offending driver is contained in, and then double-click on the device. Select the Driver tab, and then click Roll Back Driver (see Figure 12.1).

Figure 12.1   Click on the Roll Back Driver button to revert to the previous version of the driver.

You will be asked if you want to overwrite the existing driver. Select Yes to roll back to the previous version. Windows will locate the previous version of the driver, and automatically install it on your system (at the same time it removes the existing driver). In same cases Windows will inform you that the system must be restarted for the change to take effect.

There are a few limitations to the Device Driver Roll Back option. You can revert only one iteration of the driver, meaning that if you have used more than two versions, you cannot choose any other version than the one that was installed most recently. Also, you cannot roll back printer drivers. Installing printers is done through the Printers and Faxes (Windows XP) or Printers (Windows Vista) applet in Control Panel, and this applet does not support the Device Driver Roll Back function. Finally, you cannot use the Device Driver Roll Back option to completely uninstall a driver. If you want to uninstall a driver, click Uninstall on the device's property dialog instead of Roll Back Driver (refer to Figure 12.1).

Uninstalling Software Through the Windows Control Panel

If the Windows startup problem is related to a recently installed software program, you can remove the offending program after you have started Windows in Safe mode. To do so, open Control Panel in Classic view and double-click on the Add/Remove Programs applet (Windows XP) or the Programs and Features applet (Windows Vista). Select the program you want to uninstall from the list of installed software that appears, and select Remove.

Although these applets in Control Panel are supposed to remove all traces of a program, this is not always the case. If you remove a program in this fashion and the same problem continues to occur, there is a chance that the program still has data left in the Windows Registry.

In this case, you will need to open the Windows Registry and remove any entries pertaining to the offending program. For more information on how to edit the Windows Registry, refer to Chapter 5, "Tweaking and Tuning Windows," in this book.

Using the System Restore Tool with Windows XP and Vista

The System Restore tool, which is included in both Windows XP and Windows Vista, can be very useful in recovering a system that has become unreliable for fails to boot properly. The System Restore service monitors the status of certain key files and settings. Every so often, this service takes a snapshot of certain aspects of your computer's current status. These snapshots are referred to as *restore points*. You can use the System Restore tool to roll back your machine to one of the recorded restore points.

Caution

The System Restore tool is not a substitute for an antivirus or spyware solution, nor is it a data backup strategy. System Restore does not save your documents, email, or other such files. It can, however, be used to restore a Windows installation to a previous point in time when it was working properly.

If your Windows XP or Windows Vista–based PC will not start normally, there are two alternative methods you can use to access the System Restore tool. One method is used if you are able to start Windows in normal Safe mode, the other should be used if you can only start Windows in Safe Mode with Command Prompt. Windows Vista also adds a third method if the system won't start in Safe Mode: running System Restore from the Windows Vista Recovery Environment.

◄◄ For more general information on how System Restore works and how it's configured, **see** "System Restore," **p. 500**.

System Restore in Safe Mode

If you are able to start Windows in Safe mode and get to the Windows GUI, you can initiate the System Restore tool from the Help and Support option in the Start menu. To do this, follow these steps in Windows XP:

1. From the Start menu, select Help and Support.

2. In the Help and Support Center, under Pick a Task, click on Undo Changes to Your Computer with System Restore.

3. You will now see the Welcome to System Restore screen. Select Restore My Computer to an Earlier Time, and click Next (see Figure 12.2).

4. You will be asked to choose the restore point you want to use: Restore points are listed with a date and description. Select the restore point you want, and click Next.

5. This takes you to the Confirm Restore Point Selection page. Ensure that the settings you've chosen are correct and click Next.

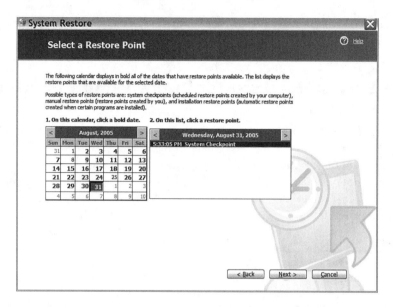

Figure 12.2   Select the desired restore point from the calendar and click Next.

The System Restore tool will reinstate the settings and key system files from the restore point you selected, and will then restart the computer. If you decide for whatever reason that the restore did not accomplish what you wanted it to, you can reverse the process by going back into the System Restore tool and selecting the Undo My Last Restoration option.

With Windows Vista, follow this procedure:

1. When the system starts in Safe mode, the Help and Support Center opens automatically. Click the What Is System Restore link.

2. From the What Is System Restore dialog, open the Click to Open System Restore link.

3. You will now see the Restore System Files and Settings dialog. By default, the most recent restore point is selected. To use this restore point, click Next and go to step 5. To see a list of other restore points, click Choose a Different Restore Point and then click Next.

4. You will be asked to choose the restore point you want to use. Note that by default, Windows Vista displays only the last five days' worth of restore points. To see older restore points, click the Show Restore Points Older Than 5 Days check box. Restore points are listed with a date and description. Select the restore point you want, and click Next.

5. This takes you to the Confirm Restore Point Selection page. Ensure that the settings you've chosen are correct and click Finish. The system restarts, and resets your computer to the selected configuration.

System Restore in Safe Mode with Command Prompt

If you are unable to start Windows in Safe mode, you can still access the System Restore tool if you are able to start Windows with the Safe Mode with Command Prompt option. The System

Restore tool can be launched from the command prompt by using the following syntax in Windows XP:

```
%systemroot%\system32\restore\rstrui.exe
```

In this instance, %*systemroot*% is the directory where the Windows installation exists. With Windows XP, this directory is named WINDOWS unless the default selection was changed during the installation process.

When Windows Vista is started in Command Prompt mode, it opens to the %systemroot%\ system32 folder. Use the following commands to open System Restore:

```
CD restore
```

This command changes your current location to the restore folder, which is one level below the system32 folder. Then type

```
rstrui.exe
```

After you have launched the rstrui.exe file, the command-line version of the System Restore tool starts. If there is an administrative password for the Windows installation, you will be asked to enter it before you can proceed with the restore. You will then be asked to choose a specific restore point to start the restore process. The restore process begins by passing the command to the System Restore service, which accesses the System Restore change logs. The System Restore service uses the change logs to create a restore map, which enables the service to re-create the specific system state you have selected. The restore map is then processed, the system restarts, and the new Registry and dynamic data stores are loaded.

Note

For more information on using environment variables, refer to Chapter 9, "Windows Commands and Scripting."

Caution

For the System Restore tool to function, the System Restore service must be enabled in Windows. By default, this service is enabled when Windows is installed. However, the service can be disabled either through the System applet in Control Panel, or via the Services option in the Administrative Tools applet in Control Panel.

Using System Restore from the Windows Recovery Environment

Windows Vista offers System Restore as one of the options available from the Windows Recovery Environment (Windows RE), which is available as a fallback startup method on some computers, or can be run from the Windows Vista distribution DVD.

◀◀ For details, **see** "Windows Recovery Environment," this chapter, **p. 780**.

The System Restore tool can be the best procedure to use if you are unsure which driver or program may be causing the problem, or if uninstalling the driver or program doesn't solve the problem.

Recovery Console for Windows XP

One of the lesser-known maintenance features of Windows XP and Windows 2000 that's very useful in fixing a Windows system that won't fully boot is the Recovery Console. It's an interesting animal—rather than a management tool that you run from Windows, the Recovery Console is a completely independent, standalone, utterly minimal installation of Windows with "plain vanilla" device drivers, a very limited command-line interface, and no GUI. The idea is that no matter how badly messed up your main Windows installation might get, due to bad or incorrect drivers, weird hardware, missing files, or incorrect Registry entries, the Recovery Console should still be able to boot up and work.

Although Microsoft recommends that you try Safe mode first, the Recovery Console gives you a Command Prompt window from which you may be able to bring a nonbootable system back to life. You can use it to disable a device driver that crashes Windows before it can start up, delete a virus or spyware program, install fresh copies of system files that have become corrupted, and manage disk partitions. Under certain circumstances you can also use the Recovery Console to extract urgently needed files from a nonbootable system without going to the trouble of moving the hard disk to another computer or reinstalling Windows. However, this takes advance preparation.

Recovery Console Access Restrictions

By default, Recovery Console commands can only be used to read, write, and modify files in selected folders of your hard drives:

- The Windows folder (the `%systemroot%` folder) and its subfolders
- The root folders of your hard drives
- The folder from which the Recovery Console booted (`c:\cmdcons` if it was installed on your hard drive)
- Removable media such as CDs, DVDs, and floppy disks

Thus, using default settings, you cannot use Recovery Console to view, modify, or copy in user profile folders or any other folders; attempts to do so will result in an Access Denied error message.

Furthermore, by default, you can copy files from one hard drive to another (subject to the limitations just mentioned), and from removable media to hard drives, but you cannot copy files from a hard disk to a floppy disk, so you cannot use Recovery Console to salvage user files from a non-bootable computer.

You can configure Recovery Console so that it *can* access any folder, and *can* copy files out of the computer to removable media. But the `set` command, which is used to relax access restrictions, is available only if you make an adjustment to your computer's Security Policy before you boot the Recovery Console, and thus this has to be done before you run into trouble.

If you think you will ever want to be able to use the Recovery Console to copy files out of an unbootable computer to a floppy disk, you should enable the `set` command *now*. It's best if you also install the Recovery Console on your hard disk at the same time. You can also make the Security Policy changes without installing to disk—the procedure is described in steps 5 through 11 in the next section—but I recommend preinstallation.

Installing Recovery Console on Your Hard Disk

If you plan ahead, you can install Recovery Console on your hard disk, and it will appear as a boot-time option. The advantage of doing this is that you won't have to hunt for your Setup CD when you need to use Recovery Console. At the same time, you can choose to enable the set command that relaxes Recovery Console's access restrictions, or you can make it possible to use the Console without having the Administrator password.

Caution

You should not both enable the **set** command *and* remove the requirement for the Administrator password. With both of these options enabled, anyone with physical access to your computer would be able to access and view, delete, or take a copy of any file, without having to know any password at all.

Note

If your computer is a member of a domain network, Group Policy settings may be used to override Local Security policy, so your network administrator may prevent your use of the Recovery Console, or your attempt to relax its security restrictions. Likewise, Group Policy can also be used to enable access.

Note

If you have set up software mirrored or RAID disks using the Windows Disk Management console, you must break the mirror before installing the Recovery Console, and you cannot re-create the mirror unless your disks have been converted from Basic to Dynamic disks. See Microsoft Knowledge article support.microsoft.com/kb/229077 for details.

To install the Recovery Console on your hard disk, follow this procedure:

1. Log on as a Computer Administrator and insert your Windows Setup CD.

   On Windows XP, if your Setup CD has the original or Service Pack 1 version of XP, and you have subsequently installed Service Pack 2, you cannot use your original Setup CD. You must find and use an XP Setup CD that has SP2 preinstalled. You might be able to borrow a Setup CD from a friend with a newer computer.

2. Wait for the Windows Setup window to appear, and close it.

3. Open a Command Prompt window, and type the following command:

   `d:\i386\winnt32 /cmdcons`

   but type the letter corresponding to your CD drive in place of *d*.

4. Let Windows Setup complete the installation, and then remove the CD. Close the Command Prompt window.

5. If you want to enable the `set` command, which will let you bypass Recovery Console's access restrictions, proceed with step 6. Otherwise, skip ahead to step 8.

6. To enable the `set` command, open the Control Panel, select Performance and Maintenance, open Administrative Tools, and then open Local Security Policy.

7. In the left pane, open Security Settings, Local Policies, and select Security Options. In the right pane, double-click Recovery Console: Allow Floppy Copy. Select Enabled, and then click OK. Repeat with Recovery Console: Access to All Drives and All Folders. Now, skip ahead to step 11.

8. To eliminate the requirement that you enter the Administrator password to manage this Windows installation using the Recovery Console, proceed with step 9. Otherwise, skip ahead to step 12.

9. To disable the Administrator password requirement, open the Control Panel, select Performance and Maintenance, open Administrative Tools, and then open Local Security Policy.

10. In the left pane, open Security Settings, Local Policies, and select Security Options. In the right pane, double-click Recovery Console: Allow Automatic Administrative Logon. Select Enabled, and then click OK.

11. Close the Local Security Settings window and the Control Panel.

12. Click Start, right-click My Computer, and select Properties. Select the Advanced tab, and under Startup and Recovery, click Settings.

13. Be sure that the default operating system is *not* Microsoft Windows Recovery Console; if it is, select an appropriate default operating system option.

14. Ensure that Time to Display List of Operating Systems is checked, and set the number of seconds to 5. Finally, click OK to close the dialog.

Now, the next time you restart your computer, the Windows loader will display a boot menu, as shown in Figure 12.3. If you make no choice, after five seconds Windows will go ahead and start up as usual. If you need to use the Recovery Console, immediately press the down-arrow key to stop the clock, and then highlight Microsoft Windows Recovery Console and press Enter.

Note

The `boot.ini` entry for the Recovery Console is

```
C:\CMDCONS\BOOTSECT.DAT="Microsoft Windows Recovery Console" /cmdcons
```

although the drive letter may be different on your installation. This is handy to know in case you accidentally remove it from your `boot.ini` file or if you delete and have to replace `boot.ini`.

Caution

If you install Recovery Console on your hard disk and later convert the hard disk from FAT to NTFS format, you must reinstall Recovery Console. Until you do, the bootable version will not work, and you will only be able to start Recovery Console from your Setup CD.

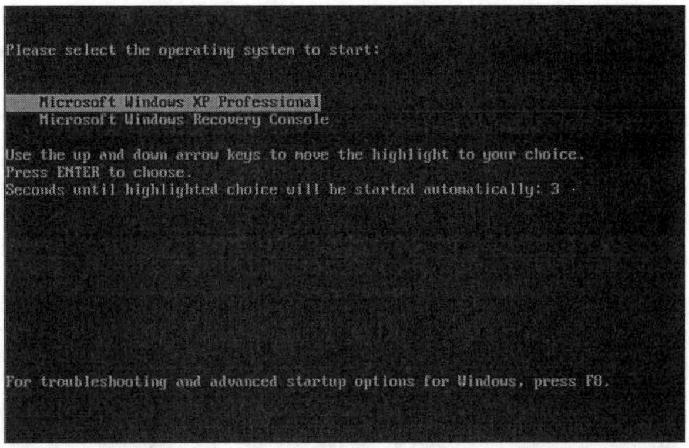

Figure 12.3   After installation, the Recovery Console appears as a boot option.

Starting Recovery Console from Your Setup CD

If you need to use the Recovery Console to repair a broken Windows installation but you did not preinstall it on your hard disk, you can start it by booting from your Windows Setup CD, using this procedure:

1. Insert your Windows Setup CD into your CD or DVD drive, and restart your computer. You may need to enter your BIOS Setup program to change the Boot Order setting so that booting from the CD drive is enabled, and the CD drive is checked before the hard drive.

2. When the Welcome to Setup screen appears, select R to Repair, and if prompted to do so, C to run the Recovery Console.

3. While the Recovery Console is starting, you will see the prompt Press F6 if you need to install a third party SCSI or RAID driver. If your disk drive interface requires a nonstandard driver, press F6 and follow the same procedure you used during Windows Setup to select an alternate driver.

4. The Recovery Console will ask you to select a Windows installation.

Now, proceed as described in the next section.

Note

If your computer is set up for network booting and your organization uses Remote Installation Services, you can also boot Recovery Console through RIS. See Microsoft Knowledgebase article support.microsoft.com/kb/222478 for instructions.

Using the Recovery Console

To start the Recovery Console, if you have installed the Recovery Console on your hard disk, restart your computer and select Microsoft Windows Recovery Console from the boot options menu. Otherwise, boot from your Windows XP Setup CD as described in the previous section.

When the Recovery Console has loaded, there will be a five-second window in which you can press Enter to select an alternative keyboard layout. The default is US English Qwerty.

The Recovery Console will then examine your hard disks for any Windows installations it can find, and it will display them in a numbered list, even if only one is found, as shown in Figure 12.4. Enter the number corresponding to the Windows installation you want to repair and press Enter.

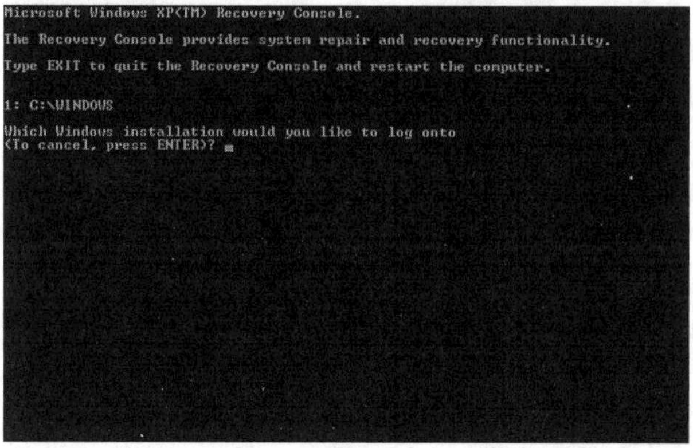

Figure 12.4 When it starts, Recovery Console lets you select from any detected Windows installations.

If your Windows folder is not displayed, either its disk is inaccessible, or the installation is too corrupted to continue; in this case you need to fix the hardware, or reinstall Windows. You can press Enter to exit the Recovery Console and restart the computer.

Note

If your computer is set up for multibooting into Windows XP, 2000, or NT, be careful. You could damage your Windows installation if you try to use the Windows XP Recovery console on a Windows 2000 installation, or vice versa. Although all Windows installations are listed, work only with installations that match the version of the Recovery Console you're using. Boot from the other OS setup CD to get the right version, if necessary.

If a password is set for your Administrator account, and if you haven't disabled the need for the Administrator logon by modifying Security Policy, as discussed earlier, you will be prompted for the Administrator password.

◀◀ If you cannot remember the password to the Administrator account, **see** "Dealing with a Lost Password," **p. 452**.

The Recovery Console window works almost exactly like the Command Prompt window. You can use the cd command to change directories and dir to list directory contents; many of the usual commands like copy and del are available to let you manage files; and as usual, uppercase and lowercase do not matter when entering commands or options. However, there are also some distinct differences:

- Command-line editing functions are minimal. Filename completion is not available. You can use the up- and down-arrow keys to recall previously typed commands, but you cannot use the left- and right-arrow keys to move the cursor around in a command line for editing. To make changes, you must use the Backspace key to erase characters and then retype the rest of the line.

- The Recovery Console supports only a small list of built-in commands. No other programs (.EXE files) can be run.

- The input and output redirection operations > and < and the pipeline operator | are not supported.

- Output never scrolls off the screen. If a listing fills the screen it automatically pauses; you can press the spacebar to display the next screen, or Esc to cancel the listing.

- Most commands that accept a filename argument will not accept wildcard specification using ? or * unless you use the set command to enable the AllowWildCards option.

- Spaces are required between arguments. Although the normal command prompt accepts cd\windows as a valid command, Recovery Console doesn't—you must type cd \windows instead.

- As mentioned previously, the Recovery Console's default settings prohibit access to folders other than the Windows folder and root folders, and prohibit copying files to floppy disk. If you need to relax these restrictions, use the set command to enable the AllowAllPaths option.

The next sections show some useful examples. After the examples is a reference of all Recovery Console commands.

Repair the Boot Loader

If you install another operating system such as Linux, MS-DOS, or Windows 98 or Me, the OS setup program will overwrite the boot sector and master boot record boot code and you will not be able to load Windows XP. If you want to dual-boot with Linux, you can use LILO, GRUB, or other Linux loaders as the primary loader, so this may be okay, but in most cases, you will want to reinstall the Windows XP loader. To do this, start the Recovery Console and issue the commands **fixboot** and **fixmbr**. Then type **quit** to restart the computer.

Disable a Buggy Driver or Service

If a buggy device driver (or less likely, a service) is preventing Windows from booting, you may be able to boot after disabling it using the Recovery Console. In some cases, the Blue Screen of Death (BSOD), which displays information about the CPU's state at the time of a Windows crash, lists the name of the device driver that caused the problem, and you will know which driver to disable or roll back. Sometimes, however, the BSOD doesn't display the driver name. In this case, you should start by disabling the driver for any newly installed devices first, before proceeding to try disabling nonessential devices one at a time.

Tip

If Windows automatically reboots after a crash so quickly that you can't see what the Blue Screen of Death says, or it reboots over and over, and you have Windows XP Service Pack 2 or later, you're in luck. Press F8 while Windows is starting to display the Advanced Options Startup menu. Select Disable Automatic Restart on System Failure, and then select Start Windows Normally. This should let you see the crash report. You'll need to power the computer off and back on to restart it if the BSOD is displayed. Ctrl+Alt+Del won't budge it.

Before using the Recovery Console, try booting in VGA mode, and then in Safe mode, and then in Last Known Good mode, in that order, using the F8 boot options menu discussed earlier in the chapter. If Windows starts with one of these selections, you can probably disable the problematic device or update its driver using the GUI Device Manager.

If this doesn't help, use the Recovery Console `listsvc` command to get a listing of all installed device drivers and services. The listing starts like this:

```
drivername         startupmode
    descriptive name
6to4               Auto
    IPv6 Helper Service
Abiosdsk           Disabled

abp480n5           Disabled

ACPI               Boot
    Microsoft ACPI Driver
ACPIEC             Disabled

adpu160m           Disabled

aec                Manual
    Microsoft Kernel Acoustic Echo Canceller
```

Look for device drivers with the Boot or System startup mode. Use the `disable` startup selection to disable one or two at a time, and *write down the name and original startup mode of each driver you disable*, so you can later re-enable them if you determine that they are not the ones causing the problem.

Disable Spyware, Adware, or Viruses

Most virus spyware and adware programs go to great lengths to prevent you from uninstalling them. Some of the measures include detecting your attempt to install antivirus or antispyware software and blocking the installation program, keeping executable files open and locked so that they cannot be deleted, monitoring the Registry so that startup entries can be immediately replaced if you delete them, renaming their own executable files to make them more difficult to find, and more.

Usually, if you boot your computer in Safe mode these programs do not start up, and you can then delete them manually, or install antispyware software to delete them.

If these programs continue to thwart you even in Safe mode, boot up the Recovery Console. Locate the executable files for these programs and delete them or rename them so that they will not be started. The commands to use are `cd`, to change directories, and `ren`, to rename the executable file. For example, if you found that a program named `malware.exe` was starting up with Windows, and that it was located in folder `\windows\system32`, you could use these commands to thwart it:

```
cd \windows\system32
rename malware.exe malware.bad
quit
```

When Windows restarts, the commands used to run `malware.exe` will not find this file, so it will not start.

Replace a Missing *boot.ini*

If you inadvertently delete the `boot.ini` file from the root folder of your first hard drive, Windows will scan through your drives looking for the first Windows installation it can find. If this is not the right folder, Windows will not boot, and you will need to re-create `boot.ini` before you can start Windows. You can do this with the Recovery Console.

Because you have no `boot.ini` file, you will need start the Recovery Console by booting from your Windows XP Setup CD, as described earlier. On Windows XP, you can type the command

```
bootcfg /rebuild
```

`bootcfg` will scan your hard drives for Windows installations. For each located installation, `bootcfg` will prompt:

- **Add installation to boot list? (Yes/No/All)** — Press Y to add the Windows folder as a startup selection, N to skip it, or A to add it and all other identified installations. If you press N, `bootcfg` will search for another installation.

- **Enter Load Identifier** — Enter a name for this Windows installation. Whatever you type will appear as a selection in the boot menu. Something like `Windows XP Professional on C Drive` might be appropriate.

- **Enter OS Load Options** — It's safest to simply press Enter and not enter any load options. You can, however, add any of the options listed earlier in the discussion of `boot.ini`. If you add more than one, put a space between each option. Some useful possibilities include the following:

`/fastdetect`	Speeds up detection of COM ports, helpful for normal home or office workstations, where you are not using the headless-server option.
`/noexecute=optin`	Sets Windows Data Execution Protection to monitor Windows plus explicitly listed applications.
`/SOS`	Makes `ntldr` print out the name of each device driver it loads, to help identify a failed driver.

After setting up all desired Windows installations, remove your Windows Setup CD and enter the quit command to restart your computer.

On Windows 2000, `bootcfg` is not available. You will have to use the `map` command to see a list of all disk drives in ARC format, using the command

```
map arc
```

Then construct a `boot.ini` file manually on another computer using the examples shown earlier in this chapter in the discussion of `boot.ini`, copy it to a floppy disk, and then copy it to the disabled computer using the Recovery Console. First, if the disabled computer has an existing `boot.ini` file, you can delete it with the commands

```
c:
cd \
copy boot.ini boot.ini.bak
attrib -r boot.ini
del boot.ini
```

Then copy the new version from the floppy disk:

```
copy a:boot.ini c:\
attrib +s boot.ini
attrib +h boot.ini
attrib +r boot.ini
```

Back Up `boot.ini`

If you are going to use Recovery Console to modify your `boot.ini` file, you should first make a backup copy by typing these commands:

```
c:
cd \
copy boot.ini boot.ini.bak
```

Then, if you have to revert to the original version, use these commands:

```
c:
cd \
copy boot.ini.bak boot.ini
Overwrite boot.ini (Yes/No/All): y
attrib +s boot.ini
attrib +h boot.ini
attrib +r boot.ini
```

Recovery Console Command Summary

This section lists the Recovery Console commands. Each entry includes a syntax description. In the syntax description, several characters are used to indicate optional parts of the command line and are *not* meant to be typed literally:

[ ]	Brackets surround optional arguments
|	A vertical bar separates alternate choices
italics	Indicate placeholder names that are to be replaced with actual names appropriate for your system
boldface	Indicates text to be typed literally

`attrib`—Change Attributes on a File or Directory

Syntax: **attrib +r\|-r\|+s\|-s\|+h\|-h\|+c\|-c** *filename*

The `attrib` command is used to set or clear file attributes. The +*x* arguments set attributes, and the -*x* arguments clear them, where *x* can be any of the following letters:

r   Read-only

s   System

h   Hidden

c   Compressed

You can only specify one +*x* or -*x* argument. If you have to change several attributes, you have to issue separate commands for each. Typing the attrib command without a +*x* or -*x* argument doesn't display the file's current attributes as you might expect, but results in an error message. To view a file's attributes, use the dir command.

batch—*Execute Commands from a Text File*

Syntax: **batch** *inputfile* [*outputfile*]

The batch command instructs the Recovery Console to read the specified file named *inputfile* and interpret its contents as Recovery Console commands. Because there is no edit command in the Recovery Console, to be useful, you must have prepared a batch input file in advance, or must place it on a floppy disk. The output of the commands will be written to the screen unless the optional *outputfile* argument is specified. This command is not available in the Windows 2000 Recovery Console.

bootcfg—*Modify* boot.ini *Startup and Recovery Options*

Syntax: **bootcfg /add**

             bootcfg /rebuild

             bootcfg /scan

             bootcfg /list

             bootcfg /disableredirect

             bootcfg /redirect [*port baudrate*] | [**usebiossettings**]

bootcfg modifies file boot.ini on the boot drive, which contains the list of operating system choices. It's especially helpful with the /rebuild option to replace your boot.ini file if it was inadvertently deleted. This command is not available in the Windows 2000 Recovery Console.

There are six different versions of the command:

/add   Scans all hard disks for Windows installations and prompts for one to be added to boot.ini. Prompts for a Load Identifier (name to display on the boot menu) and OS Load Options, which are arguments like /SOS as described earlier in this chapter; can be left blank.

/rebuild   Scans all hard disks for Windows installations, and prompts for those to be added to boot.ini. The selected installations are added to any already in boot.ini, so this option is best used only to replace a missing boot.ini. Also, see the discussion on backing up boot.ini earlier in this section.

(continues)

/scan	Displays a list of Windows installations found on your hard disks; does not modify `boot.ini`.
/list	Lists the boot entries already in your `boot.ini` file.
/default	Prompts for a `boot.ini` boot choice to be set as the default boot choice.
/redirect	The /redirect and /disableredirect options apply only to Windows 2003 Server, and are used to manage boot monitoring over a serial port for "headless" servers with no display adapter.

cd and *chdir*—Display or Change Current Directory

Syntax: **cd** [[*drive:*]*path*]

The `cd` command changes the default directory on the current or specified drive. The path may be specified as an absolute path (starting with \) or a relative path. The name .. stands for the parent directory.

(To change the default drive, enter a command line consisting of just a drive letter followed by a colon, as in d:.)

Without any arguments, `cd` displays the current drive and directory. With a drive letter but no path, `cd` displays the default directory for the specified drive.

Use quotation marks around any path name containing spaces. For example, cd "\windows\ profiles\username\programs\start menu".

By default, `cd` operates only in the restricted set of folders listed earlier in this chapter. To permit access to other folders, the set command must have been enabled, and you must have used the set command to enable the AllowAllAPaths option.

chkdsk—Check Disk Format for Errors

Syntax: **chkdsk** [*drive:*] [/P|/R]

The `chkdsk` command checks the boot drive or the specified drive for errors and prints a report of unlinked sectors and so on. By default, `chkdsk` will not run unless a drive is marked as *dirty*; that is, if Windows was shut down without properly dismounting the drive. The /P option forces `chkdsk` to check the drive even it was correctly dismounted. The /R option makes `chkdsk` read every sector on the disk and check for errors; this can take quite a long time. The /R option implies /P.

cls—Clear the Screen

Syntax: **cls**

Clears the screen.

copy—Copy a File

Syntax: **copy** *sourcefile* [*destinationfile*]

The copy command copies a file. The file to be copied, the *sourcefile*, can be specified using a path and filename, or just a filename, in which case it is located in the current directory.

The destination file can be specified as a full path, a folder name, a filename, or it can be omitted, in which case the file is copied to the current directory using its original name.

The copy command option has some restrictions unless you have used the set command to remove them. The default restrictions are as follows:

- The source and destination folders must be in the limited list (Windows folder and subfolders, root folders, cmdcons folder, removable media) unless the AllowAllPaths option is enabled.
- The destination cannot be on removable media, unless the AllowRemovableMedia option has been enabled.
- The filename must be fully spelled out, unless the AllowWildcards option has been set.
- If the destination file exists, you will be asked if you want to overwrite it, unless the NoCopyPrompt option is enabled.

Compressed files on the Windows installation CD usually have an underscore as the last character of their filename extension, for example, .EX_ or .DL_. When copying a compressed file to the hard disk to replace a corrupted file, the Recovery Console will automatically decompress it as it is copied, but you must specify the desired extension in the destination filename—for example, .EXE or .DLL.

del and *delete*—Delete a File

Syntax: **del** [*drive:*][*path*]*filename*

The del or delete command is used to delete a file. You can specify the filename with or without a path. If the path is omitted, the file is deleted from the current directory.

The filename must be fully spelled out, unless the AllowWildcards option has been set. See the set command for more details.

Caution

There is no undelete option and no Recycle Bin available in the Recovery Console—if you delete a file, it's gone forever. If you want to disable a bad driver or suspected virus program, it might be safer to use the disable command, or rename the file to something like badprogram.exe.xxx, before taking the more drastic step of deleting it.

dir—List Files and Subdirectories

Syntax: **dir** [*drive:*][*path*][*filename*]

The dir command lists all files, including hidden and system files, in the current or specified directory. The listing has five columns, which list the file's modification date, modification time, attributes, size in bytes, and name.

The attributes column uses the following letters:

d   Directory

a   Archive (changed since backup)

r   Read-only

h   Hidden

s   System file

c   Compressed

e   Encrypted

p   Reparse point

You can specify wildcards in the filename specification for the dir command. If the list fills the screen, the Recovery Console automatically pauses the listing. Press the spacebar to display the next page or Esc to cancel the listing.

disable—Disable a Service or Device Driver

Syntax: **disable** *servicename*

The disable command disables a device driver or service by setting its startup mode to SERVICE_DISABLED. Disable prints the driver or service's previous startup mode before changing it. You should make a note of the old mode, in case you need to enable the drive or service again.

The listsvc command lists the names of all installed drivers and services. Use listsvc to find the correct spelling of the driver or service's name and type it on the disable command line.

diskpart—Manage Hard Disk Partitions

Syntax: **diskpart** [/**add**|/**delete**] [*device*|*drive*|*partition*] [*size*]

diskpart adds partitions to or deletes partitions from a hard disk. You can add or delete partitions based on the disk's device name, drive letter, or partition name (the map command can be used to list device names).

However, unless you need to use diskpart in a Recovery Console batch file, the easiest way to manage partitions in Recovery Console is to type diskpart with no arguments. This displays the interactive partition editor used during Windows Setup, as shown in Figure 12.5.

Caution

Do not use the **diskpart** command to manage a disk that you have upgraded from a basic disk to a dynamic disk. **diskpart** could destroy your partition table and make your data inaccessible. To manage the partitions on a dynamic disk, boot Windows and use Disk Manager.

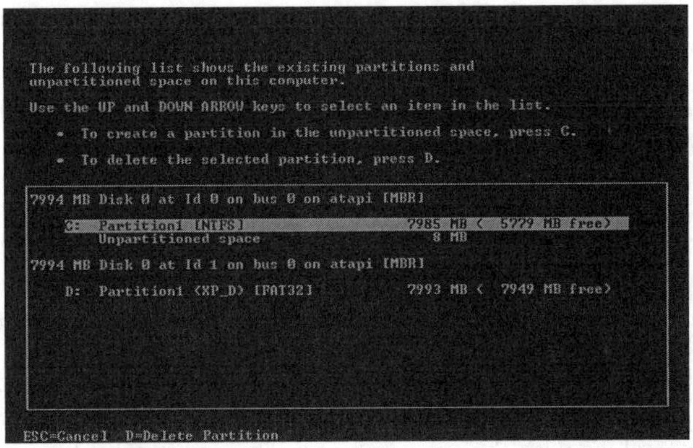

Figure 12.5   The `diskpart` command with no arguments displays a simple partition editor.

enable—*Enable a Service or Device Driver*

Syntax: **enable** *servicename* [*mode*]

The `enable` command changes the boot mode of a specified device driver or service. Service and device driver names can be listed using the `listsvc` command.

With no *mode* specified, `enable` displays the service or driver's current startup mode. The mode can be changed by specifying one of the following keywords: `SERVICE_BOOT_START`, `SERVICE_SYSTEM_START`, `SERVICE_AUTO_START` (corresponds to Automatic in the Services Management console), or `SERVICE_DEMAND_START` (corresponds to Manual).

Be very careful when changing driver or service boot modes. Disable services and drivers with the `disable` command, and record the original setting in case you must enable it again.

exit—*Quit the Recovery Console and Reboot*

Syntax: **exit**

The `exit` command closes the Recovery Console and restarts the computer.

expand—*Expand or List a Compressed* `.CAB` *File*

Syntax: **expand** *sourcefile* [/**F:***filename*] [*destination*] [/**Y**]
        expand *sourcefile* [/**F:***filename*] /**D**

The `expand` command is used to extract files from `.CAB` files (Microsoft's version of the `.ZIP` file, used mainly on installation disks and in the `\windows\system32` folder to hold large numbers of installable device drivers).

The *sourcefile* argument specifies a `.CAB` file. The command operates on all files in the `.CAB` file unless the /F option is used to name a specific file. Wildcards can be used in the /F filename specification.

With the /D option, the command lists the files in the .CAB file (or the specified file(s) specified with /F).

Without /D, the command expands the .CAB file(s) and copies them to the destination folder or file specified in the *destination* argument. If the *destination* argument is omitted, the file(s) are copied to the current directory.

If the destination file(s) already exist, expand asks you if it should overwrite them. You can respond with the letter N for no, Y for yes, or A to overwrite all files. Alternatively you can add /Y to the command line, in which case expand will be allowed to overwrite existing files without asking.

The destination path must be in the Windows folder or a root folder unless the AllowAllPaths option has been enabled with the set command. The destination path cannot be on removable media unless the AllowRemovableMedia option has been enabled.

The destination file cannot be read-only. Use the attrib command to remove the read-only attribute before using expand to overwrite a read-only file.

fixboot—Rewrite the Boot Sector of the Boot Drive

Syntax: **fixboot** [*drive:*]

The fixboot command writes the Windows boot loader into first sector on the boot (active) partition, as specified by its drive letter. This is the program that locates and starts ntldr.exe. You can use fixboot if the boot loader gets overwritten by another operating system's installation procedure. If you don't specify a drive letter, the current boot drive is used.

Caution

Damage to your boot sector *could* have been caused by a virus or hardware problem. Microsoft recommends running an antivirus check before using the **fixboot** command.

fixmbr—Rewrite the Master Boot Record of the Boot Drive

Syntax: **fixmbr** [*devicename*]

The fixmbr command replaces the boot loader contained in the boot partition's first block, called the Master Boot Record (MBR). The boot loader precedes the partition table, which is also stored in the Master Boot Record.

The boot drive can be specified using one of the device names displayed by the map command. If omitted, the current boot drive is used.

If fixmbr detects an invalid or nonstandard partition table signature, it will prompt you before rewriting the master boot record.

Caution

Damage to your Master Boot Record *could* have been caused by a virus or hardware problem. Microsoft recommends running an antivirus check before using the **fixmbr** command.

format—Format a Disk Volume

Syntax: **format** [*drive:*] [/**Q**] [/**FS:***filesystem*]

The Recovery Console's `format` command can format hard disk volumes (partitions) but not removable media. You should specify the partition's drive letter and the desired /FS value explicitly. The *filesystem* value can be FAT (for FAT-16), FAT32, or NTFS. The /Q option specifies a quick format, which creates an empty file system but does not test every block. It can be used to speed the format process but should be used only on a drive that is known not to have any defects.

Caution

Do not use the **format** command on a volume on a disk that you have upgraded from a basic disk to a dynamic disk. To manage the partitions on a dynamic disk, boot Windows and use Disk Manager.

help—Print Help Information

Syntax: **help** [*command*]

Help by itself lists all the Recovery Console commands (except set!). To print the syntax and description of a specific command type **help** followed by the command name.

listsvc—List All Device Drivers and Services

Syntax: **listsvc**

The `listsvc` command lists all available services and device drivers. The listing will pause when it fills the screen. Press the spacebar to display the next screen or Esc to cancel the listing. You can use the names listed in the left column with the `enable` and `disable` commands.

logon—Select a Windows Installation

Syntax: **logon**

The `logon` command lets you select a different Windows installation to administer. As when the Recovery Console starts, `logon` lists the detected installations and lets you select one by entering a number. You will be prompted for the Administrator password, if one is set, unless Security Policy for the installation does not require the Administrator password. See the instructions for installing Recovery Console on the hard disk for a mention of this policy setting.

map—Display Disk Devices and Drive Letter Mappings

Syntax: **map** [**arc**]

`map` lists the drive letter to physical device mappings that are currently active. This is a typical output printout from `map`:

```
C: NTFS      7986MB     \Device\Harddisk0\Partition1
D: FAT32     7993MB     \Device\Harddisk1\Partition1
A:                      \Device\Floppy0
E:                      \Device\CdRom0
```

The optional parameter arc tells map to display ARC paths instead of Windows device paths. The output from map arc shows the drive names as they are specified in boot.ini, as in this example:

```
C: NTFS      7986MB     multi(0)disk(0)rdisk(0)partition(1)
D: FAT32     7993MB     multi(0)disk(0)rdisk(1)partition(1)
A:                      \Device\Floppy0
E:                      \Device\CdRom0
```

md and mkdir—Create a Directory

Syntax: **mkdir** [*drive:*]*path*

The mkdir command creates a new folder. By default, mkdir can create folders only within the Windows folder or its subfolders, the root directory of any hard disk partition, or removable media. You can remove this restriction by enabling the AllowAllPaths option with the set command.

more and type—Display a Text File on the Screen

Syntax: **more** *filename*

                type *filename*

The more and type commands are equivalent in the Recovery Console. Both display a text file on the screen. If the listing fills the screen, the display pauses. Press the spacebar to display the next screen, or Esc to cancel the listing.

net use—Torment Windows XP Users with False Hopes

The Windows XP Recovery Console's net use command is described in the help listing and in numerous Microsoft support documents, and like its regular Command Prompt counterpart it is supposed to be able to let you access a network shared folder. However, it doesn't work—no network adapter or protocol drivers are loaded with the Recovery Console.

rd and rmdir—Delete a Directory

Syntax: **rmdir** [*drive:*]*path*

rmdir deletes the specified folder. The folder must be empty. It works only on folders in the system directories of the current Windows installation, the root directory of hard disks, and removable media, unless you have used the set command to enable the AllowAllPaths option.

ren and rename—Rename a File

Syntax: **rename** [*drive:*][*path*]*filename newname*

You cannot specify a drive or folder path as part of the destination filename.

rename works only on files in the system directories of the current Windows installation, the root directory of hard disks, and removable media, unless you have used the set command to enable the AllowAllPaths option.

set—Enable or Disable a Recovery Console Option

Syntax: `set AllowWildCards = true|false`

`set AllowAllPaths = true|false`

`set AllowRemovableMedia = true|false`

`set NoCopyPrompt = true|false`

The `set` command is available only if you edited Local Security Policy or Group Policy for the selected Windows installation prior to booting the Recovery Console, and enabled `Recovery Console: Allow floppy copy and access to all drives and all folders`, as described earlier in the section "Installing Recovery Console on Your Hard Disk."

When enabled, the `set` command can be used to relax Recovery Console's access restrictions. The default settings for the four options is `false`. To gain increased access you can set any or all of these values to `true`:

`AllowWildCards`	If set to `true`, you can specify wildcards (* and ?) in Recovery Console's copy and `delete` commands.
`AllowAllPaths`	If set to `true`, you can access all folders on all drives, rather than just the root and Windows folders.
`AllowRemovableMedia`	If set to `true`, you can copy files from the hard drives to floppy disks and other removable media.
`NoCopyPrompt`	If set to `true`, Recovery Console will not prompt before overwriting an existing file.

You must separate the words and the equal sign with spaces, otherwise Windows will print `"The parameter is not valid"`, which is a fairly unhelpful remark. A correctly entered command looks like this:

```
set allowallpaths = true
```

Caution

These options compromise Windows security, so you should be sure you want to make this possible before you enable access to the **set** command by editing the Registry. You should not enable the **set** command *and* allow Recovery Console to open Windows without the Administrator password; otherwise, anyone with physical access to your computer will be able access any file without knowing any passwords.

systemroot—Change to the Windows Folder

Syntax: `systemroot`

Sets the current directory to the Windows folder of the currently selected Windows installation—for example, `C:\windows`. This is handy if you've changed to another directory and want to get back to the original drive and folder.

Command Prompt in Windows Recovery Environment

Windows Vista includes a full-featured command prompt mode as part of the Windows Recovery Environment, rather than the limited subset of commands available as part of the Windows 2000/XP Recovery Console (see previous section). Likewise, the Windows Vista command prompt can work with any folder and drive visible to the system, including USB and other types of external and removable-media drives.

Most of the commands listed in the previous section work in the Windows RE or Vista's standard command prompt mode (but are not limited the way they are in Windows XP), but a few have been replaced by other commands, as shown in Table 12.2.

Table 12.2   **Windows Vista Equivalents for Recovery Console Commands**

Recovery Console Command	What It Does	Windows Vista Equivalent Command(s)	Notes
BootCfg	Repairs boot configuration Bcdedit	BootRec /ScanOS BootRec /Rebuild BCD the	BootRec is available only in Windows RE. Bcdedit can run from standard command prompt only if you start command prompt as Administrator: right-click Command Prompt and select Run as Administrator, and provide credentials as required.
FixBoot	Rewrites boot sectors	BootRec/FixBoot	BootRec is available only in Windows RE.
FixMBR	Repairs master boot record	BootRec/FixMBR	BootRec is available only in Windows RE.
Map	Displays disk partitions	DiskPart	Requires administrator credentials when run from the standard command prompt.
Systemroot	Switches the working folder to the default Windows folder (usually C:\Windows)	CD\Windows or Chdir\Windows	Substitute the correct folder name if your Windows installation uses a different folder than \Windows.

The Recovery Console commands `Logon`, `Listsyc`, `Enable`, and `Disable` have no equivalent in Windows Vista.

◀◀ For more information about the command prompt in Windows XP and Windows Vista, see Chapter 9, "Windows Commands and Scripting."

Automated System Recovery with Windows XP

If you have exhausted all the options discussed in the previous sections, there is one final, last resort, a "Break Glass in Case of Emergency" tool you can use to attempt to access a Windows XP installation that won't start up. Windows XP Professional offers a feature in its Backup tool (NTBACKUP.EXE) that can be used to create Windows startup emergency disks that can be used when all other methods have failed. This feature of Windows Backup is known as the *Automated*

System Recovery (ASR) tool. Microsoft created the ASR tool to replace the Emergency Repair Disk that was a part of Windows NT and Windows 2000—although Microsoft also recommends that the ASR tool should be used only if there are no other disaster recovery options available to you.

ASR consists of two parts: a backup of critical files that is made to a local (recommended) or remote storage device, and a floppy disk containing three files critical to the restoration phase.

The files that are backed up include the system state data and all files stored on the system volume. *System state* refers to all the components that determine the current state of the operating system (hence the clever name) and includes user accounts, hard drive configuration, network configuration, video settings, hardware configuration, software settings, and various other critical files that are required to run Windows XP Professional properly. Additionally, the system state includes files that are required to start the operating system properly, including those that are found in the %systemroot% directory and boot files such as ntldr and ntdetect.

The floppy disk contains three files: asr.sif, asrpnp.sif, and setup.log. If you're thinking that the .SIF extension sounds familiar, you're right. .SIF files are used as answer files to customize unattended installations of Windows XP Professional. The functions of these three files are outlined as follows:

- Asr.sif contains information about your computer's storage devices including hard drives, partitions, volumes, and removable storage devices. A portion of the asr.sif file is shown in Figure 12.6.

- Asrpnp.sif contains information about the plug and play information installed in your computer.

- Setup.log contains a listing of all system state and critical files that were backed up. It aids in the restoration of these files when you invoke ASR recovery.

◄◄ To learn more about answer files, **see** "Using Interactive Answer Files for Installation of Windows XP," **p. 180**.

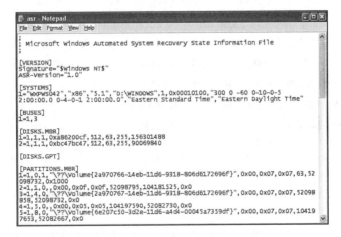

Figure 12.6   asr.sif contains information about hard drives and removable storage.

Tip

Although not the intended purpose of `asr.sif` and `asrpnp.sif`, these files provide a great wealth of information about installed devices and configurations for exploration into Microsoft product activation.

The Automated System Recovery process is one that is not to be taken lightly. You should not consider using ASR until you have unsuccessfully tried to use other recovery methods, such as Driver Roll Back, System Restore, Parallel Installations, Last Known Good Configuration, Recovery Console, Safe Mode, or restoration using Windows XP Professional Backup. ASR restores only the system state and other critical files that were backed up at the time of its creation.

Tip

The frequency with which you make your ASR backups is critical to having a successful experience when using ASR for recovery. Make them regularly, at least weekly—more often if you make frequent changes to the computer.

The Automated System Recovery tool is accessed as a wizard within Windows Backup. From the Start menu, go to All Programs, Accessories, System Tools, and then click Backup. After the Backup program launches, click Advanced Mode, and then click the Automated System Recovery Wizard. The wizard prompts you to provide a floppy disk and removable media, which it uses to create an ASR floppy and ASR backup media set. The ASR media set can consist of backup tapes, recordable CDs or DVDs, or other IDE or SCSI hard disks. You cannot restore an ASR backup set from a network share.

Note

Although Windows XP Home includes Backup as an optional program that can be installed from the installation CD, XP Home's version of Backup does not include ASR.

The process to create an Automated System Recovery set is outlined here.

1. Start the Windows XP Backup utility by clicking Start, All Programs, Accessories, System Tools, Backup.

2. If the Wizard view appears, as shown in Figure 12.7, click Advanced Mode.

3. Click the Automated System Recovery Wizard button.

4. Click Next to dismiss the opening page of the ASR Wizard.

5. From the Backup Destination page, shown in Figure 12.8, configure the location where the backed up files are to be placed. For best results, a local storage location is preferred over a network location that may not be available later. After configuring your location, click Next to continue.

6. On the Completing the Automated System Recovery Preparation Wizard page, click Finish to initiate the ASR creation process.

7. When prompted, insert a blank 3-1/2 inch 1.44MB floppy disk in the A: drive of your computer. Click OK to create the floppy disk portion of the ASR set.

8. Label and store the floppy disk in a safe, secure location for future use.

Figure 12.7   The Windows XP Professional Backup utility in Wizard mode.

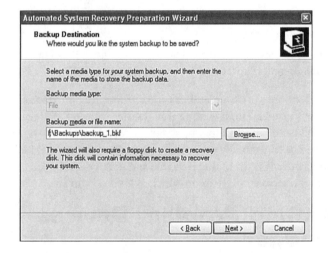

Figure 12.8   Configuring the backup destination.

Should the day come when you need to use ASR to recover your computer, proceed as outlined here:

1. Start your computer with the Windows XP Professional Setup CD-ROM.

2. When prompted to press a key to boot from the CD-ROM, do so. If your computer does not support booting from a CD-ROM, you will need to use Setup floppy disks to start the process.

3. When prompted to press F2 to start Automated System Recovery, as shown in Figure 12.9, do so. You will be prompted to supply your ASR floppy disk.

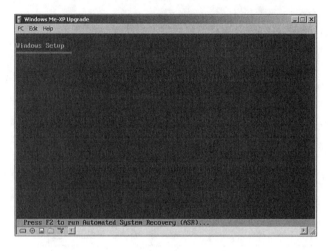

Figure 12.9   Starting ASR.

4. Provide the backup media set when prompted.

5. Specify a destination directory for the restore (generally C:\Windows).

6. ASR restores your data.

7. After ASR completes, restore other backups and reinstall programs to bring your system back to full operational status.

Because the ASR tool only backs up and restores the files that are necessary to restore the system state of a Windows installation, it is not a true disaster recovery strategy. It is also important to note that although using the ASR tool may repair a Windows installation to the point that you can start Windows, it can actually overwrite or destroy your personal files on the hard disk during the restore process. It is for that reason that the ASR tool is the last option you should consider when trying to recover a system on which Windows won't start.

Troubleshooting Problem Devices with Device Manager

The key to troubleshooting devices is interpreting the messages that Device Manager provides. Between the message the Device Manager provides, the event log, and the information displayed in the following sections, you should be able to narrow down the source of the problem. I can tell you that in almost all cases, it's the device driver's fault.

To use this section, open the problem device's properties page in Device Manager, and view the General tab. Look at the error message displayed under Device Status, locate it in the lists of error messages that follow in this section, and then follow the corresponding fix-it procedure.

Note

If the addition of a new hardware device has damaged Windows so badly that you can't get it to start up, go to the end of this chapter and follow the instructions under "System Restore."

Bad Driver or Incorrect Driver

Device Status says:

This device is not configured correctly. (Code 1)

The *bustype* device loader(s) for this device could not load the device driver. (Code 2)

The driver for this device might be corrupted, or your system may be running low on memory or other resources. (Code 3)

The driver for this device might be bad, or your system may be running low on memory or other resources. (Code 3)

This device is not working properly because one of its drivers may be bad, or your Registry may be bad. (Code 4)

The driver for this device requested a resource that Windows does not know how to handle. (Code 5)

The drivers for this device need to be reinstalled. (Code 7)

This device is not working properly because Windows cannot load the file *name* that loads the drivers for the device. (Code 8)

This device is not working properly because Windows cannot find the file *name* that loads the drivers for the device. (Code 8)

This device is not working properly because the file *name* that loads the drivers for this device is bad. (Code 8)

Device failure: Try changing the driver for this device. If that doesn't work, see your hardware documentation. (Code 8)

This device is not working properly because the BIOS in your computer is reporting the resources for the device incorrectly. (Code 9)

Windows stopped responding while attempting to start this device, and therefore will never attempt to start this device again. (Code 11)

The driver information file *name* is telling this child device to use a resource that the parent device does not have or recognize. (Code 17), where *<name>* is the .INF file for the device.

Reinstall the drivers for this device. (Code 18)

The drivers for this device need to be reinstalled. (Code 18)

Windows cannot start this hardware device because its configuration information (in the Registry) is incomplete or damaged. To fix this problem you can first try running a troubleshooting wizard. If that does not work, you should uninstall and then reinstall the hardware device. (Code 19)

Your Registry may be bad. (Code 19)

Windows could not load one of the drivers for this device. (Code 20)

This display adapter is not functioning correctly. (Code 23)

The loaders for this device cannot load the required drivers. (Code 23)

Windows can't specify the resources for this device. (Code 27)

The drivers for this device are not installed. (Code 28)

Windows cannot install the drivers for this device because it cannot access the drive or network location that has the setup files on it. (Code 32)

Windows cannot initialize the device driver for this hardware. (Code 37)

Windows cannot load the device driver for this hardware. The driver may be corrupted or missing. (Code 39)

Windows cannot access this hardware because its service key information in the Registry is missing or recorded incorrectly. (Code 40)

The software for this device has been blocked from starting because it is known to have problems with Windows. Contact the hardware vendor for a new driver. (Code 48)

Fix: Click on the device's Driver tab. Click the Driver Details button. If no driver has been installed click the Update Driver button. This will invoke the Hardware Update Driver Wizard and walk you through installing a driver for the device.

If this fails, close the dialog, right-click the device, and click Uninstall. You may need to install a driver manually using your manufacturer-supplied software. Usually this means executing a program (often called `setup.exe` or `install.exe`) that will install a driver on the computer. See "Forcing Detection and Reinstallation," earlier in this section.

Code 39 may also indicate a problem with your hard disk itself; you might use `CHKDSK` to perform a disk check before continuing.

Bad Bus Detection

Device Status says:

> Windows could not load the driver for this device because the computer is reporting two *bustype* bus types. (Code 2)

> Your computer's system firmware does not include enough information to properly configure and use this device. To use this device, contact your computer manufacturer to obtain a firmware or BIOS update. (Code 35)

Fix: Check with your computer or motherboard manufacturer for a BIOS update.

Resource Conflict

Device Status says:

> Another device is using the resources this device needs. (Code 6)

> This device cannot find enough free resources that it can use. If you want to use this device, you will need to disable one of the other devices on this system. (Code 12)

> This device is causing a resource conflict. (Code 15)

> Windows cannot identify all the resources this device uses. (Code 16)

> Windows could not identify all the resources this device uses. (Code 16)

> Windows cannot determine which resources are required for this device. (Code 33)

> This device is requesting a PCI interrupt but is configured for an ISA interrupt (or vice versa). Please use the computer's system setup program to reconfigure the interrupt for this device. (Code 36)

Fix: A resource (I/O port, interrupt, or DMA channel) conflict has occurred. It can also occur if a required resource was not allocated to the device, or if an incorrect device driver was selected.

Verify that the resources requested by the device are available using the Device Manager or System Information tool (`WinMSD.EXE` on XP, `msinfo32.exe` on 32-bit versions of Vista). If another device is using the requested resources, you can resolve the problem by disabling the conflicting device, reconfiguring either the conflicting device or the failed device using Device Manager, or reconfiguring the conflicting or failed device using your BIOS configuration program.

Verify that the BIOS is not disabling a required interrupt or DMA channel or not reserving a resource for a legacy device. Resource problems of this type usually fall into three categories:

- **USB devices**—Verify that interrupts have not been disabled for the USB controller in the BIOS.
- **PCI bus devices**—Verify that the requested interrupt or DMA channel has not been reserved for a specific legacy (ISA) device.
- **ISA bus devices**—Verify that the required interrupt or DMA channel has been reserved by the BIOS for the device.

If the steps under "Bad Driver or Incorrect Driver" do not resolve the problem, you may need to manually configure resources, disable the conflicting device, or remove it physically from the computer.

Failed Hardware, Missing Hardware, or Incorrect Driver

Device Status says:

> This device cannot start. (Code 10)
>
> This device is either not present, not working properly, or does not have all the drivers installed. (Code 10)
>
> This device is either not present, not working properly, or does not have all the drivers installed. (Code 13)
>
> This device is not present, is not working properly, or does not have all its drivers installed. (Code 24)
>
> This device is not working properly because Windows cannot load the drivers required for this device. (Code 31)
>
> This device is not working properly because <device> is not working properly. (Code 31)
>
> Windows successfully loaded the device driver for this hardware but cannot find the hardware device. (Code 41)
>
> Currently, this hardware device is not connected to the computer. (Code 45)

Fix: First, the peripheral may have failed or may not be installed correctly. To check for this possibility, remove the peripheral in question and physically reinstall it. If the peripheral is an internal peripheral on the PCI or ISA bus, clean the copper contacts using an eraser before reinstalling it. If the peripheral is connected via a cable, verify that all cable connections are clean, not damaged, and that the cables themselves are not routed by any device that may cause interference (power supply, monitor, speakers, and so on).

Second, the peripheral may have a resource conflict. Verify that the resources requested by the device are available. This can be accomplished using the Device Manager or System Information tool (WinMSD.EXE on XP, msinfo32.exe on 32-bit versions of Vista). If another device is using the requested resources you can resolve the problem by disabling the conflicting device, reconfiguring either the conflicting device or the failed device using Device Manager, or reconfiguring the conflicting or failed device using your BIOS configuration program.

Finally, the device driver may not be installed correctly, or the wrong device driver (such as one designed for a prior version of Windows) may be installed. To resolve the former, first uninstall the device driver and then reinstall it as described previously for Error Code 1.

Restart Required

Device Status says:

> This device cannot work properly until you restart your computer. (Code 14)
>
> Windows is in the process of setting up this device. (Code 26)
>
> Windows cannot gain access to this hardware device because the operating system is in the process of shutting down. (Code 46)

Fix: Restart Windows. If the problem persists after a restart, right-click the device, select Uninstall, and have Device Manager scan for new devices to reinstall it.

Device Driver Shutdown Problem

Device Status says:

> Windows is removing this device. (Code 21)
>
> Windows cannot load the device driver for this hardware because a previous instance of the device driver is still in memory. (Code 38)
>
> Windows cannot load the device driver for this hardware because there is a duplicate device already running in the system. (Code 42)

Fix: Wait for 15 seconds or so. If the device entry still appears, reboot the computer. If the problem persists, uninstall and reinstall the device driver as discussed in previous entries.

Disabled Device

Device Status says:

> This device is disabled. (Code 22)
>
> This device is not started. (Code 22)

Fix: Right-click the device in question and choose Enable from the pop-up menu.

Incomplete Windows Setup

Device Status says:

> Windows is in the process of setting up this device. (Code 25)

Fix: Thiserror message usually occurs during the initial setup of Windows during the first or second reboots. It usually indicates an incomplete file copy. Restart the computer. If that fails to resolve the situation, reinstall Windows.

Device Disabled by BIOS

Device Status says:

> This device is disabled because the firmware of the device did not give it the required resources. (Code 29)

> This device is disabled because the BIOS of the device did not give it the required resources. (Code 29)

Fix: Refer to the onscreen message provided by the peripheral's BIOS during startup (for example, Adaptec SCSI controllers may display a message instructing you to press Ctrl+A to access its BIOS setup), or refer to the peripheral documentation to enable the device.

Disabled Service

Device Status says:

> A driver (service) for this device has been disabled. An alternate driver may be providing this functionality. (Code 32)

Fix: If the driver is actually a service, you can edit the startup value in the Registry by using the Service MMC snap-in to resolve the problem. For a device, you can either uninstall and then reinstall the driver as described for Error Code 18, or edit the Registry directly and change the start type.

Manual Device Configuration Required

Device Status says:

> Windows cannot determine the settings for this device. Consult the documentation that came with this device and use the Resource tab to set the configuration. (Code 34)

Fix: Manually allocate the resources for this device.

Device Reported Problems

Device Status says:

> Windows has stopped this device because it has reported problems. (Code 43)

> An application or service has shut down this hardware device. (Code 44)

Fix: Restart the computer. Errors of this nature should be logged in the System or Application event log. If the error continues, review the event log to determine the cause of the error. If that doesn't help, request help from the manufacturer or try to get an updated driver.

Device Prepared for Removal

Device Status says:

> Windows cannot use this hardware device because it has been prepared for "safe removal," but it has not been removed from the computer. (Code 47)

Fix: Remove and reinsert the peripheral, or restart the computer.

Registry Size Limit Exceeded

Device Status says:

> Windows cannot start new hardware devices because the system hive is too large (exceeds the Registry Size Limit). (Code 49)

Fix: Your best bet is to add more memory (RAM) to your computer.

Parallel Windows Installation

As I mentioned earlier in this chapter, there are times when you may want to give up on a malfunctioning Windows installation, and rebuild the machine from scratch. However, if the hard disk contains valuable data that you want to back up before you rebuild the machine, you won't want to remove the existing partitions and reformat the hard disk. In this instance, you should consider doing a parallel Windows installation.

A parallel Windows installation is sometimes the only way to recover data from a machine that you can't repair through Last Known Good Configuration, Safe mode, or Recovery Console. The goal of performing a parallel Windows installation isn't to repair a system, but it does provide a way for you to access your crucial data and back it up before rebuilding the system from scratch.

To do a parallel Windows installation, reboot the computer with the Windows XP or Vista installation disc in the CD or DVD drive. Boot the machine from the CD or DVD, and begin the Windows Setup installation process. If there is more than one usable partition on the hard disk, Windows Setup will show you a list of the existing partitions. You can use the same partition that the current Windows installation resides on, or choose a different partition. When Windows Setup presents you with formatting options, you should choose Leave the Current File System Intact (No Changes). This will prevent your existing data from being lost during the installation process. For more information on the Windows installation process, see Chapter 3, "Installing Windows."

After Windows Setup is complete, boot the computer into the new installation of Windows. You should then be able to access the contents of the hard drive and back up the desired data before formatting and rebuilding the machine.

Caution

Do *not* perform a repair installation to the same partition as the existing Windows installation if you are attempting to retrieve data that has been deleted or been lost through disk corruption or repartitioning. If disk sectors containing data are marked as available, they may be overwritten by a parallel installation, or indeed by *any* files being written to the disk.

To retrieve deleted or corrupted files, use a file retrieval program designed to scan the disk directly, such as Ontrack Easy Recovery Data Recovery, and specify a different drive than the Windows system drive as the location to store retrieved files.

The Blue Screen of Death: Interpreting STOP Error Messages

At the beginning of this chapter, we split Windows problems into three primary classifications. You've looked at how to solve problems encountered during Windows installation, and problems related to Windows startup; let's turn our attention to dealing with problems that occur when Windows is already up and running.

Although there are a number of different errors that can occur after Windows XP or Vista has started up, the most damaging and frustrating is the dreaded STOP error, or Blue Screen of Death (BSOD), which is the first symptom listed in Table 12.1 earlier in this chapter.

Note

The specific shade of blue in the BSOD is the subject of some debate. I have one friend who insists that it is a shade of *periwinkle*. Far be it from me to cast aspersions on her color sense, but we'll just leave it at basic blue for the purposes of brevity.

The appearance of a STOP error screen is always an unwelcome sight (see Figure 12.10). It indicates that the operating system encountered something so catastrophic or destabilizing that it was unable to continue running. As noted earlier, a STOP error screen can appear during Windows installation, during Windows startup, while you are in the Windows GUI, or even during Windows shutdown. Given that it is one of the more common symptoms of a Windows problem, it is important to know more about what information a STOP error screen contains, and how to interpret it.

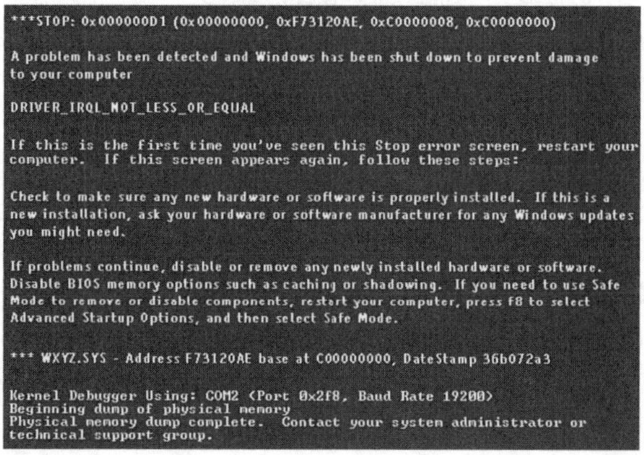

Figure 12.10   A Blue Screen of Death.

Let's go through the content of the BSOD shown here, and see what information you can glean from it.

The top line of the screen contains what Microsoft refers to as *bugcheck information*. This includes a hexadecimal code for the STOP error, followed by a number of error parameters. The parameters (which appear in parentheses) are also written in hexadecimal.

This line is followed by a friendly message informing you, in case you hadn't noticed, that Windows has been shut down. Under this message is additional bugcheck information in the form of a *symbolic name*. The symbolic name is often what you will use to look up more information on the error, including possible solutions.

Under the symbolic name is a suggested course of action for you to take. Microsoft refers to this information as the *recommended user action*. Depending on the nature of the STOP error, the recommended user action can sometimes actually be useful. However, it is fairly generic information, and you will often need to do more investigation in order to isolate the cause of the problem.

After the recommended user action, you will find (if applicable) the name of the driver or program that's associated with the STOP error. This information can be very valuable when trying to determine the source of the error, although in some cases it could be a red herring.

Finally, the last section of the STOP error screen shows information pertaining to debugging tools and memory dump files. If you have a computer running a kernel debugger hooked up to the malfunctioning system via a COM port, this information will be noted in the last section of the error screen. Also, if Windows was configured to create a memory dump file in the event of a system crash (an option that's configured using the Advanced tab in the System applet in Control Panel), the success or failure of this action will be reported here.

Tip

There is a very important setting that affects the behavior of STOP errors that's configured through the System applet in Windows XP's Control Panel. On the Advanced tab, click the Settings button in the Startup and Recovery section. On the Startup and Recovery dialog, in the section labeled System Failure, you will see an option that reads Automatically Restart. If this check box is filled, the system will display the STOP error screen only for as long as it takes to write the memory dump file, after which it will automatically restart the computer. If you want STOP error screens to stay in place until you manually restart the system (this is almost always the case), you should clear the check box for this option.

To access the Advanced tab in Windows Vista, open the System and Maintenance category in Control Panel and click Advanced System Settings in the task pane.

Make a Record of STOP Errors

When a STOP error screen appears, before you do anything—before you touch a single key on the keyboard or button on the front of the PC—grab a piece of paper and a pen and write down the contents of the STOP error screen in its entirety.

This cannot be stressed enough: If you fail to write down the information from the STOP error screen before rebooting, you may lose a valuable clue that indicates the source of the problem. Don't be in a hurry to press the Reset button; take the time to start documenting the problem so that you have all the information available at your disposal. If you have a digital camera that can take close-up pictures, use it to capture the STOP screen. (Windows screen capture cannot be used to capture a STOP screen.)

Common STOP Errors

As is often the case with computer-related issues, there are certain problems that are more common to Windows XP or Vista than others. This means that there are certain messages that appear on STOP error screens with greater frequency than others.

In this section, you will find a list of the most common STOP error messages (and their probable causes) that appear in the event of a system crash. Each STOP error is listed with its bugcheck information and symbolic name, one or more associated explanations for the STOP error, and a number of possible resolutions.

STOP: 0x0000000A

IRQL_NOT_LESS_OR_EQUAL

This STOP error message is often caused by a flawed device driver or system firmware. If the device driver is listed in the STOP error message, try disabling it or rolling back to the previous version.

If this STOP error occurs while you are doing an upgrade installation of Windows XP or Vista, you should do a compatibility check of the system by using the Windows XP Upgrade Advisor or Windows Vista Upgrade Advisor. This error can also occur if there is antivirus or antispyware software running on the system you are trying to upgrade. Be sure to shut down any instances of these types of software before upgrading a previous version of Windows.

STOP: 0x0000001E

KMODE_EXCEPTION_NOT_HANDLED

This STOP error is related to unknown or illegal processor instructions. This error can be caused by a flawed device driver, or by memory or IRQ conflicts. If a driver is mentioned in the error message, disable it or roll back to a previous version.

This particular error can also be caused by a third-party "remote control" software program. This is usually indicated by the mention of the file WIN32K.SYS. If this is the case, try to disable the software in question by restarting Windows in Safe mode.

STOP: 0x00000024

NTFS_FILE_SYSTEM

This message indicates a problem with the NTFS.SYS driver file that is responsible for reading and writing to NTFS file systems. Possible causes for this error are malfunctioning SCSI and/or ATA hard drives or the drivers for such devices.

Another possible cause of this error is if you are using certain utilities that access the hard drive in a specific manner, and if these utilities are incompatible with Windows XP or Windows Vista. Examples of such programs include antivirus, antispyware, backup, and disk-defragmenting software. Check the compatibility of any such programs by looking them up online in the Windows Catalog on the Microsoft website.

STOP: 0x0000002E

DATA_BUS_ERROR

This STOP error message is related to problems with system memory. Types of memory that can cause this error include RAM modules, the Level 2 cache on the CPU, and video memory on a display adapter. Use a third-party utility to test the system RAM, processor, and display adapter memory. Earlier, I mentioned the Windows Memory Diagnostic from Microsoft, which you can use to check system RAM. Another great hardware diagnostic utility is Sandra (**S**ystem **AN**alyser, **D**iagnostic, and **R**eporting **A**ssistant) from SiSoftware. You can download the free Sandra Lite version of this tool at http://www.sisoftware.net/.

This error can also indicate that there is a damaged or defective component on the systemboard. If all the memory checks out as okay, visually inspect the systemboard for any cracks, scratches, or burn marks.

STOP: 0x0000003F

NO_MORE_SYSTEM_PTES

This error message is related to Page Table Entries (PTEs). Specifically, it indicates that the system's PTEs are either depleted or damaged. This can be caused by a flawed device driver, or by an application that is allocating too much kernel memory.

If a device driver is listed, try disabling it, rolling it back to a previous version, or replacing it with a newer version. Other possible suspects include recently installed backup programs, multimedia applications, antivirus software, and CD mastering utilities.

STOP: 0x00000050

PAGE_FAULT_IN_NONPAGED_AREA

Faulty memory, including RAM, processor L2 cache, and video card RAM, are often the culprits behind this STOP error. Test your memory if possible, or if you suspect that a recently installed piece of hardware is the issue, try removing it and see if that solves the problem.

STOP: 0x00000077

KERNEL_STACK_INPAGE_ERROR

This error is caused when Windows kernel data that's located in the virtual memory page file cannot be found. Possible causes include defective memory modules, bad sectors within the page file on the hard drive, or a disk controller error.

More information on this error can be found in the first parameter that appears in parentheses at the top of the STOP error message. Possible entries include

0xC000009A	Lack of nonpaged pool resources.
0xC000009C	Bad sectors in the page file (hard drive).
0xC000009D	Damaged power or data cables or connections; faulty SCSI termination; problem with hard drive or hard drive controller.

0xC000016A   Bad sectors in the page file (hard drive).

0xC0000185   This code can mean a number of things, including a defective hard drive controller, faulty SCSI termination, damaged cables or loose connections, or it may indicate that two devices attempted to use the same system resources.

STOP: 0x00000079

MISMATCHED_HAL

This STOP error is displayed when the system tries to use out-of-date versions of the NTOSKRNL.EXE or HAL.DLL files. (HAL stands for *Hardware Abstraction Layer.*) This error can occur after you have made repairs using Recovery Console.

There are two versions of the NTOSKRNL.EXE and HAL.DLL files on the Windows XP installation CD; one version is for single-processor systems, the other is for multiprocessor systems. If you copy the wrong version of either of these files to your system, the MISMATCHED_HAL STOP error will occur.

The multi-processor versions of these files are NTKRNLMP.EXE and HALMPS.DLL.

STOP: 0x0000007A

KERNEL_DATA_INPAGE_ERROR

This STOP error is extremely similar to the KERNEL_STACK_INPAGE_ERROR message listed previously in this section. It relates to Windows kernel data that is supposed to be in the page file, but cannot be found or written into memory. Treat this error the same as a KERNEL_STACK_INPAGE_ERROR message.

STOP: 0x0000007B

INACCESSIBLE_BOOT_DEVICE

This error is specific to Windows startup. It indicates that Windows was unable to initialize the file system. This could be caused by a hard drive failure, a damaged hard drive controller, or incorrect settings in the BOOT.INI startup file.

If all the hardware is functioning normally, it is still possible that the startup files have become corrupted, or that the Master Boot Record has become damaged. Follow the instructions in the "Using Recovery Console" section of this chapter to restore these files.

STOP: 0x0000007F

UNEXPECTED_KERNEL_MODE_TRAP

The most common cause of this STOP error is defective memory such as RAM modules, L2 processor cache, or video card memory. It can also be caused by an overheating system; make sure that all cooling fans, particularly CPU heatsink fans, are working properly.

STOP: 0x0000009F

DRIVER_POWER_STATE_FAILURE

This error is based on power-related activities such as shutting down the system, or suspending/resuming from standby or hibernation mode. Check the driver that's named in the error message, and try replacing it or rolling back to a previous version.

STOP: 0xBE

ATTEMPTED_WRITE_TO_READONLY_MEMORY

This is another "bad driver" error. It occurs when a software driver attempts to write to a section of read-only memory. Replace, roll back, or delete.

STOP: 0xC2

BAD_POOL_CALLER

No, this error has nothing to do with a snarky lifeguard. It has everything to do with a flawed piece of software or device driver trying to do memory operations in ways that it's not supposed to. If it is a software program causing the error, remove it. If it is a device driver, replace, roll back, or delete.

Stop: 0x000000CE

DRIVER_UNLOADED_WITHOUT_CANCELLING_PENDING_OPERATIONS

Another issue related to a misbehaving driver. In this instance, a driver exited without canceling pending operations. Replace, roll back, or delete.

STOP: 0x000000D1

DRIVER_IRQL_NOT_LESS_OR_EQUAL

This error is commonly caused by a flawed driver trying to access pageable memory using an improper IRQL. Replace, roll back, or delete.

STOP: 0x000000D8

DRIVER_USED_EXCESSIVE_PTES

This error is essentially identical to the NO_MORE_SYSTEM_PTES error listed earlier in this section. Follow the same steps that were given for that STOP error message.

STOP: 0x000000EA

THREAD_STUCK_IN_DEVICE_DRIVER

Driver trouble again...although this error is almost always linked specifically to the video card display driver. Check with the manufacturer for a driver compatible with your version of Windows.

STOP: 0x000000ED

UNMOUNTABLE_BOOT_VOLUME

This STOP error occurs when the input/output subsystem fails to mount the boot volume. This can be due to a damaged file system, but in certain instances can also be caused by a conflict between the disk controller and the hard drive cable.

If the system uses an Ultra Direct Memory Access (UDMA) PATA (ATA/IDE) controller, and the hard drive is plugged in with a standard 40-wire cable rather than the necessary 80-wire UDMA cable, the end result can be the 0x000000ED UNMOUNTABLE_BOOT_VOLUME STOP error.

However, if the first parameter to appear in parentheses at the top of the STOP error is 0xC0000032, the problem is being caused by a damaged file system. Try using the CHKDSK /R command from Recovery Console; if this doesn't solve the problem, try using the FIXBOOT command. (You will take a closer look at the CHKDSK tool later in this chapter.)

STOP: 0x000000F2

HARDWARE_INTERRUPT_STORM

This error is related to interrupt requests (IRQs); specifically, this error occurs when a hardware device fails to comply with an interrupt release signal sent by a device driver. It can also occur if a flawed device driver doesn't send an interrupt release signal to a device, or if the flawed driver claims an IRQ that's assigned to a different device.

The HARDWARE_INTERRUPT_STORM error most commonly occurs just after installing a new piece of hardware. Remove the new device, and see if that solves the problem. If it does, check and see if the device appears in the Windows Catalog as a compatible device. You can also look at the manufacturer's website to see if it has any information concerning Windows XP compatibility issues, or if there are newer drivers available for the device.

STOP: 0xC000021A

STATUS_SYSTEM_PROCESS_TERMINATED

This STOP error is usually caused by a recently installed device driver or software program. If the STOP error lists a driver or program file, try removing the driver or program in order to solve the issue.

This error can also be caused by restoring system data from a backup set, but the backup program doesn't restore certain files that it believes are currently in use on the system. This can be avoided by ensuring that your backup software is compatible with Windows XP.

STOP: 0xC0000221

STATUS_IMAGE_CHECKSUM_MISMATCH

This error message is usually attributable to a damaged system file or device driver. The name of the file causing the error will usually appear as part of the STOP message. Try using Safe mode or Recovery Console to replace the file with a new copy from the Windows XP installation CD.

Windows XP and Windows Vista Troubleshooting Tools

Not every problem encountered within Windows XP or Windows Vista will bring the entire system to a crashing halt. There are a number of minor problems that can occur that range from the inability to use a peripheral device such as a printer or a gamepad, to a software program that is unable to run without crashing, to a malfunctioning system device such as a modem or an audio card.

Windows XP and Windows Vista include a number of built-in tools and resources for troubleshooting minor errors that occur within the operating system. Some of these troubleshooting tools and resources are

- The Windows Event Log, for Windows XP and Vista
- Dr. Watson (debugging program), for Windows XP
- Windows Troubleshooters, for Windows XP
- CHKDSK (also referred to as CheckDisk), for Windows XP and Windows Vista
- DirectX Diagnostic Tool, for Windows XP and Windows Vista
- Program Compatibility Wizard, for Windows XP and Windows Vista
- System Configuration Utility, for Windows XP and Windows Vista

Troubleshooting tools exclusive to Windows Vista are discussed in "Windows Vista Troubleshooting Tools," p. 780.

Reading the Event Log

The Windows Event log is a sort of collective blog written by Windows, its services, and applications as they go about their business, and it records errors, warnings, and observations that aren't necessarily displayed on the desktop or in message boxes. To read these messages, open the Event Viewer by right-clicking [My] Computer, select Manage, and then select Event Viewer in the left pane. Alternatively, type **eventvwr.msc** at the command prompt or in Vista's start menu Search box. With Windows Vista, you must provide Administrator-level credentials to run Event Viewer unless User Account Control has been disabled.

Tip

It's a good idea to check the event logs for Warning and Error events every week or two, even if you're not noticing any problems. For example, read or write errors reported by the disk system may warn you of an impending hard disk failure well before the disk fails entirely. And if you've been having problems with networking, software crashes, or driver malfunctions, start your troubleshooting by scanning through the System and Application logs, again looking primarily at Warning and Error messages.

The Event Viewer displays at least three different log sections:

- **Application log**—Contains events logged by applications or programs running on the computer. For example, a program might record a file error in the application log. Each program's developer decides which, if any, events to record.

- **Security log**—Records security events such as valid and invalid logon attempts as well as audit events related to resource use such as creating, opening, or deleting files. The administrator can specify which events will be recorded in the Security log by enabling specific logging actions.

- **System log**— Contains events logged by Windows system components. For example, the failure of a driver or other system component to load during startup is recorded in the System log.

On Windows Vista, there are dozens of additional log sections. The three primary logs just mentioned are displayed in the Windows Logs folder, along with two other log categories:

- **Setup**—Records events related to software installation, updates, and Windows updates, performed by the Windows Installer service.

- **Forwarded Events**—Records events received from other computers through the Subscriptions system, through which you can instruct Windows to monitor other computers for specific events or categories of events.

In the Applications and Services Logs folder, there are several more major sections:

- **DFS Replication**—Monitors files that are downloaded or uploaded from domain servers through the Distributed File System mechanism.

- **Hardware Events**—Records events related to hardware management, malfunctions and diagnostics.

- **Internet Explorer**

- **Key Management Service**

- **Media Center**—Records events related to Windows Media Center (present only if Media Center is included in your version of Vista).

- **Microsoft**—This is a folder containing quite a number of subfolders (54, on one of my computers running Vista Ultimate) for a wide range of Windows services and applications such as Backup, Bits-Client (the Windows Update downloading service), DiskDiagnostic, OfflineFiles and so on. Each of these files in turn has one or more logs, named, variously: Operational, Admin, Analytic, Verbose, Debug and Diagnostic. (To see the Analytic and Debug logs, right-click in the left pane, select View, Show Analytic and Debug Logs.)

Other logs may be created if you install optional Windows components (such as Windows PowerShell) or third-party applications.

In addition, there are folders for custom views, which are filtered collections of events from other logs, and subscriptions, which are lists of computer names and events that you want your computer to collect from other systems on your network.

All users of a computer can view the Application and System logs, but only Administrators can view the Security log. Log entries are categorized into one of five event types, which are listed in Table 12.3.

Table 12.3   Windows Event Types

Event Type	Description
Error	Indicates that a serious problem has occurred, such as a loss of data or degradation in usability or reliability. A service that fails to load or a domain controller that is unavailable for contact will cause an Error event. More often than not, you will receive an onscreen warning concerning the Error event.
Warning	Indicates that a less serious event has occurred that should not normally have an immediate adverse effect on the computer. Low disk space or failure to contact a time server to update the clock might cause a Warning event.
Information	Indicates the successful completion of a task or the successful operation of an application, device, or service. Many occurrences will create an Information event, such as the starting of a network service or the loading and configuring of a driver.
Success Audit	Indicates that an action that was configured for success auditing was attempted and was successful. Auditing can monitor access to files or folders, logging on to the network, use of privileges, and so on.
Failure Audit	Indicates that an action that was configured for failure auditing was attempted and was unsuccessful. Failure audit events can be used to identify users who are attempting to gain access to files or privileges for which they are not authorized.

So, how do you use the Event log for troubleshooting purposes? On XP, the Application and System logs provides you with information about most software and hardware problems. On Vista, in addition, the Administrative Events section under Custom Views can provide additional troubleshooting clues. The Security log records attempts by software or users to perform restricted actions, so the Security log can alert you to attempts by others to hack your computer. It can also tell you exactly what files or folders a program or service is having trouble accessing, if you're finding that a user or program is being prevented from doing something it should be able to do.

You can easily scan through these logs for events that might shed light on a problem you're investigating, or events that may predict an upcoming problem. On Vista, the entry's details will appear in the preview pane. On XP, double-click an entry to view detailed information.

Some of other possible activities include the following:

- To save a log file for archival purposes, select Save Log File As. You will need to select from three file types: .EVT, .TXT, or .CSV. If you plan on opening the log later in the Event Viewer, you should save it in .EVT format. If you save a log in .TXT (plain text) or .CSV (comma-delimited) format, you can import the data into a spreadsheet or database for further processing.

- To open a saved log file, select Open Log File. This comes in handy if you've saved and cleared out Event logs.

- Click New Log View (Windows XP) to create a copy of the selected log, allowing you to create a custom view of it without changing the view of the original.

- Click Create Custom View (Windows Vista) to create a customized view you can save for reuse. This feature enables you to view the log in its normal mode or a customized mode.

- After you've archived a log, you can Clear All Events in the log to start with a clean slate again.

- Export List is a nice feature that allows you export a log file to a text file for easy transport and viewing in any text editor.

You can configure maximum log size and specify event retention polices by right-clicking a log name in the left pane and selecting Properties. Figure 12.11 shows the General tab, from which you can configure most of the basic options for a log.

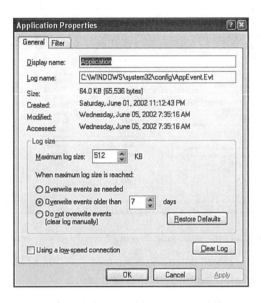

Figure 12.11 You can configure log sizes and event retention limits.

Caution

A common hacker trick is to do something improper, and then flood the log with innocuous entries to flush out any record of their misdeeds. On important servers, then, it's a common security practice to disable automatic overwriting of the security log. However, if you disable the overwriting of old events and your log grows to the maximum configured size, the logging of new events will not occur. Always pay careful attention to your logs when you have selected to manually clear log entries.

Security Logging and Auditing

By default, security logging is turned off and must be enabled through Local Security Policy, or on a domain network, Group Policy. Security logging can record attempts to log on with incorrect passwords.

The Administrator can also set auditing policies to enable logging of auditing events, which can help you determine whether an application or service is failing because it cannot gain access to needed files, or which can help you watch for attempts by people to access things they shouldn't. Files and folders to be so monitored must be stored on NTFS-formatted disks, and must be marked separately for auditing using their Advanced Security Properties dialogs. In addition, Simple File Sharing must be turned off. Auditing is not available on Windows XP Home Edition.

To enable Security logging, log on as a Computer Administrator, open the Administrative Tools menu from the Start menu or Control Panel, and select Local Security Policy. Alternatively, at the command prompt, type the command **gpedit.msc**. View Local Policies, Audit Policy, as shown in Figure 12.12.

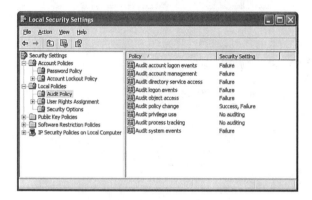

Figure 12.12   Enable Security and Audit logging from the Local Security Policy editor.

To have the Security log record failed logon attempts, set Audit Logon Events to Failure. To record all logons, set Audit Logon Events to Success, Failure.

To permit the recording of file and folder audit activity, set Audit Object Access to Failure, or Success, Failure. Then, modify the Security permissions of the files and/or folders you want to monitor. To do this, follow these steps:

1. Use Windows Explorer to locate and right-click the file or folder you want to audit. Select Properties.

2. Select the Security tab. (If it does not appear, either the file is on a FAT-formatted disk or Simple File Sharing has not been disabled.)

3. Click the Advanced button and select the Auditing tab. (If Auditing does not appear, you are not logged on as a Computer Administrator.) Click Add.

4. You may select specific users and groups to be monitored. Enter a username, group name, or Everyone to monitor all access.

5. Select the type of activity you want to monitor (see Figure 12.13), and click the check box in the Successful and/or Failed column. Only the selected activities and results will be considered for logging in the Event log, and then, only the result types for Object Access set earlier in the policy editor will actually be recorded.

6. Save the changes by clicking OK.

When you have enabled auditing for debugging purposes, it's best to disable it immediately after solving the problem to avoid having the Security log grow unnecessarily large.

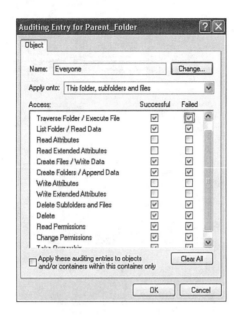

Figure 12.13   Select access types and results for auditing.

Dr. Watson

Dr. Watson is a software-debugging program used in Windows XP that, in the event of an application crash, writes debugging information to a log file that can be used by a programmer or software technical support expert to troubleshoot the application. To view the Dr. Watson setup dialog box from the Start menu, select Run, type **DRWTSN32**, and press Enter (see Figure 12.14).

You can configure a number of options in the Dr. Watson dialog box. The changes that you make using this interface are saved in the Windows Registry key HKEY_LOCAL_MACHINE\SOFTWARE\Microsoft\DrWatson.

The first time you open the Dr. Watson dialog box, the program automatically creates a folder that it uses to store any log files it creates. By default, the path to this folder is Documents and Settings\All Users\Application Data\Microsoft\Dr Watson. You can select a different location for this folder by using the Log File Path setting at the top of the Dr. Watson dialog box.

In addition to the log files, Dr. Watson is capable of creating a binary dump file that a programmer can load into a software debugger program to troubleshoot the error. Activate this option by checking the Create Crash Dump File check box in the Options section of the Dr. Watson dialog box. As with the log files, you can indicate a different default path for the crash dump file by entering it into the Crash Dump line near the top of the Dr. Watson screen.

The Number of Instructions entry tells Dr. Watson how many instructions it should disassemble before and after the program counter for each thread state dump. (A *program counter* is a register that holds the memory location for a thread's point of execution.) The Number of Errors to Save entry sets a limit on the number of errors Dr. Watson will save in a log file.

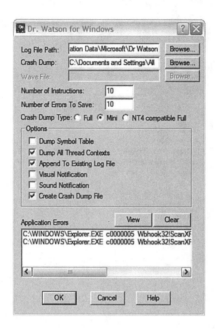

Figure 12.14 Use the Dr. Watson dialog box to configure how debugging data is generated.

In the Options section of the Dr. Watson dialog box, you can check or uncheck six variables to switch them on or off. Dump Symbol Table configures Dr. Watson to include the symbol table for each software module. Activating this option can cause your dump files to become very large. Activating Dump All Thread Contexts causes Dr. Watson to log a state dump for every thread in the program that is crashing. If this option is left unchecked, Dr. Watson creates a state dump for only the thread that is causing the error in the program. The Append to Existing Log File option decides whether Dr. Watson should add error data to the end of the existing DRWTSN32.LOG file, or create a new log file for each program error. If you check this option, you should monitor the size of the DRWTSN32.LOG file, as it can grow to a cumbersome size. You can check the Visual Notification and Sound Notification options if you want to receive visual or audible cues when Dr. Watson detects a program error. Finally, there is the Create Crash Dump File option that I mentioned earlier in this section.

Unless you are a software programmer, the log and dump files created by Dr. Watson will be of limited personal use. However, these files can be sent to a Microsoft support specialist or to the creator of the software that is experiencing errors. Usually, a programmer uses the information in these files to determine the exact point in the program's lines of code where the error is taking place, and to examine the specific variables in the code that might be responsible for causing the problem.

Windows Vista replaces Dr. Watson with the Problem Reports and Solutions tool, which is found in the System and Maintenance portion of Control Panel.

Windows Troubleshooters

Windows Troubleshooters are mini-programs that are used to troubleshoot a minor problem with normal Windows XP operations. The Windows Troubleshooters are similar in design and function to expert systems. An *expert system* is a software program that contains knowledge gathered from one or more human experts. When the program is run, it asks a series of questions to collect information from the user, and then uses this information in concert with its internal knowledge to diagnose a problem or analyze a given situation. An expert system possesses an internal logic structure that enables it to follow a deductive process, much as a person would when troubleshooting a Windows problem.

Windows XP offers to open a Windows Troubleshooter when you encounter certain specific problems. However, you can always access the full list of Troubleshooters by selecting the Help and Support option from the Start menu.

In the Help and Support Center, type `List of Troubleshooters` into the Search box located in the top-left corner of the screen and press Enter. In the Search Results box, click on the List of Troubleshooters link that appears.

Table 12.4 lists all the Windows Troubleshooters and what each one should be used for.

Table 12.4   Windows Troubleshooters

Windows Troubleshooter Name	Subject Area Covered
Digital Video Discs (DVDs)	DVD-ROM drives and decoders
Display	Display adapters, monitors, and drivers
Drives and Network Adapters	Hard drives, floppy drives, CD and DVD drives, network adapters, tape drives
File and Print Sharing	Workgroups and networks, sharing files and print devices, logon issues
Hardware	Covers a wide variety of hardware, including input devices, USB devices, modems, audio cards, and so on
Home Networking	Home network setup, file and print sharing, Internet connections
Input Devices	Mice, keyboards, trackballs, cameras, and scanners
Internet Connection Sharing (ICS)	Sharing an Internet connection between two or more computers
Internet Explorer	Using Internet Explorer as your web browser
Modem	Internal and external modem connections and operation
Multimedia and Games	Games, multimedia programs, DirectX, audio, and controllers
Outlook Express	Using Outlook Express as your email client
Printing	Installing and operating print devices
Sound	Audio and audio adapters
Startup/Shutdown	Starting and shutting down a system, standby mode, and hibernation mode
System Setup	Installing and configuring Windows
USB	All USB hubs and peripherals

Note

There is a fair amount of crossover between the various Windows Troubleshooters in terms of what subject area each Troubleshooter covers. You should always try to use the Troubleshooter that is most specific for the problem you are working on. For example, if you are dealing with a malfunctioning modem, you should choose the Modem Troubleshooter over the Hardware Troubleshooter because the first troubleshooter is more relevant to the issue.

With certain Windows Troubleshooters, you may be asked to restart the computer or to exit out of the Troubleshooter before completing a step. It is therefore recommended that you manually track your progress through the Troubleshooter on a piece of paper, making a note of the questions asked and your responses to each question. By doing this, you can restart the Troubleshooter after closing it and get back to where you were.

CHKDSK

CHKDSK is a tool you can use to check the integrity of a Windows XP or Windows Vista file system, and possibly repair any errors that the tool finds. CHKDSK can be used as a command-line tool, or is available through the Windows GUI (although the GUI version doesn't include all the functionality of the command-line version).

There are a number of switches you can use to determine how CHKDSK will function. If you just type **CHKDSK** at the command prompt and press Enter without any switches, the program will run as a read-only diagnostic. It will report any errors it finds, but it will not attempt to repair them.

Here is a list of the switches you can use with CHKDSK for Windows XP and Vista:

/f   CHKDSK attempts to fix any errors that it finds.

/v   On a FAT or FAT32 file system volume, CHKDSK will display the name and full path of every file on the disk. On an NTFS volume, this switch displays relevant information on any actions CHKDSK performs.

/r   CHKDSK attempts to locate bad sectors and recover any readable data from them.

/x   Attempts to dismount the volume you want CHKDSK to scan. This switch will not work on the boot volume (the volume that contains the Windows operating files).

/i   Forces CHKDSK to use a less complex scan of index entries, which reduces the amount of time CHKDSK takes to run. This switch is relevant for NTFS volumes only.

/c   Similar to the /i switch; it forces CHKDSK to skip over verifying the cycles in the folder structure of the volume being scanned, which reduces the amount of time CHKDSK takes to run.

Windows Vista's version of CHKDSK adds the following switches:

/l:size   Changes the log file size to the specified number of Kilobytes (KB); if size is not specified, shows current value. For NTFS volumes only.

/b   Reevaluates bad clusters (allocation units) on the volume (use with the /r switch).

Before you use CHKDSK to try to correct a problem with a Windows file system volume, you should make an attempt to back up the data on the volume. Also, if the volume you are scanning is fairly large and contains a lot of data, you may want to have a cup of coffee and a magazine handy; CHKDSK can take a very long time to complete when dealing with large volumes. Using the /i and /c switches can help to reduce the time it takes for CHKDSK to complete its scan of NTFS-based volumes.

There is a version of CHKDSK you can run from within the Windows GUI. Double-click My Computer or select it from the Start Menu, and right-click on the volume you want to scan. Click Properties, select the Tools tab, and click Check Now (see Figure 12.15).

Figure 12.15 Running the GUI version of CHKDSK while Windows is running.

From here, you can select three options:

- Run CHKDSK in read-only mode (finds errors but doesn't repair them) by clicking Start.
- Run CHKDSK with the Automatically Fix File System Errors check box selected. This is the equivalent of running CHKDSK with the /f switch.
- Run CHKDSK with the Scan For And Attempt Recovery Of Bad Sectors check box selected. This is the equivalent of running CHKDSK with the /r switch.

◀◀ For more information on CHKDSK and other disk utilities, **see** "File System Utilities," **p. 672**.

DirectX Diagnostic Tool (*DXDIAG.EXE*)

DirectX is a suite of multimedia-related application programming interfaces (APIs) built into the Windows operating system. Microsoft first created DirectX for the release of Windows 95. DirectX provides software developers with a standardized platform for multimedia application development, which enables them to create software that can access specialized hardware features, without having to write hardware-specific code. DirectX provides improved communication between software and hardware devices, and interacts with practically everything on a Windows PC that involves video, audio, and input devices. As of this writing, the most current version of DirectX for Windows XP is 9.0c, which was released in August 2004. DirectX 9.0c is compatible with Windows 9x/Me/2000/XP. DirectX 10 is included as part of Windows Vista, and is compatible only with Windows Vista. Windows Vista SP1 updates DirectX 10 to DirectX 10.1, adding improved 3D rendering options.

Both versions of Windows include a diagnostic tool that you can use to troubleshoot issues related to DirectX. The DirectX Diagnostic Tool tells you which version of DirectX is installed on your system. It also displays information regarding the various DirectX-related drivers, and the version supplied with DirectX 9.0c provides a series of user-initiated diagnostic tests you can use to determine if DirectX and the hardware devices it interacts with are functioning normally. This can be a valuable tool for troubleshooting Windows problems related to audio and video problems, and input devices such as gamepads.

The DirectX Diagnostic Tool does not appear in the Start menu. To launch it, go to the Start menu, select Run, and type **DXDIAG.EXE**. With Windows Vista, type Dxdiag into the instant desktop search box and press Enter when the Dxdiag program appears.

You can navigate through the DirectX Diagnostic Tool using the tabs at the top of the screen, or by using the Next Page button at the bottom of the screen to go through each tab sequentially. The list of tabs found in DirectX Diagnostics for both Windows XP and Windows Vista include the following:

- The System tab displays a list of information related to your system configuration. This information includes the current date and time, your computer's name and operating system version, the language setting, the system manufacturer and model, your system BIOS version, the type of processor you have installed, the amount of system RAM, page file statistics, and the version of DirectX that's currently installed on your system.

- The Display tab gives you detailed information on your video adapter, including its name and manufacturer, the chip and digital-to-analog (DAC) type, the amount of onboard video memory, your current display mode, and the type of monitor you have installed. This screen also lists the driver files being used for your video adapter. Below this information, the DirectX 9.0c version includes three diagnostic tests you can run on your system. The first diagnostic tests DirectDraw acceleration, which controls display memory management. The second test checks Direct3D acceleration, which provides 3D graphics support via the video adapter hardware. The third diagnostic checks the AGP texture acceleration, which is a graphics feature that only exists on certain video cards. Below these three diagnostic tests is a dialog box that displays any warning messages generated by the tests.

- The Sound tab contains information on your system's audio components. This includes the name and device ID of your sound card, a manufacturer and product ID, and the drivers associated with the device. If you are using the DirectX 9.0c version, this screen offers one diagnostic that's used to test DirectSound, a DirectX component that controls how audio is presented on your system. Again, error messages are displayed in a dialog box near the bottom of the screen.

- The Input tab shows a list of all the input devices you have attached to your system, including keyboards, mice, and other input devices such as gamepads, joysticks, and trackballs. There are no diagnostics you can perform on this screen, but a dialog box displays any error messages that the DirectX Diagnostic Tool detects.

Because DirectX 10 has undergone an extensive redesign, its version of DirectX Diagnostics lacks the following tabs found in the DirectX 9.0c (and earlier) version:

- The DirectX Files tab shows you all the installed files that are related to DirectX. Also displayed are the version numbers for each file, the date they were created, and the size of each file on the hard disk. Below the file list is a Notes box that displays any error messages that the diagnostic tool generates concerning any of the files.

- The Music tab is similar to the Sound tab, but is more specialized in that it focuses on a DirectX component called DirectMusic. On this screen, you'll find information on any Musical Instrument Digital Interface (MIDI) devices you have configured on your system, and a diagnostic that tests the functionality of DirectMusic.

- The Network tab offers information on DirectPlay components. DirectPlay is a networking API that controls networking services at the transport and session protocol levels. DirectPlay is responsible for moderating the function of network-based games such as massive multiplayer role-playing games (MMPORGs). The Network tab displays a list of registered DirectPlay service providers, a list of registered DirectPlay applications, and two diagnostic tests. The first test checks the DirectPlay Voice functionality, which is used with games that offer players the ability to speak to each other using headsets. The second diagnostic tests the DirectPlay function of DirectX.

- The More Help tab offers four options that are accessed by clicking onscreen buttons. The first option launches the DirectX Windows Troubleshooter. The second button launches the Audio Windows Troubleshooter. (You took a closer look at Windows Troubleshooters earlier in this chapter.) The third button loads the Microsoft System Information Tool, which provides an extremely detailed look at your system's overall hardware, software, and Internet configurations. The fourth button is used to override the default refresh rate used by DirectDraw. Generally speaking, you should leave this button alone, unless you are absolutely sure of what you're doing.

Program Compatibility Wizard

The Program Compatibility Wizard is used as a workaround for compatibility issues with a program that was released for an earlier version of Windows that has trouble functioning under Windows XP or Windows Vista.

In Windows XP, the Program Compatibility Wizard can be launched from the Start menu by choosing All Programs, Accessories. In Windows Vista, start it from Control Panel, Programs, Programs and Features, Use an Older Program with This Version of Windows. Alternatively, you can right-click on a program's launch file or shortcut, select Properties, and then click on the Compatibility tab.

The Windows XP version can be used to run a program in one of the compatibility modes for Windows 95, 98, Me, NT4.0 (SP5), and 2000. The Windows Vista version adds a compatibility mode for Windows XP Service Pack 2.

Both versions of the Program Compatibility Wizard also offer three display options for older programs:

- Run in 256 Colors
- Run in 640×480 Screen Resolution
- Disable Visual Themes

The Windows Vista version offers the same option, and adds two additional options:

- Disable desktop composition, which turns off transparency and other advanced features
- Disable display scaling on high-DPI settings

The Windows Vista version also adds another option to run the program as an administrator. This option is visible only on Administrator accounts. If there is more than one user on a computer, you see an option to show settings for all users. This option is not visible if User Account Control has been disabled.

Tip

If you are running an application in a Windows Compatibility mode, you should close any active antivirus and antispyware programs. These programs can cause problems when running an application in Windows Compatibility mode.

System Configuration Utility

The System Configuration Utility is a powerful troubleshooting tool that allows you to configure a number of Windows startup variables (see Figure 12.16). To access the System Configuration Utility from the Start menu, select Run, and enter **MSCONFIG**.

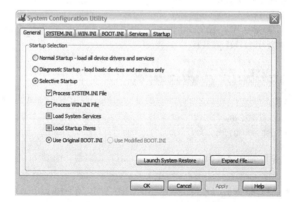

Figure 12.16   Using the Microsoft System Configuration Utility to manually set startup variables.

From the General tab, you can choose to alter the startup method that Windows will use the next time you reboot the machine. Diagnostic Startup is essentially the same as Safe mode; you can further configure this option by selecting which services you want to start by clicking on the Services tab. Selective Startup allows you to further customize startup on a more granular level.

The SYSTEM.INI and WIN.INI tabs in the Windows XP version contain services and programs that are primarily meant to provide backward compatibility for programs designed for earlier versions of Windows. The SYSTEM.INI and WIN.INI files are not necessary to run Windows XP, but may be required by older drivers and programs.

The Boot.INI tab in the Windows XP version of MSConfig has been replaced by the Boot tab in the Windows Vista version. This tab is used to configure boot options.

◄◄ For details, **see** "Adjusting Boot Options with MSConfig," **p. 76**.

The Services tab can be used to enable or disable specific services. This can be very useful if you are troubleshooting a Windows startup problem, and want to disable services without uninstalling the associated software. You can view only the third-party services in the list by clicking on the Hide All Microsoft Services check box.

The Startup tab allows you to enable or disable software programs that are started when Windows is started. Common examples of such programs include antivirus software, instant message clients, and third-party control panels for display adapters and audio cards. Again, disabling all unnecessary programs and enabling them one at a time can help to isolate and identify the cause of a Windows startup problem.

If you would like to know what some of the more cryptically named startup items are, you can try looking them up at www.sysinfo.org.

The Tools tab is included by default as part of MSConfig in Windows Vista. On systems running Windows XP SP2, the Tools tab can be added to MSConfig by installing the update discussed in Knowledge Base article 906569, available at http://support.microsoft.com.

The Tools tab can be used to start the tools listed in Table 12.5; select the tool and click Launch to start it. As a bonus, the Tools tab shows the correct syntax to run each command from the command line.

Table 12.5   Programs Available on the MSConfig Tools Tab

Tool Name	Description on the Tools Tab	Default Command	Available Versions
About Windows	Shows the version of Windows currently installed on the system.	C:\WINDOWS\system32\winver.exe	XP, Vista
Command Prompt	Opens a Command Prompt window.	C:\WINDOWS\system32\cmd.exe	XP, Vista
Event Viewer	Displays monitoring and troubleshooting messages from Windows and other programs.	C:\WINDOWS\system32\Eventvwr.msc	XP, Vista
Internet Options	Internet Explorer settings.	C:\WINDOWS\system32\inetcpl.cpl	XP, Vista
Internet Protocol Configuration	IPCONFIG is a command-line tool used to control network connections on Windows-based computers.	C:\WINDOWS\system32\cmd.exe /k C:\WINDOWS\system32\ipconfig.exe	XP, Vista

(continues)

Table 12.5   Continued

Tool Name	Description on the Tools Tab	Default Command	Available Versions
Network Diagnostics	Network Diagnostics scans your system to gather information about your hardware, software, and network connections.	C:\WINDOWS\system32\netsh.exe diag gui	XP, Vista*
Programs	Add or remove programs and Windows components.	C:\WINDOWS\system32\appwiz.cpl	XP, Vista
Registry Editor	Make changes to the Windows Registry.	C:\WINDOWS\regedit.exe	XP, Vista
Security Center	Configure Automatic Updates, Windows Firewall, and Internet properties settings.	C:\WINDOWS\system32\wscui.cpl	XP, Vista
System Information	View advanced information about hardware and software settings.	C:\ProgramFiles\CommonFiles\MicrosoftShared\MSInfo\msinfo32.exe	XP, Vista
System Properties	View basic information about your computer's system settings.	C:\WINDOWS\system32\sysdm.cpl (XP) C:\WINDOWS\system32\control.exe system (Vista)	XP, Vista
System Restore	Restore computer to a previous state.	C:\WINDOWS\system32\restore\rstrui.exe	XP, Vista
Task Manager	Provides details about programs and processes running on your computer.	C:\WINDOWS\system32\taskmgr.exe	XP, Vista
Remote Assistance	Receive help from (or offer help to) a friend over the Internet.	C:\WINDOWS\system32\msra.exe	Vista
Computer Management	View and configure system settings and components.	C:\WINDOWS\system32\compmgmt.msc	Vista
Internet Options	View and change Internet Explorer settings.	C:\WINDOWS\system32\inetcpl.cpl	Vista
Performance Monitor	Monitors reliability and performance of local or remote computers.	C:\WINDOWS\system32\perfmon.exe	Vista
Disable UAC	Disables User Account Control (requires reboot).	C:\Windows\System32\cmd.exe /k %windir%\System32\reg.exe ADDHKLM\SOFTWARE\Microsoft\Windows\CurrentVersion\Policies\System /v EnableLUA /t REG_DWORD /d 0 /f	Vista
Enable UAC	Enables User Account Control (requires reboot).	C:\Windows\System32\cmd.exe /k %windir%\System32\reg.exe ADD HKLM\SOFTWARE\Microsoft\Windows\CurrentVersion\Policies\System/v EnableLUA /t REG_DWORD /d 1 /f	Vista

This tool is not available in Windows Vista Home Basic or Home Premium editions.

Note

You can disable User Account Control for administrators only by using the Local Security Policy on Windows Vista Ultimate and Business editions. For details, see http://www.howtogeek.com/howto/windows-vista/disable-user-account-controluac-for-administrators-only/.

To disable User Account Control for administrators only on Windows Vista Home Basic and Home Premium editions, a Registry fix is required. A preconfigured Registry fix is available from the website just referenced.

Tip

You can customize the Tools menu in Windows XP by creating an XML file called `Mccfgtlc.xml`. For details, see Microsoft Knowledge Base article 906569, available at http://support.microsoft.com.

Installing Additional Windows XP Support Tools

As you have seen, there are a number of troubleshooting tools and resources available in a normal Windows XP installation. However, Microsoft has also provided a large collection of additional programs known as the Windows Support Tools. These tools are meant for use by Microsoft support specialists and experienced Windows users to help diagnose and solve Windows issues. The Windows Support Tools are not installed by default when you install Windows XP, but they can be installed at a later time from the Windows XP installation CD.

To install Windows Support Tools, place the Windows XP installation CD into your system while Windows is running. Open the contents of the CD in My Computer or Windows Explorer and browse to the `Support\Tools` folder. Double-click the `SETUP.EXE` file to install the Windows Support Tools.

Note

If you are running Windows XP Service Pack 2, you should not install the Windows Support Tools from the Windows XP installation disk. Microsoft has an updated version of this package, *Windows XP Service Pack 2 Support Tools*, available as a free download on its website. To download this newer version, visit http://www.microsoft.com/downloads/details.aspx?FamilyID=49ae8576-9bb9-4126-9761-ba8011fabf38&displaylang=en.

There are nearly fifty different command-line programs available in the Windows Support Tools. Thankfully, a help file that describes each tool in depth is placed in the Windows Support Tools item created in the Start menu after installation. Each entry in the help file includes an overview of the support tool, notes on how to use the tool from the command line, the syntax you should use when typing the command as well as all the available switches, one or more examples of the tool's functionality, and a list of related support tools that may be applicable to the issue you are troubleshooting.

Here are some examples of the types of tools included in the Windows Support Tools:

- **Dependency Walker (DEPENDS.EXE)**—Dependency Walker displays a hierarchical diagram showing all of the child modules that a parent module (such as an .EXE, .DLL, or .SYS file) is dependent on in order to function properly. This tool can be used to troubleshoot Windows errors that are based on module load issues. When Dependency Walker scans a parent module such as an .EXE file, it automatically detects and reports several common application errors such as missing modules, invalid modules, and circular dependency errors.

- **Disk Manager Diagnostics (DMDIAG.EXE)**—Disk Manager Diagnostics displays the system state and configuration data related to disk storage. This information includes the computer name and the operating system installed, the physical disk type, any existing hard disk mount points, drive letter usage, and disk partition configuration. You can write all the information produced by this diagnostic to a text file by including a directory path and filename as part of the command (for example, type `dmdiag > C:\diskinfo\diskinfo.txt` at the command line, and the tool will write the information to a file named diskinfo.txt in the C:\diskinfo directory).

- **Pool Byte Monitor (POOLMON.EXE)**—Pool Byte Monitor is used to monitor memory tags such as total paged and nonpaged pool bytes. This tool is most commonly used to attempt to detect possible memory leaks. Memory leaks occur when a program or service reserves memory for itself, but doesn't relinquish it when it is finished running. Eventually, a memory leak will result in inadequate memory being available for the operating system to function properly, resulting in system errors or lockups. Pool Byte Monitor can be used to track which memory tag's byte levels are increasing over time without being released, which is a common symptom of a memory leak.

In addition to the Windows XP Support Tools you can install from the Windows XP CD, you can also download Network Diagnostics for Windows XP from http://support.microsoft.com/kb/914440. This tool analyzes the results of the following tests: IP configuration, default gateway, Winsock, DNS, firewall, and Internet connectivity validation. It installs to \Windows\network diagnostic\xpnetdiag.exe. It uses Internet Explorer to display the diagnostic log after it runs.

The Windows Memory Diagnostic, a standard feature in Windows Vista, is also available as a downloadable utility for Windows XP.

◀◀ For details, **see** "Memory Diagnostic," **p. 786**.

Windows Vista Troubleshooting Tools

Although Windows Vista carries over a number of troubleshooting tools from Windows XP, it also adds a number of newly developed tools, many of which are easier to use and more powerful than those in Windows XP. These include

- Windows Recovery Environment (Windows RE)
- Problem Reports and Solutions
- Reliability and Performance Monitor
- System Health Report

Each of these tools is discussed in the following sections.

Windows Recovery Environment

The Windows Recovery Environment (Windows RE) is a set of troubleshooting tools designed to solve the most common problems with Windows Vista startup. Some systems with preinstalled

Windows Vista automatically start Windows RE if Vista does not boot, whereas other systems might include Windows RE on a bootable CD or DVD. You can also start Windows RE from the Windows Vista distribution DVD. Use it as a boot device, click Next on the initial dialog, and click Repair Your Computer on the Install Now dialog.

When Windows RE starts, it first looks for the location of the Windows Vista installation to repair. Click Next after it locates the installation, and the System Recovery Options dialog shown in Figure 12.17 appears.

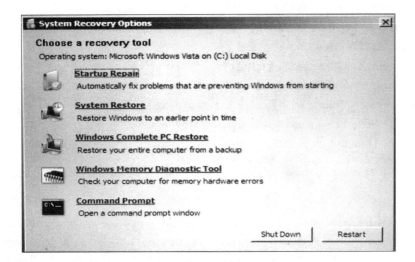

Figure 12.17 System Recovery Options in Windows RE.

Note

You can create a Windows Vista Recovery Environment CD with the Create a Recovery Disc option in Windows Vista Service Pack 1.

If you are using Windows AIK as part of the deployment process for Windows Vista, you can create a Windows RE CD with Windows AIK.

Some computer vendors preinstall Windows RE on the hard disk in a special partition. In some cases, you must press F8 at system startup and select Repair as the boot option to start Windows RE. If a system fails to boot Vista, some systems are configured to run Windows RE automatically. Contact your system manufacturer for details.

Command Prompt

The command prompt available in the Windows Vista Recovery Environment enables full access to all accessible drives connected to the computer at startup. Unlike the limited Windows XP Recovery Console, which was primarily designed for restoring system files to a crashed system, the Windows Vista command prompt can use any command prompt program, including multiple file-and-folder copy programs such as xcopy and robocopy. Command prompt enables you to copy data from a crashed system to another drive, including external USB drives. You can even format CD and DVD media from Command Prompt and copy files to the media.

Here are some of the commands you may find useful to run from the Recovery Environment command prompt (these same commands also work from a command prompt in Windows Vista):

- **regedit**—Views and edits the Windows Vista Registry.
- **robocopy**—Powerful file- and folder-copying utility (better than Xcopy).
- **format**—Erases and prepares blank media for use. Use the /fs:UDF option to format CD or DVD media.
- **bcdedit**—Displays and configures boot settings.
- **chkdsk**—Checks drives for errors.
- **exit**—Closes the command prompt.
- **tasklist**—Lists running tasks.
- **taskkill**—Kills a specified task.
- **tree**—Displays a graphical chart of a folder (directory) structure.
- **shutdown**—Shuts down a local or remote system.
- **net**—Versatile network client configuration tool.
- **dir**—Lists files and folders.

To get help with any command-prompt program, type the program name and add /?.

Startup Repair

Startup Repair is designed to solve problems with missing or corrupt drivers, system files, boot configuration settings, Registry settings, or disk metadata. When you run Startup Repair, it analyzes your drive to determine which repairs are necessary. You then see the following options:

- Repair and Restart
- View Details

Before you click Repair and Restart, you can see the repairs that will be made by clicking the View Details link. A new window opens (see Figure 12.18 for a typical example).

After reviewing the repairs, click Close, click Repair and Restart, and then Finish to complete the repair process and restart your system. The repair process takes just a few seconds in most cases.

Click Repair and Restart, click Finish, and your system is repaired and restarts automatically.

It may be necessary to run Startup Repair repeatedly to fix some problems. Each time you run it, it performs additional repairs. You can use Startup Repair up to five times on a system that does not boot. If the system does not boot after the fifth time, you need to perform manual repairs using the Command Prompt.

Note

If you have a USB flash memory drive connected to your computer, remove it before you run Startup Repair. According to Microsoft Knowledge Base article 934540, Startup Repair might analyze the USB drive instead of the hard disk and conclude your system is working. This could happen if you use a USB flash memory drive for storage, as part of an implementation of BitLocker, or if you use a USB-based fingerprint reader that also includes a flash memory drive.

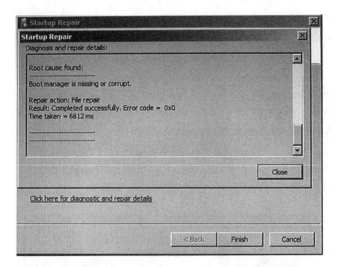

Figure 12.18 Viewing the details of a startup problem with Startup Repair.

System Restore

If your computer cannot boot after you install new hardware or software, restoring your system to its condition before the change can help the system to work properly. To restore your computer's configuration to an earlier time from Windows RE, follow these steps:

1. Select System Restore from the System Repair Options dialog.

2. Click Next on the opening dialog.

3. Select a restore point from those listed. Click Next to continue.

4. Select the drive(s) you want to restore. The system disk is selected automatically. Click Next to continue.

5. The system displays the restore point you chose. To select a different restore point, click Back. Click Finish to restart the computer and restore your system to the restore point specified.

Tip

Before running System Restore, try removing the last device installed, especially if it is a device connected via the USB or FireWire (IEEE-1394) ports. You can remove these devices without dismantling the computer. If the system starts normally after removing a USB or FireWire-based device, update drivers for the device before reconnecting it.

Windows Complete PC Restore

Windows RE for Vista Business, Enterprise, and Ultimate editions includes Windows Complete PC Restore, which restores backups made with Windows Complete PC Backup. Windows Complete PC Backup creates an image backup of the entire system, so when you run Windows Complete PC Restore, you can use it to recover from a crashed hard disk, even if you have replaced the hard disk.

Restoring to the Same Hard Disk or a Same-Size Replacement

If you are restoring a Windows Complete PC Backup to the same hard disk or a replacement hard disk of the same capacity, follow this procedure:

1. Connect your backup drive to the computer and make sure it is turned on before you start Windows Complete PC Restore. If you used a DVD or other removable media to contain the backup, make sure you have inserted the last disc or cartridge into the drive.

2. Select Windows Complete PC Restore from the System Recovery Options dialog.

3. To restore the most recent backup, click Next on the opening dialog (see Figure 12.19). To restore an earlier backup, select Restore a Different Backup, then Click Next. Select the backup to restore.

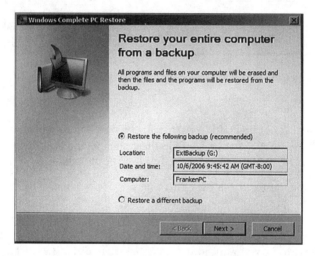

Figure 12.19   Preparing to restore the most recent Complete PC Backup image.

4. If you do not want to reformat the hard disk, click Finish to start the restoration process. To repartition the hard disk to match the drive partitions contained in the backup, select the Format and Repartition Disks option, then click Finish (see Figure 12.20).

5. If you are restoring from DVD or other removable media, swap media as directed until the restore process is complete.

6. The system reboots after the restore process is complete. To bring your system back to its most recent configuration, restore data backups that took place after the last image backup was performed.

Restoring to a Larger Hard Disk

Windows Complete PC Restore is designed primarily to restore a working system to the same hard disk or the same-capacity hard disk. If you attempt to use Windows Complete PC Restore to restore a working system to a larger-capacity hard disk, you may see the following error:

```
There are too few disks on this computer or one or more of the disks is too small.
Add or change disks so they match the disks in the backup and try the restore
again. (0x80042401)
```

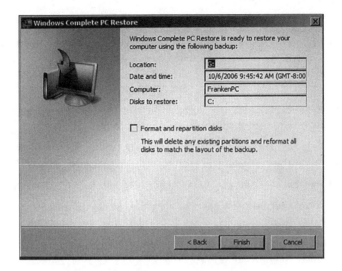

Figure 12.20   Reviewing restoration options.

If you see this error, rerun the restore process and select the option to format and repartition disks (refer to Figure 12.20). However, if the error persists, you must manually create a partition on the new hard disk that matches the size of the existing partition before you run Windows Complete PC Restore. The hard disk you use as a restore target should be unpartitioned.

To ensure that the hard disk contains no existing partitions, you can use Diskpart's Clean command or a third-party disk maintenance program. Diskpart can also be used to create the partition. Diskpart is a command-line utility that can be run from Windows Vista's command prompt.

The following procedure for cleaning up existing disk partitions and creating new ones is adapted from a procedure developed by Thiti V. Sintopchai and posted as a comment at http://professionalinsight.net/VistaBackup.aspx. In this example, the Windows Complete PC Backup image is of a C: drive on a 75GB partition.

1. After starting command prompt from Windows RE's System Recovery Options menu, type **Diskpart** and press Enter; the DISKPART> prompt appears.

2. Type **List Disk** and press Enter. Available hard disk drives are displayed. Typically, the system hard disk is Drive 0.

3. Type **Select Disk=0** and press Enter to select Drive 0.

4. Type **List Partition** and press Enter. A new hard disk should list no partitions. If you see any partitions, use a different hard disk (if the partition might contain data you need) or remove the partition.

5. To remove any existing disk partitions, type **clean** and press Enter.

6. Type **create partition primary size=76800** and press Enter to create a 75GB partition. Substitute the size of the partition.

Tip

Before you have a system problem, use DISKPART or the properties sheet for your current hard disk to determine the size of the system partition. Record this information so that you can use it to create a partition of the correct size with Diskpart if you need to install a larger hard disk and use Windows Complete PC Restore to restore your system.

7. Type `List Partition` and press Enter; note the number of the partition you created. If the disk is new or unpartitioned, this number should be 0.

8. Type `Select Partition=0` and press Enter to make this partition active (substitute the correct number if the partition you created is a different number).

9. Type `format fs=ntfs label="Vista"` and press Enter.

10. Type `list volume` and press Enter to view the list of volumes. Note the number of the NTFS partition with the label "Vista." It is identified as *x* in step 11.

11. Type `select volume=x` and press Enter (substitute the number of the volume from step 10 for *x*) to make the new volume active.

12. Type `assign letter=C` and press Enter to assign the volume labeled "Vista" to drive C:.

13. Type `Exit` and press Enter to exit Diskpart.

14. Type `Exit` and press Enter to exit the command prompt.

15. Attach your backup drive and run Complete PC Restore.

Memory Diagnostic

If your system won't boot, in many cases problems with memory could be to blame. You can test your system's memory modules with the Windows Memory Diagnostic Tool, which you can run from three different locations:

- Windows RE's System Recovery Options menu.
- The Windows Boot Manager (displayed when you press F8 at system startup).
- The Administrative Tools folder in the Control Panel. This option requires you to restart the system.

The Windows Memory Diagnostic Tool runs before the Windows Vista GUI starts, enabling it to test all your system's memory. During the test, a progress display, shown in Figure 12.21, shows test progress.

To adjust how the tool tests memory, press F1 to display the Options dialog. Options include:

- **Test type**—Basic (performs three different memory tests); Standard (performs eight different memory tests; default setting); Extended (performs 17 different memory tests)
- **Cache configuration**—Off (disables memory caching for all tests); On (enables memory caching for all tests); Default (caching on for some tests and off for others)

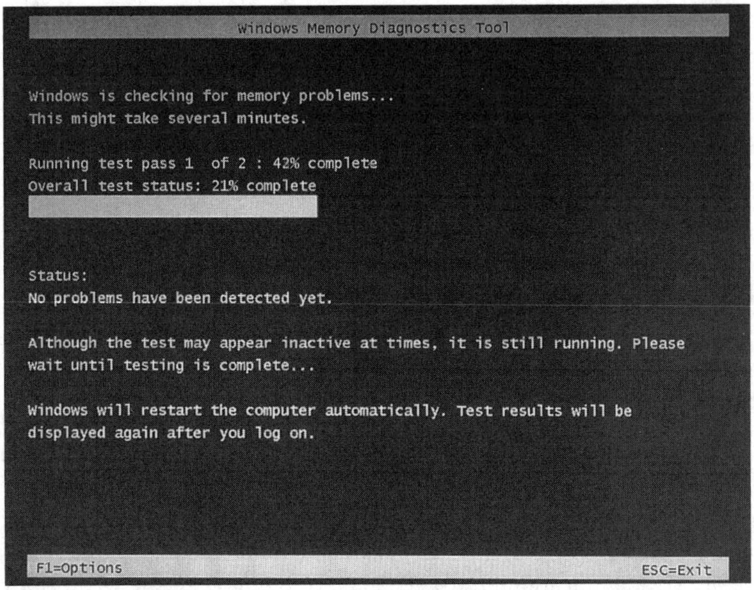

```
                    Windows Memory Diagnostics Tool


   Windows is checking for memory problems...
   This might take several minutes.

   Running test pass 1  of 2 : 42% complete
   Overall test status: 21% complete



   Status:
   No problems have been detected yet.

   Although the test may appear inactive at times, it is still running. Please
   wait until testing is complete...

   Windows will restart the computer automatically. Test results will be
   displayed again after you log on.




   F1=Options                                                          ESC=Exit
```

Figure 12.21   The Windows Memory Diagnostic Tool.

Tip

Memory cache on modern systems is built into the processor. To help determine whether memory problems are found in main memory or the processor's cache memory, use the Extended test type, which performs some tests with cache enabled and some tests with cache disabled. If the system fails tests with cache enabled but not with cache disabled, the processor's onboard cache might be faulty, requiring a processor swap.

You can also enable cache or disable cache for all tests by using the Cache Configuration option. The default option enables cache for some tests, and disables it for some tests. To determine which tests use memory caching or disable it, open the Options menu and select each test type.

■ **Number of test passes**—2 is the default. Select from 0 (infinite test passes) to 99. Use a higher value to help find memory problems that may take place only after the system has been running for some time.

To stop testing, press Esc.

Tip

If your system uses ECC memory, disable ECC support in the system BIOS before performing tests if possible. This helps ensure that single-bit errors that ECC corrects automatically can be detected.

If your system has more than 4GB of RAM, keep in mind that Windows Memory Diagnostic Tool can test only up to 4GB of RAM. To test all the RAM in such a system, remove enough RAM to reduce the total memory size to less than 4GB, run the tool, and then test the remainder of the memory separately.

If there are any problems with memory, Windows Vista reports them during testing and lists problems detected in Problem Reports and Solutions.

Note

Windows XP users can also use the Windows Memory Diagnostics Tool. It's available as a download from the Microsoft Online Crash Analysis website at http://oca.microsoft.com/en/windiag.asp. This web page also has instructions on how to make a bootable CD or floppy disk containing the tool.

Problem Reports and Solutions

The Microsoft Online Crash analysis feature is familiar to many Windows XP users. It prompts you to report your problem to Microsoft. Unfortunately, it does not provide an easy way to determine whether the problem is ever resolved. To determine what problems you've had on a particular system, it's necessary to scroll through the Event Viewer, which is cluttered with computer events that are not problems as well as actual problems.

Windows Vista replaces the Online Crash Analysis feature with the new Problem Reports and Solutions applet in Control Panel. When Vista detects a problem (sometimes even one so slight it might not display a notification message), details of the problem are recorded in Problem Reports and Solutions (see Figure 12.22).

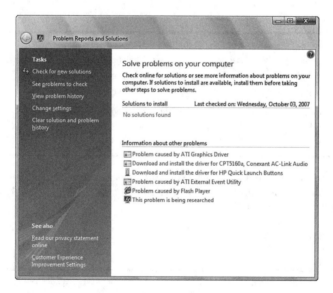

Figure 12.22   The new Problem Reports and Solutions tool.

In the main pane, current solutions to install (if any) are listed, along with problems caused by both Microsoft and third-party applications. Click each link to see the status of the problem. By default, Windows Vista automatically checks for solutions.

The left pane provides additional tools:

- *Check for New Solutions* checks the Microsoft website for solutions to problems detected on your computer. To learn more about a specific problem, click View Problem Details and open the links provided. You may be prompted to upload additional information to assist in finding a solution. To upload additional information, click Yes when prompted.

- *See Problems to Check* lists all problems that have not yet been uploaded. Select problems; then click Check for Solutions to upload the problems for analysis.

- *View Problem History* displays a list of detected problems. Boldfaced items have not yet been uploaded (see Figure 12.23).

- *Change Settings* provides two options: Automatic checks for Solutions (the default) or Ask Windows Vista to Check for Solutions. If you select the latter option, you need to use the Check for New Solutions option to receive solutions.

- *Clear Solution and Problem History* discards the current history information.

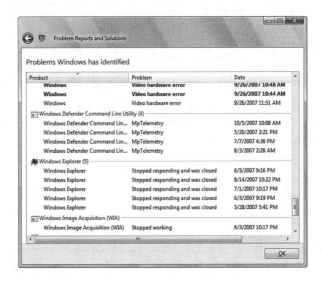

Figure 12.23   A sample list of identified problems.

Reliability and Performance Monitor

The Reliability and Performance Monitor is located in the Advanced Tools section of Performance Information and Tools in the Control Panel's System and Maintenance category. This tool might remind you of the Performance Monitor (`perfmon.msc`) in Windows XP, but it is both more powerful and easier to use. The Resource Overview, shown in Figure 12.24, provides real-time performance information about your processor, disk drives, network, and memory subsystems.

◄◄ To learn more about using the Performance Monitor module, **see** "Monitoring Your System to Identify Bottlenecks," **p. 310**.

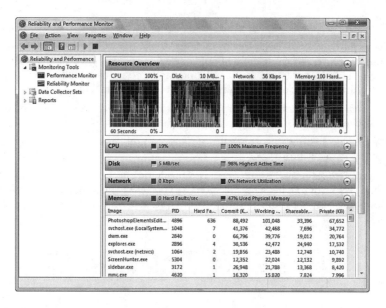

Figure 12.24   Viewing the details of memory usage with the Resource Overview.

To determine the reliability of your system over time, open the Reliability Monitor node. The Reliability Monitor's System Stability Chart, shown in Figure 12.25, tracks the following events on a daily basis:

- Application failures
- Hardware failures
- Windows failures
- Miscellaneous failures

The frequency and severity of these failures are used to calculate a reliability index, shown at the upper-right corner of the chart. The System Stability Chart also tracks the following:

- Driver installs
- Driver uninstalls
- Application installs
- Application uninstalls
- Driver and application version information

To view the details for any date, select it from the pull-down menu or scroll to it and click it. Only categories with activity are expanded in the System Stability Report visible below the chart.

Note

A yellow ! symbol in the Reliability Monitor indicates a failed application or driver install, whereas a red X symbol indicates other types of failures. A blue information (i) symbol indicates software or driver installation or uninstallation.

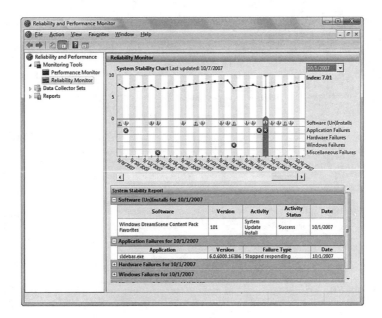

Figure 12.25 Reliability Monitor tracks application, hardware, Windows, and miscellaneous failures to calculate a reliability index.

Approximately three months of information is displayed in the System Stability Chart, enabling you to see trends in system stability, and to determine whether particular programs or devices are frequently causing problems.

System Health Report

The Reliability and Performance Monitor can also analyze the health of your entire system. To create a System Diagnostics report (also known as the *system health report*):

1. Open the System and Maintenance category in Control Panel

2. Click Performance Information and Tools

3. Click Advanced Tools in the Tasks pane

4. Click Generate a System Health Report

To view the report, open the Reports node, the System node, the System Diagnostics node, and click the report shown. Figure 12.26 shows a portion of a typical report.

Note

The name of the report is created from the date run and the number of reports run on that date. For example, a report named 20070202_0001 is the first report run on February 2, 2007.

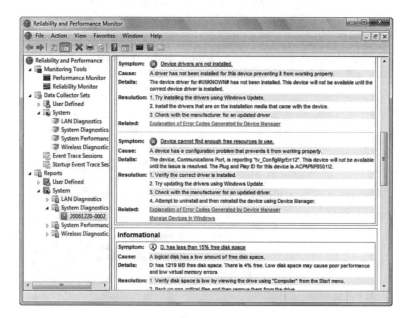

Figure 12.26 A portion of a typical System Diagnostics report.

System Diagnostics provides a one-stop reporting resource for all the following:

- Software configuration
- Hardware configuration
- CPU, disk, memory, and network subsystems
- Disabled devices
- Device drivers
- The status of antivirus and firewall protection
- Resource usage
- System services
- Startup programs
- IDE SMART disk status
- Windows Experience score
- Network interfaces

Using the Microsoft Knowledge Base

At the beginning of this chapter, I mentioned that part of being a good troubleshooter is knowing where to look for relevant knowledge and information. There are a number of online resources you can (and should) access when you are troubleshooting a Windows problem. One of the most relevant online resources comes from the makers of Windows itself: the Microsoft Help and Support site, home of the Microsoft Knowledge Base (MSKB). The MSKB contains hundreds of thousands of articles offering technical support for every available Microsoft product, including Windows XP and Windows Vista. These articles include troubleshooting tips, how-to articles, coverage of new security updates and Service Packs, and columns that are geared towards software developers.

To visit the Microsoft Help and Support site, point your browser to

> http://support.microsoft.com/

From this page, you can access a number of different Windows information resources. You can do a search of the Knowledge Base, visit one of the product-specific solution centers, or browse to the Microsoft newsgroups, an online community of users who share their knowledge of Microsoft products.

Every article that appears in the Knowledge Base is assigned an Article ID number (see Figure 12.27). This number serves as the primary reference point for each article. For example, it's possible that you have encountered a sentence like this before:

"For more information, see KB article 933173."

Alternatively, this reference is sometimes abbreviated to simply read "KB933173." In this example, this is the Article ID of the Knowledge Base article #933173, "The computer does not recognize the Windows Vista installation disc."

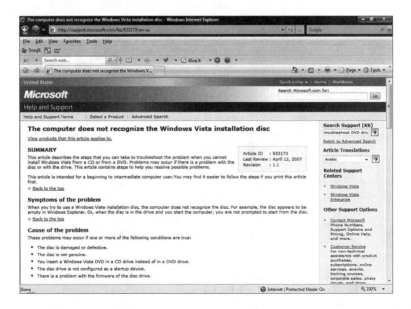

Figure 12.27 Viewing an article in the Microsoft Knowledge Base.

Knowledge Base articles follow a common section structure. Each article opens with a high-level summary of the material it contains. Next to the summary is an information box with the article ID number, the last review date, and the revision number. Depending upon the article, it might contain a list of symptoms, typical causes of the problem, and steps to resolve the problem, or it might contain an introduction and the main body of the article. All types of articles end with a list of software products or services that the article applies to, and finally, a list of keywords associated with the article.

If you want to read a specific article in the Knowledge Base and you know its article ID, you can browse directly to it by typing the following URL in the Address bar of Internet Explorer:

> http://support.microsoft.com/?kbid=(Article ID #)

Alternatively, you can also use Help and Support in the Windows Start menu to open a Knowledge Base article. Open Help and Support, and type the letters **KB** followed by the number of the article into the Search box near the top of the screen (see Figure 12.28).

The Microsoft Knowledge Base also offers a Basic Search, as well as an Advanced Search functionality.

If you would like to keep up with new articles as they are added to the Knowledge Base, Microsoft offers *Really Simple Syndication* or *RSS feeds* that you can use to receive notification of new articles. Each RSS feed is based on a specific product, so you can pick and choose which Microsoft products you want to monitor for new Knowledge Base articles. To select RSS feeds based on products, go to http://support.microsoft.com/selectindex/?target=rss.

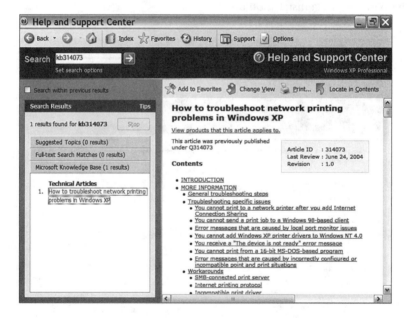

Figure 12.28   You can use the Help and Support feature in Windows XP or Windows Vista to view Knowledge Base articles.

INDEX